FAYETTE COUNTY, GEORGIA
PROBATE RECORDS

Volume II

ANNUAL RETURNS
INVENTORIES
SALES
BONDS

1845–1897

Jeannette Holland Austin

HERITAGE BOOKS
2012

HERITAGE BOOKS
AN IMPRINT OF HERITAGE BOOKS, INC.

Books, CDs, and more—Worldwide

For our listing of thousands of titles see our website
at
www.HeritageBooks.com

Published 2012 by
HERITAGE BOOKS, INC.
Publishing Division
100 Railroad Ave. #104
Westminster, Maryland 21157

Copyright © 1996 Jeannette Holland Austin

All rights reserved. No part of this book may be reproduced or transmitted in any form or by any means, electronic or mechanical, including photocopying, recording or by any information storage and retrieval system without written permission from the author, except for the inclusion of brief quotations in a review.

International Standard Book Numbers
Paperbound: 978-1-58549-609-9
Clothbound: 978-0-7884-9217-4

table of contents

Fayette County Ordinary Mixed Records
Inventories, Appraisements, Sales and Returns
Book D (1845-1853)   Page 1-72

Fayette County Administrators and Guardians Bonds
Book B (1850-1877)   Page 73-191

Fayette County Ordinary Mixed Records
Inventories, Appraisements, Sales and Returns
Book F (1856-1859)   Page 192-243

Fayette County Ordinary Mixed Records
Inventories, Appraisements, Sales and Returns
Book G (1859-1862)   Page 244-299

Fayette County Ordinary Mixed Records
Inventories, Appraisements, Sales and Returns
Book I (1871-1878)   Page 300-359

Fayette County Ordinary Mixed Records
Inventories, Appraisements, Sales and Returns
Book J (1878-1885)   Page 360-393

Fayette County Ordinary Mixed Records
Inventories, Appraisements, Sales and Returns]
Book K (1886-1889)   Page 394-415

Fayette County Ordinary Mixed Records
Inventories, Appraisements, Sales and Returns
Book L (1891-1897)   Page 416-443

Comments

The information contained herein was abstracted from the original records at Fayette County Courthouse in Fayetteville, Georgia. A concerted effort was made to abstract all pertinent genealogical data which might prove helpful in research, however, this should not reclude the researcher from examining the records themselves for further clarification. Generally, the mere mention of an annual return without data means that none was given. This is particularly true of annual returns or guardian's returns which were filed from year to year.

There are some numbering inconsistencies which exist in the numbering system. These errors are noted in their proper place.

Standard genealogical abbreviations are used, such as Admr Administrator), Admx (Administratrix), LWT (Last Will and Testament), etc.

Jeannette Holland Austin

Fayette County Ordinary Mixed Records
Inventories, Appraisements, Sales and Returns
Book D (1845-1853)

Note: No vouchers were included, except where indicated.

Inventory of the Goods, Chattels, Lands and Tenaments of William Whaley, decd, taken on 12 Oct 1844
Page 1-2

Includes a list of the property sold on 15 Nov 1845. Appraisers: Elizabeth Whaley, Josiah Whaley, Samuel Whaley, Thomas Johnson, Reuben Wallis, William Jackson, Mathew Leyle and Fanny Hutcherson.

The Following is an Inventory of the Property that was Appraised of the Estate of Reuben Millsaps, Sr., late of said county, decd, this 29 Nov 1844
Page 3-5

Appraisers: Stephen Smith, Edward Moore, William Irvings
Negroes: Silsey and child, Andrew, Auston, Any and child, Arthur, Green, Sarah (girl), George (boy), Lissy (girl), Eveline (girl) and Delah (girl).
 Part of Lot No. 193, 4th District of Fayette Co., 150 acres
Lot No. 255, 4th District of Fayette Co.
Lot No. 1, 5th District of Fayette Co. ("the above Lot as returned is found to be wrong number")

At the sale of the property, some of the purchasers were: Hiram Millsaps, Reuben Millsaps, Partheny Millsaps and Larkin Millsaps.

List of Negroes Sold:
Anny and infant child sold to Jessy L. Blalock
Andrew sold to Phillip Fitzgerald
Arthur sold to Thomas B. Gay
Green sold to Phillip Fitzgerald
George sold to William H. Blalock
Melissa sold to Pete E. McLeroy
Eveline and Delila sold to Edward Moore
Recorded: 3 Apr 1845

Return No. 9, Hubbard Stubbs, Orphan of William Stubbs in Account Current with John O. Dickson, Gdn, from 1 Jan 1844 up to 31 Dec 1844 inclusive
Page 6
Filed: 5 May 1845

Return No. 5, Turner and Sarah, Orphans of G. Deadsil, in Account Current with John O. Dickson, Gdn, from 1 Jan 1844 up to 31 Dec 1844 inclusive
Page 6. Filed: 5 May 1845

Estate of John Palmer, decd, in Account Current with Mary Palmer, Admx, from 1 Jan 1844 up to 31 Dec 1844 inclusive
Page 6-7 Filed: 13 May 1845

Return No. 3, Rebecca, William D., Nancy, Susan, Joseph, Francis, Margaret and Emiline, minor children of Josiah Swainy, in Account Current with Josiah Swainy, Gdn, from 1 Jan 1843 up to 31 Dec 1844 inclusive
Page 7

Filed: 13 May 1845

Return No. 1, Wilie A., minor child of Herrod Pate, decd, in Account Current with Herrod Pate, Gdn, from 1 Jan to 31 Dec 1844 inclusive
Page 7-8

Filed: 13 May 1845

Return No. 4, Mary A., Orphan of I. Fitzgarrell, decd, in Account Current with P. Fitzgarrold, Gdn, from 1 Jan up to 31 Dec 1844 inclusive

Page 8. Filed: 13 May 1845

Estate of H. Hubbard, in Account Current with P. Fitzgarrell, Admr, from 1 Jan to 31 Dec 1844 inclusive
Page 8

Recorded: May Term 1845

Return No.___, Estate of Augustus R. Beall, decd, in Account Current with P. O. Beall, Admr, 9 Aug 1843 up to 12 May 1845 inclusive
Page 9

To amount paid Lewis Hobgood on Lot. Filed 13 May 1834

Return No. 1, Francis M., Orphan of Thomas Carroll, decd, in Account Current with A. McBride, Gdn, from 1 Jan 1844 up to 31 Dec 1944 inclusive
Page 9. Recorded: 7 Jul 1845

Return No. 1, Emily J., Orphan of Thomas Carroll, decd, in Account Current with A. McBride, Gdn, from 1 Jan to 31 Dec 1844 inclusive
Page 9

7 Jul 1845 - By 2 negroes received from Exrs of Estate of Thomas Carroll, decd, one by the name of Frank, a man, and the other a boy by the name of Jourdan.

Return No. 4, the Estate of Archibald Boothe, in Account Current with Zacariah Petty, Admr
Page 9-10

To cash paid out to the atty of Levi Turner in the case of said Turner against me, as Admr, in Fayette Inferior Court (voucher #1). /s/Zacariah Petty
Filed: 18 Feb 1845

Return No. 4, Estate of Thomas Carroll, decd, in Account Current with A. McBride, Exr, 1 Jan to 31 Dec 1844 inclusive
Page 10-11
20 vouchers.
To hire of negro boy, Clark, to A. McBride
To hire of negro boy, Frank, to A. McBride
To hire of negro boy, Guy, to Eli Edmondson
To hire of negro boy, George, to William Herring
To hire of negro boy, Ben, to Mr. Jackson
To hire of negro girl, Leny, to Mr. Jackson
Recorded: Jul 1845

An Inventory of the Goods, Chattels, Lands and Tenements of Bryan Griggs, late of Fayette Co., decd, 15 Jul 1845
Page 11-13

Negroes - Sutton (man), Brussillar (woman), Milley (girl), Sarah (girl), Sarah (girl), Gabe (boy).
60 acres.

Appraisers: Burrell Brown, A. Jennings, N. Stinchcomb, William Craig, William Whatley, sworn 15 Jul 1845. Recorded: 12 Aug 1845
Sale of Personal Property - among the purchasers were: Rocella Griggs (primary purchaser).
Recorded: 27 Jul 1844

Georgia, Washington Co., Estate of Michael Ikener, Inventory and Appraisement
Page 14-19

Negro Men - Spencer, Jacob, Bob, Hardy, Doctor, Ceasor, Bill, Bull, John Henry
Negro Women - Mary and child, Adam, Hannah, Suckey, Viney and child, India Ann, Sarah and child, Mark, Nancy, Betsey, Leman and child, Mitchell, Nelly and two children, George and Harry, Lucinda (girl), Eve, Roan, Caly, Jinney, Martha, Mary, Tilpha, Marah.
Negro Boys - Reuben, Jim, Jesse, Harvey, Elleck
Appraisers: Bolin Luptot, John Hodges, William Hall
Sale of Personal Property. Among the purchasers were: Arthur Johnson, Daniel McCoy, James Wood, Simeon Bland, John F. Achord, D. R. Tucker, Dennis Stubbs, George Hodges, D. R. Tucker.
2800 acres sold to Daniel R. Tucker on the first Tues. in Dec 1844 before the courthouse door at Sandersville, Ga. 49 vouchers. /s/Rowland Stubbs, Admr.
Recorded: 26 Aug 1845

We do hereby certify that the foregoing contains a true Appraisement and Valuation of the Negroes belonging to the Estate of Thomas Carroll, decd, as produced to us by Andrew McBride and Seaborn I. Mann, qualified Exrs, on 4 Dec 1844
Page 19

John D. Stell, William Miles, Robert Holliday, Thomas B. Gay, Phillip Fitzgarrold, appraisers.
Recorded: 1 Nov 1845

Negroes Sold -
Ben to M. L. Carroll
George and Clark to A. McBride
Harvey to Mary Hammock
Frank to Emily Jane Carroll
Guy to Marcus L. Carroll
Jesse and Bobb to S. I. Weaver
Feb and her 4 children to Francis M. Carroll
Tab and her 1 child to Mary Hammock
Lezzy and Jourdan to A. McBride and E. I. Carroll
Phebe, old and infirm
Martha, Orphan of Jonathan Mann, in Account Current with Zachariah Mann, Gdn, from 1 Jan 1843 up to 31 Dec 1844 inclusive
Page 20
5 vouchers. Recorded: 1 Nov 1845

Return No. 12, Estate of Thomas Bennett, decd, in Account Current with William Bennett, Admr, to 1 Nov 1845
Page 20. Recorded: 17 Nov 1845

Isaac Hightower, Gdn, in Account Current with Hilliard Hightower
Page 21. Recorded: 17 Nov 1845

Inventory and Appraisement of the Estate of Elizabeth Whaley, late of Fayette Co., decd
Page 21-23

Appraisers: Cainey Strickland, Little Berry Jackson, Zachariah Mann. Recorded: 17 Nov 1845
List of Property Sold - among purchasers were: William P. Whaley, Josiah Whaley and Samuel Whaley
Fayette Co. Inferior Court Ordered to Distribute to Asbury Hull Tilghman, heir and distributee of Aaron Gilghman, late of Fayette Co., decd, his proportionable part of Estate, the first Mon. in Nov. 1845
Page 23

Commissioners: William Bennett, George Ware, John Graves (x, his mark).
Recorded: 17 Jan 1846

A List of the Appraisement of the Perishable Property Belonging to the Estate of William Osborn, decd, this 22 Day of Oct 1845
Page 23-25
Commissioners sworn 22 Oct 1845 - W. P. Allen, W. H. Flowers, Seaborn Jones

A List of the Personal Property Sold 22 Oct 1845. Among purchasers were: Martha Osborn, Mary Osborn, James Osborn, I. Osborn. Recorded: 24 Jan 1846

The Estate of Thomas Carroll, in Account Current with Seaborn J. Weaver, one of the Exrs, from 1 Jan to 31 Dec 1844 inclusive
Page 26

Sale of 4 Lots in Carroll Co.
To hire of negroes - Lizzie, Ben, Harry, Bob, George, Tab, Jesse

Legatees: Mary Hammock, James Carroll, Thomas Carroll, John Carroll, Elizabeth Carroll
Recorded: 24 Jan 1846

Inventory and Appraisement of the Goods and Chattels of Samuel Thompson, Sr., late of Fayette Co., decd
Page 26-28
T. Mathews, J. A. Smith, E. Moore, Drewry B. Mays, appraisers

Return No. 5, the Estate of Thomas Carroll, decd, in Account Current with A. McBride, Exr, from 1 Jan to 31 Dec 145 inclusive
Page 28-31

Recorded: 7 Mary 1846

Return No. 3, Estate of F. G. Stewart, decd, in Account Current with Martin N. Burch, Admr, Dec 1835 to date
Page 31

Recorded: 4 Mar 1846

Return No. 5, Estate of Thomas Carroll, decd, in Account Current with A. McBride, Exr, 1 Jan to 31 Dec 1845 inclusive
Page 31
Legatees: Thomas Carroll and Sterling Elder for Joshua Carroll

Inventory and Appraisement of Estate of John McLeroy, decd
Page 32-33

Reuben Wallis, Philip Fitzgerald, John M. Murphy, John Jackson (x, his mark), Appraisers.

Account of Personal Property on 21 Nov 1845. Purchasers were: Martha McLeroy, Thomas King, A. McBride, John M. Murphy and Birde Jackson.
Recorded: 2 Apr 1846

Return No. 1, Estate of Bryan Griggs, decd, in Account Current with George Ware, one of the Admrs from 1st Jul to 31st Dec 1845 inclusive
Page 33

Recorded: 2 Apr 1844

Estate of Pitt W. Milner, decd, in Account Current with Adaline M. Cowan, formerly Milner, Admx, from 6 Jun 1845 to 1 Dec 1845 inclusive
Page 34

To hire of negroes - Burrell, Anthony, Squire and William
Recorded: 3 Apr 1844

An Account of the Sale of the Personal Property of Pitt W. Milner, decd, late of Alabama, Sold 24 Mar 1846 in the Town of Fayetteville, Ga.
Page 34-35

Among the purchasers: Joseph S. Cowen.
Recorded: 11 Apr 1844

Estate of Michael Ikener, decd, in Account Current with Roland Stubbs, Admr, from 1 Jan to 31 Dec 1845 inclusive
Page 36-37

14 vouchers. Recorded: 13 Apr 1844

Return No. 1, Estate of Reuben Millsaps, decd, in Account Current with John Williams, Admr, and Perthena Millsaps, Admr, from 1 Sept 1844 to 31 Dec 1845 inclusive. Page 36-37

18 vouchers. Voucher #6 to T. M. Millsaps.
Recorded: 16 Apr 1844

Mary Ann, minor heir of James Fitzgerald, in Account Current with Philip Fitzgerald, Gdn, from 1 Jan to 31 Dec 1845 inclusive
Page 38-39

Cash paid for tuition. Recorded: 29 Jun 1846

Estate of Elisha Check, decd, in Account Current with Philip Fitzgerald, Admr, from 1 Jan to 31 Dec 1845 inclusive
Page 38-39

9 vouchers. Recorded: 29 Jun 1844

James D., minor of James Fitzgerald, decd, in Account Current with Philip Fitzgerald, from 1 Jan 1844 to 31 Dec inclusive
Page 38-39
8 vouchers. Recorded: 27 Jun 1844

Estate of Wright Martin, decd, in Account Current with Nancy Martin, Showing the
Condition of the Estate from the time of appointmen to May Term of 1844 of the
Court of Ordinary
Page 40-49

Sold negroes - Frank and Sellar (woman). Old negro woman, Polly, deceased.
Negroes: Peter, Randall, Stephen, Frank, Rachael, Phebea, Ann, Hiram, Ebenezer,
Emily, Eady. Hannah was bought.

Recorded: 29 Jun 1844

Estate of Aaron Tilghman, decd, in Account Current with William Miles, Exr, from
1 Jan to 31 Dec 1845 inclusive
Page 40-41

Sale of Negroes -
Boy, Joe, to Jeptha Landrum
Boy, Sandford, to E. Moon
Boy, Richmond, to Benjamin Starr
Boy, Ellick, to Williamson Jenkins.
Recorded: 29 Jun 1844

Wiley A., minor child of H. Pate, in Account Current with H. Pate from 1 Jan to
31 Dec 1845 inclusive
Page 42-43

Recorded: 29 May 1844

Return No. 5, Estate of John Brogden, decd, in Account Current with Alfred Brown
Page 42-43

4 vouchers. Recorded: 29 May 1844

Helen M. and John C., Orphans of Samuel W. Cox, in Account Current with John D.
Stell, Admr, from 1 Jan 1843 up to 31 Dec 1845 inclusive
Page 42-43

Recorded: 25 Jul 1844

Estate of William Whaley, decd, in Account Current with William Jackson, Admr de
bonis non, from 1 Jan to 31 Dec 1845 inclusive
Page 42-43

3 vouchers. Recorded: 25 Jul 1844

Amanda, Orphan of M. T. Bishop, in Account Current with James Graves, Gdn, from
the 1st Jan 1842 to 31 Dec 1845 inclusive
Page 44-45

Recorded: 9 Sept 1844

Return No. 4, Martha, Elizabeth and Elisha G., minors, in Account Current with
Elisha Hill, Gdn, from 1 Jan 1844 to 31 Dec 1845 inclusive
Page 44-45

Recorded: 9 Sept 1844
Return No. 2, Estate of Isaiah Warren, in Account Current with G. and B.
Westbrook, from 1 Jan to 31 Dec 1845 inclusive
Page 44

Recorded: 21 Sept 1844

Return No. 6, Turner and Sarah Bedsil, in Account Current with John O. Dickson,
Gdn, from the 1st of Jan to 31st Dec 1845 inclusive
Page 45

3 vouchers. Recorded: 21 Sept 1844

Return No. 5, Estate of Joh Nichols, decd, in Account Curret with Benjamin
Neal, Admr, from 1 Jan 1844 to 31 Dec 1845 inclusive
Page 46

4 vouchers. Recorded: 21 Sept 1844

A list of the Perishable Property of Samuel Thompson, decd, Sold on 29th, 30th
and 31st days of Dec 1845
Page 47-50

Among the purchasers were: John Smith, William Whatley, Dennis Stubbs, Benjamin
G. Fortson, Oliver Spradlin. Recorded: 12 Oct 1844

Return No. 4, Estate of Drury May, decd, in Account Current with James E. May
and Lovzinski Glass, Admrs, 1 Jan 1844 to 1 Jan 1845 inclusive
Page 50

10 vouchers. Legatees: L. Glass and J. V. May. Recorded: 13 Nov 1844

Martha E., minor child of John Hays, decd, in Account Current with David Haney,
Gdn, from 1 Jan to 2 Mar 1844 inclusive
Page 50-5

Recorded: 13 Nov 1844

Inventory and Appraisement of Estate, Both Real and Personal, of Avington B.
Williams, late of Fayette Co., decd
Page 51

Includes Lots No. 118, 119, 140, and 1/2 of Lot No. 116.

Negroes - Morris, Bile, Viney, Hannah, Alsey, Caroline and Henry

Inventory and Appraisement of the Estate of Oliver McLean, decd
Page 52-53

Appraisers: William Brassell, Jesse Jones and John C. Brassell. Recorded: 1 Jan 1847

Estate of William Osborn, decd, in Account Current with Gay Upchurch, Admr, from 1 Jan to 31 Dec 1846 inclusive
Page 54

10 vouchers. To cash paid - A. Poole, F. M. Jones, Guy Upchurch, A. Tomlinson, Frazier & Moon, Seaborn Smith, Robert Miller, M. H. Flowers, and B. Flowers. Recorded: 28 Jan 1847

Estate of J. T. L. Barnes, decd, in Account Current with Gay Upchurch, Admr, from 1 Jan 1845 to 31 Dec 1846 inclusive
Page 54-55

13 vouchers. To cash paid - Michael Barnes, William B. Hardeman, W. D. Barns, W. E. Crumbie, T. M. Jones and Robert Holliday. Recorded: 28 Jan 1849

Martha Ann, minor child of John Hayes, in Account Current with David Hayes, Gdn, from 1 Jan to 31 Dec 1844 inclusive
Page 55

by amount of - Cynthia Hays, Samuel G. Pegg and Samuel G. Jones, Jesse Lasseter, James Davis, James Spence, E. Haines, S. W. Parham and Ambrose Blackwell. Recorded: 28 Jan 1847

Estate of John Brogden, in Account Current with Alfred Brown, Admr, from 1 Jan to 31 Dec 1846 inclusive
Page 56
Recorded: 28 Jan 1847

Estate of Aaron Tilghman, decd, in Account Current with William Miles, Exr, from 1 Jan to 31 Dec 1846 inclusive
Page 56
To cash paid - Thomas Byrne. Recorded: 28 Jan 1847

Inventory and Appraisement of the Goods, Chattels and Credits of the Estate of John Sellers, decd, as produced us by the Admr of said Estate on the 14th and 15th Jan 1847
Page 57-58

Appraisers: Paschal E. Collins, J. M. Barfield, Jordan & Goodson, Jared I. Whitaker, and Thomas B. Gay.
Recorded: 28 Jan 1847

A List of the Sale of the Perishable Property of A. B. Williams, decd, sold on 13th Nov 1846
Page 59-60
Among the purchasers were: Widow, James M. Barfield, Robert R. Freeman, William Jacobs, William A. Reeves and Allen Reeves. Recorded: 30 Jan 1847

Return No. 2, Estate of Reuben Millsaps, decd, in Account Current with John Williams, Admr, from 1 Jan to 31 Dec 1846 inclusive
Page 60-61

23 vouchers. Legatees: P. Millsaps, O. Millsaps, L. Millsaps, H. Millsaps, W. H. Blalock, I. Williams.
Recorded: 15 Mar 1847

Estate of David J. Berry, decd, in Account Current with E. P. Allen, Admr, 1 Jan 1845 to 31 Dec 1846 inclusive
Page 61
Recorded: 15 Mar 1847

Mary Ann, Orphan of James Fitzgerald, decd, in Account Current with P. Fitzgerald, Gdn, from 1 Jan to 31 Dec 1846 inclusive
Page 62

8 vouchers. To cash paid - T. Byrom, W. F. Herring, I. H. Johnson, Thomas H. Whitley, M. Vincent Mahoney and P. Fitzgerald. Recorded: 15 mar 1847

Helen M. and John C., Orphans of Samuel W. Cox, decd, in Account Current with John D. Stell, Gdn, from 1 Jan to 31 Dec 1846 inclusive
Page 62
Recorded: 15 Mar 1847

Meriman P. Champion, Orphan of Abner M. Champion, in Account Current with William C. Champion, Gdn, from 1 Jan to 31 Dec 1845 inclusive
Page 63

6 vouchers. Recorded: 15 Mar 1847

Synthia A. Champion, Orphan of Abner M. Champion, in Account Current with William C. Champion, Gdn, from 1 Jan to 31 Dec 1845 inclusive
Page 63

6 vouchers. Recorded: 15 Mar 1847

Adison Champion, Orphan of Abner M. Champion, in Account Current with William C. Champion, Gdn, from 1 Jan to 31 Dec 1845 inclusive
Page 63
Recorded: 15 Mar 1847

Abner G. Champion, Orphan of Abner M. Champion, in Account Current with William C. Champion, Gdn, from 1 Jan to 31 Dec 1845 inclusive
Page 64
Recorded: 15 Mar 1847

Meriman P. Champion, Orphan of Abner M. Champion, in Account Current with
William C. Champion, Gdn, from 1 Jan to 31 Dec 1846 inclusive
Page 64

Recorded: 15 Mar 1847

Synthia Champion, Orphan of Abner M. Champion, in Account Current with William
C. Champion, Gdn, from 1 Jan to 31 Dec 1846 inclusive
Page 64-65

Recorded: 15 Mar 1847

Adison C. Champion, Orphan of Abner M. Champion, in Account Current with William
C. Champion, Gdn, from 1 Jan to 31 Dec 1846 inclusive
Page 65

Recorded: 15 Mar 1847

Abner G. Champion, Orphan of Abner M. Champion, in Account Current with William
C. Champion, Gdn, from 1 Jan to 31 Dec 1846 inclusive
Page 65

Recorded: 15 Mar 1847

Emily I., Orphan of Thomas Carroll, decd, in Account Current with A. McBride,
Gdn, from 1 Jan to 31 Dec 1845 inclusive
Page 66

7 vouchers. To cash paid - 1845 taxes, T. Byrne, M. M. Tidwell, J. F. Johnson,
A. McBride
Recorded: 15 Mar 1847

James P., minor heir of James Fitzgerald, decd, in Account Current with P.
Fitzgerald, from 1 Jan to 31 Dec 1846 inclusive
Page 66

7 vouchers. Recorded: 15 Mar 1847

Return No.1, Estate of Samuel Thompson, decd, in Account Current with Lewis
Thompson, Exr, from date of Letters to 31 Dec 1846 inclusive
Page 67

20 vouchers. Legatees: L. T. Thompson and Ellen Thompson. Recorded: 16 Mar 1849

Estate of Bryan Griggs, decd, in Account Current with George Ware and Rocella
Griggs, Admrs, from 1 Jan to 31 Dec 1846 inclusive
Page 68

7 vouchers. Recorded: 1 Mar 1847

List of Sales of Town Property and Negroes Belonging to the Estate of Pitt W.
Milner, Sold on the 1st Tues. in Feb 1847
Page 68

Negroes sold -

Antony to Parker Eason
Squire to William G. Brown
Burrell to William Herring
William to John H. Milner
Frank to M. M. Tidwell
Lucy to Henry McLeroy
Henry to B. O. Jones
(women) Charity and Lemas to William N. Shell

Recorded: 16 Mar 1847

Francis M., Orphan of Thomas Carroll, decd, in Account Current with A. McBride,
Gdn, from 1 Jan to 31 Dec 1845 inclusive
Page 69

5 vouchers. Recorded: 6 Jun 1847

Estate of Michael Ikenor, decd, in Account Current with Roland Stubbs, Admr, up
to 31 Dec 1846
Page 69

5 vouchers. Recorded: 6 Jun 1847

Ira B. Meadors, minor of A. Meadors, decd, in Account Current with E. P.Allen,
Gdn, from 1 Jan 1845 to 31 Dec 1846 inclusive
Page 70

Property on hand - Negro boy, Robert, about 5, Fannie, about 12, and Robert.
Received for hire of negro girl, Fassey, for 1846. Recorded: 6 Jun 1847

Inventory and Appraisement of the Perishable Property of Albert G. Hancock, late
of Fayette Co., decd
Page 70-71

Appraisers: Gay Upchurch, John M. Osborn, William Shadrick. Recorded: 6 Jun 1847

A List of the Property of A. G. Hancock, decd
Page 71

Recorded: 9 Jul 1847

Return No. 1, Estate of A. B. Williams, decd, in Account Current with James H.
Williams, Admr, from 1 Jan 1846 to 31 Dec 1846 inclusive
Page 72
4 vouchers. Recorded: 9 Jul 1847

Orphans of Josiah Warren, decd, in Account Current with G. and B. Westbrook, from 1 Jan to 31 Dec 1846 inclusive
Page 72
2 vouchers. Recorded: 9 Jul 1847

An Account Credit with E. P. Allen, Admr of A. Meadors, decd, from 1 Jan 1846 to 31 Dec inclusive
Page 73

9 vouchers. To cash paid - M. Bozee, B. J. Hill, P. Fitzgerald, A. J. Brown, E. P. Memor, S. Fuller, L. Petills, S. W. Minor, S. Plier, I. T. Meadors, P. J. Morrow, Fi.Fa. Clerk of Superior Court.
/s/I. T. Meadors, former Admr

Estate of Abraham Meadors, decd, in Account Current with Elijah P. Allen, Admr, from the time of appointment to 31 Dec 1845 inclusive
Page 74
11 vouchers. Recorded: 9 Jul 1847

Inventory and Appraisement of Estate of Isaac Hughs, decd
Page 74-75

Appraisers: Andrew McBride, Robert Holliday, Sr. and Almond Stratton.
One negro woman, Aggy, one judgment against Daniel R. Thomas and George Allen obtained a the March Term 1846 of the Superior Court of Fayette Co.

Inventory and Appraisement of the Estate of W. H. Cavender, taken 9 Jul 1847
Page 75-77

Lots 16 and 163 in 4th District of Fayette, Co., 65 acres. Recorded: 17 Aug 1847

An Account of the Sale of the Personal Estate of R. Beall, decd, 1 Nov 1838
Page 78-81

Among purchasers were: Thadeus Beall, P. O. Beall, Mrs. M. A. H. Beall.
To hire of negroes, Ben to James W. Alford, Violet and child and Lizi and 3 children to James W. Alford, and renting of plantation to Jesse Pope. Town Lot to Eli Edmondson. Recorded: 21 Sept 1847

Inventory and Appraisement of the Estate of Thomas Watson, late of Fayette Co., decd
Page 81-82

Includes Lot 22 in 7th District of Fayette Co.
Appraisers sworn 7 May 1847: D. D. Denham, R. C. Ellington, Williamson Jenkins
Recorded: 22 Sept 1847

A List of the Sale of the Perishable Property of Thomas Watson, decd, on 18 Jun 1847. Page 83-85

Among purchasers were: Widow, William Watson, John Watson, and W. Watson.
Recorded: 22 Sept 1847

Estate of Augustus R. Beall, decd, in Account Current with P. O. Beall, Admr, from 12 May 1845 to 31 Dec 1847 inclusive
Page 85

3 vouchers. Recorded: 22 Sept 1847

Sale of the Property of W. H. Cavender, decd, Sold 21 Sept 1847
Page 85-87

Among the purchasers was: Delilah Cavender. Recorded: 26 Oct 1847

Sale of the Property of Oliver McLean, decd, Sold 22 Dec 1846
Page 88-89

Among the purchasers: Mary McLean. Recorded: 12 Jan 1848

Temporary Inventory of the Estate of Dempsey A. Reeves, late of Fayette Co., decd
Page 89

Recorded: 13 Jan 1848

Estate of Oliver McLean, decd, in Account Current with John McLean, decd, from the date of Ltrs Nov Term 1846 to 31 Dec 1847 inclusive
Page 90

17 vouchers. Legatee: John McLean. Recorded: 13 Jan 1848

Return No. 1, Estate of Wade H. Cavender, decd, in Account Current with John C. Brassell, Admr, from date of Ltrs at Jul Term 1847 to 31 Dec 1847 inclusive
Page 91

9 vouchers. Recorded: 27 Jan 1848

William N. Hill, Gdn of Mary Elisabeth and Susan Adaline, minor heirs of Pitt W. Milner, decd, from 3 May to 31 Dec 1847 inclusive
Page 91-92
6 vouchers. Recorded: 27 Jan 1848

Meriman P. Champion, minor of Abner Champion, decd, in Account Current with William C. Champion, Gdn, from 1 Jan 1847 to 31 Dec 1847 inclusive
Page 92
4 vouchers. Recorded: 27 Jan 1848

Cynthia A. Champion, minor of Abner Champion, decd, in Account Current with William C. Champion, Gdn, from 1 Jan 1847 to 31 Dec 1847 inclusive
Page 92-93
6 vouchers. Recorded: 27 Jan 1848

Adison I. Champion, minor of Abner Champion, decd, in Account Current with William C. Champion, Gdn, from 1 Jan 1847 to 31 Dec 1847 inclusive
Page 93

5 vouchers. Recorded: 27 Jan 1848

Abner G. Champion, minor of Abner Champion, decd, in Account Current with William C. Champion, Gdn, from 1 Jan 1847 to 31 Dec 1847 inclusive
Page 93-94

5 vouchers. Recorded: 27 Jan 1848

Elisabeth, minor child of Elisha Hill, in Account Current with Elisha Hill, Gdn, from 1 Jan to 31 Dec 1847 inclusive
Page 94

Recorded: 27 Jan 1848

Inventory and Appraisement of Estate, Both Real and Personal, of Dempsey A. Reeves, decd, with the necessary certificates annexed, to-wit:
Page 95

Appraisers: William Reeves, Allen Reeves, William T. Bates. Recorded: 24 Feb 1848

Inventory of the Property, Real and Personal, of Robert R. Smarr, decd
Page 96-97

500 1/4 acres in 4th District of Fayette Co.
320 acres in Chambers Co., Alabama
40 acres in Cass Co.
Negroes - Winston, Aarron, Nelson, Tour, Bashr,, Joseph, Henry, Malissa, Mary, Delila and child Hamilton, Ailsey, Emma, Sally, Isabela, Harriet, Eliza.

Appraisers: William Reeves, Alfred Brown, I. H. Crittendon, John I. Whitaker
Recorded: 24 Feb 1848

List of Sale of the Personal Property of P. A. Reeves, decd, Sold 1 Jul 1848
Page 98

Among the purchasers were: E. Reeves, W. D. Reeves, Wyatt D. Reeves, A. M. Reeves, William B. Reeves, and J. F. Reeves.

Estate of William Osborn, decd, in Account Current with Gay Upchurch, Exr, from 1 Jan to 31 Dec 1847 inclusive
Page 99

6 vouchers. Legatees: James R. D. Osborn, William G. Osborn, Robert Miller, Huie Jackson and W. P. Smith.

Recorded: 28 Mar 1848

Return No. 1, Estate of Atha Jarrott, decd, in Account Current with Benjamin Starr, Exr, from the time of Receiving of Ltrs to 31 Dec 1846
Page 99

Paid legatees in full of their distributive shares of said estate as per Voucher No. 1.
Recorded: 29 Mar 1848

Estate of Pitt W. Milner, late of Alabama, decd, in Account Current with James F. Johnson, Admr de bonis non from the 31st day of Dec 1846 to 31st day of Dec 1847 inclusive
Page 100-101

Paid T. H. Whitley, tuition for: Sophronia, Elisabeth, John, Pitt, James.
Recorded: 29 Mar 1848

Return No. 1, Estate of John McLeroy, decd, in Account Current with Martha McLeroy, Admx, 1 Jan 1846 to 31 Dec 1846 inclusive
Page 102

10 vouchers. Martha McLeroy received support for herself and child for one year.
Recorded: 3 Apr 1848

A List of the Sale of a Part of the Perishable and Personal Property of the Estate of John Sellers, decd, Sold on the 13th day of Mar 1847
Page 103-106
Among the purchasers were: Widow Sellers, Willis Champion, Ishmael Dunn.

A Bill of the Sale of the Balance of the Perishable Property. The major purchasers were: Paschal E. Collins and Willis A. Jordan.
Recorded: 6 Apr 1848

Estate of Albert G. Hancock, decd, in Account Current with A. L. Huie, Admr, from 1 Mar to 31 Dec 1849
Page 106
2 vouchers. Recorded: 6 Apr 1848

Orphans of Isaiah Warren, decd, in Account Current with Gainy Westbrook, Gdn, from 1 Jan to 31 Dec 1849 inclusive
Page 107
2 vouchers. Recorded: 6 Apr 1848

Helen M. and John C. Cox, Orphans of Samuel W. Cox, decd, in Account Current with John D. Stell, Gdn, from 1 Jan to 31 Dec 1847 inclusive
Page 107
2 vouchers. Recorded: 6 Mar 1848

Elisa, Orphan of Matthew T. Bishop, decd, in Account Current with William G. Smith, Gdn, from 1 Jan to 31 Dec 1847 inclusive
Page 108
2 vouchers. Recorded: 6 Apr 1848

Estate of Samuel Thompson, decd, in Account Current with Lewis H. Thompson, Exr, from 1 Jan to 31 Dec 1847 inclusive
Page 108-109

19 vouchers. To cash paid legatees - Allen Thompson, Elisabeth Thompson, Samuel Thompson, Jeremiah Thompson, I. T. Wheatlen, Larkin Millsaps and L. T. Thompson. Recorded: 10 Apr 1848

Inventory and Appraisement of the Estate of William P. Whaley, late of Fayette Co.
Page 109-110

Appraisers sworn on 13 Apr 1848: Zachariah Mann, Thomas Simpson, George Stewart and Thomas F. Brown. Recorded: 4 May 1848

The Following is a List of the Sale of the Personal Property of William P. Whaley, decd, late of Fayette Co., Sold on 19th day of Apr 1848
Page 110-111

Among the purchasers were: S. R. Whaley, Hiram Whaley, Josiah Whaley and Samuel Whaley.
Recorded: 4 May 1848

Inventory and Appraisement of the Estate of Kinchen Strickland, decd, 21 Apr 1848. Page 112-113

A. I. Mundy, Admr. Appraisers: Jesse Ware, I. T. Anthony, and I. C. Williams
Recorded: 8 May 1848

Inventory and Appraisement of the Estate of Francis M. Carroll, decd, as produced to us by Eli Edmondson, Admr
Page 113

Negroes - Feb and infant child, Matilda, Charles, Rachael, George, Allen. Appraisers: John D. Stell, W. N. Hill, Robert Holliday, Sr. and Almond Stratton. Recorded: 8 Jun 1848

Inventory and Appraisement of the Estate of Francis Price
Page 113-114

Negroes - Esther (girl), Lewis, Jordan, James, Anna and child, Charlotte, Lucinda. Lot Nos. 98, 95, 96 and 67. Appraisers: James E. May, Hiram Travis, T. C. Mathis. Recorded: 8 Jun 1848

Nancy T., Orphan of M. T. Bishop, in Account Current with Jesse Ward, Gdn, from time of his appointment to 31 Dec 1847 inclusive
Page 115

1 voucher. To cash received from James Graves and L. C. Smith. Recorded: 23 Aug 1848

Thomas C., Orphan of I. Bosworth, decd, in Account Current with Josiah R. Bosworth, Gdn, from 1 Jan 1843 to 31 Dec 1847 inclusive
Page 115

12 vouchers. To cash paid - Sarah Reese, I. H. Johnson, William Hadden, Josiah R. Bosworth, A. N. Clardy, Thomas Byrom, and B. O. Jones.

Recorded: Jul Term 1848

An Account Current with E. Paller, Admr of Abram Meadors, decd, from 1 Jan to 31 Dec 1847
Page 116

To cash paid Oliver Chase and W. B. Fuller. Recorded: 23 Aug 1848

An Account Current with Elijah P. Allen, Gdn of Ira B. Meadors, minor of A. Meadors, decd, from 1 Jan 1847 to 31 Dec inclusive
Page 116

Received of William McKown for hire of a negro girl, Nancy
Received of I. H. Niblet for hire of a negro boy, Robert
Recorded: 23 Aug 1848

Estate of Michael IKenor, decd, in Account Current with Roland Stubbs, Admr, from 1 Jan to 31 Dec 1847 inclusive
Page 116-117

8 vouchers. Sarah Stubbs, legatee. Recorded: 28 Aug 1848

Estate if A. B. Williams, decd, in Account Current with James H. Williams, Admr, from 1st Jan to 31st Dec 1847 inclusive
Page 117-118

20 vouchers. To cash paid - John McLean, S. W. Bloodworth, James I. Stell, 1847 tax, Moses Williams, James Spurlin, William Brasley, Drury Nicholls, James H. Williams, John D. Stell, William Reeves, Murray & Logan, William T. Baks, J. B. Sargent & co., J. Y. Reeves, Green Page, and John M. Faulkner.

Recorded: 28 Aug 1848

Estate of Bryan Griggs, decd, in Account Current with George Mann, Admr, from 1st Jan to 31st Dec 1847 inclusive
Page 118-119

17 vouchers. Recorded: 3 Jul 1848

Estate of Oliver McLean, in Account Current with John McLean, Exr, from 1st Jan to 31st Dec 1848 inclusive
Page 119

8 vouchers. To cash paid - George H. Page, W. B. Fuller, Miles Ward, Thomas H. Duffell, Mary McLean, Anny Pranson, Hiram Moses and John McLean.

Recorded: 15 Dec 1848

Martha A., Orphan of Sterling Elder, decd, in Account Current with Charles Clements, Gdn, from 1st Jan 1843 to 31st Dec 1846 inclusive
Page 120

9 vouchers. To cash paid - Bosworth Landrum, T. Byrum, William Whatley, M. M. Tidwell, I. H. Johnson and Watts & Minafer. Recorded: 15 Dec 1848

Martha E. Hays, minor, in Account Current with David Haynes, Gdn, from 1 Jan to 31 Dec 1847 inclusive
Page 120

Recorded: 15 Dec 1848

Estate of John Whaley, decd, in Account Current with Patrick H. Allen, Admr, from 1 Jan 1847 to 1 Nov 1848 inclusive
Page 121

5 vouchers. To cash paid - John W. Wilkins, W. H. Blalock, Mary Whaley, I. Johnson, and W. B. Fuller. Recorded: 15 Dec 1848

Estate of William H. Avera, decd, in Account Current with Isaac B. Avera, Admr, from date of Ltrs to 31 Dec 1847 inclusive
Page 121

7 vouchers. To cash paid - R. M. Avera, Mrs. R. Avera, S. W. Minor, and 1847 tax. Recorded: 4 Sept 1848

Inventory and Appraisement of the Estate of John T. Storey, decd on 1 Feb 1848
Page 122

M. M. Tidwell, Admr
Appraisers: J. L. Blalock, W. N. Hill, W. N. Blalock, Almond Stratton.
Recorded: 18 Dec 1848

List of Sale of the Personal Property of John T. Storey, decd
Page 122

Purchasers were: W. N. Hill, W. J. Russell, James A. Newton, E. E. Cleckler, John O. Dickson, M. M. Tidwell, Barnard Lamb and T. M. Millsaps.

Inventory and Appraisement of the Estate of William F. M. Elder, minor of Joshua Elder, decd
Page 123

Negroes - William, age 18, Daniel, age 16, Clemency, age 10, Pamelia, age 7, and Mariah, age 40
Appraisers: Josiah H. Elder, Charles Clements, Marberry Sparks
Recorded: 22 Jan 149

Appraisement of the Estate of John Westmoreland, decd, taken 16 Dec 1848
Page 123-125

Appraisers: Thomas Coppedge, Parry Hicks, Hiram Travis and A. Gray
Recorded: 22 Jan 1849

The Following is a True and Perfect Inventory of the Estate of William Attkisson, decd
Page 125-127

Appraisers: Samuel Pyle, L. B. Jackson and Counsel Rentfrow
Jesse Attkisson, Admr
Recorded: 22 Jan 1847

Inventory of Sale of the Perishable Property Belonging to the Estate of William Attkisson, Sold on a Credit until 25 Dec 1849
Page 127-128

Among the purchasers were: Counsel Rentfrow, J. Ward, J. Attkisson, Sarah Attkisson, H. Buffington, F. M. Wakefield. Recorded: 22 Jan 1849

Inventory and Sale of Perishable Property of Kinchen Strickland, decd, Sold on Friday, 28th of Sept 1848
Page 129-131

Among the purchasers were: Widow Kinchen, Harry Strickland, James Smith, Seaborn Smith, John R. Waldroup, Caney Strickland. Recorded: 22 Jan 1849

Inventory and Appraisement of the Estate of Jesse Lasseter, decd
Page 131-133

Included was - Negro woman, Eliza.
Appraisers: Caleb Simmons, Samuel G. Pegg, W. E. Tucker
Recorded: 22 Jan 1849

Meriman P. Champion, minor of Abner Champion, decd, in Account Current with William Champion, Gdn, from 1st Jan to 31st Dec 1848 inclusive
Page 133

2 vouchers. Recorded: 23 Jan 1849

Synthia A. Champion, minor of Abner Champion, decd, in Account Current with William Champion, Gdn, from 1st Jan to 31st Dec 1848 inclusive
Page 133

5 vouchers. Recorded: 23 Jan 1849

Adison Champion, minor of Abner Champion, decd, in Account Current with William Champion, Gdn, from 1st Jan to 31st Dec 1848 inclusive
Page 134

5 vouchers. Recorded: 23 Jan 1849

Abner G. Champion, minor of Abner Champion, decd, in Account Current with William Champion, Gdn, from 1st Jan to 31st Dec 1848 inclusive
Page 134

3 vouchers. Recorded: 23 Jan 1849

Estate of Robert R. Smarr, decd, in Account Current with Martha C. Cox, Admx, from 10 Jan 1848 to 1 Dec 1848 inclusive
Page 135-136

22 vouchers. To cash paid - T. Byrom, Chapman Hill & Cox, J. H. Johnson, B. W. Doo, Daniel Long, Richardson & Merrit, Sims & Threlkeld, William Blackman, William G. Edwards, William Cline, M. Glass, William Pollard, H. Rentfrow & Co., John H. Reeves and Martha C. Smarr, Admx.

Recorded: 23 Jan 1849

January 1849. P. Eason, Gdn for Mary Elisabeth Milner and William Milner, minors of Pitt W. Milner
Page 136

Recorded: 23 Jan 1849

Mary Ann, Orphan of James Fitzgerald, decd, in Account Current with Phillip F. Fitzgerald, Gdn, from 1 Jan to 31 Dec 1847 inclusive
Page 136-137

5 vouchers. To cash paid - J. H. Johnson, T. Stratton, M. V. Mahoney, T. Byrne, and Gdn.
Recorded: 23 Jan 1849

James P., minor of James Fitzgerald, decd, in Account Current with Phillip F. Fitzgerald, Gdn, from 1 Jan to 31 Dec 1847 inclusive
Page 137

8 vouchers. To cash paid - Nancy Fitzgerald, P. Stratton, J. H. Johnson, S. D. Dorsey, T. H. Whitley, T. Byrne, and R. Roberts. Recorded: 23 Jan 1849

Alexander L. Huie, Admr of the Estate of Albert G. Hancock, decd, from 1 Jan 1848 to 31 Dec 1848 inclusive
Page 138

10 vouchers. To cash paid - Mary Hancock, C. T. Hancock, R. C. Huie, Murray & Logan, C. Bowlin, W. P. Allen, A. L. Huie, 1847-1848 tax.
Recorded: 23 Jan 1849

Estate of Aaron Tilghman, decd, in Account Current with William Miles, Exr, from 1 Jan to 31 Dec 1847 inclusive
Page 138-139

7 vouchers. To hire of negro boy, Joe, to William Whatley. To hire of negro boy, Rich, to J. Landrum. Legatee: Seaborn Phillips
Recorded: 23 Jan 1849

Eliza, Orphan of Matthew T. Bishop, decd, in Account Current with William G. Smith, Gdn, from 1 Jan to 31 Dec 1848 inclusive
Page 139

2 vouchers. Recorded: 23 Jan 1849

William N. Hill, Gdn of Susan Adaline, Orphan of Pitt W. Milner, decd, from 1 Jan to 31 Dec 1848 inclusive
Page 140

3 vouchers. Recorded: 23 Jan 1849

Estate of Thomas Watson, decd, in Account Current with William Watson, Admr, from the time of appointment, 1 Mar 1847 to 31 Dec inclusive
Page 141

15 vouchers. By sale of negro man, Milton. Recorded: 24 Jan 1849

Inventory and Appraisement of Estate of Joseph Anthony, decd
Page 142-144

Appraisers: Samuel G. Pegg, W. A. Beorny, A. J. Brown
Recorded: 15 Mar 1849

Return No. 2, Nancy, Orphan of Mathew T. Bishop, in Account Current with Jesse Ward, Gdn, from 1 Jan t 31 Dec 1848 inclusive
Page 144

Recorded: 16 Mar 1849

John C. Cox, minor heir of Samuel W. Cox, decd, in Account Current with John D. Stell, Gdn, from 1 Jan to 31 Dec 1848 inclusive
Page 144

2 vouchers. Recorded: 2 Apr 1849

Estate of Wade H. Cavender, decd, in Account Current with John O. Brassell, Gdn, from 1 Jan to 31 Dec 1848 inclusive
Page 145

To cash paid - P. H. Brassell, James E. May, A. Gray, R. B. Bridges, A. McBride, Oliver M. Pearson, Joshua Grace, G. H. Page and Delilah Cavender.
Recorded: 2 Apr 1849

Martha E., minor of John M. Haze, decd, in Account Current with David Hains, Gdn, from 1 Jan to 31 Dec 1848 inclusive
Page 145

Recorded: 2 Apr 1849

Estate of William Osborn, decd, in Account Current with Gay Upchurch, Admr, from 1 Jan to 31 Dec 1848 inclusive
Page 146

3 vouchers. To cash paid - William McMichael, M. E. Jackson.
Recorded: 16 Apr 1849

Orphan of Josiah Warren, decd, in Account Current with Gainey Westbrook, Gdn, from 1 Jan to 31 Dec 1848 inclusive
Page 146

4 vouchers. To cash paid - Henry Rentfrow, David Partlow, Nancy Partlow, Abram Warren.
Recorded: 11 Apr 1849

Estate of Bryan Griggs, decd, in Account Current with George Ware, Admr, from 1 Jan to 31 Dec 1848 inclusive
Page 147

8 vouchers. Recorded: 16 Apr 1849

Estate of Dempsey A. Reeves, in Account Current with Wyatt S. Reeves, Admr, from 1 Jan t 31 Dec 1848 inclusive
Page 147

2 vouchers. Recorded: 17 Apr 1849

Estate of A. B. Williams, decd, in Account Current with James B. Williams, Admr, from 1 Jan to 31 Dec 1848 inclusiveb
Page 148

12 vouchers. To cash paid - Thomas C. Mathews, Gdn, Martin C. Smarr, M. Reed, Jacob Bently, J. M. Word, M. Westmoreland, John R. Jones, Mary Logan.

Legatee: P. Williams.
Recorded: 17 Apr 1849

Estate of Reuben Millsaps, decd, in Account Current with John Williams, Admr, from 1 Jan to 31 Dec 1847 inclusive
Page 149

14 vouchers. To cash paid legatees: John Williams, P. Millsaps, Larkin Millsaps, Olive Millsaps, Hiram Millsaps, Williams Millsaps.
Recorded: 18 Apr 1849

Return No. 3, Emily J., Orphan of Thomas Carroll, decd, in Account Current with A. McBride, Gdn, from 1 Jan to 31 Dec 1846 inclusive
Page 150

4 vouchers. Recorded: 18 Apr 1849

Emily J., Orphan of Thomas Carroll, decd, in Account Current with A. McBride, Gdn, from 1 Jan to 31 Dec 1847 inclusive
Page 150

4 vouchers. Recorded: 18 Apr 1849

Emily J., Orphan of Thomas Carroll, decd, in Account Current with A. McBride, Gdn, from 1 Jan to 31 Dec 1848 inclusive
Page 150-151

4 vouchers. Recorded: 18 Apr 1849

Return No. 3, Francis A., Orphan of Thomas Carroll, in Account Current with A. McBride, Gdn, from 1 Jan to 31 Dec 1846 inclusive
Page 151

5 vouchers. Recorded: 18 Apr 1849

Return No. 4, Francis A., Orphan of Thomas Carroll, in Account Current with A. McBride, Gdn, from 1 Jan to 31 Dec 1847 inclusive
Page 151-152

9 vouchers. Recorded: 18 Apr 1849

Return No. 6, Estate of Thomas Carroll, decd, in Account Current with Andrew McBride, one of the Exrs., from 1 Jan to 31 Dec 1846 inclusive
Page 152

5 vouchers. Recorded: 18 Apr 1849

Return No. 7, Estate of Thomas Carroll, decd, in Account Current with Andrew McBride, one of the Exrs, from 1 Jan to 31 Dec 1847 inclusive
Page 153

2 vouchers. Recorded: 18 Apr 1849

Return No. 8, Estate of Thomas Carroll, decd, in Account Current with Andrew McBride, one of the Exrs, from 1 Jan to 31 Dec 1848 inclusive
Page 153

3 vouchers. Recorded: 18 Apr 1849

Inventory and Appraisement of the Estate of Isaac S. Kimberly, decd
Page 154-155

Appraisers sworn 21 Feb 1849: Henry Rentfro, Caswell Kite, Marcus Long
Recorded: 18 Apr 1849

Inventory and Appraisement of the Estate of Edward Bearden, late of Fayette Co., decd
Page 156-157

Negro boy - Alek
Negro girl - Lena
Negro woman - Jane and child, Jim
Negro woman - Mary and 3 children, viz: Cintha, Mary and Caroline

355 acres, Lots 156 and 157, Fayette Co.

Appraisers: John L. Elder, James Loyd, Samuel Swanson, Sarah H. Ellison, Nathaniel Stinchcomb
Recorded: 18 Apr 1849

Georgia, Fayette Co., We, whose names are hereunto subscribed, being appraisers appointed by the Honorable Court of Ordinary of said County, do hereby certify the following is a true Inventory and Appraisement of the personal effects of Holland Leopard, decd, on 29 Sept 1849, as produced to us by Jeptha Landrum, the Exr
Page 158-159

Appraisers: John Watson, J. J. Wood, J. Palmer, Bryan Allen
Recorded: 12 May 1849

Return No. 4, Account Current 1848 of Elijah P. Allen with Estate of A. Meadows, decd
Page 160

Receipt of E. P. Allen, Gdn for Ira B. Meadows, to hiring of negro girl and boy.
State of Louisaiana, Parish of Jackson, Elijah P. Allen swears the above is a true and correct Return and voucher, on 21 Feb 1849.

To amount received from Margaret Meadows, Gdn of M. Meadows, minor.
To amount collected of George C. Hightower.
To amount received from E. P Allen, Gdn of Ira B. Meadows, minor.

Recorded: 12 May 1849

Inventory and Sale of Property of Joseph Anthony, late of Fayette Co., decd, 12 Jan 1849
Page 160-162

Among the purchasers were: I. M. Anthony, Barr B. Anthony, Bob Anthony, S. M. Anthony
Recorded: 12 May 1849

The Following is a List of the Personal Property of Estate of Francis Price Sold 15 Apr 1848
Page 162-163

Among purchasers were: Samuel Price, Q. S. Price
Recorded: 12 May 1849

Inventory of the Lands and Credits of Wyatt McQuirt, decd, 17 May 1849

Appraisers: Eli Edmondson, Z. Blaylock, Thomas R. Pearson.
Recorded: 25 May 1849

Inventory and Appraisement of Estate of Stephen Smith
Page 164-165

Negroes - Fanny, Hannah, Juda, Seley, Phoeby, James, Fredrick, Clarry, Lizan, Uchee, Mary, Clive, Lucinda, Joseph, Henry, Luois, Emily, Sarah, Betty, Jeff, Joseph and Alsy.

Appraisers: Z. Blaylock, E. Y.Moore, James S. Towson, Harbert Travis (x, his mark)
Recorded: 28 Jun 1849

Inventory and Appraise of Estate of George Ware, decd
Page 165-170

Negroes as follows:

Joe, age 50
Jacob, age 40
Lamb, age 34
Big Jim, age 24
William, age 22
Little Jim, age 21
John, age 20
Peter, age 18
Gabe, age 22
Willie, age 14
Toby, age 11
Nelly, age 40 and child (boy, 2 months old)
Martha, age 25 and girl, age 2
Polly, age 24
Liddy, age 16
Harriet, age 11
Mary, age 9
Booker, age 6
Ben, age 4
Fanny, age 4

Lot No. 125, Fayette Co., includes Millsand improvements
Lot No. 100, Fayette Co.
Lot No. 131, Fayette Co.
1/2 of Lot No. 126, Fayette Co.
1/2 of Lot No. 45, Fayette Co.
Lot No. 66, Fayette Co.
Lot No. 124, Fayette Co.
1/8th of Lot 101, Fayette Co.
160 acres and 4 acres in Floyd Co.

Also includes 60 accounts against a number of people.
Appraisers: B. O. Jones, Nathaniel Stinchcomb, Samuel Swanson and John Elder, sworn 27 Jul 1849

John S. Holliday, Admr. Recorded: 25 Sept 1849

Inventory and Appraisement of the Goods, Chattels and Credits of Isaiah Smith, decd
Page 171-172

Includes 300 acres. Negroes: Henry, Clary, Rachel and child (Willis)
Appraisers: W. P. Allen, William J. Barnes, Cornelius Beavers.
Recorded: 25 Sept 1849

Inventory and Appraisement of the Personal Effects and Real Estate of Thomas Herring, decd, as produced to us by Admr of said Estate, to-wit: Allen Jennings and Mary Ann Herring on 11 Jul 1849

202 1/2 acre, Lot No. 40, 6th District, Fayette Co.
202 1/2 acres, Lot No. 37, 6th District, Fayette Co.
101 1/4 acres, Lot No. 41, 6th District, Fayette Co
202 1/2 acres, Lot No. 49, 6th District, Fayette Co.

Appraisers: Jeptha Landrum, Sr., Nathaniel Stinchcomb, William Jennings, James A.Jennings
Recorded: 25 Sept 1849

Georgia, Fayette Co., Inventory of T. R. Persons, decd, this 15th Sept 1849
Page 174-175

4 Lots of Land on which the farm is situated, 5th District, Fayette Co.
Negroes - Phil, Calvin, Tide, Isaak, John, Silvey, Elizer and child, Antionette, Mariah and Texanah, Mary, Delila, Everlina and child, Abram, Washington, Stephen, Jesse.

Appraisers: Z. Blaylock, C. E. Bennett, L. T. Thompson, sworn 15 Sept 1849

Recorded: 25 Sept 1849

Inventory and Appraisement of Estate of James Loyd, decd
Page 176-179

Negroes - Henry, Anthony, Luois, Nelson, Nicey, Aggey, Jane

Appraisers: John D. Stell, Nathaniel Stinchcomb, D. D. Denham, Charles J. Robinson, sworn on 14 Aug 1849

Inventory and Schedule of money, books of accounts, notes, bonds and judgments of James Loyd, decd includes many notes, 6 Fi.Fas. Recorded: 25 Sept 1849

Inventory and Appraisement of the Goods and Chattels, Lands and Tenements of Rocella Vernon, late of said county, decd, taken on 30 Jul 1849
Page 180

Appraisers sworn on 30 Jul 1849 - Marcus Varner, Nathaniel Stinchcomb, John A. Jennings
Recorded: 25 Sept 1849

Estate of Pitt W. Milner, decd, in Account Current with James F. Johnson, Admr de bonis non, from 1 Jan to 31 Dec 1848 inclusive
Page 181

10 vouchers. Recorded: 25 Sept 1849

Estate of Kinchen Strickland, decd, in Account Current with A. J. Munday, Admr, from the time of his appointment, Jan 1848 to 31 Dec 1848 inclusive
Page 181-183

26 vouchers. Recorded: 25 Sept 1849

James P., minor of James Fitzgerald, decd, in Account Current with Philip Fitzgerald, Gdn, from 1 Jan 1848 to 31 Dec inclusive
Page 183

4 vouchers. Recorded: 28 Nov 1849

Mary A., minor of James Fitzgerald, decd, in Account Current with Philip Fitzgerald, Gdn, from 1 Jan 1848 to 31 Dec inclusive
Page 184

3 vouchers. Recorded: 28 Nov 1849

Estate of Holland Leopard, decd, in Account Current with Jeptha Landrum, Exr, from 3 Jul 1848 to 31 Dec inclusive
Page 184

Recorded: 28 Nov 1849

Estate of Edward Bearden, decd, in Account Current with Jeptha Landrum, Admr, from 6 Nov 1848 to 31 Dec 1848 inclusive
Page 185

Recorded: 25 Nov 1849

Sale of Personal Property of Thomas Herring, decd, by Mary Ann Herring, Admx, on 10 Dec 1849
Page 186-187

Among purchasers: Mary Ann Herring. Recorded: 10 Jan 1850

Sale Bill of Personal Property of Isaac S. Kimberly, decd
Page 1881-190

Among the purchasers were: Widow Kimberly, William Kimberly, E. Kimberly, Edward Kimberly, Mrs. Kimberly. Recorded: 10 Jan 1850

Inventory and Appraisement of Estate of Allen Jennings, decd
Page 190-193

Lot No. 64, 7th District, Fayette Co., 202 1/2 acres
Lot No. 63, 7th District, Fayette Co., 202 1/2 acres
Lot No. 39, 7th District, Fayette Co., 202 1/2 acres
Lot No. 67, 7th District, Fayette Co., 202 1/2 acres
Lot No. 68, 7th District, Fayette Co., 202 1/2 acres
Lot No. 34, 7th District, Fayette Co., 202 1/2 acres
Lot No. 93, 7th District, Fayette Co., 202 1/2 acres
Lot No. 94, 7th District, Fayette Co., 202 1/2 acres
Lot No. 33, 7th District, Fayette Co., 64 acres

3 Lots in Cherokee Co. - Lot No. 1146, 2d District, 2d Section, 40 acres
                        Lot No. 937, 15th Dist., 2d Section, 40 acres
                        Lot No. 319, 9th Dist., 2d Section, 160 acres

Estate of Allen Jennings, contd....

Negroes -

Jack, age 20
Gust, age 29
Aaron, age 40
Squin, age 40
Simm, age 16
Philis, age 16
Charles, age 11
John, age 6
Alfred, age 10
Mac, age 5
Boston, age 5
Lucas, age 3
Henry, age 8 months
Dick, age 8 months
Jenny, age 39
Milly, age 62
Rose, age 40
Martha, age 28
Phillis, age 18
Hailey, age 19
Caroline, age 10
Mary, age 8
Harriet, age 5
Hannah, age 4
Mariah, age 2
Milly and child

Appraisers: Jeptha Landrum, Sr., Nathaniel Stinchcomb, B. O. Jones, sworn 28 Nov 1849
Recorded: 10 Jan 1850

Jonesboro, Ga., 22 Dec 1848, An Account of the Sale of the Property and Land and Lots as was Advertised by James Hanes, Exr, of the Estate of Jesse Lasseter, late of Fayette Co., decd
Page 194-196

Among purchasers: Jesse Lasseter, Jacob F. Lasseter
Recorded: 10 Jan 1850

Sale of the Property of James Loyd, decd, 3 Jan 1850
Page 197-199

Among purchasers: Milton Loyd, William M. Spear, Widow Loyd, John Loyd, John Loyd, Marion Loyd, James Loyd.

Recorded: 15 Nov 1850

Return No. 16, Estate of Aaron Tilghman, decd, in Account Current with William Miles, Exr, 1 Jan to 31 Dec 1848 inclusive
Page 199-200

John B. Allen, Legatee
One negro boy (Richmond) delivered to John Allen, legatee, appraised by George Ware, John Graves and Eli Edmondson.

To hire of Joe to William Whatley and Williamson Jenkins. Recorded: 21 Jan 1850

Return No. 17, Estate of Aaron Tilghman, decd, in Account Current with William Miles, Exr, from 1 Jan to 31 Dec 1849 inclusive
Page 200

3 vouchers. Recorded: 14 Nov 1850

The Final Return of William G. Smith, Gdn of Eliza Bishop, Orphan of Matthew T. Bishop, decd
Page 200

Recorded: 14 Jan 1850

Estate of Francis M. Carroll, in Account Current with Eli Edmondson, Admr, from 6 Mar 1848, the date of Granting Letters up to 31 Dec 1849 inclusive
Page 201

16 vouchers. Legatees: John Carroll, Marcus L. Carroll, Thomas Carroll, James Carroll, Joshua Elder.
Received of A. McBride for hire or negro girl, Matilda and boy.
Sale of negroes, Sept 1849, as follows -
Feb and 2 children and George sold to Andrew McBride
Matilda sold to Thomas Duffell
Rachel sold to S. J. Weaver
Allen sold to Eli Edmondson

Recorded: 21 Jan 1850

Estate of George Ware, decd, to John S. Holliday, Admr
Page 202

36 vouchers. Taxes for 1849, etc. Recorded: 21 Jan 1850

Estate of John Lassiter, in Account Current with James Harris, Jr., Exr, from the date of Letters Testamentary, to 31 Dec 1849 inclusive
Page 204

14 vouchers. To cash paid Seppy Lasseter, and Jacob Lasseter, legatee
Recorded: 21 Jan 1850

Estate of Michael Ikener, decd, in Account Current with Rowland Stubbs, Admr, from Jan 1848 to 31 Dec 1849 inclusive
Page 205

19 vouchers. To cash paid Sarah Stubbs, legatee. Recorded: 31 Jan 1850

Nancy, Orphan of Martha T. Bishop, in Account Current with Jesse Ward, 1 Jan to 31 Dec 1849 inclusive
Page 206

2 vouchers. To cash paid Samuel G. Pegg. Recorded: 31 Jan 1850

John C. Brassell, Admr, Estate of Wade H. Cavender, in Account Current from the 1st Jan 1849 to 31 Dec 1849 inclusive
Page 206

5 vouchers. To cash paid - James T. Travis, James Henson, Henry Rentfrow, P. H. Brassell, Gdn. Recorded: 31 Jan 1850

Estate of William Atkinson, in Account Current with Jesse Atkinson, from 4 Nov 1848 to 31 Dec 1849 inclusive
Page 207

8 vouchers. To Fi.Fa. against Henry Hill. Recorded: 31 Jan 1850

Estate of William F. Elder to Joshua Elder, Gdn
Page 208

5 vouchers. Hire of sale of negro boy, Bill, in 1850. Recorded: 31 Jan 1850

Sarah Bedsil, in Account Current with John O. Dickson, Gdn, from 1 Jan 1848 to 31 Dec 1849 inclusive
Page 208

3 vouchers. Recorded: 31 Jan 1850

Estate of John McLeroy, decd, in Account Current with Martha McLeroy, Admr, from 1 Jan 1847 to 31 Dec 1847 inclusive
Page 209

3 vouchers. Recorded: 31 Jan 1850

Martha E. Hays, Orphan of John Hays, in Account Current with Lemuel M. Murphy, Gdn, from 5 Mar 1849 to 31 Dec inclusive
Page 209

Recorded: 31 Jan 1850

Thomas C., Orphan of James Bosworth, in Account Current with Josiah R. Bosworth, Gdn, from 1 Jan to 31 Dec 1848 inclusive
Page 210

4 vouchers. To cash paid - M. P. Kellogg, J. H. Johnson, J. R. Bosworth. Recprded: 31 Jan 1850

Thomas C., Orphan of James Bosworth, in Account Current with Josiah R. Bosworth, Gdn, from 1 Jan to 31 Dec 1849 inclusive
Page 210211

2 vouchers. To cash paid - J. R. Bosworth. Recorded: 31 Jan 1850

Parker Eason, in Account Current with Estate of Pitt W. Milner, decd
Page 311-212

Recorded: 31 Jan 1850

Return No. 3, Estate of Pitt W. Milner, in Account Current with James F. Johnson, Admr de bonis non, 1 Jan 1849 to 31 Dec 1849 inclusive
Page 212

4 vouchers. To cash paid - John J. Calwell, William N. Hill, Gdn. Recorded: 15 Mar 1850

Estate of Dempsey A. Reeves, in Account Current with W. S. Reeves, Admr, from 1 Jan 1849 to 31 Dec inclusive
Page 213

14 vouchers. To cash paid - M. Westmoreland, W. D. Reeves, John M. Falkner, 1849 taxes, Willis Champion, Mitchel Henderson, James A. McGee, Marry & Logan, William T. Bates, William S. Herrondale, A. M. Reeves.

Sale of 75 acres by John W. Reeves. Recorded: 15 Mar 1850

Estate of Kinchen Strickland, in Account Current with Andrew J. Munday, Admr, from 1 Jan to 31 Dec 1849 inclusive
Page 214

15 vouchers. To cash paid - Caney Strickland, Isaac Strickland, Charles Whaley, Jesse T. Anthony, A. B. Reeves, William R. Blackwell, A. M. Parker, James A. Smith, L. B. Jackson, James Wyatt, Thomas Brown, Abner Camp, Samuel G. Pegg.

Recorded: 15 Mar 1850

Estate of A. B. Williams, in Account Current with W. H. Blalock, Admr, from the time of appointment to 31 Dec 1849
Page 215-216

7 vouchers. To cash paid - James Floyd, Elizabeth Smith, Sarah Ann Smith, John Brassell, William H. Blalock, Jesse Hodges.
Recorded: 15 Mar 1850

Meriman P. Champion, Orphan of Abner Champion, decd, in Account Current with William C. Champion, Gdn, from 1 Jan 1849 to 31 Dec inclusive
Page 216

2 vouchers. Recorded: 15 Mar 1850

Cintha P. Champion, Orphan of Abner Champion, decd, in Account Current with William C. Champion, Gdn, from 1 Jan 1849 to 1 Dec inclusive
Page 216

5 vouchers. Recorded: 15 Mar 1850

Adison J. Champion, Orphan of Abner Champion, decd, in Account Current with William C. Champion, Gdn, from 1 Jan 1849 to 1 Dec inclusive
Page 217

4 vouchers. Recorded: 15 Mar 1850

Abner G. Champion, Orphan of Abner Champion, decd, in Account Current with William C. Champion, Gdn, from 1 Jan 1849 to 1 Dec inclusive
Page 217

2 vouchers. Recorded: 15 Mar 1850

Georgia, Fayette Co., We, whose names are hereunto subscribed, being appointed by the Honorable Court of the Ordinary of said County, do hereby certify to that the following is a true inventory and appraisement of the personal effects and real estate of Thomas Herring, decd, produced to us by William Russell, Admr de bonis non of said decd, to-wit: Thomas Herring, this 28th day of Jan 1850 was appraised as follows, to-wit11/11/94
Page 218-219

202 1/2 acres, Lot No. 40, 6th District, Fayette Co.
202 1/2 acres, Lot No. 39, 6th District, Fayette Co.
101 1/4 acres, Lot No. 41, 6th District, Fayette Co.
202 1/2 acres, Lot No. 49, 6th District, Fayette Co.

Negroes - Charles and Mary

A List of the Sale of the Personal Property. Among the purchasers were: Mary A. Herring, widow, D. D. Denham, John Lee.
Recorded: 14 Mar 1850

Inventory and Appraisement of the Estate of Alexander Smith, on 26 Apr 1850
Page 219-220

Appraisers sworn on 24 Apr 1850 - T. C. Matthews, Z. Blalock, Edward Moor.

Recorded: 1 May 1850

Inventory and Appraisement of the Estate of Daniel S. Waterson, decd
Page 221

249 1/2 acres.
Negroes - Lise (woman), Green, Hanson, Sarah, Lena.
Appraisers: Reubin Wallis, Jesse Ward, J. H. Waldrop, sworn 29 Mar 1850

Recorded: 1 May 1850

Inventory and Appraisement of the Property of the Estate of Joseph Anthony, decd
Page 222-225

Lot No. 242, 5th District, Fayette Co.
Negroes - Kesiah and child, Jane, Matilda, James and Micajah

Appraisers: Caney Strickland, William E. Tucker, L. M. Murphy, sworn on 3 May 1850
Among purchasers at Sale - Thomas Jennings, Howell L. Elder, Larkin Millsaps, Charles Wiliford, William Jones, L. Stokes, William Smith and E. Brown.

Negroes sold -
Milly sold to Marcus Varner
Jenny sold to Thomas Jennings
Philis sold to William Jennings
Milly sold to A. M. Parker
Haley sold to Jesse Jones
Caroline sold to A. M. Parker

Estate of James Murphy - By Virtue of (Commission) Warrant of Appraisement to us Directed at Honorable Inferior Court of Fayette Co. Sitting for Ordinary Purposes, makes the following inventory and appraisement, to-wit:
Page 225-233

Lot No. 50, 5th District, Fayette Co.
E. 1/2 of Lot No. 23, 3rd District, Henry Co.
E. 1/2 of Lot No. 47, 5th District, Fayette Co.
W. half of Lot No. 18, 5th District, Fayette Co.
25 acres, being part of Lot No. 48, 5th District, Fayette Co.
Lot No. 107, 5th District, Fayette Co.
N. 1/2 of Lot 16, 5th District, Fayette Co.

Slaves - Benjamin, Jason, Samuel, Henry, Green, Susan and child, Hannah, Nancy, Liza, Jane, Mary, Jack, Charles, Quin (girl), Benny and Margaret.

Includes a long list of Notes and accounts.

Appraisers: Elijah Glass, William N. Hill, John O. Dickson, sworn on 19 Mar 1850
Recorded: 19 Mar 1850

Inventory and Appraisement of the Estate of James Loyd, decd, so far as was produced to us by William J. Russell, Admr de bonis non on the Estate of the deceased
Page 234-237

202 1/2 acres, Lot No. 102, 7th District, Fayette Co., includes Mill Lot
202 1/2 acres, Lot No. 70, 7th District, Fayette Co.
101 1/4 acres, Lot No. 71, 7th District, Fayette Co.
101 1/4 acres, Lot No. 92, 7th District, Fayette Co.
50 acres, Lot No. 91, 7th District, Fayette Co.
50 acres, Lot No. 27, 7th District, Fayette Co.
10 acres, Lot No. 28, 7th District, Fayette Co.
91 1/4 acres, Lot No. 28, 7th District, Fayette Co.

Estate of James Loyd, contd....

Negroes - Henry, Anthony, Lewis, Nelson, Nicy, Aggy and child about 3 months old, Jane. Includes several Fi Fas. on Gainy Westbrook and D. Kelly, as well as a list of Notes.

Appraisers: D. D. Durham, Nathaniel Stinchcomb, Samuel H. Ellison. Recorded: 15 May 1850

A Sale Bill of the Personal Property of James Loyd Sold by William J. Russell, Admr de bonis non on the Estate of James Loyd, decd, 9 May 1850
Page 238-239

Among the purchasers: Marion Loyd, James Loyd, Milton Loyd, John W. Spear, Jeptha Landrum, Washington Landrum, Jaabez M. Rhodes.

Recorded: 15 May 1850

Inventory and Appraisement of the Estate of Mitchel Henderson, decd
Page 240-246

Negroes - Randsom, Paul, William, Joseph, Easter, Nancy, Malissa, Daniel, Elizabeth, Caroline, Mary, Willis, Abraham, Mariah, Isaac, Robert, Thomas and Harriett

Appraisers: Allen Reeves, Joseph Williams, Elijah Ballard, Hope H. O'Glilm (x, his mark)

Among purchasers at the public sale on 21 Mar 1850 - David P. Elder, Joshua Elder, Thomas Henderson, Andrew Henderson and Rutha Henderson.

Recorded: 15 May 1850

Administrator's Sale of two negroes, to-wit: John (a man) and Mary (a woman) Sold as the Property of Pitt W. Milner, late of the State of Alabama, Sold this day by James F. Johnson, Admr de bonis non
Page 247

John sold to M. M. Tidwell
Mary sold to Thomas M. Jones

Recorded: 15 Jul 1850

Estate of Holland Leopard, in Account Current with Jeptha Landrum, Exr, from 31 Dec 1848 to 31 Dec 1849 inclusive
Page 247

7 vouchers. To cash paid - Watts & Minifree, J. B. Cook, Samuel Thompson, Gainey Westbrook, Elisha Baker, Jeptha Landrum.

Recorded: 15 Jul 1850

Estate of Joseph H. Cavender, decd, in Account Current with P. H. Brassell, Gdn. from 5 Mar 1849 to 31 Dec 1849 inclusive
Page 247

2 vouchers. Recorded: 15 Jul 1850

Estate of Edward Bearden, decd, in Account Current with Jeptha Landrum, Admr, from 31 Dec 1848 to 31 Dec 1849 inclusive
Page 248

15 vouchers. Voucher #5 paid Aaron Bearden.
Recorded: 15 Jul 185

An Account Current with Mrs. Martha W. Dunn, former Mrs. Martha W. Sellers, for her actings and doings while acting as Admr on the Estate of John Sellers, late of said county, decd, from 11 Jan 1847 until her intermarriage with her present husband, Ishmael Dunn, inclusive
Page 249

9 vouchers. Recorded: 15 Jul 1850

Estate of Thomas J. Williams, Idiot, in Account Current with John H. Williams, Gdn, from the time of appointment to 31 Dec 1849 inclusive
Page 249

Recorded: 15 Jul 1850

Estate of Thomas Watson, decd, in Account Current with William Watson, Admr, from 1 Jan to 31 Dec 1849 inclusive
Page 250

3 vouchers. To cash paid - William Watson, T. M. Millsaps (cost), and Mary Watson.
Recorded: 15 Jul 1850

Estate of A. G. Hancock, in Account Current with A. L. Huie, Admr, from 1 Jan to 31 Dec 1849 inclusive
Page 250

Recorded: 15 Jul 1850

Estate of Robert R. Smarr, decd, in Account Current with Mrs. Martha C. Smarr, Admx, from 1 Jan 1849 to 31 Dec inclusive
Page 251-252

32 vouchers. Recorded: 15 Jul 1850

Miss Jane E. Griggs, Orphan of Bryan Griggs, decd. in Account Current with B. O. Jones, Gdn, from 8 May 1849 to 31 Dec inclusive
Page 252

6 vouchers. Recorded: 16 Jul 1850

Miss Mary M. Griggs, Orphan of Bryan Griggs, decd, in Account Current with B. O. Jones, Gdn, from 8 May 1849 to 31 Dec inclusive
Page 252

2 vouchers. Recorded: 16 Jul 1850

William G. Griggs, Orphan of Bryan Griggs, decd, in Account Current with B. O. Jones, Gdn, from 8 May 1849 to 31 Dec inclusive
Page 252

Recorded: 16 Jul 1850

John W. Griggs, Orphan of Bryan Griggs, decd, in Account Current with B. O. Jones, Gdn, from 8 May 1849 to 31 Dec inclusive
Page 253

3 vouchers. Recorded: 16 Jul 1850

An Account Current with Ishmael Dunn, Admr of the Estate of John Sellers, decd, from 11 Jan 1847 to 31 Dec 1849 inclusive
Page 253-255

70 vouchers. To hire of negroes - Ceasor, Caty, Mary and child, Bob, Caroline, Caty, Faby, Fanny
Recorded: 16 Jul 1850

An Account Current with Ishmael Dunn, Gdn, for the Person and Property of Louisa W. Sellers, minor of John Sellers, from the Granting of Letters to-it: 7 May 1849 to 31 Dec inclusive
Page 256

23 vouchers. Recorded: 16 Jul 1850

Sale of Perishable Property of Rocella Vernon, decd, Sold 25 Dec 1849 by James F. Johnson, Admr
Page 257-258

Major purchasers: Epps Brown and William Smith
Recorded: 16 Jul 1850

Estate of Andrew Shelnut, in Account Current with John Shelnut, Admr - Arbitrators appointed by the Inferior Court of Fayette Co. to Appraise the Property, 17 Aug 1850
Page 258

Appraisers: John Ward, James M. Oakely, Jabex M. Rhodes
Recorded: 20 Aug 1850

A List of the Sale of I. Smith, decd, 22 Oct 1849
Page 258-260

Major purchasers: James McConnel, William Shaddick, John M. Chapman, Thomas P. Jones, James Davis, Elizabeth Smith and Seaborn Smith.

Recorded: 20 Aug 1850

Inventory and Appraisement of the Estate of James J. Stell, late of said county, decd
Page 261-262

Robert M. Stell, Admr

Appraisers: William B. Fuller, Abner Coker, M. M. Tidwell, sworn 20 Aug 1850

Inventory and Appraisement of Mary Waldroup, decd
Page 263

Henry Simpson, Admr.
Appraisers: John M. Murphy, Ralph Jackson, E. M. Murphy, sworn on 7 Sept 1850

Inventory and Appraisement of the Estate of Simon P. Murphy, decd
Page 264-265

Appraisers: Elijah Glass, Reuben Walls, Henry McLeroy and E. M. Murphy
Recorded: 9 Sept 185

Inventory and Appraisement of the Estate of James Hunter, decd, as produced to us by Andrew J. Sweat, Admr, this 20th day of Jun 1850
Page 265-266

125 acres, Lot No. 86, 5th District, Fayette Co.
40 acres, Lot No. 410, 16th District, 2d Section, Cobb Co., originally Cherokee Co.

Appraisers: Elijah Glass, James Turner, Thomas W. King, Ephraim Sweat
Recorded: 9 Sept 1850

Inventory and Appraisement of the Estate of John Dorman, decd
Page 267-271

Lot No. 73, 5th District, Fayette Co., 252 1/2 acres
Appraisers: Moses Padgett, Hugh D. Nuncey (x, his mark), Charles Johnson (x, his mark), sworn on 31 Jul
1850. Alford Dorman, Admr.
Recorded: 9 Sept 1850

Sale of a Portion of the Personal Estate on 8 Oct 1851

Among the purchasers were: Richmond Dorman, William P. King, S. F. Banks, Alfred Dorman and Robert R. King.

Appraisement Bill. Negroes - John, Leroy, Ceasor, Liza, Vilet, Margaret, Ann, Isaac, Liusa, Betsey, Dinah, Lewis, Sarah. Appraisers: S.T. Whitaker, Allen Reeves, H. H. Ogletree (x, his mark)

Recorded: 19 Oct 1850

The Heirs of James Loyd, in Account Current with James Loyd to the time of his death, by William J. Russell, Admr
Page 271-272

Recorded: 25 Feb 1851

A List of the Sale of the Personal Property of William R. Head
Page 273-274

The major purchasers at sale were: James Head, Frank Head and O. G. Head
Recorded: 25 Feb 1851

A Sale of the Personal Property Sold under the Will of Simon P. Murphy, Admr, 15 Nov 1850
Page 274

Purchasers: J. H. Murphy, Nathan Eason, John Nash, J. I. Whitaker, L. M. Murphy
Recorded: 25 Feb 1851

A List of the Appraisement of the Goods and Chattels, Lands and Tenements of Paschal E. Collins, decd, 12 Nov 1850
Page 275-279

Negroes - Bill, Stephen, Aron, Rhoda, Sally, Taressa, William, Charles, Peter, Harriet
Appraisers: L. H.Jordan, B. Y. Evans, D. R. Askew, Jordan Goodson, sworn 27 Jan 1849

Inventory and Schedule of the Money, Books, Accounts, etc. on 12 Nov 1850.
Recorded: 13 Nov 1850

Order of the Inferior Court, Sept Term 1850 to Distribute Estate of the late James Murphy, decd, among the Distibutees, to-wit:
Page 280-281

Joseph Murphy, Elizabeth Murphy, John Murphy, James P. Murphy, Arthur Robertson, and Andrew Murphy, legatees of said decd, assigned Nos. 1-6 for drawing of negroes.

Recorded: 26 Aug 1851

By virtue of an Order of the Court of Ordinary for Sept Term 1850 to make distribution of the Negroes belonging to the Estate of the late Allen Jennings, decd, among the Distributees, to-wit:
Page 281-283

Judy Ann Craig, wife of William M. Craig, daughter of said decd - negroes, Jack, Nelly and Henry

Rhoda Sophrona, now wife of Reuben Milsapps, daughter of said decd - negroes, Alfred, Dick, Augustus and Mahala

Lucy Ann, wife of Anderson M. Parker, daughter of said decd - Negroes, Mariah, Haney, Milly and child

Elizabeth Jane Jennings, a minor, daughter of said decd - Negroes, Bastin and Hannah

William Jennings, son of decd, of full age - Negroes, Mary, Susan, Caroline, Charles and Philly

Thomas Jennings, son of decd - Negroes, Mark, Harriett, Thelsey Jane, Charles

Commissioners: B. O. Jones, Jeptha Landrum, Murphy Brown, Nathaniel Stinchcomb, John Phillips

An Account of the Sale of James Austin, decd, on 3 Dec 1850
Page 283-284

Andrew J. Sweat, Admr. Recorded: 27 Feb 1851

Inventory and Appraisement of the Estate of John McLean, late of Fayette Co., decd
Page 284-287

Lot No. 187, 21st District, Fayette Co.
Lot No. 198, 21st District, Fayette Co.
Lot No. 199, 21st District, Fayette Co.
50 acres, Lot No. 219, 21st District, Fayette Co.

Negroes - Salene and child, Roland and Stephen (child)

Appraisers: Eli Edmondson, Andrew McBride, Nelson Weally, sworn 20 Dec 1850

Estate of Francis Price, decd, in Account Current with Elizabeth Price, Admr, from the time of Granting Letters, 31 Dec 1846 inclusive
Page 287

15 vouchers. To cash paid Elizabeth Price (x, her mark)
Recorded: 27 Feb 1851

Henry P. Fitzgerald, Orphan of James Fitzgerald, decd, in Account Current with Philip Fitzgerald, Gdn, from 1 Jan to 31 Dec 1849 inclusive
Page 288

Recorded: 27 Feb 1851

The Estate of Francis Price, decd, in Account Current with Elizabeth Price, Admx, from 1 Jan 1849 to 31 Dec inclusive
Page 288

5 vouchers. Recorded: 27 Feb 1851

Mary A., Orphan of James Fitzgerald, decd, in Account Current with Philip Fitzgerald, from 1 Jan 1849 to 26 Sept 1850 inclusive
Page 289

Recorded: 27 Feb 1851

The Estate of Isaiah Smith, decd, in Account Current with M. P. Smith, Admr, from the date of Letters of Admn to 31 Dec 1849 inclusive
Page 289-290

16 vouchers. Recorded: 28 Feb 1851

Estate of Thomas R. Parson, decd, with Sterling J. Elder, Admr, from the time of Granting of the Letters to 31 Dec 1849 inclusive
Page 290-291

31 vouchers. Recorded: 28 Feb 1851

Estate of John Dorman, decd, in Account Current with Alfred Dorman, Admr, from 1 Jul 1850 to 31 Dec inclusive
Page 291-292

6 vouchers. Recorded: 28 Feb 1851

Estate of Thomas Watson, decd, in Account Current with William Watson, Admr, from 1 Jan to 31 Dec 1850 inclusive
Page 293

6 vouchers. To cash paid - John Watson (legatee), John DeVaughn, Robert Watson, May Watson, William Watson, and William Watson (grandson).

Recorded: 28 Feb 1851

Estate of Francis M. Carroll, decd, in Account Current with Eli Edmondson, from 1 Jan 1850 to 31 Dec inclusive
Page 293-294

11 vouchers. Legatees: Thomas Carroll and John Elder
Recorded: 28 Feb 1851

Thomas Watson, minor of Thomas Watson, decd, in Account Current with William Watson, Gdn, from 1 Jan 1850 to 31 Dec inclusive
Page 294

Recorded: 28 Feb 1851

Return No. 1, Eswtate of Rocella Vernon for the year 1850 up to 31 Dec inclusive
Page 295-296

24 vouchers. Recorded: 28 Feb 1851

Estate of Bryan Griggs, decd, for Jan 1850
Page 296

16 vouchers. Recorded: 28 Feb 1851

Parker Eason, Gdn of May E. Milner, Estate of Pitt W. Milner, decd, to 31 Dec 1850 inclusive
Page 297

7 vouchers. Recorded: 1 Mar 1851

John W., Orphan of Pitt W. Milner, decd, in Account Current with William N. Hill, Gdn, from 1 Jan to 31 Dec 1849 inclusive
Page 298

Recorded: 1 Mar 1851

Susan Adaline, Orphan of Pitt W. Milner, decd, in Account Current with William N. Hill, Gdn, from 1 Jan to 31 Dec 1849 inclusive
Page 298

Recorded: 1 Mar 1851

Pitt W. Milner, Orphan of Pitt W. Milner, in Account Current with William N. Hill, Gdn, from 1 Jan to 31 Dec 1849 inclusive
Page 298

Recorded: 1 Mar 1851

James M. Milner, Orphan of Pitt W. Milner, in Account Current with William N. Hill, Gdn, from 1 Jan to 31 Dec 1849 inclusive
Page 299

Recorded: 1 Mar 1851

An Account Current with Joseph A. Murphy, one of the Admrs of the Estate of Simon P. Murphy, decd, from 1 Jan 1850 to 31 Dec inclusive
Page 300

6 vouchers. Recorded: 1 Mar 1851

Estate of Isaac S. Kimball, decd, in Account Current with William D. Kimberly, Admr, from the time of granting Letters of Admn to 31 Dec 1849 inclusive
Page 300-301

18 vouchers. Recorded: 1 Mar 1851

An Account Current with Jared J. Whitaker, Gdn of the Property of Jasper Loyd, minor of James Loyd, from the date of Letters to 31 Dec inclusive
Page 302

Recorded: 1 Mar 1851

In Account Current with Jared J. Whitaker, Gdn of the Property of Newton Loyd, minor of James Loyd, from the date of Letters to 31 Dec inclusive
Page 302

Recorded: 1 Mar 1851

Estate of Allen Jennings to William Jennings, Admr
Page 303-304

30 vouchers. Recorded: 1 Mar 1851

Parker Eason, Gdn of William L. Milner, in Account Current with the Estate of Peter W. Milner, decd, to 31 Dec 1850 inclusive
Page 304-305

Recorded: 1 Mar 1851

An Account Current with William C. Champion, Gdn of Cynthia A. Champion, minor of Abner Champion, decd, from 1 Jan 1850 to 31 Dec inclusive
Page 305

3 vouchers. To cash paid - Henry Renfro and Elizabeth A. Champion (ward).
Recorded: 1 Mar 1851

An Account Current with William C. Champion, Gdn of Allison J. Champion, minor of Abner Champion, decd, from 1 Jan 1850 to 31 Dec inclusive
Page 305

Recorded: 1 Mar 1851

An Account Current with William C. Champion, Gdn of Abner G. Champion, minor of Abner Champion, decd, from 1 Jan 1850 to 31 Dec inclusive
Page 306

Recorded: 1 Mar 1851

Estate of Robert R. Smarr, decd, in Account Current with Martha C. Smarr, Admx, from 1 Jan 1850 to 31 Dec inclusive
Page 306-308

21 vouchers. Recorded: 1 Mar 1851

Estate of James Murphy, decd, in Account Current with John Murphy, Admr, from 21 Mar 1850 to 31 Dec inclusive
Page 30-310

37 vouchers. Legatees (distribution of Negroes):

John Murphy given Nancy and child, Ellen and Dock
Andrew Murphy given Jason and Jane
James P. Murphy given Hannah and child, Margaret and Mary and Green
Elizabeth Murphy given Henry and Eliza
Joseph H. given Tom, Mary and Cheely
Arthur Robinson given Ben and Flesan? and her 3 children

Estate of Andrew Shelnut, decd, in Account Current with John Shelnut, Admr, from Letters of Admn to 31 Dec 1850 inclusive
Page 311

Recorded: 4 Mar 1851

Archibald J. Hayes, Orphan of Lewis Hayes, decd, in Account Current with P. E. Allen, Admr, from 8 Jan 1849 to 31 Dec 1850 inclusive
Page 312

5 vouchers. Recorded: 4 Mar 1851

Estate of Thomas J. Williams, in Account Current with John H. Williams, Gdn, from 1 Jan to 31 Dec 1850 inclusive
Page 312-313

Recorded: 5 Mar 1851

Estate of Mary Waldroup, in Account Current with Mary Simpson, Admr, from time of appointment in 1850 to 31 Dec 1851 inclusive
Page 313-314

3 vouchers. Recorded: 3 Mar 1851

Estate of Michael Ikener, decd, in Account Current with Rowland Stubbs, Admr, from 1 Jan 1850 to 31 Dec inclusive
Page 314-315

6 vouchers. Recorded: Mar Term 1851

John D., Orphan of John Anthony, decd, in Account Current with Rowland Hutcheson, from the time of appointment, as Gdn in 1848 up to 31 Dec 1850 inclusive
Page 315

Recorded: 5 Mar 1851

Estate of John Westmoreland, in Account Current with Mark W. Westmoreland, from 19 Nov 1849 to 31 Dec 1850 inclusive
Page 316

Recorded: 5 Mar 1851

Thomas E., Orphan of James Loyd, decd, in Account Current with John Loyd, Gdn, from 1 Jul 1850, the date of Ltrs to 31 Dec inclusive
Page 316-317

Recorded: 5 Mar 1851

Sarah Frances, Orphan of James Loyd, in Account Current with John Loyd, Gdn, from 1 Jul 1850 to the time of Ltrs to 31 Dec inclusive
Page 317

Recorded: 5 Mar 1851

M.? M. Elder, minor of Joshua Elder, in Account Current with Joshua Elder, Gdn, from 1 Jan to 31 Dec 1850 inclusive
Page 318

4 vouchers. Recorded: 5 Mar 1851

Joseph W., Orphan of Wade H. Cavender, in Account Current with Philip H. Brassell, Gdn, from 1 Jan to 31 Dec 1850 inclusive
Page 318-319

Recorded: 5 Mar 1851

Estate of Dempsey A. Reeves, decd, in Account Current with Wyatt S. Reeves, Admr, from 1 Jan to 31 Dec 1850 inclusive
Page 319-320

6 vouchers. To cash paid - John W. Reeves, legatee, John W. Reeves, Gdn, and Allen Reeves for J. A. G. Reeves. Recorded: 5 Mar 1851

Return No. 1, Estate of William Buse, decd, in Account Current with John Buse, Admr, from the time of appointment to 31 Dec 1850
Page 320

Recorded: 5 Mar 1851

Estate of James Martin, decd, in Account Current with Andrew J. Sweat, Admr, from 3 Jun 1850, time of granting Ltrs to 31 Dec 1850 inclusive
Page 321

3 vouchers. Recorded: 5 Mar 1851

Samuel, Orphan of James Loyd, decd, in Account Current with James Loyd, Gdn, from the time of Letters up to 31 Dec 1850 inclusive
Page 321-322

Recorded: 5 Mar 1851

Return No. 3, Miss Jane E. Griggs, Orphan of Bryan Griggs, decd, in Account Current with B. O. Jones, Gdn, from 1 Jan to 31 Dec 1850 inclusive
Page 322

2 vouchers. Recorded: 6 Mar 1851

Return No. 3, Sarah W. Griggs, Orphan of Bryan Griggs, decd, in Account Current with B. O. Jones, Gdn, from 1 Jan to 31 Dec 1850 inclusive
Page 322-323

Recorded: 6 Mar 1851

Estate of Jesse Lasseter, in Account Current with James Haines, Exr, from 1 Jan to 31 Dec 1850 inclusive
Page 323-324

7 vouchers. Recorded: 6 Mar 1851

Sale of Part of the Perishable Property Belonging to the Estate of Jesse Lasseter, Sold on the 13th day of Sept 1850
Page 325

Among the purchasers: Jesse Lasseter, James Haynes, Robert Craig, Thomas J. Lasseter, William Jackson

Martha M., Orphan of Wade H. Cavender, decd, in Account Current with John C. Brassell, Gdn, from 14 Jan from the time of appointment to 31 Dec 1850 inclusive
Page 325-326

Recorded: 6 Mar 1851

Estate of Wade H. Cavender, decd, in Account Current with John C. Brassell, Admr, from 1 Jan 1850 to 31 Dec inclusive
Page 326-327

Recorded: 6 Mar 1851

Estate of Kinchen Strickland decd, in Account Current with A. J. Munday, Admr, from 1 Jan 1850 to 31 Dec inclusive
Page 327

8 vouchers. Recorded: 6 Mar 1851

Estate of A. B. Williams, decd, in Account Current with James H. Williams, Admr, from 1 Jan 1851 to 31 Dec inclusive
Page 328

17 vouchers. Legatees: William R. Moseley, Z. Williams, Lewis E. Moseley.
To boarding of Celesta, Elizabeth, Cintha and Marcey.
Recorded: 7 Mar 1851

Estate of James Loyd, decd, in Account Current with William J. Russell, Admr de bonis non, from 21 Mar 1850 to 31 Dec inclusive
Page 329, then misnumbered to begin with Page 340-341

19 vouchers. To cash paid - Milton Loyd, distributee, John Loyd, Gdn, Sarah Loyd, widow, John Loyd, distributee, James Loyd, distributee, Jared J. Whitaker, Gdn, and John M. Akins, legatee.

Recorded: 7 Mar 1851

Estate of Thomas Herring, decd, in Account current with William I. Russell, Admr de bonis non from the date of Letters to 31 Dec 1850 inclusive
Page 341-343

To cash paid - Mary Ann Herring for support

Recorded: 7 Mar 1851

Estate of James J. Stell, decd, in Account Current with R. M. Stell, Admr, from 1 Jul 1850 to 31 Dec inclusive
Page 343-344

7 vouchers. Recorded: 7 Mar 1851

A List of Property Sold at the Residence of John Westmoreland, decd, on 3 Jan 1849
Page 344-346

Purchasers: M. W. Westmoreland, C. F. Westmoreland, Mrs. E. Westmoreland

Recorded: 8 Mar 1851

A Sale Bill of the Negro Property Belonging to the Estate of John Westmoreland, decd, Sold by T. C. Mathews, Admr
Page 346-347

Sales as follows:

Tom and wife, Mary, and George to Elizabeth Westmoreland
Old negro woman to Mark Westmoreland
Mary and Jack to Stephen D. Wilson
Dice, Elizabeth and 2 children to Thomas C. Mathews
Henry, Dudley, Caroline, Sam, Nice to M. W. Westmoreland
Rose, Ziletha to Westley Westmoreland
Alna to C. S. Westmoreland
Steward, Julia to M. J. Westmoreland
Hal, Daniel and Olive to William Mathews
Bill to M. Westmoreland

Estate of John Westmoreland, contd....

Edi to Thomas Westmoreland
Martin to Henry C. Mathews

Recorded: 8 Mar 1851

Return Book D, page 346-347

Inventory and Appraisement of the Real and Personal (ready money) of Wright Martin, decd
Page 348-349

Negroes as follows:
Peter, age 45
Stephen, age 30
Randle, age 34
Hiram, age 22
Ebenezer, age 20
Henry, age 15
Rachel, age 40
Pheba, age 32
Sarah, age 25
Ann, age 27
Ede, age 19
Nancy, age 36
Qean, age 13
Harriet, age 13
Mariah, age 15
Martha, age 12
Hannah, age 9
Manena, age 25
Emilia Ann, age 5
Margaret, age 9
Susan, age 4
Francis, age 4
Rhoda, age 8
Caroline, age 1
Tom, age 12
Bob, age 11
Crawford, age 10
Jim, age 10
Wesley, age 8
John, age 7
Warren, age 1
John, age 6
Jim, age 3
Emily and child

202 1/2 acres including York Lot
607 1/2 acres including the homestead
Appraisers: John D. Stell, John Palmer, Mathew Yates, sworn 4 Feb 1857
Jesse L. Blalock and James Hobgood, Admrs de bonis now, with Will annexed
Recorded: 4 Jun 1851

Sale of the Perishable Property of Wright Martin, decd, 17 Mar 1851
Page 350-351

Among purchasers: Jackson Martin, J. Martin, Jack Martin and William Martin

Recorded: 18 Jun 1851

An Appraisement of the Estate of James Turner, late of Fayette Co., decd
Page 352

Negroes - Sarah and child, Ellen, and John

15 Feb 1851 - Produced by Elijah Glass and James Turner, Jr., Admrs.
Appraisers: Hubbard Stubbs, Thomas Turner, Robert D. Dickson and Ephraim Sweat

Recorded: Jun 1851

Sale of the Negroes Belonging to the Estate of A. B. Williams, decd, on the first Tues. in Mar 1850 by James H. Williams, Admr
Page 353

Negroes sold as follows:

Bill to William R. Moseley
Caroline, Henry, George, Viney and Hannah to W. H. Williams
Alsey to Thomas C. Matthews

Sale of Morris being postponed - he was sold on the first Tues. in May 1850 to W. R. Moseley.

Recorded: 18 Jun 1851

A Sale Bill of the Land and Negroes of W. R. Head, Sold on the first Tues. in Jan 1851 by Oliver J. Head and David P. Elder, Admrs
Page 353

Negroes sold as follows:

Leroy and Ceasor to O. J. Head
Elijah and Dinah to A. L. F. Head
Vilet and Viney to James M. head
Margaret and Isaac to David P. Elder
Ann and Ceans to Jane Head, widow
Woman and child, Elizabeth, and Lewis to Robert A. Head

Recorded: 18 Jun 1851

A List of the Sale of the Perishable Property Belonging to the Estate of George Ware, decd, on 30 Oct 1851
Page 354-359

Among the purchasers: Mildred Ware, G. W. Ware, B. A. Ware, George W. Ware

Recorded: 21 Jun 1851

Estate of George Ware, continued......

Order to Distribute to Heirs:
Page 359-361

Mildred Ware, widow
Burrell A. Ware
George W. Ware
Louisa L. Ware
John S. Holliday
Emily F. Ware, represented by John S. Holliday, Gdn for said minors
Catherine and James Ware, represented by Burrell A. Ware
Ann and Richard Ware, represented by Mildred Ware, Gdn and mother

Lots drawn on 28 Dec 1850 for Negroes, as follows:

Jack and Harriet to Mildred Ware, Gdn for Richard Ware
Jim and Mary to Burrell A. Ware, Gdn of James Ware
Daniel and Foley to John S. Holliday, Gdn for Emily F. Ware
Liddy, Ben and Joe to George W. Ware
Nelly, Fanny, Peter to Mildred, Gdn of Ann Eliza Ware
John and Tom to Burrell A. Ware, Gdn for Catherine Ware
Bill and Lucy to Mildred Ware
Martha and Susan and Wilie to John S. Holliday
Gale and Book to Burrell A. Ware
Polly and Big Jim to Louisa L. Ware

Recorded: 21 Jun 1851

Account of the Sale of the Land of the Estate of James Murphy, decd, Sold on the first Tues. of Nov. 1850
Page 361

Lot No. 50, 5th District, 202 1/2 acres (and Mills), Fayette Co. - Sold to James P. Murphy
Lot No. 47, 5th District, 202 1/2 acres, Fayette Co. - Sold to William N. Hill
1/2 of Lot No. 18, 5th District, 101 1/4 acres, Fayette Co. - Sold to John Murphy
1/2 of Lot No. 16, 5th District, 101 1/4 acres, Fayette Co. - Sold to James P. Murphy
1/2 of Lot No. 23, 3rd District, Henry Co., 101 1/2 acres, Fayette Co. - Sold to Shockley Gibson
25 acres, S. E. corner of Lot No. 48, 5th District, Fayette Co. - Sold to James P. Murphy

Recorded: 21 Jun 1851

Account of the Sale of the Perishable Property of the Estate of James Murphy, decd, Sold on the 7th day of Nov 1850
Page 361-364

Among purchasers: Andrew Murphy, James P. Murphy, Joseph H. Murphy, John H. Murphy, Elizabeth Murphy, J. M. Murphy, I. H. Murphy.

Recorded: 23 Jun 1851

Sale of the Perishable Property of James Turner, Sr., decd, Sold on the 17th day of Feb 1851 by Elijah Glass and James Turner, Admrs
Page 365

Recorded: 25 Jun 1851

Estate of Thomas R. Persons, decd, in Account Current with Sterling J. Elder, Admr, from 1 Jan to 31 Dec 1850 inclusive
Page 366-367

42 vouchers. Recorded: 27 Aug 1851

Claborn A., Orphan of James G. Christian, decd, in Account Current with Gideon F. Mann, Gdn, from the time of appointment to 31 Dec 1850 inclusive
Page 367

To cash paid - Harriett Christian for boarding and clothing, tuition
Filed: 5 May 1851. Recorded: 27 Aug 1851

James L, Orphan of James G. Christian, decd, in Account Current with Gideon F. Mann, Gdn, from the time of appointment to 31 Dec 1850 inclusive
Page 368

To cash paid - Harriett Christian for boarding and clothing, tuition
Filed: 5 May 1851. Recorded: 27 Aug 1851

John A., Orphan of James G. Christian, decd, in Account Current with Gideon F. Mann, Gdn, from the time of appointment to 31 Dec 1850 inclusive
Page 368

To cash paid - Harriett Christian for boarding and clothing, tuition
Filed: 5 May 1851. Recorded: 28 Aug 1851

Lucy J., Orphan of James G. Christian, decd, in Account Current with Gideon F. Mann, Gdn, from the time of appointment to 31 Dec 1850 inclusive
Page 369

To cash paid - Harriett Christian for boarding, clothing, tuition
Filed: 5 May 1851. Recorded: 28 Aug 1851

William M., Orphan of James G. Christian, decd, in Account Current with Gideon F. Mann, Gdn, from the time of appointment to 31 Dec 1850 inclusive
Page 370

To cash paid Harriett Christian for boarding, clothing, tuition
Filed: 5 May 1851. Recorded: 28 Aug 1851

Morgan F., Orphan of James G. Christian, decd, in Account Current with Gideon F. Mann, Gdn, from the time of appointment to 31 Dec 1850 inclusive
Page 370

To cash paid Harriett Christian for boarding, clothing, tuition
Filed: 5 May 1851. Recorded: 28 Aug 1851

Sarah Ann, Orphan of James G. Christian, decd, in Account Current with Gideon F. Mann, Gdn, from the time of appointment to 31 Dec 1850 inclusive
Page 370

To cash paid Harriet Christian for boarding, clothing, tuition
Filed: 5 May 1851. Recorded: 28 Aug 1851

Estate of Isaiah Smith, decd, in Account Current with William P. Smith, from 1 Jan 1850 to 9 Oct 1850 inclusive
Page 371

10 vouchers. Recorded: 28 Aug 1851

Estate of D. S. Waterson, decd, in Account Current with Kisiah Waterson, Admx, from the time of Letters of Admn to 31 Dec 1850
Page 371

2 vouchers. By one negro child borned since the appraisement. /s/Kiziah Waterson (x, her mark)
Filed: 5 Mar 1851. Recorded: 28 Aug 1851

A Sale Bill of the Real Estate of James Loyd, decd, together with the Negro Property Sold on the 6th day of Jan 1851 and first Tues. by William J. Russell, Admr de bonis non on said Estate on time til the 25th day of Dec 1851
Page 372

13 vouchers.

50 acres, Lot No. 27, Fayette Co. - sold to Jeptha Landrum
10 acres, Lot No. 28, Fayette Co. - sold to Jeptha Landrum
201 acres, Lot No. 102, Mill Lot, Fayette Co. - sold to James Loyd
135 1/2 acres, Lot No. 70, Fayette Co. - sold to John Loyd
101 1/4 acres, Lot No. 71, Fayette Co. - sold to John Loyd

Sale of Negroes:

Nicy, age 50, to Milton loyd
Henry, age 26, to Milton Loyd
Anthony, age 22 or 23, to J.Lasseter
Nelson, age 21, to Milton Loyd
Lewis, age 21, to Jeptha Landrum
Aggy and child, Mary, age 18 and 1 year, to G. F. Mann
Jane, age 15, to Thomas Duffel

Cotton Gin sold to William Bennett
Thrasher and patent farm sold to James J.Spier

Recorded: 28 Aug 1851

A Sale Bill of the Real Estate Belonging to the Estate of Thomas Herring, decd, Sold on the first Tues. in Dec 1850 and the 3rd day of the month and also the Negroes Belonging to said Estate Sold on the first Tues. in Jan 1851 and the 6th day of the month.
Page 372

Lot No. 37, 7th District, Fayette Co., sold to William Jennings
Lot No. 40, 7th District, Fayette Co., sold to James R. Jennings
1/2 of Lot No. 41, Fayette Co., sold to William May
Lot No. 49, Fayette Co., sold to Isaac P. Gay

old negro man sold to Joseph Speer

/s/William J. Russell, Admr de bonis non
Recorded: 28 Aug 1851

A Sale Bill of Real Estate Belonging to Mitchel Henderson, decd, Sold on the 5th day of Nov 1850
Page 373

Lot No. 143, 4th District, Fayette Co. to William Reeves
Lot No. 142, 4th District, Fayette Co. to John H. Starr
Lot No.141, 4th District, Fayette Co. to Thomas Henderson
1/2 of Lot No. 116, 4th District, Fayette Co. to Lemuel G. Shipp

Negroes sold -

Bill, Joseph and Easter to John Faulkner
Paul to Daniel H. Pounder
Nancy and children to Rutha Henderson
Old negro woman, Mary to Thomas Henderson

Recorded: 28 Aug 1851

Estate of Benjamin Folsom, in Account Current with Mathew Gates, Admr, from 1 Jan 1842 to 31 Dec inclusive
Page 373

2 vouchers. To cash paid - Jane Forston, Jane Wickett and John Wickette
Recorded: 29 Aug 1851

An Account with Ishmael Dunn, Admr of the Estate of John Sellers, decd, from 1 Jan 1850 to 31 Dec 1850 inclusive
Page 374-375

16 vouchers. Negro girl, Caroline, died in 1848. Negro girl, Fanny, died in 1849

Hire of Negroes - Ceasor, Bob, Peter, Fenly, Caty, Mary and 5 children for 1850

The Negroes of said Estate were divided out by Ishmael Dunn, in right of his wife and Christopher C. Bowen, in right of his wife, by the consent of Ishmael Dunn, Admr. on 31 Dec 1850 as follows:

Negroes to Ishmael Dunn -

Caty, age 65
Bob, age 21

Estate of John Sellers, contd.....

Mary, age 40
Rachel, age 5
Andrew, age 4
Singleton, age 13 (being since appraisement)

Negroes to Christopher C. Bowen -

Ceasor, age 70
Fenly, age 15 (woman)
Peter, age 13
Isaac, age 10
Thomas, age 8

Recorded: 29 Aug 1851

Louisa W. Sellers, Orphan of John Sellers, decd, in Account Current with Ishmael Dunn, Gdn, from 1 Jan 1850 to 31 Dec inclusive
Page 376

22 vouchers. Recorded: 29 Aug 1851

Estate of William P. Whaley, decd, in Account Current with Jesse Ward, Admr, from 1 Jan to 31 Dec 1850 inclusive
Page 377

10 vouchers. Recorded: 29 Aug 1851

The Estate of William P. Whaley, in Account Current with Jesse Ward, Admr, from 18 Jan 1849 to 31 Dec inclusive
Page 378

14 vouchers. To cash paid - S. D. Whaley (vouchers #5, 7 and 8), Josiah Whaley (vouchers #10 and 11).
Recorded: 29 Aug 1851

Estate of Pitt W. Milner, decd, in Account Current with James H. Johnson, Admr de bonis non, from 14 Jan to 31 Dec 1850 inclusive
Page 379

11 vouchers. Includes John S. Holliday's Fi.Fa.
Recorded: 1 Sept 1851

Martha E. Hayes, Orphan, in Account Current with L. M. Murphy, Gdn, from 1 Jan to 31 Dec 1850 inclusive
Page 380

4 vouchers. To cash paid - William I. Russell, C. C. O., R. Rogers (for tuition, boarding)
Recorded: 1 Sept 1851

The Estate of Aaron Tilghman, decd, in Account Current with William Miles, Exr, from 1 Jan to 31 Dec 1850 inclusive

Page 380

2 vouchers. To cash paid - Henry Rentfrow, M. H. Westbrook (legatee, in right of his wife, Elizabeth). Also, one negro boy, Joel.

Recorded: 1 Sept 1851

Estate of George Ware, decd, in Account Current with 1 Jan 1850 to 31 Dec inclusive
Page 381-382

43 vouchers. To John S. Holliday, Admr and Mildred Ware, Admx.
Recorded: 2 Sept 1851

An Account Current with the Estate of Vicy Bearden, a minor, with William W. Bearden, Gdn of said minor, 4 Mar 1850 to 31 Dec 1850 inclusive
Page 382

To cash paid JohnN.Smith for tuition
Recorded: 2 Sept 1851

Estate of Edward Bearden, decd, in Account Current with Jeptha Landrum, Admr, on said Estate, 31 Dec 1849 to 31 Dec 1850 inclusive
Page 383-384

21 vouchers. William W. Bearden, Gdn for Vicy Bearden.

Legatees - William W. Bearden, Solomon Bearden, Aaron Bearden, Walter J. Campbell, Thomas E. Campbell, Thomas J. Head, Miss Louisa E. Campbell, and Mrs. Frances Bearden.

Recorded: 2 Sept 1851

Estate of Holland Leopard, decd, in Account Current with Jeptha Landrum, Exr, from 31 Dec 1849 to 31 Dec 1850 inclusive
Page 384

6 vouchers. Recorded: 2 Sept 1851

Return No. 3, Orphan of William B. Wootton, late of Fayette Co., decd, in Account with Lucinda Wooten, Gdn, from 1 Jan 1843 to 31 Dec 1850 inclusive
Page 385

1 Lot of Land in Cherokee Co.
1850 sale of land in Fayette Co.
11 vouchers. Young L. Wootton, distributee (voucher #11)
Recorded: 2 Sept 1852

Estate of J. Anthony, decd, in Account Current with William Sparkman, Admr, from the time of appointment to 31 Dec 1850 inclusive
Page 385

Recorded: 2 Sept 1851

Estate of Francis Price, decd, in Account Current with Elizabeth Price, Admx, from 1 Jan to 31 Dec 1850 inclusive
Page 386

3 vouchers. Recorded: 4 Sept 1851

Estate of William Atkinson, in Account Current with Jesse Atkinson, Admr, from 1 Jan to 31 Dec 1850 inclusive
Page 386-387

6 vouchers. To cash paid - Sarah Atkinson (voucher #1), Liles Newton, Henry Hill, Thomas A. Latham, D. Holcomb and William Cline.
Recorded: 4 Sept 1851

Estate of Wyatt McGuirt, in Account Current with William H. Blalock, Admr, from 1 Jan 1850 to 31 Dec 1850 inclusive
Page 387

6 vouchers. To cash paid - Thomas Byrne, J. H. Johnson, I. L. Blalock, Thomas M. Millsaps, William I. Russell, P. H. Brassell.

Recorded: 4 Sept 1851

Sarah A., Orphan of Pitt W. Milner, decd, in Account Current with William N. Hill, Gdn, from 1 Jan 1850 to 31 Dec 1850 inclusive
Page 388

2 vouchers. Recorded: 4 Sept 1851

Pitt W. Milner, Orphan of Pitt W. Milner, decd, in Account Current with William N. Hill, Gdn, from 1 Jan 1850 to 31 Dec 1850 inclusive
Page 388

2 vouchers. Recorded: 4 Sept 1851

John H. Milner, Orphan of Pitt W. Milner, decd, in Account Current with William N. Hill, Gdn, from 1 Jan 1850 to 31 Dec 1850 inclusive
Page 389

1 voucher. Recorded: 4 Sept 1852

James M. Milner, Orphan of Pitt W. Milner, decd, in Account Current with William N. Hill, Gdn, from 1 Jan 1850 to 31 Dec 1850 inclusive
Page 389

1 voucher. Recorded: 4 Sept 1851

Inventory and Appraisement of the Estate of Silas G. Eastin, decd
Page 390

Negroes - Simon, George, Lucy, Reese and Jordan
Appraisers: John D. Stell, Charles Graves (x, his mark), N. Easton, sworn 1 Oct 1851
Recorded: 27 Oct 1851

List of the Sale of the Perishable Property Belonging to the Estate of S. G. Eastin Sold by Elijah Cleckler, Exr, on 15 Oct 1851
Page 390

Purchasers: W. B. Gosden, Edward W. Leach, Mathew Yates, Charles Graves, Jordan Lord, Samuel Jackson, William Spraggins, Williamson Jenkins, William A. Jones, Blake Jackson, Isaac Hartley and M. Waldroup.

Recorded: 27 Oct 1851

Sale of the Land and Negroes Belonging to the Estate of James Turner, decd, Sold 4 Nov 1851 (with the exception of Sarah and child sold for $400)
Page 391

66 acres, Lot No. 85, Fayette Co. - sold to William Jennings
66 acres, Lot No. 76, Fayette Co. - sold to William Jennings

Sarah and child, Catherine - sold to Elijah Glass
Joe - sold to Elijah Glass
Ellen - sold to Gilbert Gay
John - sold to William Glass

Recorded: 17 Nov 1851

12 Nov 1851, The Following is a List and Appraisement of the Goods, Chattels of Sarah Stubbs, as produced to us by Dennis Stubbs and Simon T. Whitaker, Admr
Page 391-397

Slaves - Spencer, Bill, Henry, Ellick, Bob, Nancy, Mary, Caty, Jincy, Sarah and child, Zilphey, Mack, Wright, Louisa and Jane.

Appraisers: T. D. King, Elijah Glass and Charles Johnson (x, his mark), sworn 12 Nov 1851
Recorded: 17 Nov 1851

Property Sold at the Sale of the Admrs of Sarah Stubbs, decd, at her late Residence on 18 and 19 Dec 1851
Page 397

Among purchasers: Hubbard Stubbs, and H. Stubbs
Recorded: 17 nov 1851

Inventory and Appraisement of the Estate of William Reeves, decd
Page 397-402

Appraisers: James H. Williams, Thomas B. Gay, John M. Faulkner, Elijah Ballard, sworn 3 Jul 1851
Filed: 5 Jul 1851

Inventory and Schedule of Money notes and Accounts of William Reeves, decd, recorded: 17 Nov. 1851

An Account of the Sale of a Portion of the Personal Estate of William Reeves, Sold 5 Nov 1851 - Among purchasers: Widow Reeves, J. M. Reeves, Allen Reeves, A. W. Reeves, Miss M. C. Reeves, Miss L. A. Reeves, W. S. Reeves and W. B. Reeves.
Recorded: 17 Nov 1851

Appraisement of the Goods and Chattels of Morris Harris, decd, on 30 Jan 1852 by Abner Camp, Exr
Page 403-407

Appraisers: Jesse Ward, John R. Waldroup, Seaborn Harris, sworn 30 Jan 1852

Inventory of the Notes and Credits of Morris Harris, decd, recorded: 27 Feb 1852

Among purchasers of articles - Abner Camp, John Camp, Seaborn Camp, Feiney Hutcheson, Zachariah Mann.

Sale of 125 acres in Fayette Co., Lot No. 86 in 5th District and Lot No. 410 in Cobb Co. sold on first Tues. in Jan of 1851.

Inventory and Appraisement of Estate of Mark Smallwood, decd
Page 407-409

Appraisers: Jeptha Landrum, A. Chandler, Nathaniel Stinchcomb, Johnson Waters, sworn 2 Oct 1851

An Account of the Personal Property of Mark Smallwood Sold at Public Outcry on 3rd Dec 1851 by Samuel H. Ellison, Admr
Page 409-413

Among purchasers: Harriet Smallwood, Riley Smallwood, Milligan Smallwood, M. P. Smallwood

Return of the Sale of the Land and hire of Negroes -

Lot No. 165, Fayette Co. -sold to Littleton Stokes
Lot No. 166, Fayette Co. - sold to Littleton Stokes
Negro girl, Eady, sold to Littleton Stokes
50 acres on Lot No. 156, Fayette Co. - sold to William J.Campbell

Negroes sold as follows -

James and Eady to Littleton Stokes
Mills to M. P. Smallwood
Eliza to Reuben Millsaps
Henry to Washington Brown
John to L. H. Ellison
Charles to Johnston Whatley
Wesley to Willis Landrum
Edom to Seaborn Shropshire
Patsey to Harriet Smallwood
Lizes to Jeptha Landrum, Jr.
Saline and 3 children to Harriet Smallwood

Mary Ann, Orphan of Dempsey A. Reeves, in Account Current with John W. Reeves, Gdn, from the time of appointment of Gdn to 31 Dec 1850 inclusive
Page 413

Recorded: 13 Jul 1852

Allison, Orphan of Abner Champion, decd, in Account Current with William C. Champion, Gdn, from 1 Jan 1851 to 31 Dec inclusive
Page 414

Recorded: 13 Jul 1852

Abner G., Orphan of Abner Champion, decd, in Account Current with William C. Champion, Gdn, from 1 Jan 1851 to 31 Dec inclusive
Page 414

Recorded: 13 Jul 1852

Mary Ann, Orphan of Abner Champion, decd, in Account Current with William C. Champion, Gdn, from 1 Jan 1851 to 31 Dec inclusive
Page 415

Recorded: 13 Jul 1852

Parker Eason, Gdn for William L. Milner, Orphan of Pitt W. Milner, decd, to 31 Dec 1851 inclusive
Page 415-416

To recording bond for apprenticeship. Recorded: 13 Jul 1852

Sarah Frances Loyd, Orphan of James Loyd, decd, Orphan of James Loyd, decd, in Account Current with John Loyd, Gdn, from 1 Jan 1851 to 31 Dec inclusive
Page 416

3 vouchers. M. A. Rainey gave receipt for tuition of Sarah Loyd, and M. P. Byington gave receipt for tuition for Sarah Loyd.

Recorded: 13 Jul 1852

Thomas Emery Loyd, Orphan of James Loyd, decd, in Account Current with John Loyd, Gdn, from 1 Jan 1851 to 31 Dec inclusive
Page 417

3 vouchers. Receipt from M. A. Rainey for tuition of Sarah Loyd, and from M. P. Byington for tuition of Sarah Loyd.

Recorded: 13 Jul 1852

Estate of James J. Stell, decd, in Account Current with R. Manson, Admr, from 1 Jan 1851 to 31 Dec inclusive
Page 418-421

13 vouchers. To cash paid - Mrs. E. R. Stell. Includes a Fi.Fa. of Asa Chandler vs. Martha Ogilby and Eli Edmondson (Clerk after Appeal). Also, John Meadows, Admr vs. George C. Hightower as princ. & solomon Woodruff, Sec., Clerk, Sheriff, J.Landrum, Fi.Fa. Also, The Officers of the Court vs. William McPherson and J. J. Stell, his atty, Clerk, atty, Fi. Fa.

The above Fi.fas. were paid by R. Manson Stell, Admr.
Voucher #12 was signed by Elizabeth Stell for $20 for use of family of decd.

Recorded: 14 Jul 1852

Archabald J. Hays, Orphan of Lewis Hayes, decd, in Account Current with P. H. Allen, Gdn, from 1 Jan to 31 Dec inclusive
Page 421-422

Recorded: 14 Jul 1852

Samuel Loyd, Orphan of James Loyd, decd, in Account Current with James Loyd, Gdn, from 1 Jan to 31 Dec 1851 inclusive
Page 422

4 vouchers (included with the Return). Receipt of M. P. Byington for tuition.
Recorded: 14 Jul 1852

Estate of Edward Bearden, in Account Current with Jeptha Landrum, Admr, from 31 Dec 1850 to 31 Dec 1851 inclusive
Page 423

Legatee - Washington Bearden.
2 vouchers. Recorded: 14 Jul 1852

Estate of Holland Leopard, in Account Current with Jeptha Landrum, Exr, from 31 Dec 1854 to 31 Dec 1851 inclusive
Page 424

Filed: 5 Jun 1852. Recorded: 15 Jul 1852

Morgan F., Orphan of James C. Christian, in Account Current with Gideon F. Mann, Gdn, from 1 Jan 1851 to 31 Dec inclusive
Page 424-425

1 voucher. Filed: 29 Mar 1852. Recorded: 15 Jul 1852

John A., Orphan of James C. Christian, in Account Current with Gideon F. Mann, Gdn, from 1 Jan 1851 to 31 Dec inclusive
Page 425

1 voucher. Filed: 29 Mar 1852. Recorded: 15 Jul 1852

Claborn A., Orphan of James C. Christian, in Account Current with Gideon F. Mann, Gdn, from 1 Jan 1851 to 31 Dec inclusive
Page 426

1 voucher. Filed: 29 Mar 1852. Recorded: 15 Jul 1852

Lucy J., Orphan of James C. Christian, in Account Current with Gideon F. Mann, Gdn, from 1 Jan 1851 to 31 Dec inclusive
Page 426

2 vouchers. Filed: 29 Mar 1852. Recorded: 15 Jul 1852

James J., Orphan of James C. Christian, in Account Current with Gideon F. Mann, Gdn, from 1 Jan 1851 to 31 Dec inclusive
Page 427

2 vouchers. Filed: 29 Mar 1852. Recorded: 15 Jul 1852

Sarah Ann, Orphan of James C. Christian, in Account Current with Gideon F. Mann, Gdn, from 1 Jan 1851 to 31 Dec inclusive
Page 427

1 voucher. Filed: 29 Mar 1852. Recorded: 15 Jul 1852

Ann Eliza Ware, Orphan of George Ware, decd, in Account Current with Mildred Ware, Gdn, from time of appointment to 31 Dec 1851 inclusive
Page 428

By 3 negroes - Peter, Nelly and Fanny
Filed: 2 Jun 1852. Recorded: 15 Jul 1852

Richard Ware, Orphan of George Ware, decd, in Account Current with Mildred Ware, Gdn, from time of appointment to 31 Dec 1851 inclusive
Page 428

By 2 negroes Jack and Harriet, hired out in 1851
Recorded: 15 Jul 1852

James E. Ware, Orphan of George Ware, decd, in Account Current with Mildred Ware, Gdn, from time of appointment to 31 Dec 1851 inclusive
Page 429

By hire of 2 negroes, Jim and Mary, during 1851. 4 vouchers.
Recorded: 15 Jul 1852

Francis, Orphan of Thomas Herring, decd, in Account Current with W. J. Russell, Gdn, from 7 Jul 1851, the time of appointment, to 31 Dec 1851 inclusive
Page 430

1 voucher. Filed: 28 May 1852. Recorded: 15 Jul 1852

Marcus, Orphan of Thomas Herring, decd, in Account Current with W. J. Russell, Gdn, from 7 Jul 1851, the time of appointment, to 31 Dec 1851 inclusive
Page 430

1 voucher. Filed: 28 May 1852. Recorded: 15 Jul 1852

Jonathan, Orphan of Thomas Herring, decd, in Account Current with W. J. Russell, Gdn, from 7 Jul 1851, the time of appointment, to 31 Dec 1851 inclusive
Page 431

1 voucher. Filed: 28 May 1852. Recorded: 15 Jul 1852

Nancy, Orphan of Mathew T. Bishop, in Account Current with Jesse Ward, Gdn, from 1 Jan 1851 to 31 Dec inclusive
Page 431

Filed: 29 Apr 1852. Recorded: 15 Jul 1852

James W., Orphan of P. Milner, decd, in Account Current with William N. Hill, Gdn, from 1 Jan to 31 Dec 1851 inclusive
Page 432

1 voucher. Filed: 29 May 1852. Recorded: 15 Jul 1852

Pitt W., Orphan of P. Milner, decd, in Account Current with William N. Hill, Gdn, from 1 Jan to 31 Dec 1851 inclusive
Page 433

2 vouchers Filed: 29 May 1852. Recorded: 15 Jul 1852

John H., Orphan of P. Milner, decd, inAccount Current with William N. Hill,Gdn, from 1 Jan to 31 Dec 1851 inclusive
Page 433

2 vouchers. Voucher #2, Received of William N. Hill, Gdn of John H.Milner, Orphan of Pitt W. Milner, decd, late of Alabama. $500 payment in full of the trust fund received by him from the hands of James F. Johnson, Admr de bonis non on Estate of said decd, this 18 Jan 1851. /s/John H Milner, legatee

Filed: 29 May 1852. Recorded: 14 Jul 1852

Susan A. Milner, Orphan of P. Milner, decd, in Account Current with William N.Hill,Gdn, from1 Jan to 31 Dec 1851 inclusive
Page 434-435

2 vouchers. Filed: 29 May 1852. Recorded: 14 Jul 1852

John H., Orphan of Wade H. Cavender, decd, in Account Current with Jabez M. Brassell,Gdn,from the time of his appointment, 14 Jan 1850 to 31 Dec 1851 inclusive
Page 435

Filed: 4 Jun 1852. Recorded: 16 Jul 1852

Inventory and Appraisement of the Estate of John W. Pledger, decd, so far as was produced to us by Council Rentfrow, Admr
Page 436-437

Thomas J. Foster, William A. Cavender, H. Buffington, Appraisers, sworn 5 May 1852
Recorded: 14 Jul 1852

Martha M., Orphan of Wade H. Cavender, in Account Current with John C. Brassell, Gdn, from 1 Jan 1851 to 31 Dec 1851 inclusive
Page 437

3 vouchers. Recorded: 17 Jul 1852

An Account Current with the Estate of Vicy Bearden, a minor, with William W. Bearden, Gdn, from 1 Jan 1851 to 31 Dec 1851 inclusive
Page 438

2 vouchers. Paid Francis Bearden for board and clothing
Filed: 24 May 1852. Recorded: 17 Jul 1852

Estate of Benamin Folsom, in Account Current with Mathew Yates, Admr, from 1 Jan 1851 to 3 May 1852 inclusive
Page 438-439

3 vouchers. Advertised Letters of Dismission in *Georgia Jeffersonian*.
Recorded: 19 Jul 1852

Joseph H., Orphan of Wade H. Cavender, in Account Current with Phillip S. Brassell, Gdn, from 1 Jan 1851 to 31 Dec inclusive
Page 439-440

2 vouchers. Recorded: 19 Jul 1852

Estate of Jesse Lasseter, in Account Current with James Hanes, Exr, from 1 Jan to 31 Dec 1851 inclusive
Page 440-441

2 vouchers. Receipt from Seppers Lasseter (x, her mark), for $200. for use of family
Recorded: 19 Jul 1850

Miss Elizabeth Jennings, in Account Current with William Jennings, Gdn, from 14 Nov 1850 to 31 Dec 1851 inclusive
Page 441-443

9 vouchers. Includes cash paid to Elizabeth by the Gdn.
Recorded: 20 Jul 1852

Estate of Kinchen Strickland, in Account Current with Andrew J. Munday, Admr, from 1 Jan to 31 Dec 1851 inclusive
Page 443-444

4 vouchers. To cash paid - Cany Westbrook, Gdn for Elizabeth, Martha, Francis and Catharine, orphans and legatees. To cash paid Susan Strickland, widow, for her full share as widow.

Thomas Watson, minor of Thomas Watson, decd, in Account Current with William Watson, Gdn, from 1 Jan to 31 Dec 1851 inclusive
Page 445-446

3 vouchers. Filed: 5 Apr 1852. Recorded: 21 Jul 1852

Estate of Silas G. Eastin, in Account Current with Elijah Cleckler, Exr, from 5 May to 31 Dec 1851 inclusive
Page 446-447

3 vouchers. Recorded: 21 Jul 1852

Estate of John Dorman, in Account Current with Alford Dorman, Admr, from 1 Jan to 31 Dec 1851 inclusive
Page 447-449

8 vouchers. includes Heirs receipts as follows -

Godfrey J. Betsill, son-in-law of John Dorman
William P. King
Richmond Dorman
S. F. Banks (x, his mark)
Hiram Dorman
Filed: 29 Mar 1852. Recorded: 22 Jul 1852

Estate of Avington B. Williams, decd, in Account Current with James H. Williams, Admr, from 1 Jan 1851 to 31 Dec 1851 inclusive
Page 449-450

Lewis E. Mosley, distributee
Thomas C. Matthews, Gdn of minor children
Recorded: 22 Jul 1852

Wilson A. Willerford, decd, in Account Current with Charles W. Willerford, Admr, from 1 Jan 1851 to 31 Dec 1851 inclusive
Page 451

3 vouchers. To cash paid - Martha E. Wilkinson, Gdn,for schooling and board
To cash paid - Westley Wilerford, Gdn for Wilson A. Wilerford, orphan
To cash paid - Charles W. Wilerford, Gdn for Wilson A. Wilerford, orphan
Recorded: 22 Jul 1852

Miss Jane E. Griggs, Orphan of Bryan Griggs, decd, in Account Current with B. O. Jones, Gdn from 1 Jan to 31 Jan 1851 inclusive
Page 452-453

4 vouchers. (included) Filed: 19 May 1852. Recorded: 22 Jul 1852

Estate of Simon P. Murphy, decd, in Account Current with Joseph H. Murphy and Rebecca Murphy, Admrs, from the 1st of Jan 1851 to 31 Dec 1851 inclusive
Page 453-455

6 vouchers (included). Filed: 3 May 1852. Recorded: 22 Jul 1852

Amanda C. Ware, Orphan of George Ware, decd, in Account Current with Burrell A. Ware, Gdn, from the time of appointment in 1850 to 31 Dec 1851 inclusive
Page 455-458

9 vouchers (included).
By 2 negroes - John, a man and Tom, a boy.
Vou. #1, Received of Burrell A. Ware, Gdn for Catherine Ware, Orphan of George Ware, decd, $3.12 in full of her part of expense in appointng his guardian thid 30th Dec 1851. /s/William J. Russell, C. C. O.
Receipt from M. A. Raney and Daniel Evans (tuition for Catherine Ware).
Receipt from John Holliday (tuition fo Amanda Catherine Ware).
Filed: 2 Jun 1852. Recorded: 23 Jul 1852

Estate of Burrell Ware, decd, in Account Current with Amherst W. Stone, Admr de bonis non from 1 Jan 1851 to 31 Dec 1851 inclusive
Page 458-459

1851. Dec. 10. By amount received from John Holliday, Admr and Mildred Ware, Admx of George Ware, decd, it being money received by said George Ware in his lifetime fo sale of negroboy, Sam, for $340 ....and negro girl, Ann, $280.00.../s/D. B. More

Fi.Fa. against Amherst W. Stone, Admr, for several sums of money, due John Holliday and Mildred Ware, Admrs.

3 vouchers (included). Includes expenses of Admr to Paulding Co.
Filed: 5 Apr 1852. Recorded: 23 Jul 1852

Estate of Michael Ikener, decd, in Account Current with Rowland Stubbs, Admr, from 1 Jan to 31 Dec 1851 inclusive
Page 460

3 vouchers (included). Filed: 3 May 1852. Recorded: 23 Jul 1852

Estate of Allen Jennings, in Account Current with William Jennings, Admr, with the Will annexed from 1 Jan 1851 to 31 Dec 1851 inclusive
Page 461-463

9 vouchers (included). To cash paid 1849-1851 taxes, Thomas M. Millsaps, B. O. Jones, Murry & Logan, William N. Hill, Cynthia Jennings.

By Sale of Land -

Lot No. 39, 7th District, Fayette Co.
Lot No. 64, 7th District, Fayette Co.
Lot No. 63, 7th District, Fayette Co.
Lot No. 94, 7th District, Fayette Co.
1/2 of Lot No. 67, 7th District, Fayette Co.
1/2 of Lot No. 68, 7th District, Fayette Co.
1/2 of Lot No. 93, 7th District, Fayette Co.
14 acres of Lot No. 33, 7th District, Fayette Co.
Lot No. 34, 7th District, Fayette Co.

Filed: 5 May 1852. Recorded: 23 Jul 1852.

Martha E., Orphan of John Hayes, decd, in Account Current with Lemuel E. Murphy, Gdn, from 1 Jan to 31 Dec 1851 inclusive
Page 464-465

4 vouchers (included). Filed: 5 Jul 1852. Recorded: 24 Jul 1852

Estate of Aaron Tilghman, decd, in Account Current with William Miles, Exr, from 1 Jan 1851 to 31 Dec 1851 inclusive
Page 465-466

6 vouchers (included).

2 Lots of land paid legatees as per voucher #6 -Received of William Miles, Exr of the Estate of Aaron Tilghman, decd. the title and possession of 2 lots of land, to-wit: Lot No. 255 in 16th District, 1st Section, Cherokee Co., Lot No. 808 in the 2d District, 3rd Section, Cherokee Co., which fully discharges him from administrating in said 2 lots of land as aforesaid of said estate, said lots have been sold and distributed among the legatees, this the -- day of May 1851. /s/Williamson Jenkins, John B. Allen, Sebon J. Files, A. H. Tilghman and Marshal H. Westbrooks.

Filed: 5 Apr 1852. Recorded: 24 Jul 1852

Estate of William Attkinson, decd, in Account Current with Jesse Attkinson, Admr, from 1 Jan 1851 to 31 Dec 1851 inclusive
Page 466-468

9 vouchers (included). To cash paid - Harrison Walker (for several judgments, William Atkinson vs. George Peters & Aaron Godwon, Guardianship, William Atkinson vs. George Peters and Elisa, the old fi fa. 26 Apr 1845,and Thomas A. Lathram's fi.fas. against William Atkinson (1846), Wiley Banks & Co. vs. William Atkinson, William Atkinson vs. George Peters, and William Wakefield vs. William A. Atkinson.), William Cline (advertising citation for dismuission from said estate).

To heirs as follows (for their full shares) -

John Ward , William L. Smith, Sarah Attkinson, William Attkinson, John D. and Joseph Attkinson, Jesse Attkinson.

Filed: 30 Mar 1852. Recorded: 24 Jul 1852

An Account Current with Jared I. Whitaker, Gdn for the person and property of Jasper Loyd, minor of James Loyd, decd, from 1 Jan to 31 Dec 1851 inclusive
Page 469-471

8 vouchers (included). To cash paid - Daniel Evans, James A. Newton, William Bennett, Piety Philips, R. K. Holliday & Co., J. L. Blalock, and Jared I. Whitaker (Gdn, for boarding and lodging for said ward in 1851).

Filed: 2 Jun 1852. Recorded: 26 Jul 1852

An Account Current with Jared I. Whitaker, Gdn for the person and property of Newton loyd, minor of James Loyd, decd, from Jan 1851 to 31 Dec inclusive
Page 471

2 vouchers (included). Filed: 2 Jun 1852. Recorded: 26 Jul 1852

Estate of Thomas Herring, decd, in Account Current with William Russell, Admr de bonis non, from 1 Jan to 31 Dec 1851 inclusive
Page 472-475

9 vouchers (included). To cash paid - Conner & Stone, attys, Thomas Byrne, F. M. Harrell, Mary A. Herring (legatee), James D. Parnell (in right of his wife, Mary, formerly Mary Herring, legatee), William J. Russell, Gdn for Johnathan Marcus and Francis Herring, minors and legatees of Thomas Herring, decd.

Filed: 5 Apr 1852. Recorded: 2 Jul 1852

Estate of James Turner, Sr., decd, in Account Current with Elijah Glass, one of the Admrs, from the time of appointment to 31 Dec 1851 inclusive
Page 475-483

19 vouchers (included). Receipt of Margaret A. D. Russell for tuition of children. 12 months' support given the widow, Anna Turner (x, her mark) for support of family for 1851, there being 12 in the family.

Filed: 3 Apr 1852. Recorded: 27 Jul 1852

Estate of George Ware, decd, in Account Current with John S. Holliday and Mildred Ware, Admrs, from 1 Jan to 31 Dec 1851 inclusive
Page 484-488

17 vouchers (included). Voucher #14 To Amherst W. Stone, Admr de bonis non of Burrell Ware, late of Texas, decd, to sale of negro girl, Anna, about 6 years old, the property of said Burrell Ware, sold by said George Ware as Admr of Burrell 1 Jun 1847 for cash of $280....to amount of cash received from James Ware for sale of negro boy, Sam, the property of said Burrell Ware sold 1 Jun 1847 on 12 months' credit for $680 1/2 in hands of said George Ware as Admr, the other 1/2 in collectd by hm...../s/Amherst W. Stone.

Voucher #16, receipt from Louisa L. Ware for part payment of her legacy

Filed: 25 May 1852. Recorded: 28 Jul 1852

Emily F. Ware, Orphan of George Ware, decd, in Account Current with John L. Holliday, Gdn, from time of appointment ot 31 Dec 1851 inclusive
Page 489-494

16 vouchers (included).

By hire of 2 negroes-to-wit, Lamb and Tob, received from the Admr of John L. Holliday and Mildred Ware.

By hire of Lamb for 1851
By hire of Tob for 1851

Filed: 25 May 1852. Recorded: 28 Jul 1852

Estate of James Loyd, decd, in Account Current with William J. Russell, Admr de bonis non from 1 Jan 1851 to 31 Dec inclusive
Page 495-501

23 vouchers (included).

Legatees: John W. Spear (in right of wife, Emily Spear, formerly Emily Loyd), Sarah Loyd, widow, Milton Loyd, John Loyd, Gdn of Sarah Frances Loyd and Thomas Emory Loyd, James Loyd, F. M. Loyd, Jared I. Whitaker, Gdn of Newton and Jasper Loyd.

Filed: 25 May 1852. Recorded: 9 Aug 1852

An Account Current with Robert C. Porter, Gdn, for the person and property of Andrew M. Henderson, a minor son of Mitchel Henderson, late of Fayette Co., decd, from date of Letters to 31 of Dec 1851 inclusive
Page 501-503

4 vouchers (included). To cash paid - Elisha P. Bolton, Wooton & Co., William J. Russell, Clerk, H. Harington, R. C. Porter, Gdn, board, etc.

Filed: 2 Jun 1852. Recorded: 9 Aug 1852

Estate of Mitchel Henderson, decd, in Account Current with Robert C. Porter, Exr of said Estate, from 1 Jan 1851 to 31 Dec inclusive
Page 503-516

45 vouchers (included). Filed: 3 Jun 1852. Recorded: 10 Aug 1852

Estate of James Murphy, late of said county, decd, in Account Current with John Murphy, Admr, from 1 of Jan 1851 to 31 Dec inclusive
Page 517-524

39 vouchers (included).

Legatees as follows -

Andrew Murphy
James P. Murphy
Elizabeth Murphy
John Murphy

Filed: 2 Jun 1852. Recorded: 10 Aug 1852

Estate of Thomas R. Persons, decd, in Account Current with Sterling J. Elder, decd, from 1 day of Jan to 31 Dec 1851
Page 525-535

37 vouchers (included). Filed: 2 Jun 1852. Recorded: 12 Aug 1852

Estate of John Westmoreland, decd, in Account Current with Thomas C. Mathews and C. L. Westmoreland, Admrs, from time of appointment to present date, 11 Dec 1851
Page 536-556

46 vouchers (included).

Legatees as follows -

Thomas C. Mathews
C. S. Westmoreland
M. Westmoreland
Robert J. Westmoreland
Westley Westmoreland
Stephen E. Wilson
Elizabeth Westmoreland, widow
Mark W. Westmoreland
Mark W. Westmoreland, Gdn for Sarah J. Westmoreland

Elizabeth Westmoreland (x, her mark) receipt for boarding one negro woman and 10 children in 1849.
Filed: 29 Mar 1852. Recorded: Jul Term 1852

Estate of John Westmoreland, Decd, in Account of Hotchpotch with C. S. Westmoreland and Thomas C. Mathews, Admrs, as Return by Legatees -
Page 556-557

John Westmoreland paid Thomas C. Mathews, C. S. Westmoreland, M. Westmoreland, S. E. Wilson, William Mathews, Mark J. Westmoreland, Robert J. Westmoreland, Westley Westmoreland (legatees) received cash and negroes

Filed: 29 Mar 1852. Recorded: 26 Aug 1852

Gideon F. Mann, Gdn
Page 557-558

(only vouchers)

Voucher No. 2, Received of Gideon F. Mann, Gdn of Morgan F. Christian, Claborn A. Christian, Lucy J. Christian, J. A Christian, orphans of J. G. Christian, decd......clothing and tuition this 30 Dec 1851 /s/Harriet C. Christian

Recorded: 6 Oct 1852

Inventory and Appraisement of the Estate of William Stubbs, decd, No. 1
Page 558

As produced by Rowland Stubbs, Admr

"The dower whereon Sarah Stubbs resided at the time of her death appraised to be worth $750.00."

Appraisers: Elijah Glass, Charles Johnson (x, his mark), Gilbert Gay, Jr.
Recorded: 8 Oct 1852

Inventory and Appraisement of the Estate of John W. Pledger, decd
Page 559

Not dated.

Account of the Sale and a portion of the personal Estate of Paschal E. Collins, decd, Sold on the 8th and 9th of Jan 1851
Page 560-566

To rent of a portion of land to Mrs. Emiline Collins, support to contain 26 acres at 50 per acre

Support to contain 40 acres to W. J. Grant, 50 acres to Seaborn Page, 31 acres to Henderson King, 5 acres to D. Shell and 30 acres to Emiline Collins

To hire of negroes, Bill, Stephen, Aaron, Rhoda, Sally, Tarissa, William, Charles, Peter and Harriet

Sale of Negroes -

Aaron to Jared I. Whitaker
Sally to Q. L. Price
Stephen to Q. L. Price
Rhoda to Mrs. E. Collins
Bill to Smith Griffin
Peter to Mrs. E. Collins
Charles to Mrs. E. Collins
William to Mrs. E. Collins
Katy to Mrs. E. Collins
Frank to Peter McLeroy
Teresa and her child, Jane to Peter McLeroy

Recorded: 21 Oct 1852

Inventory and Appraisement of Estate of William W. Kennedy, decd
Page 566-567

Appraisers: Robert C. Huie, James Mc Kown, Robert McKown, Alex L. Huie, sworn 8 Oct 1852
Recorded: 21 Oct 1852

Inventory and Appraisement of the Estate of James A. Newton, decd
Page 567-576

Appraisers: T. M. Jones, W. H. Blalock, K. Holliday, C. C. Shell
Recorded: 22 Oct 1852

Sale of personal property. Among purchasers: Sarah Newton, William N. Hill, William Glass, J. B. Avera, etc.

Recorded: 21 Oct 1852

Estate of Bryant Griggs, decd, in Account Current with James F. Johnson, Admr de bonis non from 31 Dec 1850 to 31 Dec 1851 inclusive
Page 576-577

5 vouchers.

Heir receipt, as follows:
Epps Brown, in right of wife, Lenah W. Brown

Recorded: 26 Oct 1852

Return No. 2, Estate of Rocella Vernon, decd, in Account Current with James F. Johnson, admr, from 31 Dec 1850 to 31 Dec 1851 inclusive
Page 577

No vouchers.
Filed: 2 Aug 1852. Recorded: 24 Oct 1852

Estate of Pitt W. Milner, decd, in Account Current with James F. Johnson, Admr de bonis non from 31 Dec 1850 to 31 Dec 1851 inclusive
Page 578-579

5 vouchers. To cash paid - W. N. Hill, (Gdn of Pitt W. L. Milner, James M. Milner and Susan A. Miler, minors, for their distributive shares), William T. Griffin, John H. Milner (legatee), C. C. Shell, and William J. Russell, C. C. O., and E. M. Callaway.

Filed: 3 Jul 1852. Recorded: 29 Oct 1852

John H. Cox, minor heir of Samuel W. Cox, decd, n Account Current with John D. Stell, Gdn, from 1 Jan 1846 to 31 Dec inclusive
Page 579

Filed: 4 Jul 1852. Recorded: 29 Oct 1852

Jesse Lasseter, Admr of Miles L. Scott, late of South Carolina, decd, in Account Current from 1 day of Dec 1851 to 31 Dec inclusive
Page 580

Sale of Lot No. 123 in 13th District of Fayette Co.
Filed: 5 Jul 1852. Recorded: 29 Oct 1852

Estate of A. G. Hancock, in Account Current with A. L. Huie, Admr, from 1 Jan 1850 to 31 Dec 1851 inclusive
Page 581-582

5 vouchers. Includes Fi.Fa. against Alexander Huie, Admr, in favor of William Gilbert.
Recorded: 6 Nov 1852

The Estate of John Sellers, decd, in Account Current with Ishmael Dunn, Admr, from 1 Jan 1851 to 31 Dec 1851 inclusive
Page 583-586

9 vouchers (included). Includes Fi.Fa., John D. McCrae vs.Ishmael Dunn, Admr of John Sellers, decd, in Fayette Superior Court.

Filed: 5 Aug 1852. Recorded: 6 Nov 1852

Estate of William Reeves, decd, in Account Current with Allen Reeves, Admr, from Granting Letters of Admn to 1st day of Jan 1852
Page 586-592

21 vouchers (included). To cash paid - William J. Russell, C. C. O., Conner & Stone, M. C. Smarr, James M. Morris, James M. Couch, M. L. Heath, Mary Clizbe, William S. Herington, Thomas B. Gay, H. H. Carroll, H.Thornton (tax), Allen Reeves, M. P. Maleer, S. D. Hablett, J. H. Williams, G. W. Norman, C. H. Johnson & Co., Sargent & Co.

Recorded: 13 Nov 1852

Estate of Paschal E. Collins, decd, in Account Current with C. C. Bowen from 1 Jan 1851 to 31 Dec 1851 inclusive
Page 593-616

39 vouchers (included). Filed: 6 Jul 1852. Recorded: 9 Dec 1852.

Estate of Wright Martin, decd, in Account Current with James L. Hobgood, one of the Admrs de bonis non with Will annexed from date of his appointment to 31 Dec 1851 inclusive
Page 617-625

17 vouchers (included). To cahs paid - W. W. Hobgood, R. K. Holliday & Co., John W. Wilkins, W. H.Blalock, Austell & Camp, L. Blalock. M. M. Tidwell,etc.

Includes some fi.fas. in Fayette Superior Court.
Filed: 22 Jun 1852. Recorded: 11 Dec 1852

Inventory and Sale of the Personal Property of William W. Kennedy, late of said county, decd
Page 626-627

Purchasers: John Kennedy, E. Kennedy, George R. Kennedy, Alexander L. Huie, Jesse G. Smith, R. C. Huie.

Not dated.

Inventory and Appraisement of the Estate of Elbert Bishop, late of Fayette Co., decd
Page 627-630

Includes 50 acres of land.
Appraisers: T. J. Milner, Bogan Mask, Johnathan Mitchel, Benjamin F. Rhodes, sworn 12 Nov 1852
Jesse Hubbard, Admr.

Sale of personal property.Among purchasers: Henry Hubbard, Jesse Hubbard, Bogan Mask, Moses Turner, Jr., Wiseman Banks, Berry Phillips, etc. Not dated.

Miss S. J. Westmoreland, Orphan of John Westmoreland, decd, in Account Current with Mark W. Westmoreland, from 1 Jan 1851 to 31 Dec inclusive
Page 630-632

5 vouchers. Filed: 30 Sept 1852. Recorded: 2 Dec 1852

Thomas M., Orphan of William Gamage, decd, in Account Current with Floyd Gamage, from the time of appointment to 31 Dec 1851 inclusive
Page 633

By amount received of James H. Smith, former guardian
Filed: 21 Sept 1851. Recorded: 2 Dec 1852

Inventory and Appraisement of the Estate of James Brassell, decd, 13 Dec 1852
Page 634

Appraisers: P. H. Brassell, W. W. Mathews, John C. Brassell, sworn 13 Dec 1852
Recorded: 18 Dec 1852

Appraisement of the Goods, Chattels (money only excepted) of David Graves, decd, 13 Jan 1853
Page 635-637

Appraisers: Bryan Allen, Hillery Cleckler, John Graves (x, hismark) and Minton Graves, sworn 13 Jan 1853
Recorded: 9 Feb 1853

A List of the Sale of the Perishable Property. Purchasers: Matilda Graves, Wiley Graves, James F. Formby.

Recorded: 9 Feb 1853

Inventory and Sale of the Perishable Property of Estate of James Brassell, late of Fayette Co., decd, this 14th Jan 1853
Page 637-639

Among purchasers: P. H. Brassell, J. C. Brassell, L. D. Padgett, W. W. Mathews, etc.
Recorded: 7 Feb 1853

A List of the Sale of a portion of the Real Estate of William Stubbs, late of said county, decd. Sold 7 Dec 1852
Page 640

155 acres, being parts of Lots No. 74 and 75 in 5th District of Fayette Co., being 117 1/2 acres off of N. 1/2 of Lot 70 and 17 1/2 acres off of NW corner of Lot 75, it being the dower of Sarah Stubbs, sold as the property of William Stubbs, decd, to Hubbard Stubbs.

/s/Rowland Stubbs, Admr de bonis non

Recorded: 28 Feb 1853

END OF BOOK D

Fayette County Administrators and Guardians Bonds
Book B (1850-1874)

Guardian's Bond of Robert C. Porter
Page 1

Robert C. Porter, principal, and Andrew M. Henderson, give $1850 bond on 1 May 1850 upon the condition that Robert C. Porter this day be apptd Gdn of Andrew M. Henderson, orphan of Mitchel Henderson, decd.
/s/Robert C. Porter
/s/Hugh Porter
Recorded: 9 May 1850

Admr's Bond, John Buse, Admr of Estate of William Buse, late of Mexico, decd
Page 1-2

John Buse and William Wiggins give bond for $500 upon the condition that John Buse make inventory, etc.
Recorded: 9 May 1850.
/s/John Buse
/s/William Wiggings

Admr's Bond of P. B. Cox, Admr de bonis non of Catherine Molder, late of said county
Page 2-3

Date: 6 May 1850. Bond for $500.
/s/P. B. Cox
/s/Almond Stratton
Recorded: 9 May 1850

Admr's Bond of J. Sweat, Admr of James Hunter, late of Fayette Co.
Page 4

Date: 3 Jun 1850. Bond for $1850.00. Admr to make inventory, etc.
/s/Andrew J. Sweat
/s/Ephraim Sweat
Recorded: 6 Jun 1850

Guardian's Bond, Ishmael Dunn appointed Gdn of Sarah Baily, a person deaf and dumb
Page 5

Date: 3 Jun 1850. Bond for $1850.00.
/s/Ishamel Dunn
/s/Chrit Bowen
Recorded: 6 Jun 1850

Guardian's Bond, Hiram Travis appointed Gdn of Richard and Thomas Humphrey, Orphans of William Humphrey
Page 5-6

Date: 3 Jun 1850. Bond for $1850.00.
/s/Hiram Travis
/s/James Jones (x, his mark)
Recorded: 6 Jun 1850

Temporary Letters of Adm to R. Manson Stell of Goods, Chattels, Rights and Credits of James J. Stell
Page 6

Date: 15 Mar 1850.. Bond for $2000.00
/s/R. Manson Stell
/s/John D. Stell
Recorded: 6 Jun 1850

Admrs' Bond of R. Manson, Admr of James J. Stell, late of Fayette Co.
Page 7

To make true and perfect infentory of said estate.
Date: 1 Jul 1850. Bond for $1500.00
/s/R. Manson Stell
/s/John D. Stell
/s/T. D. King
Recorded: 5 Jul 1850

Admrs' Bond of O. I. Head and David P. Elder, Admrs of William R. Head, decd
Page 8

David P. Elder, Joshua Elder and Thomas Whitaker make Bond for $7000 upon the condition that O. I. Head and David P. Elder be appointed Admrs of William R. Head, decd, late of Fayette Co., 1 Jul 1850.
/s/O. J. Head
/s/David P. Elder
/s/Joshua Elder (x, his mark)
Simon T. Whitaker
Recorded: 5 Jul 1850

Admr's Bond of Alfred Dorman, Admr of Estate of John Dorman
Page 9-10

Alfred Dorman and Tandy D. King give bond for $1000 upon the condition that Alfred Dorman be appointed Admr of Estate of John Dorman, decd, late of Fayette Co.
/s/Alfred Dorman
/s/T. D. King
Recorded: 5 Jul 1850

Admr's Bond of John Shelnut, Admr of Andrew Shelnut
Page 10-11

John Shelnut and John Ward give bond for $500 upon the condition that John Shelnut be appointed Admr of Andrew Shelnut, decd, late of Fayette Co.
/s/John Shelnut
/s/John Ward
Recorded: 5 Jul 1850

Guardian's Bond of Jared I. Whitaker
Page 11

Bond of Jared I. Whitaker and Simon T. Whitaker for $6000 on 1 Jul 1850 upon the condition that Jared I. Whitaker be appointed Gdn of Jasper Loyd and Newton Loyd, Orphans of James Loyd.
/s/Jared I. Whitaker
/s/John J. Whitaker
/s/Simon T. Whitaker
Recorded: 5 Jul 1850

Admrs' Bond of Joseph H. and Rebecca Murphy, Admrs of Simon P. Murphy
Page 12

Bond of Joseph H. Murphy, Rebecca Murphy, Jeptha Murphy, Thomas E. Murphy, Nathan Eason and Emanuel Murphy for $6000 dated 1 Jul 1850, upon the condition that Joseph H. Murphy and Rebecca Murphy, Admrs with LWT annexed of Simon P. Murphy, decd, late of Fayette Co.
/s/Joseph H. Murphy
/s/Rebecca Murphy
/s/Jeptha Murphy
/s/Thomas E. Murphy
/s/Nathan Eason
/s/E. Murphy
Recorded: 5 Jul 1850

Guardian's Bond of John Loyd
Page 13

John Loyd, Sarah Loyd, Mary Fernander James Loyd, and Jeremiah S. Jones, bond for $6000 dated 1 Jul 1850 upon the condition that John Loyd be appointed Gdn this day to Thomas Embry Loyd and Sarah Frances Loyd, Orphans of James Loyd, decd.
/s/Mary Fernander
/s/James Loyd
/s/J. S. Jones
Recorded: 5 jul 1850

Admrs' Bond of Henry Simpson, Admr of Mary Waldroup
Page 14

Henry Simpson, Reubin Wallis and Jordan Lord give bond for $500 dated 2 Sept 1850 upon the condition that Henry Simpson be appointed Admr of Mary Waldroup, decd, late of Fayette Co.
/s/Henry Simpson
/s/Reubin Wallis
/s/Jordan Loyd
Recorded: 4 Sept 1850

Admrs' Bond of Amherst W. Stone, Admr of Burrell Ware
Page 15

Amherst W. Stone and John S. Holliday give bond for $1000 on 4 Nov 1850 upon the condition that Amherst W. Stone be appointed Admr de bonis non of Burrell Ware, late of Texas.
/s/Amherst W. Stone
/s/John S. Holliday
Recorded: 5 Nov 1850

Guardian's Bond of John S. Holliday
Page 16

John S. Holliday and Robert K. Holliday give bond for $5000 on 4 Nov 1850 upon the condition that John S. Holliday is this day appointed Gdn of Emily F. Ware, Orphan of George Ware.
/s/John S. Holliday
/s/Robert K. Holliday
Recorded: 5 Nov 1850

Guardian's Bond of William Jennings, Jr.
Page 16-17

William Jennings, Jr., Nathaniel Stinchcomb and Burrell A. Ware give bond for $5000 on 4 Nov 1850 upon the condition that William Jennings be appointed this day Gdn to Elizabeth Jennings, Orphan of Allen Jennings.
/s/William Jennings, Jr.
/s/Nathaniel Stinchcomb
/s/Burrell A. Ware
Recorded: 5 Nov 1850

Admrs' Bond of Christopher C. Bowen
Page 17-18

Christopher C. Bowen and Emeline Collins give bond for $6000 on 4 Nov 1850 upon the condition that C. C. Bowen be appointed Admr of Paschal E. Collins, decd, late of Fayette Co.
/s/C. C. Bowen
/s/Emeline Collins (x, her mark)
Recorded: 5 Nov 1850

Guardian's Bond of James Loyd
Page 18

James Loyd, John Loyd, Sarah Loyd, William Whatley and Walter J. Campbell give $3000 bond on 4 Nov 1850 upon the condition that James Loyd be apptd Gdn to Samuel Loyd, orphan of James Loyd, decd.
/s/James Loyd
/s/John Loyd
/s/Sarah Loyd
/s/William Whatley
/s/Walter J. Campbell
Recorded: 5 Nov 1850

Guardian's Bond of Burrell A. Ware
Page 19

Mildred Ware, John S. Holliday and Burrell A. Ware give bond for $10,000 upon the condition that Mildred Ware this day be appointed Gdn to Richard and Ann Eliza Ware, Orphans of George Ware, decd.
/s/Mildred Ware
/s/John S. Holliday
/s/Burrell A. Ware
Recorded: 5 Nov 1850

Guardian's Bond of Burrell A. Ware
Page 19-20

Burrell A. Ware, John S. Holliday and Nathaniel Stinchcomb give bond on 4 Nov 1850 for $10,000 upon the condition that Burrell A. Ware be appointed this day Gdn to James and Catherine Ware, Orphans of George Ware, decd.
/s/Burrell A. Ware
/s/John S. Holliday
/s/Nathaniel Stinchcomb
Recorded: 5 Nov 1850

Admrs' Bond of Warren N. Glass
Page 20-21

Warren N. Glass, George M. Berry, Wiley W. Glass give $8000 bond on 4 Nov 1850 upon the condition that Warren N. Glass be appointed Admr of Uriah Glass, decd, late of Fayette Co.
/s/Warren N. Glass
/s/George M. Berry
/s/Wiley W. Glass
Recorded: 5 Nov 1850

Admrs' Bond of Jesse Lasseter
Page 21-22

Jesse Lasseter and William H. Flowers give bond for $500 on 22 Nov 1850 upon the condition that Jesse Lasseter be appointed Gdn of Miles L. Scott, late of South Carolina.
/s/Jesse Lasseter
/s/William H. Flowers
Recorded: 22 Nov 1850

Guardian's Bond of Zadok Blalock
Page 22-23

Zadok Blalock, Isaac B. Avera give bond for $100 on 6 Nov 1850 upon the condition that Zadock Blalock be appointed Gdn to Barbary, Elizabeth Anne and Mary Jane Avera, orphans of William H. Avrea, decd.
/s/Zadok Blalock
/s/Isaac B. Avrea
Recorded: 22 Nov 1850

Guardian's Bond of Talton Holland
Page 23

Talton Holland and Lewis C. Smith give bond for $500 on 7 Jan 1851 upon the condition that Talton Holland be appointed Gdn this day of the heirs of Talton and Susan Holland, children of said Talton and Susan Holland.
/s/Talton Holland
/s/Lewis C. Smith
Recorded: 8 Jan 1851

Admrs' Bond of Elijah Glass and James Turner
Page 34

Elijah Glass and James Turner and John Murphy and William N. Hill give $9000 bond on 13 Jan 1851 upon the condition that Elijah Glass and James Turner be appointed Admrs of James Turner, late of this county, decd.
/s/Elijah Glass
/s/James Turner
/s/John Murphy
/s/William N. Hill
Recorded: Jan 1851

Admrs' Bond of James L. Hobgood and Jesse L. Blalock
Page 25

James L. Hobgood, Jesse L. Blalock, Lewis Hobgood, William H. Blalock and Jackson Martin, give bond for $30,000 on 13 Jan 1851 upon the condition that James L. Hogbood and Jesse L. Blalock be appointed Admrs with LWT annexed of Wright Martin, decd. late of said county.
/s/James L. Hobgood
/s/Jesse L. Blalock
/s/Lewis Hobgood
/s/William H. Blalock
/s/Jackson Martin
Recorded: 3 Jan 1851

Guardian's Bond of Charles W. Wiliford
Page 26

Charles W. Wiliford and D. D. Denham give $7000 bond on 13 Jan 1851 upon the condition that Charles W. Wiliford be appointed Gdn this day of Wilson A. Wiliford, orphan of Wilson P. Wiliford, decd.
/s/Charles W. Wiliford
/s/D. D. Denham
Recorded: 14 Jan 1851

Guardian's Bond of Edmond Knowls
Page 26-27

Edmond Knowls and Eli Edmondson and Andrew McBride give for $100 on 13 Jan 1851 upon the condition that Edmond Knowls be appointed Gdn to Benjamin F. Knowls, orphan of Benjamin E. Knowls, decd.
/s/Edmond Knowls (x, his mark)
/s/Eli Edmondson
/s/Andrew McBride
Recorded: 14 Jan 1851

Guardian's Bond of Floyd Gammage
Page 27

Floyd Gammage and Francis M. Nix give bond for $320.00 on 3 Mar 1851 upon the condition that floyd Gammage be appointed this day Gdn to Thomas M. Gammage, orphan of William Gammage, decd.
/s/Floyd Gammage
/s/F. M. Nix
Recorded: 7 Mar 1857

Admrs' Bond of Allen Reeves
Page 28

Allen Reeves and James H. Williams and Oliver J. Head give $4000 bond on 5 May 1851 upon the condition that Allen Reeves be appointed Admr of William Reeves.
/s/Allen Reeves
/s/James H. Williams
/s/O. J. Head
Recorded: 6 May 1851

Guardian's Bond of Washington Wilson
Page 29

Washington Wilson and John S. Holliday give $400 bond on 7 Jul 1851 upon the condition that Washington Wilson be appointed this day Gdn to Nancy and John Wilson, children of the said Washington Wilson.
/s/Washington Wilson
/s/John S. Holliday
Recorded: 8 Jul 1851

Admrs' Bond of Abner Camp
Page 29-30

Abner Camp and John Camp, security, give $15,000 bond on 1 Sept 1851 upon the condition that Abner has obtained Temp. Letters of Admr of Morris Harris, decd.
/s/Abner Camp
/s/John Camp, sec.
Recorded: 5 Sept 1851

Admrs' Bond of Samuel H. Ellison
Page 30-31

Samuel H. Ellison, D. D. Denham, Littleton Stokes and Jarrot Handly give $15,000 bond on 1 Sept 1851 upon the condition that Samuel H. Ellison be appointed Admr of Mark Smallwood, late of this county.
/s/Samuel H. Ellison
/s/D. D. Denham
/s/Littleton Stokes
/s/Jarrot Handly
Recorded: 5 Sept 1851

Admrs' Bond of Jesse L. Blalock and James L. Hobgood
Page 31-32

Jesse L. Blalock and James L. Hobgood, Jabez M. Brassell and Andrew McBride give $2000 bond on 1 Sept 1851 upon the condition that Jesse L. Blalock and James L. Hobgood be appointed Admrs of Wright Martin.
/s/Jesse L. Blalock
/s/James L. Hobgood
/s/Jabez M. Brassell
/s/Andrew McBride
Recorded: 5 Sept 1851

Admrs' Bond of Simon T. Whitaker and Dennis Stubbs
Page 32-33

Simon T. Whitaker and Dennis Stubbs give bond for $12,000 on 3 Nov 1851 upon the condition that Simon T. Whitaker and Dennis Stubbs be appointed Admrs of Sarah Stubbs.
/s/S. T. Whitaker
/s/Dennis Stubbs
/s/O. J. Head
/s/John O. Dickson
/s/John D. Stell

Guardian's Bond of Parker Eason
Page 33-34

William T. Griffin, prinicpal and Parker Eason, security, give bond for $500 on 3 Nov 1851 upon the condition that Parker Eason be appointed this day Gdn fo William S. Milner, a minor of Pitt W. Milner, decd, that the annual interest of the estate of said ward was not sufficient to educate and maintain said ward and that he was unable to control said ward and he should be granted an order binding said ward with the Griffin for and until he arrives to the full age of 21 years upon his giving bond and security in the sum of $500.
/s/William T. Griffin
/s/Parker Eason
Recorded: 4 Nov 1851

Guardian's Bond of William J. Russell
Page 34-35

William J. Russell and Charles Clements give bond for $5000 on 29 Feb 1851 upon the condition that William J. Russell was appointed Gdn on 7 Jul to John Herring, Marcus Herring and Frances Herring, Orphans of Thomas Herring, decd.
/s/William J. Russell
/s/Charles Clements
Recorded: 29 Dec 1851

Admrs' Bond of Rowland Stubbs
Page 35

Rowland Stubbs and Robert K. Holliday, security, give bond for $1000 on 5 May 1852 upon the condition that Rowland Stubbs be appointed Admr of William Stubbs
/s/Rowland Stubbs
/s/Robert K. Holliday, sec.
Recorded: 8 Jul 1852

Admrs' Bond of Zadok Blalock
Page 36

Zadok Blalock and William H. Blalock, security, give $1500 bond on 3 May 1852 upon the condition that Zadok Blalock be appointed Admr of Barbary McDonald.
/s/Zadock Blalock
/s/William H. Blalock
Recorded: 8 Jul 1852

Admrs' Bond of Council Rentfrow
Page 37

Council Rentfrow and Elijah Glass, security, give $1000 bond on 3 May 1852 upon the condition that Council Rentfrow be appointed Admr of John W. Pledger.
/s/Council Rentfrow
/s/Elijah Glass, sec.
Recorded: 9 Jul 1852

Admrs' Bond of Christopher C. Bowen
Page 37-38

Christopher C. Bowen, S. T. Whitaker and L. H. Griffin and William H. Blalock make $10,000 bond on 7 Jun 1852 upon the condition that Christopher C. Bowen be appointed Admr of Paschal E. Collins.
/s/Christopher C. Bowen
/s/S. T. Whitaker
/s/L. H. Griffin
/s/William H. Blalock
Recorded: 9 Jul 1852

Admrs' Bond of William N. Hill
Page 38-39

William N. Hill, principal, and William J. Russell and William H. Blalock, give $800 bond on 7 Jun 1852 upon the condition that William N. Hill be apptd Admr of James A. Newton, decd, late of Fayette Co.
/s/W. N. Hill
/s/William J. Russell
/s/W. H. Blalock
Recorded: 9 Jul 1852

Guardian's Bond of Edmond Knoles
Page 39-40

Edmond Knoles and William H. Hill give $100 bond on 5 Jul 1852 upon the condition that Edmond Knoles be appointed Gdn of James M. Knoles, minor son of Benjamin E. Knoles, decd.
/s/Edmond Knoles (x. his mark)
/s/William N. Hill
Recorded: 9 Jul 1852

Admrs' Bond of William Malone
Page 40

William Malone and Calvin S. Westmoreland give $1000 bond on 5 Jul 1852 upon the condition that William Malone be appointed Admr of William W. Bishop, late of Montgomery Co., Alabama.
/s/William Malone
/s/C. S. Westmoreland
Recorded: 9 Jul 1852

Admrs' Bond of Jesse Hubbard
Page 41

Jesse Hubbard and John O. Dickson, security, give $600 bond on 22 Sept 1852 upon the condition that Jesse Hubbard be appointed temporary Admr of Elbert Bishop, decd.
/s/Jesse H. Hubbard (x, his mark)
/s/John O. Dickson
Recorded: 6 Dec 1852

Admrs' Bond of James L. Hobgood
Page 42

James L. Hobgood, J. C. W. Gosdin, A. J. Martin, William Martin, Lewis Hobgood and Nathan Camp, securities, give $20,000 bond on 4 Oct 1852 upon the condition that James L. Hogbood be appointed Admr of Wright Martin, decd.
/s/James L. Hobgood
/s/Lewis Hobgood
/s/J. C. W. Gosdin
/s/Jackson Martin
/s/William Martin
/s/Nathan Camp
Recorded: 6 Oct 1852

Admrs' Bond of James L. Hobgood
Page 43

James L. Hogbood, Admr de bonis non and Lewis Hobgood and J. C. W. Gosden, A. J. Martin, William Martin and Andrew McBride, securities, give $2000 bond on 4 Oct 1852 upon the condition that James L. Hobgood be appointed Admr de bonis non of Wright Martin
/s/James L. Hogbood
/s/Lewis Hobgood
/s/J. C. W. Gosden
/s/A. J. Martin
/s/William Martin
/s/Andrew McBride
Recorded: 6 Oct 1852

Admrs' Bond of Drury B. May
Page 44

Drury B. May, principal, and Jeptha V. May, security, gives $1000 bond on 4 Oct 1852 upon the condition that Drury B. May be appointed Admr of Hiram Moses.
/s/Drury B. May
/s/Jeptha V. May, security. Recorded: 6 Oct 1852

Admr's Bond of John B. Kennedy
Page 45

John B. Kennedy, Admr, principal, and George R. Kennedy and William Y. Conine, securities, give $2000 bond on 4 Oct 1852
/s/John B. Kennedy
/s/George R. Kennedy, sec.
/s/William Y. Conine, sec.
Recorded: 6 Oct 1852

Admrs' Bond of Christopher C. Bowen
Page 46

Christopher C. Bowen, principal and John Bowen, security, give $1000 bond on 6 Dec 1852 upon the condition that Christopher C. Bowen be appointed Admr of Paschal E. Collins.
/s/Christopher C. Bowen
/s/John Bowen, sec.
Recorded: 6 Dec 1852

Admrs' Bond of Jesse Hubbard
Page 47

Jesse Hubbard, principal and John O. Dickson, security, give $600 bond on 1 Nov 1852 upon the condition that Jesse Hubbard be appoibnted Admr of Elbert Bishop.
/s/Jesse Hubbard
/s/John O. Dickson, sec.
Recorded: 1 Nov 1852

Guardian's Bond of William Jennings
Page 48

William Jennings and James Jones, security, give $170 bond on 10 Nov 1852 upon the condition that William Jennings be appointed this day Gdn of the person and property of Emily Turner, orphan of James Turner.
/s/William Jennings
/s/James Jones, sec.
Recorded: 10 Jan 1853

Guardian's Bond of Lorenzo D. Padgett
Page 48-49

Lorenzo D. Padgett and Alfred Brown give $150 bond on 10 Jan 1853 upon the condition that Lorenzo D. Padgett be appointed Gdn of James T. Brassell, minor of James Brassell.
/s/L. D. Padgett
/s/Alfed Brown
Recorded: 10 Jan 1853

Admrs' Bond of Matilda Graves
Page 49-50

Matilda Graves, principal and Minto Graves, John Graves and Hilery Cleckler and Jesse Ward, securities, give $2000 bond on 10 Jan 1853 upon the condition that Matilda Graves be appointed Admx of David Graves.
/s/Matilda Graves (x, her mark)
/s/Minton Graves
/s/John Graves
/s/Hilery Clackler
/s/Jesse Ward
Recorded: 10 Jan 1853

Guardian's Bond of William H. Blalock
Page 50-51

William H. Blalock and William J. Russell and Zadock Blalock give $5000 bond on 7 Mar 1853 upon the condition that William H. Blalock be this day appointed Gdn to Jefferson Bearden, Quiller Bearden, Larkin Bearden, Parthena Bearden, Sarah Ann Bearden and Asa J. Bearden.
/s/William H. Blalock
/s/William J. Russell
/s/Z. Blalock
Recorded: 30 Apr 1853

Guardian's Bond of Nicholas F. Powers
Page 51

Nicholas F. Powers and George Powers, security, give $700, $900 and $49 bond on 7 Mar 1853 upon the condition that Nicholas F. Powers be appointed Gdn to Thomas M. G. Powers.
/s/N. F. Powers
/s/George Powers
Recorded: 30 Apr 1853

Guardian's Bond of Marcus E. McIntosh
Page 52

Marcus E. McIntosh and A. C. McIntosh give $150 bond on 6 Jun 1853 upon the condition that Marcus E. McIntosh this day be appointed Gdn of Andrew J. McBride and Lachland L. McBride, minors of William McBride.

No signatures

Guardian's Bond of Jesse Barintine
Page 52-53

Jesse Barintine, Jr. and James F. Johnson, security, give $400 bond on 3 May 1853 upon the condition that Jesse Barintine, Jr. be appointed this day Gdn of James Thompson.
/s/Jesse Barintine, Jr.
/s/James F. Johnson, sec.
Recorded: 9 Aug 1853

Admrs' Bond of Andrew J. Mundy and Reuben T. Mundy
Page 53-54

Andrew J. Mundy and Reuben T. Mundy, principal, and John O. Dickson and William J. Russell, securities, give $4000 bond on 4 Jul 1853 upon the condition that Andrew J. Mundy and Reuben T. Mundy be appointed Admrs of Jesse Lasseter.
/s/A. J. Mundy
/s/R. T. Mundy
/s/John O. Dickson
Recorded: 9 Aug 1853

Guardian's Bond of Elijah Glass
Page 54

Elijah Glass and John O. Dickson, security, give $800 bond on 4 Jul 1853 upon the condition that Elijah Glass be appointed this day Gdn to Nathan, Fdrick, Sampson and Zachariah Turner, orphans of James Turner, decd, late of Fayette Co.
/s/Elijah Glass
/s/John O. Dickson, sec.
Recorded: 9 Aug 1853

Guardian's Bond of Charles Whaley
Page 55

Charles Whaley as principal and Madison Whaley and Reuben Wallis as securities give $500 bond on 4 Jul 1853 upon the condition that Charles Whaley, by virtue of an order of said court at July term of 1853 appointed a person to whom Daniel Whaley an orphan child of John Whaley, late of said county, decd, about 13 years of age is bound until said orphan shall be 21 years of age.
/s/Charles Whaley (x, his mark)
Madison Whaley
Reuben Wallis
Recorded: 10 Aug 1853

Guardian's Bond of William B. Fuller
Page 55-56

William B. Fuller, principal, and Mial M. Tidwell, John O. Dickson and John S. Holliday, security, give $2500 bond on 4 Oct 1853 upon the condition that William Be. Fuller be appointed this day Gdn of the property of Martha Thompson and Mary Thompson, minor children of Allen Thompson.
/s/William B. Fuller
/s/M. M. Tidwell
/s/John O. Dickson
/s/John S. Holliday
Recorded: 13 Dec 1853

Guardian's Bond of Wyatt S. Reeves.
Page 56-57

Wyatt S. Reeves and Allen Reeves, security give bond for $180 on 7 Nov 1853 upon the condition that Wyatt S. Reeves has been this day appointed Gdn to Letha Ann Reeves, orphan of William Reeves.
/s/Wyatt S. Reeves
/s/Allen Reeves
Recorded: 13 Dec 1853

Guardian's Bond of Samuel Kerlen
Page 57

Samuel Kerlen and Allen Reeves give $500 bond on 7 Nov 1853 upon the condition that Samuel Kerlen be appointed Gdn to John H. Mathews, orphan of Doctor N. Mathews.
/s/Samuel Kerlen
/s/Allen Reeves
Recorded: 13 Dec 1853

Guardian's Bond of Marcellus E. McIntosh
Page 57-58

Marcellus E. McIntosh and C. McIntosh, security, give $150 bond on 6 Jun 1853 upon the condition that Marcellus E. McIntosh has been this day appointed Gdn of the persons and property of Andrew J. McBride and Lachland McBride, minors of William McBride.
/s/M. E. McIntosh
/s/A. C. McIntosh
Recorded: 28 Jan 1854

Guardian's Bond of Martha A. Reeves
Page 58

Martha A. Reeves and Joshua H. Starr and Wyatt S. Reeves give bond for $4000 on 7 Nov 1853 upon the condition that Martha A. Reeves has been this day appointed Gdn to William F. Reeves, Henry C. Reeves, Amos W. Reeves, Robert H. Reeves, Sarah Ann Reeves and Martha W. Reeves.
/s/Martha A. Reeves
/s/Joshua H. Starr
/s/Wyatt S. Reeves
Recorded: 28 Jan 1854

Admrs' Bond of Allen Reeves
Page 59

Allen Reeves, principal, and Samuel Kerlen, security, give $4000 bond on 5 Sept 1853 upon the condition that Allen Reeves be appointed Admr of William Reeves, late of said county, decd.
/s/Allen Reeves
/s/Samuel Kerlen
Recorded: 13 Dec 1853

Admrs' Bond of William H. Flowers
Page 60

William H. Flowers, principal, and Ephraim M. Pool, security, give $550 bond on 7 Nov 1853 upon the condition that William H. Flowers be appointed Admr de bonis non of the goods and chattels, rights, credits and lands of Miles Scott, late of the State of South Carolina, decd, to make inventory, etc.
/s/William H. Flowers
/s/E. M. Pool
Recorded: 13 Dec 1853

Admx' Bond of Sarah Jennings
Page 61

Sarah Jennings, principal, and James R. Jennings, security, give $7000 bond on 5 Dec 1853 upon the condition that Sarah Jennings be appointed Admx with the nuncupative Will annexed of John A. Jennings.
/s/Sarah F. Jennings
/s/James R. Jennings
Recorded: 13 Dec 1853

Temporary Admrs' Bond of A. J. Mundy
Page 62

Andrew J. Mundy and Reuben Wallis, security, give $7000 bond on 8 Dec 1853 upon the condition that A. J. Mundy has this day applied and obtained Temporary Letters of Admn of Francis M. Jones, decd.
/s/A. J. Mundy
/s/Reuben Wallis
Recorded: 28 Jun 1854

Admrs' Bond of Andrew J. Mundy
Page 63

Andrew J. Mundy, principal, and Reuben T. Mundy and James H. Waldrup, securities, give $7000 bond on 9 Jan 1854 upon the condition that Andrew J. Mundy be appointed Admr of Francis Jones, late of said co., decd.
/s/A. J. Mundy
/s/J. H. Waldrup
/s/B. T. Mundy
Recorded: 28 Jan 1854

Temporary Admrs' Bond of Hugh Porter
Page 64

Hugh Porter and Eli Edmondson, security, give bond for $2000 on 15 Dec 1853 upon the condition that Hugh Porter has obtained Temporary Letters of Admn on Sansom W. Roberts, decd.
/s/Hugh Porter
/s/Eli Edmondson
Recorded: 22 Feb 1854

Admrs' Bond of Hugh Porter
Page 65

Hugh Porter, principal, and H. F. Underwood, security, give $2000 bond on 6 Feb 1854 upon the condition that Hugh Porter be appointed Admr of Sansom W. Roberts, decd.
/s/Hugh Porter
/s/H. F. Underwood
Recorded: 22 Feb 1854

Guardian's Bond of Mathew Jones
Page 66

Mathew Jones, principal, and William J. Russell, security, give $1200 bond on 4 Oct 1854 upon the condition that Mathew Jones has this day been apptd Gdn to William Tompson, minor son of Allen Tompson.
/s/Mathew Jones
/s/William J. Russell
Recorded: 22 Feb 1854

Guardian's Bond of Martha Owens
Page 66-67

Martha Owens and William Owens, security, give bond for $1850 on 9 Jan 1854 upon the condition that Martha Owens has been appointed this day Gdn to Martha Amanda, Sarah Elizabeth, Matilda C., Lucinda Caroline and Robert Martin Owens.
/s/Martha Owens
/s/W. J. Owens
Recorded: 20 Feb 1854

Guardian's Bond of James Hanes
Page 67

James Hanes and Samuel T. W. Minor, security, give $250 bond on 6 Feb 1854 upon the condition that James Hanes has been this day appinted Gdn to Elisha Lasseter and Elizabeth Lasseter.
/s/James Hanes
/s/S. T. W. Minor. Recorded: 22 Feb 1854

Guardian's Bond of Hugh Porter
Page 68

Hugh Porter and H. F. Underwood, security, gibe $1200 bond on 6 Feb 1854 upon the condition that Hugh Porter be appointed this day Gdn to Mary A. Roberts and William Roberts.
/s/Hugh Porter
/s/H. F. Underwood
Recorded: 22 Feb 1854

Admrs' Bond of Haywood Ozburn
Page 68-69

Haywood Ozburn, principal, and Henry Rentfrow, security, give $300 bond on 7 Mar 1854 upon the condition that Haywood Ozburn be appointed Admr of William K. Ozburn, late of said co., decd.
/s/S. H. Ozburn
/s/Henry Rentfrow
Recorded: 30 May 1854

Admrs' Bond of Andrew J. McBride
Page 69-70

Andrew McBride as principal and Edward Connor, security, give $500 bond on 6 Mar 1854 upon the condition that Andrew McBride be appointed Admr of Estate of Samuel Martin, late of said county, decd.
/s/Andrew McBride
/s/Edward Connor
Recorded: 30 May 1854

Admrs' Bond of Jeptha Landrum
Page 70-71

Jeptha Landrum, principal and Willis F. Landrum bie $500 bond on 4 May 1854 upon the condition that Jeptha Landrum, Sr. be appointed Admr of Richmond Jones, late of said county, decd.
/s/Jeptha Landrum
/s/W. F. Landrum
Recorded: 31 May 1854

Admrs' Bond of Sidney D. Mann
Page 71-72

Sidney D. Mann, principal, and Reuben Wallis, security, give $500 bond on 1 May 1854 upon the condition that Sidney D. Mann be appointed Admr de bonis non of Peter Mann, late of said county, decd.
/s/S. D. Mann
/s/Reuben Wallis
Recorded: 31 May 1854

Guardian's Bond of Hugh Porter
Page 72-73

Hugh porter and H. F. Underwood, security, give $2500 bond on 1 May 1854 upon the condition that Hugh Porter is this day appointed Gdn to Sarah T. Roberts, Lewis E. H. Roberts, James S. Roberts and Griffin A. Roberts.
/s/Hugh Porter
/s/H. F. Underwood
Recorded: 31 May 1854

Guardian's Bond of James W. Tally
Page 73

James W. Tally, Jordan Williams and James L. Lovejoy, security, give $4000 bond on 1 May 1854 upon the condition that James W. Tally has been this day apptd Gdn to Kindrick D. Little, minor orphan of Zabud Little, decd.
/s/James W. Tally
/s/Jordan Williams
/s/James L. Lovejoy
Recorded: 31 May 1854

Guardian's Bond of John A. F. Hawkins
Page 74

John A. F. Hawkins and John I. Whitaker and Simon T. Whitaker, securities, bond for $5000 on 5 Jun 1854 upon the condition that John A. F. Hawkins has been this day apptd Gdn to Michael A. E. Collins, Romulus D. Collins, Emily C. Collins, James A. Collins and Paschal Collins, Martin Collins and Elizabeth N. Collins.
/s/John A. F. Hawkins
/s/John I. Whitaker
/s/S. T. Whitaker
Recorded: 20 Jul 1854

Guardian's Bond of Simon T. Whitaker
Page 75

Simon T. Whitaker, principal, and John I. Whitaker and Oliver J. head, security, give $6000 bond on 5 Jul 1854 upon the condition that Simon T. Whitaker has this day been appointed Gdn to Francis A. E. Neel, John Neel, Amelia H. Neel, Benjamin F. Neel, Sarah Jane Neel, Pocahonta Neel and James Neel.
/s/S. T. Whitaker
/s/John I. Whitaker
/s/Oliver J. Head
Recorded: 20 Jul 1854

Admrs' Bond of Mel M. Mathews
Page 76

Mel M. Mathews, principal, and Samuel Kerlen, security, give $150 bond on 5 Jun 1854 upon the condition that Mel M. Mathews is appted Admr of Rachael A. Mathews, late of said county, decd, to make inventory, etc.
/s/M. M. Matahews
/s/Samuel Kerlen
Recorded: 20 Jul 1854

Guardian's Bond of Robert Iverson
Page 77

Robert Iverson and Albert G. Brooks, security, give $20,000 on 2 Oct 1854 upon the condition that Robert Iverson has been appointed Gdn to person and property of George W. Brooks and John N. Brooks, minor of Ivey Brooks.
/s/Robert Iverson
/s/Albert G. Brooks
Recorded: 17 Nov 1854

Guardian's Bond of Albert G. Brooks
Page 77-78

Albert G. Brooks and Robert Iverson, security, give $10,000 bond on 2 Oct 1854 upon the condition that Albert G. Brooks has been this day apptd Gdn of Harriet T. Brooks, minor orphan of Ivey Brooks, decd.
/s/Albert G. Brooks
/s/Robert Iverson
Recorded: 7Nov 1854

Admrs' Bond of George J. Miles
Page 78

George J. Miles, principal, and William Miles, security, give $2000 bond on 7 Aug 1854 upon the condition that George J. Miles be apptd Admr of Thura Z. Miles, late of said county, decd.
/s/George J. Miles
/s/William Miles
Recorded: 17 Nov 1854

Admrs' Bond of John I. Whitaker
Page 79

John I. Whitaker and Simon T. Whitaker give $1000 bond on 4 Sept 1854 upon the condition that John I. Whitaker be appointed Admr of Elbert Harris, late of this co., decd.
/s/John I. Whitaker
/s/Simon T. Whitaker
Recorded: 17 Nov 1854

Admrs' Bond of Newton M. Fitts
Page 81

Newton M. Fitts and Francis Patterson, security give $200 bond on 2 Oct 1854 upon the condition that Newton M. Fitts be apptd Admr of the Estate of Walker Fitts, late of this county, decd.
/s/N. M Fitts
/s/Francis Patterson. Recorded: 7 Nov 1854

Guardian's Bond of Delila Moses
Page 81

Delila Moses and John C. Brassell, Phillip Brassell and Jabez M.Brassell, security, give $508 on 2 Oct 1854 upon the condition that Delila Moses be appointed Gdn to Martha M. Cavender, orphan of Wade H. Cavender, decd.
/s/Delila Moses
/s/John C. Brassell
/s/P.H. Brassell
/s/J. M. Brassell
Recorded: 18 Nov 1854

Admr's Bond of James L. Hobgood
Page 81-82

James L. Hobgood, Jackson Martin, Wright Martin, Samuel R. Hobgood and Leiws Hobgood give $10,000 bond on 6 Nov 1854 upon the condition that J. L. Hobgood be apptd Admr de bonis non of the Estate of Wright Martin, late of this county, decd, to make inventory, etc.
/s/James L. Hobgood
/s/Wright Martin
/s/Jackson Martin
/s/Samuel R. Hobgood
/s/Lewis Hobgood
Recorded: 18 Nov 1854

Admrs' Bond of William B. Fuller
Page 83

William B. Fuller, Mial M.Tidwell, security, give bond for $1200 on 6 Jul 1854 upon the condition that William B. Fuller be appointed Admr with the Will annexed of the Estate of Mary Cockrell, late of Alabama, decd.
/s/WilliamF. Fuller
/s/M. M. Tidwell
Recorded: 14 Dec 1854

Admrs' Bond of William E. Tucker
Page 84

William E. Tucker and Whitmel P. Allen, security, give bond for $8000 on 4 Dec 1854 upon the condition that William E. Tucker be appointed Admr of the Estate of Joshua S. Calloway, late of this county, decd.
/s/William E. Tucker
/s/W. P. Allen
Recorded: 14 Dec 1854

Guardian's Bond of Mathew Jones
Page 85

Mathew Jones and Samuel S. W. Minor and Alfred Brown, security, give $1000 bond on 4 Dec 1854 upon the condition that Mathew Jones be appointed Gdn to William Thompson, minor of Allen Thompson.
/s/Mathew Jones
/s/S. T. W. Minor
/s/A. Brown
Recorded: 14 Dec 1854

Guardian's Bond of Phillip H. Brassell
Page 85-86

Phillip H. Brassell and John C. Brassell, security, give $500 bond on 4 Dec 1854 upon the condition that Phillip H. Brassell be appointed Gdn to John H. Cavender, orphan of Wade H. Cavender, decd.
/s/P. H. Brassell
/s/John C. Brassell
Recorded: 14 Dec 1854

Admrs' Bond of Wiley Rountree
Page 86-87

Wiley Rountree, principal, and William A. Fuller and David Hanes, securities, give bond for $800 on 8 Jan 1855 upon the condition that Wiley Rountree be appted Admr of Francis M. Roberts, late of said county, decd.
/s/Wiley Rountree
/s/William A. Fuller
/s/David Hanes (x, his mark)
Recorded: 14 Feb 1855

Guardian's Bond of Martha McLeroy
Page 87

Martha McLeroy, principal, and Patrick H. Allen, Whitmell P. Allen, William E. Luckie and M. B. DeVaughan, securities, give bond for $18,000 on 5 Feb 1855 upon the condition that Martha McLeroy has been this day apptd Gdn to Martha F. McLeroy, Pitt M. McLeroy, Emily H. McLeroy and Thomas E. B. McLeroy.
/s/Martha McLeroy
/s/W. E. Tucker
/s/Patrick H.Allen
/s/M. B. DeVaughan
/s/W. P. Allen
Recorded: 14 Feb 1855

Guardian's Bond of M. B. DeVaughan
Page 88

M. B. DeVaughan, principal and Patrick H. Allen, Whitmel P. Allen and William E. Luckie, securities, give $4,500 bond on 5 Feb 1855 upon the condition that M. B. DeVaughan has been apptd Gdn to Wiley H. McLeroy.
/s/M. B.DeVaughan
W. P.Allen
/s/Patrick H. Allen
/s/William E. Tucker
Recorded: 14 Feb 1855

Guardian's Bond of William M. Spearr
Page 88-89

William M. Spearr, principal, and Joseph Spearr, Nathaniel Stinchcomb, security, give $40000 bond on 6 Feb 1855 upon the condition that William M.Spearr has this day been apptd Gdn to Green Griggs.
/s/William M. Spearr
/s/Joseph Spearr
/s/Nathaniel Stinchcomb
Recorded: 14 Feb 1855

Admx' Bond of Mary Waldrup
Page 89-90

Mary Waldrup, principal and Winslow G. Norton and Miles Norton, securities, give $800 bond on 5 Mar 1855 upon the condition that Mary Waldrup be apptd Admx of Thomas D. Waldrup, late of said county, decd.
/s/Mary Waldrup (x, her mark)
/s/Winslow G. Norton (x, his mark)
Recorded: 8 May 1855

Admrs' Bond of James McConnell
Page 90-91

James McConnell, principal and Milligan B. DeVaughan and Elijah Glass, securities, give bond for $2000 on 5 Mar 1855 upon the condition that James McConell be apptdd Admr of Emily McLeroy, late of the State of Louisiana.
/s/James McConnell
/s/M. B. DeVaughan
/s/Elijah Glass
Recorded: 8 May 1855

Admrs' Bond of William N. Hill
Page 91-92

William N. Hill, principal and John B. Allen, security, give $200 bond on 2 Apr 1855 upon the condition that William N. Hill be appted Admr of Sophrona P. Hill, wife of William N. Hill, late of said county, decd.
/s/William N. Hill
/s/John B.Allen
Recorded: 8 May 1855

Guardian's Bond of James Hanes
Page 92

James Hanes, principal, and James F. Johnson, security, give $100 bond on 2 Apr 1855 upon the condition that James Hanes be apptd Gdn this day of Sophia Lasseter.
/s/James Hanes
/s/James F. Johnson
Recorded: 8 May 1855

Admrs' Bond of Jesse Barintine
Page 93

Jesse Barrintine, principal and William H. Blalock, security, give $500 bond on 5 Mar 1850 upon the condition that Jesse Barintine be apptd Admr of Sarah Elizabeth Barintine, late of said county, decd.
/s/Jesse Barrintine (x, his mark)
/s/William H. Blalock
Recorded: 8 May 1855

Admrs' Bond of Thomas L. Long and Isham Long
Page 94-95

Thomas L. Long and Isham Long, principal,and William J. Russell, security, give $10,000 bond on 4 Jun 1855 upon the condition that Thomas L. Long and Isham Long be apptd Admrs of Estate of Marcus Long, late of said cunty, decd.
/s/Thomas L. Long
/s/Isham T. Long
/s/William J. Russell
Recorded: 4 Jun 1855

Guardian's Bond of William J. Russell
Page 95

William J. Russell and Jeptha Landrum, Jr., security, give bond for $10 on 5 Jun 1855 upon the condition that William J. Russell be apptd Gdn of the person and property of William Baggett.
/s/William J. Russell
/s/Jeptha Landrum
Recorded: 12 Jun 1855

Admrs' Bond of Oliver M. Pearson
Page 96-97

Oliver M. Pearson, principal, and Thomas C. Matthews, John C. Brassell, Willis Brassell and John I. Whitaker, securities, give $6000 bond on 2 Jul 1855 upon the condition that Oliver M. Pearson be apptd Admr of Olive McLane, late of said county, decd.
/s/Oliver M. Pearson
/s/T.C.Matthews
/s/John C. Brassell
/s/Willis Brassell
/s/John I. Whitaker
Recorded: 23 Jul 1855

Admrs' Bond of Oliver M. Pearson
Page 97-98

Oliver M. Pearson, principal,and Thomas C. Matthews, John C. Brassell, Willis Brassell, John I. Whitaker,security, give $5000 bond on 2 Jul 1855 upon the condition that Oliver M. Pearson be apptd Admr of Mary McLane, late of said county, decd.
/s/Oliver M. Pearson
/s/S. C. Matthews
/s/JohnC. Brassell
/s/Willis Brassell
/s/John I. Whitaker
Recorded: 23 Jul 1855

Admrs' Bond of Oliver M. Pearson
Page 98-99

Oliver M. Pearson, principal, and Thomas O. Matthews, John C. Brassell, Willis Brassell, and John I. Whitaker, securities, give $1000 bond on 2 Jul 1855 upon the condition that Oliver M. Pearson be apptd Admr of Mary McLane, late of said county, decd, to make inventory, etc.
/s/Oliver M. Pearsn
/s/T. C. Matthews
/s/John C. Brassell
/s/John I. Whitaker
Recorded: 23 Jul 1855

Temporary Admrs' Bond of Francis L. Lord
Page 100

Francis L. Lord, Rice Eason and John Harrison, securities, give $200 bond on 18 Sept 1855 upon the condition that Francis L. Long has obtained temporary Letters of Admn on Henry Lord, decd.
/s/Francis L. Lord
/s/Rice Eason
/s/John Harrison
Recorded: 22 Oct 1855

Guardian's Bond of John O. Dickson
Page 101

John O. Dickson and Robert D. Dickson give $800 bond on 8 Oct 1855 upon the condition that John O. Dickson is this day apptd Gdn to Sampson Turner, Frederick Turner, Nathan Turner and Zachariah Turner, orphans of James Turner, decd.
/s/John O. Dickson
/s/Robert D. Dickson

Admrs' Bond of Francis L. Lord
Page 102

Francis L. Lord, principal, and Rice Eason and T. W. Miner, security, give $200 bond on 5 Nov 1855 upon the condition that Francis L. Lord be apptd Admr of Henry Lord, late of said county, decd.
/s/Francis L. Lord
/s/S. T. W. Miner
/s/Rice Eason
Recorded: 6 Mar 1856

Admrs' Bond of Hansford D. Palmer
Page 103

Hansford D. Palmer, principal, and Charles W. Smith and Spencer T. Wellborn, securities, give bond for $4500 on 5 Nov 1855 upon the condition that Hansford D. Palmer be apptd Admr of John Palmer, late of said county, decd.
/s/Hansford D. Palmer
/s/C. W. Smith
/s/Spencer T. Wellborn

Guardian's Bond of William W. Bearden
Page 104

W. W. Bearden and Thomas J. Head, William Head, James Head, securities, give bond for $800 on 3 Dec 1855 upon the condition that W. W. Bearden has been apptd Gdn to Vicey Bearden, orphan of Edward Bearden.
/s/William W. Bearden (x, his mark)
/s/Thomas J. Head
/s/William Head
/s/James W. Head
Recorded: 28 Dec 1855

Admrs' Bond of Archibald M. Smith
Page 104-105

Archibald M. Smith, principal, and Benjamin B. Dykes, security, give $500 bnd on 3 Dec 1855 upon the condition that Archibald M. Smith be aptd Admr of Rodrick D. M. Avrea, late of Texas, decd.
/s/A. M. Smith
/s/BenjaminB. Dykes
Recorded: 28 Dec 1855

Guardian's Bond of John F. Mann
Page 106

John F. Mann and Gideon F. Mann, security, give $225 bond on 17 Dec 855 upon the condition that John F. Mann has this day been apptd Gdn to the person and property of Clayburn S. Mann, minor orphan of John D. Mann, late of said county, decd.
/s/J. F. Mann
/s/G.F. Mann
Recorded: 28 Dec 1855

Admx' Bond of Louisa L. Stell
Page 107-108

Louisa L. Stell, principal, and Mildred Ware, security, give $3000 bond on 3 Dec 1855 upon the condition that Louisa L. Stell be apptd Admx of Rufus T. Stell, late of said county, decd.
/s/Louis Stell
/s/Mildred Ware
Recorded:28 Dec 1855

Admrs' Bond of John B. Allen
Page 108-109

John B. Allen, principal, and Lewis F. Blalock, Henry F. Underwood and Jabez M. Brassell, securities, give $4000 on 4 Dec 1855 upon the cndition that John B. Allen be apptd Admr of Silas G. Eastin, late of said co., decd, to make inventory, etc.
/s/John B. Allen
/s/Lewis F. Blalock
/s/H. F. Underwood
/s/Jabez M. Brassell
Recorded: 28 Dec 1855

Admx' Bond of Rachel Eason
Page 109-110

Rachel Eason, principal, and Thomas Simpson, security, give $1200 bond on 3 Dec 1855 upon the condition that Rachel Eason is apptd Admx of Richard B. Eason, late of said co., decd
/s/Rachel Eason (x, her mark)
/s/Thomas Simpson
Recorded: 28 Dec 1855

Guardian's Bond of Nathan Camp
Page 110

Nathan Camp and Mial Tidwell, security, give $7500 bond on 4 Feb 1856 upon the condition that Nathan Camp has been apptd Gdn of person and property of James T. Jennings, William J. Jennings, Rhoda E. Jennings and Morgan Jennings, minor orphans of John A. Jennings, decd.
/s/Nathan Camp
/s/M. M. Tidwell
Recorded: 18 Jan 1856

Admrs' Bond of James L. Hobgood
Page 111

James L. Hobgood and Jackson Martin, Lewis C.Smith, securities, give $2500 on 14 Jan 1856 upon the condition that James L. Hobgood be apptd Admr of Samuel R. Hobgood, late of this county, decd.
/s/James L. Hobgood
/s/Jackson Matin
/s/Lewis C. Smith
Recorded: 13 Feb 1856

Guardian's Bond of Joseph Speer
Page 112

Joseph Speer and William Speer, security, give $6000 on 14 Jan 1856 upon the condition that Joseph Speer has been this day apptd Gdn to Thomas C. Speer, minor of the said Joseph Speer.
/s/Joseph Speer
/s/William M. Speer
Recorded: 13 Feb 1856

Admrs' Bond of Herod Thornton
Page 112-113

Herod Thornton, principal, and Blackman Thornton and Haywood Thornton, securities, give bond for $7800 on 1 Jan 1856 upon the condition that Herod Thornton be apptd Admr of Herod Thornton, Sr.,decd.
/s/Herod Thornton
/s/Blackman Thornton
/s/Haywood Thornton
Recorded: 13 Feb 1856

Admrs' Bond of Zadock Connor
Page 114

Zadock Connor and Edward Connor, security, give bond for $600 on 3 Mar 1856 upon the condition that Zadock C Connor be apptd Admr of Elisabeth Mulkey, late of this county, decd.
/s/T. C. Connor
/s/Edward Connor
Recorded: 19 Apr 1856

Admrs' Bond of William Alexander
Page 115

William Alexander and John P. Copeland, security, give $1000 on 3 Mar 1856 upon the condition that William Alexander be apptd Admr of James W. Copeland, late of this county, decd.
/s/William Alexander
/s/John P. Copeland
Recorded: 19 Apr 1856

Guardian's Bond of Mathew Yates
Page 116

Mathew yates and Counsel Rentfrow, security, give $2000 bond on 3 Mar 1856 upon the condition that Mathew Yates has been this day apptd Gdn to persons and property of Sophrona J. Yates and Emily M. Yates, orphans and minors of George M. Yates, decd.
/s/Mathew Yates
/s/Counsel Rentfrow. Recorded: 17 Apr 1856

Guardian's Bond of Counsel Rentfrow
Page 116-117

Counsel Rentfrow and Mathew Yates, security, give $1600 bond on 3 Mar 1856 upon the cndition that Counsel Rentfrow has been this day apptd Gdn to the property of Joseph P. Pledger, orphan of JohnW. Pledger, late of said county, decd.
/s/Counsel Rentfrow
/s/Mathew Yates
Recorded.19 Apr 1856

Temporary Admrs'Bond of Simon T. Whitaker and Dennis Stubbs
Page 117

Simon T. Whitaker and Dennis Stubbs, principal and John I. Whitaker, security, give $5000 bond on 24 Apr 1856 upon the condition that Simon T. Whitaker and Dennis Stubbs be apptd temp. Letters of Admns on William Stubbs, decd.
/s/S. T. Whitaker
/s/Dennis Stubbs
/s/John I. Whitaker
Recorded: 26 Apr 1856

Admrs' Bond of Mathew Yates
Page 118

Mathew Yates and Counsel Rentfrow, security, give $2000 bond on 3 Mar 1856 upon the condition that Mathew Yates be apptd Admr of George M. Yates, late of said county, decd.
/s/Mathew Yates
/s/Counsel Rentfrow
Recorded: 26 Apr 1856

Guardian's Bond of John S. Holliday
Page 119

John S. Holliday, principal, and John O. Dickson and Mial M. Tidwell give $2000 bond on 5 May 1856 upon the condition that John S. Holliday be apptd Gdn to property of Mary and Martha Thompson, minor children of Allen Thompson.
/s/John S. Holliday
/s/John O. Dickson
/s/M. M. Tidwell
Recorded: 10 May 1856

Guardian's Bond of Andrew J. Pollard
Page 119-120

Andrew J. Pollard, principal, and Lewis T. Thompson, security, give $325 bond on 5 May 1856 upon the condition that Andrew J. Pollard has been this day apptd Gdn to person and property of Mary E. Moses and William N. Moses, minor orphans of Hiram Moses, decd.
/s/Andrew J. Pollard
/s/LewisT. Thompson
Recorded: 10 May 1856

Guardian's Bond of Varney A. Gaskill
Page 120

Varney A. Gaskill, principal, and Jared I. Whitaker and William May, securities, give $600 bond on 5 May 1856 upon the condition that Varney A. Gaskill has this day been apptd Gdn to person and property of Jeffrey Hillsman.
/s/Varney A. Gaskill
/s/Jared Irwin Whitaker
/s/William May
Recorded: 10 May 1856

Admrs' Bond of John O. Brown
Page 121

John O. Brown, principal, and Cornelius Bennett and L. F. Blalock, Samuel T. W. Minor, security, give $2000 bond on 5 May 1856 upon the condition that John O. Brown be apptd Admr of Alfred Brown, to make inventory, etc.
/s/John O. Brown
/s/L. F. Blalock
/s/C. E. Bennett
Recorded: 10 May 1856

Guardian's Bond of Roxanna J. Mundy
Page 123

Roxanna J. Mundy and A. J. Mundy, security, give $200 on 5 May 1856 upon the condition that Roxanna J. Mundy has been this day apptd Gdn to property of Reuben T Mundy, Amanda A. Mundy and Julia Ann Mundy.
/s/Roxanna J. Mundy
/s/A. J.Mundy
Recorded: 19 Jul 1856

Guardian's Bond of Delila Moses
Page 123-124

Delila Moses, principal, and John C. Brassell and Phillip H. Brassell, security, give $300 bond on 2 Jun 1856 upon the condition that Delila Moses has been this day apptd Gdn to person and property of Phillip B. Moses and Hiram D. Moses
/s/Delila Moses
/s/John C. Brassell
/s/P. H. Brassell
Recorded: 19 Jul 1856

Guardian's Bond of Andrew J. Pollard
Page 124

Andrew J. Pollard, principal, and Lewis T. Thompson, security, give $165 bond on 3 Jun 1856 upon the conditon that Andrew J. Pollard has this day been apptd Gdn to JohnL. Moses.
/s/Andrew J. Pollard
/s/L. T. Thompson
Recorded: 19 Jul 1856

Admx' Bond of Nancy Stubbs
Page 124-125

Nancy Stubbs, principal,and Elijah Glass, John Huie, Edward Connor, Wilham S. Chambers and Daniel McLucas, securities, give $7000 bond on 4 Jun 1856 upon the condition that Nancy Stubbs be apptd Admx of William Stubbs, late of said county decd.
/s/Nancy Stubbs (x, her mark)
/s/Elijah Glass
/s/John Huie
/s/Edward Connor
/s/William S.Chambers
/s/Daniel McLucas
Recorded: 17 Jul 1856

Admrs' Bond of Edward Connor
Page 126

Edward Connor, Andrew McBride and Thomas H. Stephens give bond for $7000 on 9 Jun 1856 upon the condition that Edward Connor obtain letters of Admn pursuant to an Order of the goods and chatiels, rights and credits of William Stubbs...to collect and preserve from waste all goods, chattels, etc.
/s/Edward Connor
/s/Andrew McBride
/s/Thomas W. Stephens (x, his mark)
Recorded: 19 Jul 1856

Admrs' Bond of Edward Connor
Page 126

Edward Connor, Andrew McBride and Thomas H. Stephens, securities, give $7000 bond on 9 Jun 1856 upon the condition that Edward Connor be apptd Admr of William Stubbs, decd.
/s/Edward Connor
/s/Andrew McBride
/s/Thomas H. Stephens (x, his mark)
Recorded: 19 Jul 1856

Admrs' Bond of William May
Page 126-127

William May, principal, and Isaac P. Gay and Thomas C. Mathews, security give $40,000 on 8 Jul 1856 upon the condition that William May be apptd Admr of William Jennings, late of said co., decd.
/s/William May
/s/Isaac P. Gay
/s/Thomas C. Mathews
Recorded: 21 Jul 1856

Guardian's Bond of C. E. Bennett
Page 127-128

C. E. Bennett and Jeptha Landrum, Sr., security give $1800 bond on 7 Jul 1856 upon the condition that C. E. Bennett is this day apptd Gdn of the person and property of Russell C. Strickland, orphan of Simeon Strickland.
/s/C. E. Bennett
/s/Jeptha Landrum, Sr.
Recorded: 21 Jul 1856

Guardian's Bond of Barbary Palmer
Page 128

Barbary Palmer and John Watson, security, give $1800 on 4 Aug 1856 upon the condition that Barbary Palmer be apptd Gdn of the person and property of James M. Palmer, Joseph S. Palmer and Sarah E. Palmer, orphans of John Palmer.
/s/Barbary Palmer (x, her mark)
John Watson
Recorded: 7 Aug 1856

Guardian's Bond of James McConnell
Page 129

James McConnell and Stephen G. Dorsey, security, give $3000 bond on 4 Aug 1856 upon the condition that James McConnell has been this day apptd Gdn of the person and property of Morris H. Allen, orphan of Coleman A. Allen, decd.
/s/James M. Connell
/s/Stephen G. Dorsey
Recorded: 7 Aug 1856

Admrs' Bond of Joshua Elder
Page 129-130

Joshua Elder and Charles Clements, security give $2000 bond on 7 Jul 1856 upon the condition that Joshua Elder be apptd Admr of Howell Elder, late of this co., decd.
/s/Joshua Elder
/s/C. Clements
Recorded: 7 Aug 1856

Guardian's Bond of Jeptha Landrum, Sr.
Page 131

Jeptha Landrum, Sr., S. T. W. Minor, Sandford Adams and Ucibious Slayton give $8000 bond on 1 Sept 1856 upon the condition that Jeptha Landrum, Sr. has this day been apptd Gdn of the property of H. D. L. Elder, minor of Joshua Elder.
/s/Jeptha Landrum
/s/S. T. W. Minor
/s/A. Adams
/s/Mcibious Slayton (x, his mark)
Recorded: 2 Oct 1856

Guardian's Bond of Nathan Camp
Page 131-132

Nathan Camp and Sterling Elder, security, give $4000 bond on 1 Sept 1856 upon the condition that Nathan Camp has been this day apptd Gdn of the property of Mary F. P. Strickland, minor child of Barney Strickland.
/s/Nathan Camp
/s/Sterling Elder
Recorded: 2 Oct 1856

Temporary Admrs' Bond of Killis Brown
Page 132

Killis Brown and William Thames, security, give $5000 bond on 4 Oct 1856 upon the condition that Killis Brown has this day obtained temporary Letters of Admn of Mason Gentry, decd.
/s/Killis Brown
/s/William Thames
Recorded: 28 Oct 1856

Guardian's Bond of Rowland Stubbs
Page 133

Rowland Stubbs and John S. Holliday, security, give $10,000 bond on 6 Oct 1856 upon the condition that Rowland Stubbs be apptd Gdn of the person and property of James J. Newton.
/s/Rowland Stubbs
/s/John S. Holliday
Recorded: 28 Oct 1856

Guardian's Bond of William N. Hill
Page 133-134

William N. Hill, Mial M. Tidwell and Rowland Stubbs, securities, give $4800 bond on 6 Oct 1856 upon the condition that William N. Hill has been apptd Gdn to the persons and property of Pitt W. Milner, James M. and Susan A. Milner, orphans of Pitt W. Milner.
/s/William N. Hill
/s/M. M. Tidwell
/s/Rowland Stubbs
Recorded: 28 Oct 1856

Guardian's Bond of William M. Spear
Page 134

William M. Spear and Joseph Spear and John Spear give $2200 bond on 7 Oct 1856 upon the condition that William M. Spear has been appointed Gdn of the person and property of Green Griggs, minor orphan of Bryant Griggs, decd.
/s/W. M. Spear
/s/Joseph Spear
Recorded: 28 Oct 1856

Admrs' Bond of John Edmondson
Page 134-135

John Edmondson, principal, and Mial M. Tidwell give $700 bnd on 6 Oct 1856 upon the condition that John Edmondson be apptd Admr of Silas Brown, late of said co., decd., make inventory, etc.
/s/John Edmondson
/s/Mial M. Tidwell
Recorded: 28 Oct 1856

Admrs Bond of Miles Norton
Page 135-136

Miles Norton, principal, Tinnytine Norton, security give $1000 on 6 Oct 1856 upon the condition that Miles Norton be apptd Admr of Eardly Norton, late of said co., decd, to make inventory, etc.
/s/Miles Norton
/s/Tinnytine Norton
Recorded: 30 Oct 1856

Admrs' Bond of Rowland Stubbs
Page 136-137

Rowland Stubbs, principal and Mozee Harp and John S. Holliday, securities, give $7000 bond on 15 Oct 1856 upon the condition that Rowland Stubbs be apptd Admr of William Stubbs, late of said co., decd, to make inventory, etc.
/s/Rowland Stubbs
/s/Mozee Harp
/s/John S. Holliday
Recorded: 30 Oct 1856

Guardian's Bond of James F. Johnson
Page 138

James F. Johnson, principal, and Sherod H. Gay, security, give $4000 bond on 4 Nov 1856 upon the condition that James F. Johnson has been this day apptd to the guardianship of the persons and property of Franklin B. Jones and Sarah F. Jones, orphans of Francis M. Jones.
/s/James F. Johnson
/s/Sherod H. Gay
Recorded: 5 Nov 1856

Admrs' Bond of Thomas J. Camp

Page 138-139

Thomas J. Camp, Admr and Alfred Austell and Benjamin Camp, security, give $15,000 bond on 27 Nov 1856 upon the condition that Thomas J. Camp has this day applied and obtained Letters of Admn of Nathan Camp, decd.
/s/Thomas J. Camp
/s/A. Austell
/s/Benjamin Camp
Recorded: 27 Nov 1856

Admrs' Bond of Killis Brown
Page 139-140

Killis Brown and William Thames, security give $4000 bond on 1 Dec 1856 upon the condition that Killis Brown, Admr of Mason Gentry, late of said co., decd, do make inventory, etc.
/s/Killis Brown
/s/William Thames
Recorded: 26 Dec 1856

Guardian's Bond of Joseph McLean
Page 140-141

Joseph M. McLean and John O. Brown, security, give bond for $600 on 2 Dec 1856 upon the condition that Joseph M. McLean has this day been apptd Gdn to the persons and property of John M. McLean, Juan Fernander McLean and Hamden Sidney McLean.
/s/Joseph Mc. Lean
/s/John O. Brown
Recorded: 24 Dec 1856

Admrs' Bond of Thomas J. Camp
Page 141-142

Thomas J. Camp, Alfred Austell and Benjamin Camp, securities, give $1200 bond on 13 Jan 1857 upon the condition that Thomas J. Camp be apptd Admr of Nathan Camp, late of this county, decd.
/s/Thomas J. Camp
/s/Benjamin Camp
/s/A. Austell
Recorded: 30 Jan 1857

Guardian's Bond of Benjamin B. Dykes
Page 142

Benjamin B. Dykes, Mathew Read and Counsel Rentfrow, security, give $600 bond on 13 Jan 1857 upon the condition that B. B. Dyke has been appointed Gdn to person and property of William M. Whitlow, orphan of Warren Whitlow, decd.
/s/Benjamin B. Dykes
/s/Mathew Read
/s/Counsel Rentfrow
/s/30 Jan 1857

Temporary Admrs' Bond of George Creal
Page 143

George Creal, principal, and William Creal and George Mundy, securities, give $3000 bond on 9 Dec 1856 upon the condition that George Creal obtain temporary Letters of Admn of William Bray, decd.
/s/George Creal (x, his mark)
/s/William Creal (x, his mark)
/s/George W. Mundy
Recorded: 30 Jan 1857

Guardian's Bond of Oliver M. Pearson
Page 144

Oliver M. Pearson and L. F. Blalock, security, give $400 bond on 12 Jan 1857 upon the condition that Oliver M. Pearson has this day been apptd Gdn of the property of Elizabeth A. Reeves.
/s/Oliver M. Pearson
/s/L. F. Blalock
Recorded: 5 Feb 1857

Admrs' Bond of Perry Hicks
Page 144-145

Perry Hicks, William W. Mathews and Allen Reeves, securities, give $1500 bond on 12 Jan 1857 upon the condition that Perry Hicks be apptd Admr of Christopher Cline, late of this county, decd.
/s/Perry Hicks
/s/William W. Mathews
/s/Allen Reeves
Recorded: 6 Feb 1857

Guardian's Bond of Chambers E. Bennett
Page 145-146

Chambers E. Bennett and William Bennett, security, give $2200 bond on 12 Jan 1857 upon the condition that Chambers E. Bennett has this day been apptd Gdn to the property of Sarah J. Elkins, Thomas W. Elkins, Mary E. Elkins, Elizabeth F. Elkins and Emeline Elkins, minor children of James Elkins.
/s/C. E. Bennett
/s/William Bennett
Recorded: 6 Feb 1857

Guardian's Bond of Allen Reeves
Page 146

Allen Reeves, Phillip H. Brassell, William W. Mathews and Joseph M. McLean, securities, give $225 bond on 12 Jan 1857 upon the condition that Allen Reeves has been this day apptd Gdn to the property of Oliver A. Reeves, minor child of said Allen Reeves.
/s/Allen Reeves
/s/William W. Mathews
/s/P. H. Brassell
/s/J. M. McLean
Recorded: 11 Feb 1857

Guardian's Bond of Joseph McLean
Page 147

Joseph McLean and Allen Reeves, security, give $500 bond on 12 Jan 1857 upon the condition that Joseph M. McLean has been this day apptd Gdn to person and property of Rebecca McLean, William McLean and Alison McLean.
/s/J. M. McLean
/s/Allen Reeves
Recorded: 6 Feb 1857

Guardian's Bond of James M. Pate
Page 147-148

James M. Pate and John I. Whitaker, security, give $200 bond on 4 Dec 1856 upon the condition that James M. Pate has been this day apptd Gdn to property of John W. Pate.
/s/James M. Pate
/s/John I. Whitaker
Recorded: 6 Feb 1857

Temporary Admrs' Bond of Robert C. Huie
Page 148

Robert C. Huie and John M. Huie, security, give $1000 bond on 27 Jan 1857 upon the condition that Robert C. Huie has this day applied and obtained temporary Letters of Admn of Robert Huie, decd.
/s/Robert C. Huie
/s/John M. Huie
Recorded: 6 Feb 1857

Admrs' Bond of George Creal
Page 149

George Creal and Isham T. Long, security, give $1500 bond on 2 Jan 1857 upon the condition that George Creal be apptd Admr of William Bray, late of this county, decd, to make inventory, etc.
/s/George Creal (x, his mark)
/s/Isham T. Long
Recorded: 6 Feb 1857

Guardian's Bond of Matilda Graves
Page 150

Matilda Graves and Jesse Ward, security, give $1200 bond on 2 Feb 1857 upon the condition that Matilda Graves has been this day apptd Gdn to the property of Lear Oleva Graves and Salena Graves.
/s/Matilda Graves (x, her mark)
/s/Jesse Ward
Recorded: 6 Feb 1857

Guardian's Bond of Phillip H. Brassell
Page 150-151

Phillip H. Brassell, principal, and Wiley J. Gay, Willis Brassell, Lorenzo D. Padgett and John C. Brassell, securities, give $16,000 bond on 2 Mar 1857 upon the condition that Phillip H. Brassell has this day been apptd Gdn of the person and property of William Jennings, James T., Roda E. and Mary Ann Jennings.
/s/P. H. Brassell
/s/Wiley J. Gay
/s/Willis Brassell
/s/L. D Padgett
/s/John C. Brassell
Recorded: 2 Mar 1857

Temporary Admrs' Bond of Peter E. McLeroy
Page 151-152

Peter E. McLeroy and Joseph H. Murphy, security, give $6000 bond on 7 Apr 1857 upon the condition that Peter E. McLeroy has applied and obtained temporary Letters of Admn of James McLeroy, decd.
/s/Peter E. McLeroy
/s/Joseph H. Murphy
Recorded: 10 Apr 1857

Admrs' Bond of Robert C. Huie
Page 152

Robert C. Huie and John M. Huie, securities give $1400 bond on 6 Apr 1857 upon the condition that Robert C. Huie be apptd Admr of Robert Huie, late of said county, decd, to make inventory, etc.
/s/Robert C. Huie
/s/John M. Huie
Recorded: 10 Apr 1857

Guardian's Bond of W. P. Allen
Page 154

W. P. Allen and Elijah Glass, security, gibve $1400 bnd on 6 Apr 1857 upon the condition that W. P. Allen has this day been apptd Gdn of property and person of Martha Long.
/s/W. P. Allen
/s/Elijah Glass. Recorded: 10 Apr 1857

Guardian's Bond of P. H. Allen
Page 154-155

P. H. Allen and Elijah Glass, security, give $2000 bond on 6 Apr 1857 upon the condition that P. H. Allen has been this day apptd Gdn of person and property of Susan Milner, minor orphan of Pitt W. Milner, decd.
/s/P. H.Allen
/s/Elijah Glass
Recorded: 10 Apr 1857

Guardian's Bond of Willis C. Beavers
Page 155

Willis C. Reeves and Whitmel P. Allen, security, give $3200 on 1 Jun 1857 upon the condition that Willis Reeves has been this day apptd Gdn to Reuben M. Lasseter, Seppa Lasseter, James T. Lasseter, Elleanor Lasseter, Sarah J. Lasseter and Malinda Lasseter.
/s/Willis C. Beavers
/s/W. P. Allen
Recorded: 1 Jun 1857

Guardian's Bond of Robert R. King
Page 155-156

Robert R. King, principal, and Thomas J. King, security, give bond for $1400 on 12 Oct 1857 upon the condition that Robert R. King has been this day apptd Gdn of the person and property of Hail, an idiot of said county.
/s/R. R. King
/s/Thomas J. King
Recorded: 24 Oct 1857

Admx' Bond of Julia Burnside
Page 156-157

Julia Burnside, principal, and C. C. McIntosh and A. Burnside, security, give $5000 bond on 12 Oct 1857 upon the condition that Julia Burnside be apptd Admx of Thomas Burnside, late of this county, decd.
/s/Julia A. Burnside
/a/A. Burnside
/s/A. C. McIntosh
Recorded: 24 Oct 1857

Admrs' Bond of William F. Eason
Page 157-158

William F. Eason and John Nash and Rasbury Eason, securities, give $4000 bond on 9 Nov 1857 upon the condition that William F. Eason be apptd Admr of Miles Norton, late of this county, decd. to make inventory, etc.
/s/William F. Eason
/s/John C. Nash
/s/Rasbury Eason

Guardian's Bond of Joshua A. Cook
Page 158-159

Joshua A. Cook and Mial Tidwell, security, give $9000 bond on 2 Nov 1857 upon the cnondition that Joshua A. Cook has been this day apptd Gdn to person and property of Rebecca P., Thomas. E. and George Cook, orphans of Harbert Cook, decd
/s/Joshua A. Cook (x, his mark)
/s/M. M. Tidwell
Recorded: 10 Nov 1857

Temporary Admrs' Bond of Thomas C. Mathews
Page 159

Thomas C. Mathews, principal, and Patsy T. Smith and William W. Mathews, securities, give $10,000 bond on 2 Nov 1857 upon the condition that Thomas C. Mathews has applied and redceived temporary Letters of Admn of Nelly G. Evans, decd.
/s/T. C. Mathews
/s/Patsy T. Smith
/s/W. W. Mathews
Recorded: 10 Nov 1857

Temporary Admrs' Bond of Thomas C. Mathews
Page 160

Thomas C. Mathews, principal, and Patsy T. Smith and William W. Mathews, security, give bond for $11,000 on 2 Nov 1857 upon the condition that Thomas C. Mathews has this day applied and obtained temporary Letters of Admn of Gincy E. Smith, decd.
/s/T. C. Mathews
/s/Patsy T. Smith
/s/W. W. Mathews
Recorded: 10 Nov 1857

Admrs' Bond of Mary W. Hutcherson and Jesse T. Anthony
Page 161

Mary W. Hutcherson and Jesse T. Anthony and Willis Beavers and L. C. Hutcherson, securities, give $5000 bond on 23 Nov 1857 upon the condition that Mary W. hutcherson and Jesse T. Anthony has this day applied and obtained Letters of Admn on Rowland Hutcherson, decd.
/s/Mary M. Hutcherson
/s/J. T. Anthony
/s/Willis Beavers
/s/L. C. Hutcherson
Recorded: 1 Dec 1857

Admrs' Bond of Zadock Blalock
Page 162

Zadock Blalock and William H. Blalock, security, give $4000 bond on 7 Dec 1857 upon the condition that Zadock Blalock be apptd Admr of Flora Sanders, decd.
/s/Zadock Blalock
/s/William N. Blalock
Recorded: 10 Dec 1857

Admrs' Bond of L. F. Blalock
Page 163

L. F. Blalock and W. W. Bosworth and William Glass, security, give $1000 bond on 7 Dec 1857 upon the condition that L. F. Blalock be apptd Admr de bonis non of Eardly Norton, late of this county, decd, and make inventory, etc.
/s/L. F. Blalock
/s/W. W. Bosworth
/s/William Glass
Recorded: 10 Dec 1857

Temporary Admrs' Bond of John M. Huie
Page 164

John M. Huie and John Huie, security, give $1000 bond on 12 Dec 1857 upon the condition that John M. Huie be granted temporary Letters of Admn of Lucy Hill, late of this county, decd.
/s/John M. Huie
/s/John Huie
Recorded: 15 Dec 1857

Temporary Letters of Admn of Ellison Rush and H. D. Palmer
Page 165

Ellison Rush and H. D. Palmer, principal, and Windsor G. Norton and Jackson Martin, securities, give $5000 bond on 23 Dec 1857 upon the condition that Ellison Rush and H. D. Palmer have this day applied and been granted temporary Letters of Admn on John Watson, decd.
/s/H. D. Palmer
/s/Ellison Rush
/s/Jacksn Martin
/s/Winslow G. Norton (x, his mark)
Recorded: 26 Dec 1857

Temporary Admrs'Bond of John Rush
Page 166

John Rush and J. P. Shropshire, security, give $500 bond on 5 Jan 1858 upon the condition that John Rush has this day applied for temporary Letters of Adm (and been granted) on William T. Rush, decd.
/s/John Rush
/s/J. P. Shropshire
Recorded: 5 Jan 1858

Orphans of Mason Gentry
Page 167

Georgia, Fayette Co.} By J. L. Blalock, Ordinary of said county, to Young L. Wooton of said county, Greeting.

Whereas, Emily and Mary Gentry, minor orphans of Mason Gentry, decd, and possessed in their own right of a considerable estate, by means where of the power of granting the guardianship of the said Emily and Mary Gentry to me known manifestly to belong,and for the better security the estate and more ample maintainance and education of the said orphans, and from the integrity and confidence...; I do humbly commit the tuition, educationand guardianship....to you, the said Young L. Wooton.........this 13 Feb 1858.
/s/J. L. Blalock, Ordinary

Admrs' Bond of Young L. Wooton
Page 168-169

Young L. Wooton, principal, and M. M. Tidwell and P. H. Allison, securities, give $1000 bond on 25 Dec 1857 upon the condition that Young L. Wooton be apptd Admr of estate of James W. Milner, late of said countyk, decd, make inventory, etc.
/s/Young L. Wooton
/s/M.M. Tidwell
/s/P. H. Allison
Recorded: 27 Feb 1858

Admrs' Bond of H. D. Palmer and Ellison Rush
Page 169-170

H. D. Palmer and Ellison Rush, principals, and I. M. Austin and William S. Thurmond, securities, give $5000 bond on 11 Jan 1858 upon the condition that H. D. Palmer and Ellison Rush be apptd Admrs of John Watson, late of this county, decd.
/s/Ellison Rush
/s/H. D. Palmer
/s/William S. Thurmond
/s/I. M. Austin
Recorded: 27 Feb 1858

Temporary Admrs' Bond of John W. Hill
Page 171

John W. Mill and Mozee Harp, security, give $8000 bond on 1 Jan 1858 upon the condition that John W. Hill be granted temporary Letters of Admn of W. N. Hill, decd.
/s/John W. Hill
/s/Mozee Harp
Recorded: 27 Feb 1858

Admrs' Bond of E. H. Kirksey and G. W. Ware
Page 172

E. H. Kirksey and George W. Ware, principals, and John Holliday, security, give $600 bond on 11 Jan 1858 upon the condition that E. H. Kirksey and G. W. Ware be apptd admrs de bonis non of Thomas Waldroup, late of said county, decd.
/s/E. H. Kirksey
/s/George W. Ware
/s/John S. Holliday
Recorded: 27 Feb 1858

Admrs' Bond of Mary W. Hutcherson and Jesse T. Anthony
Page 173

Mary A. Hutchinson, Jesse T. Anthony, principals, and Leander Hutcherson and Willis Beavers, securities, give $5000 bond on 11 Jan 1858 upon the condition that Mary W. Hutcherson and Jesse T. Anthony be apptd admrs of Rowland Hutcherson, late of this county, decd.
/s/Mary W. Hutcherson
/s/J. T. Anthony
/s/Willis Beavers
/s/S.C. Hutcherson
Recorded: 27 Feb 1858

Admrs' Bond of Zadok Blalock
Page 174

Zadok Blalock and Andrew McBride, security give $4000 bond on 11 Jan 1858 upon the condition that Zadok Blalock, Admr with the LWT annexed of Flora Sanders, decd, to make an inventory, etc.
/s/Z. Blalock
/s/Andrew McBride
Recorded: 27 Feb 1858

Admrs' Bond of Wiley W. Bosworth
Page 175

W. W. Bosworth and L. F. Blalock, security, give $400 bond on 11 Jan 1858 upon the condition that Wiley W. Bosworth be apptd Admr of Daniel Long, late of said co., decd.
/s/Wiley W. Bosworth
/s/L. F. Blalock
Recorded: 27 Feb 1858

Admrs' Bond of John Rush
Page 176-177

John Rush and Benamin B. Dykes, security, give $500 bond on 1 Mar 1858 upon the condition that John Rush be apptd Admr of William T. Rush, late of this county, decd.
/s/John Rush
/s/Benjamin B. Dykes
Recorded: 6 Mar 1858

Admrs' Bond of Charles E. Kimberly
Page 177-178

Charles E. Kimberly, principal, and James M. Kimberly, security, give bond for $550 on 16 Mar 1858 upon the condition that Charles E. Kimberly be apptd Admr of Sarah E. Kimberly, late of this county, decd., to make inventory, etc.
/s/Charles E. Kimberly (x, his mark)
/s/J. M. Kimberly
Recorded: 24 Mar 1858

Admrs' Bond of Alfred Austell, Benjamin Camp and Simeon Zellars
Page 178-179

Alfred Austell, Benjamin Camp, Simeon Zellars, principal, and John A. Smith and William B. Swann, securities, give bond for $39,000 on 13 Mar 1858 upon the condition that Alfred Austell, Benjamin Camp and Simeon Zellars be apptd Admrs of Nathan Camp, late of said county, decd, and make inventory, etc.
/s/A. Austell
/s/Benjamin Camp
/s/SimeonZellars
/s/John Smith
/s/W.B. Swann
Recorded: 24 Mar 1858

Admrs' Bond of John M. Huie
Page 179-180

John M. Huie and Patrick H. Allen, security, give $600 bond on 5 Apr 1858 upon the condition that John M. Huie be apptd Admr of Lucy A. Hill, late of this county, decd, and make inventory, etc.
/s/John M. Huie
/s/P. H. Allen
Recorded: 7 Apr 1858

Guardian's Bond of J. F. Johnson
Page 181

James F. Johnson, principal, and Whitmel P. Allen, security, give $4000 bond on 29 Apr 1858 upon the condition that J. F. Johnson has been apptd Gdn to the persns and property of Franklin B. Jones and Sarah F. Jones, orphans of Francis M. Jones.
/s/James F. Johnson
/s/W. P. Allen
Recorded: 1 May 1858

Guardian's Bond of Wright Martin
Page 181-182

Wright Martin, principal, and Jackson Martin and Nancy Hobgood, securities, give $6000 bond on 18 Apr 1858 upon the conditionthat Wright Martin has been apptd Gdn to property of Willis W. Hobgood and Selina Hobgood, minor orphans of Samuel R. Hobgood, late of said county, decd.
/s/Wright Martin
/s/Jackson Martin
/s/Nancy Hobgood
Recorded: 1 May 1858

Admrs' Bond of John I. Whitaker
Page 182-183

John I. Whitaker, principal, and Willis R. Whitaker, security, give $1000 bond on 3 May 1858 upon the condition that John I. Whitaker, as Admr de bonis non with Will annexed of Mary McLean, late of said county, decd, do make an inventory, etc.
/s/John I. Whitaker
/s/William R. Whitaker
Recorded: 4 May 1858

Admrs' Bond of John I. Whitaker
Page 183-184

John I. Whitaker, principal, and Willis R. Whitaker, security, give $2000 bond on 3 May 1858 upon the condition that John I. Whitaker, Admr de bonis non with Will annexed of Oliver McLean, decd, do make an inventory, etc.
/s/John I. Whitaker
/s/Willis R. Whitaker
Recorded: 4 May 1858

Guardian's Bond of Martha A. Reeves
Page 184

Martha A. Reeves, principal, and John I. Whitaker, security, give $4000 bond on 3 May 1858 upon the condition that Martha A. Reeves has been apptd Gdn to William P. Reeves, Sarah Ann Reeves and Martha W. Reeves.
/s/Martha A. Reeves
/s/John I. Whitaker
Recorded: 4 May 1858

Admrs' Bond of Mathew Read
Page 185

Mathew Read, principal, and Benjamin B. Dyke, security, give $4000 on 24 Apr 1858 upon the condition that Mathew Read be apptd Admr with LWT annexed of John Burk, decd, to make inventory, etc.
/s/Mathew Read
/s/BenjaminB. Dyke
Recorded: 4 May 1858

Admrs' Bond of C. E. Bennett
Page 186-187

C. E. Bennett, principal, and William Bennett, security, give $400 bond on 7 Jun 1858 upon the condition that C. E. Bennett be apptd admr of Sarah J. Elkins, late of said county, decd, and make inventory, etc.
/s/C. E. Bennett
/s/William Bennett
Recorded: 19 Jun 1858

Guardian's Bond of Charity A. Ramsey
Page 187

Charity A. Ramsey, principal, and Thomas M. Jones and Noah Smith give $4000 bond on 7 Jun 1858 upon the condition that Charity A. Ramsey has been this day apptd Gdn to property of James E., Eli W., Julia F. and Nancy I. C. Ramsey.
/s/Charity A. Ramsey
/s/T. M. Jones
/s/Noah Smith
Recorded: 22 Jun 1858

Admrs' Bond of Thomas I. King
Page 188-189

Thomas I. King, principal and L. F. Blalock, security, give bond for $1600 on 7 Jun 1858 upon the condition that Thomas I. King be apptd Admr of William P. King, late of said county, decd.
/s/Thomas I. King
/s/L. F. Blalock
Recorded: 22 Jun 1858

Guardian's Bond of Jackson Martin
Page 189

Jackson Martin, principal, and James L. Hobgood and Wright Martin, securities, give $5000 bond on 5 Jul 1858 upon the condition that Jackson Martin has been this day apptd Gdn to property of Nancy Jane, William Henry and Kemler Guinett Gosden.
/s/Jackson Martin
/s/J. L. Hogbood
/s/Wright Martin
Recorded: 17 Jul 1858

Admrs' Bond of James J. Newton
Page 189-190

James J. Newton, principal and Edward Connor and Rowland Stubbs, securities, give $1200 bond on 5 Jul 1858 upon the condition that James J. Newton be apptd Admr of William Stubbs, said of said county, decd.
/s/James J. Newton
/s/Rowland Stubbs
/s/Edward Connor
Recorded: 17 Jul 1858

Admrs' Bond of Dempsey Brown
Page 191

Dempsey Brown, principal, and John S. Holliday, security, give $200 bond on 2 Aug 1858 upon the condition that Dempsey Brown be apptd Admr of Benjamin Brown, late of said county, decd, to make inventory, etc.
/s/Dempsey Brown
/s/John S. Holliday
Recorded: 4 Aug 1858

Admrs' Bond of William N. McConnell
Page 192

William N. McConnell and James McConnell, as security give bond of $1000 on 6 Aug 1858 upon the condition that William N. McConnell be apptd Admr of William S. Allen, late of the State of Louisiana, decd, and make inventory, etc.
/s/William N. McConnell
/s/James W. McConnell
Recorded: 9 Aug 1858

Admrs' Bond of Richard B. Humphrey
Page 193-194

Richard B. Humphrey, principal, and Josiah H. Murphy and J. F. Blalock, securities, give $500 bond on 6 Sept 1858 upon the condition that Richard B. Humphrey be apptd Admr of Susan Wish, late of said county, decd, make inventry, etc.
/s/R. B. Humphrey
/s/J. H. Murphy
/s/J. H. Murphy
/s/J. F. Blalock
Recorded: 11 Sept 1858

Admx' Bond of Nancy Stephens
Page 194-195

Nancy Stephens and James G. Smith, securities, give $1600 bond on 6 Sept 1858 upon the condition that Nancy Stephens be apptd Admx of John Stephens, late of the State of Arkansas, decd, and make inventory.
/s/Nancy Stephens
/s/James G. Smith
/s/R. W. Morrow
Recorded: 11 Sept 1858

Admrs' Bond of James J. Newton and Edward Connor
Page 195-196

James J. Newton and Edward Connor, principals, and Thomas H. Stephens, security, give $10,000 bond on 8 Oct 1858 upon the condition that James J. Newton and Edward Connor be apptd Admrs of William Stubbs, late of this county, decd., to make inventory, etc.
/s/James J. Newton
/s/Edward Connor
/s/Thomas H. Stephens
Recorded: 8 Oct 1858

Guardian's Bond of Mary Jane Rush
Page 197

Mary Jane Rush, principal, and Jarod Handley, and Larkin L. Handley give $500 bond on 1 Nov 1858 upon the condition that Mary Jane Rush has been this day apptd Gdn to property of Mary E. and Sarah F. Rush.
/s/Mary Jane Rush
/s/Jarod Handley
/s/L. L. Handley

Admrs' Bond of Phillip H. Brassell
Page 198-199

Phillip H. Brassell, principal and W. W. Bosworth, security, give $100 bond on 1 Nov 1858 upon the condition that Phillip H. Brassell be apptd Admr of Joanah Sims, late of said county, decd.
/s/Phillip H. Brassell
/s/W. W. Bosworth
Recorded: 1 Nov 1858

Guardian's Bond of John B. Long
Page 199

John B. Long, principal, and William Long and Moses Daniel, security, give $1200 bond on 6 Dec 1858 upon the condition that John R. Long has been appointed guardianship of the person and property of Martha Jane Long, orphan of Mark Long, decd.
/s/John B. Long
/s/Moses Daniel
/s/W. H. Long
Recorded: 7 Dec 1858

Admrs' Bond of Archibald Smith and Seaborn Smith
Page 200-201

Archibald Smith and Seaborn Smith, principal, and Daniel Hanes, security give $10,000 bond on 6 Dec 1858 upon the condition that Archibald Smith and Seaborn Smith be apptd Admrs of Joseph Scates, late of said county, decd, and make inventory, etc.
/s/Archibald Smith
/s/Seaborn Smith
/s/Daniel Hanes (x, his mark)
Recorded: 7 Dec 1858

Guardian's Bond of Benjamin B. Dykes
Page 201

Benjamin Dykes, principal, and Mathew Read, security, give $4400 bond on 6 Dec 1858 upon the condition that Benjamin B. Dykes has this day been apptd Gdn of the person and property of Martha E. Whitlow, orphen of Warren Whitlow.
/s/Benjamin B. Dykes
/s/Mathew Read
Recorded: 7 Dec 1858

Admr's Bond of John Williams and Solomon Bridges
Page 202-203

John Williams and Solomon Bridges, principal, and William H. Blalock, security, give $200 bond on 6 Dec 1858 upon the condition that John Williams and Solomon Bridges be apptd Admrs of Travis Nichols, late of said county, decd, and make inventory, etc.
/s/S. T. Bridges
/s/John Williams
/s/William H. Blalock
Recorded: 7 Dec 1858

Guardian's Bond of Joshua Cook
Page 203

Joshua Cook, principal and J. M. Trimble, security give $25000 bond on 6 Dec 1858 upon the condition that Joshua Cook formerly has been apptd Gdn to the person and property of Becky Ann Cook and Thomas Elbert Cook, George M. Cook, orphans of Harbard Cook, decd.
/s/Joshua Cook (x, his mark)
/s/J. M. Trimble
Recorded: 7 Dec 1858

Temporary Admrs' Bond of John S. Holliday and George W. Ware
Page 204

John S. Holliday and George Ware, principal, and George C. King, security, give $7000 bond on 22 Dec 1858 upon the condition that John S. Holliday and George Ware have this day applied for and obtained temporary Letters of Admn of Howel Vaughan, decd.
/s/John S. Holliday
/s/George W. Ware
/s/George C. King
Recorded: 22 Dec 1858

Guardian's Bond of Lucy Ann Smith
Page 205

Lucy Ann Smith, principal, and Thomas Dewberry and John W. Smith, security, give $3000 bond on 10 Jan 1859 upon the condition that Lucy Ann Smith has been this day apptd Gdn to person and property of Margaret M. J. Smith.
/s/Lucy Ann Smith
/s/John W. Smith
Recorded: 10 Jan 1859

Guardian's Bond of James T. Thames
Page 205-206

James T. Thames, principal, and Thomas M. Jones and William Thames, security give $3000 bond on 10 Jan 1859 upon the condition that James T. Thames has been this day apptd Gdn to person and property of James Thames, Mary Thames, John Thames and Cintha C. Thames, minor children of John Thames.
/s/James T. Thames
/s/Thomas M. Jones
/s/William Thames
Recorded: 10 Jan 1859

Admrs' Bond of Andrew McBride
Page 206-207

Andrew McBride, principal, and William H. Blalock, security, give $3000 bond on 10 Jan 1859 upon the condition that Andrew McBride be apptd Admr of John A. McBride, late of said county, decd.
/s/Andrew McBride
/s/William H. Blalock
Recorded: 10 Jan 1859

Guardian's Bond of John I. Whitaker
Page 207-208

John I. Whitaker, principal, and Simon T. Whitaker, security, give $600 bond on 28 Jan 1859 upon the condition that John I. Whitaker has this day been apptd Gdn to M. A. E. Collins, R. D. Collins, Emily Collins, James A. Collins, Paschal Collins and Martin H. Collins, orphans of Pascal E. Collins, late of said county, decd.
/s/John I. Whitaker
/s/W. R. Whitaker
Recorded: 7 Mar 1859

Guardian's Bond of William W. Sibley
Page 210-211

William W. Sibley, principal, and Eli Edmondson, security, give $400 bond on 7 Mar 1859 upon the condition that William W. Sibley has been apptd Gdn to person and property of Robert Hail, Idiot.
/s/W. W. Sibley
/s/Eli Edmondson
Recorded: 7 Mar 1859

Admrs' Bond of Francis P. Jones
Page 211-212

Francis P. Jones, principal, and John L. Jones, security, give $2000 bond on 4 Apr 1859 upon the condition that Francis P. Jones be apptd Admr of Daniel K. Gilmer, late of said county, decd, to make inventory, etc.
/s/Francis P. Jones
/s/John L. Jones
Recorded: 4 Apr 1859

Guardian's Bond of Josiah Hilsman
Page 212-213

Josiah Hilsman, John T. Gray and V. A. Gaskill give $4000 bond on 2 May 1859 upon the condition that Josiah Hilsman has been this day apptd Gdn to Jeremiah, Josiah, Amanda, Lucy, Jeffrey, Ella and James Hilsman, minor orphans of James Hilsman, decd.
/s/Josiah Hilsman
/s/John T. Gray, by his atty in fact, Josiah Hilsman
/s/V. A. Gaskin
Recorded: 5 May 1859

Guardian's Bond of Josiah Hilsman
Page 215

Josiah Hilsman is about to apply for Guardianship of Jeremiah, Josiah, Amanda, Lucy, Jeffrey, Ella and James Hilsman, minor children of James Hilsman, decd. There are therefore to authorize and impower the said Joshua Hilsman to sign my name as security for him..../s/John T. Gay
Recorded: 5 May 1859

Admrs' Bond of Malinda McEachern
Page 214-215

Malinda McEachern, principal, and John Fields, security, give $800 bond on 9 May 1859 upon the condition that Malinda McEachern be apptd Admr of Martin McEachern, late of said county, decd, to make inventory, etc.
/s/Malinda McEachern
/s/John Field
Recorded: 12 May 1859

Guardian's Bond of William Ballard
Page 215

William Ballard, principal, and Jesse Cook, security, give $800 bond on 6 Jun 1859 upon the condition that William Ballard has been this day apptd Gdn to person and property of Rebecca > P. Cook.
/s/William Ballard
/s/Jesse Cook (x, his mark)
Recorded: 10 Jun 1859

Admrs' Bond of George W. Ware and John S. Holliday
Page 215-216

George W. Ware and John S. Holliday, principals, and George C. King, security, give bond for $6000 on 6 Jun 1859 upon the cndition that George W. Ware and John S. Holliday be apptd Admrs of Howell Vaughn, decd.
/s/John S. Holliday
/s/George W. Ware
/s/George C. King
Recorded: 10 Jun 1859

Guardian's Bond of Joshua Cannon
Page 217

Joshua Cannon, principal, and C. A. Hardin, Z. Blalock, and William H. Blalock, securities, give $10,000 bond on 4 Jul 1859 upon the condition that Joshua Cannon has been this day apptd Gdn to property of Augustin E. Harden, a minor child of John H. Harden and C. A. Harden.
/s/Joshua Cannon
/s/C. A. Harden
/s/Z. Blalock
/s/William H. Blalock
Recorded: 7 Jul 1859

Guardian's Bond of M. M. Tidwell
Page 217-218

M. M. Tidwell and William P. Chandler and William T. Thurman, securities, give $4000 bond on 4 Jul 1859 upon the condition that M. M. Tidwell has this day been apptd Gdn to person and property of Crissa Miles, orphan of William Miles, late of said county, decd.
/s/M. M. Tidwell
/s/William P. Chandler
/s/William T. Thurman
Recorded: 7 Jul 1859

Guardian's Bnd of John S. Holliday
Page 218-219

John S. Holliday and George W. Ware, security, give $4000 bond on 4 Jul 1859 upon the condition that John S. Holliday has been this day apptd Gdn to John L. Miles, orphan of William Miles, late of said county, decd.
/s/John S. Holliday
/s/George W. Ware
Recorded: 7 Jul 1859

Admrs' Bond of William P. Chandler
Page 219-220

William P. Chandler, principal, and Burrell A. Ware, Edward Leach, Wyat Chandler, William Glass and M. M. Tidwell, sec., $40,000 bond on 5 Jul 1859 that William P. Chandler be apptd Admr of Estate of William Miles.
/s/William P. Chandler
/s/Wit Chandler
/s/E. W. Leach

Admrs' Bond of William P. Chandler, contd....

/s/B. A. Ware
/s/William Glass
/s/M. M. Tidwell, Recorded: 7 Jul 1859

Admrs' Bond of S. T. W. Minor
Page 220-221

S. T. W. Minor and William Bennett, security, give $500 bond on 5 Jul 1859 upon the condition that S. T. W. Minor be apptd Admr of William R. Wilkinson, late of this county, decd, to make inventory, etc.
/s/S. T. W. Minor
/s/William Bennett
Recorded: 7 Jul 1859

Admrs' Bond of Francis P. Jones
Page 221-222

Francis P. Jones, principal, and John L. Jones, security, give $225 bond on 5 Sept 1859 upon the condition that Francis P. Jones be apptd Admr of John Jones, late of said county, decd, to make inventory, etc.
/s/Francis P. Jones
/s/John L. Jones
Recorded: 6 Sept 1859

Admrs' Bond of Solomon T. Bridges
Page 222-223

Solomon T. Bridges, principal, and Thomas B. Gay, security, give $30,000 bond on 5 Sept 1859 upon the condition that Solomon T. Bridges be apptd Admr of John T. Macey, late of said county, decd, to make inventory, etc.
/s/S. T. Bridges
/s/Thomas B. Gay
Recorded: 6 Sept 1859

Admx' Bond of Patsey T. Smith
Page 224

Patsy T. Smith, Thomas C. Mathews and R. L. G. Bozeman, securities, give $1450 bond on 15 Sept 1859 upon the condition that Patsey T. Smith be apptd Admx with LWT annexed of Jane E. Smith, decd, and to make inventory, etc.
/s/Patsey T. Smith
/s/T. C. Maathews
/s/R. L. G. Bozeman
Recorded: 14 Oct 1859

Guardian's Bond of William Trantham
Page 225

William Trantham and Andrew McBride, security give $200 bond on 5 Oct 1859 upon the condition that William Trantham be apptd Gdn to person and property of Nathan Turner.
/s/William Trantham
/s/Andrew McBride
Recorded: 14 Oct 1859

Admr's Bond of Richard B. Humphrey
Page 225-226

Richard B. Humphrey, principal, and William J. Russell, S. D. Dorsey, L. F. Blalock and William H. Blalock, securities, give $8000 bond on 23 Sept 1859 upon the condition that Richard B. Humphrey be apptd Admr of Estate of Susannah West, late of said county, decd, to make inventory, etc.
/s/R. B. Humphrey
/s/William J. Russell
/s/S. D. Dorsey
/s/L. F. Blalock
/s/William H. Blalock
Recorded: 14 Oct 1859

Admrs' Bond of Lewis F. Blalock
Page 227-228

Lewis F. Blalock, principal, and William H. Blalock, Solomon D. Dorsey and Hardaway Smith, securities, give $6000 bond on 5 Dec 1859 upon the condition that Lewis F. Blalock be apptd Admr of Charles Clements, late of said county, decd.
/s/Lewis F. Blalock
/s/Hardaway Smith
/s/S. D. Dorsey
/s/William H. Blalock
Recorded: 12 Dec 1859

Admx' Bond of Malinda McEachern
Page 228-229

Malinda McEachern, principal, and Isaac Field and Samuel T. W. Minor, securities, give $200 bond on 11 Dec 1859 upon the condition that Malinda McEachern be apptd Admr of Martin P. McEachern, late of said county, decd, to make inventory, etc.
/s/Malinda McEacher
/s/I. M. Field
/s/S. T. W. Minor
Recorded: 12 Dec 1859

Admrs' Bond of Hansford D. Palmer
Page 229-230

Hansford D. Palmer, principal, and Charles W. Smith and Spencer T. Wilborn, securities, give $4500 bond on 5 Nov 1855 upon the condition that Hansford D. Palmer be apptd Admr of John Palmer, late of said county, decd, to make inventory, etc.
/s/Handsford D. Palmer
/s/C. W. Smith
/s/Spencer T. Wilborn
Recorded: 15 Feb 1860

Admrs' Bond of Daniel D. Denham and Permelia Russell
Page 230-231

Daniel D. Denham and Permelia Russell, principals, and L. F. Blalock, security, give $1000 bond on 13 Feb 1860 upon the condition that Daniel D. Denham and Permelia Russell have this day applied and obtained Letters of Admn on William Russell, decd.
/s/D. D. Denham
/s/Permelia Russell
/s/L. F Blalock, Recorded: 13 Feb 1860

Admrs' Bond of James W. Bozeman
Page 231-232

James W. Bozeman, principal, and Thomas C.Mathews and William W. Mathews, securities, give $12,000 bond on 5 Mar 1860 upon the condition that James W. Bozeman be apptd Admr with LWT annexed of Nelley G. Evans, late of said county, decd, to make inventory, etc.
/s/James W. Bozeman
/s/T. C. Mathews
/s/William W. Mathews
Recorded: 30 Mar 1860

Admrs' Bond of Samuel T. W. Minor
Page 232-233

Samuel T. W. Minor, principal, and Young L. Wooton, security, give $500 bond on 5 Mar 1860 upon the condition that Samuel T. W. Minor be apptd Admr of Berry Norton, late of said county, decd, to make inventory, etc.
/s/Samuel T. W. Minor
/s/Young L. Wooton
Recorded: 30 Mar 1860

Admrs' Bond of Vines Graves
Page 233-234

Vines Graves, principal, and Solomon D. Dorsey and Williamson Jinkins, securities, give $3000 bond on 2 Apr 1860 upon the condition that Vines Graves be apptd Admr of Matilda Graves, late of said county, decd, to make inventory, etc.
/s/Vines Graves
/s/S.D. Dorsey
/s/William Jinkings
Recorded: 4 Apr 1860

Admrs' Bond of Daniel D. Denham and Parmelia Russell
Page 234-235

Daniel D. Denham and Parmelia Russell, principals, and L. F. Blalock, security, give $600 bond on 2 Apr 1860 upon the condition that Daniel D. Denham and Parmelia Russell be apptd Admrs of William Russell, late of said county, decd, and give inventory, etc.
/s/Daniel D. Denham
/s/Parmelia Russell (x. her mark)
L. F.Blalock
Recorded: 4 Apr 1860

Vines Graves applies for Letters of Admn on Estate of Wiley Graves, decd, 14 Apr 1860
Page 236-237

Vines Graves, principal and Williamson Jenkins, security, give $2000 bond on 4 Jun 1860 upon the condition that Vines Graves be apptd Admr of Wiley Graves, late of said county, decd, make inventory, etc.
/s/Vines Graves
/s/Williamson Jenkins
Recorded: 7 Jun 1860

C. E. Bennett applies for Letters of Dismission from the Guardianship of R. G. Strickland
Page 236

(nothing follows)

William Head applied for Letters of Guardianship of Person and Property of the minor orphans of James W. Head, decd
Page 236

(nothing follows)

Admrs' Bond of Patrick H. Allen
Page 237-238

Patrick H. Allen, principal, and Young L. Wootton, security, give $500 bond on 4 Jun 1860 upon the condition that Patrick H. Allen be apptd Admr of James W. Milner, late of said county, decd, to make inventory, etc.
/s/P. H. Allen
/s/Y. L. Wootten
Recorded: 7 Jun 1860

Guardian's Bond of James M. Camp
Page 238-239

James M. Camp, principal, and Jesse L. Blalock, security, give $4000 bond on 4 Jun 1860 upon the condition that James M. Camp has been this day apptd Guardian of property of Caroline D. Camp.
/s/James M. Camp
/s/Jesse L. Blalock
Recorded: 7 Jun 1860

Guardian's Bond of Eli Edmondson
Page 239

Eli Edmondson, principal, and John Huie, security, give $3000 bond on 2 Jul 1860 upon the condition that Eli Edmondson has been this day apptd Gdn to George W. Neal, Rachael P. Neal, James T. Neal, Benjamin F. Neal and Emily J. Neal.
/s/Eli Edmondson
/s/John Huie
Recorded: 2 Jul 1860

Guardian's Bond of James J. Carson
Page 239-240

James J. Carson, principal, and John C. Brassell, security, give $600 bond on 2 Jul 1860 upon the condition that James J. Carson has been this day apptd Gdn to John P. Neal.
/s/James J. Carson
/s/John C. Brassell
Recorded: 2 Jul 1860

Guardian's Bond of William Head
Page 240-241

William Head, principal, and William Watson, security, give $1000 bond on 6 Aug 1860 upon the condition that William Head has this day been apptd Gdn to property of Sarah Jane, Nancy Ann Luticia, Edney Ann Francina, Americus L. and William Thomas T. Head, orphans of James W. Head, decd.
/s/William Head
/S/William Watson
Recorded: 6 Aug 1860

Guardian's Bond of Francis M. Lester
Page 241

Francis M. Lester, principal, and Jackson Martin, Charles W. Smith, William J. Russell and Lewis F. Blalock, security, give $7000 bond on 1 Oct 1860 upon the condition that Francis M. Lester has this day been apptd Gdn of person and property of Sarah Ann Clements.
/s/F. M.Lester
/s/Jackson Martin
/s/C. W. Smith
/s/William J. Russell
/s/L. F. Blalock
Recorded: 2 Oct 1860

Guardian's Bond of Lewis F. Blalock
Page 242

Lewis F. Blalock, principal, Andrew McBride, Jackson Martin and William J. Russell, securities, give $7000 bond on 1 Oct 1860 upon the condition that Lewis F. Blalock has this day been apptd Gdn to person and property of Roxey Clements.
/s/L. F. Blalock
/s/Andrew McBride
/s/Jackson Martin
/s/William J. Russell
Recorded: 2 Oct 1860

Guardian's Bond of Adam Clements
Page 242-243

Adam Clements, principal, and Josiah H. Elder, Charles W. Smith and Lewis F. Blalock, security, give $14000 bond on 1 Oct 1860 upon the condition that Adam Clements has been this day apptd Gdn to person and property of Mallissa E. Clements and William Clements.
/s/Adam Clements
/s/Josiah H. Elder
/s/C. W. Smith
/s/L. F. Blalock. Recorded: 2 Oct 1860

Temporary Admrs' Bond of Thomas M. Jones and Richard M. Everitt
Page 243-244

Thomas M. Jones and Richard M. Everitt, principals and James L. Hobgood, security, give $25000 bond on 9 Oct 1860 upon the condition that Thomas M. Jones and Richard M. Everitt has this day applied to and obtained temporary Letters of Admn on Estate of Noah Smith, decd.
/s/Thomas M. Jones
/s/R. M. Everitt
/s/J. L. Hobbood
Recorded: 29 Oct 1860

Admrs' Bond of Robert M. Jinnings
Page 244-245

Robert M. Jinnings, principal, and Marcus W. Swanson and J. L. Blalock, securities, give $12000 bond on 6 Nov 1860 upon the condition that Robert M. Jinnings be apptd Admr de bonis non with LWT annexed of John A. Jinnings, decd, to make inventory, etc.
/s/Robert M. Jinnings
/s/M. W. Swanson
/s/J. L. Blalock
Recorded: 6 Nov 1860

Guardian's Bond of Francis Bishop
Page 245

Francis Bishop, principal, Thomas Ellis and William M. Bishop, securities, give $8000 bond on 3 Dec 1860 upon the condition that Francis Bishop has this day been apptd Gdn to person and property of Sarah P. Bishop, Lavonia Bishop, Amandy Caroline Bishop, Josephen Bishop, and Prometia Thomas Bishop.
/s/Francis Bishop (x, *her* mark)
/s/Thomas Ellis
/s/Willis M. Bishop

Guardian's Bond of Elizabeth J. Harper
Page 246

Elizabeth J. Harper, principal, and John J. Gilbert, security, give $5000 bond on 5 Dec 1860 upon the condition that Elizabeth J. Harper has been this day apptd Gdn to person and property of Mathew G. Harper and Susanah G. Harper.
/s/Elizabeth J. Harper (x, her mark)
/s/John J. Gilbert
Recorded: 3 Dec 1860

Guardian's Bond of James L. Hobgood
Page 246-247

James L. Hobgood, principal, and Jackson Martin, security, give $5000 bond on 3 Dec 1860 upon the condition that James L. Hobgood has this day been apptd Gdn to person and property of Priscilla Jannett Hobgood.
/s/J. L. Hobgood
/s/Jackson Martin
Recorded: 3 Dec 1860

Admrs' Bond of Thomas M. Jones and Richard M. Everitt
Page 247-248

Thomas M. Jones and Richard M. Everitt, principals, and James T. Thames and Enock G. Jones, securities, give $3000 bond n 3 Dec 1860 upon the condition that Thomas M. Jones and Richard M Everitt be apptd Admrs of Noah Smith, late of said county, decd, make inventory, etc.
/s/Thomas M. Jones
/s/Richard M. Everitt
/s/J. F. Thames
/s/E. G. Jones
Recorded: 3 Dec 1860

Temporary Admrs' Bond of Jesse Barintine
Page 248-249

Jesse Barintine, principal, and Jesse L. Blalock, security, give $1000 bond on 14 Dec 1860 upon the condition that Jesse Barintine applied for and received temporary Letters of Admn on estate of Daniel Barintine, decd
/s/Jesse Barintine (x, his mark)
/s/J. L. Blalock
Recorded: 14 Dec 1860

Guardian's Bnd of Joshua A. Milner
Page 249-250

Joshua A. Milner, principal, and Andrew McBride and Elijah Glass, securities, give $12,000 bond on 24 Dec 1860 upon the condition that Joshua A. Milner has been this day apptd Gdn to person and property of Thomas J. Milner, a lunatic of said county.
/s/Joshua A. Milner
/s/Andrew McBride
/s/Elijah Glass
Recorded: 4 Jan 1861

Admrs' Bond of William Bennett
Page 250-251

William Bennett, principal, and C. E. Bennett, security, give $3000 bond on 14 Jan 1861 upon the condition that William Bennett be apptd Admr of Minton Graves, Jr., late of said county, decd, and make inventory.
/s/William Bennett
/s/C. E. Bennett
Recorded: 14 Jan 1861

Temporary Admrs' Bond of Harriet H. Miers and Samuel T. W. Minor
Page 251

Harriet H. Miers and Samuel T. W. Minor, principal, and Edmond Jackson, security, give $2000 bond on 14 Jan 1861 upon the condition that Harriet H. Miers and Samuel T. W. Minor has this day applied for and obtained temporary Letters of Admn of Andrew J. Miers, decd.
/s/Harriet H. Miers
/s/Samuel T. W. Minor
/s/Edmond Jackson
Recorded: 14 Jan 1861

Admrs' Bond of Richard B. Humphrey
Page 252

Richard B. Humphrey, principal, and James M. Camp and Jackson Martin, security, give $3500 bond on 14 Jan 1860 upon the condition that Richard B. Humphrey be apptd Admr of Susanah West, late of said county, decd, to make inventory, etc.
/s/R. B. Humphrey
/s/James M. Camp
/s/Jackson Martin
Recorded: 14 Jan 1860

Admrs' Bond of Harriet H. Miers and Samuel T. W. Minor
Page 253

Harriet H. Miers and Samuel T. W. Minor, principals, and Edmond Jackson, security, give $2000 bond on 4 Mar 1861 upon the condition that Harriet H. Miers and Samuel T.W. Minor be apptd Admrs of Andrew J. Miers, late of said county, decd, make inventory, etc.
/s/Harriet Miers (x, her mark)
/s/S. T. W. Minor
/s/Edmond Jackson
Recorded: 4 Mar 1861

Admrs' Bond of William H. Wooton
Page 254

William H. Wooton, principal, and John W. Truett, security, give $600 bond on 4 Mar 1861 upon the condition that William H. Wooton be apptd Admr de bonis non of James W. Milner, late of said county, decd, and make inventory, etc.
/s/William H. Wooton
/s/John W. Truett
Recorded: 4 Mar 1861

Admrs' Bond of William B. Standfield
Page 255

William B. Standfield, principal, and Dennis Stubbs, security, give $600 bond on 6 May 1861 upon the condition that William B. Standfield be apptd Admr of Martin Bellile, late of said county, decd.
/s/William B. Standfield (x, his mark)
/s/Dennis Stubbs
Recorded: 6 May 1861

Admrs' Bond of Jesse Barintine
Page 256-257

Jesse Barintine, principal, and J. L. Blalock, security, give $1500 bond on 3 Jun 1861 upon the condition that Jesse Barintine be apptd Admr of David Barintine, late of said county, decd, make inventory, etc.
/s/Jesse Barintine (x, his mark)
/s/J. L. Blalock
Recorded: 3 Jun 1861

Temporary Admrs' Bond of Phillip H. Brassell and Willis Brassell
Page 257-258

Phillip H. Brassell and Willis Brassell, principals, and Thomas C. Mathews, Jesse L. Blalock and William Glass, securities, give $30,000 bond on 25 Jun 1861 upon the condition that Phillip H. Brassell and Willis Brassell have applied for and receivd temporary Letters of Admn on William Brassell, decd.
/s/P. H. Brassell
/s/Willis Brassell
/s/T. C. Matthews
/s/J. L. Blalock
Recorded: 25 Jun 1861

Guardian's Bond of John T. Cooper
Page 258

John T. Cooper and Robert Iverson, security, give $15,000 bond on 6 Aug 1861 upon the condition that John T. Cooper be apptd Gdn to Harriett T. Brooks.
/s/John T. Cooper
/s/Robert Iverson
Recorded: 6 Aug 1861

Admrs' Bond of Philip H. Brassell and Willis Brassell
Page 259

Philip H. Brassell and Willis Brassell as principals and Jesse L. Blalock, Thomas C. Mathews and Jemerson Alford as securities give $30,000 bond on 2 Sept 1861 upon the condition that Philip H. Brassell and Willis Brassell be apptd Admrs of William Brassell, decd, make inventory, etc.
/s/Philip H. Brassell
/s/Willis Brassell
/s/J. L. Blalock
/s/T. C. Mathews
/s/Jemerson Alford
Recorded: 2 Sept 1861

Admrs' Bond of Haney Porter and John M. Porter
Page 260-261

Haney Porter and John M. Porter, principals, and John I. Whitaker, Andrew McBride, James McBride and Rowland Stubbs, securities, give $50,000 bond on 7 Oct 1861 upon the condition that Haney Porter and John m. Porter be apptd Admrs of Hugh Porter, decd, and make inventory, etc.
/s/Haney Porter
/s/John M. Porter
/s/John I. Whitaker
/s/Andrew McBride
/s/James McBride
/s/Rowland Stubbs
Recorded: 7 Oct 1861

Admrs' Bond of L. F. Blalock
Page 261

L. F. Blalock, principal, and William J. Russell and Andrew McBride, securities, give $15,000 bond on 9 Oct 1861 upon the conditin that L. F. Blalock this day be apptd Admr with LWT annexed of Silas G. Eastin, decd.
/s/L. F. Blalock
/s/William J. Russell
/s/Andrew McBride
Recorded: 9 Oct 1861

Guardian's Bond of Haney Porter
Page 262

Haney Porter, principal, and Oliver P. McLean and William Glass, securities, give $2000 bond on 7 Nov 1861 upon the condition that Haney Porter is this day apptd Gdn to Sarah T. Roberts, James G. Roberts and Griffin A. Roberts, orphans of Sampson W. Roberts, decd.
/s/Haney Porter
/s/Oliver P. McLean
/s/William Glass, Recorded: 7 Dec 1861

Guardian's Bond of Willis R. Whitaker
Page 265

Willis R. Whitaker, principal, and John I. Whitaker, securities, give $35,000 bond on 7 Nov 1861 upon the condition that Willis R. Whitaker be apptd Gdn to Andrew J., William S., Benjamin F., and Sarah Francis Whitaker, orphans of Simon T. Whitaker, decd.
/s/Willis R. Whitaker
/s/John I. Whitaker
Recorded: 7 Nov 1861

Admrs' Bond of John J. Gilbert
Page 265-266

John J. Gilbert, principal, and Samuel W. Marshman, security, give $3000 bond on 2 Dec 1861 upon the condition that John J. Gilbert be apptd Admr of George H. Jackson, decd.
/s/J. J. Gilbert
/s/S. W. Marshburn
Recorded: 7 Dec 1861

Temporary Letters of Admn of Elizabeth L. Spratlin
Page 267

Elizabeth L. Spratlin, principal, and C. G. Tanner, securit, give $40,000 bond on 1 Dec 1861 upon the condition that Elizabeth L. Spratlin be granted temporary Letters of Admn on Estate of Jesse M. Spratlin, decd.
/s/Elizabeth L. Spratlin
/s/C. G. Tanner
Recorded: 21 Dec 1861

Admrs' Bond of Jesse Barrintine
Page 268

Jesse Barrintine, principal, and L. F. Blalock, security give $1000 bond on 13 Jan 1862 upon the cndition that Jesse Barintine be apptd Admr of William S. Elkins, decd, give inventory, etc.
/s/Jesse Barrintine (x, his mark)
/s/L. F. Blalock
Recorded: 16 Jan 1862

Admrs' Bond of James T. Travis
Page 269

James T. Travis, principal, and Edward Moon, security, give $5000 bond on 3 Mar 1862 upon the condition that James T. Travis be apptd Admr of Washington Duffell, decd.
/s/James T. Travis
/s/Edward Moon
Recorded: 3 Mar 1862

Benjamin M. Jackson's Admrs' Bond
Page 270

Benjamin M. Jackson, principal and John J. Gilbert, security, give $500 bond on 3 Mar 1862 upon the condition that Benjamin M. Jacksn be apptd Admr of Jefferson F. Jackson, decd, ldate of Fayette Co.
/s/B. M. Jackson
/s/J. J. Gilbert
Recorded: 3 Mar 1862

William H. Wootton's Admrs' Bond
Page 271

William H. Wootton, principal, and John J. Gilbert, security, gives $2400 bond on 3 Mar 1862 upon the condition that William H. Wootton be apptd Admr of C. C. Shell, late of said co., decd.
/s/William H. Wootton
/s/John J. Gilbert
Recorded: 3 Mar 1862

Guardian's Bond of William M. Speer
Page 272

William M. Speer and Joseph Speer give $4000 bond on 7 Apr 1862 upon the condition that William M. Speer is apptd Gdn to John W. Griggs, Orphan of Bryant Griggs, decd.
/s/William M. Speer
/s/Joseph Speer
Recorded: 16 Jun 1862

Admrs' Bond of Jeptha M. Murphy and Sarah E. Murphy
Page 272-273

Jeptha M. Murphy and Sarah E. Murphy, principals, and James M. Austin, security, give $200 bond on 7 Jul 1862 upon the condition that Jeptha M. Murphy and Sarah E. Murphy be apptd Admrs of William P. Murphy, decd, and make inventory, etc.
/s/Jeptha M. Murphy
/s/S. A. Murphy
/s/J. M. Austin
/s/William Bennett
Recorded: 7 Jul 1862

Temporary Letters of Admn Bond of Milligan B. DeVaughan
Page 273-274

Milligan B. DeVaughn, principal, and John Lester, security, give $28,000 bond on 28 Jul 1862 upon the condition that Milligan B. DeVaughn obtain temporary Letters of Admn on John DeVaughan, decd.
/s/M.B. DeVaughan
/s/John Lester
Recorded: 28 Jul 1862

Guardian's Bond of James P. Moon
Page 274-274 (should be 274-275)

James P. Moon, principal, and G. W. Souter give $1800 bond on 5 Aug 1862 upon the condition that James P. Moon be apptd Gdn to person and property of Emma J. Ansley, Orphan of John Ansley, decd.
/s/James P. Moon
/s/G. W. Souter
Recorded: 5 Aug 1862

Temporary Admrs' Bond of Nathaniel Stinchcomb
Page 274 (misnumbered)

Nathaniel Stinchcomb, principal, and John S. Holliday, security, give $1000 bond on 22 Sept 1862 upon the condition that Nathaniel Stinchcomb be apptd Admr of James W. Edmondson, decd
/s/Nathaniel Stinchcomb
/s/John S. Holliday
Recorded: 23 Sept 1862

Admrs' Bond of Mathew Baker
Page 275

Mathew Baker, principal, and Isaac Hartley, security, gives $500 bond on 6 Oct 1862 upon the condition that Mathew Baker be apptd Admr of James Baker, decd.
/s/Mathew Baker
/s/Isaac Hartly
Recorded: 6 Oct 1862

Admrs' Bond of Jesse Carter
Page 276

Jesse Carter (principal) and L. F. Blalock, security, give $200 bond on 6 Oct 1862 upon the condition that Jesse Carter be apptd Admr of Jesse H. Carter, decd.
/s/Jesse Carter
/s/L. F. Blalock
Recorded: 6 Oct 1862

Temporary Letters of Admn Bond of James Boyd
Page 276-277

James Boyd, principal, and Joshua P. Shropshire, security, give $3000 bond on 22 Oct 1862 upon the condition that James Boyd be granted temporary Letters of Admn on Wilson Spence, decd.
/s/James Boyd
/s/J. P. Shropshire
Recorded: 22 Oct 1862

Admrs' Bond of Isham Hicks
Page 277-278

Isham Hicks, principal, and Perry Hicks, security, give $200 bond on 3 Nov 1862 upon the condition that Isham Hicks be apptd Admr of James T. W. Hicks, decd, to make inventory, etc.
/s/Isham hicks
/s/Perry Hicks
Recorded: 3 Nov 1862

Admrs' Bond of Lewis C. Smith
Page 278-279

Lewis C. Smith, principal, and Elijah Glass, security, give $200 bond on 3 Nov 1862 upon the condition that Lewis C. Smith be apptd Admr of Daniel McEachern, decd.
/s/Lewis C. Smith
/s/Elijah Glass
Recorded: 3 Nov 1862

Admrs' Bond of Nathaniel Stinchcomb
Page 279

Nathaniel Stinchcomb, principal, and Elijah Glass, security, give $1000 bond on 3 Nov 1862 upon the condition that Nathaniel Stinchcomb be apptd Admr of James W. Edmondson, decd, to make inventory.
/s/Nathaniel Stinchcomb
/s/Elijah Glass
Recorded: 3 Nov 1862

Admrs' Bond of John I. Whitaker
Page 280

John I. Whitaker, principal, and Willis R. Whitaker and C. C. Sams, securities, give $14,000 bond on 3 Nov 1862 upon the condition that John I. Whitaker be apptd Admr of William J. Sams, decd.
/s/John I. Whitaker
/s/W. R. Whitaker
/s/C. C. Sams
Recorded: 3 Nov 1862

Guardian's Bond of Edmond Segraves
Page 281

Edmond Segraves, principal, and Haney Segraves, John I. Whitaker, Tilmon Fuller, W. R. Whitaker and Robert Holliday, securities, give $60,000 bond on 3 Nov 1862 upon the condition that Edmond Segraves be apptd Gdn of the person and property of Archibald R. Porter, John H. Porter and Ophelia J. Porter, orphans of Hugh Porter, decd.
/s/Edmond Segraves
/s/Haney Segraves
/s/John I. Whitaker
/s/Tilmon Fuller
/s/W. R. Whitaker
/s/Robert Holliday
Recorded: 18 Nov 1862

Admrs' Bond of John S. Holliday and Henry B. Holliday
Page 282

John S. Holliday and Henry B. Holliday, principals, and John I. Whitaker, security, give $20,000 bond on 18 Nov 1862 upon the condition that John S. Holliday and Henry B. Holliday are apptd Admrs of Robert Holliday, decd.
/s/John S. Holliday
/s/Henry B. Holliday
/s/John I.Whitaker
Recorded: 18 Nov 1862

Admrs' Bond of James Boyd
Page 283

James Boyd, principal, and L. F. Blalock, security, give $3000 bond on 1 Dec 1862 upon the condition that James Boyd be apptd Admr of Wilson Spence, decd.
/s/James Boyd
/s/L. F. Blalock
Recorded: 1 Dec 1862

Admrs' Bond of John M. Murphy, Sr.
Page 283-284

John M. Murphy, Sr., principal, and John J. Gilbert, security, give $5000 bond on 1 Dec 1862 upon the condition that John M. Murphy, Sr. be apptd Admr of John M. Murphy, Jr., decd.
/s/John M. Murphy, Sr.
/s/John J. Gilbert
Recorded: 1 Dec 1862

Temporary Letters of Admn of Seaborn Pate
Page 284

Seaborn Pate, principal, and William Jackson, security, give $2500 bond on 24 Dec 1862 upon the condition that Seaborn Pate has applied this day and received temporary Letters of Admn of Martin Collins, decd.
/s/Seaborn Pate
/s/William Jackson
Recorded: 24 Dec 1862

Admx' Bond of Rhoda F. Handley
Page 285

Rhoda F. Handley, principal, and Jarot Handley, security, give $3000 bond on 12 Dec 1863 upon the condition that Rhoda F. Handley be apptd Admx of Thomas J. Handley, decd.
/s/rhoda E. Handley
/s/Jarot Handley
Recorded: 14 Jan 1863

Guardian's Bond of Harriet H. Miers
Page 285-286

Harriet H. Miers, principal, and William Miers and William P. Eason, security, give $300 bond on 12 Jan 1863 upon the condition that Harriet H. Miers be apptd Gdn of the person and property of Sarah Ann Permelia, Mary Jane, Lucinda E. and John E. Miers, Orphans of Andrew J. Miers, decd.
/s/Harriet H. Miers
/s/William Miers (x, his mark)
William P. Eason
Recorded: 12 Jan 1863

Guardian's Bond of John J. Gilbert
Page 286

John J. Gilbert, principal, and L. F. Blalock, security, give $3000 bnd on 12 Jan 1863 upon the condition that John J. Gilbert be apptd Gdn to persons and property of Mathew G. Harper and Susan G. Harper, orphans of William Harper, late of Henry Co., Ga.
/s/John J. Gilbert
/s/L. F. Blalock
Recorded: 12 Jan 1863

William E. Archer's Admrs' Bond
Page 286-287

William E. Archer and Allen Reeves, security, give bond for $1200 on 12 Jan 1863 upon the condition that William E. Archer be apptd Admr of Fleming J. Hodges, decd, make inventory, etc.
/s/William E. Archer (x, his mark)
/s/Allen Reeves
Recorded: 14 Jan 1863

Temporary Admrs' Bond of Lorenzo D. Padgett
Page 287-288

Lorenzo D. Padgett, principal, and Willis Brassell, seurity, give $3000 bond on 19 Jan 1863 upon the condition that Lorenzo D. Padgett receive temporary Letters of Admn on Stephen H. King, decd.
/s/Lorenzo D. Padgett
/s/Willis Brassell
Recorded: 19 Jan 1865

Admrs' Bond of John S. Holliday
Page 288

John S. Holliday, principal, and George W. Ware, security, give bond $20,000 on 2 Feb 1865 upon the condition that John S. Holliday be apptd Admr of Robert Holliday, decd.
/s/John S. Holliday
/s/George W. Ware
Recorded: 4 Feb 1865

Admrs' Bond of Joseph S. Speer, Sr.
Page 289

Joseph Speer, Sr., principal, and Lorenzo D. Padgett, seurity, give $1000 on 2 Feb 1863 upon the condition that Joseph Speer, Sr. be apptd Admr of Randel T. Osburn, decd.
/s/Joseph Speer, Sr.
/s/L. D. Padgett
Reorded: 4 Feb 1863

Admrs' Bond of Rowland Stubbs
Page 289-290

Rowland Stubbs, principal, and Elijah Glass, security, give $2000 bond on 2 Mar 1863 upon the condition that Rowland Stubbs be apptd Admr of Westley Turner, decd
/s/Rowland Stubbs
/s/Elijah Glass
Reorded: 4 Mar 1863

Guardian's Bond of Peter E. McLeroy
Page 290

Peter E. McLeroy, principal, and Elijah Glass, security, give $800 bond on 2 Mar 1863 upon the condition that Peter E. McLeroy has this day been apptd Gdn to the property of Francis H. Jones, Charlotta T. Jones, Emily A. Jones, Nancy R. Jones and Gaskey C. Jones, minors of Mathew Jones.
/s/Peter E. McLeroy
/s/Elijah Glass
Recorded: 4 Mar 1863

Admrs' Bond of Seaborn Pate
Page 291

Seaborn Pate, principal, and William Jackson, security, give $2500 bnd on 2 Mar 1863 upon the condition that Seaborn Pate be apptd Admr of Martin Collins, decd, make inventory, etc.
/s/Seaborn Pate
/s/William Jackson
Recorded: 4 Mar 1863

Temporary Admrs' Bond of John C. Brassell
Page 291-292

John C. Brassell, principal, and Raman R. Rogers, security, give $2000 bond on 2 Mar 1863 upon the condition that John C. Brassell obtain temporary Letters of Admn of James J. Carson, decd.
/s/John C Brassell
/s/R. R. Rogers
Recorded: 4 Mar 1863

Admrs' Bond of Lorenzo D. Padgett
Page 292

Lorenzo D. Padgett, principal,and John C. Brassell, security, give bond for $3000 on 2 Mar 1863 upon the condition that Lorenzo D. Padgett be apptd Admr of Stephen H. King, decd.
/s/L. D. Padgett
/s/John C. Brassell
Recorded: 4 Mar 1863

Admrs' Bond of L. F. Blalock
Page 293

L. F. Blalock, principal,and William H. Blalock, security, give $600 bond on 2 Mar 1863 upon the condition that L. F. Blalock be apptd Admr of Elijah P. Eastin, decd.
/s/L. F. Blalock
/s/W. H. Blalock
Recorded: 4 Mar 1863

Temporary Admrs' Bond of Blackman Thornton
Page 293-294

Blackman Thornton, principal,and Herod Thornton, security, give bond for $1500 on 11 Mar 1863 upon the condition that Blackman Thornton obtain temporary Letters of Admn on Hiram H. Thornton, decd.
/s/Blackman Thornton
/s/Herod Thornton
Recorded: 11 Mar 1863

Admrs' Bond of James Bottoms
Page 294-295

James Bottoms, principal, and John J. Gilbert, security, give bond for $1200 on 6 Apr 1863 upon the condition that James Bottoms be apptd Admr of Elisha F. Jackson, decd.
/s/James Bottoms
/s/John J. Gilbert
Recorded: 6 Apr 1863

Guardian's Bond of Lucinda C. Jackson
Page 295

Lucinda C. Jackson, principal, and James Bottoms, security, give $500 bond on 6 Apr 1863 upon the conditionthat Lucinda C. Jackson is this day apptd Gdn of persons and property of James I. B. Jackson, Francis Marion Jackson, and Martha Ann Eliza Jackson, Orphans of Elisha F. Jackson, decd.
/s/Lucinda C. Jackson
/s/James Bottoms
Recorded: 6 Apr 1863

Admr's Bond of L. F. Blalock
Page 296

L. F. Blalock, principal, and S. D. Dorsey, security, give bond for $3000 on 4 May 1863 upon the condition that L. F. Blalock be apptd Admr of Willis M. Bishop, decd.
/s/L. F. Blalock
/s/S. D. Dorsey
Recorded: 5 May 1863

Admrs' Bond of John C. Brassell
Page 296-297

John C. Brassell, principal, and R. R. Rogers, security, give bond for $3000 on 4 May 1863 upon the condition that John C. Brassell be apptd Admr of James J. Carson, decd.
/s/John C. Brassell
/s/R. R. Rogers
Recorded: 5 May 1863

Guardian's Bond of Isaac A. Haisten
Page 297

Isaac A. Haisten, principal, and Arthur Robinson, security, give $2000 bnd on 4 May 1863 upon the cndition that Isaac A. Haisten is this day apptd Gdn to property of Joseph Bishop and Henry Bishop, orphans of Willis M. Bishop, decd.
/s/Isaac A. Haisten
/s/Arthur Robinson
Recorded: 5 May 1863

Temporary Admrs' Bond of L. F. Blalock
Page 298

L. F. Blalock, principal, and William H. Blalock, security, give bond for $16,000 on 18 May 1863 upon the condition that L. F. Blalock obtain temporary Letters of Admn of Thomas J. Milner, decd.
/s/L. F. Blalock
/s/William H. Blalock
Recorded: 18 May 1863

Admrs' Bond of Blackman Thornton
Page 298-299

Blackman Thornton, principal, and Herod Thornton, security, give bond for $1500 on 1 Jun 1863 upon the condition that Blackman Thornton be apptd Admr of Hiram H. Thornton, decd, to make inventory, etc
/s/Blackmon Thorntn
/s/Herod Thornton
Recorded: 2 Jun 1863

Admrs' Bond of Isaac A. Haisten
Page 299-300

Isaac A. Haisten, principal, and Leroy M. Cobb, security, give $8000 bond on 1 Jun 1863 upon the condition that Isaac A. Haisten is apptd Admr of John T. Bagwell, decd.
/s/I. A. Haisten
/s/L. M. Cobb
Recorded: 2 Jun 1863

Admrs' Bond of James D. Murphy
Page 300

James D. Murphy, principal, and M. M. Tidwell and L. F. Blalock, securities, give $8000 bond on 1 Jun 1863 upon the condition that James D. Murphy be apptd Admr de bonis non of John M. Murphy, Jr., decd, make inventory, etc.
/s/James D. Murphy
/s/M. M. Tidwell
/s/L. F. Blalock
Recorded: 2 Jun 1863

Admrs' Bond of William J. Russell
Page 301

William J. Russell, principal, and L. F. Blalock, security, give $5000 bond on 1 Jun 1863 upon the condition that William J. Russell be apptd Admr of Jones Cochran, decd.
/s/William J. Russell
/s/L. F. Blalock
Recorded: 2 Jun 1863

Temporary Admrs' Bond of James M. Austin
Page 301-302

James M. Austin, principal, and C. E. Bennett, security, give $8000 bond on 5 Jun 1863 upon the condition that James M. Austin be granted temporary Letters of Admn of A. R. Graves, decd.
/s/J. M. Austin
/s/C. E. Bennett
Recorded: 5 Jun 1863

Guardian's Bond of James M. Camp
Page 302

James M. Camp and William H. Blalock, security, give $1000 bond on 6 Jul 1863 upon the condition that James Boyd is this day apptd Gdn of the persons and property of Ida, Victoria and Elizabeth Spence, orphans of Wilson Spence, decd.
/s/James Boyd
/s/James M. Camp
/s/W. H.Blalock
Recorded: 7 Jul 1863

Guardian's Bond of Eli Edmondson
Page 303

Eli Edmondson, principal, Andrew McBride and William W. Mathews, security, give $30,000 bond on 6 Jul 1863 upon the condition that Eli Edmondson is this day apptd Gdn to persons and property of Joseph A. Cofield and Uriah P. Cofield, orphans of Warner Cofield, decd.
/s/Eli Edmondson
/s/Andrew McBride
/s/William W. Mathews
Recorded: 7 Jul 1863

Admrs' Bond of Juan F. McLane
Page 304

Juan F. McLane, principal, and John C. Brassell and Eli Edmondson, securities, give $6000 bond on 6 Jul 1863 upon the condition that Juan F. McLane be apptd Admr de bonis non with LWT annexed of John McLane, decd.
/s/J. F. McLane
/s/Eli Edmondson
/s/John C. Brassell

Temporary Admrs' Bond of Robert C. Bridges
Page 304-305

Robert C. Bridges, principal, and Eli Edmondson and Hillery Brooks, security, give $6000 bond on 6 Jul 1863 upon the condition that Robert C. Bridges has obtained temporary Letters of Admn of Eli Burgamy, decd.
/s/R. C. Bridges
/s/Eli Edmondson
/s/Hillery Brooks
Recorded: 7 Jul 1863

Temporary Admrs' Bond of John I. Whitaker
Page 305

John I. Whitaker, principal, and Willis R. Whitaker, security, give $800 bond on 9 Jul 1863 upon the condition that John I. Whitaker obtain temporary Letters of Admn of Terry Runnels, decd.
/s/John I. Whitaker
/s/W. R. Whitaker
Recorded: 9 Jul 1863

Admrs' Bond of Joshua A. Milner
Page 306

Joshua A. Milner, principal, and Willis Beavers, William Shadrick, Jesse Ward, and Joshua W. Lyle, securities, give $8000 bond on 3 Aug 1863 upon the condition that Joshua A. Milner be apptd Admr with LWT annexed of Thomas J. Milner, decd.
/s/J. A. Milner
/s/Willis Beavers
/s/William Shadrick
/s/Jesse Ward
/s/Joshua W. Lyle (x, his mark)
Recorded: 6 Aug 1863

Admrs' Bond of William H. Blalock
Page 307

William H. Blalock, principal, M. M. Tidwell and L. F. Blalock, securities, give $3000 bond on 3 Aug 1863 upon the condition that William H. Blalock be apptd Admr of Martha Owens, decd, make inventory, etc.
/s/W. H. Blalock
/s/M. M. Tidwell
/s/L. F. Blalock
Recorded: 6 Aug 1863

Temporary Admrs' Bond of Hillery Brooks
Page 307-308

Hillery Brooks, principal, and Robert C. Bridges, security, give $3000 bond on 3 Aug 1863 upon the condition that Hillery Brooks be granted temporary Letters of Admn on Estate of Thomas J. Henderson, decd.
/s/Hillery Brooks
/s/R. C. Bridges
Recorded: 6 Aug 1863

Admrs' Bond of James M. Austin
Page 308-309

James M. Austin, principal, and Nathan Eason, security, give $8000 bond on 5 Aug 1863 upon the condition that James M. Austin be apptd Admr of A. R. Graves, decd.
/s/J. M. Austin
/s/Nathan Eason
Recorded: 6 Aug 1863

Admrs' Bnd of Nathan Eason and Martha Graves
Page 309-310

Nathan Eason and Martha Graves principals, and James M. Austin, security, give $3000 bond on 4 Aug 1863 upon the condition that Nathan Eason and Martha Graves be apptd Admrs of Vines Graves, to make inventory, etc.
/s/Nathan Eason
/s/Martha Graves
/s/J. M. Austin
Recorded: 6 Aug 1863

Temporary Admrs' Bond of E. T. Humperly
Page 310

E.T. Humperly, principal, and W. J. Abercrombie, security, give $1000 bond on 12 Aug 1863 upon the condition that E. T. Hemperly has obtained temporary Letters of Admn of Edward Hemperly, decd
/s/E. T. Hemperly
/s/W. J. Abercrombie
Recorded: 12 Aug 1863

Admx' Bond of Frances Jane Burgamy
Page 311

Frances Jane Burgamy, principal, and Charles Bailey, security, give $10,000 bond on 7 Sept 1863 upon the condition that Frances Jane Burgamy be apptd Admx of Eli Burgamy, decd.
/s/Frances J. Burgamy
/s/Charles Bailey
Recorded: 10 Sept 1863

Admrs' Bond of John J. Gilbert
Page 311-312

John J. Gilbert, principal, and Peter E. McLeroy, security, give $4000 bond on 7 Sept 1863 upon the condition that John J. Gilbert be apptd Admr of Trustin Turner, decd.
/s/John J. Gilbert
/s/Peter E. McLeroy
Recorded: 10 Sept 1863

Guardian's Bond of Eli Edmondson
Page 312

Eli Edmondson, principal, and Thomas C. Mathews, Isaac P. Gay and William W. Mathews, security, give $60,000 bond on 7 Sept 1863 upon the condition that Eli Edmondson be apptd Gdn to persons and property of Martha Ann, Anneleza and Exor Cofield, orphans of Uriah Cofield, decd.
/s/Eli Edmondson
/s/T. C. Mathews
/s/Isaac P. Gay
/s/William W. Mathews
Recorded: 10 Sept 1863

Guardian's Bond of Eli Edmondson
Page 313

Eli Edmondson, principal, and T. C. Mathews, William W. Mathews, securities, give $5000 bond on 7 Sept 1863 upon the condition that Eli Edmondson is this day apptd Gdn of person and property of Pearch O. Burgamy, orphan of Eli Burgamy, decd.
/s/Eli Edmondson
/s/T. C. Mathews
/s/William W. Mathews
Recorded: 10 Sept 1863

Admrs' Bond of L. F. Blalock
Page 313-314

L. F. Blalock, principal, and Solomon S. Dorsey, security, give $4000 bnd on 7 Sept 1863 upon the condition that L. F. Blalock be apptd Admr of Edward Hemperly, decd, make inventory, etc.
/s/L. F. Blalock
/s/S. D. Dorsey
Recorded: 10 Sept 1863

Admx' Bond of Tanissa Wootton
Page 314

Tanissa Wootton, principal, and M. M. Tidwell and James Hanes, security, give $4000 bond on 7 Sept 1863 upon the condition that Tanissa Wootton be apptd Admx of Young L. Wootton, decd.
/s/Tanissa Wootton
/s/M. M. Tidwell
/s/James Hanes
Recorded: 10 Sept 1863

Admrs' Bond of John I. Whitaker
Page 315

John I. Whitaker, principal, and Willis R. Whitaker, security, gives $1000 bond on 7 Sept 1863 upon the condition that John I. Whitaker be apptd Admr of Terry Runnells, decd.
/s/John I. Whitaker
/s/Willis R. Whitaker
Recorded: 10 Sept 1863

Admrs' Bond of Williamson Jenkins
Page 315-316

Williamson Jenkins, principal, and Solomon D. Dorsey, security, give $2300 bond on 7 Sept 1863 upon the condition that Williamson Jenkins be apptd Admr de bonis non of Matilda Evans, decd.
/s/Williamson Jenkins
/s/Solomon D. Dorsey
Recorded: 10 Sept 1863

Admrs' Bond of James Boyd
Page 316-317

James Boyd, principal, and William Milner, security, give $2000 bnd on 5 Oct 1863 upon the condition that James Boyd be apptd Admr of M. H. Boyd, decd.
/s/James Boyd
/s/William Milner
Recorded: 6 Oct 1863

Temporary Admrs' Bond of Josiah Pyron and H. F. Longino
Page 317

Josiah Pyron and H. F. Longino, principals, and Robert C. Bridges and Hillery Brooks, securities, give $8000 bond on 5 Oct 1863 upon the condition that Josiah Pyrum and H. F. Longin be issued temporary Letters of Administration of the Estate of Madison King, decd.
/s/Josiah Pyron
/s/H. F. Longino
/s/Robert C. Bridges
/s/Hillery Brooks. Recorded: 6 Oct 1863

Admrs' Bond of Hillery Brooks
Page 318

Hillery Brooks, principal, and Robert C. Bridges, security, give $3000 bond upon the condition that Hillery Brooks be apptd Admr of Thomas J. Henderson, decd.
/s/Hillery Brooks
/s/Robert C. Bridges
Recorded: 6 Oct 1863

Admrs' Bond of John C. Brassell
Page 318-319

John C. Brassell, principal, and Lorenzo D. Padgett, security, give $4000 bond on 5 Oct 1863 upon the condition that John C. Brassell be apptd Admr of Joseph McLane, decd.
/s/John C. Brassell
/s/Lorenzo D. Padgett. Recorded: 6 Oct 1863

Admrs' Bond of Jesse Ward
Page 319-320

Jesse Ward, principal, and Reuben Wallis, security, give $3000 bond on 5 Oct 1863 upon the condition that Jesse Ward be apptd Admr of James Ward, decd.
/s/Jesse Ward
/s/Reuben Wallis
Recorded: 6 Oct 1863

Guardian's Bond of Martha Graves
Page 320

Martha Graves, principal, and Rice Eason, security, give $1000 bond on 5 Oct 1863 upon the condition that Martha Graves be apptd Gdn of the person and property of Wiley V. Graves, orphan of Vines Graves decd.
/s/Martha Graves
/s/Rice Eason
Recorded: 6 Oct 1863

Guardian's Bond of Caroline M. Boyd
Page 321

Caroline M. Boyd, principal, and James Boyd and William Milam, securities, give $1000 bond on 5 Oct 1863 upon the condition that Caroline M. Boyd be apptd Gdn of the person and property of William H. Boyd, orphan of William H. Boyd, decd.
/s/Caroline M. Boyd
/s/James Boyd
/s/William Milam
Recorded: 6 Oct 1863

Guardian's Bond of Martha Ann Turner
Page 321-322

Martha Ann Turner, principal, and Lorenzo D. Padgett, security, gives $2500 bond on 12 Nov 1863 upon the condition that Martha Ann Turner be apptd Gdn of William B. Turner, orphan of Trustin Turner, decd.
/s/Martha Ann Turner
/s/Lorenzo D. Padgett
Recorded: 13 Nov 1863

Guardian's Bond of Nettie Ann Banks
Page 322

Nettie Ann Banks, principal, and Lorenzo Morgan and Eli Edmondon, securities, give $5000 bond on 2 Nov 1863 upon the condition that Nettie Ann Banks be apptd Admx of Kinnan Banks, decd.
/s/Nettie Ann Banks
/s/Lorenzo Morgan
/s/Eli Edmondson
Recorded: 3 Nov 1863

Admrs' Bond of Daniel D. Denham
Page 323

Daniel D. Denham, principal, and Lewis C. Smith and Williamson Jenkins, securities, give $4000 bond on 2 Nov 1863 upon the condition that Daniel D. Denham be apptd Admr of William Watson, decd.
/s/Daniel D. Denham
/s/Lewis C. Smith
/s/Williamson Jenkins
Recorded: 3 Nov 1863

Admrs' Bond of Edward Connor
Page 324

Edward Connor, principal, and Elijah Glass, security, give bond on 7 Dec 1863 upon the condition that Edward Connor be apptd Admr of Thomas H. Stephens, decd.
/s/Edward Cnnor
/s/Elijah Glass
Recorded: 8 Nov 1863

Guardian's Bond of L. F. Blalock
Page 324-325

L. F. Blalock, principal, and John J. Gilbert, security, give $500 bond n 7 Dec 1863, upon the condition that L. F. Blalock be apptd Gdn of the property of Arthur Minnick, Idiot.
/s/L. F. Blalock
/s/John J. Gilbert
Recorded: 8 Dec 1863

Admrs' Bond of Josiah Pyron and H. F. Longino
Page 325-326

Josiah Pyron and H. F. Longino, admrs with LWT annexed, principals, and Robert C. Bridges and Hillery Brooks, securities, give bond on 7 Dec 1863 upon the condition that Josiah Pyron and H. F. Longino make a true and perfect inventory, etc. on Madison King, decd.
/s/Josiah Pyron
/s/H. F. Longino
Recorded: 8 Dec 1865

Admrs' Bond of Emma Field and James R. Bailey
Page 326

Emma Field, Admx and James R. Bailey, Admr, principals, and James D. Murphy, security, give $5000 bond on 7 Dec 1863 upon the condition that Emma Field and James R. Bailey be apptd Admrs of Isiah M. Field, decd, to make inventory, etc.
/s/Emma Field
/s/James R. Bailey
/s/James D. Murphy
Recorded: 8 Dec 1863

Guardian's Bond of Martha A. Murphy
Page 327

Martha A. Murphy, principal, and James D. Glass and Elijah Glass, securities, give $20,000 bond on 7 Dec 1863 upon the condition that Martha A. Murphy be apptd Gdn of the person and property of George N. Murphy and Joseph R. Murphy, orphans of John M. Murphy.
/s/Martha A. Murphy
/s/James D. Glass
/s/Elijah Glass
Recorded: 8 Dec 1863

Admrs' Bond of Daniel D. Denham
Page 327-328

Daniel D. Denham, principal, and John Phillips and L. F. Blalock, securities, give $2000 bond on 11 Jan 1864 upon the condition that Daniel D. Denham be apptd Admr of Thomas A. Watson, decd.
/s/Daniel D. Denjam
/s/John Phillips
/s/L. F. Blalock
Recorded: 12 Jan 1864

Guardian's Bond of Elizabeth Thornton
Page 328

Elizabeth Thornton, principal, and Blackman Thornton and H. C. Spier, securities, give $800 bond on 11 Jan 1864 upon the condition that Elizabeth Thornton be apptd Gdn of the person and property of David L. Thornton, orphan of Hiram H. Thornton, decd.
/s/Elizabeth Thornton
/s/Blackman Thornton
/s/H. C. Spier
Recorded: 12 Jan 1864

Guardian's Bond of Samuel R. Jones
Page 329

Samuel R. Jones principal, and Charles Jones, security, give $2000 bond on 10 Jan 1864 upon the condtion that Samuel R. Jones be apptd Gdn of the person and property of William F. McLane.
/s/Samuel R. Jones
/s/Charles Jones
Recorded: 12 Jan 1864

Guardian's Bond of Williamson Jenkins
Page 329-330

Williamson Jenkins, principal, and William W. Wilkins, security, give $400 bond on 7 Mar 1864 upon the condition that Williamson Jenkins be apptd Gdn of the property of Rozey Graves and Rufus Graves, orphans of Wiley Graves, decd.
/s/Williamson Jenkins
/s/William W. Wilkins
Recorded: 8 Mar 1864

Guardian's Bond of William H. Persons
Page 330

William H. Persons, principal, and Lewis T. Thompson, security, give $5000 bond on 7 Mar 1864 upon the condition that William H. Persons be apptd Gdn of the person of Misouri Duffell, orphan of Washington D. Duffell, decd.
/s/William H. Persons
/s/Lewis T. Thompson
Recorded: 8 Mar 1864

Admrs' Bond of Williamson Jenkins
Page 330-331

Williamson Jenkins, principal, and William W. Wilkins, security, give $1600 bond on 7 Mar 1864 upon the conditin that Williamson Jenkins be apptd Admr of Wiley Graves, decd.
/s/Williamson Jenkins
/s/William W. Wilkins
Recorded: 8 Mar 1864

Bond of Clerk of the Inferior Court
Page 331

L. F. Blalock, principal, and C. U. Boatright and J. C. Yates, give $3000 bond on 4 Mar 1864 upon the condition that L. F. Blalock was on 6 Jan 1864 elected Clerk of the Inferior Court of said county of Fayette.
/s/L. B. Blalock
/s/C. U. Boatright
/s/J. C. Yates
Recorded: 8 Mar 1864

Guardian's Bond of Nancy Watson
Page 332

Nancy Watson, principal, and James Black, security, gives $2000 bond on 15 Mar 1864 upon the condition that Nancy Watson be apptd Gdn of the person and property of Virginia Ann Watson, orphan of Thomas W. Watson, decd.
/s/Nancy Watson
/s/James Black
Recorded: 15 Mar 1864

Temporary Letters of Admn of Nathan Eason
Page 332-333

Nathan Eason, principal, and S. T. W. Minor, security, gives $4000 bond on 15 Mar 1864 upon the condition that Nathan Eason be granted temporary Letters f Admn of Major Kite, decd.
/s/Nathan Eason
/s/S. T. W. Minor
Recorded: 15 Mar 1864

Admrs' Bond of Nathan Eason
Page 333-334

Nathan Eason, principal, and S. T. W. Minor, saecurity, gives $1400 bond on 2 May 1864 upon the condition that Nathan Eason be apptd Admr of Major Kite, decd.
/s/Nathan Eason
/s/S. T. W. Minor
Recorded: 5 May 1864

Admrs' Bond of S. T. W. Minor
Page 334

S. T. W. Minor, principal, and John Huie, security, give $200 bond on 2 May 1864 upon the condition that S. T. W. Minor be apptd Admr of Charlton S. Minor, decd.
/s/S. T. W. Minor
/s/John Huie
Recorded: 3 May 1864

Admrs' Bond of Mary Martin and Joseph G. Yates
Page 335

Mary Martin and Joseph G. Yates, principals, and L. F. Blalock and W. P. Redwine, securities, give $35,000 bond on 4 Jul 1864 upon the condition that Mary Martin and Joseph G. Yates be apptd Admrs of Jackson Martin, decd.
/s/Mary Martin
/s/Joseph G. Yates
/s/L. F. Blalock
/s/W. P. Redwine
Recorded: 5 Jul 1864

Temporary Admrs' Bond of Kerdeliau C. Swanson
Page 336

Kerdeliau C. Swanson, principal, and John Lester and M. W. Swanson, securities, give $60,000 bond on 8 Jul 1864 upon the condition that Kerdeliau C. Swason be issued temporary Letters of Admn of Estate of Andrew P. Swanson, decd.
/s/Kerdeliau C. Swanson
/s/John Lester
/s/M. W. Swanson
Recorded: 8 Jul 1864

Guardian's Bond of William H. Persons
Page 337

William H. Persons, principal, and John T. Hewell and John Lester, give $8000 bond on 1 Aug 1864 upon the condition that William H. Persons be apptd Gdn of person and property of Mary Terisa, Rebecca, Millard Hill, Exer Ann, Pallestine and Francis Drury Patterson, orphans of Francis M. Patterson.
/s/William H. Persons
/s/John T. Hewell
/s/John Lester

Admrs' Bond of W. H. Persons
Page 337-338

William H. Persons, principal, and John T. Hewell, security, give $1500 bond on 1 Aug 1864 upon the condition that William H. Persons be apptd Admr with LWT annexed of Samuel Cox, decd.
/s/William H. Persons
/s/John T. Hewell

Admrs' Bond of Robert C. Elington
Page 339

Robert C. Elington, principal, and Lewis C. Smith and Sanford Adams, securities, give $10,000 bond on 1 Aug 1864 upon the condition that Robert C. Elington be apptd Admr of David W. Elington, decd.
/s/Robert C. Elington
/s/L. C. Smith
/s/S. Adams

Temporary Admrs' Bond of Mary Travis
Page 340

Mary Travis, principal, and Edward Moon, security, gives $5000 bond on 1 May 1865 upon the condition that Mary Travis be granted temporary Letters of Admn of Howard C. Travis, decd.
/s/Mary Travis
/s/Edward Moon
Recorded: 3 May 1865

Temporary Admrs' Bond of Martha Ann Duffell
Page 340-341

Martha Ann Duffell, principal, and Edward Moore, principal, give $2000 bond on 1 May 1865 upon the condition that Martha Ann Duffell be granted temporary Letters of Admn of L. Duffell, decd.
/s/Martha Ann Duffell
/s/Edward Moore
Recorded: 3 May 1865

Guardian's Bond of Henry J. Hughie
Page 341

Henry J. Hughie, principal, and John T. Hewell and William M. Pyron, securities, give $10,000 bond on 1 May 1865 upon the condition that Henry J. Hughie be apptd Gdn of Mary Clark, orphan of L. B. Clark, decd.
/s/H. J. Hughie
/s/John T. Hewell
/s/W. M. Pyron. Recorded: 4 Mar 1865

Guardian's Bond of Francis E. Carson
Page 342

Francis E. Carson, principal, and Robert Neel and William Whatley, securities, gives $400 bond on 1 May 1865 upon the condition that Francis E. Carson be apptd Gdn to orphans of James J. Carson, decd.
(unnamed)
/s/Francis E. Carson
/s/Robert Neel
/s/William Whatley. Recorded: 13 May 1865

Admx' Bond of Mary Travis
Page 342-343

Mary Travis, principal, and John T. Howell, security, gives $4000 bond on 5 Jun 1865 upon the condition that Mary Travis be apptd Adx of Howard C. Travis, decd.
/s/Mary Travis
/s/John T. Howell

Admrs' Bond of Sarah S. Fitts
Page 303

Sarah S. Fitts, principal, and W. W. Mathews, security, gives $500 bond on 5 Jun 1865 upon the condition that Sarah F. Fitts be apptd Admx of John B. Fitts, decd.
/s/Sarah S. Fitts
/s/W. W. Mathews
Recorded: 8 Jun 1865

Admrs' Bond of Juan F. McLane
Page 344

Juan F. McLane, principal, and Edmond Seagraves and H. S. McLane, securities, give $2500 bond on 5 Jun 1865 upon the condition that Juan F. McLane be apptd Admr of Oliver P. McLane, decd.
/s/Juan F. McLane
/s/Edmond Seagraves
/s/H. S. McLane
Recorded: 12 Jun 1865

Admrs' Bond of Jane and John Edmondson
Page 344-345

Jane Edmondson and John Edmondson, principals, and W. W. Mathews and Burket Rentfrow, securities, give $50,000 bond on 5 Jun 1865 upon the condition that Jane and John Edmondson be apptd Admrs of Eli Edmondson, decd.
/s/Jane Edmondson
/s/John Edmondson
/s/W. W. Mathews
/s/Burket Rentfrow
Recorded: 12 Jun 1865

Admrs' Bond of George M. Davis
Page 345-346

George M. Davis, principal, and Elijah Glass and Wesly M. Davis, securities, give $3000 bond on 5 Jun 1865 upon the condition that George M. Davis be apptd Admr of John W. Davis, decd.
/s/George M. Davis
/s/Elijah Glass
/s/Wesly M. Davis
Recorded: 12 Jun 1865

Guardian's Bond of Thomas J. Edmondson
Page 346

Thomas J. Edmondson, principal, and John W. Kelly, William W. Matthews and John Edmondson, securities, give $30,000 bond on 5 Jun 1865 upon the condition that Thomas J. Edmondson be apptd Gdn of Martha, Annah and exor Cofield, orphans of Uriah Cofield, decd.
/s/Thomas J. Edmondson
/s/John W. Kelly
/s/William W. Matthews
/s/John Edmondson
Recorded: 12 Jun 1865

Admrs' Bond of Oliver Thompson
Page 347

Oliver Thompson, principal, and William H. Blalock give $1000 bond on 3 Jul 1865 upon the condition that Oliver Thompson be apptd Admr of James S. Thompson, decd.
/s/Oliver Thompson (x, his mark)
/s/William H. Blalock
Recorded: 4 Jul 1865

Admrs' Bond of Cordelian C. Swanson
Page 348

Cordelian C. Swanson, principal, and John Lester, security, gives $3000 bond on 4 Sept 1865 upon the condition that Cordelian C. Swanson be apptd Admr of Andrew V. Swanson, decd.
/s/Kordelian C. Swanson
/s/John Lester
Recorded: 8 Sept 1865

Admrs' Bond of A. R. Smith
Paage 348-349

A. R. Smith, principal, and James M. Oakly, security, gives $2000 bond on 4 Sept 1865 upon the condition that A. R. Smith be apptd Admr of Henry C. Spier, decd.
/s/A. R. Smith
/s/James M. Oakly
Recorded: 8 Sept 1865

Admx' Bond of Mary E. Loyd
Page 349-350

Mary E. Loyd, principal, and Sarah Loyd, security, gives $3000 bond on 2 Oct 1865 upon the condition that Mary E. Loyd be apptd Admx of John Loyd, decd.
/s/Mary E. Loyd
/s/Sarah Loyd
Recorded: 9 Oct 1865

Admrs' Bond of William Whatley
Page 350

William Whatley, principal, and John C. Brassell and Johnston Whatley, securities, gives $4000 bond on 4 Sept 1865 upon the condition that William Whatley be apptd Admr with LWT annexed of Allen West, decd.
/s/William Whatley
/s/Johnston Whatley
/s/T. S. Price
Recorded: 10 Oct 1865

Temporary Admrs' Bond of Needham Jackson
Page 351

Needham Jackson, principal, and Herod Thornton, security, gives $600 bond on 23 Sept 1865 upon the condition that temporary Letters of Admn be granted to Jordan Jackson, decd.
/s/Needham Jackson
/s/Herod Thornton
Recorded: 11 Oct 1865

Temporary Admrs' Bond of John S. Miles
Page 351-352

John S. Miles, principal, and William P. Redwine, security, gives $600 bond on 14 Oct 1865 upon the condition that John S. Miles be granted temporary Letters of Admn of Agnes Miles, decd.
/s/John S. Miles
/s/William P. Redwine
Recorded: 24 Oct 1865

Admx' Bond of Martha A. Duffell
Page 352-353

Martha A. Duffell, principal, and Edward Moore and James T. Travis, securities, give $3000 bond on 6 Nov 1865 upon the condition that Martha A. Duffell be apptd Admx of Thomas L. Duffell, decd.
/s/Martha A. Duffell
/s/Edward Moore
/s/James T. Travis
Recorded: 12 Nov 1865

Temporary Admrs' Bond of Seaborn Pate
Page 353

Seaborn Pate, principal, and Leroy M. Cobb, security, gives $5000 bond on 6 Nov 1865 upon the condition that temporary Letters of Admn be issued to Henry M. Pate, decd.
/s/Seaborn Pate
/s/L. M. Cobb
Recorded: 17 Nov 1865

Temporary Admrs' Bond of Isaac A. Haisten
Page 353-354

Isaac A. Haisten, principal, and Thomas C. Matthews, security, gives $4000 bond on 17 Nov 1865 upon the condition that temporary Letters of Adm be granted to Isaac A. Haisten on Estate of Charles Baily, decd.
/s/Isaac A. Haisten
/s/Thomas C. Matthews. Recorded: 21 Nov 1865

Temporary Admrs' Bond of Philip H. Brassell
Page 354-355

Philip H. Brassell, principal and George W. Ware, security, gives $1000 bond on 6 Dec 1865 upon the condition that Philip H. Brassell be granted temporary Letters of Admn of Charles C. Shell, decd.
/s/P. H. Brassell
/s/George W. Ware
Recorded: 14 Dec 1865

Temporary Admrs' Bond of Allison Spier
Page 355-356

Allison Spier, principal, and Benjamin F. Spier give $2000 bond on 27 Nov 1865 upon the condition that Allison Spier be granted temporary Letters of Admn on Allison Spier, decd.
/s/Allison Spier
/s/Benjamin F. Spier
Recorded: 15 Dec 1865

Admrs' Bond of Needham Jackson
Page 356-357

Needham Jackson, principal, and Samuel T. W. Minor, security, gives $3000 bond on 1 Dec 1865 upon the condition that Needham Jackson be apptd Admr of Jordan Jackson, decd.
/s/Needham Jackson
/s/Samuel T. W. Minor
Recorded: 15 Dec 1865

Admrs' Bond of John S. Miles
Page 357

John S. Miles, principal, and M. M. Tidwell and Richmond Dorman, securities, gives $700 bond on 4 Dec 1865 upon the condition that John S. Miles be apptd Admr of Agness Miles, decd.
/s/John S. Miles
/s/M. M. Tidwell
/s/Richmond Dorman
Recorded: 15 Dec 1865

Guardian's Bond of George W. Edmondson
Page 358

George W. Edmondson, principal, and John T. Mathews and John Edmondson, securities, gives $3000 bond on 1 Dec 1865 upon the condition that George W. Edmondson be apptd Gdn to Eli Edmondson, orphan of Eli Edmondson, decd.
/s/George W. Edmondson
/s/John T. Mathews
/s/John Edmondson
Recorded: 11 Dec 1865

Guardian's Bond of Gainey Westbrook
Page 358-359

Gainey Westbrook, principal, and Nathaniel Stinchcomb and James W. Johnson, give $2000 bond on 4 Dec 1865 upon the condition that Gainey Westbrook be apptd Gdn to Louisa J. Edmondson, orphan of James W. Edmondson, decd.
/s/Gainey Westbrook
/s/Nathaniel Stinchcomb
/s/James W. Jackson
Recorded: 11 Dec 1865

Guardian's Bond of P. Romulus Collins
Page 359

P. Romulus Collins, principal, and John W. Kelly, security, gives $1600 bond on 4 Dec 1865 upon the condition that P. Romulus Collins be apptd Gdn to Paschal and Emily Collins, orphans of Paschal Collins.
/s/P. R. Collins
/s/J. W. Kelly
Recorded: 19 Dec 1865

Temporary Admrs' Bond of John M. Ward
Paage 359-360

John M. Ward, principal, and John O. Brown and James G. Morris, securities, give bond for $1600 on 14 Dec 1865 upon the condition that John M. Ward be granted temporary Letters of Admn of Miles Ward, decd.
/s/John M. Ward
/s/John O. Brown
/s/James O. Morris
Recorded: 19 Dec 1865

Guardian's Bond of Stephen Rentfrow
Page 360-361

Stephen Rentfrow, principal, and Burket Rentfrow, security, gives $600 bond on 4 Dec 1865 upon the condition that Stephen Rentfrow be apptd Gdn to Susan S. T. Duffell, orphan of Thomas L. Duffell.
/s/Stephen Rentfrow
/s/Burket Rentfrow
Recorded: 20 Dec 1865

Temporary Admrs' Bond of John W. Smith
Page 361

John W. Smith, principal, and Joseph G. Yates, security, gives $1000 bond on 5 Jan 1866 upon the condition that temporary Letters of Admn be issued to John W. Smith on Estate of Jane Landrum, decd.
/s/John W. Smith
/s/Joseph G. Yates
Recorded: 9 Jan 1866

Admrs' Bond of John I. Whitaker
Page 362

John I. Whitaker, principal, and Willis R. Whitaker, security, gives $1000 bond on 8 Jan 1866 upon the condition that John I. Whitaker be apptd Admr of Henry M. Pate, decd.
/s/John I. Whitaker
/s/Willis R. Whitaker. Recorded: 15 Jan 1866

Admrs' Bond of Isaac A. Haisten
Page 362-363

Isaac A. Haisten, principal, and Leroy M. Cobb, security, give $7000 bond on 8 Jan 1866 upon the conditin that Isaac A. Haisten be appd Admr of Charles Baily, decd.
/s/Isaac A. Haisten
/s/L. M. Cobb
Recorded: 15 Jan 1866

Guardian's Bond of Mary S. Bagwell
Page 363

Mary S. Bagwell, principal, and Leroy M. Cobb, security, give $1000 bond on 8 Jan 1866 upon the condition that Mary S. Bagwell be apptd Gdn to John W. Bagwell, orphan of John T. Bagwell, decd.
/s/Mary S. Bagwell
/s/L. M. Cobb
Recorded: 15 Jan 1866

Admrs' Bond of Williamson P. Redwine
Page 364

Williamson P. Redwine, principal, and Lewis F. Blalock, security, give $1000 bond on 8 Jan 1866 upon the condition that Williamson P. Redwine be apptd Admr of William H. Wootton, decd
/s/W. P. Redwine
/s/L. Blalock
Recorded: 15 Jan 1866

Admrs' Bond of Allison Spier, Jr.
Page 364-365

Allison Spier, Jr., principal, and (blank) give bond for $1200 on 8 Jan 1866 upon the condition that Allison Spier, Jr. be apptd Admr of Allison Spier, Sr.
No signatures
Recorded: 16 Jan 1866

Admrs' Bond of John W. Smith
Page 365

John W. Smith, principal, and Joseph G. Yates, security, give $2000 bond on 5 Jan 1866 upon the condition that John W. Smith be apptd Admr de bonis non with LWT annexed of Larkin Landrum, decd.
/s/John W. Smith
/s/Joseph G. Yates
Recorded: 13 Feb 1866

Admrs' Bond of John H. Smith
Page 366

John H. Smith, principal, and Joseph G. Yates, security, give $1000 bond on 5 Feb 1866 upon the condition that John H. Smith be apptd Admr of Jane Landrum, decd.
/s/John H. Smith
/s/Joseph G. Yates
Recorded: 13 Feb 1866

Admrs' Bond of Phillip H. Brassell
Page 366-367

Phillip H. Brassell, principal, and George W. Ware, security, give $1000 bond on 5 Feb 1866 upon the condition that Phillip H. Brassell be apptd Admr de bonis non of Charles C. Shell, decd.
/s/Phillip H. Brassell
/s/George W. Ware
Recorded: 13 Feb 1866

Admrs' Bond of Phillip H. Brassell
Page 367

Phillip H. Brassell, principal, and John T. Hewell, John C. Brassell and Thomas J. Edmondson, securities, give $2000 bond on 5 Feb 1866 upon the condition that Phillip H. Brassell be apptd Admr of James T. Jennings, decd.
/s/Phillip H. Brassell
/s/John T. Hewell
/s/John C. Brassell
/s/Thomas J. Edmondson
Recorded: 13 Feb 1866

Admrs' Bond of John M. Ward
Page 368

John M. Ward, principal, and James G. Morris, security, give $3000 bond on 5 Feb 1866 upon the condition that John M. Ward be apptd Admr of Miles Ward, decd.
/s/John M. Ward
/s/James G. Morris
Recorded: 15 Feb 1866

Admx' Bond of Mary A. R. Horn
Page 368-369

Mary A. R. Horn, principal, and John C. Brassell, security, give $1000 bnd on 5 Mar 1866 upon the condition that Mary A. R. Horn be apptd admx of Thomas H. Horn.
/s/Mary A. R. Horn
/s/John C. Brassell
Recorded: 8 Mar 1866

Admrs' Bond of William M. Speer
Page 369-370

William M. Speer principal, and James W. Johnson, security, give $1000 bond on 5 Mar 1866 upon the condition that William M. Speer be apptd Admr of John W. Griggs, decd.
/s/William M. Speer
/s/James W. Johnson
Recorded: 8 Mar 1866

Admrs' Bond of William Eason
Page 370-371

William Eason, principal, and Rice Eason, security, give $2000 bond on 5 Mar 1866 upon the condition that William Eason be apptd Admr of John Denton, decd.
/s/William Eason
/s/Rice Eason
Recorded: 8 Mar 1866

Admx' Bond of Martha Wilkinson
Page 371

Martha Wilkinson, principal, and ephraim Sweat and Bradford Banks, securities, give $1000 bond on 5 Mar 1866 upon the condition that Martha Wilkinson be apptd Admx of Elbert Wilkinson, decd.
/s/Martha Wilkinson
/s/Ephraim Sweat
/a/Bradford Banks
Recorded: 8 Mar 1866

Admrs' Bond of James M. Padgett
Page 372

James M. Padgett, principal, and Lorenzo D. Padgett and John C. Brassell, securities, give $2000 bond on 5 Mar 1866 upon the condition that James M. Padgett be apptd Admr of John M. McLane, decd.
/s/James M. Padgett
/s/Lorenzo D. Padgett
/s/John C. Brassell
Recorded: 9 Mar 1866

Guardian's Bond of William Whatley
Page 372-373

William Whatley, principal, and Rachel Neal and B. F. Neal, securities, give $2000 bond, upon the condition that William Whatley be apptd Gdn this day of George F., James F. and R. P. Neal, orphans of Benjamin F. Neal, decd.
/s/William Whatley
/s/Rachel Neal
/s/B. F. Neal
Recorded: 9 Mar 1866

Guardian's Bond of William G. Bishop
Page 373

William G. Bishop, principal, and James W. Linch, security, give $3000 bond on 5 Mar 1866 upon the condition that William G. Bishop be apptd Gdn this day of Charles, Jefferson and Dorah Baily, orphans of Charles Baily, decd.
/s/William G. Bishop
/s/James W. Linch
Recorded: 9 Mar 1866

Guardian's Bond of Isaac A. Haisten
Page 373-374

Isaac A. Haisten, principal, and James W. Linch, security, give $2000 bond on 5 Mar 1866 upon the conditon that Isaac A. Haisten be apptd this day Gdn to John C. and Mary C. Baily, orphans of Charles Baily, decd.
/s/Isaac A. Haisten
/s/James W. Linch
Recorded: 9 Mar 1866

Guardian's Bond of Nancy Landrum
Page 374

Nancy Landrum, principal, and Samuel Ellison, security, give $600 bond on 21 Apr 1866 upon the conditon that Nancy Landrum this day be apptd Gdn of William W., Ulissa A. F. and Edelia L. Landrum, orphans of Willis Landrum, decd.
/s/Nancy Landrum
/s/Samuel Ellison
Recorded: 23 Apr 1866

Admrs' Bond of John T. Stephens
Page 374-375

John T. Stephens, principal, and William A. Brooks and Jesse L. Wade, securities, give $2000 bond on 2 Apr 1866 upon the condition that John T. Stephens be apptd Admr of John Stephens, decd.
/s/John T. Stephens
/s/William A. Brooks
/s/Jesse L. Wade
Recorded: 23 Apr 1866

Admrs' Bond of John J. Handly
Page 375

John J. Handly, principal, and Joseph G. Yates, security, give $600 bond on 7 Mary 1866 upon the condition that John J. Handly be apptd Admr de bonis non of Thomas J. Handly, decd.
/s/John J. Handly
/s/Joseph G. Yates
Recorded: 9 May 1866

Admx' Bond of Jane Jones
Page 376

Jane Jones, principal and Nathaniel Miller and Francis Patterson, give $3000 bond on 7 Mary 1866 upon the condition that Jane Jones be apptd Admx of Francis P. Jones, decd.
/s/Jane Jones
/s/Nathaniel Miller
/s/Francis Patterson
Recorded: 9 May 1866

Admrs' Bond of William Shadrick
Page 376-377

William Shadrick, principal, and Sarah A. Norton, security, give $2000 bond on 4 Jun 1866 upon the condition that William Shadrick be apptd Admr of Winslow Norton, decd.
/s/William Shadrick
/s/Sarah A. Norton
Recorded: 12 Jun 1866

Guardian's Bond for William S. Milner
Page 377

William S. Milner, principal, and Nathan Eason, security, give $1000 bond on 7 Mar 1866 upon the condition that William S. Milner be apptd this day Gdn to Benjamin J. Griggs
/s/William S. Milner
/s/Nathan Eason
Recorded: 12 Jun 1866

Admrs' Bond of James M. Palmer
Page 378

James M. Palmer, principal, and Joseph G. Yates, security, give $2000 bond on 4 Jun 1866 upon the condition that James M. Palmer be apptd Admr of H. D. Palmer, decd.
/s/James M. Palmer
/s/Joseph G. Yates
Recorded: 12 Jun 1866

Admrs' Bond of Robert H. Whitlock
Page 379

Robert H. Whitlock, principal, and Beasly Whitlock, security, give $1000 bond on 2 Jul 1866 upon the condition that Rovert H. Whitlock be apptd Admr of Daniel Whitlock, decd.
/s/Robert H. Whitlock
/s/Beasly Whitlock
Recorded: 5 Jul 1866

Temporary Admrs' Bond of Josiah J. Morgan
Page 379-380

Josiah J. Morgan, principal, and Thomas J. Heard, security, give $3000 bond on 9 Jul 1866 upon the condition that Josiah J. Morgan be issued temporary Letters of Administration on the Estate of Joshua W. Morgan, decd.
/s/Josiah J. Morgan
/s/Thomas J. Heard
Recorded: 10 Jul 1866

Guardian's Bond of Emily J. Pate
Page 380

Emily J. Pate, principal, and Charles Pyron, security, give $1000 bond on 6 Aug 1866 upon the condition that Emily J. Pate be this day apptd Gdn to Stephen J., orphan of Henry M. Pate, decd.
/s/Emily J. Pate
/s/Charles Pyron
Recorded: 7 Aug 1866

Admrs' Bond of Charles J. Robinson
Page 381

Charles J. Robinson, principal, and Samuel T. W. Minor, security, give $2000 bond on 6 Aug 1866 upon the condition that Charles J. Robinson be apptd Admr de bonis non with LWT attached of Zadock Davis, decd.
/s/C. J. Robinson
/s/S. T. W. Minor
Recorded: 7 Aug 1866

Admrs' Bond of Herod Thornton
Page 381-382

Herod Thornton, principal, and Blackman Thornton, security, give $1000 bond on the condition that Herod Thornton be apptd Admr with LWT annexed of Haywood Thornton, decd.
/s/Herod Thornton
/s/Blackman Thornton
Recorded: 6 Sept 1866

Guardian's Bond of Isaac A. Haisten
Page 382

Isaac A. Haisten, principal, and Elizabeth T. Kendall, security, give $3000 bond on 10 Sept 1866 upon the condition that Isaac A. Haisten be apptd this day Gdn of the person and property of Emory G. Burgamy, orphan of John Burgamy.
/s/Isaac A. Haisten
/s/Elizabeth T. Kendall
Recorded: 12 Sept 1866

Admrs' Bond of David McLucas
Page 382-383

David McLucas, principal, and Daniel McLucas, security, give $2000 bond on 3 Sept 1866 upon the condition that David McLucas be apptd Admr of Andrew McLucas, decd.
/s/David McLucas
/s/Daniel McLucas
Recorded: 12 Sept 1866

Guardian's Bond of William S. Milner
Page 383

William S. Milner, principal, and John Thweat and John T. Hewell, securities, give $1500 bond on 28 Aug 1866 upon the condition that William S. Milner be this day apptd Gdn of Jeffrey E. and Ellah G. Hillsman, minors and orphans of James Hillsman, decd.
/s/William S. Milner
/s/John Thweat (x, his mark)
/s/John T. Hewell. Recorded: 12 Sept 1866

Guardian's Bond of Jeremiah Hillsman
Page 384

Jeremiah Hillsman, principal, and Nathan Eason and William S. Milner, securities, give $1500 bond on 28 Aug 1866 upon the condition that Jeremiah Hillsman be apptd this day Gdn of Lucy T. and James L. Hillsman, minor orphans of James Hillsman, decd.
/s/Jeremiah Hillsman
/s/Nathan Eason
/s/William S. Milner
Recorded: 13 Sept 1866

Guardian's Bond of William J. Grant
Page 384

William J. Grant, principal, and William G. Bishop, give $1000 bond on 5 Nov 1866 upon the condition that William J. Grant be apptd this day Gdn of the persons and property of the minors and orphans of Francis Patterson, decd. (unnamed orphans)
/s/William J. Grant
/s/William G. Bishop
Recorded: 6 Nov 1866

Admrs' Bond of Victor Stinchcomb
Page 385

Victor Stinchcomb, principal, and Nathaniel Stinchcomb, securit, give $3000 bond on 3 Nov 1866 upon the condition that Victor Stinchcomb be apptd Admr of John Loyd, decd.
/s/Victor Stinchcomb
/s/Nathaniel Stinchcomb
Recorded: 23 Nov 1866

Admrs' Bond of Emily J. Rentfrow
Page 386

Emily J. Rentfrow, principal, and John W. Mason, security, give $2000 bond on 7 Jan 1867 upon the condition that Emily J. be apptd Admr of Henry Rentfrow.
/s/Emily J. Rentfrow
/s/John W. Mason
Recorded: 8 Jan 1867

Guardian's Bond of Susan Long
Page 387

Susan Long, principal and William Hartsfield, security, give $500 bond on 7 Jan 1867 upon the condition that Susan Long be apptd Gdn of the personal property of Henry A. U. Long, minor orphan of George D. Long.
/s/Susan Long
/s/William Hartsfield
Recorded: 8 Jan 1867

Admrs' Bond of Lewis B. Griggs
Page 387-388

Lewis B. Griggs, principal, and William M. Speer, security, give $2000 bond on 7 Jan 1867 upon the condition that Lewis B. Griggs be apptd Admr with LWT annexed of wiley W. Bosworth, decd.
/s/Lewis B. Griggs
/s/William M. Speer
Recorded: 8 Jan 1867

Guardian's Bond of William M. Speer
Page 388

William M. Speer, principal, and Lewis B. Griggs, security, gives $500 bond on 7 Jan 1867 upon the condition that William M. Speer be this day apptd Gdn to Benjamin F. Osborn, orphan of John Osborn, decd.
/s/William M. Speer
/s/Lewis B. Griggs
Recorded: 8 Jan 1867

Guardian's Bond of Daniel A. McLucas
Page 388-389

Daniel A. McLucas, principal, and L. F. Blalock and Richmond Dorman securities, give $600 bond on 4 Feb 1867 upon the condition that Daniel A. McLucas be this day apptd Gdn of Emmah Elkins, minor orphan of James Elkins, decd.
/s/Daniel A. McLucas
/s/L. F. Blalock
/s/Richmond Dorman
Recorded: 7 Feb 1867

Temporary Admrs' Bond of Jeptha Landrum
Page 389

Jeptha Landrum, principal, and Ucebius Slayton, security, give $1000 bond on 18 Feb 1867 upon the condition that Jeptha Landrum be granted temporary Letters of Admn on Estate of Washington Landrum, decd.
/s/Jeptha Landrum
/s/Ucebius Slaytn (x, his mark)
Recorded: 19 Feb 1867

Temporary Admrs' Bond of A. J. Vickers
Page 390

A. J. Vickers, principal, and James R. Vickers and J. W. Meeks, securities, give $500 bond on 23 Jan 1867 upon the condition that A. J. Vickers be apptd temporary Admr of Estate of Simeon A. Minick, decd.
/s/A. J. Vickers
/s/James R. Vickers
/s/J. W. Meeks
Recorded: 19 Feb 1867

Temporary Admrs' Bond of A. J. Vickers
Page 390-391

A. J. Vickers, principal, and James R. Vickers and J. W. Meeks, securities, give $500 bond on 23 Jan 1867 upon the condition that A. J. Vickers be issued temporary Letters of Admn of James Wesly Minick, decd.
/s/A. J. Vickers
/s/James R. Vickers
/s/J. W. Meeks
Recorded: 19 Feb 1867

Admx' Bond of Mary E. Carter
Page 391-392

Mary E. Carter, principal, and John Phillips and James Loyd, securities, give $1200 bond on 4 Mar 1867 upon the condition that Mary E. Carter be apptd Admx of John W. Carter, decd.
/s/Mary E. Carper
/s/John Phillips
/s/James Loyd
Recorded: 7 Mar 1867

Guardian's Bond of Lucy Stephens
Page 392

Lucy Stephens, principal, and William J. Brooks, security, give $300 bond on 4 Mar 1867 upon the condition that Lucy Stephens be this day apptd Gdn of George T., Martha C., Alexander, Jefferson and Mary Stephens, orphans of John W. Stephens, decd.
/s/Lucy Stephens (x, her mark)
/s/William J. Brooks
Recorded: 5 Mar 1867

Guardian's Bond of Mary E. Landrum
Page 392-393

Mary E. Landrum, principal, and Samuel H. Ellison, security, gives $600 bond on 1 Apr 1867 upon the condition that Mary E. Landrum this day be apptd Gdn of Anna A., Joseph B., Laura, Theoher, Napoleon B. and Jeptha Tidwell Landrum, orphans of Jeptha Landrum, decd.
/s/Mary E. Landrum
/s/Samuel H. Ellison
Recorded: 5 Apr 1867

Power of Attorney
Page 393

Georgia, Fayette Co) Samuel H. Ellison appoints D. C. Stokes as my lawful attorney to sign my name to a bond for Mary E. Landrum as Gdn for the minor children of Jeptha Landrum, Jr.
/s/Samuel H. Ellison
Recorded: 5 Apr 1867

Admrs' Bond of A. J. Vickery
Page 393-394

A. J. Vickery, principal, and James R. Vickery and J. W. Meeks, security, give bond for $300 on 1 Apr 1867 upon the condition that A. J. Vickers be apptd Admr of James R. Minnick, decd.
/s/A. J. Vickery
/s/James R. Vickery
/s/J. W. Meeks
Recorded: 15 May 1867

Admrs' Bond of Jeptha Landrum
Page 395-396

Jeptha Landrum, principal, and Eusebeus Slaton, security, gives $2000 bond on 3 Jun 1867 upon the condition that Jeptha Landrum be apptd Admr of Washington Landrum, decd.
/s/Jeptha Landrum
/s/Eusebeus Slaton (x, his mark)
Recorded: 3 Jun 1867

Admrs' Bond of William S. Milner
Page 396

William S. Milner, principal, and Lewis W. Smith and J. L. Hillsman, securities, give $800 bond on 3 Jun 1867 upon the condition that William S. Milner be appid Admr of Susan A. Griggs, decd.
/s/William S. Miler
/s/Lewis W. Smith
/s/J. L. Hillsman
Recorded: 5 Jun 1867

Admrs' Bond of Jesse L. Blalock
Page 397

Jesse L. Blalock, principal, and Lewis F. Blalock, security, gives $500 bond on 5 Aug 1867 upon the condition that Jesse L. Blalock be apptd Admr of John L. Blalock, decd
/s/Jesse L. Blalock
/s/Lewis F. Blalock. Recorded: 17 Aug 1867

Temporary Admrs' Bond of Calvin J. Fall
Page 398

Calvin J. Fall, principal, and Thomas C. Spear, security, gives $2000 bond on 19 Aug 1867 upon the condition that temporary Letters of Admn be issued to Calvin J. Fall on Estate of Joseph Spear, decd.
/s/C. F. Fall
/s/T. C. Spear
Recorded: 20 Aug 1867

Temporary Admrs' Bond of James M. Palmer
Paage 398-399

James M. Palmer, principal, and Edwin W. Burge, security, for $500 for 23 Aug 1867, upon the condition that James M. Palmer be issued temporary Letters of Admn of Barbary Palmer, decd.
/s/James M. Palmer
/s/Edwin W. Burge
Recorded: 23 Aug 1867

Temporary Admrs' Bond of Mary Spier
Page 399-400

Mary Spier, principal, and James J. Spier, security, gives $2000 bond on 11 Sept 1867, upon the condition that Mary Spier be issued temporary Letters of Admn of William M. Spier.
/s/Mary Spier
/s/James J. Spier
Recorded: 12 Sept 1867

Admrs' Bond of Solomon T. Bridges
Page 400-401

Solomon T. Bridges, principal, and Isaac P. Gay and Wiley J. Gay, securities, gives $20,000 bond on 7 Oct 1867 upon the condition that Slomon T. Bridges be apptd Admr of Thomas B. Gay.
/s/Solomon T. Bridges
/s/Isaac P. Gay
/s/Wiley J. Gay
Recorded: 8 Oct 1867

Admrs' Bond of Calvin J. Fall
Page 401-402

Calvin J. Fall, principal, and Thomas C. Spier, security, gives bond for $2000 on 7 Oct 1867 upon the condition that Calvin J. Fall be apptd Admr of Joseph Spier, decd.
/s/C. J. Fall
/s/Thomas C. Spier
Recorded: 8 Oct 1867

Admrs' Bond of James M. Palmer
Page 402

James M. Palmer, principal and Edward M. Burge and James Black, securities, give $1000 bond on 7 Oct 1867 upon the condition that James M. Palmer be apptd Admr of Barbery Palmer.
/s/James M. Palmer
/s/Edward M. Burge
/s/James Black. Recorded 8 Oct 1867

Temporary Admrs' Bond of Thomas A. Adams
Page 403

Thomas A. Adams, principal, and R. B. Shell, security, gives $5000 bond on 28 Nov 1867 upon the condition that temporary letters of administration of Arthur Robinson, decd.
/s/Thomas A. Adams
/s/R. B. Shell
Recorded: 29 Nov 1867

Admx' Bond of Rachel Neal
Page 403-404

Rachel Neal, principal, and William Whatley and Benjamin F. Neal, securities, give $500 bond on 2 Dec 1867 upon the condition that Rachel Neal be apptd Admx of Francis Carson, decd.
/s/Rachel Neal
/s/William Whatley
/s/Benjamin F. Neal
Recorded: 3 Dec 1867

Guardian's Bond of M. Jane Jones
Pagae 404-405

M. Jane Jones, principal and Wilson C. Reeves, security, give $300 bond on 2 Dec 1867 upon the condition that M. Jane Jones be apptd Gdn of Emily J., James H., Matthew F., Missouri A. and William F. Jones, orphans of Francis P. Jones, decd.
/s/M. Jane Jones
/s/Wilson C. Reeves
Recorded: 3 Dec 1867

Admx' Bond of Mary Speir
Page 405

Mary Speir, principal, and James J. Speir, security, gives $3000 bond on 2 Dec 1867 upon the condition that Mary Speir be apptd Admx of William M. Spier, decd.
/s/Mary Speir
/s/James J. Speir
Recorded: 8 Jan 1868

Admrs' Bond of Thomas A. Adams
Page 406

Thomas A. Adams, principal, and R. B. Shell and Samuel Robinson and Leroy M. Cobb, securities, give $5000 bond on 6 Jan 1868 upon the condition that Thomas A. Adams and R. B. Shell be apptd Admrs of Arthur Robinson, decd.
/s/Thomas A. Adams
/s/R. B. Shell
/s/Samuel Robinson
/s/L. M. Cobb

Guardian's Bond of John R. Brooks
Page 407

John R. Brooks, principal, and George W. Brooks, security, gives $1000 bond on 3 Feb 1868 upon the condition that John R. Brooks be apptd Gdn to John C. Baily, orphan of Charles Baily, decd.
/s/John R. Brooks
/s/George W. Brooks
Recorded: 4 Feb 1868

Guardian's Bond of George W. Brooks
Page 407

George W. Brooks, principal, and John R. Brooks, security, gives $1000 bond on 3 Feb 1868 upon the condition that George W. Brooks be apptd Gdn to Mary C. Baily, orphan of Charles Baily, decd.
/s/George W. Brooks
/s/John R. Brooks
Recorded: 4 Feb 1868

Admrs' Bond of Alvin F. Guice
Page 408

Alvin F. Guice, principal, and John Guice, security, gives $500 bond on 2 Mar 1868 upon the condition that Alvin F. Guide be apptd Admr of Peter Guide, decd.
/s/Alvin F. Guide
/s/John Guice
Recorded: 4 Mar 1868

Guardian's Bond of Oliver Thompson
Page 409

Oliver Thompson, principal, and William H. Blalock, give $1000 bond on 2 Mar 1868 upon the condition that Oliver Thompson be apptd Gdn this day to George C. K. and Robert H., orphans of James S. Thompson, decd.
/s/Oliver Thompson
/s/William H. Blalock
Recorded: 4 Mar 1868

Guardian's Bond of A. J. Hand
Page 409-410

A. J. Hand, principal, and James E. Haisten, security, give $3000 bond on 2 Mar 1868 upon the condition that A. J. Hand be apptd Gdn to Jefferson, Charles and Dorah Baily, orphans of Charles Baily, decd.
/s/A. J. Hand
/s/James E. Haisten
Recorded: 4 Mar 1868

Guardian's Bond of Mary Jane Elizabeth Palmer
Page 410

Mary Jane Elizabeth Palmer, principal, and William P. Head, security, gives $130 bond on 28 Mar 1868 upon the condition that Mary Jane Elizabeth Palmer this day be apptd Gdn of Thomas A., Laura E. and Mary S. Palmer, orphans of J. S. Palmer, decd.
/s/Mary Jane Elizabeth Palmer
/s/William P. Head (x, his mark)

Recorded: 28 Mar 1868

Guardian's Bond of James Thames
Page 410-411

James Thames, principal, and John A. Parker, security, gives $3300 bond on 6 Apr 1868 upon the condition that James Thames be apptd Gdn to Mary, John and Cynthia Thames, minor children of John Thames.
/s/J. Thames
/s/J. A. Parker
Recorded: 9 Apr 1868

Admrs' Bond of Zadok Blalock
Page 411-412

William H. Blalock, principal, and William J. Russell, security, gives $2000 bond on 4 Jun 1868 upon the condition that William H. Blalock be apptd Admr of Zadok Blalock, decd.
/s/W. H. Blalock
/s/W. J. Russell
Recorded: 5 Jun 1868

Admrs' Bond of James M. Palmer
Page 412-413

James M. Palmer, principal, and W. M. Cook and Samuel E. Christopher, securities, give $1000 bond on 6 Jul 1868 upon the condition that James M. Palmer be apptd Admr de bonis non of John Palmer, decd
/s/James M. Palmer
/s/W. M. Cook
/s/Samuel E. Christopher. Recorded: 6 Jul 1868

Tax Collector's Bond of Spencer Harvey
Page 413

Spencer Harvey, principal, and James Bradberry, S. T. W. Minor and C. A. Harvey, securities, give $3900 bond on 14 Sept 1868....that Spencer Harvey was on 24 Apr 1868 elected Tax Collector of Fayette Co.
/s/Spencer Harvey
/s/James Bradberry
/s/S. T. W. Minor
/s/C. A. Harvey
Recorded: 15 Sept 1868

Receiver of Tax Returns Bond of L. Harrison
Page 414

L. Harrison, principal, and T. D. King, J. T. Travis and Daniel A. McLucas, securities, give $1440 on 14 Sept 1868 upon the condition that L. Harrison was elected Receiver of Tax Returns of Fayette Co.
/s/L. Harrison
/s/T. D. King
.s.J. T. Travis
/s/Daniel A. McLucas
Recorded: 15 Sept 1868

County Treasurer's Bond of B. Thornton
Page 414-415

B. Thornton, principal and Herod Thornton and Felix Thornton, securities, give $6000 bond on 3 Sept 1868....that B. Thornton was elected County Reasurer of Fayette Co.
/s/B. Thornton
/s/Herod Thornton
/s/Felix Thornton
Recorded" 21 Sept 1868

Coroner's Bond of E. Sweat
Page 415

E. Sweat, principal, and Q. C. Guice, Mozee Harp and James C. Hightower, securities, give $500 bond on 8 Sept 1868 ....that E. Sweat was elected on 24 Apr 1868 Coroner of Fayette Co.
/s/E. Sweat
/s/Q. C. Guice
/s/Mozee Harp
/s/James C. Hightower
Recorded: 31 Sept 1868

Bond of Clerk of the Superior Court
Page 416

A. E. Stokes, principal, and M. M. Tidwell, Z. B. Blalock, J. L. Blalock and Davis C. Stokes, give $3000 bond on 12 Sept 1868....that on 24 Apr 1868 A. E. Stokes was elected Clerk of the Superior Court of Fayette Co.
/s/A. E. Stokes
/s/M. M. Tidwell
/s/Z. B. Blalock
/s/J. L. Blalock
/s/Davis C. Stokes
Recorded: 12 Sept 1868

Sheriff's Bond of W. L. Ellison
Page 416-417

W. L. Ellison, principal, and E. W. Leach, M. W. Swanson, J. P. Shropshire, John Favor and Edward Moore, securities, give $10,000 bond on 15 Sept 1868...that W. L. Ellison was elected Sheriff of Fayette Co.
/s/W. L. Ellison
/s/E. W. Leach
/s/M. W. Swanson
/s/J. P. Shropshire
/s/John Favor
/s/Edward Moore
Recorded: 21 Sept 1868

Admrs' Bond of Bennett Adams
Page 417-418

Bennett Adams, principal, and Amy Adams and Elias Adams and A. McEachern, securities, give $1600 bond on 7 Sept 1868 upon the condition that Bennett Adams be apptd Admr of Sanford Adams, decd.
/s/Bennett Adams
/s/Amy Adams
/s/Elias Adams
/s/A. McEacher
Recorded: 31 Sept 1868

Admx' Bond of S. Elizabeth Edmondson
Page 418-419

S. Elizabeth Edmondson, principal, and Thomas J. Edmondson, security, gives $1000 bond on 5 Oct 1868 upon the condition that S. Elizabeth Edmondson be apptd Admx of John Edmondson, decd.
/s/S. Elizabeth Edmondson
/s/Thomas J. Edmondson
Recorded: 5 Oct 1868

Admrs' Bond of Robert K. Horton
Page 419-420

Robert K. Horton, principal, and M. M. Tidwell, security, give $1000 bond on 2 Nov 1867 upon the condition that Robert K. Horton be apptd Admr of John C. Horton, decd.
/s/Robert K. Horton
/s/M. M. Tidwell
Recorded: 2 Nov 1868

Admx' Bond of Louisa Phillips
Page 420-421

Louisa Phillips, principal, and Calvin J. Fall, security, give $1600 bond on 7 Dec 1868 upon the condition that Calvin J. Fall be appt Admx of John Phillips, decd.
/s/Louisa Phillips
/s/C. J. Fall
Recorded: 8 Dec 1868

Admx' Bond of Susan Long
Page 421-422

Susan Long, principal, and James N. Lynch and Nathaniel L. Collins, securities, give $1600 bond on 7 Dec 1868 upon the condition that Susan Long be apptd Admx of George D. Long, decd.
/s/Susan Long
/s/James N. Lynch
/s/Nathaniel L. Collins
Recorded: 8 Dec 1868

Surveyor's Bond of John R. Robinson
Page 422

John R. Robinson, principal, and Charles J. Robinson and Richmond Dorman, securities, give $1000 bond on 18 Dec 1868....that John R. Robinson was elected Surveyor of Fayette Co. on 24 Apr 1868.
/s/John R. Robinson
/s/Charles J. Robinson
/s/Richmond Dorman
Recorded: 18 Dec 1868

Guardian's Bond of Amanda J. Spier
Page 423

Amanda J. Spier, principal, and Edward C. Bustin, security, gives $354 bond on 19 Dec 1868 upon the condition that Amanda J. Spier be apptd Gdn to John W. T. Spier, orphan of John T. Spier, decd.
/s/Amanda J. Spier
/s/Edward C. Bustin

Admr's Bond of P. H. Brassell
Page 423-424

P. H. Brassell, principal, and John T. Howell, security, gives, $500 bond on 4 Jan 1869 upon the condition that P. H. Brassell be apptd Admr of Lorenzo D. Padgett, decd.
/s/P. H. Brassell
/s/John T. Howell

Temporary Admrs' Bond of Matthew Yates
Page 424

Matthew Yates, principal, and Lewis C. Smith, security, gives $1000 bond on 5 Jan 1869 upon the condition that temporary Letters of Admn be issued to Matthew Yates on Estate of Charles O. Thames, decd.
/s/Matthew Yates
/s/Lewis DC. Smith

Admrs' Bond of Jeptha Landrum
Page 425

Jeptha Landrum, principal, and Joseph H. Farr, security, give $1500 bond on 1 Feb 1869 upon the condition that Jeptha Landrum be apptd Admr de bonis non of Larkin Landrum, decd.
/s/Jeptha Landrum
/s/John H. Farr
Recorded: 5 Feb 1869

Admrs' Bond of Jeptha Landrum
Page 425-426

Jeptha Landrum, principal, and John H. Farr, security, give $400 bond on 1 Feb 1869 upon the condition that Jeptha Landrum be apptd Admr de bonis non of Jane Landrum, decd.
/s/Jeptha Landrum
/s/John H. Farr
Recorded: 5 Feb 1869

Guardian's Bond of John R. Brooks
Page 426

John R. Brooks, principal and A. J. Hand, security, give $1000 bond on 1 Feb 1869 upon the condition that John R. Books be apptd Gdn this day of John C. Baily, orphan of Charles Baily.
/s/John R. Brooks
/s/A. J. Hand
Recorded: 5 Feb 1869

Guardian's Bond of John R. Brooks
Page 426

John R. Brooks, principal, and A. J. Hand, security, gives $1000 bond on 1 Feb 1869 upon the condition that John R. Brooks be apptd this day Gdn of Mary C. Baily, orphan of Charles Baily, decd.
/s/John R. Brooks
/s/A. J. Hand
Recorded: 5 Feb 1869

Guardian's Bond of Blackman Thornton
Page 427

Blackman Thornton, principal, and John Faver, security, give $830 bond on the condition that Blackman Thornton be this day apptd Gdn to George W. and Allison C. Speer, orphans of Henry C. Speer, decd.
/s/Blackman Thornton
/s/John Faver
Recorded: 5 Feb 1869

Guardian's Bond of A. R. Smith
Page 427-428

A. R. Smith, principal, and C. W. Smith, security, give $1225 bond on 1 Mar 1869 upon the condition that A. R. Smith be apptd Gdn to Emily Ann, David W. and Martha A. L. Speer, orphans of Henry C. Speer, decd.
/s/A. R. Smith
/s/C. W. Smith
Recorded: 4 Mar 1869

Temporary Admrs' Bond of James Graves
Page 428

James Graves, principal, and Jasper Graves, security, give $2000 bond on 4 Mar 1869 upon the condition that temporary Letters of Admn be granted to James Graves on Estate of Minton Graves, decd.
/s/James Graves
/s/Jasper Graves
Recorded: 4 Mar 1869

Admrs' Bond of James Graves
Page 429

James Graves, principal, and Lewis C. Smith and John Graves, securities, give $2000 bond on 12 Apr 1869 upon the condition that James Graves be apptd Admr of Minton Graves, decd.
/s/James Graves
/s/Lewis C. Smith
/s/John Graves

Admrs' Bond of S. T. W. Minor, Jr.
Page 430

S. T. W. Minor, Jr., principal, and Charles J. Robinson, security, give $1500 bond on 2 Aug 1869 upon the condition that S. T. W. Minor, Jr. be apptd Admr of Edward Connor, decd.
/s/S. T. W. Minor, Jr.
/s/Charles J. Robinson

Admx' Bond of Mary E. Pollard
Page 431

Mary E. Pollard, principal, and E. W. Leach, security, give $3000 bond on 2 Aug 1869 upon the condition that Mary E. Pollard be apptd Admx of C. F. Pollard, decd.
/s/Mary E. Pollard
/s/E. W. Leach

Guardian's Bond of William J. Russell
Page 432

William J. Russell, principal, and Jesse Barentine and L. F. Blalock, securities, give $5000 on 2 Aug 1869 upon the condition that William J. Russell be apptd this day Gdn to Wesley S. Thomas M. J., Gen. William R. L., Mary C., Gen. Beauregard, and Hester Ann Medorah Russell, orphans of William J. Russell, parent and natural guardian.
/s/William J. Russell
/s/Jesse Barentine
/s/L. F. Blalock

Guardian's Bond of A. J. Hand
Page 433

A. J. Hand, principal, and John R. Brooks, security, give $400 bond on 30 Jul 1869 upon the condition that A. J. Hand be this day apptd Gdn of Charles Jefferson and Madora Baily, orphans of Charles Baily.
/s/A. J. Hand
/s/John R. Brooks

Guardian's Bond of Stephen Rentfrow
Page 433-434

Stephen Rentfrow, principal, and W. S. Brown and L. G. Tinsley, securities, give $1000 bond on 15 Sept 1869 upon the condition that Stephen Rentfrow be apptd natural Gdn to Charley D. Rentfrow, minor of Stephen Rentfrow, decd.
/s/Stephen Rentfrow
/s/W. S. Brown
/s/L. G. Tinsley

Guardian's Bond of Mary E. Speir
Page 434

Mary E. Speir, principal, and J. B. Cook and Ellison Rush, securities, give $500 bond on 30 Oct 1869 upon the condition that Mary E. Speer be this day apptd Gdn to Young Rountree and Synthia E. Rountree, orphans of Ephraim Roundtree, decd.
/s/Mary E. Sper
/s/J. B. Cook
/s/Ellison Rush

Guardian's Bond of Allison Speir
Page 435

Allison Speir, principal, and B. F. Speir, security, gives bond on 1 Nov 1869 upon the condition that Allison Speir be this day apptd gdn to Mary E. and Lela V., orphans of Martin V. Speir, decd.
/s/Allison Speir
/s/B. F. Speir
Recorded: 17 Nov 1869

Guardian's Bond of Mildred Ann Kenedy
Page 435-436

Mildred Ann Kenedy, principal, and James L. Kenedy, security, give $600 bond on 8 Nov 1869 upon the condition that Mildred Ann Kenedy is this day apptd Gdn to Theodolia McLane, orphan of James McLane, decd.
/s/Mildred Ann Kenedy
/s/J. L. Kenedy
Recorded: 18 Nov 1869

Guardian's Bond of Anna Robinson
Page 436-437

Anna Robinson, principal, and G. G. Grant, security, give $4000 bond on 11 Jan 1869 upon the condition that Anna Robinson is this day apptd Gdn to Margaret S., E. W. F., Luisa and Samuel J. Robinson, orphans of Arthur Robinson.
/s/Anna Robinson
/s/G. G. Grant
Recorded: 22 Nov 1869

Guardian's Bond of James McEachern
Page 437

James McEachern, principal, and W. J. Robinson, security, give $50 bond on 5 Jan 1870 upon the condition that James McEachern this day be apptd Gdn of the person and property of Elijah M. McEachern, orphan of Daniel McEachern, decd.
/s/James McEachern
/s/W. J. Robinson
Recorded: 8 Jan 1870

Guardian's Bond of M. A. Palmer
Page 438

M. A. Palmer, principal, and Ellison Rush, security, give $400 bond on 4 Jan 1870 upon the condition that M. A. Palmer is this day apptd Gdn of the person and property of John S. Palmer and Lula H. Palmer, minor orphans of H. D. Palmer, decd.
/s/M. A. Palmer
/s/Ellison Rush
Recorded: 8 Jan 1870

Guardian's Bond of Cicero H. Eastin
Page 438-440 (page 439 skipped)

Cicero H. Eastin, principal, and John Faver, security, give $1200 bond on 5 Jun 1870 upon the condition that Cicero H. Eastin is this day apptd Gdn of Permelia G. Eastin, minor orphan of S. G. Eastin, decd.
/s/Cicero H. Eastin
/s/John Faver
Recorded: 8 Jan 1870

Admrs' Bond of R. N. Smith
Page 440-441

R. N. Smith, principal and W. R. Silman and W. R. Daniel, securities, give $1000 bond on 5 Jan 1870 upon the condition that R. N. Smith be apptd Admr of A. R. Smith, decd.
/s/R. N. Smith
/s/W. R. Silman
/s/W. R. Daniel
Recorded: 8 Jan 1870

Guardian's Bond of Luisa M. Harper
Page 441-442

Luisa M. Harper, principal, and J. W. Harper, security, give $200 bond on 7 Jul 1870 upon the condition that Luisa M. Harper is this day apptd Gdn of the personal property of W. E., Nancy L., Susan, J. E., W. A., Q. A. and Charley P. Harper, minor orphans of Wyatt A. Harper, decd.
/s/Luisa M. Harper
/s/J. W. Harper
Recorded: 8 Jan 1870

Guardian's Bond of Elizabeth Graves
Page 442

Elizabeth Graves, principal, and John B. Robinson, security, give $30 bond on 11 Jan 1870 upon the condition that Elizabeth Graves is this day apptd Gdn of the personal property of George W. Graves, orphan children of Charley Graves, decd.
/s/Elizabeth Graves
/s/John B. Robinson

Admrs' Bond of R. N. Smith
Page 443

R. N. Smith, principal, and W. R. Daniel and W. R. Silman, securities, give $3000 bond on 7 Feb 1870 upon the condition that R. N. Smith be apptd Admr with LWT annexed of A. R. Smith, decd.
/s/R. N. Smith
/s/W. R. Daniel
/s/W. P. Silman
Recorded: 17 Feb 1870

Guardian's Bond of William Guice
Page 444

William Guice, principal, and A. F. Guice, security, give $200 bond on 7 Mar 1870 upon the condition that William Guide is this day apptd Gdn of the persons and property of Linton S. and Margaret E. Guice, orphans of Peter Guice, decd.
/s/William Guice
/s/A. F. Guice
Recorded: 13 Mar 1870

Temporary Admrs' Bond of Azariah Mims
Page 444-445

Azariah Mims, principal, and Sanford C. Oliver and William B. Ballard, securities, give $500 bond on 23 Mar 1870 upon the condition that temporary Letters of Admn be issued to Azariah Mims on Estate of William Ballard, decd.
/s/Azariah Mims
/s/Sanford C. Oliver
/s/William B. Ballard

Guardian's Bond of Joseph F. McLane
Page 446

Joseph F. McLane, principal, and John I Whitaker and W. L. Whitaker and Haney Segraves, securities, give $1000 bond on 6 Apr 1870 upon the condition that Joseph F. McLane be apptd Gdn of the person and property of Archabal R. Porter, orphan of Hugh Porter, decd.
/s/Joseph F. McLane
/s/John I Whitaker
/s/W. L. Whitaker
Recorded: 12 Apr 1870

Admrs' Bond of Azariah Mims
Page 447-448

Azariah Mims, principal, and Sanford C. Oliver and William B. Ballard, securities, give $2730 bond on 2 May 1870 upon the condition that Azariah Mims be apptd Admr of William Ballard, decd.
/s/Azariah Mims
/s/Sanford C. Oliver
/s/William B. Ballard
Recorded: 4 mar 1870

Guardian's Bond of T. C. Speer
Page 448-449

T. C. Speer, principal,and Nathaniel Stinchcomb, security, give $700 bond on 2 May 1870 upon the condition that T. C. Speer be apptd Gdn of person and property of J. W. F. Speer, orphan of John W. Speer, decd.
/s/T. C. Speer
/s/Nathaniel Stinchcomb
Recorded: 4 May 1870

Admrs' Bond of James T. Travis
Page 449-450

James T. Travis, principal, and L. B. Blalock, security, give $1000 bond on 2 May 1870 upon the condition that James T. Travis be apptd Admr of Edward Moore, decd.
/s/James T. Travis
/s/L. B. Blalock
Recorded: 3 Jun 1870

Admx' Bond of Martha M. Padgett
Page 450-451

Martha M. Padgett, principal, and Joseph F. McLane, security, give $500 bond on 6 Jun 1870 upon the condition that Martha M. Padgett be aptd Admx of John M. McLane, decd.
/s/Martha M. Padgett
/s/J. F. McLane
Recorded: 4 Jun 1870

Admr's Bond of E. W. Leach
Page 451-452

E. W. Leach, principal, and Nathaniel Stinchcomb and W. A. Leach, securities, give $5000 bond on 6 Jun 1870 upon the condition that E. W. Leach be apptd Admr de bonis non of the LWT of Isaac H. Smith, decd.
/s/E. W. Leach
/s/Nathaniel Stinchcomb
/s/W. A. Leach
Recorded: 6 Jun 1870

Guardian's Bond of S. S. Trimble
Page 453-454

S. S. Trimble, principal, and P. M. Trimble, security, gives $600 bond on 4 Jul 1870 upon the condition that S. S. Trimble be apptd Gdn of the person and property of Sarah C. Ballard, orphan of William Ballard, decd.
/s/S. S. Trimble
/s/P. M. Trimble
/s/H. G. Trimble
/s/J. A. Chapman
Recorded: 7 Jul 1870

Temporary Admrs' Bond of J. J. Gilbert
Page 454-455

J. J. Gilbert, principal, and H. M. Roggers, sedcurity, give $1000 bond on 16 Jul 1870 upon the condition that temporary Letters of Admn be issued to J. J. Gilbert on Estate of Bird M. Jackson, decd.
/s/J. J. Gilbert
/s/H. M. Roggers

Admrs' Bond of James T. Travis
Page 455-457

James T. Travis, principal, and B. Rentfro and C. S. Jones, securities, give $2800 bond on 1 Aug 1870 upon the condition that James T. Travis be apptd Admr of Edward Moore, decd.
/s/James T. Travis
/s/B. Rentfro
/s/C. S. Jones
Recorded: 4 Aug 1870

Admrs' Bond of N. B. Robinson
Page 457-458

N. B. Robinson, principal, and John R. Robinson, security, give $300 bond on 1 Aug 1870 upon the condition that N. B. Robinson be apptd Admr of Mary McLeroy, decd.
/s/N. B. Robinson
/s/John R. Robinson
Recorded: 4 Aug 1870

Guardian's Bond of Joseph F. McLane
Page 458-459

Joseph F. McLane, principal, and John Whitaker and W. R. Whitaker, securities, give $2000 bond on 5 Sept 1870 upon the condition that Joseph P. McLane be this day apptd Gdn of the person and property of John H. and Ophelia J. Porter.
/s/J. F. McLane
/s/John Whitaker
/s/W. R. Whitaker
Recorded: 8 Sept 1870

Guardian's Bond of John M. Porter
Page 459-460

John M. Porter, principal, and D. A. McLucas and A. B. Avera, securities, give $500 bond on 5 Sept 1870 upon the condition that John M. Porter be apptd Gdn of the person and property of Martha Ann Jackson, orphan of Bird M. Jackson.
/s/John M. Porter
/s/D. A. McLucas
/s/A. B. Avera
Recorded: 8 Sept 1870

Admrs' Bond of John J. Gilbert
Page 460-461

John J. Gilbert, principal, and Peter E. McLeroy, H. M. Roggers and Daniel A. McLucas, securities, give $7000 bond on 7 Sept 1870 upon the condition that John J. Gilbert be apptd Admr of Bird M. Jackson, decd.
/s/John J. Gilbert
/s/Peter E. McLeroy
/s/H. M. Roggers
/s/Daniel A. McLucas
Recorded: 9 Sept 1870

Guardian's Bond of H. C. Fisher
Page 461-462

H. C. Fisher, principal, and E. W. Leach, Nathaniel Stinchcomb and J. L. Smith, securities, give $4000 bond on 3 Oct 1870 upon the condition that H. C. Fisher be apptd Gdn of the person and property of Minia G., Sallie A. and Norah H. Smith, orphans of Z. H. Smith, decd.
/s/H. C. Fisher
/s/E. W. Leach
/s/Nathaniel Stinchcomb
/s/J. L. Smith
Recorded: 8 Oct 1870

Admrs' Bond of M. L. Yates
Page 462-463

M. L. Yates, principal, and B. F. Head, security, give $1000 bond on 7 Nov 1870 upon the condition that M. L. Yates be apptd Admr of James W. Head, decd.
/s/M. L. Yates
/s/B. F. Head
Recorded: 9 Nov 1870

Guardian's Bond of J. A. Chapman
Page 463-464

J. A. Chapman, principal, and P. M. Trimble and S. S. Trimble, securities, give $500 bond on 2 Jan 1877 upon the condition that J. A. Chapman be apptd Gdn of the person and property of Mary Indiana E. Ballard, orphan of William Ballard.
/s/J. A. Chapman
/s/P. M. Trimble
/s/S. S. Trimble
/s/H. G. Trimble
Recorded: 5 Jan 1871

Guardian's Bond of Rebecca C. Smith
Page 464-465

Rebecca C. Smith, principal, and Blackman Thornton and Ezekiel M. Gardner, give $1600 bond on 6 Feb 1871 upon the condition that Rebecca C. Smith is this day apptd Gdn of the person and property of A. C., Emily A., David C. and Mary A. S. Speer, orphans of Henry W. Speer, decd.
/s/Rebecca C. Smith
/s/Blackman Thornton
/s/Ezekiel M. Gardner
Recorded: 8 Feb 1871

Guardian's Bond of W. W. Bearden
Page 465-466

W. W. Bearden, principal, and E. W. Leach, security, give $250 bond on 6 Mar 1871 upon the condition that W. W. Bearden is this day apptd Gdn of the person and property of Martha A. E., Mary J. E., Susan F., Evaline S., Edward, Y. H. and Willis N. Bearden, children of W. W. Bearden.
/s/W.W. Bearden
/s/E. W. Leach

Admx' Bond of Mary Kirksey
Page 466-467

Mary Kirksey, principal, and J. L. H. Waldrop and George Mansfield, securities, give $4000 bond on 4 May 1871 upon the condition that Mary Kirksey is this day apaptd Admx of John G. Norton, decd.
/s/Mary Kirksey
/s/J. L. H. Waldrop
/s/George Mansfield
Recorded: 5 May 1871

Guardian's Bond of George N. Davis
Page 467-468

George N. Davis, principal, and J. L. Blalock and L. F. Blalock and John Lester, securities, give $1400 bond on 1 May 1871 upon the condition that George N. Davis is this day apptd Gdn of the person and property of M. L., B. W., A. E., M. C., G. A., B. L. and E. W. Davis, orphans of John W. Davis, decd.
/s/George N. Davis
/s/J. L. Blalock
/s/John Lester
Recorded: 5 May 1871

Guardian's Bond of John L. Hobgood
Page 468-469

John L. Hobgood, principal, and James M. Palmer and W. M. Cook, securities, give $1500 bond on 4 Sept 1871 upon the condition that John L. Hobgood be apptd Gdn of the person and property of Nancy J., William H. and Cornilla J. Gasden, orphans of Jackson Gasden, decd.
/s/James L. Hobgood
/s/James M. Palmer
/s/William M. Cook
Recorded: 7 Sept 1871

Guardian's Bond of T. C. Malone
Page 469

T. C. Malone, principal, and William Malone, security, give $2000 bond on 2 Oct 1871 upon the condition that t. C. Malone is this day apptd Gdn of the person and property of L. M. Malone, minor of William Malone, decd.
/s/T. C. Malone
/s/William Maone
Recorded: 4 Oct 1871

Admrs' Bond of Herod Thornton
Page 470

Herod Thornton, principal, and Needham Jackson, security, give $600 bond on 2 Oct 1871 upon the condition that Herod Thornton be apptd Admr of Pheraby Thornton, decd.
/s/Herod Thornton
/s/Needham Jackson
Recorded: 5 Oct 1871

Guardian's Bond of L. B. Griggs
Page 471

L. B. Griggs, principal, and T. D. King, security, give $300 bond on 6 Nov 1871 upon the condition that L. B. Griggs is this day apptd Gdn of the person and property of Wyley Bosworth, orphan of W. W. Bosworth, decd.
/s/L. B. Griggs
/s/T. D. King
Recorded: 8 Nov 1871

Admrs' Bond of William Shadrick
Page 471-472

William Shadrick, principal, and W. G. C. Jones, security, give $1250 bond on 6 Nov 1871 upon the condition that William Shadrick be apptd Admr of W. G. Norton, decd.
/s/William Shadrick
/s/W. G. C. Jones
Recorded: 8 Nov 1871

Admrs' Bond of J. E. H. Ware
Paage 473

J. E. H. Ware, principal, and G. W. Ware, security, give $3000 bond on 6 Nov 1871 upon the condition that J. E. H. Ware be apptd Admr with LWT annexed of R. D. Ware, decd.
/s/J. E. H. Ware
/s/G. W. Ware
Recorded: 8 Nov 1871

Guardian's Bond of E. W. Leach
Page 473-474

E. W. Leach, principal, and W. A. Leach and H. C. Fisher, securities, give $3000 bond on 4 Dec 1871 upon the condition that E. W. Leach be apptd Gdn of the person and property of J. Q., J. L. and J. D. Landrum, orphans of Washington Landrum, decd.
/s/E. W. Leach
/s/W. A. Leach
/s/H. C. Fisher
Recorded: 8 Dec 1871

Guardian's Bond of S. T. W. Minor
Page 474-475

S. T. W. Minor, principal, and James M. Austin and M. M. Tidwell, securities, give $800 bond on 5 Feb 1872 upon the condition that S. T. W. Minor be apptd Gdn of the person and property of Manirva, Stanley and Green Norton, orphans of W. G. Norton, decd.
/s/S. T. W. Minor
/s/James M. Austin
/s/M. M. Tidwell
Recorded: 9 Feb 1872

Temporary Admrs' Bond of J. M. Austin
Page 475-476

J. M. Austin, principal, and G. W. Ware, security, give $1600 bond on 26 Feb 1872 upon the condition that J.M. Austin be issued temporary Letters of Admn of Estate of John Graves, decd.
/s/J. M. Austin
/s/G. W. Ware

Guardian's Bond of Emily E. Head
Page 476

Emily E. Head, principal, and Robert Kirlin and L. C. Smith, securities, give $64.20 bond on 4 Mar 1872 upon the condition that Emily E. Head is this day apptd Gdn of the person and property of M. L. and William T. Head, orphans of James W. Head.
/s/Emily E. Head
/s/Robert Kirlin
/s/L. C. Smith
Recorded: 8 Mar 1872

Guardian's Bond of E. C. W. Smith
Page 477

E. C. W. Smith, principal, and G. W. Edmondson, E. W. Leach and T. C. Speer, securities, give $2000 bond on 1 Apr 1871 upon the condition that E. C. W. Smith is this day apptd Gdn of the person and property of Sarah F. and Thomas C. Speer, orphans of John W. Smith, decd.
/s/E. C. W. Smith
/s/G. W. Edmondson
/s/E. W. Leach
/s/T. C. Speer
Recorded: 5 Apr 1872

Guardian's Bond of Martha A. Duffell
Page 478

Martha A. Duffell, principal, and John E. Travis, security, give $700 bond on 1 Apr 1872 upon the condition that Martha A. Duffell is this day apptd gdn of the person and property of Thomas E. and Columbus W., orphans of Thomas L. Duffell, decd.
/s/Martha A. Duffell
/s/John E. Travis
Recorded: 5 Apr 1872

Admrs' Bond of James M. Austin
Page 479

James M. Austin, principal, and W. B. DeVaughn and S. T. W. Minor, securities, give $17,000 bond on 1 Apr 1871 upon the condition that James M. Austin be apptd Admr of John Graves, decd.
/s/James M. Austin
/s/W. B. DeVaughn
/s/S. T. W. Minor
Recorded: 6 Apr 1872

Temporary Admrs' Bond of Samuel Loyd
Page 480

Samuel Loyd, principal, and Z. B. Blalock and Bennett Adams, securities, give $800 bond on 8 Jul 1872 upon the condition that temporary Letters of Admn be issued to Samuel Loyd on Estate of Sarah Loyd, decd.
/s/Samuel Loyd
/s/S. B. Blalock
/s/Bennett Adams
Recorded: 9 Jul 1872

Admrs' Bond of Samuel Loyd
Page 481-482

Samuel Loyd, principal, and C. F. Fall and E. W. Leach, securities, give bond for $2300 on 7 Sept 1872 upon the condition that Samuel Loyd be apptd Admr of Sarah Loyd, decd.
/s/Samuel Loyd
/s/C. F. Fall
/s/E. W. Leach
Recorded: 5 Sept 1872

Admrs' Bond of Phillip Stinchcomb
Page 482-483

Phillip Stinchcomb, principal, and J. W. Johnson and J. O. Stinchcomb, give $4000 bond on 6 Sept 1872 upon the condition that Phillip Stinchcomb be apptd Admr of G. W. Stinchcomb, decd.
/s/Phillip Stinchcomb
/s/J. W. Johnson
/s/J. O. Stinchcomb
Recorded: 10 Sept 1872

Admrs' Bond of T. B. Swanson
Page 483-484

T. B. Swanson, principal, and E. W. Leach and William T. Glower, securities, give $12,000 bond on 7 Oct 1872 upon the condition that T. B. Swanson be apptd Admr of Samuel Swanson, decd.
/s/T. B. Swanson
/s/E. W. Leach
/s/William T. Glower

Guardian's Bond of T. C. Speer
Page 484-485

T. C. Speer, principal, Samuel Loyd and W. T. Glower, securities, give $700 bond on 7 Oct 1872 upon the condition that T. C. Speer be apptd Gdn of the person and property of Joseph M. Speer, orphan of John W. Speer, decd.
/s/T. C. Speer
/s/Samuel Loyd
/s/W. T. Glower
Recorded: 9 Oct 1872

Guardian's Bond of E. W. Leach
Page 485-486

E. W. Leach, principal, and D. C. Stokes and W. L. Elison, securities, give $2000 bond on 4 Nov 1872 upon the condition that E. W. Leach is this day apptd Gdn of the person and property of Joseph Stolon and Lara T. and Napoleon B. Landrum, orphans of Jeptha Landrum, Jr.
/s/E. W. Leach
/s/D. C. Stokes
/s/W. L. Elison
Recorded: 8 Nov 1872

Admrs' Bond of Samuel Loyd
Page 486-487

Samuel Loyd, principal, and Z. B. Blalock, security, give $200 bond on 3 Dec 1872 upon the condition that Samuel Loyd be apptd Admr of James Loyd, decd.
/s/Samuel Loyd
/s/Z. B. Blalock
Recorded: 8 Dec 1872

Admrs' Bond of E. W. Leach
Page 487-488

E. W. Leach, principal, and Samuel Loyd and William Ellison, securities, give $2000 bond on 1 Jan 1873 upon the condition that E. W. Leach be apptd Admr of Larkin Landrum, decd.
/s/E. W. Leach
/s/Samuel Loyd
/s/William Ellison
Recorded: 8 Jan 1873

Admrs' Bond of E. W. Leach
Page 488-489

E. W. Leach, principal, and Samuel Loyd and William C. Ellison, give $500 bond on 6 Jan 1873 upon the condition that E. W. Leach be apptd Admr of Jeptha Landrum, decd.
/s/E. W. Leach
/s/Samuel Loyd
/s/William C. Ellison
Recorded: 8 Jan 1873

Guardian's Bond of Phillip Stinchcomb
Page 489-490

Phillip Stinchcomb, principal, and Nathaniel Stinchcomb, security, give $1600 bond on 3 feb 1873 upon the condition that Phillip Stinchcomb this day be apptd Gdn of the person and property of G. P. and Lizzie, orphans of G. W. Stinchcomb, decd.
/s/Phillip Stinchcomb
/s/Nathaniel Stinchcomb
Recorded: 7 Feb 1873

Guardian's Bond of J. O. Stinchcomb
Page 490-491

J. O. Stinchcomb, principal, and Nathaniel Stinchcomb, security, give $1600 bond on 3 Feb 1873 upon the condition that J. O. Stinchcomb is this day apptd Gdn of the person and property of Tululah and Marietta, orphan children of G. W. Stinchcomb, decd.
/s/J. O. Stinchcomb
/s/Nathaniel Stinchcomb
Recorded: 7 Feb 1873

Guardian's Bond of C. B. Nipper
Page 491

C. B. Nipper, principal, and E. K. Fortson and James A. Chambers, securities, give $1500 bond on 7 Apr 1873 upon the condition that C. B. Nipper be apptd Gdn of the person and property of Simon T. Whitaker, orphan of John I. Whitaker, decd.
/s/C. B. Nipper
/s/E. K. Fortson
/s/James A. Chambers
Recorded: 11 Sept 1873

Admrs' Bond of J. N. McEachern
Page 492

J. N. McEachern, principal, and W. P. Redwine, security, give $800 bond on 7 Apr 1873 upon the condition that J. N. McEachern be apptd Admr of Nazareth Norton, decd.
/s/J. N. McEachern
/s/W. P. Redwine
Recorded: 11 Apr 1873

Admr's Bond of Samuel Loyd
Page 493-494

Samuel Loyd, principal, and T. C. Speer, security, give $2000 bond on 7 Apr 1873 upon the condition that Samuel Loyd be apptd Admr de bonis non of James Loyd, decd.
/s/Samuel Loyd
/s/T. C. Speer
Recorded: 11 Apr 1873

Guardian's Bond of Allen Reeves
Page 494

Allen Reeves, principal, and J. F. McLane, security, give $75 bond on 7 Apr 1873 upon the condition that Allen Reeves is this day apptd Gdn of the person and property of Nancy Reeves, orphan of Allen Reeves, decd.
/s/Allen Reeves
/s/J. F. McLane
Recorded: 11 Apr 1873

Temporary Admrs' Bond of C. B. Nipper
Page 495

C. B. Nipper, principal, and W. R. Whitaker and M. W. Swanson, securities, give $1400 bond on 5 May 1873 upon the condition that temporary Letters of Admn be issued to C. B. Nipper on Estate of John I. Whitaker, decd.
/s/C. B. Nipper
/s/W. R. Whitaker
/s/M. W. Swanson
Recorded: 7 May 1873

Admrs' Bond of C. B. Nipper
Pagae 496-497

C. B. Nipper, principal, and E. H. Fortson, James A. Chambers, A. O. Gay, J. F. McLane, W. R. Whitaker, John Nipper, E. W. Leach, B. L. Johnson, M. W. Swanson and W. T. Glower, securities, give $8000 bond on 7 Apr 1873 upon the condition that C. B. Nipper be apptd Admr of John I. Whitaker, decd.
/s/C. B. Nipper
/s/E. H. Fortson
/s/James A. Chambers
/s/A. O. Gay
/s/J. F. McLane
./s/W. R. Whitaker
/s/John Nipper
/s/E. W. Leach
/s/B. L. Johnson
/s/M. W. Swanson
/s/W. T. Glower
Recorded: 4 Jun 1873

Admrs' Bond of W. W. Swanson
Page 497-498

W. W. Swanson, principal, and E. W. Leach and Burket Rentfrow, securities, give $1700 bond on 2 Jun 1873 upon the condition that W. W. Swanson be apptd Admr of Marcus Varner, decd.
/s/W. W. Swanson
/s/E. W. Leach
/s/Burket Rentfrow
Recorded: 4 Jun 1873

Admrs' Bond of W. S. Milner
Page 498-499

W. S. Milner, principal, and William P. Eason and W. W. Wilkins, securities, give $2000 bond on 2 Jun 1873 upon the condition that W. S. Milner be apptd Admr of Junia L. Hillsman, decd.
/s/W. S. Milner
/s/William P. Eason
/s/W. W. Wilkins
Recorded: 4 Jun 1873

Admrs' Bond of G. W. Slaton
Page 499-500

G. W. Slaton, principal, and Usibious Slaton, E. W. Leach and W. T. Glower, securities, give $7500 bond on 2 Jun 1873 upon the condition that G. W. Slaton be apptd Admr of W. T. Chandler, decd.
/s/G. W. Slaton
/s/Usibious Slaton (x. his mark)
/s/E. W. Leach
/s/W. T. Glower
Recorded: 2 Jun 1873

Admrs' Bond of W. L. Williams
Page 501

W. L. Williams, principal, and J. L. Blalock, security, give $2000 bond on 2 Jun 1873 upon the condition that W. L. Williams be apptd Admr of William Johnson, Sr.
/s/W. L. Williams
/s/J. L. Blalock
Recorded: 6 Jun 1873

Admr's Bond of A. J. Shropshire
Page 502

A. J. Shropshire, prinfcipal, and E. W. Leach and B. L. Johnson, securities, give $12,000 bond on 2 Jun 1873 upon the condition that A. J. Shropshire be apptd Admr of J. P. Shropshire, decd.
/s/A. J. Shropshire
/s/E. W. Leach
/s/B. L. Johnson
Recorded: 6 Jun 1873

Guardian's Bond of Gainy Westbrook
Page 503

Gainy Westbrook, principal and J. W. Johnson and Phillip Stinchcomb, give $600 bond on 2 May 1874 upon the condition that Gainy Westbrook be apptd Gdn of the property of Eliza, Ann and John Loyd, orphans of John Loyd, decd.
/s/Gainy Westbrook
/s/J. W. Johnson
/s/Phillip Stinchcomb
Recorded: 9 May 1874

"The first bond was insufficient and the bond was given in lieu of the first bond. /s/L. B. Griggs, Ordinary"

Temporary Admrs' Bond of C. E. Bennett
Page 504

C. E. Bennett, principal, and R. H. Bennett and R. T. Dorsey, securities, give $5000 bond on 16 Jul 1873 upon the condition that temporary Letters of Adm be issued to C. E. Bennett on the Estate of William Burrell, decd.
/s/C. E. Bennett
/s/R. H. Bennett
/s/R. T. Dorsey
Recorded: 17 Jul 1873

Temporary Admrs' Bond of Nathan Eason
Page 505

Nathan Eason, principal, and William P. Eason, security, give $600 bond on 21 Jul 1873 upon the condition that temporary Letters of Admn be issued Nathan Eason on Estate of Rice Eason, decd.
/s/Nathan Eason
/s/William P. Eason
Recorded: 2 Jul 1873

Admrs' Bond of Jesse Blalock
Page 505-506

Jesse Blalock, principal, and W. L. Williams, security, give $200 bond on 4 Aug 1873 upon the condition that Jesse Blalock be apptd Admr of Sarah Ann Burke, decd.
/s/Jesse Blalock
/s/W. L. Williams
Recorded: 6 Aug 1873

Admrs' Bond of James M. Bridges
Page 506-507

James M. Bridges, principal, and W. W. Mathews, security, give $4000 bond on 4 Aug 1873 upon the condition that James M. Bridges be apptd Admr of R. E. Bridges, decd.
/s/James M. Bridges
/s/W. W. Mathews
Recorded: 6 Aug 1873

Admrs' Bond of John J. Gilbert and W. L. Williams
Page 507-508

John J. Gilbert and W. L. Williams, principals, and J. L. Blalock and John C. Nash, securities, give $4000 bond on 4 Aug 1873 upon the condition that John J. Gilbert and W. L. Williams be apptd Admrs of H. M. Rogers, decd.
/s/John J. Gilbert
/s/W. L. Williams
/s/J. L. Blalock
/s/John C. Nash
Recorded: 6 Aug 1873

Guardian's Bond of Martha A. Stinchcomb
Page 508-509

Martha A. Stinchcomb, principal, and B. T. Harken, security, give $1000 bond on 24 Jul 1873 upon the condition that Martha A. Stinchcomb be apptd Gdn of the person and property of Georgia A. Stinchcomb, orphan of George W. Stinchcomb, decd.
/s/Martha A. Stinchcomb
/s/B. T. Harken
Recorded: 4 Sept 1873

Guardian's Bond of Blakely Bagwell
Page 509-510

Blakely Bagwell, principal, and A. M. Tankersly and Seaborn Pate, secrities, give $4000 bond on 7 Oct 1873 upon the condition that Blakely Bagwell is this day apptd Gdn of the person and property of John Bagwell, orphan of John Bagwell, decd.
/s/Blakely Bagwell
/s/A. M. Tankersly
/s/Seaborn Pate
Recorded: 9 Oct 1873

Guardian's Bond of William J. Gay
Page 510

William J. Gay, principal, and S. T. Bridges and C. F. Fall, securities, give $18,000 bond on 6 Oct 1873 upon the condition that William J. Gay be this day apptd Gdn of the personal property of Isaac P. Gay, an incompetent and insane person.
/s/William J. Gay
/s/S. T. Bridges
/s/C. F. Fall
Recorded: 9 Oct 1873

Admrs' Bond of Blakely Bagwell
Page 511

Blakely Bagwell, principal, and A. M. Tankersley and Seaborn Pate, securities, give $4000 bond on 6 Oct 1873 upon the condition that Blakely Bagwell be apptd Admr of Mary Bagwell, decd.
/s/Blakely Bagwell
/s/A. M. Tankersley
/s/Seaborn Pate
Recorded: 9 Oct 1873

Temporary Admrs' Bond of Tilmon Fuller
Page 512

Tilmon Fuller, principal, and James B. Hunnicutt, security, give $1000 bond on 22 Oct 1873 upon the condition that temporary Letters of Admn be issued to Tilmon Fuller on Estate of Permelia M. Maynard, decd.
/s/Tilmon Fuller
/s/James B. Hunnicutt
Recorded: 23 Oct 1873

Admx Bond of Aley Eason
Page 513

Aley Eason, principal, and James N. McEachern, J. S. Blalock and G. W. Clark, securities, give $3000 bond on 8 Oct 1873 upon the condition that Aley Eason be apptd Admx of Rice Eason, decd.
/s/Aley Eason
/s/James N. McEachern
/s/J. S. Blalock
/s/G. W. Clark
Recorded: 12 Nov 1873

Guardian's Bond of N. Norton
Page 514

N. Norton, principal, and S. T. W. Minor, securities, give $550 bond on 1 Dec 1873 upon the condition that N. Norton this day be apptd Gdn of the persons and property of G. W., J. H. and C. F. Norton, orphans of Nazareth Norton,d ecd.
/s/N. Norton
/sw/S. T. W. Minor
Recorded: 8 Dec 1873

Guardian's Bond of M. M. Collier
Page 515

M. M. Collier, principal, and t. Jaskew, secrity, give $150 bond on 2 Dec 1873 upon the condition that M. M. Collier is this day apptd Gdn of Ida C., orphan of Madison Collins, decd.
/s/M.M. Collier
/s/T. Jaskew
Recorded: 8 Jan 1874

Guardian's Bond of A. J. Shropshire
Page 515-516

A. J. Shropshire, principal, and B. L. Johnson, securities, give $2300 bond on 6 Jan 1874 upon the condition that A. J. Shropshire this day be apptd Gdn of the persons and property of Newman? and Johnie Shropshire, orphans of J. W. Shropshire, decd.
/s/A. J. Shropshire
/s/B. L. Johnson
Recorded: 10 Jan 1874

Guardian's Bond of N. Norton
Pagae 516-517

N. Norton, principal, and S. T. W. Minor, security, gives $180 bond on 6 Dec 1874 upon the condition that N. Norton this day be apptd Gdn of the person and property of A. J. Norton, orphan of Nazareth Norton, decd.
/s/N. Norton
/s/S. T. W. Minor
Recorded: 10 Jan 1874

Admrs' Bond of A. A. Turner
Page 517-518

A. A. Turner, principal, and Hinson Turner and W. B. Jones, securities, give $1500 bond on 2 Feb 1874 upon the condition that A. A. Turner be apptd Admr of Loduska Turner, decd.
/s/A. A. Turner
/s/Hinson Turner
/s/W. B. Jones
Recorded: 7 Feb 1874

Guardian's Bond of Amanda M. Johnson
Page 518-519

Amanda W. Johnson, principal, and W. T. Glower, security, give $150 bond on 25 Mar 1874 upon the condition that Amanda M. Johnson be this day apptd Gdn of person and property of William J., James M. and John H., orphans of John J. Johnson, decd.
/s/Amanda W. Johnson
/s/W. T. Glower
Recorded: 7 Mar 1874

Guardian's Bond of Willis W. Hobgood
Page 519

Willis W. Hobgood, principal, and J. L. Blalock and W. L. Williams, securities, give $5000 bond on 6 Apr 1874 upon the condition that Willis W. Hobgood this day be apptd Gdn of the person and property of Salina J. Hobgood, orphan of Samuel R. Hobgood, decd.
/s/Willis W. Hobgood
/s/J. L. Blalock
/s/W. L. Williams
Recorded: 8 Apr 1874

Guardian's Bond of T. C. Spear
Page 520

T. C. Spear, principal, and M. W. Swanson, security, give $1000 bond on 1 Jun 1874 upon the condition that T. C. Spear this day be apptd Gdn of the person and property of Emma Loyd, orphan of Milton Loyd, decd.
/s/T. C. Spear
/s/M. W. Swanson
Recorded: 6 Jun 1874

Guardian's Bond of J. P. Graves
Page 520-521

J. P. Graves, principal, and John L. Graves, security, give $2300 bond on 1 Jun 1874 upon the condition that J. P. Graves be this day apptd Gdn of personal property of S. C. Graves, orphan of John Graves, decd.
/s/J. P. Graves
/s/John L. Graves
Recorded: 6 Jun 1874

Guardian's Bond of E. W. Leach
Page 521-522

E. W. Leach, principal and Burket Rentfrow and W. T. Glower, securities, give $2000 bond on 3 Apr 1874 upon the condition that E. W. Leach be this day apptd Gdn of the person and property of Martha E. M. Swanson and Marshal N. Swanson, orphans of Samuel Swanson, decd.
/s/E. W. Leach
/s/Burket Rentfrow
/s/W. T. Glower
Recorded: 6 Jun 1874.

END OF BOND BOOK B

Fayette County Ordinary Mixed Records
Inventories, Appraisements, Sales and Returns
Book F (1856-1859)

Ann E. Ware, Orphan of George Ware, decd, in Account Current with Mildred Ware, from 1 Jan 1855 to 31 Dec 1855 inclusive
Page 1-3

4 vouchers.
Filed: 25 Jun 1856. Recorded: 2 Oct 1856

Richard Ware, Orphan of George Ware, decd, in Account Current with Mildred Ware from 1 Jan 1855 to 31 Dec 1855 inclusive
Page 2-8

Received of Mildred Ware, Gdn for Richard Ware, $5.00 in full of the above account, 31 Dec 1855.
/s/Holliday & Ware

Recorded: 5 Oct 1856

Texas, Bastrop Co...Know all men by these presents that we, John H Henon and Martha F. Henon and Elizabeth Dicty, his wife, and Mary Almannia Ware by her Gdn, Paul Deitz, heirs at law of Burrel Ware, decd, and heirs at law of James Ware, decd, late of Floyd Co., Ga., and heirs at law of Letty Ware, decd, late of Floyd Co., Ga. have made, constituted and appointed......Burrel H. Ware of Floyd Co., Ga., as true and lawful attorney.. to collect such sums of money or property whatsoever...payable or belonging to us as heirs of the said Burrel Ware, decd, from the Estate of said James Ware, decd, or from the Estate of the said Letty Ware, decd, in Floyd Co......which may be due John H. Henon and Martha F. Henon, his wife, Paul Dietz and Elizabeth Dietz, his wife, and Mary Almannia Ware by her Gdn, Paul Dietz....5 Apr 1855.

Estate of Green Griggs, Orphan of Bryant Griggs, decd, in Account Current with William Spear from the time of apointment to 31 Dec 1855 inclusive
Page 9

2 vouchers. For 2 negro boys recd from James F. Johnson, Admr de bonis non on the Estate of Bryant Griggs, decd, 1 Apr 1855 - Sutton, a boy about 7 years of age and Allen, a boy about 7 years of age

Filed: 30 May 1856. Recorded: 3 Oct 1856

In Account Current with Jesse Barrentine, Gdn of James Thompson from the date of his appointment to 31 Dec 1855
Page 9-10

Filed: 6 May 1856. Recorded: 3 Oct 1856

Emily, Orphan of James Turner, decd, in Account Current with William Jennings, Gdn, from 1 Jan 1855 to 31 Dec inclusive
Page 10-11

2 vouchers. Filed: 8 May 1856. Recorded: 3 Oct 1856

Estate of Walker Fitts in Account Current with Newton M. Fitts, Admr, from 1 Jan 18555 to 7 May 1856 inclusive
Page 11-17

22 vouchers. To cash paid - A. G. Crutch, J. M. Brassell, N. M. Fitts, N. V. Pitts, Oliver M. Persons, Jr., Thompson Jacobs, Huie & Conner, attys, George C. King, F. L. Landrum (tax collector), William S. Reeves, N.M.Fitts, W. F. Landrum, D. E. Drury, W. F. Landrum, J. L. Blalock, D. E. Drury, Frances M. Patterson, Brassell & May, George C. King
Filed: 7 May 1856. Recorded: 4 Oct 1856

Estate of James Turner, decd, in Account Current with Elijah Glass, Admr, from 1 Jan 1855 to 31 Dec inclusive
Page 17-18

3 vouchers. To cash paid - George C. King, J. D. Norton (legatee), and Peter Turner (legatee)
Filed: 30 May 1856. Recorded: 4 Oct 1856

Harriet T. Brooks, minor Orphan of Ivey Brooks in Account Current with A. G. Brooks, Gdn from the date of his Letters to 31 Dec 1855 inclusive
Page 18-19

7 vouchers. Filed: 13 May 1856. Recorded: 4 Oct 1856

An Account Current with Simon T. Whitaker one of the Admrs of Sarah Stubbs, decd, from 1 Jan 1855 to 31 Dec 1855
Page 20-21

William Stubbs, legatee
Filed: 20 May 1855. Recorded: 4 Oct 1856

William B. Fuller, Gdn of Martha Thompson
Page 22-23

Vou. #1, Received of William B. Fuller, Gdn of Martha Thompson $4.25 payment in full of his part of the expenses of the appointment of guardianship this 3 Dec 1855.

Heirs: William Stubbs (x, his mark)
Recorded: 8 Nov 1856

Mary Thompson, minor Allen Thompson, in Account Current with William B. Fuller, Gdn, from date of appointment to 31 Dec 1855
Page 24-25

5 vouchers. Recorded: 8 Nov 1856

Estate of Harbert Cook, decd, in Account Current with William N. Cook, Exr, from 1 Jan 1855 to 31 Dec
Page 25

4 vouchers. To cash paid - Charles E. Kimberly, J. L Blalock (Ordinary), Joshua Cook and Franklin Landrum (tax collector)
Recorded: 8 Nov 1856

Estate of Moses Williams, decd, in Account Current with James H. Williams, Exr from Qualifying as Exr
Page 26-27

10 vouchers. Legatees - James M Spurlin, John H. Williams, Allen Reeves, Elizabeth Killum, James H. Williams
Filed: 28 Jun 1856. Recorded: 8 Nov 1856

Estate of Sansom W. Roberts in Account Current with Hugh Porter from 1 Jan 1855 to 31 Dec 1856
Page 28-29

To cash paid -

Oliver McLane in right of wife, Mary
Hugh Porter, Gdn of William H. Roberts, Sarah T. Roberts, E. H. G. Roberts, James S. Roberts, Griffin A. Roberts
Hugh Porter, in right of his wife, Nancy Roberts

Filed: 27 Mar 1856. Recorded: 22 Nov 1856

An Account Current with John I. Whitaker, Admr of Elbert Harris, late of Fayette Co., decd, from 1 Jan 1855 to 31 Dec 1855
Page 30-32

7 vouchers. Filed: 28 Jun 1856. Recorded: 7 Jul 1856

An Account Current with Oliver M. Pearsons, Admr with the Will annexed of Mary McLane from appointment to 31 Dec 1855
Page 32-36

22 vouchers. To cash paid - T. C. Mathews, Holliday & Ware, T. L. Duffel, Dr. P. H. Brassell, Allen Reeves, William Vernon, Ann Pearson, Brassell & May.

Sale of negro, Anthony
Sale of 160 acres of land
Filed: 30 May 1856. Recorded: 22 Nov 1856

An Account Current with O. M. Pearson, Admr of Oliver McLean, decd, from appointment to 31 Dec 1855
Page 36-37

7 vouchers. Filed: 30 May 1856. Recorded: 22 Nov 1856

Estate of William Reeves, decd, in Account Current with Allen Reeves, Admr, from 1 Jan 1855 to 31 Dec 1855 inclusive
Page 38-39

7 vouchers. Filed: 30 Jun 1856. Recorded: 27 Nov 1855

James E. C. Ware, Orphan of George Ware, decd, in Account Current with Burrell A. Ware, Gdn, from 1 Jan 1855 to 31 Dec 1855 inclusive
Page 40-41

5 vouchers. Filed: 30 Jun 1856. Recorded: 29 Nov 1856

Inventory and Appraisement of Estate of James W. Head, decd
Page 41-42

Appraisers: William Watson, Berry L. Johnson, James L. Hobgood, Thomas P. Johnson
Recorded: 13 Dec 1856

Inventory and Appraisement of the Estate of Mason Gentry, late of Fayette Co., decd
Page 42-44

Negroes -

Annah, age 65
John, age 29
Kisey, (woman) age 17

Appraisers: John J. Patterson, William Thomas, James Young, sworn 9 Oct 1856
Estate includes a list of notes.
Recorded: 13 Dec 1856

An Account Current with Abner Camp as Exr of LWT of Morris Harris, late of Fayette Co., decd, from 1 Jan 1855 to 31 Dec 1855 inclusive
Page 44-45

2 vouchers. Recorded: 13 Dec 1856

Peter W. Milner, Orphan of Pitt W. Milner, decd, an Account Current with William N. Hill, Gdn. from 1 Jan 1855 to 31 Dec 1856
Page 46

Filed: 30 Jun 1856. Recorded: 26 Dec 1856

Susan A. Milner, Orphan of Pitt W. Milner, decd, in Account Current with William N. Hill, Gdn. from 1 Jan 1855 to 31 Dec 1856
Page 47

3 vouchers. To cash paid - George C. King, Julia Ann Simmons and Adeline M. Cowan and Caleb Simmons
Recorded: 26 Dec 1856

James M. Milner, Orphan of Pitt W. Milner, decd, in Account Current with William N. Hill, Gdn. from 1 Jan 1855 to 31 Dec 1856
Page 48-49

6 vouchers. Filed: 3 Jun 1856. Recorded: 26 Dec 1856

Estate of James A. Newton in Account Current with William N. Hill, Admr, from 1 Jan 1855 to 31 Dec 1855 inclusive
Page 49-50

Vou. #4, Townsen Crow vs. James A. Newton and Jesse L. Blalock, $43.12, 27 Mar 1856; Received of William N. Hill, Admr of Estate of James A. Newton, decd. /s/A. W. Stone, Atty for Plaintiff
4 vouchers. Filed: 20 Jun 1856. Recorded: 26 Sept 1856

Sale Bill of Land and Negroes Belonging to Estate of William Jinnings, late of Fayette Co., decd. Sold at the Court House door....on first Tues. in Dec 1856 on a credit of 12 months
Page 51

Lot of Land No. 38, 6th District, Fayette Co. bought by William May
Lot of Land No. 57, 6th District, Fayette Co. bought by William J. Russell
Lot of Land No. 25, 6th District, Fayette Co. bought by William Glass
Lot of Land No. 24, 6th District of Fayette Co., bought by Thomas G. Gay

Negroes as follows -

Julie Ann, age 10
Sterling, age 12
Mary, age 10
Jesse, age 12
Mulatto boy, Andrew, age 8
Prince, age 9
Jerry, age 5
Sarah and 5 children
Polly, age 10
Dilsey, age 9
Josiah, age 54 and Miney, his wife
Dick, age 19
Squire, age 25
Dennis, age 21
Wiley, age 17
Mary, age 27
Lendy, age 25 and child
Landy, age 7
Phillip, age 17

Recorded: 26 Dec 1856

George W. Brooks, Orphan, in Account Current with Robert Iverson, Gdn, from time of appointment to 31 Dec 1855 inclusive
Page 51-52

6 vouchers. Filed: 24 Jun 1856. Recorded: 24 Dec 1856

John N. Brooks, Orphan, in Account Current with Robert Iverson, Gdn, from time of appointment to 31 Dec 1855 inclusive
Page 53-54

5 vouchers. Recorded: 26 Dec 1856

An Account Current with William Jinnings as Admr for Allen Jinnings, late of Fayette Co., decd, from 1 Jan 1855 to 31 Dec 1855
Page 54-56

9 vouchers. To cash paid legatees - A. M. Parker, Reuben Millsaps for R. Sophrody Millsaps, William Jennings, and William Jinnings, Gdn of Elizabeth Jinnings, Thomas Jinnings, William M. Craig and Oney Parker and A. M. Parker.
Recorded: 26 Dec 1856

James P., Orphan of James Fitzgerald, decd, in Account Current with Phillip Fitzgerald, Gdn, from 14 of Jan 1855 to 14 Aug 1856 inclusive
Page 57-59

7 vouchers. Filed: 14 Aug 1856. Recorded: 24 Dec 1856

An Account Current with Sterling J. Elder, Admr of T. R. Pearsons, decd, from 1 Jan 1855 to 31 Dec 1855
Page 59-70

31 vouchers. Filed: 27 May 1856. Recorded: 26 Dec 1856

In Account Current with Thomas C. Mathews, Gdn of Collecta, Marcus L. and Elizabeth L. Williams, minors, from 1 Jan 1855 to 31 Dec 1855
Page 71-74

Cash paid A. B. Lovejoy, in right of his wife, Elizabeth
7 vouchers. Recorded: 26 Dec 1857

Estate of Jesse Lasseter, decd, in Account Current with A. J. Mundy, Admr, from 1 day of Jan 1855 to 31 Dec 1855 inclusive
Page 74-77

8 vouchers. Recorded: 26 Dec 1856

Estate of Bryan Griggs, decd, in Account Current with James F. Johnson, Admr de bonis non from 1 Jan 1854 to 30 Jun 1856 inclusive
Page 77-78

6 vouchers. Filed: 30 Jun 1856. Recorded: 26 Dec 1856

Estate of George Ware, decd, in Account Current with John S. Holliday and Mildred Ware, Admrs, from 1 Jan 1854 to 31 Dec 1855 inclusive
Page 79-88

28 vouchers.
Voucher #17. Georgia, Fayette Co., To Reuben Millsaps Greeting: You are hereby commanded that laying all other business aside, you be and appear at the Superior Court....then and there to testify and the truth to say between Daniel R. Thomas, Plaintiff and John S. Holliday and Mildred Ware, Defendant, in behalf of the defendant....This 18 Sept 1855. /s/Samuel T. W. Minor, Clerk, Superior Court
Filed: 25 Jun 1856. Recorded: 27 Dec 1856

An Account Current with Francis L. Lord, Admr of Estate of Henry Lord, decd, from date of his Letters to 31 Dec 1855 inclusive
Page 89-90

4 vouchers. Filed: 4 May 1856. Recorded: 27 Dec 1856

Estate of Mark Smallwood, decd, in Account Current with Samuel H. Ellison, Admr, from 1 Jan 1855 to 31 Dec 1855 inclusive
Page 91-92

6 vouchers. To cash paid - Harriet Ann Smallwood (x, her mark), Martin C. Smallwood, Tolbert Smallwood, Jasper Landrum.
Recorded: 27 Dec 1856

W. M. Matthews, Admr of Estate of Rachael Mathews, decd, in Account Current with said Estate from 1 Jan 1855 to 15 Jul 1856 inclusive
Page 92-94

4 vouchers. Recorded: 27 Dec 1856

Estate of Wright Martin, decd, in Account Current with James L. Hobgood, Admr de bonis non with the Will annexed, from 1 Jan to 31 Dec 1855 inclusive
Page 94-98

18 vouchers. Filed: 24 Jun 1856. Recorded: 27 Dec 1856

In Account Current with James P. Fitzgerald, Exr of Ann Fitzgerald, decd, from date of Letters to 31 Dec 1855 inclusive
Page 99-101

8 vouchers. Heir - Rody Carew.
Recorded: 27 Dec 1856

Larkin Bearden, Orphan of Edward Bearden, decd, in Account Current with William H. Blalock, Gdn, from 1 Jan 1855 to 31 Dec inclusive
Page 102

Filed: 25 Jun 1856. Recorded: 28 Dec 1856

Asa J. Bearden, Orphan of Edward Bearden, decd, in Account Current with William H. Blalock, Gdn, from 1 Jan 1855 to 31 Dec 1855 inclusive
Page 102-103

Filed: 28 Jun 1856. Recorded: 28 Dec 1856

Sarah A. Bearden, Orphan of Edward Bearden, decd, in Account Current with William H. Blalock, Gdn, from 1 Jan 1855 to 31 Dec 1855 inclusive
Page 103

Filed: 21 Jun 1856. Recorded: 28 Dec 1856

Perthena Bearden, Orphan of Edward Bearden, decd, in Account Current with William H. Blalock, Gdn, from 1 Jan 1855 to 31 Dec 1855 inclusive
Page 103

Filed: 23 Jun 1855. Recorded: 28 Dec 1856

Jefferson Bearden, Orphan of Edward Bearden, decd, in Account Current with William H. Blalock, Gdn, from 1 Jan 1855 to 31 Dec 1855 inclusive
Page 103-104

3 vouchers. Recorded: 28 Dec 1856

Quiller Bearden, Orphan of Edward Bearden, decd, in Account Current with William H. Blalock, from 1 Jan 1855 to 31 Dec 1855 inclusive
Page 105-106

Recorded: 28 Dec 1856

Inventory and Appraisement of the Property of John Pearce, late of said county, decd
Page 106

Appraisers: James M. Pate, Daniel K. Gilmer, John L. Jones, sworn 1 Nov 1856
Recorded: 28 Dec 1856

Inventory and Sale of the Real Estate of Herod Thornton, Sr., late of Fayette Co., decd, Sold on first Tues. in Nov 1856
Page 107

157 7/8 acres, Lot 49, 7th District, bought by Felix and John B. Thornton
59 acres, Lot 256, 7th District, bought by Blackmon Thornton
40 acres, Lot 226, 7th District, bought by John Favor
101 1/4 acres, W half of Lot 19, 9th District, bought by Rebecca Brogdon
101 1/4 acres, W half of Lot 19, 9th District, bought by Needham Jackson
50 acres, E half Lot 254 in 15th District, bought by Blackmon Thornton
101 1/4 acres, W half of Lot 255 in 7th District, bought by Pheriby Thornton
101 1/4 acres, E half of Lot 255, 7th District, bought by Haywood Thornton

Recorded: 14 Feb 1857

Inventory and Appraisement of the Estate of William Bray, decd
Page 107-108

Appraisers: George W. Munday, Elisha Walden, William Creel (x, his mark), Henry Niles (x, his mark)
Recorded: 28 Feb 1857

In Account of Sale of Personal Property of William Bray, decd, Sold at Public Auction on 23 Dec 1856
Page 108-110

Appraisers: T. B. Gay, T. D. King, G. W. Souter, A. W. Gray
Recorded: 28 Feb 1857

Sale of the Perishable Property of the Estate of Elisha Hill, decd, late of Fayette Co., 23 Jun 1857
Page 110-113

Recorded: 28 Feb 1857

Inventory and Appraisement of the Estate of Robert Huie, decd, of Fayette Co.
Page 113-117

Appraisers: W. Y. Conine, James McKean, W. P. Allen, Daniel Norman, Seaborn Smith
Recorded: 6 Mar 1857

Return of the Perishable Property. Recorded: 19 May 1857

Inventory and Appraisement of the Estate of Christopher Cline, decd
Page 117-119

Appraisers: Jacob Bowers, B. C. Bridges, Daniel Mitchell (x, his mark)
Recorded: 21 May 1857

The commissioners appointed Perry Hicks, Admr of Christopher Cline, decd.
Commissioners: W. W. Sibly, Jacob Bowers, R. Iverson. Recorded: 20 May 1857
Purchasers: Mrs. Cline, James Dorsey, R. C. Bridges, L. J. Bowers, Charles Bailey, Robert Iverson, Thomas Humphey, Thomas Drake, etc.
Recorded: 20 May 1857

Inventory and Sale of the Personal Property Belonging to the Estate of Mason Gentry Sold 20 Oct 1856
Page 120-122

Among purchasers: A. F. Yancy, A. J. Poole, E. M. Lasseter, William McPeak, D. Norman, M. Brown, etc.
Recordede: 26 May 1857

In Account Current with James Hanes, Jr., as Gdn of Elizabeth Lasseter from 1 Jan 1856 to 31 Dec 1856 inclusive
Page 123

Vou. #2, Received of James Hanes, Jr. as Gdn of Elizabeth Lasseter, formerly but now Elizabeth M. Welch, in right of my wife, the said Elizabeth M...... this 15 Nov 1856. /s/J. J. Welch /s/Elizabeth M. Welch
Recorded: 10 Jun 1857

An Account Current with James Hanes, Jr. as Gdn of Elisha Lasseter from 1 Jan 1856 to 31 Dec 1856 inclusive
Page 124

Filed: 11 Apr 1857. Recorded: 10 Jun 1857

An Account Current with James Hanes, Jr., Gdn of Sophia Lasseter from 1 Jan 1856 to 31 Dec 1856 inclusive
Page 124-125

Filed: 6 Apr 1857. Recorded: 10 Jun 1857

Orphans of William B. Wooton, decd, in Account Current with Lucinda Wooton, Gdn, from 1 Jan 1855 to 31 Dec 1856 inclusive
Page 125-126

3 vouchers. Recorded: 10 Jun 1857

Sale Bill of Real Estate of Evans Westley by Mathew Yates, Exr
Page 126-127

Bill of Articles Sold as Property of G. A. Yates, decd, 27 Mar 1856. Some purchasers: A. N. Yates, J. J. Hartley, J. G. Yates, A. P. Johnson, R. N. Harris, etc.
Recorded: 10 Jun 1857

Estate of Marcus Long, decd, in Account Current with Thomas Long and Isham Long, Admrs from 1 Jan 1856 to 31 Dec 1856 inclusive
Page 127-129

5 vouchers. Filed: 6 Apr 1857. Recorded: 10 Jun 1857

Sarah F. Roberts, minor of Sampson W. Roberts, decd, in Account Current with Hugh Porter, Gdn, from 1 Jan 1856 to 31 Dec inclusive
Page 129-130

Filed: 10 Apr 1857. 4 vouchers. Recorded: 11 Jun 1857

W. H. Roberts, minor of Sansom W. Roberts, decd, in Account Current with Hugh Porter, Gdn, from 1 Jan 1856 to 31 Dec inclusive
Page 130-131

Heir receipts - W. H. Roberts
Filed: 10 Apr 1857. Recorded: 11 Jun 1857

Ishmael Dunn, Gdn for Louisa W. Sillers
Page 131-132

Vou. #1, Received of Ishmael Dunn, Admr of Estate of John Sillers, late of said county, decd, $368.10 in part of Louisa W. Sillers distributive share of said estate. 31 Dec 1849. /s/Ishmael Dunn, Gdn for Louisa W. Sillers
Recorded: 11 Jun 1857

Estate of Vicy Bearden, Orphan of Edwin Bearden, decd, in Account Current with W. W. Bearden, BGdn, from 1 Jan 1856 to 31 Dec 1856 inclusive
Page 133-134

2 vouchers. Recorded: 4 Jun 1857

Estate of Elbert Bishop, decd, in Account Current with Jesse Hubbard, Admr, from 1 Jan 1856 to 31 Dec 1856 inclusive
Page 134-135

2 vouchers. Recorded: 11 Jun 1857

Estate of R. D. Little in Account Current with James W. Talley, Gdn, from 1 Jan 1856 to 31 Dec 1856
Page 136

7 vouchers. Recorded: 11 Jun 1857

Estate of E. H. Roberts, minor orphan of Sansom W. Roberts in Account Current with Hugh Porter, Gdn, from time of appointment up to 31 Dec 1856
Page 136

Filed: 10 Apr 1857. Recorded: 12 Jun 1857

Griffin Roberts, minor son of Sansom W. Roberts, decd, to Hugh Porter, Gdn, from 1 Jan 1856 to 31 Dec inclusive
Page 136-137

4 vouchers. Recorded: 12 Jun 1857

Estate of James S. Roberts, minor orphan of Sansom W. Roberts, decd, to Hugh Porter, Gdn, from time of appointment to 31 Dec 1856 inclusive
Page 137

Recorded: 12 Jun 1857

Estate of John L. Moses, Orphan of Hiram Moses, decd, in Account Current with Andrew J. Pollard, Gdn, from date of his Letters to 2nd Feb 1857 inclusive
Page 137-138

Vou. #3. Received of Andrew J. Pollard, Gdn of John L. Moses, Orphan of Hiram Moses, decd, $177.00 in full of all the money in my hands as Gdn of said John L. Moses, this the 3rd day of Feb 1857. /s/John L. Moses

Filed: 2 Feb 1857. Recorded: 12 Jun 1857

Estate of Green Griggs in Account Current with William Spear, Gdn, from 1 Jan 1856 to 31 Dec inclusive
Page 139-140

Filed: 7 May 1857. Recorded: 7 Jun 1857

Estate of John Palmer in Account Current with H. Q. Palmer, Admr, from time of his appointment to 31 Dec 1856
Page 140-171

132 vouchers.
Filed: 2 Mar 1857

An Inventory of Assets Belonging to Alfred Austin in Account with Nathan Camp, 1/2 of which belongs to N. Camp Estate when divided or sold
Page 171-173

202 1/2 acres known as B. Nealy Lot
202 1/2 acres known as Joseph Green Lot
100 acres known as Thomas Yarbough
100 acres known as George Yarbough
150 acres known as C. Yarbough
260 acres known as Shulers
202 1/2 acres known as J. B. Silvey
100 acres known as Noah
166 acres known as Hollan

Sale of Personal Property of Nathan Camp, decd, sold on 1st day of Nov 1857
Includes Inventory of Deeds to lots and parcels of land belonging to Nathan Camp, decd
Recorded: 30 Jun 1857

An Account of Sale of Negroes Belonging to Estate of James Brassell, decd, Sold at private sale this 6 day of Feb 1857
Page 173

Negroes sold -
Joseph sold to James T. Brassell
George sold to James T. Brassell
Peter sold to Willis Brassell
Sopa sold to Willis Brassell
Dick sold to Willis Brassell
Caroline sold to L. D. Padgett

Recorded: 30 Jun 1857

An Account Current with Joseph McLane, one of Exrs of LWT of John McLean, late of Fayette Co., from 1 Jan 1856 to 31 Dec 1856
Page 174-182

31 vouchers. Filed: 18 May 1857. Recorded: 21 Jul 1857

Estate of Evans Westley in Account Current with Mathew Yates, Exr, from time of his appointment to 1 Jun 1857
Page 182-185

18 vouchers. To cash paid - Jackson Westly (his share), G. L. Westly (his share), William S. Westly (his share), Joseph W. Spradlin (his share), Norris Pope (his share), Andrew J. Davis (his share), John Youngblood (share of wife, Martha), Mrs. May Pope (her share)

Filed: 4 Jun 1857. Recorded: 21 Jul 1857

Estate of John W. Pledger in Account Current with Counsel Rentfrow from 1 Jan 1856 to 31 Dec 1856 inclusive
Page 186-187

Recorded: 25 Jul 1857

John H. Orphan of Wade H. Cavender, decd, in Account Current with Phillip H. Brassell, Gdn, from 1 Jan 1856 to 31 Dec 1856 inclusive
Page 187

Filed: 1 Jun 1857. Recorded: 26 Jul 1857

Joseph H., Orphan of Wade H. Cavender, decd, in Account Current with Phillip H. Brassell, Gdn, from 1 Jan to 31 Dec 1856 inclusive
Page 188

Filed: 1 Jun 1857. Recorded: 23 Jul 1857

Martha M. Cavender, Orphan of Wade H. Cavender, decd, in Account Current with Delilah Moses, Gdn, from 1 Jan to 31 Dec 1856 inclusive
Page 189

3 vouchers. Filed: 10 Jun 1857. Recorded: 2 Jul 1857

Hiram D. Moses, Orphan of Hiram Moses, decd, in Account Current with Delilah Moses, Gdn from 1 Jun to 31 Dec inclusive
Page 190

2 vouchers. Filed: 10 Jan 1857. Recorded: 24 Jul 1857

Phillip B. Moses, Orphan of Hiram Moses, decd, in Account Current with Delilah Moses, Gdn, from 3 day of Jun to 31 Dec inclusive
Page 191

2 vouchers. Filed: 10 Jun 1857. Recorded" 24 Jul 1857

Estate of William N. Moses in Account Current with A. J. Pollard from time of appointment to 31 Dec inclusive
Page 192

1 voucher. Filed: 10 Jun 1857. Recorded: 24 Jul 1857

Estate of Mary Moses in Account Current with A. J. Pollard, Gdn, from time of his appointment to 31 Dec inclusive
Page 192-193

1 voucher. Filed: 10 Jun 1857. Recorded: 24 Jul 1857

Estate of Thomas C. Speer in Account Current with Joseph Speer, Gdn, from time of his appointment to 1 Jan 1857 inclusive
Page 193

Received of Joseph Speer, Gdn, $2277.33, it being in full of all my distributive share of my father's estate coming to James Loyd, decd, in right of m wife, formerly Sarah F. Loyd, now Sarah F. Speer, this 18 Mar 1857. /s/Thomas C. Speer in right of my wife, formerly Sarah F. Loyd, now Sarah F. Speer

Filed: 2 Jun 1857. Recorded: 24 Jul 1857

Russell G. Strickland, Orphan of Simon Strickland, decd, in Account Current with C. E. Bennett, Gdn, from time of his Letters to 31 Dec 1856 inclusive
Page 194-195

3 vouchers. Filed: 4 Dec 1856. Recorded: 24 Jul 1857

Estate of Alfred Brown in Account Current with John O. Brown, Admr, from time of appointment to 31 Dec 1856
Page 195-197

6 vouchers. Filed: 1 Jun 1857. Recorded: 24 Jul 1857

Estate of Thomas D. Waldroup, decd, in Account Current with Mary Waldroup, Admx, from time of her appointment to 31 Dec 1856
Page 197-200

5 vouchers. Filed: 1 Jun 1857. Recorded: 24 Jul 1857

An Account Current with William May as Admr of William Jennings, late of Fayette Co., decd, from time of his appointment to 31 Dec 1856
Page 200-205

Notes on James B. Jennings, John A. Jennings, R. Millsaps, M. M. Harrell, Burrell Brown, J. G. Giles and William May.

12 vouchers. Filed: 12 Jun 1857. Recorded: 25 Jul 1857

Estate of Joshua S. Calloway, decd, in Account with William E. Tucker, Admr, from 1 Jan 6o 31 Dec 1856
Page 205-210

17 vouchers. Filed: 6 May 1857. Recorded: 28 Jul 1857

Richard Ware, Orphan of George Ware, decd, in Account Current with Mildred Ware, Gdn, from 1 Jan 1856 to 31 Dec 1856 inclusive
Page 211

5 vouchers. Filed: 30 Jun 1857. Recorded: 14 Aug 1857

Ann E. Ware, Orphan of George Ware, decd, in Account with Mildred Ware, Gdn, from 1 Jan 1856 to 31 Dec 1856 inclusive
Page 213-214

7 vouchers. Filed: 30 Jun 1857. Recorded: 14 Aug 1857

Estate of Moses Williams, decd, in Account Current with James H. Williams, Exr, from 1 Jun 1856 to 31 Dec 1856 inclusive
Page 214-215

2 vouchers. Filed: 18 Jun 1856. Recorded: 15 Aug 1857.

An Account Current with Jesse Barrentine, Gdn of James Thompson, from 1st Jan 1856 to 31 Dec 1856 inclusive
Page 215-216

Filed: 30 Jun 1857. Recorded: 15 Aug 1857

William, minor son of Allen Thompson, in Account Current with Mathew Jones, Gdn, from 1 Jan 1856 to 31 Dec 1856
Page 216

2 vouchers. Filed: 29 Jun 1857. Recorded: 15 Aug 1857

An Account Current with Joseph H. Murphy, one of the Admrs of Simon P. Murphy, decd, from 1 Jan 1856 inclusive showing the gross amount of Estate and the debts and administrative expenses with the distributive share of cash legatees
Page 216-221

Amount of sale of negro man, Andrew
Heirs receiving shares - J. H.Murphy, C. P. Murphy, M. J.Murphy, Nathan Eason, J.M. Murphy, L. T. Doyal, trustee for Jemina L. McKinny, John Humphrey, R. B. Humphrey, Charlotte Murphy, David L. Duffey, Receckah Murphy (x, her mark).

Heirs receiving during the lifetime of Simon P. Murphy - Joseph H. Murphy, C. P.Murphy, M. J. Murphy, Thomas E. Murphy (son of Simon P. Murphy), Jeptha M. Murphy in right of his wife, Nancy, M. McKinny, in right of his wife, Lucinda, dau. of Simon P. Murphy, John Humphrey and Nathan Eason.
Filed: 22 Jun 1857. Recorded: 15 Aug 1857

Estate of William W. Kennedy, in Account Current with John B. Kennedy, Admr, from 1 of Jan 1854 to 31 Dec 1856 inclusive
Page 222

4 vouchers. Filed: 18 Jun 1856. Recorded: 17 Aug 1857

An Estate of James Brassell, decd, in Account Current with Willis Brassell, Exr, from 1 Jan 1856 to 1 Jul 1857 inclusive
Page 223-224

Heirs -
Samuel Pruitt, for his wife, Mary Pruitt (Polly) by the LWT of said James Brassell, decd.
William Brassell, bequest from LWT
L. D. Padgett in right of his wife, Elizabeth, by the LWT
James T. Brassell, by the LWT
Willis Brassell, by the LWT

8 vouchers. Filed: 1 Jul 1857. Recorded: 17 Aug 1857

Samuel Loyd, Orphan of James Loyd, decd, in Account Current with James Loyd, Gdn, from 1 Jan 1856 to 31 Dec 1856 inclusive
Page 225-226

6 vouchers. Recorded: 17 Aug 1857

Zachariah, Orphan of James Turner, decd, in Account Current with John O. Dickson, Gdn, from 1 Jan 1856 to 31 Dec 1856 inclusive
Page 226

3 vouchers. To cash paid Ann Turner (x, her mark) for boarding orphan in 1856
Filed: 30 Jun 1857. Recorded: 17 Aug 1857

Nathan, Orphan of James Turner, decd, in Account Current with John O. Dickson from 1 Jan to 31 Dec 1856 inclusive
Page 227

Filed: 30 Jun 1857. Recorded: 17 Aug 1857

Frederick, Orphan of James Turner, decd, in Account Current with John O. Dickson, Gdn, from 1 Jan to 31 Dec 1856 inclusive
Page 227-228

3 vouchers. To cash paid Ann Turner (x, her mark) for boarding orphan.
Recorded: 17 Aug 1857

Sampson, Orphan of James Turner, decd, in Account Current with John O. Dickson, Gdn, from 1 Jan to 31 Dec 1856 inclusive
Page 228

2 vouchers. To cash paid Ann Turner (x, her mark) for boarding orphan.
Filed: 30 Jun 1857. Recorded: 17 Aug 1857

Estate of Silas G. Eastin in Account Current with John B. Allen, Admr, from 1 Jan 1856 to 31 Dec 1856 inclusive
Page 229-230

To hire of boy, Simon, for 1856
To hire of boy, George, for 1856

4 vouchers. Filed: 30 Jun 1856. Recorded: 17 Aug 1857

Estate of Mark Smallwood, decd, in Account Current with Samuel H. Elison, Admr, from 1 Jan 1856 to 31 Dec inclusive
Page 230-231

3 vouchers. Filed: 30 Jun 1857. Recorded: 17 Aug 1857

Estate of Harbert Cook, decd, in Account Current with William N. Cook, Exr, from 1 Jan 1856 to 31 Dec 1856 inclusive
Page 231

2 vouchers. Filed: 6 Jul 1857. Recorded: 17 Aug 1857

An Account Current with John I. Whitaker as Admr of Elbert Harris, late of Fayette Co., decd, from 1 Jan 1856 to 31 Dec 1856
Page 231-232

2 vouchers. Filed: 3 Jun 1857. Recorded: 17 Aug 1857

John N. Brooks, Orphan of Ivey Brooks, decd, in Account Current with Robert Iverson, Gdn, from 1 Jan 1856 to 31 Dec 1856 inclusive
Page 232-234

9 vouchers.

Received from Daniel Smith, Admr of Ivey Brooks in 24 Mar 1856
To amount on hand for hire of boy, Jim, for 1856
To amount on hand for hire of boy, Moses, for 1856
To amount on hand for hire of girl, Sharlot, for 1856

Filed: 30 Jun 1857. Recorded: 17 Aug 1857

George W. Brooks, Orphan of Ivey Brooks, decd, in an Account Current with Robert Iverson, Gdn, from 1 Jan 1856 to 31 Dec 1856 inclusive
Page 235-237

To hire of boy, Jeff, for 1856
To hire of boy, Toby, for 1856
To hire of girl, Caroline, for 1856

10 vouchers.
Filed: 30 Jun 1857. Recorded: 17 Aug 1857

Estate of Isaac Hughs, decd, in Account with John Huie, Admr, from 1 Jan 1846 to 1 Jan 1857 inclusive
Page 237-238

6 vouchers. Filed: 2 Nov 1856. Recorded: 18 Aug 1857

An Account Current with Sterling J. Elder as Admr of Thomas R. Persons, late of Fayette Co., decd, from 1 Jan 1856 to 31 Dec 1856 inclusive
Page 239-249

36 vouchers. Filed: 1 Jun 1857. Recorded: 22 Aug 1857

Inventory and Appraisement of the Estate of Windham West, decd
Page 250-253

Appraisers sworn 11 Oct 1856 - James Boyd, Henry C. Speer, E. C. Bustin
Recorded: 24 Oct 1857

A List of Articles sold 31 Oct 1856. Purchasers: Brittain West, William Spraggins, Widow West, Kella Peters, P. M. Tidwell, J. C. Deason, Blake Jackson, Isam West, James P. Luck, Joseph West, J. J. Hartly and Willis West. Recorded: 24 Oct 1857

Marcus, Orphan of Thomas Herring, decd, in an Account Current with William J. Russell, Gdn, from 1 Jan 1855 to 31 Dec inclusive
Page 253-254

6 vouchers. Filed: 1 Jul 1856. Recorded: 6 Nov 1857

Francis, Orphan of Thomas Herring, decd, in an Account Current with William J. Russell, Gdn, from 1 Jan 1855 to 31 Dec inclusive
Page 255-256

5 vouchers. Filed: 1 Jul 1856. Recorded: 6 Nov 1857

Johnathan, Orphan of Thomas Herring, decd, in Account Current with William J. Russell, Gdn, from 1 Jan 1855 to 31 Dec inclusive
Page 256-258

7 vouchers. Filed: 1 Jul 1856. Recorded: 6 Nov 1857

Estate of James Turner, decd, in Account Current with Elijah Glass, Admr from 1 Jan to 31 Dec 1856 inclusive
Page 258
1 voucher. Filed: 30 Jun 1857. Recorded: 17 Nov 1857

Estate of George Ware, in Account Current with John L. Holliday and Mildred Ware, Admrs from 1 Jan 1856 to 31 Dec inclusive
Page 259-260

6 vouchers.

John S. Holliday and Mildred Ware } Ejectment, Appeal in said case, etc.
vs.
Epps Brown

Received of John S. Holliday Admr of George Ware, decd, $6 in full of above account, 31 Dec 1856.
/s/S.T. W. Minn, clerk

Daniel R. Thomas } Bill in Equity
vs.
John S. Holliday and
Mildred Ware

Received of John S. Holliday, Admr, acct of George Ware, decd. $16.76 in full of the above acct. 31 Dec 1856. /s/S. T. W. Minor, Clerk

Recorded: 7 Nov 1857

An Account Current with Simon T. Whitaker as one of the Admrs of Sarah Stubbs, late of Fayette Co., decd, from 1 Jan 1856 to 31 Dec inclusive
Page 260-261

Heirs -

Hubbard Stubbs
Jesse Barintine in right of his wife, Nancy
Jesse Barintine in right of his former wife, Sarah Elizabeth, decd.
Jesse Barintine, Gdn of James Thompson, minor heir of Allen Thompson

Recorded: 17 Nov 1857

Amount of Sales of Harbert Cook's Estate, late of Fayette Co., decd, 14 Aug 1857
Page 262-267

Among purchasers - Seaborn C. Cook, Joshua Cook, C. M. Cook, J. P. Cook, Rebecca P. Cook, Caleb M. Cook, etc.

Sale of land and negroes to -
Jessie L. Blalock - negro woman, Jane
J. P. Shropshire - negro boy, Tom
William Glass - negro boy, Laurence and one lot lot, No. 66 in 13th District
William P. Redwine - S half of Lot No. 63 in 13th District
James P. Cook - N half of Lot 95 in 13th District
William A. Crombie - Lot No. 67, Fayette Co.
William Denson - 3/4 Lot No. 94, 13th District
Caleb M. Cook - Lot No. 28, 13th District
A. Y. Mimms, half of Lot No. 36
Peter McLeroy, Lot No. 37
Recorded: 23 Nov 1857

Inventory and Appraisement of Thomas Faulkner, decd
Page 267-270

Negroes - Berry, Ned, Warren, Sarah and 2 children, Clarah and one child, Lucy and 2 children
445 acres of land

Appraisers: Elijah Glass, John I. Gilbert, Peter E. McLeroy, James Walker, John Barron, sworn 31 Oct 1857.
Recorded: 23 Nov 1857

Sale Bill of Personal Property of Thomas Faulkner, decd, 5 Nov 1857. Among purchasers were - Peter E. McLero, I. I. Gilbert, Joseph H. Murphy, Eliza C. Faulkner, John M. Murphy, Charles Shell, Charles Murphy, Bird Jackson, etc. Recorded: 23 Nov 1857

Johnathan herring, Orphan of Thomas Herring, decd, in Account Current with William J. Russell, Gdn, from 1 Jan 1856 to 31 Dec inclusive
Page 271-272

5 vouchers. To cash paid Mary A. Herring for boarding orphan.
Recorded: 25 Nov 1857

Francis Herring, Orphan of Thomas Herring, decd, in Account Current with William J. Russell, Gdn, from 1 Jan 1856 to 31 Dec inclusive
Page 273-274

7 vouchers. To cash paid Mary A. Herring for boarding orphan.
Filed: 30 Jun 1857. Recorded: 23 Nov 1857

Marcus Herring, Orphan of Thomas Herring, decd, in Account Current with William J. Russell, Gdn, from 1 Jan 1856 to 31 Dec inclusive
Page 274-275

6 vouchers. To cash paid Mary A. Herring for boarding orphan.
Filed: 30 Jun 1857. Recorded: 28 Nov 1857

The Estate of G. M. Yates in Account Current with Mathew Yates, Admr, from time of appointment to 31 Dec 1856
Page 276-283

17 vouchers. Recorded: 28 Nov 1857

John H. Mathews, Orphan of Doctor N. Mathews, decd, in Account Current with Samuel Kerlin, Gdn, from date of his Letters up to e1 Dec 1856 inclusive
Page 283

2 vouchers. Filed: 20 May 1857. Recorded: 28 Nov 1857

Partheny Bearden, Orphan of Edward Bearden in an Account with William H. Blalock, Gdn, from 1 Jan 1856 to 31 Dec inclusive
Page 284

Filed: July Term 1857. Recorded: 28 Nov 1857

Jefferson Bearden, Orphan of Edward Bearden in Account Current with William H. Blalock, Gdn, from 1 Jan 1856 to 31 Dec inclusive
Page 285

Filed: Jul Term 1857. Recorded: 28 Nov 1857

Sarah A. Bearden, Orphan of Edward Bearden in Account Current with William H. Blalock, Gdn, from 1 Jan 1856 to 31 Dec inclusive
Page 285-286

Recorded: 28 Nov 1857

Asa J. Bearden, Orphan of Edward Bearden, in Account Current with William H. Blalock, Gdn, from 1 Jan 1856 to 31 Dec inclusive
Page 286

Filed: July Term 1857. Recorded: 28 Nov 1857

Quiller Bearden, Orphan of Edward Bearden, in Account Current with William H. Blalock, Gdn, from 1 Jan 1856 to 31 Dec inclusive
Page 287-288

State of Alabama, Marshall County - Know all men by these presents that I, Quiller Bearden of the county and state aforesaid have this day...appoint John W. Lowsey of the county and state aforesaid my true and lawful attorney to act for me and in my name...to draw and receive from William H.Blalock, my Gdn in Fayette Co., Ga.,all the money that is coming to me from the estate of Edward Bearden of Fayette Co., Ga., decd.....this 12 Mar 1857. /s/Quiller Bearden (x, his mark)

Filed: July Term 1857 Recorded: 28 Nov 1857

Larkin Bearden, Orphans of Edward Bearden in Account Current with William H. Blalock, Gdn, from 1 Jan 1856 to 1 Dec inclusive
Page 288-289

Filed: July Term 1857. Recorded: 28 Nov 1857

An Account Current with Oliver M. Pearson as Exr of Estate of Oliver McLane, decd, from 1 Jan 1856 to 31 Dec inclusive
Page 289-291

14 vouchers.

Heirs receiving shares as follows -

O. W. Duffel for Sarah Duffell, formerly Sarah McLane
T. B. Duffell for Sarah Duffell, formerly Sarah McLane
Oliver P. McLane
Joseph McLane
Ann Pearson (her mark)
William A. Smith in right of his wife, Mary Jane Smith, formerly Mary Jane Reeves
Jacob M. Brooks in right of wife, Rachael L. Brooks, formerly Rachael L. Duffell
H. H. McLane
A.J. Pollard in right of wife, Rachal Pollard, formerly Rachal Moses
A. J. Pollard, Gdn of John L. Moses, William N. Moses and Mary E. Moses, minor children of Hiram Moses, decd
L. W. Presley in right of wife, Rachael M. Presley, formerly Rachael M. Reeves
Miles Ward, in right of wife, Liny Ward, formerly Liny McLane.

By amount of sale of negroes belonging to the Estate sold 1st Tues. in Dec 1855
Filed: 23 May 1857. Recorded: 5 Dec 1857

In Account Current with O. W. Pearson Admr with Will annexed of Mary McLane, decd, from 1 Jan 1856 to 31 Dec 1856 inclusive
Page 292-294

11 vouchers.
Heirs receiving shares -

L. W. Presley, in right of wife, Rachael M. Presley
William A. Smith, in right of wife, Mary Jane Smith, formerly Mary Jane Reeves
W. O. Duffell
Jacob M. Brooks, in right of wife, Rachel L. Brooks, formerly Rachel L. Duffell
Miles Ward, in right of wife, Liny M. Ward
A. J. Pollard
A.J. Pollard, as Gdn of John L. Moses, William N. Moses and Mary E. Moses
Ann Pearson (x, her mark)
L.W. Presley, in right of his wife, Rachael M. Presley, formerly Rachael M. Reaves
F. L. Duffell

Filed: 25 May 1857. Recorded: 5 Dec 1857

Estate of Windom West in Account Current with Britton West, Exr, from time of his appointment up to 1 Jul 1857
Page 294-305

31 vouchers.
Filed: 1 Jul 1857. Recorded: 9 Dec 1857

Inventory and Sale of the Land Belonging to Estate of Elisha Hill, late of said county, decd, sold first Tues. in Sept 1857
Page 305

Lot of Land No. 243 sold to B. H. Fortson
100 acres off of Lot No. 244 sold to John H. Starr
50 acres off of Lot No. 14 sold to G. W. Soutee
50 acres off of Lot No. 156 sold to R. Stubbs

Recorded: 12 Dec 1857

James E. H. Ware, Orphan of Geroge Ware, decd, in Account Current with Burrell A. Ware, Gdn, from 1 Jan 1856 to 31 Dec inclusive
Page 306-307

8 vouchers. Filed: 28 May 1857. Recorded: 12 Dec 1857

Estate of F. M. Jones in Account Current with Andrew J. Mundy from 1 Jan 1856 to 31 Dec inclusive
Page 308-311

19 vouchers. Filed: 27 Feb 1857. Recorded: 17 Dec 1857

An Account Current with Martha McLeroy, Gdn of Martha F. McLeroy, Pitt L. McLeroy, Emily U., Thomas E. B. McLeroy, Orphans of Henry McLeroy, decd, from 31 Dec 1855 to 31 Dec 1856
Page 311-312

2 vouchers. Filed: 2 Jun 1857. Recorded: 17 Dec 1857

An Account Current with M. B. DeVaughan as Gdn of Wiley H. McLeroy, minor of Henry McLeroy, decd, from 31 Dec 1855 to 31 Dec 1856
Page 312

Filed: 2 Jun 1857. Recorded: 17 Dec 1857

Estate of Henry McLeroy, decd, in Account and Credits with William B. DeVaughan, Exr of the LWT from 31 Dec 1855 to 31 Dec 1856
Page 313-314

4 vouchers. Filed: 2 Jun 1857. Recorded: 17 Dec 1857

Martha Thompson in Account Current with John S. Holliday, Gdn, from 1 Jan 1856 to 31 Dec 1846 inclusive
Page 314-315

2 vouchers. Filed: 30 Jun 1857. Recorded: 17 Dec 1857

Sarah F., Orphan of James Loyd, decd, in Account Current with John Loyd, Gdn, from 1 Jan 1856 to 6 Feb 1857 inclusive
Page 315-316

4 vouchers. Filed: 4 May 1857. Recorded: 26 Dec 1857

Thomas Ewen, Orphan of James Loyd, decd, in Account Current with John Loyd, Gdn, from 1 Jan 1856 to 31 Dec 1856 inclusive
Page 316

2 vouchers. Filed: 4 May 1857. Recorded: 26 Dec 1857

Parker Eason, Gdn of William S. Milner, minor orphan of Pitt W. Milner, decd, from 31 Dec 1856 inclusive
Page 317

Filed: 30 Jun 1857. Recorded: 26 Dec 1857

Estate of Mason Gentry, decd, in Account with Killis Brown, Admr
Page 317-318

5 vouchers. Filed: 22 May 1857. Recorded: 26 Dec 1857

Estate of David Graves, decd, in Account Current with Matilda Graves, Admx, from 1 Jan 1855 to 31 Dec 1856 inclusive
Page 319-321

2 vouchers. Legatees - Wiley Graves, Vines Graves, Kitey Ann Graves, Francis W. Graves, Matilda Graves, and Matilda Graves for Salena Graves and Leah Oliva Graves, minors of David Graves

Recorded: 26 Dec 1857

An Account Current with Allen Reeves, Admr of William Reeves, late of Fayette Co., decd, from time of appointment to 1 Dec 1856
Page 322-323

5 vouchers. Recorded: 26 Dec 1857

An Account Current with Herod Thornton as Admr of Herod Thornton, late of Fayette Co. from time of his appointment to 1 Jan 1857
Page 324-326

14 vouchers. Widow received 12 months' support.
Heirs -
Herod Thornton
Blackmon Thornton
Rebecca Brogdon
Pherily Thornton
Haywood Thornton
Needham Jackson
Coleman Hartley
Felix Thornton
John B. Thornton
Filed: 20 May 1857. Recorded: 26 Dec 1857

Emily, Orphan of James Turner, decd, in Account Current with William Jennings, Gdn, from 1 Jan 1856 to 31 Dec inclusive
Page 326-327

1 voucher. Recorded: 26 Dec 1857

Mary Thompson in Account Current with John S. Holliday, Gdn, from 1 Jan 1856 to 31 Dec inclusive
Page 327-328

Filed: 30 Jun 1857. Recorded: 26 Dec 1857

Lucy J., Orphan of James G. Christian, decd, in Account Current with Gideon F. Mann, Gdn, from 1 Jan 1856 to 31 Dec 1856 inclusive
Page 328

3 vouchers. Filed: 3 Jun 1857. Recorded: 26 Dec 1857

Morgan F., Orphan of James G. Christian, decd, in Account Current with Gideon F. Mann, Gdn, from 1 Jan 1856 to 31 Dec 1856 inclusive
Page 329

2 vouchers. Filed: 3 Jun 1857. Recorded: 26 Dec 1857

In Account Current with S. T. Whitaker, Gdn of minor children of B. F. Neal, late of Fayette Co., decd, from time of appointment to 1 Jan 1857
Page 330-333

Distributive share of J. J. Carson in right of his wife paid
Accounts of minors, viz: B. F. Neal, Emily J. Neal, John P. Neal, George F. Neal, J. F. Neal, R. P. Neal, H.Neal

Filed: 9 Jun 1857. Recorded: 26 Dec 1857

In Account Current with Rachael Eason, Admx in Estate of Richard B. Eason, decd, from time of appointment to 1 Dec 1856 inclusive
Page 334-339

Received funds from notes of Abraham Eason, Cane Simpson and R. Morrow.
11 vouchers. Recorded: 26 Dec1857

Martha E. Hays, Orphan of John Hays, decd, in Account Current with Lemuel Murphy, Gdn, from 1 Jan 1856 to 27Aug1857 inclusive
Page 339

Received of Lemuel M. Murphy, Gdn of Martha E. Hays formerly, now Martha E. Daniel, $1147.48 in full of all moneyscfoming from him as Gdn aforesaid to the said Martha E. Hays, now Martha E. Daniel.
/s/Thomas R. Daniel, in right of my wife, Martha E. Daniel.
Filed: 27 Aug 1857. Recorded: 24 Dec 1857

John A., Orphan of James G. Christian, decd, in Account Current with Gideon F. Mann from 1 Jan 1856 to 10 Feb 1857, date of settlement
Page 340

To cash paid - John A.Christian Filed: 3 Jun 1857. Recorded: 26 Dec 1857.

Claborn A., Orphan of James G. Christian, decd, in Account Current with G. F. Mann, Gdn, from 1 Jan 1856 to 31 Dec 1856 inclusive
Page 341-342

Filed: 5 Jun 1857. Recorded: 24 Dec 1857

Sale Bill of Real Estate of William Bray, decd, Sold first Tues. in Feb 1858
Page 342

1 Lot of Land No. 153 in 15th District and bought by William E. Tucker. Received this 27 Feb 1858. /s/George C. King, Dept. C. C. O,

Inventory and Appraisement of Estate of Johnathan Smith, decd
Page 342

Negroes appraised - Ann, Sarah, Harriet, Caroline, Adaline, Dick, Elizabeth, William, Davy, Madison and Jackson.
Appraisers: Stephen W. Allen, Miles Ward and Johnson W. Gant, sworn 30 Dec 1857
Recorded: 27 Feb 1858

Account of Portion of Personal Property Belonging to Estate of Johnathan Smith, decd, Sold on 31 Dec 1857
Page 343-346

Among purchasers: John L. Patterson, Samuel Robinson, J. H. Starr, W. Power, etc.
Appraisers: J. C. Nash, Bird M. Jackson and J. J. Elbert, sworn 16 Dec 1857
Recorded: 27 Feb 1858

The Perishable Property of Miles Norton, late of said county, decd, sold on 17 Dec 1857 by Willaim F. Eason, Admr, to come due to 1 Oct next
Page 346-348

Among purchasers - John J. Gilbert, James Elkins, Ephraim Sweat, S. S. Sweat, James Elkins, Jesse Barintine, Rasbury Eason, etc.

Sale Bill of Real Estate of Christopher Cline, late of Fayette C., decd
Page 348

W half of Lot No. 65 in 6th Dist., and N half of Lot 63 same district, sold 1st Tues. in Nov last Perry Hicks as Admr. Recorded: 27 Feb 1858

An Appraisement of Property Belonging to Estate of James W. Milner, late of Fayette Co., decd
Page 348-352

Appraisers: R. K. Holliday, Lee K. Johnson, William W. McConnell, sworn 2 Dec 1857.
Recorded: 27 Jul 1858

Sale Bill, 6 Jan 1858. Purchasers were: P. W. Milner and J. H. Milner.
Recorded: 27 Feb 1858

Estate of Emily McLeroy, decd, wife of Thomas W. McLeroy, in Account Current with James McConnell, Admr of said Estate from time of Letters of Admn to 31 Dec 1857 inclusive
Page 353-354

3 vouchers. Voucher #2, Vernon Jackson Parish, La. Mar 16, 1857. Received of James McConnell, Admr on Estate of Emily McLeroy, decd, the sum of $112 out of and as a part of verdict in the case, Thomas W. McLeroy and wife vs. Elijah Cleckler. /s/Thomas W. McLeroy

Recorded: 20 Mar 1858

Inventory and Appraisement of Estate (personal) of William N. Hill, decd
Page 354-356

Appraisers: Q. C. Grice, Moze Harp, Young L. Wooton, sworn 4 Feb 1858

Sale of Personal Property. Among purchasers: Moze Harp, W. H. Blalock, R. D. Humphrey, A. Parrot, William Glass, M. M. Tidwell, etc. Recorded: 23 Mar 1858

Inventory and Appraisement of Daniel Long Estate
Page 356-360

Appraisers: George C. King, L. F. Blalock, M. M. Tidwell, sworn 13 Jan 1858.
Recorded: 25 Mar 1858

A List of the Sale of the Perishable Property, sold 25 Jan 1858. Among purchasers: J. L. Blalock, William Bradley, R. Dorman, M. M. Tidwell, J. B. Allen, J. S. Holliday, William R. Padgett, etc.
Recorded: 25 Mar 1858

Inventory and Appraisement of Propert of William T. Rush, decd
Page 360-361

Appraisers: L. H. Griffin, T. M. Handley, C. W. Smith
Recorded: 25 Mar 1858

An Account of the Sale of the Perishable Property, 16 Jan 1858, includes notes on John Rush, A. Slayton, J. W. Smith and J. Handley. Recorded: 25 Mar 1858

The Following is List of the Appraisement of Personal and Real Property of Thomas Hales, decd
Page 362-363

Negroes -

Tamer, age 38
Nelson, age 32
Isham, age 23
Minea (girl), age 17 and child, Martha
Richard, age 15
Matilda, age 10
Mahaly, age 8

270 acres of land. Includes notes of M. T. Travis and Thomas J. King
Appraisers: N. W. Mathews, Charles Bailey, I. P. Gay, Lorenzo Morgan, T. C. Mathews.
Recorded: 25 Mar 1858

Account of Sale of Personal Property, 6 Nov 1857. Among purchasers were: Charles Bailey, T. H. Horne, Joseph Hale, J.M. Jones, J. F.Spear, James Powell, etc.

Negroes sold -

Mahala, a girl, sold to R. R. King
Matilda, a girl, sold to T. . King
Tamer, a woman, sold to Tilman Burks
Nelson, a man, sold to R. R. King
Richard, a boy, sold to Joseph Hall
270 acres of land sold to J.M. Jones
Recorded: 25 Mar 1858

Inventory and Appraisement of Estate of John Watson, decd
Page 364-367

Negroes - Ann and youngest child, Martha, Hughy, Laura
Land Lot No. 148
Land Lot No. 77
Appraisers: M. J. Smith, John DeVaughan, William Watson sworn 26 Dec 1857
Recorded: 24 Mar 1858

List of Sale of Property Among purchasers: the widow, James H. Franklin, Josiah H.Elder, William J. Watson, Mathew Yates,, William Watson.

Admrs - H. D. Palmer, Ellison Rush
Recorded: 26 Mar 1858

The Following is an Inventory and Appraisement of the Property of O. M. Pearson
Page 367

E. half of Lot No. 121 in 4th District, Fayette Co.
Appraisers: James M. Spurlin, Francis P. Jones, Nathaniel Miller, Newton M. Fitts, sworn 15 Apr 1858,
Recorded: 4 May 1858

Inventory and Appraisement of Property Belonging to Estate of Rowland Hutcherson
Page 368-369

Appraisers: Willis Beavers, James M. Fletcher, Hugh Evans, Drury Coach, Hiram Adams, sworn 14 Dec 1857
Recorded: 4 May 1858

Account of the Sale of Real Estate. Among purchasers: the widow, H. T. D. Creal, N. J. Bivins, W. Beavers, Reuben Wallis, Y. S. Allen, George Creal, William Creal, Milton Hutcherson, etc.

Inventory of Property, Notes, Accounts etc. of Estate of William N. Hill, decd
Page 370-371

Negro boy, Linus
Notes.
Appraisers: H. F. Underwood, L. F. Blalock, W. W. Bosworth, Q. C. Grice, C. E. Bennett.
Recorded: 29 May 1858

Return No. 1, Thomas J. Camp, Admr of Nathan Camp, decd, from Mar Term 1858
Page 372-426

Includes notes against the estate. 81 vouchers.
Inventory of assets belonging to the estate, a list of Fi.Fas. (final settlement Mar 1858)
Appraisers: Z. B. Blalock, S. Zellars, S. Cole, William Danforth and W. H. Christian, set aside property for the widow of N. Camp, decd.
Recorded: 11 Jun 1858

Inventory of Property of Estate of Nelly G. Evans, decd
Page 426-428

Negroes -

Fanny and her children (Sophronia and Willes), Jim, Louisa, John, Tom, Nancy, Walter and Phillip
Appraisers: Seaborn Pate, James E. Haisten, Joseph B. Williams
Recorded: 22 Jun 1858

Sale Bill. Among purchasers: Isaac Haisten, Patsy S. Smith, William Mathews, etc.

Inventory of Property of Estate of Jane E. Smith, decd
Page 428-430

Negroes - Missouri and her 4 children (Vena, Nancy, Elizabeth and infant), Bob, Hannah, Nancy and her child (Cinda), Harriet, Frank, Henry, Sallie, Charles

Includes notes of William Jackson, T. C. Mathews and Hough & Fambrous
Appraisers: Seaborn Pate, James E. Haisten, Joseph B. Williams, sworn 21 Dec 1857
Recorded: 22 Jun 1858

Sale Bill. Purchasers: Patsey S. Smith, I. Calverson, H. M. Pate, I. W. Wilky, John Brassell
Recorded: 22 Jun 1858

Inventory and Appraisement of Personal Estate of Lucy A. Hill, decd
Page 430-432

Appraisers: James M. Fletcher, William Shadrick, Hugh Evans, sworn 26 Dec 1857
Recorded: 19 Jul 1858

Inventory and Sale of the personal property, sold by John M. Huie, Admr, on 26 Dec 1857.
Purchasers: Mary Hill, J. F. Mill, Willis Miles and Mary Huie.
Recorded: 19 Jul 1858

Petition of Thomas J. King, Admr of Estate of William P. King
Page 433-434

Petition shows that William P. King departed this life on 2 Mar 1858 and that the decd apptd his Admr before he died. He states that under the Act of 1856 he is to set apart five suitable persons to the widow and children of William P. King (he having left a widow and 3 children) the amount necessary for their support..... /s/William P. King

The court appointed the following commissioners: John C. Brassell, W. H. C. Dodson, Thomas L. Duffell, T. H. Horne, T. C. Mathews to set apart for years' support (above).

Schedule of the effects set apart for the widow and children listed.
Recorded: 18 Jul 1858

Inventory of the Estate includes - 60 acres of land in NW corner of Lot No. 190, etc.
Recorded: 19 Jul 1858

An Account Current with Henry Thornton as Admr of Herod Thornton, decd
Page 434-438

Sale of personal estate, see Record (blank), page 168
Heirs - Felix Thornton, Needham Jackson, Herod Thornton, Rebecca Brogden, Haywood Thornton, Blackmon Thornton, Coleman Hartley.
Filed: 6 Mar 1858. Recorded: 23 Jul 1858

Nancy Wilson, minor child of Washington Wilson in Account Current with Washington Wilson, Gdn, from 31 Dec 1852 to 31 Dec 1857
Page 438-439

2 vouchers. Recorded: 22 Jul 1858

Mary Thompson, minor in Account with John S. Holliday, Gdn, from 1 Jan 1857 to 31 Dec inclusive
Page 439-440

3 vouchers. Recorded: 23 Jul 1858

An Account Current with John W. Hill and William S. Chambers as Exrs of LWT of Elisha Hill, late of Fayette Co., decd, from time of appointment and granting Letters Testamentary to 31 Dec 1857
Page 441-449

30 vouchers. Filed: 27 Mar 1858. Recorded: 23 Jul 1858

Sarah Ann, Orphan of James G. Christian decd, in Account Current with G. F. Mann, Gdn, from 1 Jan 1857 to 31 Dec 1857
Page 449-452

Filed: 20 May 1858. Receipt of H. C. Christian for room and board. Recorded: 26 Jul 1858

An Account Current with Martha A. Reeves, Gdn of Robert W. Reeves, minor child of William Reeves, decd, from 1 Jan 1856 to 31 Dec 1857
Page 453-455

7 vouchers. To cash paid - I. Richardson, I. W. Tully, Holliday & Ware, Thomas W. Ballard
Filed: 3 May 1858. Recorded: 26 Jul 1858

An Account Current with Martha A. Reeves, Gdn of Amos W. Reeves, minor child of William Reeves, decd, from 1 Jan 1858 to 31 December
Page 456-457

5 vouchers. Recorded: 26 Aug 1858

An Account Current with Martha A. Reeves, Gdn of William P. Reeves, from 1 Jan 1857 to 1 Jan 1858
Page 457-458

6 vouchers. Recorded: 26 Jul 1858

An Account Current with Martha A. Reeves as Gdn of Henry C. Reeves from 1 Jan 1856 to 1 Jan 1857
Page 459-460

3 vouchers. Recorded: 26 Aug 1858

An Account Current with Martha A. Reeves, Gdn of Martha W. Reeves, minor child of William Reeves, decd, from 1 Jan 1856 to 31 Dec 1857
Page 460-461

2 vouchers. Filed: 3 May 1858. Recorded: 26 Jul 1858

Estate of Silas G. Eastin in Account Current with John B. Allen, Admr, from 1 Jan 1857 to 31 Dec 1857
Page 461-465

9 vouchers. Recorded: 27 Jul 1858

In Account Current with John I. Whitaker as Admr of Elbert Harris, late of Fayette Co., decd, from 1 Jan 1857 to 31 Dec inclusive
Page 466-467

7 vouchers. Includes Fi.Fa. Recorded: 31 Aug 1858

In Account of the Sale of the Property of Flora Sanders, late of Fayette Co., decd
Page 468-469

Among purchasers: Joshua Lyle, John Hunt, Joshua Malone, F. Rountree, M. McIntosh, N. C. Smith, John Lyle, Z. Blalock, etc.

Inventory and Appraisement of the Personal Property as returned by Sherod H. Gay, Joshua Lyle and I. M. Austin. Recorded: 31 Jul 1858

An Account Current with A. G. Mundy as Admr of Jesse Lasseter, Jr., decd, from 1 Jan 1856 to 1 Jan 1857 Showing a Full Settlement of Estate
Page 469-471

12 vouchers. Heirs as follows -

Seppy Lasseter
Willis Beavers in right of his wife, Martha Beavers, formerly Martha Lasseter
Willis Beavers as Gdn of Reuben, Seppy, Taylor, Ellen, Malinda and Sarah Lasseter, minor children

Recorded: 31 Jul 1858

An Account Current with R. C. Huie as Admr of Robert Cole of Fayette Co. from time of appointment up to 31 Dec 1857
Page 471-473

Recorded: 31 Jun 1858

A Statement and Account Current with Martha McLeroy, Admx of Henry McLeroy, decd
Page 474-479

Sale of negroes, see Record, page 136
To sale of personal estate, see record, page 135
6 vouchers. Heirs as follows -

James McLeroy
A. B. DeVaughan as Gdn of Wiley T. McLeroy
Martha McLeroy as Gdn of Martha H., Pitt N., Emily H and Thomas McLeroy, minors of testator
Wiley J. Gay in right of his wife
A. B. DeVaughan in right of his wife

Filed: 21 Apr 1858. Recorded: 5 Aug 1858

An Account Current with M. B. DeVaughan as Gdn of Wiley McLeroy, minor of Henry McLeroy, decd, from 31 Dec 1856 to 31 Apr 1858
Page 479-480

4 vouchers. Recorded: 5 Aug 1858

Estate of Elbert Bishop, decd, in Account Current with Jesse Hubbard, Admr, from 1 Jan 1857 to 31 Dec 1857
Page 480

1 voucher. Filed: 24 Feb 1858. Recorded: 8 Aug 1858

The Estate of Vicy Bearden, Orphan of Edward Bearden, in Account Current with W. W. Bearden, Gdn, from 31 Dec 1856 to date of settlement
Page 481-482

4 vouchers. Voucher #4. Received of William W. Bearden, Gdn of Vicy Bearden formerly, now Vicy Bradley $470.90 in full of my wife's share, this 17 Mar 1858. /s/J. P. Bradley, in right of his wife, Vicy Bradley.
Recorded: 5 Aug 1858

Ann C. Ware, Orphan of George Ware, decd, in Account Current with Mildred Ware, Gdn from 1 Jan 1857 to 31 Dec inclusive
Page 483-483

Hire of Peter and Fanny in 1857 (negros). Recorded: 6 Aug 1858

Richard P. Ware, Orphan of George Ware, decd, in Account Current with Mildred Ware, Gdn, from 1 Jan 1857 to 31 Dec inclusive
Page 484-485

4 vouchers. To cash paid - W. B. Fuller, M. H. Looney, Holliday & Ware, and George C. King, Dept. C.C.O.
Recorded: 6 Aug 1858

The Estate of Joseph P. Pledger in Account Current with Counsel Rentfrow, Gdn, from date of Letters to 31 Dec 1857
Page 485

4 vouchers. To cash paid - J. L. Blalock, John G. Jackson, Counsel Rentfrow and George C. King.
Filed: 11 Jan 1858

The Estate of John W. Pledger in Account Current with Counsel Rentfrow, Admr, from 1 Jan 1857 to 31 Dec 1857 inclusive
Page 486-487

To cash paid -
George C. King for this Return
A. G. King (legatee), in right of his wife, Martha P. King
Counsel Rentfrow, Gdn of Joseph P. Pledger, for his distributive share of estate
Filed: 11 Jan 1858.

Mary Moses, Orphan of Hiram Moses, decd, in Account Current with Andrew J. Pollard, Gdn, from 1 Jan 1857 to 31 Dec 1857
Page 487-488

To cash paid -
J. L. Blalock
M. L. Yates (in full for my charge)
George C. King (for this Return)
B. F. Logan (legatee), in right of his wife, Mary E. Logan, received funds from Andrew J. Pollard, Gdn, which he received from the Admr, Drewry B. May, of Hiram Moses, late of the said county, decd, and Oliver M. Pearson, Admr of Oliver McLain, and of May McLain, decd, this 31 Dec 1857. /s/John B. F. Logan (his mark), in right of his wife, Mary E. Logan

Filed: 7 Jan 1858. Recorded: 6 Aug 1858

The Estate of Marcus Long, decd, in Account Current with Thomas Long and Isham Long, Admrs, from 31 Dec 1856 to 31 Dec 1857
Page 488-489

1 voucher (for filing return with Clerk). Filed: 3 May 1858. Recorded: 6 Aug 1858

Estate of John Palmer in Account Current with H. D. Palmer, Admr, from 31 Dec 1856 to 31 Dec 1857 inclusive
Page 489-490

4 vouchers. To cash paid - George C. King, Samuel Thompson, Oliver M. Pearson (for taxes). Filed: 31 Dec 1857. Recorded: 6 Aug 1858

James E. H. Ware, Orphan of George Ware, decd, in Account Current with Burrell A. Ware, Gdn, from 1 Jan 1857 to 31 Dec inclusive
Page 490-492

5 vouchers. To cash paid - Holliday & Ware, William B. Fuller, M. H. Lowry, George C. King
Recorded: 6 Aug 1858

The Estate of Alfred Brown, decd, in Account Current with John O. Brown, Admr, from 1 Jan to 31 Dec 1857 inclusive
Page 492-495

4 vouchers. By amount received of T. W. Jennings in 2 Fi.Fas., from Charles Clements, A. W. Stone and Elijah Glass. Filed: 6 May 1858. Recorded: 7 Aug 1858

Wynn F. and Sarah Francis Jones, two minors of Francis M. Jones, decd, in Account Current with James F. Johnson, Gdn for said children to 31 Dec 1857
Page 495-496

7 vouchers. Recorded 7 Aug 1857

Martha M. Cavender, Orphan of Wade H. Cavender, decd, in Account Current with Delila Moses, Gdn, from 1 Jan to 31 Dec 1857 inclusive
Page 496-497

5 vouchers. To cash paid - George C. King, Dept. C. C. O., Oliver M. Pearson, tax collector, Brassell & Rodgers (acct), Blalock & Bros., P. H. Brassell.
Recorded: 7 Aug 1857

Hiram D. Moses, Orphan of Hiram Moses, decd, in Account Current with Delila Moses, Gdn, from 1 Jan to 31 Dec 1857 inclusive
Page 497

2 vouchers. Recorded: 7 Aug 1858

Russell G. Strickland, Orphan of Simon Strickland, decd, in Account Current with C. E. Brassell, Gdn, from 1 Jan 1857 to 31 Dec 1857 inclusive
Page 498-499

2 vouchers. Received of M. P. Strickland as Admr of the Estate of Simon Strickland $5.85 and interest on land one year. Received of B. G. Strickland wages for 1857.
Filed: 29 Apr 1858. Recorded: 29 Apr 1858

Mary E. Elkins, minor child of James Elkins, in Account Current with C. E. Bennett, Gdn, from date of Letters of Guardianship to 31 Dec 1857
Page 500

2 vouchers. Filed: 27 Apr 1858

Emiline Elkins, minor child of James Elkins in Account Current with C. E. Bennett, Gdn, from date of Letters of Guardianship to 31 Dec 1857
Page 501-502

2 vouchers. Filed: 27 Apr 1858. Recorded: 7 Aug 1858

Eliza F. Elkins, minor child of James Elkins in Account Current with C. E. Bennett, Gdn, from date of Letters of Guardianship to 31 Dec 1857 inclusive
Page 502

2 vouchers. Filed: 27 Apr 1858. Recorded: 7 Aug 1858

Thomas W. Elkins, minor child of James Elkins in Account Current with C. E. Bennett, Gdn, from date of Letters of Guardianship to 31 Dec 1857 inclusive
Page 503

1 voucher. Filed: 29 Apr 1857. Recorded: 7 Aug 1858

William M. Whitlow, Orphan of Warren Whitlow, decd, in Account Current with Benjamin B. Dykes, Gdn, from time of appointment to 1 Jan 1858
Page 504-506

5 vouchers. To cash paid - P. H. Brassell, Hardy & Mitchum, B. B. Dykes.
Recorded: 7 Aug 1858

Estate of James W. Head in Account Current with William T. Thurman, Exr, from date of Letters Testamentary to 1 Mar 1857 inclusive
Page 506-512

18 vouchers. Recorded: 9 Aug 1858.

Estate of Joshua S. Callaway in Account with W. E. Tucker, Admr, from 1 Jan 1857 to 31 Dec inclusive
Page 512-514

5 vouchers. Filed: 2 Feb 1858. To cash paid - Joshua Cannon for laying off widow's dower.
Georgia, Fayette Co.} Personally appeared before me, Isaac B. Huff, a Justice of the Peace in and for said county, Mrs Tabitha E. Peldon, who, being on oath, says that she is the wife of A. C. Peldon, that the above acct was contracted with her by Joshua S. Callaway before her marriage and while her name was Tabitha E. Jones...this Mar 14 1857. /s/Tabitha E. Pelden.
Recorded: 11 Aug 1858

The Estate of Christopher Cline in Account Current with Perry Hicks, Admr, from time of his appointment up to 31 Dec 1857 inclusive
Page 514-518

18 vouchers. To cash paid - widow of decd, Brassell & Rogers, W. H. Swan, W. H. Henderson, Daniel Mitchell, W. W. Sibley, W. I. Reeves, Delila Hicks
Filed: 2 Feb 1858. Recorded: 11 Aug 1858

An Account of William Jennings, late of Fayette Co., decd, from 1 Jan 1857 to 31 Dec 1857 Showing Distribution
Page 519-542

56 vouchers. To cash paid - Thomas Hale, A. B. Mitchell, B. L. Johnson, Burrell Brown, T. M. Harrell, A. Stinchcomb, I. T. Gay, William Whatley, Jeptha Landrum, W. H. F. Denson, L. T. Thompson, R. H. Jennings, Dempsey Brown, E. Shepherd, Jane Jones, William Jennings, Eason Jones.
Recorded: 12 Sept 1858

An Account Current with Francis Long, Admr of Estate of Henry Long, decd, from 1 Dec 1855 to 13 Mar 1858
Page 542-545

13 vouchers. To cash paid - F. L. Lord, George C. King, John Harrison (legatee), Jesse Brooks (legatee), Thomas L. Long (legatee), John W. Long (legatee), Penelope Long (legatee), J. C. Long (legatee), and F. L. Long (legatee).
Filed: 12 Mar 1858. Recorded: 23 Oct 1858

Estate of Mason Gentry, decd, in Account Current with Killis Brown, Admr, for year 1857
Page 545-553

23 vouchers. To cash paid - Fi.Fa. to F. T. Gayden, John G. Head, E. R. Aldings, Tidwell & Fuller, John A. Doan, May Mosely, Samuel G. Pegg, Thomas M. Damall, J. M. Kimberly, Ezzard Y Collin, C. W. McGinnis, J. J. Jones, Thomas Morris, John J. Heart, B. Atkinson, Willis Brown

By amount collecting on William Daniel's note, John B. Morris' note, and J. J. Head's note
Recorded: 23 Oct 1858

Sale of Property of Joseph Anthony Sold on 1st of Jan 1858
Page 554

150 acres of land in Lot No. 242 sold to James Anthony
Negroes sold as follows -

woman to Fanny Hutcherson
Matilda and child to Fanny Hutcherson
Micajah to Archibald Smith

Other purchasers - Jesse T. Anthony, John D. Anthony, James Brown, L. C. Hutcherson, William M. McConnel, Robert Henderson, Moab Shepherd, Thomas Mandy, William McConnell, William O. Betts, Y. L. Allen, Joseph Camp, David Harris, Daniel Hanes, T. Hutcherson, James M. Anthony, William Long.
Recorded: 8 Nov 1858

An Inventory of the Property of Susanah West, late of Fayette Co.
Page 555-558

Appraisers: Dillard Hicks, W. B. Couch, J. H. Reeves, Perry Hicks

Includes a list of notes in possession of Paschal West.
Sale Bill of Property of Susanah West. Among purchasers - R. Iverson, Perry Hicks, Thomas Humphrey, Henry Swan, A. J. Swan, William Jackson, H. Swan, Dillard Hicks, D. Hicks, W. Bishop, Lovick Bowers, T. Humphrey, D. Hicks, W. B. Couch, A. J. Swan, John Tobey, etc.
Recorded: 27 Nov 1858

Thomas Emory Loyd, Orphan of James Loyd, in Account Current with John Loyd, Gdn, from 1 Jan 1857 to 31 Dec
Page 559-560

2 vouchers. Recorded: 2 Dec 1858

Estate of John Sellers, decd, in Account Current with Ishmael Dunn, Admr, from 31 Dec 1856 to 1 Jan 1858
Page 561-562

3 vouchers. Recorded: 2 Dec 1858

Elisha Lasseter in Account Current with James Hanes, Gdn, from 1 Jan 1857 to 31 Dec 1857 inclusive
Page 562-563

2 vouchers. To cash paid - George C. King, Dept. C. C. O., and James Harris, Jr.
Recorded: 2 Dec 1858

Sarah Jane Lasseter, minor Orphan of Jesse Lasseter, decd, in Account Current with Willis Beavers, Gdn, from date of his Letters of Guardianship up to 1 Jun 1858
Page 463-564

1 voucher. Recorded: 4 Dec 1858

Eleanor Lasseter, minor Orphan of Jesse Lasseter, decd, in Account Current with Willis Beavers, Gdn, from date of his Letters of Guardianship up to 1 Jun 1858
Page 564

1 voucher. Recorded: 4 Dec 1858

Seppy Lasseter, minor Orphan of Jesse Lasseter, decd, in Account Current with Willis Beavers, Gdn, from date of his Letters of Guardianship up to 1 Jun 1858
Page 565

By amount received of Andrew J. Mundy, Admr of the Estate of Jesse Lasseter, decd, 31 Dec 1857 - $254.78
1 voucher. Recorded: 4 Dec 1858

An Account Current with Sterling J. Elders, Admr of T. R. Persons, decd. from 1 Apr 1857 to 1 May 1857
Page 566-576

To cash paid - T. C. Bennett, S. F. Blalock, Edmick Shepard, E. B. Langston, M. H. Looney, E. F. Field, M. E. Oman, M. G. Hicks, P. O. Drewry, Thomas Heard, F. O. Drewry, R. W. North, G. L. Warner (agent), Thomas Cochran, Thomas H. Wiley, J. J. Russell, Jesse Hodge, J. Bume, Page W. Heard, Blalock & Co., S. P. Elder, Holliday & Ware.
Filed: 7 May 1858. Recorded: 8 Nov 1858

An Account Current with Zadock Blalock, Admr of Flora Sanders, late of Fayette Co. with LWT annexed from time of appointment to 1 Dec 1858
Page 576-579

10 vouchers.
Recorded: 2 Dec 1858

Mahala Lasseter, minor Orphan of Jesse Lasseter, in Account Current with Willis Beavers, Gdn. from time of his Letters of Guardianship to 1 Jun 1858
Page 580

Filed: 8 Jun 1858. Recorded: 7 Dec 1858

James T. Lasseter, minor Orphan of Jesse Lasseter, in Account Current with Willis Beavers, Gdn, from time of his Letters of Guardianship to 1 Jun 1858
Page 581

By amount received of Andrew J. Mundy, Admr of Estate of Jesse Lasseter, decd, 31 Dec 1858 - $254.70.
Recorded: 7 Dec 1858

Reuben M. Lasseter, minor Orphan of Jesse Lasseter, decd, in Account Current with Willis Beavers, Gdn, from time of his Letters of Guardianship to 1 Jun 1858
Page 582

By amount received from Andrew J. Mundy, Admr of Estate of Jesse Lasseter, decd, received Dec 1858 - $254.70.
Filed: 8 Jun 1858. Recorded: 9 Dec 1858

Estate of R. D. Litter, Orphan of Zabud Litter, in Account Current with James W. Talley, Gdn, from 1 Jan 1857 to 31 Dec 1857 inclusive
Page 583

3 vouchers. Filed: 22 Jan 1858. Recorded: 9 Dec 1858

Estate of Windom West, decd, in Account current with Britton West, Exr, from 1 Jan 1856 to 10 May 1858 inclusive
Page 584-588

7 vouchers. Filed: 14 Jun 1858. Recorded: 9 Dec 1858

A List of the Property Sold as the Estate of William P. King, decd, on 17 Nov 1858 and due on 19 Nov 1859
Page 588-592

Among purchasers: A. J. Pollard, Emily King, T. D. Duffel, T. L. Duffel, I. P. Gay, T. H. Horn, H. T. Horn.
Recorded: 18 Oct 1858

An Account Current with Martha McLeroy, Gdn of Martha H., Pitt L., Emily, H. D. and Thomas E. B., minor children of Henry McLeroy, decd, from 1 Jan 1857 to 31 Dec 1857
Page 595

2 vouchers. Filed: 6 Jun 1858. Recorded: 10 Dec 1858

George W. Brooks, Orphan of Ivy Brooks, in Account Current with Robert Iverson, Gdn, from 1 Jan 1857 to 1 Jun 1858 inclusive
Page 594-596

10 vouchers. To cash paid - William R. Phillis, Favor & Rud, Ansley Moses, R. Iverson, William R. Hardy, George C. King, George Perdue and John Swan.
Recorded: 10 Dec 1858

Samuel Loyd, Orphan of James Loyd, decd, in Account Current with James Loyd, Gdn, from 1 Jan 1857 to 2 Feb 1858, the date of Testament, inclusive
Page 597-598

To cash paid - George C. King, Samuel Loyd.
Recorded: 10 Jan 1858

Estate of James Turner, decd, in Account Current with Elijah Glass, Admr, from 1 Jan 1857 to 31 Dec 1857 inclusive
Page 598

1 voucher. Filed: 22 Jun 1858.

Estate of Harbert Cook, decd, in Account Current with William N. Cook, Exr, from 31 Dec 1856 to 31 Dec 1857 inclusive
Page 599-600

6 vouchers. To cash paid - George C. King, Richard Wallis, J. L. Blalock, S. T. W. Minor
Filed: 30 Jun 1858. Recorded: 10 Dec 1858

Nathan, Orphan of James Turner, decd, in Account Current with John O. Dickson, Gdn, from 1 Jan 1857 to 31 Dec 1857
Page 600-601

2 vouchers. Filed: 30 Jun 1858. Recorded: 10 Dec 1858

Zachariah Turner, Orphan of James Turner, decd, in Account Current with John O. Dickson, Gdn, from 1 Jan 1857 to 31 Dec 1857
Page 601

2 vouchers. Filed: 30 Jun 1858. Recorded: 10 Dec 1858

Frederick Turner, Orphan of James Turner, decd, in Account Current with John O. Dickson, Gdn, from 1 Jan 1857 to 31 Dec 1857
Page 602

2 vouchers. Filed: 30 Jun 1858. Recorded: 10 Dec 1858

Estate of E. H. Roberts, minor Orphan of Sansom W. Roberts, decd, with Hugh Porter, Gdn, from 1 Jan 1857 to 31 Dec inclusive
Page 603-604

2 vouchers. Filed: 26 Apr 1858. Recorded: 10 Dec 1858

Estate of Griffin Roberts, minor Orphan of Sansom W. Roberts, decd, in Account Current with Hugh Porter, Gdn, from 1 Jan 1857 to 31 Dec inclusive
Page 604-605

2 vouchers. Filed: 26 Apr 1858. Recorded: 10 Dec 1858

Estate of Sarah T. Roberts in Account Current with Hugh Porter, Gdn, from 1 Jan 1857 to 31 Dec inclusive
Page 604-605

3 vouchers. Recorded: 10 Dec 1859

Estate of James S. Roberts, minor Orphan of Sansom W. Roberts, in Account Current with Hugh Porter, Gdn, from 1 Jan 1857 to 31 Dec inclusive
Page 605-606

2 vouchers. Recorded: 10 Dec 1859

An Account Current with S. T. Whitaker as Gdn of minor children of Benjamin F. Neal, late of Fayette Co., decd, from 1 Jan 1857 to 1 Jun 1858
Page 606

3 vouchers. Recorded: 10 Dec 1859

An Account Current with J. J. Carson, in right of his wife from 1 Jan 1857 to 1 Jun 1858
Page 606

Page 630. Credit for his share of above - $589.26
By amount due from last Return.

An Account Current with S. T. Whitaker, Gdn of R. F. Neal for 1 Jan 1857 to 1 Jun 1858 inclusive
Page 606-607

To cash paid - John Williams, Henry Banks, D. Reuben, J. Richards.

An Account Current with S. T. Whitaker, Gdn of Lucretia Neal from 1 Jan 1857 to 1 Jan 1858
Page 607

1 voucher.

An Account Current with S. T. Whitaker, Gdn of John P. Neal from 1 Jan 1857 to 1 Jan 1858
Page 607

No vouchers.

An Account Current with S. T. Whitaker, Gdn of Emily J. Neal from 1 Jan 1857 to 1 Jan 1858
Page 607-608

1 voucher.

An Account Current with S. T. Whitaker, Gdn of George F. Neal from 1 Jan 1857 to 1 Jan 1858
Page 608

To cash paid - John Wiliams, Henry Banks, B. F. Neal, Rachael Neal (the mother, for board)

An Account Current with S. T. Whitaker as Gdn of James T. Neal from 1 Jan 1857 to 1 Jan 1858
Page 608

To cash paid Henry Banks, John Williams and Rachael Neal (the mother, for board)

An Account Current with S. T. Whitaker, Gdn of B. P. Neal from 1 Jan 1857 to 1 Jan 1858
Page 609

To cash paid - Henry Banks and Richael Neal (the mother, for board)

An Account Current with S. T. Whitaker, Gdn of Harriett Neal from 1 Jan 1857 to 1 Jan 1858
Page 609-611

To cash paid - H. Banks and D. Roberts.
11 vouchers. Filed: 28 Jun 1858. Recorded: 11 Dec 1858

Estate of Araminta Hilsman in Account Current with V. A. Gaskill, Gdn, from time of his appointment to 15 Jan 1858
Page 612-614

Received of V. A. Gaskill, Gdn of the minor orphan of James Hilsman, decd, $297.26 in full of my distributive share of the Estate of Bennett Hilsman, decd, late of Hancock Co., State of Georgia. 15 Jan 1858.
/s/Joseph Neal. /s/Araminta West

Received of V. A. Gaskill, Gdn of Arminta Hilsman for boarding 1857 and 1858. /s/Amanda Hilsman

Sarah A. Milner, minor Orphan of Pitt W. Milner, decd, in Account Current with Patrick H. Allen, Gdn, from time of Letters of Guardianship to 31 Dec 1857 inclusive
Page 614

3 vouchers. To cash paid - William H. Chapman and A. G. Hudson.
Filed: 17 Aug 1858. Recorded: 10 Dec 1858

William, minor of Allen Thompson, in Account Current with Mathew Jones, Gdn, from 31 Dec 1856 to 31 Dec 1857 inclusive
Page 614-616

1 voucher.

In Account Current with V. A. Gaskill, Gdn of minor heirs of James Hilsman, decd
Page 616

To cash paid - A. J. Hilsman (for boarding minors: Bennett E. and Irene Hilsman and William Wyatt and wife, Mansell), John R. Hilsman
5 vouchers. Recorded: 10 Dec 1858

William Jennings in Account Current with Elizabeth Jennings as Gdn of now Elizabeth Swanson from 31 Dec 1854 to 1 Jan 1858 inclusive
Page 616-617

To hire of negroes, Simon and Bostin in the year of 1856
Vou. #1. Received of William Jennings, Gdn of Elizabeth Jennings formerly, now Elizabeth Swanson...in full of all claims I hold against him as my Gdn, this 11 Dec 1858. /s/Elizabeth Swanson. /s/M. W. Swanson
Recorded: 11 Dec 1858

An Account Current with Rachael Eason, Admx on Estate of Richard B. Eason, decd, from 31 Dec 1856 to 31 Dec 1856 inclusive
Page 617-619

5 vouchers. Recorded: 11 Dec 1858

An Account Current with Jesse Barintine, Admr of James Thompson, from 1 Jan 1857 to 31 Dec 1857
Page 619-620

3 vouchers. Filed: 30 Jun 1858.

John N. Brooks, Orphan of Ivey Brooks, in Account Current with Robert Iverson from 1 Jun 1856 to 1 Jun 1858 inclusive
Page 621-623

11 vouchers To cash paid - J. G. and M. F. Westmoreland, Ansley Moses, William R. Hardy, G. W. Perdue, John Swan, Frances & Redd, William R. Phillips, Robert Iverson.
Filed: 11 Jun 1858. Recorded: 11 Dec 1858

Harriet T. Brooks, minor Orphan of Ivey Brooks, decd, in Account Current with A. G. Brooks, Gdn, from 1 Jan 1857 to 31 Dec 1857
Page 623-624

5 vouchers. To cash paid - Henry Freman, A. G. Brooks, Gdn.
To hire of negroes -
boy, Break
boy, William
woman, Angeline and child
woman, Francis and children

An Account Current with T. C. Mathews, Gdn of Marcus L. Williams, minor, from 1 Jan 1857 to 1 May 1857
Page 625

To cash paid - Nicholas & Ware, John W. Attaway, J. Barr, Penelope Williams.

In Account Current with T. C. Mathews, Gdn of Miss C. Williams from 1 Jan 1856 to 1 Jul 1858
Page 625-629

Distributive shares to -

J. H. B. Williams
A. B. Lovejoy, in right of his wife, Elizabeth

William J. Russell, Gdn of Johnathan Herring, Orphan of Thomas Herring, decd, from 1 Jan to 31 Dec 1857 inclusive
Page 630

Filed: 23 Jun 1858. Recorded: 11 Dec 1858

Francis, Orphan of Thomas Herring, decd, in Account with William J. Russell, Gdn, from 1 Jan to 31 Dec 1857 inclusive
Page 630-631

5 vouchers. To cash paid - O. M. Pearson, Mary A. Herring, M. H. Looney.
Filed: 23 Jun 1858. Recorded: 11 Dec 1858

Marcus, Orphan of Thomas Herring, decd, in Account with William J. Russell, Gdn, from 1 Jan to 31 Dec 1857 inclusive
Page 631-632

5 vouchers. To cash paid - O. M. Pearson, Mary A. Herring, M. H. Looney.
Recorded: 11 Dec 1858

Parker Eason, Gdn for Willism S. Milner
Page 632-636

Recorded: 11 Dec 1858

Joseph H., Orphan of Wade H. Cavender, decd, in Account Current with P. H. Brassell, Gdn, from 1 Jan to 31 Dec 1857 inclusive
Page 637-641

4 vouchers. Filed: 10 May 1858. Recorded: 13 Dec 1858

Nathan Camp, Gdn of James T. Jennings, Orphan of John A. Jennings, decd, in Account Current with Z. B. Blalock
Page 641

Recorded: 10 Dec 1858

William J. Jinnings, Orphan of John A. Jinnings, decd, in Account CUrrent with Phillip H. Brassell, Gdn, from 2 Mar to 31 Dec 1857 inclusive
Page 641-644

Recorded: 13 Dec 1858

Mary Ann Jinnings, Orphan of John A. Jinnings, decd, in Account Current with Phillip H. Brassell, Gdn, from 1 Mar to 31 Dec 1857
Page 644-647

To cash paid - P. W. Mitcham (teacher), J. and T. J. Foster.
To amount received from William May, Admr of Estate of William Jennings, decd which is 1/4th part of $7381.60, the amount that Phillip H.. Brassell, Gdn, received, ...to be equally divided between the four minor children of Allen A. Jinnings, decd.
7 vouchers. Recorded: 13 Dec 1858

Roda E. Jinnings, Orphan of John A. Jinnings, decd, in Account Current with Phillip H. Brassell, Gdn, from 3 Mar to 31 Dec 1857 inclusive
Page 647-651

By amount received from William May, Admr on the Estate of William Jinnings, decd ...which is one fourth of $7381.60, the amount which the said Phillip H. Brassell, Gdn, received from the said william May, Admr on 10 Dec 1857 to be equally divided between the four minor children of John A. Jinnings, decd.
8 vouchers. Recorded: 13 Dec 1858

In Account Current with William Jinnings, Gdn, for Emily Turner, from 31 Dec 1857
Page 651-652

Received from William Jinnings, all my estate which is coming to me from my Guardian, William Jinnings...this 28 Oct 1857. /s/Emily Turner (x, her mark)
4 vouchers. Filed: 15 Oct 1858. Recorded: 15 Feb 1859

An Account Current with James P. Fitzgerald, Exr of Ann Fitzgerald, decd, from 31 Dec 1855 to 23 Dec 1858, the date of Settlement
Page 652-653

By amount of sale of town lot in the town of Fayetteville sold on 25 Dec 1856
Filed: 22 Dec 1858. Recorded: 15 Jul 1859

An Account Current and Statement of the Estate of Francis M. Jones, decd by the Account of A. J. Mundy from time of appointment to 1 Jan 1858
Page 654-655

To amount received in 1854 in Sale Bill, page 126
To hire of negroes for 1854 (book not given)
Return for 1854, see page 592 (book not given)

Appraised value of negroes -

girl, Polly
man, Mike
man, Jeff
woman, Flora

Received in 1856 by sale of Lot of Land in 18th District, see page 308 (book not given)
Sale of house lot in Jonesboro, see page 308 (book not given)

Filed: 31 May 1858. Recorded: 15 Feb 1859

An Appraisement of the Personal Property, Notes, etc. of Estate of William Stubbs, late of Fayette Co., decd
Page 655-656

Includes notes of Moses Turner, Hinson Turner, William S. Chambers, M. S. P. Chambers, J. P. R. Chambers, Mary McLucas, Rowland Stubbs, Jared Whitaker, William N. Hill, Eli Quick, Thomas Turner. Recorded: 19 Jul 1859.

Inventory and Appraisement of Joseph Scales, decd
Page 656-659

Appraisers: John M. Huie, Davide Evans, Hugh Evans, James Fletcher (x, his mark) and David Canes (x, his mark), sworn 7 Dec 1858. Recorded: 17 Feb 1859.

Sale Bill of Personal Property Sold by Archibald Smith and Seaborn Smith, A dmrs. on 20 Dec 1858. Some purchasers were: J. W. Smith, J. M. Huie, J. W. Lasseter, etc.

Estate of Thomas Burnside, decd
Page 660-663

Appraisers: William E. Tucker, James L. Lovejoy, Phillip Fitzgerald, J. J. Lamb, sworn 30 Oct 1857
A List of Goods sold. Some purchasers: Jackson Burnside, L. A. Mangum, William McConnell, Mrs. T. Burnside, J. C. Hightower, R. J. Huie, etc.

By an account on James Lovejoy, A. J. Brown, Wiley Berry, G. L. Warren, Zachariah Mann, John Ward, Phillip Fitzgerald, Jonathan DeVaughan, James McConnell, William McConnell, Allen Estes, James Johnson, Abner Camp and Jordan Williams.
Recorded: 23 Feb 1859

Estate of Joseph Anthony in Account Current with William Spraggins
Page 664-667

17 vouchers. To cash paid - David Hanes, Benjamin Adams, John D. Anthony, J. S. Bialock, Ordinary, Harriet Ann Anthony, Middleton M. Anthony, trustee, Polley Anthony, John M. Huie, M. M. Hutcherson. Filed: 8 Nov 1838. Recorded: 4 Mar 1859

A Statement of the Estate of Paschal Collins, decd, by the heirs at law
Page 668-672

Real estate of decd in Fayette Co. and distributed among the heirs - Lots No. 8, 25 and 26 in the 4th District to J. I. Whitaker

Emeline Collins, the widow' share of gross estate

H. T. Robinson in right of his wife's share of the gross

J. F. Hawkins in right of his wife's share of the gross

7 minor children of the deceased: John A. F. Hawkins, Gdn of said minors, to-wit: M. A. E. Collins, R. D. Collins, Emily Collins, James A. Collins, Paschal Collins, Martha H. Collins and Elizabeth A. Collins, from time of appointment to Jan 1857.

Estate of Paschal Collins contd....

J. A. H. Collins, Gdn of M. A. E. Collins from the time of appointment to Jan 1859

J. A. F. Hawkins, Gdn of R. D. Collins to 1 Jan 1859

J. A. F. Hawkins, Gdn of Emily E. Collins from time of appointment to 1 Jan 1859

J. A. F. Hawkins, Gdn of James A. Collins from time of appointment to 1 Jan 1859

John A. F. Hawkins, Gdn of Paschal Collins from the time of appointment to Jan 1859

J. A. F. Hawkins, Gdn of Martha H. Collins from time of appointment to 1 Jan 1859

Receipts from Emily Collins (x, her mark) for her share of estate given tp 31 Dec 1859.

Receipt from L. D. Haisten for his distributive share of Paschal E. Collins. 31 Dec 1858.
Received of J. A. F. Hawkins, as former Gdn of James A. Collins, M. A. E. Collins, R. S. COllins, Emily A. Collins, Paschal COllins, Martin H. Collins, the same of $1353, being their distributive share of (the children) the minor children of Paschal E. Collins.... this 25 Jan 1859. /s/John I. Whitaker.

Recorded: 4 Mar 1859

Inventory and Sale of the Land Belonging to the Estate of William Bray, decd, Sold on first Tues. in Feb 1858
Page 672

One lot of Land No. 153 in 13th District of Fayette Co. and bought by Syntha Bray.
Recorded: 15 Mar 1859

Parker Eason, Gdn for William S. Milner, Orphan of Pitt W. Milner, decd, in Account Current to 31 Dec 1858 inclusive
Page 673-674

To cash paid - J. J. Davis (tuition)
Filed: 17 Jan 1859. Recorded: 6 May 1857

Estate of Silas G. Eastin in Account Current with John B. Allen, Admr, from 1 Jan 1858 to 31 Dec 1858
Page 674-676

6 vouchers. Filed: 22 Jan 1859. Recorded: 6 Ma 1859

Estate of Avington B. Williams, decd by James B. Williams, Admr
Page 676-677

To cash paid - Andrew R. Moore, atty at law for a Fi.Fa. of Avington B. Williams, decd, $25.00 against William R. Mosby for the Estate, 4 Feb 1858
Recorded: 6 May 1859

Estate of Moses Williams, decd, in Account CUrrent with James H. Williams, Exr, from 31 Dec 1856 to 3 Feb 1859, the date of Settlement
Page 677

To cash paid - John McDonald, Gdn, A. M. Reeves (legatee), A. R. Moore, atty, Tidwell & Wooten.

Martha Thompson, minor of Allen Thompason in Account Current with John S. Holliday frn 1 Jan 1857 to 31 Dec
Page 677-679

4 vouchers.

John S. Holliday, Gdn for Martha Thompson
Page 681-683

2 vouchers. Recorded: 6 May 1859

Estate of George M. Yates in Account CUrrent with Mathew Yates, Admr, from 31 Dec 1856 to present date, 27 Jan 1859
Page 683-685

5 vouchers. To cash paid - Robert Holliday, Q. L. Summers, B. W. Brassell, George W. Ware, B. F. Fortson.
Filed: 29 Jan 1859.

An Account Current with Peter E. McLeroy, Admr of James McLeroy, (LWT), from time of appointment to 31 Dec 1858
Page 685-689

11 vouchers. To cash paid - the Editor of *The Jeffersonian*, 1857-1858 taxes, William Bradley (for coffin).

Negroes - girl, Louisa, to Gaskey Compton
        girl, Ann, to Rhoda A. Eason
        woman, Matilda to Rhoda A. Eason
To negro man, Colbert, given to the widow
To woman, Martha
To girl child, Sarah
To boy, Billy
To 150 acres of land with 50 acres given by the LWT to Peter E. McLeroy
To woman, Matilda, willed to Polly Jones
30 acres of land given by Will to Peter E. McLeroy, his part
Girl, Jane, which by the LWT to Mary McLeroy.

Recorded: 6 May 1859

Estate of Christopher Cline in Account Current with Perry Hicks, Admr, from 1 Jan 1858 to 14 Feb 1859 inclusive
Page 689-695

20 vouchers. To cash paid - Peter Knight, Howell Hubbard, Mathews & Edmondson, R. C. Bridges, E. E. Bennett, Franfcis Morgan, T. C. Mathews, S. Pate, L. D. Padgett, R. E. Bridges, Holliday & Ware, A. Gray & Harris, D. Hicks, Benjamin Gray, Q. C. Grice, J. L. Blalock, etc.
Recorded: 10 May 1859

Estate of Windom West, decd, in Account Current with Britton West, one of the Exrs, from 10 May 1858 to 10 Feb 1859 inclusive
Page 695-701

18 vouchers. To cash paid - G. W. Ray, Ann Jane West, G. W. Silvey, William Glass, A. S. Foster & Co., Smith & Silvey, Camp & Christian, C. Gorman, M. L. Yates, McKown & Strickland, Z. B. Blalock, Camp & Christian, John S. Wilkson, B. B. Dukes, J. P., and Tidwell & Wooton.

Recorded: 11 May 1859

A Statement and Account Current with Lucy Ann Smith, Executrix of LWT of Johnathan Smith, late of Fayette Co., decd, from her appointment to 1 Jan 1859
Page 701-709

29 vouchers. To cash paid - William S. Harnandex, Gay & Harris, John W. Smith, Silas Ceggans, J. A. and J. C. Banks, Willis M. Bishop, J. A. Bucks, J. W. Smith, W. Bowls (tuition), I. B. Williamsn, J. W. Smith, Josiah Pyron, etc.

Recorded: 12 May 1859

Estate of Joshua Callaway, decd, in Account with William E. Tucker, Admr, from 1 Jan to 31 Dec 1858 inclusive
Page 709-711

4 vouchers.

An Account Current with George Creel, Admr of Estate of William Bray, decd, from 1 Jan 1858 to 31 Dec 1858 inclusive
Page 712-716

11 vouchers. To cash paid - R. K. Holliday, Edward M. Taliaferro, David Hanes, J. L. Brassell, atty, J. B. Cook, Willis Beavers, Marion H. Sherling, Westley Scales.

Filed: 15 Mar 1859.

Estate of Miles Norton, decd, in Account Current with William F. Eason, Admr, from time of Admn up to 31 Dec 1858 inclusive
Page 717-723

20 vouchers. To cash paid - T. M. Jones, C. E. Bennett, David Barintine, John C. Nash, May Waldroup, Dorsey & Humphrey, Holliday & Ware, Peter Turner, W. W. Bosworth, Blalock & Bros., R. Denman, J. L. Blalock, William H. Blalock, Benjamin Norton, Tidwell & Wooten, L. F. Blalock, Admr.

By amount of Sale Bill of personal property of Miles Norton, decd and rent of land, which property was sold 17 Dec 1857.
By amount received on Dennis Stubbs' note
By amount received on Turentine Norton's note
Of land in Fayette Co. which land is contained in inventory
By amount received of sale of 40 acres of land in Spalding Co., as contained in inventory
By one negro as contained in inventory

Filed: 9 Mar 1859. Recorded: 18 Mar 1859

An Account Current and Final Settlement of Allen Reeves, as Admr of Estate of William Reeves, decd, to 31 Dec 1858
Page 724-729

To cash paid -
Martha A. Reeves, widow, for boarding children
Jason Castleberry
I. J. Ray, Clerk, Superior Court of Crawford Co., in a case of Allen Reeves, Admr. vs. Terrell A. Jackson
W. Poe, atty in the above case
William B. Miller, legatee
J. H. Starr, legatee
M. A. Reeves, widow
M. A. Reeves, Gdn of minor distributees

The Estate of Allen Jinnings, decd, in Account Current with William Jinnings, Admr, from 1 Jan 1856 to 31 Dec 1858
Page 730-736

To cash paid - Mrs. Craig, Thomas Jinnings, M. W. Swanson, Reuben Millsaps and William Jinnings (legatee).

William Craig received in lifetime of testator, negroes
A. M. Parker received in lifetime of testator (money), negroes, etc.

Recorded: 20 May 1859

An Account Current with Jesse T. Anthony and Rowland Hutcherson, Admrs of the Estate of Rowland Hutcherson from time of appointment to 1 Mar 1859
Page 737-740

14 vouchers. To cash paid - W. E. C. Jones, William McConnell, Polly Anthony, J. M. Huie, Willis Beavers, W. Scales, Huie & Connor.

Amount of estate to be divided into 8 shares -

Joseph R. Bitterton, in right of his wife, Nancy
M. A. Hutcherson
Mary M. Hutcherson, widow
Mary M. Hutcherson, Gdn of Polly, Ladson, Rowland M., Leander C. and George M. L. Hutcherson

Recorded: 24 May 1859

An Inventory and Sale of the Real Estate Belonging to the Estate of John Palmer, decd, Sold on first Tues. in Nov 1857
Page 740-744

102 1/2 acres off of Lot No. 116 in 7th District of Fayette Co. bought by J. M. Palmer
202 1/2 acres, Lot No. 107 in the 7th District of Fayette Co. bought by J. M. Palmer
Recorded: 24 May 1859

William M. Whitlow, Orphan of Warren Whitlow, decd, in Account Current with Benjamin Dykes, Gdn, from 1 Jan 1858 to 1 Jan 1859 inclusive
Page 745-747

5 vouchers. To cash paid - Byrom & Myers, J. S. and J. M. Rial, P. H. Brassell
Filed: 3 May 1859

Sale of the Perishable Property of Howell Vaughn sold on an Audit until 31 Dec 1858
Page 748-749

Among purchasers - Elizabeth Vaughn, T. H. Horn, T. L. Duffell, W. J. Jones, Marcus Varner, Benjamin Vaughn, John Bowers, W. O. Duffell, Allen Reeves, J. H. Harrell, Charles Jones, etc.

Hugh Porter, Gdn of S. T. Roberts from 1 Jan 1858 to 31 Dec 1858 inclusive
Page 750-753

3 vouchers. Filed: 24 May 1859

Richard P. Ware, minor or George Ware, in Account Current with Mildred Ware, Gdn, from 1 Jan 1858 to 31 Dec 1858
Page 754

3 vouchers. Filed: 11 May 1859. Recorded: 8 Jul 1859

Ann E. Ware, minor of George Ware, decd, in Account Current with Mildred Ware, Gdn, from 1 Jan 1858 to 31 Dec 1858
Page 755-757

5 vouchers. Filed: 11 May 1859. Recorded: 8 Jul 1859

Sarah J. Elkins, minor child of James Elkins, in Account Current with C. E. Bennett, Gdn, from the date of his Letters of Guardianship to 31 Dec 1857 inclusive
Page 758-759

To cash paid - C. E. Bennett, James Floyd, James Elkins (legatee), William T. Elkins (legatee), Susan A. Elkins (legatee), C. E. Bennett, Gdn for Ann Elkins, Emeline Elkins, Elizabeth Elkins.
Filed: 6 May 1859.

An Account Current with C.E. Bennett, Admr of Sarah J. Elkins, decd, from time of his appointment to 31 Dec 1858
Page 759-761

Heirs receipts given to C. E. Bennett, Admr of Estate of Sarah Jane Elkins, decd, as follows:

Receipt from James Elkins (x, his mark) 4 May 1857 for his distributive share of his daughter's estate.
Receipt from William T. Elkins in fulll for his distributive share of Estate of Sarah J. Elkins, 9 May 1859

Receipt of Susan A. Elkins for her distributive share of Estate of Sarah Elkins, 9 May 1859

Receipt of C. E. Bennett, Gdn of Thomas Elkins, for his distributive share of Estate of Sarah Elkins, 9 May 1859

Estate of Sarah J. Elkins contd....

Receipt of C. E. Bennett, Gdn of Emeline Elkins, for her distributive share of Estate of Sarah Elkins, 9 May 1859

Receipt of C. E. Bennett, Gdn of Elizabeth A. Elkins, for her distributive share of Estate of Sarah Elkins, 9 May 1859

Receipt of George Tankersly (x, his mark), in right of his wife Mary E. Tankersly, for her part of distributive share of Estate of Sarah Elkins, Mary E. Tankersly being formerly Mary E. Elkins, 9 May 1859.

Recorded: 9 Jul 1859

C. E. Bennett in an Account with Eliza F.Wilkins as her Gdn from 31 Dec 1857 to 31 Dec 1858
Page 762

3 vouchers. Recorded: 9 Jul 1859

An Account Current with C. E. Bennett, Gdn of Mary E. Elkins from 31 Dec 1857 to 14 May 1859
Page 763-764

6 vouchers (includes Ordinary for final Return).
Voucher #6. Received of C. E. Bennett $183.04 in full of the amount received from the Estate of grandfather, Curie? Johnson, decd, by the said Bennett as Gdn of my wife, Mary E. Elkins formerly, now Mary E. Tankersly, 14 May 1859. /s/George Tankersly (x, his mark)

Recorded: 9 Jul 1859

An Account Current with C. E. Bennett, Gdn of Emeline Elkins, from 31 Dec 1857 to 31 Dec 1858
Page 764-765

3 vouchers. Recorded: 9 Jul 1859

An Account Current with C. E. Bennett, Gdn of Thomas W. Elkins from 31 Dec 1857 to 31 Dec 1858
Page 765-766

Filed: 6 May 1859. Recorded: 9 Jul 1859

Estate of William S. Allen, decd, in Account Current with William N. McConnell, Admr, from date of his Letters to 1 Jun 1859 inclusive
Page 766-767

Filed: 1 Jun 1859. Recorded: 11 Jul 1859

Mary M. Cavender, minor Orphan of Wade H. Cavender, decd, in Account Current with Delilah Moses, Gdn, from 1 Jan to 31 Dec 1858 inclusive
Page 767-768

3 vouchers. Filed: 11 May 1859. Recorded: 11 May 1859

Phillip B. Moses, minor orphan of Hiram Moses, decd, in Account Current with Delilah Moses, Gdn, from 1 Jan to 31 Dec 1858 inclusive
Page 769

Filed: 19 May 1859. Recorded: 11 Jul 1859

Hiram D. Moses, minor Orphan of Hiram Moses, decd, in Account Current with Delilah Moses, Gdn, from time of 1 Jan 1858 to 31 Dec 1858 inclusive
Page 770

2 vouchers. Filed: 19 May 1859. Recorded: 11 Jul 1859

Estate of William Miles, decd
Page 771

Georgia, Fayette Co.} We, the undersigned appointed by the Ordinary of Fayette Co. to assess a sum for the support and maintenance of the widow and children of William Miles for twelve months from the death of William Miles......this 6 Jul 1859. /s/John Lester. /s/George W. Griffith. /s/C. M. Arnold
Recorded: 11 Jul 1859

Estate of Martin P. McEachern, decd
Page 772

Georgia, Fayette Co.} In obedience to an order of the Court of Ordinary to us directed, we do hereby certify that we have appraised the property of Martin P. McEachern, decd and that to allow andy children of deceased $90 of household furniture for use......, to-wit:.... (amount set apart for support)
/s/William Bradly
/s/L. B. Clark
/s/Charles J. Robinson, appraisers

Recorded: 12 Jul 1859

Russell G. Strickland, Orphan of Simon Strickland, decd, in Account Current with C.E. Bennett, Gdn, from 1 Jan 1858 to 31 Dec 1858 inclusive
Page 773

2 vouchers. Filed: 30 May 1859. Recorded: 23 Jul 1859

An Account Current with Jesse Barintine, Gdn of James Thompson from 1 Jan 1858 to 31 Dec 1858
Page 773-774

4 vouchers. Recorded: 25 Jul 1859

Morgan H., Orphan of James G. Christian, decd, in Account Current with G. F. Mann, Gdn, from 31 Dec 1857 to 31 Dec 1858
Page 775

3 vouchers. To cash paid H. Christian for tuition, boarding, etc.
Recorded: 25 Jul 1859

Sarah Ann, Orphan of James G. Christian, decd, in Account Current with G. F. Mann, Gdn, from 31 Dec 1857 to 31 Dec 1858
Page 775-776

3 vouchers. To cash paid H. C. Christian for board, tuition and clothing.
Recorded: 25 Jul 1859

Lucy J., Orphan of James G. Christian, decd, in Account Current with G. F. Mann, Gdn, from 31 Dec 1857 to 31 Dec 1858
Page 776-777

3 vouchers. To cash paid H. C. Christian for board, tuition, clothing.
Recorded: 25 Jul 1859

Claborn A., Orphan of James G. Christian, decd, in Account Current with G. F. Mann, Gdn, from 31 Dec 1857 to 31 Dec 1858
Page 777

3 vouchers. To cash paid H. C. Christian for board, clothing, tuition.
Recorded: 25 Jul 1859

END OF BOOK F

Fayette County Ordinary Mixed Records
Inventories, Appraisements, Sales and Returns
Book G (1859-1862)

Note: Book G begins with Page 49

A Statement of the Settlement of the Estate of Mary McLean with Exr of O. M. Pearson, decd, Showing the Amount of Estate after paying the debts and expenses and the amount due and paid to each heir
Page 49-55

4 vouchers.

Heirs, as follows:

Rachel Presley
Martha Moses
The Will gives up her share to John McLean and to Anne Pearson
John McLean
Anne Pearson

Amount paid by John I. Whitaker to children of John McLean

Oliver P. McLean
J. M. McLean
J. M. McLean, Gdn of Juan Francis, Sidney, William and Allison McLean, minor children of John McLean
U. U. McLean by J. M. McLean, Agent
John H. Harrell, in right of his wife
John McLean by O. P. McLean, Agent
James M. Pate
Leny Ward's 1/6th part of land
Miles Ward and Leny M. Ward
Elizabeth Reeves' share of land

Amount paid out by O. M. Pearson, former Admr -

William A. Smith
L. W. Presley
Allen Reeves, Gdn, in part of the distributive share of Oliver A. Reeves in the real estate of said decd as the minor children of Elizabeth Reeves, formerly Elizabeth McLean
William A. Smith, in right of his wife
L.W. Presley, in right of his wife, Rachael M. Presley
John Whitaker, Gdn
Mrs. Duffel's share of land
Martha Moses' share of land
A. J. Pollard, in right of his wife and gdn for 5 children
Callaway Walls, Gdn
Rachel M. Presley, specific legacy

Recorded: 12 Jul 1859

A Statement and Settlement of the Estate of Oliver McLean, decd, by John I. Whitaker, as Admr de bonis non from time of his appointment Showing a Full Settlement with the Heirs
Page 56-61

John McLean to his 10 children
O. P. McLean
J. M. McLean
J. M. McLean, Gdn for 3 children
U. U. McLean
J. M. McLean, Gdn for Juan Francis, Hardin Sidney and Allison McLean

Paid by John I. Whitaker, Admr -

C. P. McLean
J. M. McLean
J. M. McLean, Gdn of 4 children, Juan Francis, Hamden Sidney, William and Allison McLean
J. M. McLean, Agent for Oliver R. McLean
John McLean
John H. Harrell, in right of wife, Rachel
James M. Pate, Gdn for John W. Pate, an infant child of Miram L. Pate, formerly Miram L. McLane, now decd.

J. M. Brooks, in right of my wife, Rachel L. Duffell, now Rachel L. Brooks
W. O. Duffell
T. L. Duffell
Mrs. Duffell's share to her 5 children
Paid by James, Admr to W. O. Duffell
Paid John I. Whitaker, Admr of J. M. Brooks, in right of his wife
By James, Admr Record, page 289
W.A.Smith, in right of his wife, Mary A. Smith
Elizabeth Reeves' share to her 4 children
Paid William A. Smith, in right of his wife
By James, Admr Record, page 287
Paid L. W. Prestly, in right of his wife
Allen Reeves, Gdn of O. A. Reeves and Elizabeth Reeves
Ann Pearson
Miles Ward, in right of his wife, Linny Ward
John I. Whitaker, Gdn of Elizabeth Ann Reeves
Linny Ward's share paid by former Admr, Record 289
Martha Moses' share to 5 children
Paid by James, Admr to A. J. Pollard in right of his wife, Record, page 289
By John I. Whitaker, Admr, paid A. J. Pollard for 3 minor children of former Admr, Record page 289
A. J. Pollard for one of the children, (William N. Moses, minor son of Martha Moses, decd) the others being of age, by John I. Whitaker, Admr
A. J. Pollard, in right of his wife, Rachel M. Moses, now Rachel M. Pollard
Paid by J. I. Whitaker, Admr to J. B. F. Logan in right of one of the minors
Paid John L. Moses of age
Callaway Walls as Gdn of WilliamB. Walls, an infant child of Ann W. Walls, formerly Ann M. Moses, now decd, she being in her lifetime entitled to the 1/5th part of 1/6th share in said estate. (one of the grandchildren of Elizabeth S. Reeves (in the place of his mother)
J. B. Logan (x, his mark), in right of his wife, Mary Elizabeth Moses, now Mary Elizabeth Logan
John L. Moses
Filed: 20 May 1859

Estate of James W. Milner, decd, in Account Current with Young L. Wootton, Admr from the date of his Ltrs of Admn to 31 Dec 1858 inclusive
Page 62-73

26 vouchers. Filed: 24 May 1859. Recorded: 14 Jul 1859

Sophia Lasseter, minor orphan of Elisha Lasseter, in Account Current with James Hanes, Jr., Gdn, from 1 day of Jan 1858 to 31 Dec 1858 inclusive
Page 73-74

1 voucher. Recorded: 14 Jul 1859

Estate of Mason Gentry, decd, in Account Current with Killis Brown, Admr, for 1858
Page 74-76

8 vouchers. Recorded: 18 Jul 1859

Estate of Marcus Long, decd, in Account Current with Thomas Long and Susan Long, Admrs, from 31 day of Dec 1857 to 31 day of Dec 1858 inclusive
Page 77-79

17 vouchers.

Legatees as follows:

Nancy C. Long, widow
Marcus M. Long
William H. Long
Isham T. Long
J. B. Long
T. Y. Long
Thomas Long
J. B. Long, Gdn of Martha J. Long, minor

Recorded: 1 Jul 1859

Estate of William T. Bush, decd, in Account Current with John Bush from 1 Mar 1858 to 31 Dec inclusive
Page 80-86

20 vouchers.

To cash paid Heirs:

Mary Bush (x, her mark)
Mary Bush, Gdn for Mary E. and Sarah F. Bush, minor children

Filed: 7 Jun 1859. Recorded: 19 Jul 1859

Estate of Thomas Hales, in Account Current with Eli Edmondson and William Sibley, Exrs, from the time of their appointment up to 1st day of Jun 1859
Page 87-100

32 vouchers.
The following is a list of property willed to Susan G. hales by her husband, Thomas Hales, decd

Negroes - Isham, Minea (girl) and child Martha. /s/Susan Hales (x, her mark

Receipt from Joseph Hales (x, his mark) for one feather bed from the LWT.
Recorded: 20 Jul 1859

An Account Current with John M. Huie, as Admr of Lucy A. Hill, late of Fayette Co., decd, from the time of his appointment to 1 Jun 1859 inclusive
Page 100-107

14 vouchers. Recorded: 22 Jul 1859

Estate of Susannah West, decd, in Account Current with Rachel B. Humphrey, Admr, from the date of his Ltrs to 1 Jun 1859 inclusive
Page 108-111

8 vouchers.

Filed: 5 Jun 1859. Recorded: 22 Jul 1859

Estate of Joseph Scales in Account Current with Archabald Smith and Seaborn Smith, Admr from date of their Letters to 1st day of Jun 1859 inclusive
Page 111-116

14 vouchers. Martha M. Scales received 12 months' support as widow, for herself and children.
Recorded: 22 Jul 1859

John N. Brooks, Orphan of Ivey Brooks, decd, in Account Current with Robert Iverson, Gdn, from 1 Jun 1858 to 1 Jan 1859
Page 116-119

10 vouchers. Recorded: 27 Jul 1859

George N. Brooks, Orphan of Ivey Brooks, decd, in Account Current with Robert Iverson, Gdn, from 1 Jan 1858 to 1 Jan 1859
Page 119-123

12 vouchers. Recorded: 27 Jul 1859

An Account with Zadok Blalock Admr cum testamento annexed of Flora Sanders, decd from 1 Jan 1858 to 31 Dec 1859 inclusive
Page 124-125

7 vouchers.
Heirs receiving bequests: Edward Dodd, Young L. Wootton, and Fayetteville Baptist Church.
Recorded: 27 Jul 1859

An Account Current with Willis Beavers, as Gdn of Reuben M., Seppy, James T., Malinda, Eleanor and Sarah J. Lasseter, from 1 Jun 1858 to 31 May 1859 inclusive
Page 126-130

Filed: 24 Jun 1859. Recorded: 27 Jul 1859

Estate of Harbert Cook, decd, in Account Current with William N. Cook, Exr, from 31 Dec 1857 to 15 Jun 1859
Page 130-137

To amount on hand paid by the Exr (1855), see Record Book H, page 25. 19 vouchers.

Heirs -

Receipt of William Ballard, Gdn for Rebecca A. D. Cook, minor of Harbard Cook

Receipt of L. A. E. Cook (x, his mark), for his interest in the amount of $300 in Estate of Harbert Cook, his father.

James O. Cook (x, his mark)
William A. Crombie, as Gdn for Tempy Ann E. Cook
David D. Mims
Caleb M. Cook
John L. Ivey (x, his mark)
S. C. Cook (x, his mark)
William N. Cook
Joshua Cook
C. Y. Denson (x, his mark) and M. C. Denson (x, her mark)
Joshua A. Cook (x, his mark), Gdn for George M. C. Cook, minor and Thomas E. Cook, minor

Recorded: 28 Jul 1859

Mary Thompson, minor of Allen Thompson in Account Current with John Holliday, Gdn, from 1 Jan 1858 to 31 Dec 1858 inclusive
Page 137-138

4 vouchers. To cash paid - Holliday & Ware, James Bottoms, James Walker, and Blalock & Bros.
Recorded: 29 Jul 1859

Frederick Turner, Orphan of James Turner, decd, in Account Current with John O. Dickson, Gdn, from 1 Jan 1858 to 31 Dec 1858 inclusive
Page 139

2 vouchers. Recorded: 30 Jul 1859

Nathan Turner, Orphan of James Turner, decd, in Account Current with John O. Dickson, Gdn, from 1 Jan 1858 to 31 Dec 1858 inclusive
Page 139-140

2 vouchers. Recorded: 30 Jul 1859

Zachariah Turner, Orphan of James Turner, decd, in Account Current with John O. Dickson, Gdn, from 1 Jan 1858 to 31 Dec 1858 inclusive
Page 140-141

2 vouchers. Recorded: 30 Jul 1859

Sampson Turner, Orphan of James Turner, decd, in Account Current with John O. Dickson, Gdn, from 1 Jan 1858 to 31 Dec 1858 inclusive
Page 141-142

2 vouchers. Recorded: 30 Jul 1859

Thomas E. Loyd, Orphan of James Loyd, decd, in Account Current with John Loyd, Gdn, from 1 Jan 1858 to 31 Dec 1858 inclusive
Page 142-143

2 vouchers.Recorded: 10 Aug 1859

James E. H. Ware, minor, in Account Current with Burrell A. Ware, Gdn, from 1 Jan 1858 to 31 Dec 1858 inclusive
Page 143-144

6 vouchers. Filed: 1 Jun 1859. Recorded: 10 Aug 1859

In Account Current with Thomas C. Mathews, Gdn of M. L. Williams, Orphan of Avington B. Williams, from 1 Jul 1858 to 1 Jul 1859 inclusive
Page 145

4 vouchers.
Filed: 4 Jul 1859.

Thomas C. Mathews, Gdn of Marcus L. Williams, Orphan of Avington B. Williams
Page 146

Receipts from tax collector and J. A. Beeks.
Recorded: 10 Aug 1859

An Account Current with Simon T. Whitaker, Gdn of the minor children of B. F. Neal, decd, from 1 Jan 1858 to 31 Dec 1858 inclusive
Page 146-151

10 vouchers.
Filed: 1 Jul 1859. Recorded: 12 Aug 1859

An Account Current with John I. Whitaker, Exr of O. M. Pearson, decd, frm the time of his appointment to 1 Jul 1859
Page 151-156

17 vouchers.
Voucher #17. Received of John I. Whitaker, as Exr of O. M. Pearson, decd, $920.35, it being funds in the hands of said deceased at the time of his death belonging to the Estate of Oliver McLean, decd....this 1st Jul 1859. /s/John I. Whitaker, Admr de bonis non on the Estate of Oliver McLean, decd.
Filed: 1 Jul 1859. Recorded: 16 Aug 1859

An Account Current with Sterling J. Elder as Admr on the Estate of Thomas R. Pearson, decd, from 1 May 1858 to 1 May 1859 inclusive
Page 157-167

24 vouchers. By amount on hand May 1, 1858, see Record 566.
Recorded: 22 Aug 1859

Inventory and Appraisement of the Negroes Belonging to the Estate of Susannah West, late of Fayette Co., decd
Page 168

Appraisers: Richmond Dorman
L. F. Blalock
S. D. Dorsey

Negroes - Joshua, Ike, Jacob, John, Rhody
Recorded: 12 Oct 1859

Inventory and Appraisement of the Estate of William R. Wilkinson, decd
Page 168-170

Appraisers: Moze Hart, Robert W. Lee, Westly Turner, sworn 19 Jul 1859
Recorded: 12 Oct 1859

Elisha Lasseter, minor orphan of Elisha Lasseter, decd, in Account with James Hanes, Jr., Gdn from 31 Dec 1857 to 4 Jul 1859 inclusive
Page 170-171

2 vouchers. Recorded: 15 Oct 1859

A Statement of the Estate of Elisha Hill, decd, between the Exrs and Legatees showing first the gross estate and then the debts and Admn Expenses and the appraisement of the slaves....
Page 171-176

Debts of the Estate, see 1st Return 441.

Interest to John W. Hill as trustee to Mary Story and children
Interest to John W. Hill as trustee to Martha Lunsford and children
(Interest to the wife and children of Elias Story)
Calvin Story, one of the children of Elias Story
John Murphy, in right of his wife
A. J. Henderson, in right of his wife
Moses Hart, in right of his wife
Children of Elias Story

Paid Elias W. Story, Gdn of 5 children (vou. #15)
Paid Martha A. hoffman, one of the children (vou. #16)
Paid Lucinda Story, one of the children (vou. #17)
Paid E. W. Story, one of the children (vou. #18)
Paid Calvin Story, one of the children (vou. #19)

Recorded: 18 Oct 1859

Estate of Quiller Bearden, minor orphan of Edward Bearden, decd, in Account Current with William H. Blalock, Gdn, from 31 Dec 1856 to 30 Jun 1859 inclusive
Page 176-177

2 vouchers. Receipt from Quiller Bearden (x, hismark) for part of his distributive share as one of the legatees of the Estate of Edward Bearden, decd , 31 Dec 1857.
Recorded: 19 Oct 1859

Estate of Sarah Ann Bearden, Orphan of Edward Bearden, decd, in Account Current with William H. Blalock from 31 Dec 1856 to 31 Dec 1858
Page 177-178

3 vouchers. Filed: 30 Jun 1859. Recorded: 20 Oct 1859

Estate of Larkin Bearden, Orphan of Edward Bearden, decd, in Account Current with William H. Blalock from 31 Dec 1856 to 31 Dec 1858
Page 178-179

2 vouchers. Filed: 30 Jun 1859. Recorded: 20 Oct 1859

Estate of Asa J. Bearden, Orphan of Edward Bearden, decd, in Account Current with William H. Blalock from 31 Dec 1856 to 31 Dec 1858
Page 179-180

3 vouchers.
Filed: 30 Jun 1859. Recorded: 20 Oct 1859

Estate of Parthena Bearden, Orphan of Edward Bearden, decd, in Account Current with William H. Blalock from 31 Dec 1856 to 31 Dec 1858
Page 180-181

4 vouchers
Filed: 30 Jun 1859. Recorded: 20 Oct 1859

Estate of John Palmer, in Account Current with H. D. Palmer, Admr from 31 of Dec 1857 up to 31 of Dec 1858 inclusive
Page 181-182

3 vouchers.
Filed: 6 Jun 1859. Recorded: 12 Nov 1859

The Estate of John Watson in Account Current with Ellison Rush and H. D. Palmer, Admrs on said estate from their appointment to 1 Jun 1859
Page 183-199

47 vouchers. Fi. Fa. on Lot No. 77, 7th District, Fayette Co. as the property of John Watson, 20 Jan 1858.
Recorded: 26 Nov 1859.

Estate of Nathan Turner, in Account Current with John O. Dickson, Gdn, from 1 Jan 1859 to Oct 1859
Page 199

3 vouchers. Filed: 3 Oct 1859. Recorded: 23 Nov 1859

An Account Current with Martha A. Reeves, Gdn of Robert W. Reeves, minor child of William Reeves, decd, from 1 Jan 1858 to 31 Dec 1858 inclusive
Page 200

No vouchers. Recorded: 1 Jan 1859

An Account Current with Martha A. Reeves, Gdn of Amos W. Reeves, minor child of William Reeves, decd, from 1 Jan 1858 to 31 Dec 1858 inclusive
Page 200-201

1 voucher. Recorded: 1 Jan 1859

An Account Current with Martha A. Reeves, Gdn of William P. Reeves, minor child of William Reeves, decd, from 1 Jan 1858 to 31 Dec 1858
Page 201

1 voucher. Recorded: 1 Jan 1859

An Account Current with Martha A. Reeves, Gdn of Martha W. Reeves, orphan of William Reeves, decd, from 1 Jan 1858 to 31 Dec 1858
Page 201-203

6 vouchers. (for Returns and expenses) Recorded: 1 Jan 1859

Joseph H. Cavender, Orphan of Wade H. Cavender, decd, in Account Current with Phillip H. Brassell, Gdn, from 1st of Jan to 31 Dec 1858 inclusive
Page 203-206

5 vouchers. To cash paid - J. L. Blalock, Ordinary, Franklin Landrum, taxes, Jacob Elmore, teacher, and Jabe Brassell, Agent a/c, M. L. Keith

Recorded: 28 Nov 1859

William J. Jennings, Orphan of John A. Jennings, decd, in Account Current with Phillip H. Brassell, Gdn, from 1st Jan to 31 Dec 1858 inclusive
Page 206-209

10 vouchers. Recorded: 2 Nov 1859

James T. Jennings, minor orphan of John A. Jennings, decd, in Account Current with Phillip H. Brassell, Gdn, from 1st Jan to 31 Dec 1858 inclusive
Page 210-211

5 vouchers. Recorded: 2 Dec 1859

Mary Ann Jennings, minor orphan of John A. Jennings, decd, in Account Current with Phillip H. Brassell, Gdn, from 1st Jan to 31 Dec 1858 inclusive
Page 212-214

7 vouchers. Filed: 6 Jun 1859. Recorded: 2 Dec 1859

Roda E. Jennings, minor orphan of John A. Jennings, decd, in Account Current with Phillip H. Brassell, Gdn, from 1st Jan to 31 Dec 1858 inclusive
Page 214-217

8 vouchers. Receipt of James R. Jennings for boarding Roda.
Recorded: 10 Dec 1859

Wiley A., minor of Herod Pate, in Account Current with Herod Pate, Gdn, from 31 Dec 1845 to 31 Dec 1858 inclusive
Page 218

Includes expenses of dismission.
Filed: 6 Oct 1859. Recorded: 10 Dec 1859

Susan A. Milner, minor orphan of Pitt W. Milner, in Account Current with P. H. Allen, Gdn, from the 1st day of Jan 1858 to 31 day of Dec 1858 inclusive
Page 219-220

6 vouchers. To cash paid - Adaline M. Cowan, 1858 tax, Z. L. Wooton, atty, Hanes Key & Hanes, and W. C. Hanes.

Filed: 13 Aug 1859. Recorded: 10 Dec 1859

Estate of William N. Moses, in Account Current with A. J. Pollard, Gdn, from 31 of Dec 1857 to 15 Oct 1859 inclusive
Page 221-222

4 vouchers which include letters of dismission.
Filed: 15 Oct 1859. Recorded: 10 Dec 1859

An Account with Martha McLeroy, Gdn of Martha F., Peter L., Emily H. D. and Thomas McLeroy, minor children of Henry McLeroy, decd, from 1 Jan 1858 to 31 Dec 1858 inclusive
Page 222-223

2 vouchers, includes 1858 taxes.
Filed: 4 Jun 1859. Recorded: 10 Dec 1859

Estate of Robert Huie, in an Account Current with Robert C. Huie, decd, 31 Dec 1857 to 1 Jul 1859
Page 223-225

13 vouchers. Legatees: G. M. Millan, A. L. Huie, Mary Huie, Joseph Huie, James Huie, William M. Huie, John M. Huie, R. C. Huie.

Filed: 1 Jul 1859. Recorded: 10 Dec 1859

Estate of James Head, in Account Current with William T. Thurman, from 1st day of Mar 1858 to 1 Jun 1859 inclusive
Page 226-231

15 vouchers.
Filed: 1 Jun 1859. Recorded: 12 Dec 1859

Estate of William Stubbs, Jr., decd, in Account Current with Edward Connor, Admr, from the time of his appointment to the 1st of Jun 1859
Page 232-239

26 vouchers.

Legatee:

James J. Newton, in right of wife, Nancy J. Newton, formerly Nancy J. Stubbs, widow and relic of said William Stubbs, decd, receipt dated 30 Oct 1858

Estate of Eardly Norton, decd, in An Account Current with L. F. Blalock, Admr de bonis non from the date of his Letters to 1 Jun 1859 inclusive
Page 239-245

13 vouchers.

By amount received of sale of land, 100 acres, etc.

Fayette Inferior Court
John O. Brown, Admr
vs. Miles Norton, Admr of Eardly Norton, decd

Fi.Fa. ordered paid. Received 100 acres of land whereon Miles Newton's family lives in the 5th District of Fayette Co. adj. I. B. Avera and John Nash, 27 Feb 1858. /s/William Glass, Sheriff

Georgia, Fayette Co., Whereas, there is a matter of controversy between Elizabeth Barrentine and L.F. Blalock, Admr de bonis non on the Estate of Eardly Norton, decd relative to an open account which the said Elizabeth Barrentine claims to be due her from said Eardly Norton during his lifetime....$226.00.../s/J. L. Blalock, atty for Elizabeth Barrentine, Admr de bonis non on the Estate of Eardly Norton, decd.

The abouve account represents labor for Eardly Norton, washing, ironing clothes, etc. for 9 months. Arbitrators were appointed (L. W. Jones, W. W. Bosworth and H. F. Underwood), who awarded Elizabeth Barrentine $196.17.

Recorded: 15 Dec 1859

Estate of William N. Hill, decd, in Account Current with M. M. Tidwell, Exr, from the date of his Letters to 1 Jan 1859 inclusive
Page 246-247

Amount of sale of land and negroes...sold by M. M. Tidwell, Exr, this 2nd day of Nov 1858, the personal property having been sold by John W. Hill, temporary Admr, at the home of the plantation....

Rockaway sold to Virgil Swanson.

37 vouchers. (not included)

The Estate of Samuel R. Hobgood, decd, In Account Current with James L. Hobgood, Admr, from date of Letters to 31 Dec 1859 inclusive
Page 248-250

29 vouchers. Receipt from Adaline Cowan for boarding the children. Receipt from Mark Shipp for boarding himself and daughter, 1/6 of month. Receipt from Gary Davis for boarding daughter 4 wks.
Filed: 6 Jun 1859

Georgia, Fayette Co., Personally came before me., M. M. Tidwell, Exr of the LWT of William N. Hill, decd, who being sworn, says that the foregoing Return is true and correct.....6 Jun 1859. /s/M. M. Tidwell
Page 250-270

47 vouchers are recorded.
Recorded: 14 Dec 1859

William N. Hill, Gdn of Pitt W., James W. and Susan A. Milner, Orphans of Pitt W. Milner, decd, Current from Last Return to 25 Dec 1857 inclusive
Page 271-281

Voucher #5, Received of William N. Hill, my Gdn, $1143.09, it being the amount found to be due on settlement with him of all monies received by him from the Estate of my father, Pitt W. Milner and land father Pitt Milner, Sr., late of Monroe Co., decd. /s/James W. Milner

Voucher #6, Received of William N. Hill, my Gdn, $1167.89, it being the amount found to be due on settlement with him of all monies received by him from the Estate of my father, Pitt W. Milner and grandfather, Pitt W. Milner, Sr., late of Monroe Co. 29 Jun 1857. /s/Pitt W. Milner

Voucher #14, Received of William N. Hill, former Gdn of Susan A. Milner, orphan of Pitt W. Milner, decd, $846.00, it being the balance found to be due her on settlement of amounts received by said Hill from the Estate of Pitt W. Milner, late of Coosa Co., State of Alabama, decd, and (estate of) Pitt W. Milner, Sr., late of Monroe Co., Ga., decd..29 Jun 1857. /s/P. H. Allen, Gdn for Susan A. Milner.

Filed: 6 Jun 1859. Recorded: 15 Dec 1859

Marcus, Orphan of Thomas Herring, decd, in Account Current with William J. Russell, Gdn, from 1 Jan 1858 to 31 Dec inclusive
Page 282-283

3 vouchers. Filed: 1 Jun 1859. Recorded: 17 Jan 1860

Johnathan Herring, Orphan of Thomas Herring, decd, in Account Current with William J. Russell, Gdn, from 1 Jan 1858 to 31 Dec inclusive
Page 283-284

4 vouchers.
Filed: 1 Jun 1859. Recorded: 15 Feb 1860

Francis, Orphan of Thomas Herring, decd, in Account Current with William J. Russell, Gdn, from 1 Jan 1858 to 31 Dec inclusive
Page 285-286

5 vouchers. Filed: 1 Jun 1859. Recorded: 15 Feb 1860

Sale Bill of Estate of William R. Wilkinson, decd. Sold 30 Jul 1859
Page 287

Purchasers: Mary Wilkinson, William Bennett, William J. Wilkinson, Samuel Cox, J. T. Huie, Joel Lee, Moses Turner, G. J. Miles
Recorded: 16 Feb 1860

The Following is an inventory and Appraisement of the Estate of John A. McBride, late of Fayette Co., decd, as produced to us by Andrew McBride, Admr of said estate
Page 288-290

Appraisers: L. F. Blalock, M. M. Tidwell, T. R. Jones, sworn 8 Oct 1859
Recorded: 16 Feb 1860
Sale Bill of the Perishable Property. Primary purchasers: Mary McBride, Thos. Simpson, A. McBride, B. McBride, Benjamin McBride.

Inventory and Appraisement of the Estate of William Miles, decd, 2 Dec 1859
Page 290-291

Appraisers: C. M. Arnold, John Lester, G. W. Griffeth, sworn 2 Dec 1859
Recorded: 16 Feb 1860

Sale of the Real Estate of Joseph Scales, decd, late of Fayette Co., Sold on the 1st day of Jan 1860
Page 292

202 1/2 acres sold to Martha Scales
Negro boy, Anthony, sold to William Camp
Negro woman, Dianah, Jack and and Handy, sold to Martha Scales
Recorded: 16 Feb 1860

Georgia, Fayette Co., The Following is an Inventory and Appraisement of the Estate of Simon T. Whitaker, decd, 22 Dec 1859
Page 292-294

Negroes as follows:
Dan, Mon, Jesse, Martha, Marth, Mariah, Eliza, Emily, Mandy, Henry, Luisa, Betsy, Caroline.
Appraisers: Thomas B. Gay, William S. Sams, William Maleno, N. Milner, sworn 22 Dec 1857
Recorded: 16 Feb 1860

An Account of the Sale of the Personal Property of Simon T. Whitaker, decd, Sold at Public Outcry on 27th day of Dec 1859
Page 295-300

Among purchasers: George M. Crowder, Nathan Miller, William J. Grant, W. R. Whitaker, John I. Whitaker.
Sale of Negroes in Town of Fayetteville sold to highest bidder on first Tues. in Feb 1860 -
Martha, age 13 to William Glass
Juda, age 38 and child Betsy, age 4 to M. M. Tidwell
Amanda, age 9 to William Whitaker
Louisa, age 7 to M. M. Tidwell
Henry, age 5 to M. M. Tidwell
Martha, age 15 to Fanny Goodson
Eliza, age 15 to J. P. Shropshire
Recorded: 17 Feb 1860

Appraisement of the Estate of Charles Clements, decd
Page 300-303

Includes Negroes -
Jim, Ike, Anthony, Wenia, little Anthony, Jac, Toby, May and children (Hester and William), Nancy and child (Caroline), Julia and Lettia, Mandy and two children (Lezza and Mellia), Emily, Jane, Sterling, Easter

Appraisers: William J. Russell, Josiah H. Elder, Franklin Landrum, C. W. Smith, J. P. Shropshire sworn 12 Dec 1859
Recorded: 21 Feb 1860

Inventory and Appraisement of the Estate of Thomas Johnson, late of said county
Page 304-305

Appraisers: J. P. Shropshire, William Head, John Faver, William Watson, Hardazway Smith, sworn 25 Nov 1859
Recorded: 20 Feb 1860

Sale Bill of Charles Clements Sold 9 Jan 1860
Page 305-306

Recorded: 23 Feb 1860

James Thompson, minor of Allen Thompson, in Account Current with Jesse Barrintine, Gdn, from 31 Dec 1858 to 1 of Dec 1859 inclusive
Page 307

3 vouchers. Recorded: 28 Feb 18560

The Estate of William P. King, decd, in Account Current with Thomas J. King, Admr, from the time of appointment to 30 Dec 1859 inclusive
Page 308-312

12 vouchers. Includes notes of Thomas J. King, and Fi Fas. of Thomas W. King and Morris Jacobs, T. L. Duffie, agent for Emily King
Filed: 30 Dec 1869. Recorded: 28 Feb 1860

Francis, Levi L. and Ichabod R. May, Orphans of Levi May, decd, in Account Current with Mary May, Gdn, from 30th Dec 1840 to 31 Dec 1859 inclusive
Page 312-313

4 vouchers. To cash paid - Francis M. May, Levi L. May and Mary May, Gdn, for part of the Estate.
Recorded: 29 Feb 1860

Estate of Silas G. Eastin, decd, in Account Current with John B. Allen, Admr from 1 Jan 1859 to 31 Dec 1859 inclusive
Page 314-316

7 vouchers. To cash paid - John B. Allen, Gdn for Margaret Eastin, etc.
To hire of boy, George, for 1859
To hire of boy, Simon, for 1859
To hire of girl, Lucy, for 1859
Filed: 19 Jan 1860. Recorded: 29 Feb 1860

Martha E. Whitlow, Orphan of Warren Whitlow, in Account Current with B. B. Dykes, Gdn, from the time of his appointment to 1 day of Jan 1860 inclusive
Page 317-319

8 vouchers

Letters of Guardianship were granted to B. B. Dykes as Gdn of Martha E. Whitlow, 6 Dec 1858. (date of receipt by clerk)
Recorded: 29 Feb 1860

William M. Whitlow, Orphan of Warren Whitlow, in Account Current with B. B. Dykes, Gdn, from 1 Jan 1859 to 1 Jan 1860 inclusive
Page 319-321

8 vouchers.
Filed: 16 Jan 1860. Recorded: 1 Mar 1860

The Estate of Holland Leopard in Account Current with Jeptha Landrum, Sr., Exr of said Estate from 31 Dec 1854 to 5 Sept 1859
Page 321-324

6 vouchers. To cash paid - Samuel Brown, Jesse H. Davis, A. W. Stone, James M. Calhoun, George C. King, and Jeptha Landrum, Admr of M. W. Cooper.

Judgment obtained in Coweta Co. Superior Court against Richard Roe and Holland. Ejector- tenant in possession of Lot of land, No. 147 in 7t Dist. of said county.
Recorded: 8 Mar 1860

Sale Bill of the Goods of Thomas Johnson, decd, Sold by Berry L. Johnson, Exr, on 6 Feb 1860
Page 324-325

Purchasers: W. P. Lainer, William Watson, T. J. Head, A. W. Blalock, J. P. Shropshire, R. E. Johnson, J. W. Johnson, C. O. Thomas.
Recorded: 25 Mar 1860

A List and Inventory and Appraise Bill of the Property of John T. Macky, decd, appraised on 22nd day of Nov 1859
Page 325-326

Negroes -
Leta and children, Manda, Eliza and child, Lola, Jim, Ben, Leroy, Rosa, Lila, Minerva, Harriet, Asbury, Jane, Julian, Abner, Cidney, Levin, Morgan, Clark, Ann, Mandy, Polly, Jefferson, Wash, Easter and child, Jane.

Appraisers: Demcy Brown, P. H. Smith, Edward Shepherd. sworn 22 Nov 1859
Recorded: 27 Mar 1860

Sale Bill of Perishable Property of John T. mackey, decd, Sold on 24th Nov 1859
Page 327

Purchasers: G. M. Page, I. P. Gay, Samuel Walker, F. F. Hunter, Will I. Hening, John W. Spear, F. M Lester, Samuel Loyd, E. W. Leach, Joseph F. Spear, Lovett Warren, Lewis Brooks and Solomon T. Bridges
Recorded: 30 Mar 1860

Estate of James M. Copeland, decd
Page 327-328

William Alexander, Admr of } Bill to Marshal assets & c.
James M. Copeland, decd   } October Term 1858
vs.   }
Phineus Fillas and L. T. Doyal and others }

We, the jury, find and decree that William Alexander, Admr of Estate of James W. Copeland, decd, pay over to George M. Nolan, the auditor appointed at the last Term of Court the assets belonging to the Estate of James W. Copeland and said auditor shall pay over to creditors and assets according to the dignity of their debts..... /s/Andrew J. Glass, Foreman.

Recorded: 5 Mar 1860

Inventory and Appraisement of the Estate of James W. Copeland, decd
Page 328-329

Jonesboro, Ga. Appraisers: Young L. Wooton, Robert H. Holliday, Landford Johnson, sworn 15 Mar 1856
Recorded: 30 Mar 1860

Sale of personal property sold to - David T. Copeland, John P. Copeland, Robert H. Holliday, Eli Copeland, William Copeland, D. F. Copeland, Willis M. Copeland, James Antony, William M. Connell and William Copeland.

Recorded: 30 Mar 1860

Estate of Elbert Bishop, decd, in Account Current with Jesse Hubbard, Admr, from 1 day of Jan 1859 to 31 day of Dec 1859 inclusive
Page 329-330

Filed: 13 Feb 1860. Recorded: 5 Apr 1860

Estate of Elizabeth A. Reeves, minor child of Allen Reeves, in Account Current with John I. Whitaker, her gdn, from 1 Jan 1859 to 31 Dec 1859 inclusive
Page 330-331

3 vouchers.

By amount of legacy received from Estate of Mary McLain
By amount of legacy received from Estate of Oliver McLain

Filed: 13 Feb 1860. Recorded: 5 Apr 1860

An Account Current with John I. Whitaker, as Gdn of M. H. Collins, one of the minor children of Paschal E. Collins, decd, from time of appointment to present showing a Final Settlement
Page 331-332

5 vouchers.
Heir receiving distributive shares - M. H. Collins
Recorded: 6 Apr 1860

In Account Current with John I. Whitaker, Gdn of James Collins, one of the minor children of Paschal E. Collins, decd, from the time of appointment to 1 Jan 1860
Page 333

3 vouchers. To cash paid E. Collins for 1869 board.
Filed: 6 Feb 1860

Recorded: 6 Apr 1860

In Account Current with John I. Whitaker, Gdn of Emiline Collins, one of the minor children of Paschal E. Collins, decd, from the time of appointment to 1 Jan 1860
Page 334

Voucher #1. Received of John I. Whitaker, Gdn of Emiline Collins....$26 for board and clothing for year 1859......./s/Emiline Collins (x, her mark)

Recorded: 6 Apr 1860

An Account Current with John I. Whitaker, Gdn of Michael A. Collins, one of the minor children of Paschal E. Collins, decd, from time of appointment to 1 Jan 1860
Page 335-336

Recorded: 6 Apr 1860

An Account Current with John I. Whitaker, Gdn of Paschal Collins, one of the minor children of Paschal E. Collins, decd, from time of appointment to 1 Jan 1860
Page 336-337

Filed: 6 Feb 1860
Recorded: 6 Apr 1860

James, Mary, John and Cynthia Thomas, minor children of John Thomas, in Account Current with James T. Thomas, Gdn, from date of his Letters to 31 Jan 1860 inclusive
Page 337-339

7 vouchers.
Recorded: 6 Apr 1860

Robert Hall, Idiot, in Account Current with W. W. Sibley, Gdn, from time of his appointment to 21 Feb 1860 inclusive
Page 339-340

8 vouchers.
Recorded: 6 Apr 1860

An Account Current and Final Settlement of the Estate of Sarah Stubbs, late of Fayette Co., decd, with S. T. Whitaker, Admr
Page 341-345

Equal division in 8 Shares, the shares of each $116.97, as follows -

1. M. H. Pitman
2. S. T. Whitaker
3. Rowland Stubbs
4. W. G. Lee
5. William Stubbs
6. Hubbard Stubbs
7. Dennis Stubbs
8. Allen Thompson's children

Jesse Barrington in right of wife
Jesse Barrington, Gdn of James Thompson
W. B. Fuller, Gdn of W. Thompson
Mathew Jones, Gdn of W. Thompson

Vou. #1, L. M. Earnest, Gdn for William M. and A. J. Pitman, their share of estate
Vou. #--, D. F. H. Walker for his share
Vou. #2, S. T. Whitaker for his share
Vou. #3, Rowland Stubbs for his share
Vou. #4, Isam L. Lee, Agent of William G. Lee, for his share

State of Alabama, Coosa Co., William G. Lee appoints Isam L. Lee as his Agent, 20 Dec 1859, to receive his share

State of Georgia, Fayette Co., James J. Newton, in right of his wife, Nancy, formerly Nancy Stubbs, ..."having sold and disposed of the entire balancve of the distributive share in Estate of Sarah Stubbs, decd, to which my wife, Nancy J. Newton, formerly Nancy J. Stubbs, widow of William Stubbs, decd, to Simon T. Whitaker, for consideration, the said Simon T. Whitaker is hereby fully authorized to receive any receipt the admr of Estate of said Sarah Stubbs for the same for me, and in my name. James J. Newton, 6 Dec 1858."

Receipts from heirs-

S. T. Whitaker, assignee of J. J.Newton, Hubbard Stubbs, Dennis Stubbs,Jesse Barrintine (x, his mark) in right of wife, Sarah E. Thompson, formerly Sarah E. Barrintine, and Jesse Barrintine, Gdn of James Thompson, Aaron L. Bottoms in right of his wife, Martha, John L. Holliday, for balance due May Thompson, one of legatees, and Matthew Jones, Gdn of William Thomson.

Filed: 29 Jun 1859. Recorded: 6 Apr 1860

Samuel T. W. Minor, Admr of Berry Norton, decd
Page 345-347

Georgia, Fayette Co., Court of Ordinary, March Term 1860, The petition of Samuel T. W. Minor, Admr of Berry Norton, decd, showeth that Berry Norton, late of said county, departed this life on or about the last of Oct 1859 and your petitioner has been appointed his Admr....Therefore he prays the court as the Act of 1856 requires to appoint discrete persons to set apart to the widow and children of Berry Norton the amount necessary to maintain and support...../s/Samuel T. W. Minor, Admr of Berry Norton

12 months support ordered By George C. King, Ordinary, appoints commissioners: Charles J. Robinson, Sr., Edmond Jackson, George H. Jackson, Charles Austin and Charlton Minor.
Recorded: 8 May 1860

Appraisement of Estate (follows).

Appraisement of the Estate of William Russell, decd, of Fayette Co.
Page 348-349

Appraisers: Matthew Yates, William W. Wilkins, Blackman Thornton, William F. Franklin, Nathan Eason, J. P., sworn 24 Feb 1860

Purchasers at Sale: J. H. Franklin, William Todd, Early Brown, Mabry Whaley, Mathew Yates, A. R. Graves, Blackman Thornton, E. P. Eastin and Frederick Glass.
Recorded: 8 May 1860

Rebecca A. P. Cook, minor orphan of Harbard Cook, in Account Current with William Ballard, Gdn, from time of appointment as Gdn up to 29th day of Feb 1860 inclusive
Page 349-351

10 vouchers. To cash paid Joshua Cook (x, his mark), former Gdn and to Seaborn J. West (x, his mark) a part of his legay in right of his wife, dated 24 Jun 1859.
Recorded: 8 May 1860

Thomas E. Loyd, Orphan of James Loyd, decd, in Account Current with John Loyd, Gdn, from 31 Dec 1858 to 31 Dec 1859, the date of settlement
Page 352-353

3 vouchers. Filed: 6 Mar 1860. Recorded: 8 May 1860

Thomas Elbert, Orphan of Harbard Cook, decd, in Account Current with Joshua A. Cook, Gdn, from time of his appointment to 1st day of Dec 1859 inclusive
Page 353

Filed: 6 Mar 1860. Recorded: 8 May 1860

George M. C., Orphan of Harbert Cook, decd, in Account Current with Joshua A. Cook, Gdn, from the time of his appointment up to 31st day of Dec 1859 inclusive
Page 354

2 vouchers. Recorded: 8 May 1860

Russell G. Strickland, Orphan of Simon Strickland, decd, in Account Current with C. E. Bennett, Gdn, from 31 Dec 1858 up to 1 Jul 1859, the date of settlement
Page 355-356

3 vouchers. Receipts for shares recd: B. G. Strickland, in full share of estate, and R. G. Strickland, in full share of estate.

Filed: 5 Apr 1860. Recorded: 9 May 1860

In Account Current with C. E. Bennett, Gdn of Thomas W. Elkins, from 31 Dec 1858 to 31 Dec 1859 inclusive
Page 356

1 vouchers. Recorded: 9 May 1860

Miss Emeline Elkins, in Account Current with C. E. Bennett, Gdn, from 31 Dec 1858 to 31 Dec 1859 inclusive
Page 357

1 voucher. Recorded: 9 May 1860

C. E. Bennett, in Account Current with Eliza T. Elkins, as Gdn, from 31st of Dec 1858 up to 31st Dec 1859 inclusive
Page 357-358

Recorded: 9 May 1860

Estate of John W. Pate, in Account Current with James M. Pate, Gdn, from date of his Letters to date, this 23 Mar 1860
Page 358-359

3 vouchers.
Filed: 23 Mar 1860. Recorded: 9 May 1860

Estate of William Bray, in Account Current with George Creal, Admr, from 1 Jan 1859 to 31 Mar 1860 inclusive
Page 359-362

9 vouchers. Receipt of Cynthia Bray (x, her mark) for boardding minor children of William Bray.
Filed: 31 Mar 1860. Recorded: 10 May 1860

Solomon T. Bridges, Admr, in Account with Estate of John W. Macky
Page 362-366

8 vouchers. Recorded: 10 May 1860

Sale Bill of the Perishable Property of William Miles, Sold on 8th Dec 1859
Page 366-369

Among purchasers: Burket Rentfrow, Agnes Miles, E. J. Miles, M. M. Tidwell, Daniel McLucas, G. F. Miles, Anna Chandler, etc.

Recorded: 12 May 1860

Appraisement and Inventory of the Estate of Daniel Mitchell, late of said county
Page 369-370

100 acres of land. Appraisers: W. W. Sibley, Loenzo Morgan, Perry Hicks, John B. Fitts, Levi B. Bowers, sworn 7 Apr 1860.

Recorded: 12 May 1860

Sale Bill of Negroes Belonging to the Estate of Susannah West, late of Fayette Co., decd, Sold on 1st Tues. in Feb 1860
Page 370

Joshua, age 21 sold to William Glass
Rhoda, age 38 sold to Nancy Stephens
Isaac, age 16 sold to S. T. W. Crow
Jacob, age 10 sold to Nancy Stephens
John, age 8 sold to James G. Smith

Recorded: 22 May 1860

The Estate of Sarah T. Roberts in Account Current with Hugh Porter as Gdn from 1 Jan 1859 to 31 Dec 1859 inclusive
Page 370-371

4 vouchers. Recorded: 22 May 1860

Estate of Griffin Roberts in Account Current with Hugh Porter, Gdn, from 31 Dec 1858 to 31 Dec 1859 inclusive
Page 372

2 vouchers. Recorded: 22 May 1860

The Estate of E. H. Roberts in Account Current with Hugh Porter, Gdn, from 31 Dec 1858 to 31 Dec 1859 inclusive
Page 373

2 vouchers. Recorded: 22 May 1860

Estate of James L. Roberts in Account Current with Hugh Porter, Gdn, from 31 Dec 1858 to 31 Dec 1859 inclusive
Page 373-374

2 vouchers. Filed: 12 Apr 1860. Recorded: 22 May 1860

Morgan (Mary) F., Orphan of James G. Christian, decd, in Account Current with G. F. Mann, Gdn, from 1 Jan 1859 to 31 Dec 1859 inclusive
Page 374-375

3 vouchers. Receipt of H. C. Christian for boarding.
Filed: 16 Apr 1860. Recorded: 22 May 1860

Lucy J. Christian, Orphan of James G. Christian, decd, in Account Current with Gideon F. Mann, Gdn, from 1 Jan 1859 to 31 Dec 1859 inclusive
Page 375-376

To cash paid Lucy J. Christian in full for her distributive share of her father, James G. Christian, 31 Dec 1859.
Recorded: 22 May 1860

Sarah Ann, Orphan of James G. Christian, decd, in Account Current with Gideon F. Mann, Gdn, from 31 Dec 1858 to 31 Dec 1859 inclusive
Page 376-377

2 vouchers. Recorded: 22 May 1860

Claborn A., Orphan of James G. Christian, decd, in Account Current with Gideon F. Mann, Gdn, from 1 Jan 1859 to 31 Dec 1859 inclusive
Page 377-378

3 vouchers. Receipt from H. C. Christian for boarding.
Recorded: 22 May 1860

Inventory and Sale of the Real Estate of Thomas D. Waldroup, decd, Sold on the first Tues. in Dec 1858....
Page 378

100 acres of land, the place whereon the testator resided sold to Jesse Banister

Inventory and Appraise Bill of Estate of Matilda Graves
Page 378-380

Appraisers: S. T. W. Minor, Charles J. Robinson, Minton Graves, Sr., Williamson Jenkins and Solomon D. Dorsey, sworn 14 Apr 1860.

Recorded: 7 Jun 1860.

A List of the Personal Property - among purchasers were: Vines Graves, R. Graves, Salena Graves, and F. Graves.
Recorded: 8 Jun 1860

Mary, Elizabeth and Sarah Frances Rush, minor orphans of William T. Rush, decd, in Account Current with Mary Jane Rush, Gdn, from date of her Letters to 31 Dec 1859 inclusive
Page 380

Filed: 24 Apr 1860. Recorded: 9 Jun 1860

An Account Current with Eli Edmondson and W. W. Sibby, Exrs of Thomas Hale, decd, from 1 Jun 1859 to 1 Jun 1860
Page 381-384

10 vouchers. To cash paid - James Bynes, legatee.
Filed: 1 May 1860. Recorded: 0 Jun 1860

William P. Chandler, Admr in Account Current on Estate of William Miles from date of his Letters to 1 day Jan 1860 Inclusive
Page 385-392

17 vouchers. Received bales of cotton.
Filed: 3 May 1860. Recorded: 13 Jun 1860

An Account Current with F. P. Jones, Admr of Daniel R. Gilmer, decd, from time of appointment to 8 May 1860 Showing Final Settlement of the Estate
Page 392-398

19 vouchers.
Heirs -
Joshua Dodson, Gdn of the minors of decd, viz: Leah S. C., Elizabeth A., William E., Samuel K. and Rebecca J. Gilmer, in full for their distributive share

Joshua A. Dodson, Admr of Helena M. Gilmer, widow and relic of Daniel Gilmer, in full for her distributive share of estate.
Recorded: 13 Jun 1860

Appraisement of the Estate of Berry Norton for the purpose of setting apart 12 months' support for support and use of the widow and children, on 9 Mar 1868
Page 399

Appraisers: Charles J. Robinson, Edmond Jackson, George H. Jackson
Recorded: 13 Jun 1860

Estate of Thomas Johnson in Account Current with Bery L. Johnson, Exr, from date of Letters to 12th day of May 1860 inclusive
Page 400-402

7 vouchers. Filed: 12 May 1860. Recorded: 18 Jun 1860

An Account Current with Martha A. Reeves, Gdn of Sarah Ann Reeves, Orphan of William Reeves, decd, from 1 Jan 1859 to 31 Dec 1859 inclusive
Page 402-403

Filed: 10 May 1860.

An Account Current with Martha A. Reeves, Gdn of Henry C. Reeves, Orphan of William Reeves, decd, from 1 Jan 1859 to 31 Dec 1859 inclusive
Page 403-404

Filed: 10 May 1860. Recorded: 18 Jun 1860

Joseph H. Cavender, minor orphan of Wade H. Cavender, decd, in Account Current with Phillip H. Brassell, Gdn, from 1 Jan to 31 Dec 1859 inclusive
Page 405-407

Vouchers. Recorded: 18 Jun 1860

Patrick H. Allen, Gdn in Account Current with Susan A. Milner, from 31 Dec 1858 to 31 Dec 1859 inclusive
Page 407-408

6 vouchers. Filed: 18 May 1860. Recorded: 18 Jun 1860

An Account Current with Sterling J. Elder, as Admr on Estate of Thomas R. Persons, decd, from 1 day of May 1859 to 1st day of May 1860 inclusive
Page 409-423

34 vouchers. Filed: 11 May 1860. Recorded: 20 Jun 1860

Philip B. Moses, Orphan of Hiram Moses, decd, in Account Current with Delila Moses, Gdn, from 1 Jan to 31 Dec 1859 inclusive
Page 423-424

3 vouchers. Recorded: 29 Jun 1860

Hiram D. Moses, Orphan of Hiram Moses, decd, in Account Current with Delila Moses, Gdn, from 1 Jan to 31 Dec 1859 inclusive
Page 424-425

3 vouchers. Recorded: 29 Jun 1860

Martha A. Cavender, minor orphan of Wade H. Cavender, decd, in Account Current with Delila Moses, Gdn, from 1 Jan to 31 Dec 1859 inclusive
Page 425-426

3 vouchers. Filed: 25 May 1860. Recorded: 29 Jun 1860

Return No. 2, Estate of James W. Milner, decd, in Account Current with Young L. Wooton, Admr, from 31 Dec 1858 to 1 Jun 1860 inclusive
Page 427-432

7 vouchers. Accounts and Notes due Estate follows.
Recorded: 6 Jul 1860

Estate of William B. Wootton, decd, in Account Current with Lucinda Wootton, Admx, from date of her Letters (Last Return) of 1st day of Jun 1860 inclusive
Page 433-435

11 vouchers. To cash paid - Wilson L. Wootton, legatee, F. M. Stephens and Elizabeth Stephens, legatees, William H. Wootton, legatee, Nancy L. Wootton, legatee, and Abraham Eason and Sarah Ann Eason (x, her mark), legatees.
Recorded: 6 Jul 1860

The Estate of Thomas D. Waldroup, decd, in Account Current with George W. Ware, one of the Admrs, from date of his Letters to 31 Dec 1859 inclusive
Page 435-436

1 voucher. Filed: 4 Jun 1860. Recorded: 6 Jul 1860

Estate of John Palmer, decd, in Account Current with H. D. Palmer, Admr, from the 31st day of Dec 1858 to 31st day of May 1861 inclusive
Page 436-437

4 vouchers. Recorded: 10 Jul 1860

Estate of Joseph Scales, decd, in Account Current with Archibald Smith and Seaborn Smith, Admrs, from 1 Jun 1859 to 1 Jun 1860 inclusive
Page 437-439

5 vouchers. Filed: 1 Jun 1860. Recorded: 10 Jul 1860

Estate of John A. McBride, decd, in Account Current with Andrew McBride, Admr, from date of his Letters of Admn to 1st day of Jun 1860 inclusive
Page 439-443

10 vouchers. Filed: 3 Jun 1860. Recorded: 10 Jul 1860

Estate of John Watson, decd, in Account Current with Ellison Rush and H. D. Palmer, Admrs, from 1st day of Jun 1859 to 1st Jun 1860 inclusive
Page 443-449

20 vouchers. To cash paid - Ellison Rush, etc.
Recorded: 10 Jul 1860

Estate of Harbert Cook, decd, in Account Current with William N. Cook, Exr, from 1 Jun 1859 to 1 Jun 1860
Page 449-453

19 vouchers. Legatees: J. L. Day, T.J. West, Temperance E. Cook, William N. Cook, Caleb Cook, Charles Kimberly, James A. Cook, Gdn, David D. Mims, J. A. Cook, Gdn, J. O. Cook by W. M. Cook, Joshua A. Cook by W. M. Cook, E. Y. Denson by W. N. Cook, W. A. J. Denson by W. N. Cook, Elizabeth Cook, Joshua A. Cook for George M. Cook.
Recorded: 12 Jul 1860

An Account Current with Willis Beavers, Gdn of Reubin M., Seppy, James T., Malinda, Elleanor and Sarah J. Lasseter, minor orphans of Jesse Lasseter, late of said county, decd, from 1 Jun 1859 to 31 May 1860 inclusive
Page 453-455

Recorded: 12 Jul 1860

Estate of Mason Gentry, decd, in Account Current with Willis Brown, Admr, from 31 Dec 1858 to 31 Dec 1859 inclusive
Page 456

Filed: 8 Jun 1860. Recorded: 12 Jul 1860

Estate of Susanah West, late of Fayette Co., decd, in Account Current with Richard B. Humphey, Admr, from 1st day of Jun to 1st day of Jun 1860 inclusive
Page 457-460

12 vouchers. Recorded: 12 Jul 1860

Mary Ann Jennings, minor orphan of John A. Jennings, decd, in Account Current with Phillip H. Brassell, Gdn, from 1 Jan to 31 Dec 1859 inclusive
Page 461-462

5 vouchers. Recorded: 23 Jul 1860

James T. Jennings, minor orphan of John A. Jennings, decd, in Account Current with Phillip H. Brassell, Gdn, from 1 Jan to 31 Dec 1859 inclusive
Page 463-464

5 vouchers. Recorded: 23 Jul 1860

Roda F. Jennings, minor orphan of John A. Jennings, decd, in Account Current with Phillip H. Brassell, Gdn, from 1 Jan to 31 Dec 1859 inclusive
Page 465-466

3 vouchers. Recorded: 23 Jul 1860

William J. Jennings, orphan of John A. Jennings, decd, in Account Current with Phillip H. Brassell, Gdn, from 1 Jan to 31 Dec 1859 inclusive
Page 467-469

6 vouchers. Recorded: 23 Jul 1860

John N. Brooks, Orphan of Ivey Brooks, decd, in Account Current with Robert Iverson, Gdn, from 1 Jan 1859 to 1 Jun 1860 inclusive
Page 469-471

8 vouchers. Recorded: 30 Jul 1860

George W. Brooks, Orphan of Ivey Brooks, decd, in Account Current with Robert Iverson, Gdn, from 1 Jun 1859 to 1 Jun 1860 inclusive
Page 471-473

9 vouchers. Recorded: 31 Jul 1860

James C. H. Ware, Orphan of George Ware, decd, in Account Current with Burrell A. Ware, Gdn, from 1 Jan 1859 to 31 Dec inclusive
Page 474-475

6 vouchers.
Recorded: 30 Jan 1860

Mary Thompson, minor in Account Current with John Holliday, Gdn, from 1 Jan 1859 to 31 Dec inclusive
Page 476-477

3 vouchers. Recorded: 20 Aug 1860

Richard P. Ware, Orphan of George Ware, decd, in Account Current with Mildred Ware, Gdn, from 1 Jan 1859 to 31 Dec inclusive
Page 477-478

4 vouchers. Filed: 29 Jun 1860. Recorded: 30 Aug 1860

Ann E. Ware, Orphan of George Ware, decd, in Account Current with Mildred Ware, Gdn, from 1 Jan 1859 to 31 Dec inclusive
Page 479-481

4 vouchers.
Recorded: 20 Aug 1860

Augustin C. Harden, minor of John Harden and C. A. Harden, in Account Current with Joshua Cannon, Gdn, from the date of Letters to 1 Jun 1860 inclusive
Page 481-482

4 vouchers. To cash paid - 1859 tax, P. M. Tidwell and Joshua Cannon.
Recorded: 20 Aug 1860

Estate of Wright Martin, decd, in Account Current with James L. Hobgood, Admr, from 1 Jan 1855 to 31 Dec 1859 inclusive
Page 482-483

No business. Recorded: 21 Aug 1860

An Account Current with Zadock Blalock as the Admr of Flora Sanders, decd, with the Will annexed from 1 Jun 1859 to 1 Jun 1860
Page 483-484

4 vouchers. Recorded: 21 Aug 1860

Estate of W. S. Allen, decd, in Account Current with W. N. McConnell, Admr, from 1 Jun 1859 to 1 Jun 1860 inclusive
Page 485-488

Georgia, Clayton Co...Received of William N. McConnell, Admr upon the Estate of W. S. Allen, decd, late of Louisiana, $370.00, it being for the purchase money of the underside of 1/4th interest of 150 acres of land belonging to said estate of said deceased, situated and being in the county of Clayton, originally Henry, known as Lots of Land Numbers 213 and 214, it being the interest of owners by Morris H. Allen, Whitmill Allen and James M. Allen, all of Loisiana, in the Estate of said William S. Allen, decd, the said $370 being in full and final settlement of all the demands that Morris H. Allen, Whitmill and James M. Allen have against the said William N. McConnell, Admr....this 4th Feb 1860. /s/P. H. Allen /s/J. C. Smith

Louisiana, Parish of Jackson. Morris H. Allen, Whitmill Allen and James M. Allen acknowledge receipt of $1200 being paid by Jeptha W.Stell for their interest in Morris Harris, also the death of William S. Allen, the above lots of land in 5th District of Clayton Co. (as above), 6 Dec 1869. /s/M. H. Allen, W. H. Allen, J. M. Allen and J. W. Stell.
Filed: 3 Jun 1860. Recorded: 21 Aug 1860

Estate of Eardley Norton, decd, in Account Current with Lewis F. Blalock, Admr de bonis non from 1 Jun 1859 to 19 Jun 1860 inclusive
Page 489-490

7 vouchers. To cash paid - J. L. Blalock, Westley Femer, Turentine Norton, W. F. Eason, E. H. Kerksey and wife, George C. King, Ordinary. Paid heirs for full distributive share - Turentine Norton, W. F. Eason and E. H. Kerksey and Mary Kerksey (x, her mark). Recorded: 21 Aug 1860

Parker Eason, Gdn of William S. Milner, Orphan of Pitt W. Milner, decd, in Account Current with said Estate, from 31 Dec 1858 to 2 Jul 1860 the date of settlement
Page 491-493

12 vouchers.
Filed: 2 Jul 1860. Recorded: 21 Aug 1860

Estate of William N. Hill, decd, in Account Current with M. M. Tidwell, Exr, from 1 Jun 1859 to 31 May 1860 inclusive
Page 494-498

12 vouchers. Recorded: 25 Aug 1860

Samuel B. Hobgood Estate brought from Page 248
Page 498-508

Vouchers 1-34. Heir receiving shares - Nancy Hobgood
Filed: 30 Jun 1860. Recorded: 28 Aug 1860

Estate of Howel Vaughan, decd, in Account Current with John S. Holliday and George W. Ware, Admrs, from date of their Letters to 31 Dec 1859
Page 509-520

29 vouchers. To cash paid - F. M. Harrell, Federal Union, Marcus Varner, John T. Huie, Edward Moore, P. H. Brassell, C. E. Bennett, Dorsey & Humphrey, Blalock & Bros., John Bowers, T. C. Mathews, Burket Rentfrow, Holliday & Ware, Elizabeth Vaughn, George C. King, C. C. O.,Benjamin Vaughan, William Jones, S. T. W. Minor, Abner D. Rogers, John Vaughan, Benjamin Vaughan, Cason Jones, J. M.Blalock, atty for William Bateman, Isam White, John T. Blankenship and John T. Blankenship, atty for Emeline Wheelis

Paid heirs for their distributive shares -
John Bowers
John Vaughan
Benjamin Vaughan (x, his mark)
Cason Jones
William Bateman, Gdn for Howel T. Bateman and David R. Bateman, minor children of Eliza Bateman (the only surviving children) daughter of Howel Vaughan, late of Fayette Co., decd (J. M. Blalock of Carroll Co., Ga. appointed atty to collect their share of estate).
John T. Blankenship (x, his mark) in right of his wife, Tempy, formerly Tempy Wheelis
John T. Blankenship as atty for Emeline Wheelis (power of atty from Coosa Co., Ala.)
Filed: 30 Jun 1860. Recorded: 29 Aug 1860

Estate of Wright Martin, decd, in Account Current with James L. Hobgood, Admr de bonis non with Will annexed from 1 Jan 1856 to 31 Dec 1859 inclusive
Page 520-528

20 vouchers. Filed: 30 Jun 1860. Recorded: 31 Aug 1860

Account with Martha McLeroy, Gdn of minor children of Henry McLeroy, decd, from 1 Jan 1859 to 1 Jan 1860 Showing a Final Settlement with Benjamin Travis, in right of his wife, Martha Travis, one of the minors
Page 529-529

3 vouchers. Receipt from B. M. Travis in right of his wife, Martha, 28 Dec 1859, for full distributive share of estate.
Recorded: 31 Aug 1860

Johnathan, Orphan of Thomas Herring, decd, in Account Current with William J. Russell, Gdn, from 31 Dec 1858 to time of dismission
Page 530

Payment in full of this Return and dismission. /s/George C.King, Ordinary. 30 Aug 1860
Recorded: 31 Aug 1860

Estate of James W. Head in an Account Current with William T. Thurman, Exr, from 1 Jun 1859 to 4 Aug 1860 inclusive
Page 531-535

Voucher #13. Received of William T. Thurman, Exr of LWT of James W. Head, decd, $475.94 in full of the entire balance of estate of James W. head which is in his hands as Exr of aforesaid, which amount I, this day received as the Gdn for the persons and property of Sarah Jane, Nancy AnnLaticia, Edna Ann Francina, Americus LaFayette and William Thomas Hammond Head, minor orphans of said James W. head, decd, this 6th Aug 1860. /s/William head, Gdn for said minors

Recorded: 28 Sept 860

An Account Current with John I. Whitaker and Willis R. Whitaker, as Exrs of Simon T. Whitaker, late of Fayette Co., decd, from time of appointment to 2 Jun 1860
Page 536-549

35 vouchers.
Filed: 23 Jun 1860. Recorded: 10 Oct 1860

K. D. Little in an Account Current with James W. Talley, Gdn, from 1 day Jan 1858 to 2 Jan 1860
Page 550-552

9 vouchers.
Filed: 2 Jan 1860. Recorded: 16 Nv 1860

In Account Current with John I. Whitaker as Exr of O. W. Pearson late of Fayette Co., decd, from 1 Jul 1859 to 1 Jun 1860, it being his Final Return and Settlement
Page 552-555

To cash paid - Franklin Landrum, 1859 taxes, Oliver M. Pearson, Thomas McMahon, and George D. King, Ordinary.
Filed: 23 Jun 1860. Recorded: 16 Nov 1860

Estate of George M. Yates in Account Current with Mathew Yates, Admr, from 29 Jan 1859 to 29 Jan 1860 inclusive
Page 555

See Record Book F, page 276 (effects of George M. Yates' children)
Filed: 6 Oct 1860. Recorded: 16 Nov 1860

Sophrona Jane and Emily Martha Yates, Orphans of George M. Yates, decd, in Account Current with Mathew Yates, from date of Letters to 31 Dec 1859 inclusive
Page 556

By amount received on James R. Phillips' note, it being money coming from their grandmother (to-wit, Elijah Cleckler's wife), etc.
Recorded: 16 Nov 1860

Francis, Orphan of Thomas Herring, decd, in Account Current with William J. Russell, Gdn, from 31 Dec 1858 to 31 Dec 1859 inclusive
Page 557-559

4 vouchers. Filed: 4 Jun 1860
Recorded: 27 Nov 1860

Marcus, Orphan of Thomas Herring, decd, in Account Current with William J. Russell, Gdn, from 31 Dec 1858 to 31 Dec 1859 inclusive
Page 559-561

4 vouchers. Filed: 4 Jun 1860. Recorded: 27 Nov 1860

Order from Fayette Co. Court of Ordinary to Distribute Estate of Charles Clements, decd
Page 561-562

8 Distributees, to-wit:
Margaret Clements, widow
L. F. Blalock
F. M. Lester
Martha A. Clements, minor child
Malissa E. Clements, minor child
William J. Clements, minor child
Minor children's interests were represented by Adam Clements, Gdn
F. M. Lester represented minor child, Roxey A. Clements

Division of negroes as follows -

Mandy and 2 children to L. F. Blalock, Gdn for Roxey A. Clements
Julia and her 2 children and Melia to F. M. Lester, Gdn of Miss Sarah Ann Clements
Nancy and child to Adam Clements, Gdn of W. J. Clements
Mary and 2 children and Tobe to Martha A. Clements
Emily and little Anthony to F. M. Lester
Big Anthony and Jane to L. F. Blalock, Gdn for Roxey A. Clements
Warren and Ike to Adam Clements, Gdn for Malissa E. Clements
Old man aged about 80 years and Jack, about 18 years old and Sterling, about 6 years old and Easter, about 3 years old to widow.
Recorded: 29 Nov 1860

Inventory and Appraisement Estate of Noah Smith, decd
Page 563

Appraisers: E. C. Busting, B. F. Harper, T. J. Head, sworn 30 Oct 1860
Recorded: 22 Dec 1860

Inventory and Sale of Estate of Noah Smith, decd
Page 565

Purchasers: E. C. Bustin, E. J. Jones, J. B. Smith, A. T. Smith (claim of), J. L. Hobgood, W. Watson, J. Edmondson. Recorded: 22 Dec 1860

Inventory and Sale of the Personal Property belonging to the Estate of Danville Mitchel, 13 Oct 1860
Page 564-565

Purchasers: R. J. Chappell, James House, J. A. Haisten, T. H. Bishop, J. J. Carison, Henry Mitchell, Henry Morris, John Hubbard, Thomas Edmondson, R. Iverson, Perry Hicks, Calvin Horton and Thomas Swan.
Recorded: 22 Dec 1860

Inventory and Appraisement of Estate of Daniel Brasentine, decd
Page 565-566

Appraisers: Isaac B. Avera, A. L. Bottoms, E. Sweat, David Dorman, R. W. Tarply, sworn 21 Dec 1860
Recorded: 22 Dec 1861

Account Current with Keziah Watterson, Admx on Estate of Daniel S. Watterson, decd, from 31 Dec 1854 to 1860 inclusive
Page 567-572

18 vouchers. Distribution of Negroes to -
R. S. Watterson, Lot No. 2
Kiziah Watterson, Lot No. 2
John T. Waldroup, Lot No. 3
James J. Christian, Lot No. 4
Mary D. Watterson, Lot No. 5
William S. C. Watterson, Lot No. 6

Vouchers #13-14, receipt of Kiziah Watterson (x, her mark) for distributive share of Mary D. Watterson and William C. Watterson, minor heirs of Daniel S. Watterson, decd.

Voucher #15, receipt of Kiziah Watterson, widow, for her share of estate.

Voucher #16, receipt of R. S. Watterson for his share of estate.

Voucher #17, receipt of James J. Christian for balance due him as legatee of estate

Voucher #18, receipt of J. T. Waldrop, for balance due him as legatee of estate.

State of Georgia, Clayton Co., Order from Court of Ordinary to make distribution of Estate, the same being the estate of Daniel S. Watterson, late of Fayette Co., decd, in the hands of Kiziah Watterson, Admx. to distributees - James J. Christian, John T. Waldrop, K. L. Watterson, M. D. Watterson and W. L. C. Watterson. /s/ A. J. Mundy, R. A. Brown, Jesse Ward, commissioners, dated 7 Feb 1860.
Receipts from above heirs follow.
Filed: 8 Dec 1860 Recorded: 31 Jan 1861

Estate of Asa I. Bearden, Orphan of Edward Bearden, decd, in Account Current with William H. Blalock, Gdn, from 31 Dec 1858 to 31 Dec 1859 inclusive
Page 572-573

3 vouchers. Recorded: 31 Jan 1861

Estate of Larkin Bearden, Orphan of Edward Bearden, decd, in Account Current with William H. Blalock, Gdn, from 31 Dec 1858 to 31 Dec 1859 inclusive
Page 573-574

Filed: 30 Jun 1860. Recorded: 31 Jan 1861

Estate of Sarah Ann Bearden, Orphan of Edward Bearden, decd, in Account Current with William H. Blalock, Gdn, from 31 Dec 1858 to 31 Dec 1859 inclusive
Page 574-575

Recorded: 31 Jan 1861

Sale Bill of the Personal Property of Charles Clements, decd, Sold 19 Nov
Page 575-580

Among purchasers: Miss Mary Clements, M. A. D. Clements, Elizabeth Farr, Rachel Davis, M. E. Clements, M. A. Clements.

Recorded: 31 Jan 1861

Inventory and Appraisement of Estate of Andrew J. Mims, decd
Page 580-582

Years support allotted to widow and children.
Recorded: 2 Feb 1861

Purchasers: Rice Eason, Harriet Mims, J. M. Austin, M. McKinney, Jasper Loyd, A. McEachern, W. P. Eason.

Inventory and Appraisement of Property Belonging to Estate of Minton Graves, decd
Page 583-585

Appraisers: Young L. Wootton, C. E. Bennett, J. L. Hobgood, sworn 25 Jan 1861
Recorded: 11 Feb 1861

Sale of personal property. Purchasers: C. E. Bennett, William Bradley, Mrs. A. Clarday, Martha Graves, Daniel McEachern, Lewis C. Smith, Samuel Marshman, L. C. Smith, James Austin, R. C. Ellington, John Huiel.

Recorded: 11 Feb 1861

Thomas Elbert, Orphan of Harbard Cook, decd, in Account Current with Joshua Cook, Gdn, from 31 Dec 1859 to 1 Jan 1861 inclusive
Page 586

Recorded: 16 Feb 1861

Estate of Danville Mitchel, in Account Current with Henry Mitchel, Exr of LWT of Danville Mitchel, decd, from date of his Letters to date inclusive, which Return is Final
Page 587-588

10 vouchers. Frances Mitchel (x, her mark) for specific articles due her.
Recorded: 16 Feb 1861

Sale Bill of Land Belonging to Estate of William Miles, Sold at Public Outcry on 7 Dec 1859 in Town of Fayetteville, Fayette Co., Ga.
Page 591

Lot No. 224 in 6th District of Fayette Co. bought by William Glass
W. half of Lot No. 93 in 6th District of Fayette Co. bought by P. E. Arnold
W. half of Lot No. 45 and W. half of Lot No. 20 in 5th District, Fayette Co. bought by W. B Jones

Recorded: 23 Feb 1861

Inventory and Appraisement of Thomas J. Milner, Lunatic
Page 591-595

Negroes - Adam, Elizabeth, Henry, Pup, Albert, Aaron, Frank, Charles, Eamon, Lewis.

Appraisers: Isaac B. Avera, Andrew McLucas, Johnathan Mitchel, sworn 28 Dec 1860

Sale Bill of Perishable Property - Among purchasers: Ben Fortson, J. P. Milner, T. H. Stephens, Howell Hubbard, Moses Turner, Solomon Sweat, etc.

Recorded: 25 Feb 1861

William Thompson, minor son of Allen Thompson, in Account Current with Mathew Jones, Gdn, from 31 Dec 1857 to 31 Dec 1860 inclusive
Page 595-597

7 vouchers. To cash paid - taxes for 1859 and 1860, B. G. Strickland, George C. King, Ordinary, Aaron Bottoms.

Recorded: 12 Apr 1866

M. E. Whitlow, Orphan of William Whitlow, decd, in Account with B. B. Dykes, Gdn, from 1 Jan 1860 to 1 Jan 1861 inclusive
Page 597-599

8 vouchers. John W. Culpepper paid tuition fees.
Recorded: 12 Apr 1861

W. M. Whitlow, Orphan of Warren Whitlow, in Account with B. B. Dykes, Gdn, from 1 Jan 1860 to 1 Jan 1861 inclusive
Page 599-601

Paid B. B. Dykes for board and clothing. 8 vouchers.
Filed: 11 Mar 1861. Recorded: 12 Apr 1861

Estate of William Miles in Account Current with William P. Chandler, Admr, from 1 Jan 1860 to 1 Jan 1861 inclusive
Page 601-602

3 vouchers. To amount paid James McBride, legatee (voucher #1). Recorded: 11 Apr 1861

Solomon T. Brides, Admr, in Account Current with Estate of John T. Mackey, decd, from 1 Jan 1860 to 6 Mar 1861 inclusive
Page 603-614

Includes vouchers 9-42.
Recorded: 17 Apr 1861

Appraisal of Negroes belonging to Estate of William Miles, decd
Page 615

Appraisers: William Glass, Willis R. Whitaker, C. M. Arnold, James M. Camp, John Lester, sworn 17 Dec 1859
Recorded: 13 May 1861

Negroes appraised and divided -

Drew, Jesse and Peggy to W. P. Chandler
Dick and Chany to Sarah Miles
Henny and Len to George J. Miles
Martha, Monroe and Liza to Cressa Miles
Jim and Fayette to John S. Miles
Ann and child and Andy to Burket Rentfrow
Tom, Caroline and Rhoda to W. B. Jones
Lewis and Ellen to James McBride

Sarah Jane, Nancy Ann Laticia, Edna Ann Francina, Americus Lafayette and William Thomas Thurmand Head, Orphans of James W. Head, decd, in Account Current with William head, Gdn, from time of his appointment to 1 Jan 1861 inclusive
Page 615-616

1 voucher. Recorded: 20 May 1861

Frederick Turner, Orphan of James Turner, decd, in Account Current with John O. Dickson, Gdn, from 31 Dec 1858 to 31 Dec 1860 inclusive
Page 616-617

5 vouchers. To cash paid Ann Turner (x, her mark) for board and clothing for 1859 and 1860 and John O. Dickson, Gdn.

Recorded: 20 May 1861

Zachariah Turner, Orphan of James Turner, decd, in Account Current with John O. Dickson, Gdn, from 31 Dec 1858 to 31 Dec 1860 inclusive
Page 618-619

Receipt of Ann Turner (x, her mark) for board and clothing 1859-1860.
Recorded: 20 May 1861

Sampson Turner, Orphan of James Turner, decd, in Account Current with John O. Dickson, Gdn, from 31 Dec 1858 to 31 Dec 1860 inclusive
Page 619-620

6 vouchers. To cash paid Ann Turner (x, her mark) for board and clothing 1859-1860
Filed: 12 Apr 1861. Recorded: 20 May 1861

An Account with John I. Whitaker, Gdn of Elizabeth A. Reeves, minor child of Allen Reeves, from 31 Jan 1859 to 31 Jan 1860 inclusive
Page 621

Recorded: 20 May 1861

An Account Current with John L Whitaker, Gdn of Emelina V. Collins, one of minor children of Paschal E. Collins, decd, from 1 Jan 1860 to 1 Jan 1861 inclusive
Page 621-622

2 vouchers. Filed: 25 Mar 1861. Recorded: 20 May 1861

An Account Current with John I. Whitaker, Gdn of Romalous Collins, one of the minor children of Paschal E. Collins, decd, from 1 Jan 1860 to 1 Jan 1861 inclusive
Page 622-623

2 vouchers.
Filed: 25 Mar 1861. Recorded: 20 May 1861

An Account Current with John I. Whitaker, Gdn of Michael A. Collins, one of the minor children of Paschal E. Collins, decd, from 1 Jan 1860 to 1 Jan 1861 inclusive
Page 623-624

2 vouchers. Filed: 25 Mar 1861. Recorded: 20 May 1861

An Account Current with John I. Whitaker, Gdn of James Collins, one of the minor children of Paschal E. Collins, decd, from 1 Jan 1860 to 1 Jan 1861 inclusive
Page 624-625

3 vouchers. Filed: 25 Mar 1861. Recorded: 20 May 1861

An Account Current with John I. Whitaker, Gdn of Paschal Collins, one of the minor children of Paschal E. Collins, decd, from 1 Jan 1860 to 1 Jan 1861 inclusive
Page 625-626

2 vouchers. To cash paid Emelina Collins (x, her mark) for board and clothing
Recorded: 20 May 1861

Inventory and Sale Bill of the Personal Property of David Barintine, decd, Sold on 29 Dec 1860
Page 626-628

Among purchasers - Mary Barintine, I. B. Avera, H. Stubbs, H. Clark, etc
Recorded: 7 Jun 1861

L. F. Blalock, Admr, in Account Current with Estate of Charles Clements, decd, from date of his Letters to 31 Mar 1861 inclusive
Page 629-674

116 vouchers
Recorded: 22 Jun 1861

The Following is the Sale of the Land and Negroes Belonging to Estate of John Watson, decd
Page 674

Lot No. 77, 7th District Fayette Co.
Negro woman, Ann and child
Negro boy, Huie
40 acres lot in Floyd Co.
40 acre lot in Paulding Co.
50 acres off the lot that the widow now lives on, this 25 Dec 1860

H. D. Palmer and Ellison Rush, Admr
Recorded: 22 Jun 1861

John L. Wilson, minor child of Washington Wilson, Gdn, from 31 Dec 1852 to 13 May 1861 inclusive
Page 675.

Recorded: 25 Jun 1861

Estate of Matilda Graves in Account Current with Vines Graves, Admr, from date of his appointment to 1 May 1861 inclusive
Page 576-678

7 vouchers.
Recorded: 25 Jun 1861

Estate of Thomas Johnson in Account Current with Berry L. Johnson, Exr, from 12 May 1860 to 12 May 1861 inclusive
Page 679-682

Filed: 23 May 1861. Recorded: 25 Jun 1861

Estate of Susanah West, late of Fayette Co., decd, in Account Current with Richard B. Humphrey, Admr, from 1 Jun 1860 to 1 May 1861 inclusive
Page 682-693

13 vouchers
Recorded: 29 Jun 1861

Estate of Elbert Bishop, decd, in Account Current with Jesse Hubbard, Admr, from 31 Dec 1859 to 31 Dec 1860 inclusive
Page 693

1 vouchers. Recorded: 18 Jul 1861

An Account Current with Eli Edmondson as Gdn of B. F. Neal from time of appointment to 1 Jun 1861
Page 694-695

6 vouchers. Recorded: 18 Jul 1861

In Account Current with Eli Edmondson, Gdn of Emily J. Neel from time of appointment to 1 Jun 1861
Page 696-697

To cash paid - Cole & Malone, Brassell & McLane, Henry Banks and Rachael Neel. (board and clothing)
Filed: 29 May 1861. Recorded: 18 Jul 161

An Account Current with Eli Edmondson, Gdn of B. P. Neel from time of appointment to 1 Jun 1861
Page 697-698

3 vouchers. To cash paid Henry Banks and Rachael Neel (board and clothing)
Filed: 29 May 1861. Recorded: 18 Jul 1861

An Account Current with Eli Edmondson, Gdn of George F. Neel from time of appointment to 1 Jun 1861
Page 699-700

3 vouchers. To cash paid Henry Banks and Rachael Neel (board and clothing)
Recorded: 18 Jul 1861

Hiram D. Moses, minor orphan of Hiram Moses, decd, in Account Current with Delila Moses as Gdn from 1 Jan to 31 Dec 1860 inclusive
Page 700-701

2 vouchers. Filed: 1 Jun 1861. Recorded: 19 Jul 1861

Phillip B. Moses, minor Orphan of Hiram D. Moses, decd, in Account Current with Delila Moses as Gdn from 1 Jan to 31 Dec 1860 inclusive
Page 701-702

2 vouchers. Filed: 1 Jun 1861. Recorded: 19 Jul 1861

Martha M. Cavender, minor orphan of Wade H. Cavender, decd, in Account Current with Delila Moses, Gdn, from 1 Jan to 31 Dec 1860 inclusive
Page 702-703

2 vouchers. Recorded: 19 Jul 1861

An Account Current with W. W. Sibley as Gdn of Robert Hale Idiot, from Jan 1860 to Jun 1861 inclusive
Page 703-705

4 vouchers. Filed: 3 Jun 1861. Recorded: 19 Jul 1861

An Account Current with Martha A. Reeves, Gdn of Sarah Ann Reeves, Orphan of William Reeves, decd from 31 Dec 1859 to 31 Dec 1860 inclusive
Page 706-708

Receipts from M. A. Reeves for boarding orphan
Filed: 8 Jun 1861. Recorded: 19 Jul 1861

Sophia F. Lasseter, minor orphan of Elisha Lasseter in Account Current with James Hanes, Jr., Gdn, from 31 Dec 1858 to 22 Apr 1861 inclusive
Page 708-709

3 vouchers. Recorded: 19 Jul 1861

An Account Current with C. E. Bennett as Gdn of Emeline Elkins from 31 Dec 1859 to 31 Dec 1860 inclusive
Page 709-711

4 vouchers.
Recorded: 7 Jul 1861

An Account Current with C. E. Bennett as Gdn of Eliza F. Elkins from 31 Dec 1859 to 31 Dec 1860 inclusive
Page 711-713

3 vouchers. Filed: 29 May 1861. Recorded: 19 Jul 1861

An Account Current with C. E. Bennett Gdn of Thomas W. Elkins from 1 Jan 1860 to 31 Dedc 1860 inclusive
Page 713-714

Filed: 29 May 1861
Recorded: 19Jul 1861

Estate of Moses Gentry in Account Current with Willis Brown, Admr, from 31 Dec 1859 to 31 Dec inclusive
Page 715

3 vouchers. Recorded: 25 Jul 1861

Estate of Wright Martin, decd, in Account Current with James Hobgood, Admr, from 1 Jan 1860 to 31 Dec 1860 inclusive
Page 716

1 vouchers Recorded: 25 Jul 1861

Estate of Samuel R. Hobgood in Account Current with James L. Hobgood, Admr, from 1 Jan to 31 Dec 1860 inclusive
Page 717

2 vouchers. Tocash paid - Franklin Landrum, tax collector, and Jane Landrum (x, her mark)
Recorded: 39 Jul 1861

Estate of Wright Martin, decd, in Account with James L. Hogbood, Admr de bonis non with Will annexed from 1 Jan to 31 Dec 1860 inclusive
Page 718-721

9 vouchers.
Filed: 12 Jun 1861. Recorded: 29 Jul 1861

Estate of Joseph Scales, decd, in Account Current with Archabal Smith and Seaborn Smith, Admrs, from 1 Jun 1860 to 29 May 1861 inclusive
Page 721-723

6 vouchers.

To cash paid - S. M. Scales, J. H. Morris (tax), Blalock & Jones, attys, Martha Scales, legatee, and Archabal Smith, Gdn for May, Martha and Josephine Scales.

Recorded: 29 Jul 1861

Crissa B. Miles, Orphan of William Miles, decd, in Account Current with M. M. Tidwell, her Gdn, from date of his Letters to 31 May 1861
Page 723-725, and Page 728-729

Amount received in the division of Estate, 3 Negroes, viz: Martha, Liza, Manson, Eliza.
Recorded: 29 jUL 1861

John D. Miles, Orphan of William Miles, decd, in Account Current with John S. Holliday, Gdn, from 1 Jan 1860 to 31 Dec 1860
Page 726

Filed: 28 Jun 1861. Recorded: 1 Aug 1861

Augustine E. Harden, minor of John Harden and C. A. Harden, in Account Current with Joshua Cannon, Gdn, from 1 Jun 1860 to 1 Jun 1861
Page 727

3 vouchers. Recorded: 14 Aug 1861

Morgan F., Orphan of James G. Christian, decd, in Account Current with G. F. Mann, Gdn, from 1 Jan 1860 to 31 Dec 1860 inclusive
Page 729

2 vouchers. Recorded: 1 Aug 1861

Claborn A., Orphan of James G. Christian, decd, in Account Current with Gideon F. Mann, from 31 Dec 1859 to 31 Dec 1860 inclusive
Page 730

2 vouchers. Recorded: 1 Aug 1861

Sarah Ann, Orphan of James G. Christian, decd, in Account Current with Gideon F. Mann, from 31 Dec 1859 to 31 Dec 1860 inclusive
Page 731

2 vouchers Recorded: 1 Aug 1861

Estate of Larkin Bearden in Account Current with William H. Blalock, Gdn, from 31 Dec 1859 to 31 Dec 1860 inclusive
Page 732

2 vouchers. Recorded: 1 Aug 1861

Asa I. Bearden, Orphan of Edward Bearden, decd, in Account Current with William H. Blalock, Gdn, from 31 Dec 1859 to 31 Dec 1860 inclusive
Page 733-734

3 vouchers. Recorded: 1 Aug 1861

Estate of Sarah Ann Bearden, Orphan of Edward Bearden, decd in Account Current with William H. Blalock, Gdn, from 31 Dec 1859 to 31 Dec 1860 inclusive
Page 734-735

4 vouchers. To cash paid - 1860 taxes, Frances Bearden (for boarding said ward) and Thomas J. Cochran (his distritutive share)

Recorded: 1 Aug 1861

An Account Current with Zadock Blalock as Admr of the Will annexed of Flora Landers, decd, from 1 Jun 1860 to 1 Jun 1861 inclusive
Page 735-736

3 vouchers.
Georgia, Fayette Co. To all and singular the constables Greeting. You are hereby commanded that of the goods and chattels, lands and tenements of Samuel T. Rhoads, you levy by distress and sale thereof sufficient to make $10.35....which was adjudged againsthim at a Justice Court held in and for the 624th District G. M. on the 8th day of May 1858 in favor of Zadock Blalock, Admr of Flora Sanders.../s/S. Adams, L. C.

Filed: 25 Jun 1861.. Recorded: 1 Aug 1861

The Estate of Alford Brown, decd, in Account Current with John O. Brown, Admr, from 1 Jan 1858 to 31 Dec 1860 inclusive
Page 737

Filed: 31 May 1861. Recorded: 1 Aug 1861

Estate of John Watson, decd, in Account Current with Ellison Rush and H. D. Palmer, Admr from 1 Jun 1860 to 1 Jun 1861 inclusive
Page 738-739

Filed: 22 Jun 1861. Recorded: 1 Aug 1861

Estate of Thomas D. Waldroup, decd, in Account Current with George W. Ware, one of the Admrs, from 31 Dec 1859 to 31 Dec 1860 inclusive
Page 739-740

4 vouchers. To cash paid - George C. King, Ordinary, T. Waldroup, legatee, Sherod H. Gay, legatee and James H. Waldroup, legatee.

Recorded: 1 Aug 1861

John H. Cavender, minor orphan of Wade H. Cavender, decd, in Account Current with Phillip H. Brassell, Gdn, from 1 Jan to 31 Dec 1860 inclusive
Page 740-742

5 vouchers. Filed: 19 Jun 1961. Recorded: 12 Aug 1861

Joseph H. Cavender, minor orphan of Wade H. Cavender, decd, in Account Current with Phillip H. Brassell, Gdn, from 1 Jan to 31 Dec 1860 inclusive
Page 742-743

5 vouchers. Recorded: 17 Aug 1861

Mary Ann Jennings, alias Mary Ann Harvey, minor orphan of John A. Jennings, decd, in Account Current with Phillip H. Brassell, Gdn, from 1 Jan 1860 to 1 Jan 1861 inclusive
Page 744-757

7 vouchers. Voucher #7. Received of Phillip H. Brassell, Gdn for Mary Ann Jennings alias Mary Ann Harveny......$279.74 in full of said minor orphan's pro-rata share of the debt on which the foregoing bill was furnished, it being 1/5th part of the principal interest and cost of said debt.....ced at Fairburn, Ga. 31 May 1861.

Z. B. Blalock vs. Sarah F. Jennings and James Jennings Original but James R. Jennings Surviving defendant in Fi.Fa., Campbell Superior Court, Feb Term 1861. Received of James R. Jennings, defendant.....in full of principal and interest on this fi.fa. this 1 Sept 1860. /s/Z. B. Blalock

Georgia, Fayette Co., To Superior Court of Coweta Co. holding jurisdiction in equity. That James Jennings sometime in month of Nov 1853 and his brother, William Jennings, being advanced in years, departed this life, sharing a very large estate....That he left his only daughter, Elizabeth surviving him, who had married and was then the wife of William May, and his grandchildren-William J. Jennings, James T. Jennings, Mary Ann Jennings, Rhoda E. Jennings and Elizabeth Jennings, children of his son, John A. Jennings, who had died sometime before this, the said grandchildren standing in the place and stead of their father, John A. Jennings....That soon after the death of said William Jennings, William May and Alonzo C. McIntosh who were appointed Exrs of said LWT proceeded with probate, when the widow of said John A. Jennings, Sarah F. Jennings, employed counsel and filed caveat againstthe probate....

Numerous exhibits attached. One should read this document thoroughly in order to completely understand the transactions which transpired regarding the heirs.

Recorded: 22 Aug 1861

James T. Jennings, Orphan of John A. Jennings, decd, in Account Current with Phillip H. Brassell, Gdn, from 1 Jan 1860 to 1 Jun 1861 inclusive
Page 757-759

6 vouchers. Recorded: 27 Aug 1861

Rhoda E. Jennings, Orphan of John A. Jennings, decd, in Account Current with Phillip H. Brassell, Gdn, from 1 Jan 1860 to 1 Jun 1861 incousive
Page 760-762

Voucher #3. Received of Phillip H. Brassell, Gdn in right of my wife, Rhoda E. Jennings, $271.18 in part of a legacy coming to me in the right of my wife from her grandfather, William Jenning's Estate, this 1 Sept 1860. /s/Thomas J. Handley

Recorded: 27 Aug 1861

An Account Current with Martha McLeroy as Gdn of the minor children of Henry McLeroy from 1 Jan 1860 to 1 Jan 1861
Page 762-763

Filed: 1 Jul 1861 Recorded: 26 Oct 1861

An Account Current with Eli Edmondson and W. W. Sibley as Exrs of Thomas Hale, decd, from 1 Jun 1860 to 1 Jun 1861
Page 763-767

8 vouchers. To cash paid - 1860 taxes, James W. Burns and wife, Mary, legatees, Tilmon Burks and wife, Emily, legatees, R. R. King and wife, legatees, Thomas J. King and wife, Susannah, legatees, Joseph Hale, legatee, W. W Sibley, Gdn for Robert Hale, Idiot.

Recorded: 18 Nov 1861

Inventory and Appraisement of Real and Personal Property of William Brassell, late of Fayette Co., decd
Page 765-766

Negroes Distributed via specific legacies - Ruffin, age 24, Isaac, age 16, Madison, age 19, Moses, age 50, Tilda, age 10, Simon, age 14, Charles, about 52, Thena, about 45, Hannah and her child (17 years old), Dan, about 12, Mary, about 9, Milton, about 7, Gidon, about 5, Looney, about 3.

Other specific legacies distributed -

Land Lot No. 189 (home lot), 202 1/2 acres
Land Lot 196 (creek lot), 202 1/2 acres

Appraisers: Eli Edmondson, T. C. Mathews, L. D. Padgett, B. Rentfrow, R. R. Rogers, sworn 25 Dec 1861
Recorded: 22 Nov 1861

Inventory and Appraisement of Estate of Hugh Porter, decd
Page 767-769

Negroes as follows
Tom, Walker, Jerry, Peter, Abram, Cyrus, Milly, Sally and her child, Dick, Malissa and her child, Andy, Harriett and 2 children (Ellen and Georgian), Nancy.

700 acres of land in Fayette Co.
2 lots in Griffin containing one acre each
Appraisers: John I. Whitaker, Andrew McBride, Rowland Stubbs, sworn 22 Nov 1861
Recorded: 27 Nv 1861

Appraisement and Inventory of John Bargamy, decd, 9 Nov 1861
Page 769-770

Negroes -

Lindy, Mit, Charles, Wat, George, Bob, Nel, Bill and Mike
Appraisers: Leroy M. Cobbs, Dennis N. Strickstom, Arthur Robinson, William Jackson
Recorded: 5 Dec 1861

Estate of Harbert Cook, decd, in Account Current with William N. Cook, Exr, from 1 Jun 1860 to 1 Jun 1861
Page 771-772

4 vouchers. Recorded: 16 Dec 1861

Inventory and Appraisement of Property Belonging to Estate of Joseph H. Murphy, late of Fayette Co., deceased
Page 772-773

Negroes - America, Charles, Mariah and child, Wiley, Dennis, Henry and Faney.
Appraisers: James D. Murphy, Richmond Dorman, M. W. Pyron, sworn 20 Nov 1861
Recorded: 20 Dec 1861

Inventory of the Goods and Chattels of George M. Jackson, late of Fayette Co., decd
Page 774-775

Negro woman, Lucinda and her boy children, Daniel and Sam
Appraisers: S. T. W. Miner, Reuben Jackson, Henry J. Hughie, L. B. Clark
Recorded: 20 Dec 1861

Inventory and Sale of Property of George H. Jackson, decd, Sold 12 Dec 1861
Page 775-777

Among purchasers: Francis Jackson, R. Jackson, H. J. Jackson, widow, etc.
Recorded: 12 Dec 1862

Willis Beavers, Gdn, in Account Current with Reuben M., Seppy, James T., Malinda, Eleanor and Sarah J. Lasseter, minor orphans of Jesse Lasseter, late of Fayette Co., decd, from 31 May 1860 to 31 May 1861 inclusive
Page 777-780

Recorded: 24 Dec 1861

James E. H. Ware, Orphan of George Ware, decd, in an Account with Burrell A. Ware, Gdn, from 1 Jan 1860 to 31 Dec 1860 inclusive
Page 781-782

5 vouchers. Recorded: 24 Dec 1861

Estate of Elbert Bishop, decd, in Account Current with Jesse Hubbard, Admr, from 31 Dec 1860 to 6 Aug 1861, the date of Final Settlement
Page 783-784

6 vouchers. To cash paid heirs - William C Bishop, Moses T. Bishop, William S. Bishop and Jesse Hubbard.
Recorded: 24 Dec 1861

Estate of William Russell, decd, in Account Current with Daniel D. Durham and Pamelia Russell, Admr and Admx, from date of their Letters to 25 Jun 1861 inclusive
Page 784-786

4 vouchers. Recorded: 24 Dec 1861

Estate of John Burk, decd, in Account Current with Mathew Read, Admr, with the Will annexed from time of his appointment to 1 Jan 1861 inclusive
Page 786-789

9 vouchers. 2 Fi.Fas. settled, Thomas McGahan vs. Josh Elder and J. Landrum, Sr.. Also, Jesse Mann vs. P. H. Aldridge, John Burk. Recorded: 24 Dec 1861

An Account Current with Robert Iverson as Gdn of John N. Brooks from 1 Jun 1861 inclusive
Page 790-791

Interest realized from hire of negroes in 1860, viz: Michanic, Mon, Caroline and children, Nedd, old man, Charlotte, Rachel, Henry.

6 vouchers. Recorded: 24 Dec 1861

An Account Current with Robert Iverson as Gdn of George W. Brooks from 1 Jun 1860 to 1 Jun 1861 inclusive
Page 792-793

7 vouchers. Recorded: 24 Dec 1861

Inventory and Sale of the Real Estate of Minton Graves, decd, Sold on first Tues. in Dec 1861
Page 794

All of the inventory consists of 127 acres of land sold to William H. Blalock and one negro boy, Nelson, sold to William H. Blalock

Recorded: 8 Jan 1862

An Account Current with Jesse Barintine, Admr of Estate of David Barintine, decd, from date of his Letters to 1 Jun 1861 inclusive
Page 794-796

Recorded: 9 Jan 1862

An Account Current with Thomas M. Jones and Richard M. Everett, Admrs on the Estate of Noah Smith from the date of their Letters to 13 Nov 1861 inclusive
Page 796-797

3 vouchers. Voucher #3 from John B. Smith for 12 months' support set aside for the widow.
Recorded: 9 Jan 1862

Ann E. Ware, Orphan of George Ware, decd, in Account Current with Mildred Ware, Gdn, from 1 Jan 1860 to 31 Dec 1860 inclusive
Page 797-799

4 vouchers. Recorded: 10 Jan 1862

Richard P. Ware, Orphan of George Ware, decd, in Account Current with Mildred Ware, Gdn from 1 Jan 1860 to 31 Dec 1860 inclusive
Page 800-801

4 vouchers. Recorded: 10 Jan 1862

An Account Current with A. G. Brooks as Gdn of Harriett T. Brooks, minor child of Ivey Brooks, decde, from the year 1857 to Aug 1861 inclusive
Page 801-803

8 vouchers. To cash paid A. Moses for board and tuition and books.
Recorded: 14 Jan 1862

Inventory and Appraisement of Estate of Jesse M. Spratlin
Page 804-805

Negroes - Stephen, Click, John, Elijah, Carry, Easter, Viney, Ann and her child, John, Louisa and her children, Salina and Peter, Silvey and her child, Dorsey, Mariah and Letty.

260 acres of land in 3rd District of formerly Henry Co., now Spalding Co., Lot No. 70.
23 1/4 shares of stock of the Savannah Griffin and North Alabama Railroad

Recorded: 22 Jan 1862

Inventory and Appraisement of Estate of Washington O. Duffell, decd
Page 806-807

Negro girl, Roda. Also, other items.
Appraisers: B. Rentfrow, M. T. Travis, C. T. Jones, Z. Blalock, R. R. Rogers, sworn 4 Dec 1861
Recorded: 5 Feb 1862

Sale Bill of the Property of Washington O. Duffell, decd
Page 808-809

One negro girl, Hindy purchased by Edward Moon (who purchased most of the property)
Recorded: 5 Feb 1862

Estate of Silas G. Eastin in Account Current with John B. Allen, Admr de bonis non with the Will annexed the 1st of Oct up to 9 Oct 1861 inclusive
Page 809-814

13 vouchers. By hire of negroes - Lucy and children, Simon and George, Jordan, Ruse
Paid Joshua Cannoun for tuition of Margaret, Silas, Cicero and Permelia Eastin.
Recorded: 6 Feb 1862

Andrew McBride, Admr. in Account Current with Estate of John A. McBride, late of said county, decd, from 1 Jun 1860 to 1 Jul 1861 inhclusive
Page 815-823

15 vouchers
Filed: 29 Jan 1861.Recorded: 7 Feb 1862

An Account Current with Sterling J. Elder, as Admr of Thomas R. Persons from 1 Jun 1860 to 1 Jun 1861 inclusive
Page 823-831

28 vouchers. Recorded: 10 Feb 1862

An Account Current and Final Settlement with John I. Whitaker and Willis R. Whitaker, Exrs of Simon T. Whitaker, decd
Page 832-841

Heirs - Andrew J. Whitaker (W. R. Whitaker, his Gdn), William L. Whitaker (W. R. Whitaker, his Gdn), Benjamin F Whitaker (W. R. Whitaker, his Gdn), Sarah F. Whitaker (W. R. Whitaker her Gdn), Willis R. Whitaker as Gdn of Benjamin F. Whitaker and Sarah Frances Whitaker for specific provisions under the Will.

Receipts from Henrietta Amelia Reed, James J. Carson, in right of wife, Frances A. F. Carson, James J Carson, Gdn of John P. Neel, Eli Edmondson, Gdn of Racheal P. Neel and George W. Neel and Emily J. Neel.

Recorded: 12 Feb 1862

Sale Bill of a portion of the Personal Estate of Hugh Porter, decd, Sold 23th Dec 1861
Page 842

Among purchasers: William Glass, A. W. Reeves, Moses Turner, Jr., Allen Reeves, W. L. Reeves, etc.
Recorded: 10 Mar 1862

An Account Current and Final Settlement with John I. Whitaker Gdn of Elizabeth A. Reeves, now the wife of Henry Jones who is now of age up to 1 Jan 1862
Page 843-844

Receipt from Henry Jones for full legacy of his wife, Elizabeth A., 3 Feb 1862
Recorded: 1 Apr 1862

M. E. Whitlow, Orphan of Warren Whitlow in Account with B. B. Dykes, Gdn, from 1 Jan 1861 to 1 Jan 1862 inclusive
Page 844-845

3 vouchers. Recorded: 10 Apr 1862

W. H. Whitlow, Orphan of Warren Whitlow in Account with B. B. Dykes, Gdn, from 1 Jan 1861 to 1 Jan 1862 inclusive
Page 845

4 vouchers. Recorded: 10 Apr 1862

William J. Clements, Orphan and minor of Charles Clements, decd, in Account Current with Adam Clements Gdn, to 1 Jan 1862
Page 846

4 vouchers Recorded: 10 Apr 1862

Account Current with Adam Clements, Gdn of M. E. Clements from time of appointment to 1 Jan 1862
Page 847-850

8 vouchers. Recorded: 10 Apr 1862

Estate of Silas G. Eastin, Order to Distribute Estate
Page 850-852

Appraisers: John L. Holliday, J. P. Shropshire, D. D. Denham, Williamson Jenkins

Negroes -

Lot No. 1, Simon
Lot No. 2, George
Lot No. 3, Run and Jordan
Lot No. 4, Lucy and her 2 children, Emeline and Sarah

Heirs - Elijah P. Eastin drew Lot No. 4.
Recorded: 17 Apr 1862

Inventory and Appraisement of Estate of Jefferson F. Jackson, decd
Page 852-853

Appraisers: J. J. Gilbert, J. C. Nash, Isaac B. Avera, John Barrow, sworn 15 Mar 1862
Recorded: 5 May 1862

Sale Bill of Estate of Jefferson F. Jackson - Purchasers: Elisha Jackson, Peter E. McLeroy, Jordan Lord, R. R. Humphrey, George C. King

Set Apart for Widow and Children of C. C. Shell, decd
Page 853-860

Appraisers: W. H. Blalock, J. J. Gilbert, B. B. Humphrey, John O. Dickson

Received of William H. Wootton, Amr of C. C. Shell the within articles as set apart...this 15 Dec 1861.
/s/Sarah A. Shell, widow of C. C. Shell
Appraise Bill of Estate of C. C. Shell follows.
Recorded: 14 Dec 1861

Sale Bill of Perishable Property of Estate of C. C. Shell, decd, Sold 25 Dec 1862...
Page 861-864

Among purchasers - . J. Gilbert, Widow Shell, G. R.Shell, agent for M. L. Shell, James D. Murphy, C. P. Murphy, W. D. Mitchell, etc.
Recorded: 5 May 1862

An Account Current with John B. Long, Gdn for Martha Jane Long, Orphan of Marcus Long, decd, from time of appointment to 1 Aug 1861 inclusive
Page 865

3 vouchers. Recorded: 5 May 1862

An Account Current with H. D. Palmer, Admr of John Palmer, decd, from Jun 1861 and Showing Entire Settlement of Estate
Page 866-871

To heirs - Spencer T. Wilbourn, Jackson Martin, J. G. Yates, H. D. Palmer, S. E. Palmer, J. L. Palmer, J. M. Palmer.
Recorded: 13 May 1862

F. M. Luster, Gdn of Person and Property of Sarah A. Clements, minor Orphan of Charles Clements, late of Fayette Co., decd, in Account Current with said minor from date of Letters to 25 Dec 1861 inclusive
Page 871-872

To hire of negro woman and 3 children, 1 girl child
5 vouchers. Recorded: 14 May 1862

An Account Current with C. E. Bennett, as Gdn of Emeline Elkins from 31 Dec 1860 to 31 Dec 1861
Page 873-874

5 vouchers. Filed: 8 Apr 1862
Recorded: 14 May 1862

An Account Current with C. E. Bennett, as Gdn of Elizabeth F. Elkins from 31 Dec 1860 to 31 Dec 1861 inclusive
Page 874-875

6 vouchers. Recorded: 14 May 1862

An Account Current with C. E. Bennett, Gdn of Thomas W. Elkins from 31 Dec 1860 to 31 Dec 1861 inclusive
Page 876-877

4 vouchers. Recorded: 14 May 1862

Mary Elizabeth and Sarah Frances Smith, minor orphans of William T. Rush, decd, in Account Current with Mary Jane Rush, Gdn, from 31 Dec 1859 to 31 Dec 1861 inclusive
Page 877-878

2 vouchers. Recorded: 14 May 1862

J. M. Palmer, Orphan of John Palmer, decd, in Account Current with Barbary Palmer, Gdn, from date of Letters as of 1 Jun 1861 inclusive
Page 878-879

4 vouchers. Recorded: 14 May 1862

Sarah E., minor orphan of John Palmer, decd, in Account Current with Barbary Palmer, Gdn, from date of her Letters up to 1 Jun 1862 inclusive
Page 879-880

3 vouchers. Recorded: 14 May 1862

J. H. Palmer, Gdn of John Palmer, decd, in Account Current with Barbary Palmer, Gdn, from date of Letters up to 1 Jun 1862 inclusive
Page 880-881

2 vouchers. Recorded: 14 May 1862

Georgia, Fayette Co., An Appraise Bill of the Estate of Henderson Buffington, decd, this 12 May 1862
Page 881-883

400 acres, 9th District, Fayette Co., Lots No. 129, 81 and 82.

Negroes as follows -

Clary, about 40
Ann, 21 and her child, 5 months old
Harry, age 23
Peter, age 15
Recorded: 31 May 1862

Marcus, Orphan of Thomas Herring, decd, in Account Current with William J. Russell, Gdn, from 31 Ded 1859 to 31 Dec 1860 inclusive
Page 884-885

4 vouchers. Recorded: 16 Jun 1862

Francis Herring, Orphan of Thomas Herring, decd, in an Account Current with William J. Russell, Gdn, from 31 Dec 1859 to 31 Dec 1860 inclusive
Page 885-

3 vouchers. Filed: 1 Jul 1861. Recorded: 16 Jun 1862

An Account with John I. Whitaker, Gdn of Romalus Collins, one of the minor heirs of Paschal E. Collins, decd, from 1 Jan 1861 to 1 Jan 1862
Page 886

3 vouchers. Recorded: 20 Jun 1862

An Account Current with John I. Whitaker, Gdn of M. A Collins, one of the minor children of Paschal E. Collins, decd, from 1 Jan 1861 to 1 Jan 1862
Page 887-888

4 vouchers. Recirded: 20 Jun 1862

An Account Current with John I. Whitaker, Gdn of Emelina V. Collins, one of the minor children of Paschal E. Collins, decd, from 1 Jan 1861 to 1 Jan 1862
Page 888

1 vouchers. Recorded: 20 Jun 1862

An Account Current with John I. Whitaker, Gdn of Paschal Collins, one of the minor children of Paschal E. Collins, decd, from 1 Jan 1861 to 1 Jan 1862
Pae 889

2 vouchers. Receipt of Emelina Collins (x, her mark) for board and clothing of minor child for 1861.
Recorded: 20 Jun 1862

An Account Current with John I. Whitaker, Gdn of James Collins, minor child of Paschal E. Collins, decd,
from 1 Jan 1861 to 1 Jan 1862
Page 889-890

21 vouchers. Receipt from Emelina Collins (x, her mark) for board and clothing of minor child for 1861.
Recorded: 20 Jun 1862

Estate of William Miles in Account Current with William P. Chandler, Admr, from 1 Jan 1861 to 1 Jan 1862
Page 890-891

3 vouchers. Receipt from George J. Miles $465.72 in part of payment.
Recorded: 20 Jun 1862

Roxey, minor orphan of Charles Clements in Account Current with L. F. Blalock, Gdn, from date of Letters up to 1 Apr 1862
Page 891-893

By 1 negro man, Anthony
By 1 negro girl, Jane

4 vouchers. Filed: 14 Apr 1862. Recorded: 20 Jun 1862

Estate of Silas G. Eastin in Account Current with L. F. Blalock, Admr de bonis non with the Will annexed from 9 Oct 1861 to 9 Apr 1863 inclusive
Page 893-898

18 vouchers. To cash paid - George C. King, Ordinary, P. M. Stratton, Holliday & Ware (for Miss Margaret Eastin), William H. Wootton, Admr of C. C. Shell, Blalock & Camp (for Miss P. G. Eastin), L. F. Blalock and E. P. Eastin (legatee).

Receipts given by L. F. Blalock were for: E. P. Eastin, Miss Parmelia G. Eastin, Cicero Eastin, Miss Margaret Eastin.
Recorded: 22 Jun 1862

An Account Current with Martha A. Reeves, Gdn of Robert W. Reeves, minor child of William Reeves, decd, from 31 Dec 1860 to 31 Dec 1861
Page 898

Recorded: 22 Jun 1862

An Account Current with Martha A. Reeves, Gdn of Henry C. Reeves, from 31 Dec 1860 to 31 Dec 1861
Page 898-899

Recorded: 22 Jun 1862

An Account Current with Martha A. Reeves, Gdn of Sarah Ann Reeves, from 31 Dec 1860 to 31 Dec 1861
Page 899

Recorded: 22 Jun 1862

An Account Current with Martha A. Reeves, Gdn of Amos W. Reeves, from 31 Dec 1860 to 31 Dec 1861
Page 899-900

4 vouchers, receipt given by Martha A. Reeves, for boarding and clothing Robert W., Martha W., Henry C. and Amos W. Reeves for 1861.
Recorded: 22 Jun 1862

Morgan F., Orphan of James G. Christian, decd in Account Current with Gideon F. Mann, Gdn, from 31 Dec 186 to 1 May 1862, date of Final Settlement
Page 900-901

2 vouchers. Recorded: 22 Jun 1862

Sarah Ann, Orphan of James G. Christian, decd, in Account Current with Gideon F. Mann, Gdn, from 31 Dec 1860 to 31 Dec 1861
Page 901-902

Filed: 17 May 1862. Recorded: 22 Jun 1862

An Account Current with Thomas M. Jones and Richard M. Everett, Admrs on Estate of Noah Smith from 1 Nov 1861 to 13 May 1862
Page 902-904

Recorded: 25 Jun 1862

Estate of Thomas Johnson, decd, in Account Current with Berry L. Johnson, Exr, from 12 May 1861 to 12 May 1862
Page 904-906

7 vouchers. Recorded: 25 Jun 1862

Estate of William L. Allen, decd, in Account Current with William N. McConnell, Admr, from 1 Jun 1860 to 1 Jun 1862 inclusive
Page 906

Receipt of J. F. Thomas in full for his share of the estate, 1 Jun 1862.
2 vouchers. Recorded: 8 Jul 1862

Estate of John Watson, decd, in Account Current with Ellison Rush and H. D. Palmer, Admrs, from 1 Jun 1861 to 1 Jun 1862
Page 907

4 vouchers. To cash paid - William H. Hindman, Elisha Baker (for J. W. Baker), Nancy Watson (minor heir) and George E. King
Recorded: 8 Jul 1862

An Account Current with William N. Cook, Exr of Harbert Cook, decd, from 1 Jun 1861 to 1 Jun 1862
Page 908-909

2 vouchers. Recorded: 8 Jul 1862

Estate of Hugh Porter, decd, in Account Current with John M. Porter, Admr, from Granting of Letters of Admn to 2 Jun 1862 inclusive
Page 909-916

27 vouchers. Heirs receipts as follows -

Hany Porter, full share of legacy, as Gdn of Sarah T. Roberts (from Estate of Hugh Porter)
Hany Porter, full share of legacy, as Gdn of James L. Roberts (from Estate of Lawson W. Roberts)
Hany Porter, full share of legacy, as Gdn of Griffin Roberts (from Estate of Lawson W. Roberts)

Recorded: 18 Jul 1862

Sarah F. Whitaker, Orphan and minor of Simon T. Whitaker, decd, in Account Current with Willis R. Whitaker, Gdn, from date of his Letters to 1 Jun 1862
Page 916-917

4 vouchers. To cash paid - Jared I. Whitaker, Issabella Whitaker.
Recorded: 28 Jul 1862

Benjamin F. Whitaker, Orphan and minor of Simon T. Whitaker, decd, in Account Current with Willis R. Whitaker, Gdn, from date of his Letters to 1 Jun 1862
Page 917-919

9 vouchers. Recorded: 28 Jul 1862

Andrew J. Whitaker, orphan and minor of Simon T. Whitaker, decd, in Account Current with Willis R. Whitaker, Gdn, from date of his Letters to 1 Jun 1862
Page 920-922

10 vouchers. Recorded: 28 Jul 1862

William L. Whitaker, Orphan and minor of Simon T. Whitaker, decd, in Account Current with Willis R. Whitaker, Gdn, from the date of his Letters to 1 Jun 1862
Page 922-925

13 vouchers. Recorded: 31 Jul 1862

Augustine E. Hardin, minor of John Hardin and C. A. Hardin, in Account Current with Joshua Cannon, Gdn, from 1 Jan 1861 to 1 Jun 1862
Page 926

3 vouchers. Recorded: 31 Jul 1862

Willis Beavers, Gdn, in Account Current with Reuben Lasseter, James T., Malinda, Elenor, and Sarah J. Lasseter, minors and orphans of Jesse Lasseter, Jr., late of Fayette Co., decd, from 31 May 1861 to 31 May 1862 inclusive
Page 927-928

Recorded: 31 Jul 1862

Malinda M. Cavender, formerly but now Martha M. McLane, Orphan of Wade H. Cavender, decd, in Account Current with Delilah Moses, Gdn from 1 Jan 1861 to 1 Jun 1862 inclusive
Page 929

Received of Delilah Moses as Gdn for Martha M. Cavender formerly, but now Martha H. McLane, $241.81 in full of all moneys in her hands as such Gdn this 9 May 1862. /s/John M. McLane, in right of his wife, formerly Martha M. Cavender, but now Martha M. McLane.

Recorded: 31 Jul 1862

An Account Current with Eli Edmondson, Gdn for Emily J. Neel from 1 Jun 1861 to 1 Jun 1862 inclusive
Page 930

4 vouchers. Recorded: 12 Aug 1862

An Account Current with Eli Edmondson, Gdn of J. F. Neal from 1 Jun 1861 to 1 Jun 1862
Page 931

3 vouchers.
Recorded: 12 Aug 1862

An Account Current with Eli Edmondson, Gdn of R. P. Neel, from 1 Jun 1861 to 1 Jun 1862
Page 932

4 vouchers. Recorded.12 Aug 1862

An Account Current with Eli Edmondson, Gdn of George H. Neal from 1 Jun 1861 to 1 Jun 1862
Page 933

4 vouchers. Recorded: 12 Aug 1862

An Account Current with Jane Murphy and John J. Gilbert as Exrs of the Estate of Joseph H. Murphy, decd, from date of their Letters to 1 Jun 1862
Page 934-940

17 vouchers. Receipts from Joseph H. Murphy, Elizabeth Murphy (x, her mark), etc.
Recorded: 15 Aug 1862

Hiram D. Moses, minor orphan of Hiram Moses, decd, in Account Current with Delilah Moses as Gdn from 1 Jan to 31 Dec 1861 inclusive
Page 941

2 vouchers. Recorded: 21 Aug 1862

Phillip B. Moses, minor orphan of Hiram Moses, decd, in Account Current with Delilah Moses as Gdn from 1 Jan to 31 Dec 1861 inclusive
Page 942

2 vouchers. Recorded: 21 Aug 1862

Estate of Susannah West, late of Fayette Co., decd, in Account Current with Richard B. Humphrey, Admr, from 1 May 1861 to 1 May 1862
Page 943-944

6 vouchers.

Georgia, Cherokee Co., For value received, we, M. M. Thomson and Sarah Thompson, my wife (formerly Sarah Humphrey) hereby sell, transfer and assign to Richard B. Humphrey of the county of Fayette in said state our entire interest in the share of the estate of Joshua Stephens, late of Henry Co., decd....this 5th day of Oct 1861. /s/M. M. Thompson /s/Sarah Thompson (x, her mark)

Recorded: 21 Aug 1862

Inventory and Sale of the Real Estate Belonging to Estate of Matilda Graves and Wiley Graves, consisting of impending interest in the tract of land whereon Matilda Graves lived and died, Sold 1st Tues. in nov 1860
Page 945

Sold to - S. T. Wellin.
Recorded: 10 Sept 1862

Inventory and Appraisement of the Estate of W. P. Murphy, decd
Page 945-946

Includes imisc. items. Includes a house and lot.
Appraisers: L. F. Blalock, William Bradley and William Bennett, sworn 9 Jul 1862
Recorded: 20 Sept 1862

One years' support provided for widow and one child, setting off foodstuffs, etc.

Sale Bill and Perishable Property of W. P. Murphy, decd, Sold 23rd Jul 1862
Page 946

Misc. items
Recorded: 20 Sept 1862

Estate of Mason Gentry in Account with Killis Brown, Admr, from 31 Dec 1860 to 31 Dec 1861
Page 946-947

2 vouchers. Recorded: 23 Sept 1862

An Account with John J. Gilbert, Admr on Estate of George H. Jackson from time of his appointment to 1 Jun 1862
Page 947-948

6 vouchers. To cash paid - Richmond Dorman, William H. Blalock, taxes for 1861, George C. King, Ordinary, and Margaret F. Jackson (x, her mark), for part of her allowance..

Filed: 19 Jun 1862. Recorded: 28 Jul 1862

An Account Current with James T. Travis, Admr in Estate of Washington O. Duffell, decd, from time of appointment to 1 Jun 1862
Page 949-951

6 vouchers. Recorded: 24 Sept 1862

An Account Current with William B. Standfield, Admr on Estate of Martin Delile, decd, from date of his Letters to 1 Jun 1862
Page 951-952

5 vouchers. Recorded: 24 Sept 1862

Andrew McBride, Admr of John A. McBride in Account Current with Estate of John A. McBride, decd, from 1 Jul 1861 to 1 Jul 1862
Page 953-954

5 vouchers. Recorded: 24 Sept 1862

Georgia, Fayette Co., Inventory and Appraisement of Property of John DeVaughn, decd, to-zit:
Page 954-957

Negro man, George
Negro man, Sandy
Negro man, Jack
Negro boys - Asbury, Simon
Negro women - Rose, Nelly, Margtha

Appraisers: J. P. Shropshire, D. D. Denham, A. V. Swanson, T. J. Head, B. L. Johnson
Recorded: 23 Oct 1862

Estate of William Russell, decd, in Account Current with Daniel D. Denham and Permelia Russell, Admrs from 25 Jun 1861 to 25 Jun 1862
Page 957-958

Filed: 26 Jun 1862. Recorded: 30 Oct 1862

An Account Current with Jesse Barrentine, Admr of Estate of David Barrintine, decd, from 1 Jun 861 to 1 Jun 1862
Page 958-959

4 vouchers. To cash paid - Mary Barrentine, widow.
Recorded: 30 Oct 1862

George M. Cook, Orphan of Harbert Cook, decd, in Account Current with Joshua A. Cook, Gdn, from 1 Jan 1861 to 1 Jan 1862
Page 959-960

1 vouchers. Recorded: 24 Sept 1862

Thomas E. Cook, Orphan of Harbert Cook, decd, in Account Current with Joshua A. Cook, Gdn, from 1 Jan 1861 to 1 Jan 1862
Page 960

Filed: 24 Jun 1862. Recorded: 30 Oct 1862.

END OF BOOK G

Fayette County Ordinary Mixed Records
Inventories, Appraisements, Sales and Returns
Book I (1871-1878)

Inventory and Appraisement of the Estate of Samuel Robinson, decd
Page 1-10

Includes Lot 56, 202 1/2 acres, the N. half of Lot 40, Lot 41, being 75 acres on the West side of Lot 40.

Appraisers: Isaac A. Haisten, John A. Haisten, D. R. Askew

Sale Bill of Surplus of Property. Purchasers: G. W. Sneed, J. Sneed, John Sneed, F. A. Woods, Furman Norris and H. H. Haisten. Recorded: 11 Apr 1871

Inventory of Notes, and Sale Bill of Property Sold on 21 Dec 1868. Among the purchasers were: Jane Robinson, John Sneed, J. D. George, J. D. Jones, H. F. Patterson, Sallie Robinson, and Miss Mollie Robinson. Recorded: 3 May 1871

Inventory and Appraisement of the Estate of Jeptha Landrum, decd, of Fayette Co., Ga.
Page 10-12

Appraisers sworn 13 Dec 1870: J. P. Shropshire, W. T. Glower and Bennett Adams
Recorded: 8 May 1871

Inventory and Appraisement of Estate of John W. Speer, decd
Page 12-14

Appraisers sworn 13 Apr 1870: Lewis T. Thompson, Asa B. Mitchell, R. E. Johnson
Recorded: 9 May 1871

The Following is a True Sale Bill of the Perishable Property of J. W. Speer Sold on 10 Nov 1870
Page 14-16

Among the purchasers were: J. J. Speer, Autney Speer, George Speer, J. L. Speer, Abe Speer, Mary Ann Speer, T. C. Speer, T. E. Speer, and M. Speer. Recorded: 10 May 1871

Sale Bill of John W. Davis, decd
Page 16-17

Purchasers were: J. M. Davis, J. J. Speer, G. W. Spratlin, C. H. Knowls, L. Millsaps.
Recorded: 15 May 1871

Inventory and Appraisement of Estate of L. H. Smith, Appraised 16 Sept 1870
Page 17-19

Appraisers sworn on 16 Sept 1870: C. J. Fall, O. Wynn and W. J. Gay. Recorded: 24 May 1871

John A. Richardson, Exr of B. O. Jones, decd, makes the following Annual Return on 8 Jan 1870
Page 19-24

21 vouchers. Receipts from: Ella Jones for her share, T. W. Jones for his share (to come from the sale of 17 City lots). Recorded: 22 May 1871

In Account Current with C. H. Eastin, Gdn for Permelia G., now Mrs. Permelia G. Lister, from 7 Jan 1870 to 21 Jan 1871 and Final Settlement with said Ward
Page 25-26

9 vouchers. By amount paid to E. D. Campbell, M. L. Heath, D. A. Denham, 1870 tax, J. G. Lister and D. C. Minor. Voucher #3 receipt from M. L. Heath for 1865 and 1867 tuition. Voucher #7 $300 received of C. H. Eastin, dn for _____ now _____ (blanks) signed by J. G. Lister, 1 Jan 1871. Voucher #9 Received of C. H. Eastin $298.33 for Permelia G. Lister.

Filed: 21 Jan 1871. Recorded: 25 May 1871.

Estate of H. D. Palmer, decd, in Account Current with James M. Palmer, Admr, from 13 Jun 1868 to 8 Dec 1870
Page 26-27

To amount of sale of land sold on the first Tues. in Dec 1868, in Book H, page 774.
Filed: 20 Feb 1871. Recorded: 25 May 1871.

Estate of Berry Norton, decd
Page 27-28

Georgia, Fayette Co., We, the undersigned commissioners appointed by the Court of Ordinary of said county to assess a sum necessary for the support and maintenance of the widow and children of Berry Norton, late of said county, decd, and assessed and set apart for said purposes in addition to a certain amount assessed and set apart heretofore by a certain court of commissioners appointed by a former Court of Ordinary for that purpose, a certain parcel of land lying and being in County of Cherokee and State of Alabama, No. of Lot, page and township not now known....for 15 years. /s/J. N. McEachern /s/Edmund Jackson /s/John Eason
Recorded: 6 Jun 1871

John W. Kelly, security on Gdns Bond of Romalis E. Collins, Gdn of Paschal E. Collins, minor child of Paschal Collins, decd, in Account Current with said minor form 1 Jun 1870 to 28 Mar 1871
Page 28-29

To amount on hand 1 Jun 1870, see Book H, page (blank).
Voucher #1, Received of J. W. Kelly, security of R. E. Collins, Gdn of the minor children of P. E. Collins, decd, $295.99, it being my pro-rata share of my father's estate in full settlement of the same. 11 Jan 1871. /s/Paschal E. Collins

In Account Current with William Shadrick, Admr of Winslow G. Norton, decd, from 1 Jun 1868 to 6 Mar 1871 inclusive
Page 29-30

Rent of plantation for 1868.
Sale of 101 1/4 acres of land.
3 vouchers. Filed: 6 Mar 1871. Recorded: 8 Jun 1871.

Return of Daniel McLucas, Admr of Andrew McLucas, decd, in Account with Heir of said estate and creditors
Page 30

To rent of land for 1870. 2 vouchers. Paid heirs of said estate for their support.
Filed: 11 Mar 1871. Recorded: 9 Jun 1871

In Account Current with W. J. Grant, Gdn for F. W. Patterson, from 1 Jan 1870 up to 1 Apr 1871 inclusive
Page 31

To amount on hand from last Return - See Record Book H, page 932. 4 vouchers.
Filed: 1 Apr 1871. Recorded: 10 Jun 1871

In Account Current with W. J. Grant, Gdn for Roxana Patterson, from 1 Jan 1870 up to 1 Apr 1871 inclusive
Page 31

To amount on hand from last Return - See Record Book H, page 933. 4 vouchers.
Filed: 1 Apr 1871. Recorded 10 Jun 1871

In Account Current with W. J. Grant, Gdn for Serena Patterson, from 1 Jan 1870 to 1 Apr 1871 inclusive
Page 32-33

To amount on hand from last Return - See Record Book H, page 932. 4 vouchers.

Voucher #4 - Received of William Grant, Gdn for Ressie Patterson, $2.00 in full for medical services rendered up to date. 6 Dec 1870. /s/N. W. Gable, M. D.

Voucher #4 - Received of William Grant, Gdn for Exy Patterson. Sept 4, 1 visit, this 6 Dec 1870. /s/N. W. Gable, M. D.

Voucher #4 - Received of William Grant, Gdn for Filmore Patterson, in full for medical services rendered up to date: 6 Dec 1870. /s/N. W. Gable, M. D.

Voucher #4 - Received of William Grant, Gdn for Drury Patterson, in full for medical services rendered up to date: 6 Dec 1870. /s/N. W. Gable, M. D.

Filed: 1 Apr 1871. Recorded 10 Jun 1871

In Account Current between James Boyd, Gdn of Ida V. Spence, minor orphan of Wilson Spence, decd, from date of his Letters to the 1st of Mar 1871 inclusive
Page 33-34

To amount received from the admr of the estate $212.76, this amount being the principal and interest due on two judgments up to the first of Mar 1871, one of the said judgments being said sum of $100 principal with increst on the same from the 25th of Dec 1863 and in favor of James Boyd, as admr, the other of said admr against James W. McLeroy and George Peters, security, for the amount of $40 with interest from the 25th day of Dec 1862. Amount of judgment on Horton's Notes with interest collected. Judgment against McLeroy & Peters remains unpaid. Of the above judgments were an award made by agreement of the admr and makers of the Notes on which the award and judgments were rendered. That, in case of Horton and others Notes to the amount of $100 given for land sold in the sale of the intestates estate, were scaled down to $100 principal with interest from the 25th of Dec 1863. The case against McLeroy & Peters was likewise reduced from $120.30 to the sum of $40 principal with interest from the 25th day of Dec 1862. This being on notice given for property sold at the sale of the admr of the estate of Wilson Spence, decd vs. Stephen Horton and others.

Filed: 18 Mar 1871. Record: 10 Jul 1871

In Account Current with George W. Edmondson, Gdn of Eli Edmondson, minor of Eli Edmondson, decd, from 1 Jun 1869 up to 1 Dec 1870 inclusive
Page 35-36

6 vouchers. Voucher #6 was for Letters of Dismission of Gdn and advertising same.
Legatee receipts:
J. A. Edmondson, attorney in fact for Peter E. Edmondson
J. A. Edmondson, attorney in fact for Peter E. Edmondson

Filed: 20 Mar 1871. Recorded: 12 Jul 1871

William Guice, Gdn, in Account with Estate of Peter Guice, decd, from the time of his appointment up to 1 Sept 1871 inclusive
Page 36-37

3 vouchers. Filed: 13 Apr 1871. Recorded: 13 Jul 1871

Estate of John W. Speer, decd, in Account Current with James J. Speer, Exr, from the date of his Letters to the 1st day of Jul 1871 inclusive
Page 37-40

14 vouchers. By amount paid - C. S. Clardy, O. Winn, J. E. C. Smith, M. M. Tidwell, W. P. Chandler, I. Harrison (tax), B. F. Youngblood, Mary Ann Speer (board and clothing), Martha Carroll, C. G. Davis, J. J. Speer, Exr, Newton Loyd and G. O. Winn.

Voucher #12 paid to James J. Speer, Exr, for feather bed, etc. for J. L. Speer, orphan of John W. Speer, decd.

Filed: 31 May 1871. Recorded: 14 Jul 1871

Estate of A. R. Smith, in Account Current with B. N. Smith, Admr, from 1 Jul 1870 to 1 Jul 1871 inclusive
Page 40-43

By amount in favor of Admr, see Record Book H, page 955.
12 vouchers. By amount paid - J. G. Dorriss, M. M. Tidwell, Rebecca W. Smith, tax collector, E. M. Barge, Isaac Hartley, B. Thornton, M. M. Tidwell, atty, J. B. Avera and R. J. Dorsey

To amount of sale of 120 acres of land sold at public sale first Tues. in Jun 1871 and bid off by Rebecca W. Smith.

Voucher #5 - Received from R. N. Smith, Admr of A. R. Smith, former Gdn of the minor children of Henry Speer, decd, the sum of $626.50 in full of all moneys received by him as Gdn, this 4 Feb 1871. /s/Rebecca W. Smith, Gdn of minor children of H. C. Speer
Filed: 3 Jul 1871. Recorded: 9 Aug 1871

In Account Current with B. F. Head, Exr of the LWT of William Head, decd, from the date of his appoint in Jun of 1870 up to 3 Jul 1871 inclusive
Page 44

To amount received from the sale of land sold on the first Tues. in Nov 1870.
4 vouchers. Paid Atlanta Intelligencer for advertising, paid 1870 tax.
Filed: 3 Jun 1871. Recorded: 9 Aug 1871

Azariah Mims, Admr of Estate of William Ballard, to 16 Jun 1871
Page 45-48

To amount received from sale of personal property - See Record Book H, page 892.
11 vouchers. Paid Atlanta Daily and Weekly Intelligencer for advertising sale of land 14 May 1870.
Paid 1867 tuition to A. B. Fears for children, viz: Indiana, Sarah, Margaret A. and Lorenza Ballard.

Filed: 16 Jun 1871. Recorded: 9 Aug 1871

An Annual Account with Nathanial Stinchcomb, Exr of LWT of Guy Bannister from the time of his qualifying to 1 Jul 1871 inclusive
Page 49-51

13 vouchers. By amount paid - Dobbins & Brassell, John L. Banister (legatee), Marietta Pollard (legatee), O. T. Banister (legatee), Louisa Banister (legatee), Guy Anna Banister (legatee), Louisa Banister (legatee), 1870 tax, G. M. Davis, Gainy Westbrook, D. C. Minor, Ordinary.

Recorded: 12 Aug 1871

In Account Current with Mary S. Bagwell, Gdn of J. W. Bagwell, minor of J. S. Bagwell, decd, from 1 Dec 1870 up to 1 Jul 1871 inclusive
Page 51

To amount of last Return - See Record Book H, page 950.
Filed: 1 Jul 1871. Recorded: 13 Aug 1871

N. Stinchcomb, Secty and Agt for Victor Stinchcomb, Admr de bonis non, in Account Current with John Loyd, decd, from 1 Jul 1869 up to 1 Jul 1871 inclusive
Page 52-53

3 vouchers. Filed: 4 Jul 1871. Recorded: 13 Aug 1871

Estate of Edward Moore, decd, in Account Current with J. T. Travis, Admr, from 31 Dec 1870 up to 3 Jul 1871 inclusive
Page 53-54

6 vouchers. To cash paid - Jesse Hagges (X, his mark), D. C. Minor, Ordinary, John R. Robinson, Martha A. Duffel, Mary Travis, and Patience Duffel (X, her mark). Filed: 1 Jul 1871. Recorded: 13 Aug 1871

George M. Davis, Admr, in Account Current with John W. Davis, decd, from 1 Jul 1868 up to 1 Jul 1871 inclusive
Page 54-56

To amount on hand from last Return - See Record Book H, page 769.
5 vouchers. By amount paid - Emily H. Davis, widow, having specific articles set aside for 12 months' support and which were not on hand, she having the hogs of appraised value and balance in money.
Filed: 1 Jul 1871. Recorded: 14 Aug 1871

Annual Return of James R. Bailey, Exr of L. B. Clark, Showing Receipts and Disbursements from Jul 1870 to Jul 1871 inclusive
Page 56-57

4 vouchers. By amount paid - 1870 taxes, James R. Bailey, W. L. Waterson, atty, Temples & Stewart, attys.

Annual Return of W. W. Matthews, Exr of LWT of Alexander Smith, decd, in Account Current with the Estate of Alexander Smith
Page 57-60

By amount paid - Mooney Boyd & Co., S. Harvey for 1870 taxes, D. C. Minor, Ordinary.
Payment made to heirs for part shares, viz:

M. W. Matthews
F. F. Matthews
Mary Travis
Martha A. Duffell
H. Pope by H. H. Pope
James T. Travis for Elizabeth Travis
Nancy Pressley
Patience Duffell
William W. Matthews.
Filed: 3 Jul 1871. Recorded: 14 Aug 1871

In Account Current with Rachel Eason, Admr of R. B. Eason, decd, from 1 Jul 1868 up to 1 Jul 1871 inclusive
Page 60-61

5 vouchers. Paid 1868-1870 taxes. Filed: 17 Jun 1871. Recorded: 19 Aug 1871

Rebecca C. Smith, Gdn for H. C. Speer, minor son of Henry Speer, decd, from the time of his appointment to 1 Jul 1871 inclusive
Page 61-62

Filed: 3 Jul 1871.
Recorded: 19 Aug 1871

Annual Return of John M. Porter, Gdn of Martha A. Jackson, from date of Letters to date
Page 62-63

3 vouchers. To cash paid - D.C. Minor, Ordinary, N. B. DeVaughn, and E. L. Haynes.
Filed: 28 Jul 1871.
Recorded: 10 Sept 1871

Griffin, Ga., John Porter, Admr of Hugh Porter, decd
Page 63-65

Voucher #2, John M. Porter, Admr of Hugh Porter} Bill & c. in Spalding Superior Court
vs.
Mrs. Martha Humphris

Received of plaintiff $40 in full of my fee in the above case. Griffin, Ga., 20 Jan 1870. /s/John D. Stewart
Voucher #4, John Porter for the}   Case & c.
use of officers of court   }   Bill of Cost to Will - Includes court costs
vs.   }
Martha Humphris   }

By Amount of sale of small house and acre lot in City of Griffin, known as Humphris Place, sold to James Y. Patterson.
Filed: 28 Jul 1871. Recorded: 10 Sept 1871

In Account with John Porter, Gdn of Martha Jackson, minor of Bird M. Jackson, decd
Page 65

Voucher #1 - Received of John Porter, Gdn of Martha Jackson, minor of Bird M. Jackson, decd, $3.50 for his appointment, this 13 Feb 1871

Voucher #2 - Received of John Porter, Gdn of Martha Jackson, minor of Bird M. Jackson, decd, for Miss Martha Jackson...21 Jul 1871 /s/M. B. DeVaughn.

Inventory and Appraisement of Estate of Guy Banister, decd
Page 65-70

Appraisers: James A. Brown, Wyatt Chandler, W. A. Leach, H. W. Fisher
Sale Bill - among purchasers were: O. T. Banister, John Banister, Louanna Banister, Guyanna Banister, and Guy Banister.

Recorded: 10 Sept 1871

Inventory of Sale of Personal Property of Estate of J. Landrum, decd, 28 Feb 1871, Fayette Co.
Page 70-72

Among purchasers were: Thomas Landrum, Columbus Landrum
Recorded: 9 Oct 1871

Annual Return of W. F. and O. M. Landrum, Exrs of Estate of Jeptha Landrum, decd, showing the amount received and paid out from the time of appointment up to 1st of Jul 1871 inclusive
Page 72-98

Note: A very large estate. Large quantities of cotton sold.
See Appraise Bill, Record Book I, page 10
Copies of Notes of Jeptha Landrum to Ga. Loan & Trust Co. in amount of $1160.60 on 10 May 1870 and receipt for the payment thereof by M. G. Dobbins.

17 vouchers include a Campbell Co. Tax Fi.Fa.

Gainy Westbrook, Gdn, in Account with Luisa Jane Edmondson, minor child of James Edmondson, decd, from 1 Jul 1870 up to 8 Aug 1871 inclusive
Page 98-99

3 vouchers.
To amount on hand from last Return - See Record Book H, page 948

Filed: 8 Aug 1871. Recorded: 16 Oct 1871.

Willis R. Whitaker, Gdn, in Account Current with W. S., S. F. and B. F. Whitaker, minor children of Thomas S. Whitaker, decd, showing the entire amount of assets and the amount due each, the Notes which were compromised, and which consists in &c. from 3 Aug 1870 in the matter of S. F. and B. F. Whitaker up to 3 Aug 1871 and from 12 Jul 1869 up to 3 Aug 1871 in matter of William S. Whitaker
Page 99-103

To amount due - Sarah F. Whitaker - See Record Book H, page 817
B. F. Whitaker - See Record Book H, page 817
W. S. Whitaker - See Record Book H, page 817

Receipts for legacy from - W. S. Whitaker, John J. Whitaker (Gdn of Sarah F. Whitaker)
Filed: 28 Aug 1871. Recorded: 18 Oct 1871

C. F. Fall, Admr of Joseph Speer, decd, in Account Current with Joseph Speer, decd, from 1 Jul 1870 up to 1 Jul 1871 inclusive
Page 103-104

By amount paid as railroad fare to and from Atlanta Hotel (Bill), and for attending Bankrupt Court

To amount on hand from last Return - See Record Book H, page 914
Filed: 3 Jun 1871. Recorded: 10 Nov 1871

In Account Current with M. J. E. Palmer, Gdn of the minor children of J. S. Palmer, from 1 Dec 1870 up to 1 Sept 1871 inclusive
Page 104-105

Filed: 4 Sept 1871. Recorded: 11 Nov 1871

Estate of Haywood Thornton, decd, in Account Current with Herrod Thornton, from 1 Jul 1870 up to 2 Oct 1871 inclusive
Page 105-107

To amount on hand from last Return - See Record Book H, page 945. 3 vouchers.
Recorded: 11 Nov 1871

Estate of Jordan Jackson, in Account Current with Needom Jackson, Admr, from 1 Jul 1867 to 3 Oct 1871 inclusive
Page 107-111

To amount on hand from last Return - See Record Book 8, page 558
11 vouchers. Voucher #1 signed by Bennett Jackson on 29 Jan 1867 "....$250.00 in full satisfaction of the right, claims and interest....in and upon the estate of Jordan Jackson."

Voucher #2 signed by Caroline Cochran (X, her mark), dated 4 Nov 1867..."$250.00 in full satisfaction of the right, claims and interest....in and upon the estate of Jordan Jackson."

Voucher #3 signed by James S. Jackson, dated 4 Nov 1867"....for $250.00 in full satisfaction of the right, claims and interest...in and upon the estate of Jordan Jackson."

Voucher #4 signed by Marion Jackson dated 29 Jan 1867..."for $250.00 in full satisfaction of the right, claims and interest...in and upon the estate of Jordan Jackson."

Estate of Jordan Jackson, contd.....

Voucher #5 signed by Elizabeth Jackson (X, her mark) dated 29 Jan 1867..."for $280.00 in full satisfaction of the right, claims and interest...in and upon the estate of Jordan Jackson."

Filed: 3 Oct 1871. Recorded: 11 Nov 1871

An Account Current and Settlement with THomas A. Adams and R. B. Shell, Exrs of the Estate of Samuel Robinson, decd, showing the estate received and also the amount paid out to the heirs and creditors up to 1 Oct 1871
Page 111-123

51 vouchers of various expenses. Accounts from Griffin, Ga and Spalding Co.

Filed: 25 Oct 1871. Recorded: 18 Dec 1871

Estate of B. M. Jackson, decd, in Account Current with John J. Gilbert from the time of his appointment up to 7 Nov 1871
Page 124-133

To amount of property set aside for the widow in specific articles, See Record Book H, page (blank)
To amount of Sale Bill, See Record Book H, page (blank)

39 vouches includes accounts of A. J. Jackson, E. B. Jackson and Jesse J. Jackson

Voucher #17 - Received of J. J. Gilbert $15.00 cost and commissioners fees in the case of Levena Jackson vs. J. J. Gilbert, Admr of B. M. Jackson, decd, to 3 May 1871. /s/A. E. Stokes, Clerk

Voucher #23 - Received of J. J. Gilbert, Admr of the Estate of B. M. Jackson, decd, for the minor child of said decd, Martha Jackson, $30.00, this 22 May 1871. /s/John M. Porter, Gdn

Heirs receiving part of their share, viz:

John M. Pyron
Rebecca Pyron
Jesse J. Jackson (X, his mark)
J. J. Jackson (X, his mark)
John J. Porter, Gdn for Martha A. Jackson
W. C. Loord in right of wife, L. C. J. Loord
W. C. Loord in right of wife, Louisa C. J. Loord
E. B. Jackson (X, his mark)
William Coter (X, his mark), in right of his wife, Eveline Coter
Peter E. McLeroy for Rebecca Pyron, formerly Jackson, now Pyron (receipt dtd: 29 Sept 1871)
B. W. Tarpley, Gdn of J. J. and F. M. Jackson, minors of Elisha Jackson, decd

In Account Current with M. A. Palmer, Gdn of the minor children of H. D. Palmer, decd, from 1 Dec 1870 up to 6 Nov 1871 inclusive
Page 134

To amount on hand from last Return, See Record Book H, page 949
Filed: 6 Nov 1871. Recorded: 12 Feb 1872

In Account Current with Susan Long, Gdn of H. A. N. Long, minor of George D. Long, from 1 Jul 1870 up to 1 Dec 1871 inclusive
Page 134-136

4 vouchers. Paid 1870 tax. Voucher #3 - Georgia, Coweta Co., 1st District, To the Sheriffs and Constables of said State Greeting - You are hereby commanded that of the goods and lands and tenements of Mrs. Susan Long....you make the sum of $3.86, it being due for her State and County tax for 1870. /s/R. W. Hendrix
Filed: 11 Dec 1871. Recorded: 12 Dec 1872

Estate of John T. McKey, decd, in Account Current with Solomon T. Bridges Admr, from 28 Jul 1870 to 1 Jul 1871 inclusive
Page 136-137

By amount on hand from last Return - See Record Book H, page 920
4 vouchers. Paid tax collector, M. C. McKey, M. C. Mackey, J. H. Crumbley, furnished the minor children of John T. Mackey
Filed: 5 Dec 1871. Recorded: 12 Feb 1872

An Account Current with Matthew Jones, Gdn of William Thompson, from 1 May 1864 up to 1 Mar 1872
Page 138

To amount on hand from last Return - See Record Book H, page 351
To amount paid - William Thompson, James M. Austin, D. C. Minor, Ordinary.
Filed: 1 Mar 1872. Recorded: 14 May 1872

Georgia, Fayette Co. - Sale Bill of Real Estate of Edward Moore, decd, Sold at Public OUtcry on 3d day of Oct 1871
Page 139-141

146 1/4 acres at $7 per acre. /s/James T. Travis

The Estate of Edward Moore, decd, in Account Current and Final Settlement with James T. Travis, Admr, from 4 Jul 1871 to 5 Feb 1872 inclusive
Page 139-141

10 vouchers. By amount paid - L. Harrison, Tax Collector, R. Dorman, L. F. Blalock, Martha A. Duffell, Mary Travis, Patience Duffell, Stallings & Vaughn, J. F. Travis.
Filed: 5 Feb 1872. Recorded: 13 May 1872

In Account Current with I. A. Haisten, Admr of Charles Bailey's Estate from 7 Apr 1870 to 2 Apr 1872 inclusive
Page 141-142

By amount on hand from last Return - See Return Book H, page 904.

Heirs receiving their share, viz:

J. R. Brooks, Agt for A. J. Hand, 1 Apr 1871, for Jefferson, Charlie and Dover Bailey, minor children of Charles Bailey, decd.

J. R. Brooks, Gdn for Mary C. Bailey

Georgia, Fayette Co. - The Following is a List of the Property Sold by E. N. Leach, Admr de bonis non with Will Annexed for the benefit of Heirs and Creditors of I. H. Smith, decd, and C. G. Smith, surviving partner, each and equally interested, 15 Dec 1870
Page 142-147

Among the purchasers from the sale were: J. T. Smith, William Smith, H. C. Fisher, Sam Pinson (colored), Dick Smith, J. H. Wynn, Tuck Pinson, J. W. Arnold, J. A. Whitlock and Lewis Crafield.

Sale Bill of Personal Property of I. H. Smith, 16 Dec 1870. Among the purchasers were: Warren Smith, J. W. Smith, William Smith, Elbert Smith.

Sale Bill of the land belonging to the Estate of I. H. Smith and C. G. Smith, surviving partner - sold 1st Tues. in Nov 1870 - 626 acres of land, 1/2 of which was I. H. Smith's, decd.

Recorded: 4 Jun 1872

Georgia, Fayette County, 30 Dec 1871 } Appraise Bill of Estate of Joseph Banks, decd
Page 148

Appraisers sworn 30 Dec 1871: Bogin Mask, R. M. Henderson and Henson Turner.
Recorded: 15 Jun 1872

The Following Contains a True Inventory and Appraisement of the Goods and Chattels, Lands and tenements of the Estate of John Graves, late of said county, decd, as produced by James M. Austin, Admr
Page 149-154

Appraisers sworn 27 Feb 1872: George W. Robinson, Richmond Dorman, Y. B. Blalock and W. D. Redwine

Sale Bill of the Perishable Property dated 12 Mar 1872. Among the purchasers were: J. D. Graves and J. T. Graves. Recorded: 15 Jun 1872

Lula M. Malone, minor of William and Sarah J. Malone, in Account Current with Thomas C. Malone, Gdn, from the time of appointment to 1 Jul 1872 inclusive
Page 154

Filed: 30 May 1872. Recorded: 13 Jul 1872

Return No. 5 of B. C. Jones' Estate, John A. Richardson, Exr, makes the following Annual Return of said Estate in Fayette Co. on the 8th day of Ja 1871
Page 155-160

1870 rent of plantation
Cash received on 9 City Lots in Atlanta, subdivided into 17 Lots and sold on the 1st ues. in Nov of 1870 under Decree of Court of Chancery.

10 vouchers. Paid J. A. Richardson for boarding Bartee W. Jones in Atlanta High School, 1/4th in college, etc. Also, for boarding at Oglethorpe University (Bartee W. Jones) ending 25 Feb 1872.

B. C. Jones Estate, contd....

Heirs receiving part shares:
T. W. Jones
Miss Ella Jones

State of Georgia, Fulton County, Account of Robert O. Shields (X, his mark), John A. Richardson vs. Thomas A. Jones. Received of Robert Baugh for complaint, $9 the cost. /s/W. R. Venable, Clerk.
Filed: 11 May 1872. Recorded: 13 Jul 1872.

M. L. Yates, Admr, in Account Current with the Estate of James W. Head, on 1 Jan 1869, the same having been the date of the last Return made by William Head, decd, as the former Gdn of the minor children of James W. Head, decd, up to 1 Jan 1872 inclusive
Page 160-162

To amount from date of last Return - See Record Book H, page 881
Filed: 22 Jan 1872. Recorded: 12 Jul 1872

Estate of William Head, in Account Current with Benjamin F. Head, Exr, from 1 Jul 1871 up to 1 Jul 1872 inclusive
Page 162-168

25 vouchers. By cash paid -
Emily Head, Gdn for minor children of J. W. Head (voucher #6)
W. W. Bearden, Agt for Francis Cleckler, Levonia Miles, Eliza A. Yates, Joseph Cleckler, Julia A. Cleckler and Jacob W. Cleckler.

Legatees as follows:
G. W. Bearden
W. T. Bearden
Louticia Head
Susan Post
D. A. J. Black and S. E. Starnes
Martha Head (X, her mark)
Emily Coffee (X, her mark)
Jane Peppers
W. W. Bearden, Agt for M. J. Loblin, S. A. Thompson, D. A. J. Black and S. E. Starnes, legatees
James N. Head
Meredith W. Head
T. J. Head
W. W. Bearden (X, his mark), Gdn for his minor children
E. E. Watson (X, his mark)
E. A. Kerklin (X, his mark)
R. N. Watson
W. F. Bearden
J. A. Bearden (X, his mark)
William Watson
J. W. Watson (X, his mark)
Louisa D. Eastin

Nancy Head recovered against B. F. Head, Exr of William Head, decd, by arbitration, 4 Dec 1871, sums ordered released by the Court on 4 Dec 1871. Nancy's receipt in full for the Fi.Fa.
Filed: 1 Jul 1872. Recorded: 9 Aug 1872

P. M. Trimble, Gdn for Martha L. Ballard, minor orphan of William Ballard, decd, from the year 1871 up to 21 Jul 1872
Page 168-169

Amount received from A. Z. Mims, Admr of William Ballard, decd.
Receipt for tuition of 1871 for Walter Ballard signed by F. M. Collins
Filed: 1 Jul 1872. Recorded: 9 Aug 1872

Annual Return of James R. Bailey, Extr of L. B. Clark for 1872
Page 169-172

17 vouchers. Heirs as follows: F. J. Clark, Rilia Clark, George W. Clark, Ralph Jackson, Matildia C. Jackson, L. M. Clark, J. L. Butler, S. A. Emma Butler, Mary M. Clark, Loisa Bailey, J. R. Bailey, and H. B. Clark.
Filed: 1 Jul 1872. Recorded: 9 Aug 1872

George M. Davis, Admr, in Account Current with John W. Davis, from 1 Jul 1871 to 1 Jul 1872 inclusive
Page 172-173

To amount of interest released on sum of rent of land rented to the highest bidder for cash on the 6th day of Jun 1872...to J. W. Davis, Jr.

Filed: 13 Jul 1872. Recorded: 10 Sept 1872

S. S. Trimble, Gdn for Sarah C. Ballard, minor orphan of William Ballard, decd, for the year 1871
Page 173-175

4 vouchers. To cash paid - G. H. Holiday & Co., F. W. Collins, S. S. Trimble, Ordinary
Filed: 8 Jul 1872. Recorded: 10 Sept 1872

In Account Current with W. J. Grant, Gdn of F. M. Patterson from 1 Apr 1871 to 1 Jul 1872
Page 175

To amount on hand from last Return - See Record Book I, page 31
Filed: 6 Jul 1872. Recorded: 10 Sept 1872

In Account Current with W. J. Grant, Gdn of Drewry Patterson from 1 Apr 1871 to 1 Jul 1872
Page 175

To amount on hand from last Return - See Record Book I, page 31
Filed: 6 Jul 1872. Recorded: 10 Sept 1872

In Account Current with W. J. Grant, Gdn of Roxanna Patterson from 1 Apr 1871 to 1 Jul 1872
Page 175

To amount on hand from last Return - See Record Book I, page 31
Filed: 6 Jul 1872. Recorded: 10 Sept 1872

In Account Current with W. J. Grant, Gdn of Serena Patterson from 1 Apr 1871 to 1 Jul 1872
Page 176

To amount on hand from last Return - See Record Book I, page 32
Filed: 6 Jul 1872. Recorded: 10 Sept 1872

Edward W. Leach, Admr with LWT annexed, Estate of Isaac H. Smith, decd
Page 177-186

1870 receipt for medicine - to A. R. Wellborn

23 vouchers. Palmetto, Ga., 1870 tax.
To cash paid - Arthur Hutchison, J. F. Beckmon (Newnan) and S. E. Lowes (Coweta Co.), Mrs. S. G. Fisher, Broloz & Thomas (for Miss Emma Smith's tuitition, etc. /s/I. T. Cox), Mrs. S. S. Smith, Exr of Estate of I. H. Smith, decd, and C. G. Smith's account (includes cash for Emma Smith), H. C. Fisher, Gdn for Smith minors, viz: Minnie G., Sallie A. and Norah H. Smith, and Rufus W. Andrews for pro-rata share of Miss Emma G. Smith, heir.

Filed: 1 Jun 1872. Recorded: 10 Sept 1872

Amanda J. Speer, in Account Current with Gdn of minor children of John T. Speer up to 1 Jun 1872
Page 187

Filed: 3 Sept 1872. Recorded: 4 Dec 1872

H. C. Fisher, Gdn, in Account Current with Minnie G., Sallie A. and Nora H. Smith, minor children of Isaac H. Smith, decd, from time of appointment until 8 Aug 1872
Page 187-191

Distribution made to above minors for $607.60 each.
Includes some Senoia, Ga. accounts
Recorded: 4 Dec 1872

An Account Current and Final Settlement with Azariah Mims, Admr of William Ballard, decd, from 16 Jun 1871 to 2 Sept 1872 inclusive
Page 191-197

To amount on hand from last Return - See Record Book I, page 45
13 vouchers.

To cash paid -

C. M. Tidwell
S. Harvey, tax collector
W. M. Hathcock, Gdn for Claborn Ballard
P. M. Trimble, Gdn for Martha L. Ballard, daughter of William Ballard
J. A. Chapman
S. S. Trimble, Gdn of Sarah C. Ballard
William M. Ballard, son of William Ballard, decd, signed at Limestone Co., Texas
Margaret A. Ballard
Martha L. Ballard
S. S. Trimble, Gdn of Sarah C. Ballard, daughter of William Ballard
J. A. Chapman, Gdn of M. J. E. Ballard (dated at Campbell Co., Ga.)

Estate of John T. McKey, in Account Current with S. T. Bridges, Admr. from 1 Jul 1871 to 1 Jul 1872
Page 197-199

By amount due, See Record Book I, page 136
8 vouchers. To cash paid - M. O. McKey, Fisher & Shephard, L. Harrison, tax collector, Daniel Walker, W. T. Read, D. C. Minor, Ordinary, R. T. Dorsey, S. T. Bridges.

Filed: 17 Sept 1872. Recorded: 14 Feb 1872

William Guice, Gdn, in Account Current with Linton and Elizabeth Guice, minors of Peter Guice, decd, from 1 Apr 1871 up to 1 Dec 1872 inclusive
Page 200

To amount on hand from last Return - See Record Book I, page 36
2 vouchers.
Filed: 17 Dec 1872. Recorded: 15 Feb 1872

Sale Bill of Perishable Property of William Wyatt, decd, Sold on 25 Nov 1873
Page 201

The only purchaser was: E. W. Leach.

Inventory and Appraisement. Appraisers sworn 6 Jul 1872 - E. W. Leach, W. J. Campbell, J. A. Brown.
Recorded: 15 Mar 1873

Inventory and Appraisement of the Estate of G. W. Stinchcomb of Fayette Co., decd
Page 202

Appraisers sworn 9 Sept 1872 - D. Adams, J. W. Johnson, O. O. Baker
Recorded: 15 Mar 1872

Return of Daniel McLucas, Exr of Joseph Banks, decd, in Account Current with the Heirs of said Estate and Credited first Return on said Estate, up to 1 Jan 1873 inclusive
Page 203-204

8 vouchers. Paid - L. F. Blalock, W. H. Blalock, Camp & Blalock, J. W. Banks, Z. B. Blalock, A. J. Jones, Nancy Banks (widow of Joseph Banks - for support)

Sale Bill of Personal Property of C. DeVaughn, decd, Sold by John Farr, Exr, on 23 Oct 1872
Page 204-206

Among the purchasers were: G. Bearden, Thomas Farr, Rose DeVaughn, W. W. Walker, T. J. Askew, F. Ware and W. Coleman.
Filed 10 Mar 1873. Recorded: 21 Mar 1873

Inventory and Appraisement of the Estate of Samuel Swanson, late of Fayette Co., decd
Page 207-208

Appraisers: W. F. Glower, J. E. H. Ware, E. W. Leach, sworn 2 Nov 1872
Thomas P. Swanson, Admr

Order to set aside for 12 months support of Mrs. M. A. P. Swanson. Recorded: 18 Apr 1872

Estate of Guy Banister, decd, in Account Current with Nathaniel Stinchcomb, Exr, in Account Current and Final Settlement
Page 210-213

To amount collected of W. Wilson and J. Christopher

O. F. Banister has received $64.34, See Book I, page 67
John L. Banister is entitled to $92.17, See Book I, page 67
Mary Pollard is entitled to $71.16, See Book I, page 67
Louisa Banister is entitled to $57.12, See Book I, page 67
Total paid to Louise Banister - $960.72
Guyanna Banister is entitled to $57.12, See Book I, page 67

Filed: 22 Feb 1872. Recorded: 18 Apr 1873

Sale Bill of Estate of Samuel Swanson, decd
Page 214-216

Among the purchasers were: Simon Swanson, M. W. Swanson, W. W. Swanson, Louis Swanson, Widow Swanson, Albert Swanson.

Filed: 10 Apr 1873. Recorded: 20 Apr 1873

First Annual Return of Thomas P. Swanson, Admr of Samuel Swanson, decd
Page 216-221

19 vouchers. Voucher #5 was signed by Samuel Swanson...."By the first day of Nov next, I promise to pay W. F. Landrum, Exr of Jeptha Landrum, decd, $1393.48 as part of purchase money for Town Lot No. 1, Block B in Fairburn. Note: The exr paid off this obligation.
Years' support granted to Mrs. M. A. P. Swanson (X, her mark).
Accounts paid to T. B. Swanson.

Heirs receiving their shares:
M. W. Swanson
Mary W. Whatly and Johnston Whatly
Hillery Cleckler and Catherine E. Cleckler

Inventory and Appraisement of Personal Property of Estate of John I. Whitaker, decd
Page 222-223

Appraisers sworn 10 May 1873 - William L. Fletcher, T. W. Ballard, W. W. Mathews, J. F. McLane
Includes Lots as follows: No. 170, 184, North 1/2 of Lot 168, 185.
Filed: 20 May 1873. Recorded: 17 Jun 1873

Inventory and Appraisement of Estate of Catherine DeVaughn, late of Fayette Co., decd
Page 223-224

Estate produced by Exr.
T. J. Askew, Bennett Adams, H. Cook, appraisers sworn 7 May 1872
Filed: 10 Jul 1872. Recorded: 17 Jun 1873

James Davis, Seaborn Harris and W. J. Milner, appraisers of the N. E. 50 acres of N. Norton, Lot 230, as property of Nazareth Norton, decd
Page 224

Filed: 4 Jan 1873. Recorded: 8 Jun 1873

Inventory and Appraisement of Estate of Sarah Loyd
Page 225-228

B. Adams, J. A. Whitaker, J. L. Richardson, M. W. Swanson, W. T. Glowers apptd appraisers on 13 Jul 1872.
Sale Bill. Among the purchasers were: T. J. Askew, Bennett Adams, T. C. Speer, James Loyd, T. B. Griggs, S. N. Knowles, N. Loyd, Simon Swanson. Recorded: 5 Jul 1873

Inventory and Appraisement of Estate of Samuel H. Ellison
Page 229-232

Appraisers sworn 12 Jan 1873 - Witt Chandler, E. W. Leach and M. W. Swanson
Sale Bill of Perishable Property. Among purchasers were: W. L. Ellison, Emily Ellison
Filed: 7 Jul 1873. Recorded: 10 Jul 1873

Sale Bill of Perishable Property of G. W. Stinchcomb, decd, 7 Nov 1872
Page 233-236

Among purchasers were: N. Stinchcomb, P. Stinchcomb and Mrs. M. A. Stinchcomb
Recorded: 12 Jul 1873

Estate of Bird M. Jackson, decd, in Account Current with John J. Gilbert, Admr, 7 Nov 1871 and in full showing the entire estate and settlement of the same, this being a Final Return
Page 236-239

To total amount of estate received from all sources - See Record Book I, page 124

Heirs as follows:
A. J. Jackson (X, his mark). See Book I, page 124
Jesse Jackson, see Book I, page 124
John M. Pyron, Gdn for P. E. McLeroy
W. C. Lord and Jane Lord for P. E. McLeroy
E. B. Jackson
William Cato
R. W. Tarpley, Gdn for Bird and Marion Jackson
Filed: 3 May 1873. Recorded: 12 Jul 1873

An Account Current with W. W. Mathews, Exr of LWT of Alexander Smith, decd, from 3 Jul 1871 to 1 Jul 1872 inclusive
Page 239-246

From last Return - See Record Book I, page 57
5 vouchers
Legatees: Mary Travis, R. H. Pope, Ritter Pope

Recorded: 14 Jul 1873

An Account Current with W. W. Mathews, Exr of LWT of Alexander Smith, decd, up to 1 Jul 1873
Page 239-246

To amount received from Sale Bill, See Book I, page 58
For amount of expense, see Book I, page 57

Voucher #3 paid A. C. Noras for medicine (1867) for Patience Smith's last illness.

Heirs - shares paid to: (each receiving $109.92)
Allen Reeves, Gdn of Nancy Reeves
Susan S. Johnson, now but formerly Susan Duffel
Mary Travis
M. A. Duffel
Patience Duffel
James T. Travis
Nancy Prestley
Hardy H. Pope
W. W. Mathews
R. M. Mathews
M. W. Mathews
Alexander Reeves
Piety Reeves (X, her mark)
Allen Reeves
Recorded: 14 Jul 1873

E. W. Leach, Gdn, in Account Current with J. L. Landrum, J. Q. Landrum and Jefferson D. Landrum, minor children of Washington Landrum, decd, from time of appointment to 1 Jul 1873
Page 247-249

7 vouchers. To amount received of W. F. Landrum, Exr of Jeptha Landrum, decd, who was the Admr of Washington Landrum, settlement made and paid 25 Dec 1872 - $1415.00
To Margaret White (X, her mark), for boarding J. D. Landrum

Heirs as follows -
Jefferson D. Landrum (vouchers 3-6)...."Jefferson D. Landrum departed this life Mar 1873 and being a minor, his estate will be divided between his brother, C. J. Landrum, an adult brother who is of age, J. Q. Landrum, and J. L. Landrum, minors.
J. Q. Landrum
J. L. Landrum

Recorded: 16 Jul 1873

Inventory and Appraisement of the Goods and Chattels, Lands and Tenements of William Johnson, late of said county, decd, as produced to us by W. L. Williams, Admr of said Estate, to-wit:
Page 249-250

Includes 100 acres of land, etc.
Appraisers: J. A. Whitlock (X, his mark), C. H. Knowles, C. G. Davis, A. McEachin, John Lester, sworn 11 Jul 1873.

Filed: 11 Jul 1873. Recorded: 17 Jul 1873

Inventory and Schedule of Notes of John I. Whitlock, decd
Page 250-251

C. B. Nipper, Admr.
Filed: 7 Jun 1873

An Account Current with W. W. Bearden, Gdn of the minor children, from 1 Feb 1872 up to 1 Jul 1873 inclusive
Page 251

Estate to be divided among 6 heirs.
Receipt of M. A. E. Bearden for share of esate.

Filed: 7 Jul 1873. Recorded: 8 Aug 1873

H. C. Fisher, Gdn, in Account Current with Minnie G., Sallie A. and Nora H. Smith, minor children of I. H. Smith, decd, from 8 Aug 1872 up to 7 Jul 1873 inclusive
Page 252-254

19 vouchers. To amount paid to Sallie A. Smith from last Return - See Book I, page 187
To amount paid Norah H. Smith from last Return - See Book I, page 187

Filed: 7 Jul 1873. Recorded: 8 Aug 1873

Estate of Sarah Loyd, decd, in Account Current with Samuel Loyd, Admr, from date of appointment up to 1 Jul 1873 inclusive.
Page 255-257

To amount of sale of personal property as contained in Appraise Bill on Page 225 of Book I and returned in per Bill. See Book I, page 226. 16 vouchers.

Filed: 3 Jul 1873. Recorded: 13 Aug 1873

Mary Speer, Admx of Estate of William Speer, decd, from 22 Jul 1870 up to 1 Jul 1873 inclusive
Page 258-259

5 vouchers. Filed: 3 Jul 1873. Recorded: 13 Aug 1873

G. M. Davis, in Account Current with the Estate of J. W. Davis, from 1 Jul 1872 up to 1 Jul 1873 inclusive
Page 259-260

4 vouchers. To cash paid - D. C. Minor, E. Connor, R. T. Dorsey, I. B. Griggs
Filed: 1 Jul 1873. Recorded: 13 Aug 1873

T. C. Speer, Gdn, in Account Current with J. W. T. Speer and Joseph M. Speer, minor children of John W. Speer, decd, from date of appointment up to 1 Jul 1873 inclusive
Page 260

3 vouchers. Filed: 5 Jul 1873. Recorded: 13 Aug 1873

P. M. Trimble, Gdn for Martha L. Ballard, minor child of William Ballard, decd, from 21 Jul 1872 up to 21 Jul 1873 inclusive
Page 261

4 vouchers. Voucher #4 refers to Martha as "Mattie".
Filed: 24 Jul 1873. Recorded: 11 Sept 1873

S. S. Trimble, Gdn for Sarah C. Ballard, minor child of William Ballard, decd, from 21 Jul 1872 to 21 Jul 1873 inclusive
Page 262

4 vouchers. Filed: 29 Jun 1873 Recorded: 8 Aug 1873

An Account Current with J. E. C. W. Smith, Gdn of Sarah F. and T. C. Speer, minor children of John W. Speer, from date of appointment up to 1 Jul 1873
Page 263

Voucher #2 - Received of J. E. C. W. Smith $20.00, being amount of my fee for distribution and settlement in Fayette Superior Court, including division of rent of J. W. Speer's account, this received of said Smith as Gdn of Sarah F. and T. C. Speer, minors of John W. Speer, decd. 29 Oct 1872. /s/John D. Stewart, atty at law

Filed: 5 Jul 1873. Recorded: 13 Aug 1873

B. O. Jones' Estate, 8 Jan 1872 up to 8 Jan 1873 inclusive
Page 264-268

John A. Richardson, Exr. Return on 8 Jan 1872 includes 22 vouchers.
James Robinson's receipt for boarding Bartee W. Jones 1872 and 1873.
Voucher #8 for cemetery monument erected in the City of Atlanta Cemetery
Voucher #22 - tuition for B. W. Jones in Oglethorpe University.

Inventory and Appraisement of Estate of J. P. Shropshire, decd
Page 268-269

D. D. Durham, B. L. Johnson, C. C. Bustin, B. Head, E. W. Leach, appraisers sworn 29 Jul 1873

Includes 202 1/2 acres in 7th District of Clayt Co., Ga.
Filed: 16 Aug 1873. Recorded: 19 Aug 1873

Mathew Baker, Admr of Estate of James Baker, decd, from date of appointment to 1 Aug 1873
Page 270

Filed: 2 Aug 1873. Recorded: 11 Sept 1873

The minor children of Hugh Porter, decd, to-wit: Ophelia, A. R. and J. H. Porter, in Account Current with J. F. McLane, Gdn, from time of appointment to 23 Jul 1873
Page 271-272

Includes 7 vouchers. Maria Stripling paid tuition for children for 1870.
Filed: 22 Jul 1873 Recorded: 11 Sept 1873

Georgia, Fayette Co., Inventory and Appraisement of Estate of Marcus Varner, 21 Aug 1873
Page 273-274

James T. Travis, W. W. Mathews, Robert Jones, appraisers sworn on 21 Aug 1873.
Recorded: 22 Sept 1873

Inventory of the Property of W. P. Chandler, decd
Page 274-275

Includes 568 acres. George W. Slaton, Admr. Appraisers: Witt Chandler, William L. Wilson, E. W. Leach.
Filed: 13 Sept 1873. Recorded: 23 Sept 1873

A List of the Sale of the Goods and Chattels of John I. Whitaker, late of Fayette Co., Sold by C. B. Nipper, Admr, on 30 Jul 1873
Page 275-276

Among the purchasers were: Mrs. Whitaker, W. R. Whitaker, Shadrick Whitaker

Filed: 13 Sept 1873.
Recorded: 23 Sept 1873

James Graves, Admr, in Account Current with Estate of Minton Graves, decd, from 1 Jul 1870 up to 1 Sept 1873 inclusive
Page 276-280

28 vouchers. Heirs receiving part of their shares, as follows:

Jesse Ward
N. G. Wallis, Agt for Henry Jones
N. G. Wallis, Agt for William Bagley
N. G. Wallis, Agt for Mrs. Sallie Cobb
N. G. Wallis, Agt for Mary A. Howard
N. G. Wallis, Agt for John Mack
N. G. Wallis, Agt for Jasper Hicks
Mrs Elizabeth Graves (X, her mark) upon the power of atty of J. L. Martin
Mrs. Sarah Collier
John Graves (X, his mark)
Sally Graves
Thomas L. Jenkins
Elizabeth Graves, Gdn of George Graves
J. N. McEachin, Gdn for E. M. McEachin
J. N. McEachin, Gdn for Wiley Graves
Elizabeth Graves, Agt for James Martin
J. T. Brogdon
E. M. Graves
James Graves
J. L. Graves for Hardy Graves James P. Formby, Marion Goosley, David Jennings and Martha Graves
Filed: 30 Aug 1873. Recorded: 14 Oct 1873

W. L. Ellison, Exr of Estate of Samuel H. Ellison, from the time of his appointment to 1 Jul 1873
Page 281-183

To amount of Sale Bill of personal property, See Book I, page 230.
10 vouchers.

Heirs as follows:
F. M. and E. J. Harrell
F. M. Ellison
D. C. Stokes, Agt for S. T. Stokes
A. P. Landrum
L. A. Landrum
Filed: 3 Jul 1873. Recorded: 14 Oct 1873

Georgia, Fayette Co., By virtue of our appointment as appraisers to appraise the Estate of James L. Keilsman, decd
Page 283

Signed the Appraisers: John T. Hewell, Kellet Babb, L. B. Lewis.
Includes 87 acres. Filed: 11 Aug 1873. Recorded: 23 Oct 1873

Inventory and Appraisement of Estate of Dempsey Brown
Page 283-284

Appraisers: E. W. Leach, G. W. Slaton, William J. Guy, W. J. Campbell, T. C. Speer, sworn 20 Sept 1873
Recorded: 1 Nov 1873

Inventory and Appraisement of Estate of Mary Bagwell, decd
Page 284

J. A. Carmichael, N. Miller, J. A. Haisten, appraisers sworn on 10 Oct 1873
Includes 156 acres of land
Recorded: 1 Nov 1873

Estate of George W. Stinchcomb, in Account Current with Phillip Stinchcomb, Admr, from time of appointment to 1 Jul 1873 inclusive
Page 285-289

14 vouchers. To amount of Sale Bill of the Personal Property, See Book I, page 233
Filed: 2 Oct 1873. Recorded: 7 Nov 1873

Inventory and Appraisement of Estate of R. C. Bridges
Page 289

W. F. Kelly, N. W. Gable, J. A. Carmichael, Appraisers sworn on 10 Oct 1873.
Recorded: 12 Oct 1873

Inventory and Appraisement of Estate of H. M. Rogers
Page 289-290

Appraisers: J. H. Murphy, J. C. Nash, Mathew Orr, H. H. Simpson, Z. B. Blalock, sworn on 15 Aug 1873
Recorded: 15 Nov 1873

Inventory and Appraisement of Estate of Isaac P. Gay
Page 291

Includes 120 acres in the 6th District of Coweta Co. and a fraction of Lot No. 121.
William J. Gay, Gdn of Isaac P. Gay, certifies the inventory.
Recorded: 17 Dec 1873

Estate of Dempsey Brown, in Account Current with James H. Brown, one of the Executors, from the date of Letters to 30 Oct 1873 inclusive
Page 292-293

By amount turned over to Martha Brown (X, her mark) - $2222.51
7 vouchers. Filed: 30 Oct 1873. Recorded: 18 Dec 1873

Estate of John T. McKey, in Account Current with S. T. Bridges, Admr, from 1 Jul 1872 up to 1 Jul 1873 inclusive
Page 293-295

9 vouchers. Receipt from M. O. Mackey, the widow, for dower.
Filed: 18 Oct 1873. Recorded: 19 Dec 1873

Sale Bill of Personal and Perishable Property of J. P. Shropshire, decd, Sold by A. J. Shropshire, Admr, on 11 Dec 1873
Page 295-296

Among the purchasers were: S. J. Shropshire, M. L. Shropshire
Recorded: 20 Dec 1873

Sale Bill of the Personal Estate of Mary S. Bagwell, decd
Page 296-297

Purchasers were: L. M. Cobb, Thomas Cobb, L. T. Cobb, James Bridges, Nathan Farber, W. E. Swinny, Martha Grant and M. H. Martin

Recorded: 19 Jan 1874

Widow's Support and One child of John I. Whitaker, decd
Page 298

By appraisers: William L. Fletcher, T. W. Ballard, W. W. Mathews, Jason F. McLane, sworn on 10 May 1873
Filed: 20 May 1873. Recorded: 26 Jan 1874

12 Months' Support Set Aside for Widow of John Graves
Page 298

Appraisers: G. W. Robinson, Richmond Dorman, Z. B. Blalock, W. P. Redwine
Recorded: 26 May 1874

Sale Bill of Perishable Property of Estate of H. M. Rogers, decd, Sold by Gilbert Williams, Admrs, on 19 Dec 1873
Page 299-300

Among the purchasers were: I. B. Avera, Mrs. J. D. Rogers, J. R. Tarpley, H. H. Tarpley and Mrs. Marshburn.
Filed: 16 Feb 1874. Recorded: 10 Mar 1874

Thomas C. Malone, Gdn, in Account Current with Lola Malone, a minor, from 1 Jul 1872 to 1 Jan 1874 inclusive
Page 301-302

To amount on hand from last Return, See Book I, page 154
To cash paid - William Malone (boarding and clothing), Larkin Harrison (tax collector), C. W. Richter (tuition for 1873), G. M. Davis & Co., Stewart & Newton, L. B. Griggs, Ordinary. 7 vouchers.

Filed: 6 Jan 1874. Recorded: 10 Mar 1874

Sarah C. Ballard, in Account Current with S. S. Kimble, Gdn, from 21 Jul 1873 to date
Page 302-303

5 vouchers. Filed: 20 Jan 1874. Recorded: 10 Mar 1874

In person came before S. S. Trimble, Gdn of Sarah C. Ballard, who being sworn, says the above Return is true. 6 Jan 1874. /s/S. S. Trimble

Rachel Eason, Admx of Estate of Richard B. Eason, decd
Page 304

Heirs: Mary Eason and James Eason (x, his mark)

Georgia, Fayette Co., Inventory and Appraisement of Estate of Joel G. Godwin, late of said county, decd
Page 305

1/4th interest in Lot of Land No. 109, 9th District, Fayette Co.

Commissioners were appointed to set apart the whole of the estate for the benefit of the minor children, as follows: John Favor, J. L. Graves, W. G. Franklin, N. G. Wallis, C. H. Eastin

Georgia, Fayette Co...Isaac Hartly, Agent of the minor children of Joel G. Godwin, late of said county.

Appraisers: John Favor, Jasper L. Graves, N. G. Wallis, C. H. Eastin, W. F. Franklin
Recorded: 4 Apr 1874

William Guice, Gdn, in Account Current with Linton and Elizabeth Guice, minor children of Peter Guide, from the first day of Dec 1872 to the first day of Mar 1874 inclusive
Page 306

To amount on hand from last Return, See Book I, page 200
2 vouchers, one for tuition for Linton and Billie Guice. /s/Jeanett Howell

Inventory and Appraisement Estate of Loduska Turner, late of said county
Page 306-307

Includes 50 acres in the N. E corner of Lot No. 108, Fayette Co.

Appraisers: W. Armstrong, Ephraim Stewart, W. B. Jones and Hinson Turner (x his mark).
A. A. Turner, Admr. Recorded: 14 Apr 1874

Georgia, Fayette Co., To the Ordinary of said County - Ordered to set aside 12 months' Support for the Widow of Joshua Shropshire, decd, having met on the 29th day of Jul 1873
Page 307

Widow, Mrs. M. L. Shropshire
Commissioners: B. L. Johnson, B. F. Head, E. W. Bustin, D. D. Denham, C. W. Leach.
Filed: 16 Aug 1873. Recorded: 14 Apr 1874

Order to set aside a sum necessary for the support of the widow and children of H. M. Rogers, decd
Page 308

$800 set aside and household furniture, etc.

Commissioners: J. H. Murphy, Mathew Orr, J. C. Nash, H. W. Simpson and Z. B. Blalock
Recorded: 17 Apr 1874

Order to set aside $200 for the support of the widow of Marcus Varner, decd, on 21 Aug 1873
Page 308

Commissioners: James T. Travis, Robert Jones, W. W. Mathews
Filed: 1 Sept 1873. Recorded: 17 Apr 1874

Order to set aside for the support of the widow and children of W. P. Chandler, decd, for 12 months' support
Page 308-308

Furniture and property set apart.
Commissioners: Wit Chandler, William L. Ellis and C. W. Leach
Filed: 22 Sept 1873. Recorded: 22 Apr 1874

Order to set aside for the support of the widow and minor children of P. C. Bridges, decd, on 25 Oct 1873
Page 309

Commissioners: N. N. Gable, J. A. Carmichael, W. F. Kelly
Filed: 27 Oct 1873. Recorded: 23 Apr 1874

Sale Bill Belonging to the Estate of J. L. Hilsman, decd, Sold on the first Tues. in Nov 1873 for cash to E. C. Lewis
Page 310

Recorded: 19 May 1874

Sale of Personal Property of Marcus Varner, decd, Sold by M. W. Swanson
Page 310-311

Among purchasers: Mary Varner, Molen Shepherd, M. E. Shepherd, N. W. Swanson, Ben Wagters, Barny Arnold and Love Gay.

Recorded: 19 May 1874

Estate of Marcus Varner in Account Current with M. W. Swanson, Admr, from the time of his Letters to 24 Apr 1874 showing Final Settlement of said Estate
Page 311-312

By amount of personal property - see Book I, page 310
By amount of land - see Book I, page 311

5 vouchers. To cash paid - L. B. Griggs and Mary Varner
Filed: 3 Apr 1874. Recorded: 8 Jun 1874

Herod Thornton, Admr of Estate of Haywood Thornton, decd, from 2nd day of Oct 1871 to 29 Apr 1874
Page 313-316

By amount on hand since last Return - see Book I, page 105
16 vouchers. Filed: 29 Apr 1874. Recorded: 8 Jun 1874

W. S. Milner, Admr, in Account Current with the Estate of Jennie L. Hilsman, decd, from the time of appointment up to 27 Apr 1874
Page 316-317

$400 in full to Estate - Jennie L. Hilsman, decd, *my* wife. /s/J. W. Hilsman, husband of J. L. Hilsman

W. S. Milner, Gdn, in Account Current with Ellen G. and J. E. Hilsman, minor children of James Hilsman, decd, from 1 Jan 1873 to 28 Apr 1874
Page 317-318

To cash paid - Josiah Hilsman, former Gdn
To amount paid - Jeff Hilsman
2 vouchers.

Voucher #1, 2 Dec 1870 /s/J. E. Hilsman, son of James Hilsman, decd, for $342 in full settlement, dated at Henry Co., Ga.

Rebecca C. Smith, Gdn, in Account Current with A. C. Speer and Emily A. Barge, formerly Emily A. Speer, minors of B. C. Spear, decd, from 1 Jul 1874 to date, the same being for Final Return
Page 318-319

We take first A. C. Speer who was entitled to this sum as will appear in Book I, page 61

We now take Emily A. Barge, formerly Speer, and we find that on page 62 of Book I she and two other minors were entitled to on the first of Jul 1871

4 vouchers.
Filed: 29 May 1874. Recorded: 9 Jul 1874

2nd Annual Return of Thomas P. Swanson, Admr of the Estate of Samuel Swanson, decd, from 6 Mar 1873 to 29 May 1874
Page 319-322

To amount on hand at last Annual Return - see Book I, page 216
14 vouchers. Voucher #17, M. A. P. Swanson vs. T. B. Swanson, Admr of S. Swanson, Received $22 in full for said cases, 29 May 1874. /s/A. E. Stokes, Clerk
Filed: 29 May 1874. Recorded: 9 Jul 1874

James R. Baily, Exr of L. B. Clarke, decd, a Final Settlement with said Estate
Page 323-324

3 vouchers. Filed: 18 Jun 1874. Recorded: 7 Aug 1874
Voucher #1, Jonesboro, Ga., Received Jan 1874 of James R. Baily, Exr of L. B. Clarke, decd, $47.60 in full of W. F. Clarke's share of said estate... /s/J. M. Austin

W. F. Clarke, father of L. B. Clarke, (negro) property sold on 25 Dec in Fayette Co.
10 Negroes -

Mundy, about age 28
Henry, age 26
Susan, age 22
Martha, age 16
Adam, age 14
Barry, age 10
Charles, age 8
James, age 6
Roxy, age 5
infant, about 2

Lot of Land East of the Lot on which his late father lived known as the Starr lot, his being the 1/11th part of the above described property.

Estate of Catherine DeVaughn, in Account Current with John H. Farr, Exr, from the date of appointment to 8 Jan 1874 inclusive
Page 324-328

To amount of sale of land - see Book I, page 206
To amount of sale of personal property - see Book I, page 204
16 vouchers. Filed: 8 Jun 1874. Recorded: 8 Aug 1874

Heirs receiving part distribution, as follows:

Margaret Goodman, attorney in fact, for Thomas L. Johnson, only child of John Goodman, decd, brother of Catherine DeVaughn

T. L. Goodman, attorney in fact, for Anna O'Brien, wife of W. B. O'Brien, Anna being the only child of Catherine Doris who was one of the 6 children of Robert Gilham, decd, who was a brother of Catherine DeVaughn, decd.

Harry J. Gilham, Jr., son of Harry Gilham, Sr., decd, who was a son of Robert Gilham, decd, brother of Catherine DeVaughn, decd, the said Harry Gilham, Jr. being one of the two children of said Harry Gilham, Sr., decd, by T. L. Johnson, attorney in fact

Return No. 5 of Estate of B. O. Jones, decd, from 8 Jan 1873 to 8 Jan 1874 inclusive, with John A. Richardson, Exr
Page 328-330

7 vouchers. To cash paid J. Robinson for boarding Bartee W. Jones.
Filed: 3 Jan 1874. Recorded: 8 Aug 1874

Estate of J. P. Shropshire, in Account Current with A. J. Shropshire, from appointment to 8th Jun 1874
Page 331-338

31 vouchers (includes numerous sales of bales of cotton)

Heirs receiving part shares, as follows:

Aurelia Shropshire
M. L. Shropshire, for 12 months' support
S. Fanin Shropshire
L. M. Shropshire
A. J. Shropshire

Filed:8 Jun 1874. Recorded: 10 Aug 1874

Inventory and Appraisement of Estate of Daniel Shell of Fayette Co.
Page 338-339

Appraisers: John W. Dunbar, Charles W. Biles, Abraham Stainheimer, J. C. Grimes, N.W. Gable, sworn on 12 Jun 1874.

Recorded: 31 Aug 1874

Inventory and Appraisement of the Perishable Property of P. M. Maynard, decd
Page 339-340

Appraisers: C. P. Lynch, W. G. Bishop, James W. Lynch
Recorded: 31 Aug 1874

Sale Bill of Perishable Property of P. M. Maynard, late of Fayette Co., decd, Sold on 5th day of Nov 1843
Page 341-342

Among purchasers were: B. M. Maynard, M. Maynard, W. P. Maynard

Beds and clothing not sold turned over to minors at appraisement by Admrs, viz: Christian Maynard, Ella Maynard, Larkin Maynard,and Barto Maynard.

Recorded: 31 Aug 1874

Inventory and Appraisement of Estate of Charles Austin, late of said county, decd
Page 343

Appraisers: J. J. Gilbert, Seaborn Harris, T. P. Gray, Reubin Jackson,sworn on 17 Aug 1874
Recorded: 31 Aug 1874

Inventory and Appraisement of Estate of Wiet Chandler, late of said county, decd
Page 344

Appraisers: W. A. Leach, J. A. Brown, W. J. Campbell, sworn 15 Aug 1874
Recorded: 31 Aug 1874

Inventory and Appraisement of Estate of John Faver
Page 345-346

Includes 1860 acres with improvements. Paul Faver, Admr
Appraisers: W. P. Redwine, Isaac Hartly, C. H. Eastin, E. C. Bustin, sworn 33 Aug 1874
Recorded: 12 Sept 1874

T. C. Speer, Gdn of J. M. Speer, minor of John H. Speer, in Account Current with said minor, from 5 Jul 1873 to 6 Jul 1873 inclusive
Page 347-348

To amount on hand from last Return - see Book I, page 260
6 vouchers. Filed: 7 Jul 1874. Recorded: 12 Sept 1874

An Account Current with W. W. Bearden, Gdn of his minor children, from 1 Jul 1873 to 6 Jul 1874 inclusive
Page 348

To amount on hand from last Return - see Book I, page 251
2 vouchers. Filed: 6 Jul 1874. Recorded: 12 Sept 1874

H. C. Fisher, Gdn, in Account Current with Minnie, Sallie A. and Norah H. Smith, minor children of Isaac H. Smith, decd, from 7 Jul 1873 to 6 Jul 1874 inclusive
Page 349-351

6 vouchers. Filed: 6 Jul 1874. Recorded: 12 Sept 1874

W. L. Ellison, Exr of Estate of Samuel H. Ellison, from 1 Jul 1873 to 1 Jul 1874 inclusive
Page 351-353

10 vouchers. Heirs receiving part shares -

F. M. Ellison
L. A. Landrum (x, his mark)
N. P. Landrum
Sarah T. Stokes
David E. Stokes
E. J. Harrell

Received of William L. Ellison, Exr of Samuel H. Ellison, decd, as Gdn for the minor orphans of Jeptha Landrum. /s/E. W. Leach, Gdn

Filed: 6 Jul 1874. ecorded: 18 Sept 1874

Estate of Mary Bagwell, decd, in Account Current with Blakely Bagwell, Admr, from the time of appointment until 1 Jul 1874
Page 353-355

To amount from sale of personal property - see Sale Bill, Book I, page 297
To amount of rent of estate for the year 1873, the same having been returned for #900 lint cotton, which cotton was sold for .14 per pd.

10 vouchers. Filed: 27 Jul 1874. Recorded: 12 Sept 1874

Estate of Isaac P. Gay, Lunatic, in Account Current with W. J. Gay, Gdn, from the time of appointment until 1 Jul 1874 inclusive
Page 356-373

See Appraise Bill, Book I, page 291
53 vouchers consisting of a considerable estate. Mentions Isaac P. Gay, the ward of W. J. Gay
Filed: 21 Jul 1874. Recorded: 14 Sept 1874

Estate of John I. Whitaker, in Account Current with C. B. Nipper, Admr, from the time of his appointment up to 8 Jul 1874
Page 373-375

To amount of sale of personal property, see Sale Book Book I, page _____
To amount of sale of Lot No. 7, see Sale Book I, page _____

9 vouchers. 12 months' support granted to Levicy Whitaker, widow
Filed: 19 Jul 1874. Recorded: 14 Sept 1874

Estate of John Phillips, in Account Current with Louisa Phillips, Admx, from the time of appointment to 1 Jul 1874 inclusive
Page 375-378

To the Ordinary - The following amount is made upon the death of John Phillips in the condition of affairs the administrator, who was the wife and widow of deceased, availed herself of the provision of the condition of the state. She kept the 4 children of deceased together with some minor children of deceased's daughter on the promise of said estate and support. That no account was kept of expenses and income, as the family jointly occupied and enjoyed the entire estate.

Filed: 5 Jul 1874. Recorded: 4 Sept 1874

Sale Bill of the Personal Property of Charles Austin, decd, Sold on the 3rd day of Sept 1874 on 2 months by S. W. Clark, Temporary Admr.
Page 378-380

Among purchasers: J. M. Austin, N. Austin
Recorded: 14 Sept 1874

An Account Current with Gainy Westbrook, Gdn of Anna, Eliza and John Loyd, minor children of John Loyd, decd, from the time of appointment to 1 Jul 1874
Page 380-381

2 vouchers. Filed: 25 Aug 1874. Recorded: 10 Oct 1874

P. M. Trimble, Gdn, in Account Current with Martha L. Ballard, minor child of William Ballard, decd, from 21 Jul 1873 to 21 Jul 1874
Page 381-382

3 vouchers. To amount on hand from last Return, see Book I, page 261
Recorded: 10 Oct 1874

In Account Current with T. C. Speer, Gdn of J. W. T. Speer, minor of J. W. Speer, from 1 Jul 1873 to 27 Aug 1874, Showing a Final Settlement with said Ward
Page 382

To amount from last Return, see Book I, page 260. 2 vouchers.
Filed: 27 Aug 1874. Recorded: 14 Oct 1874

An Account Current with John L. Stephens, Admr of the Estate of John W. Stephens, decd, Showing a Final Settlement of said Estate to 28 Aug 1874
Page 383

To amount received on judgment for damages from Hillery Cleckler.
5 vouchers. Voucher #4 from G. T. Stephens for his part of money coming from Hillery Cleckler. Voucher #5, Received of John L. Stephens, Admr of John L. Stephens, my part of the money collected from Hillery Cleckler. /s/ J. T. Stephens

Filed: 28 Aug 1874. Recorded: 14 Oct 1874

Estate of A. R. Smith, in Account Current with R. N. Smith, Admr, from 1 Jul 1871 to 22 Aug 1874 Showing Final Settlement with said Estate
Page 384

To amount on hand from last Return, Book I, page 40. 4 vouchers.
Filed: 22 Aug 1874. Recorded: 14 Oct 1874

Sale Bill of the Personal Property of H. C. Travis, decd
Page 385

Purchasers: S. C. Travis, Martin Travis, C. E. Travis, Mary Travis, J. T. Travis, Fred Travis, J. V. Turner, W. D. Busbin and J. C. Grimes.

192 1/2 acres in Land Lot No. 5 was sold to S. C. Travis on the first Tues. in Oct. 1874.

Recorded: 10 Nov 1874

Inventory and Appraisement of the Estate of William J. Russell, late of said county, to-wit:
Page 386-387

Appraisers: James M. Palmer, L. L. Handly, S. E. Christopher and E. M. Barge, sworn 29 Oct 1874.
Recorded: 10 Nov 1874

Return of Daniel McLucas, Exr of Joseph Banks, decd, money received and paid out on a/c with Heirs and Creditors up to 1 Aug 1874
Page 387-388

To amount on hand from last Return, see Book I, page 203
10 vouchers. Paid Nancy Banks for support and Joseph Banks for repairing plantation.
Filed: 21 Aug 1874. Recorded: 23 Nov 1874

Inventory and Appraisement of the Estate of Mary Fernander, an Imbecile of said County
Page 389

Lot of Land No. 35 in 7th District, Fayette Co., etc.
Appraisers: F. M. Davis, A. B. Tinsley, R. E. Johnson and G. Westbrook, sworn 20 Nov 1874

Recorded: 3 Nov 1874

Sale Bill of Personal Estate of William J. Russell, decd, Sold 25 Nov 1874 for Cash
Page 390-392

Among purchasers: Len Russell, W. W. Cochran, Simon Jennings, T. J. Askew, L. T. Handley, Z. T. Barge and Rachel Davis.
Recorded: 16 Dec 1874

Inventory and Appraisement of Estate of Asa Martin, late of said county deceased, to-wit:
Page 392-396

Appraisers: N. W. Gable, Thomas Kenady and C. W. Biles, sworn 21 Oct 1874
Includes Lot No. 27 in 6th District of Fayette Co. and 50 acres, Lot No. 38 on SW corner.
Sale Bill on 12 Nov 1874. Among purchasers: J. W. Martin, Nancy Martin, A. C. Martin, M. H. Martin and J. P. Martin.
Recorded: 23 Dec 1874

James N. McEachern, in Account Current with Estate of Nazareth Norton, decd, from time of appointment and embracing a full Settlement of said Estate
Page 396-397

7 vouchers.
Voucher #1. Received of Nazareth Norton $254.94, the distributive share in full of George W., John H., Lenora C. and A. J. Norton, minors of Nazareth Norton, decd, this 21 Jan 1874. /s/N.Norton, Gdn.

Voucher #2. Received of James N. McEachern, Admr of the Estate of Nazareth Norton, $47.03, in full of my distributive share of said estate, this 24 Dec 1873. /s/Minerva Ann Cleckler /s/ T. J. Cleckler

Voucher #3. Received of James N. McEachern, Admr of the Estate of Nazareth Norton, $47.03, in full of my distributive share of said estate, this 24 Dec 1873. /s/Lucinda West (x, her mark) /s/Thomas West

Voucher #4. Received of James N. McEachern, Admr of Estate of Nazareth Norton, $47.03, in full of my distributive share of said estate, this 24 Dec 1873. /s/Olive M. Minor /s/W. B. Minor

Voucher #5. Received of James McEachern, Admr of Estate of Nazareth Norton, $47.03, in full of my distributive share of said estate, this 24th Dec 1873. /s/Martha Jane A. Parker

Voucher #6. Received of James McEachern, Admr of Estate of Nazareth Norton, $47.03, in full of my distributive share of said estate, this 24th Dec 1873. /s/Nazareth Norton

Lula M. Malone, minor, William and Sarah Malone, in Account Current with T. C. Malone, Gdn, from 1 Jan 1874 to 1 Jan 1874 inclusive
Page 397-398

To amount on hand from last Return, see Book I, page ___.

An Account Current with Mrs. M. E. Rountree as Gdn of Young and Cynthia Ella Rountree, minor children of Ephraim Rountree, decd, from 25 Jul 1870 to 7 Dec 1874
Page 398-399

To amount received from last Return, see Book H, page 919

6 vouchers. To cash paid - Young Rountree, C. E. Rountree, J. G. Lister, D. C. Minor, and Babe Mucky.
Recorded: 3 Jan 1875

Sale Bill of Real Estate of John Phillips, decd, Sold by Louisa Phillips, Admr, Sold at Fayetteville on first Tues. in Dec 1874
Page 399

50 acres off westside of lot of land No. 38 in lower 7th District of said county sold to I. B. Ivera
41 acres off E. side of W. 1/2 of Lot No. 28 in lower 7th District, sold to C. H. Knowles
Recorded: 17 Feb 1875

Sale Bill of the Personal Property of J. P. Shropshire, decd, Sold by his Admr, A. J. Shropshire, on 27 Dec 1874 for Cash
Page 400

Purchasers: D. M. Franklin, Thomas Walker, J. L. Elder, P. A. Denham, R. H. Denham and B. L. Johnson.
Recorded: 19 Feb 1875

Inventory and Appraisement of the Estate of Howell Hubbard, late of said county, decd, to-wit:
Page 400-401

Includes 50 acres, being part of Lot No. 62 in 6th District of Fayette Co.
$500 set aside for widow, Lucinda Hubbard, and her minor children

Appraisers: Jacob Bowers, L. Morgan, N. W. Gable
Recorded: 17 Feb 1875

An Account Current with M. M. Collier, Gdn of Ida C. Collier, minor of Madison Collier, decd, from time of appointment up to 1 Jan 1875
Page 402

Filed: 4 Jan 1875. Recorded: 6 Mar 1875

An Account Current with M. L. Yates, Admr de bonis non of the Estate of James W. Head, decd, from 1 Jan 1872 to 1 Jan 1875 inclusive
Page 402-403

To amount on hand from last Return. See Book I, page 161
3 vouchers
Filed: 4 Jan 1875. Recorded: 16 Mar 1875

Estate of J. P. Shropshire in Account Current with A. J. Shropshire, Admr, from 8 Jan 1874 to 2 Feb 1875 inclusive
Page 403-407

To amount on hand from last Return, see Book I, page___
To amount of sale of the personal property and which is contained in 2nd Sale Bill, see Book I, page 400
17 vouchers.
Filed: 2 Feb 1875. Recorded: 18 Mar 1875

Return of the Estate of W. P. Chandler 3 Feb 1875, Sale Bill of Personal Property
Page 408-409

Purchasers: J. Chandler, Anna Chandler, F. M Chandler, J.W. Chandler, John Chandler, Sandy DeVaughn, W. T. Glower, M. W. Simpson, Obe Quin, W. L. Ellison, M. V. Whitlock, R. H. Whitlock, J. H. Elder, G. W. Slaton, Joshua Spratlin, J. M. Davis, Tandy Key and James Ware.
Recorded: 5 Jan 1875

Inventory and Appraisement of the Estate of L. C. Smith, late of said county, to-wit:
Page 409-410

Appraisers: J. L. Graves, J.N. Wallis, Mathew Yates
Recorded: 5 Jun 1875

Sale Bill of the Personal Property of Estate of L. C. Smith, decd, Sold by M. M. Davis, Temporary Admr, on the 3rd day of Apr 1845
Page 410-411

Among purchasers: W. M. Smith, J. M. Smith, D. M. Smith
Recorded: 5 Jun 1875

Bennett Adams, in a/c with the Estate of Sandford Adams, decd, from the time of his appointment to 6 Feb 1875

By amount of personal property, see Book H, page 775
166 2/3 acres of land sold on the first Tues. in Feb 1875
12 vouchers. Fi.Fa. levied upon 50 acres in the 7th District of Fayette Co. (NW corner of Lot No. 21) on the property of Sandford Adams by deputy sheriff, J. W. Brown, on 21 May 1873

Filed: 6 Feb 1875. Recorded: 5 Jun 1875

Estate of John T. McKey, in Account Current with S. T. Bridges, Admr, from 1 Jul 1873 to 1 Apr 1875 inclusive
Page 415-419

To amount on hand from last Return, see Book I, page 293. 17 vouchers.

Voucher #12. Received of S. T. Bridges, Admr of the Estate of John T. Macky, decd, $190.00 for rest of dower and tuition of minor children, M. L. Macky and S. T. Macky, children of John T. Macky, decd, 1 Jun 1875. /s/M. O. Macky

Fi.Fa. in favor of M. L. Thomas as Admr of John M. Thomas dated 11 Nov 1873.

Filed: 6 Apr 1875. Recorded: 16 Jun 1875

An Account Current with Amanda M. Johnson, Gdn of William J., James M.and John N. Johnson, minors of John H. Johnson, decd, from time of appointment to 23 Apr 1875
Page 419-421

5 vouchers. Filed: 23 Apr 1875. Recorded: 18 Jun 1875

Inventory and Appraisement of the Estate of Jordan Lord, late of said county, decd
Page 421-422

Appraisers: G. W. Bottoms, N. C. Cato, M. Orr, H. W. Simpson, sworn 4 May 1875
Recorded: 19 Jun 1875

Sale Bill of Real Estate of W. P. Chandler, decd, Sold by G. W. Staton, Admr, on the first Tues. in Dec 1873 for Cash
Page 423

48 acres, Lot No. 158 bought by C. E. Bennett
117 acres, Lots. No. 166 and 86 bought by G. W. Ware
100 acres, Lot No. 166 bought by G. W. Ware
138 acres, part of Lot No. 165 and fraction of Lot No. 85 bought by Emmett Smith

Twelve Months' Support for Widow and 2 minor children of John Faver, decd, 22 Aug 1874
Page 423

E. C. Bustin, Isaac Hartly, W. P. Redwine, C. H. Eastin
Filed: 29 Aug 1874. Recorded: 5 Jul 1875

Appraisers Estate of W. J. Russell, decd, Set apart 12 months support for 5 minor children...Margaret H., Frank B., Charles C., G. T. and William R. Russell
Page 424

Appraisers: J. M. Palmer, S. E. Christopher, E. M. Barge and L. L. Hendly. sworn 29 Oct 1874
Filed: 31 Oct 1874. Recorded: 14 Jul 1875

Twelve Months' Support for Widow of Asa Martin
Page 424-425

Appraisers: N. W. Gable, Thomas Kennedy and Charles W. Biles,sworn 21 Oct 1874
Filed: 7 Dec 1874. Recorded: 1 Jul 1875

3rd Annual Return of Thomas B. Swanson, Admr of Estate of Samuel Sanson, from 29 May 1874 to 29 May 1875 inclusive
Page 425-428

Received for rent of storehouse in Fairburn, 25 Dec 1874
Received from sale of storehouse in Fairburn, 3 Nov 1874

9 vouchers. Receipt of M. R. Swanson (x, her mark) for dower $200, 22 Sept 1874.
Filed: 29 May 1875. Recorded: 20 Jul 1875

Estate of Catharine DeVaughn, in Account Current with John H. Farr, Exr, from 8 Jun 1874 to 8 Jun 1875 inclusive
Page 428-429

To amount from last Return, see Book 1, page 374
4 vouchers

Letters of Administration, State of Alabama, Tallapoosa County } Letters of Administration with Will annexed on the Estate of Robert Gillam, decd, granted to Elias W. Heard who has duly qualified and given bond as such...22 Dec 1875. /s/ Allen D. Sturdivant, Judge of Probate Court, Tallapoosa Co.
Page 429

Filed: 5 Jun 1875. Recorded: 22 Jul 1875

J. J. Gilbert and W. L. Williams, Admrs of the Estate of H. M. Rogers, decd, in Account Current from the commencement of this Estate in 1870 up to 1 Jun 1875
Page 430-438

27 vouchers. To cash paid - Mrs. J. D. Rogers (voucher #2), widow, for 12 months' support. Includes various notes dated at Jonesboro, Ga.

Filed: 1 Jun 1875. Recorded: 24 Jul 1875

Estate of J. P. Gay, Lunatic in a/c Current with W. J. Gay, Gdn, from 21 Jul 1874 to 1 Jul 1875 inclusive
Page 438-449

To amount to Gdn in last Return, see Book 1, page 356
31 vouchers.
Filed: 7 Jun 1875. Recorded: 26 Jul 1875

Estate of William P. Chandler, in Account Current with George H. Slaton, Admr, from time of appointment to 1 Jul 1875
Page 450-456

To amount for the sale of personal property as contained in Appraise Bill, see Book I, page 408
19 vouchers.

Voucher #13, Fi.Fa in favor of Isaiah Hollingsworth and Patsy by R. T. Doray, their attorney, $3113.00.
Voucher #14, Fi.Fa. in favor of R. G. Strickland, $246.00
Voucher #15, Fi.Fa. in favor of L. Glass & Bohannon, $291.39

An Account Current with H. C. Fisher, Gdn of Minnie G., Sally A. and Norah H. Smith, minor children of Isaac H. Smith, from 6 Jul 1874 to 5 Jul 1875 inclusive
Page 456-459

To amount due Minnie G. Smith from last Return, see Book 1, page 349
To amount due Sallie A. Smith from last Return, see Book I, page 349
To amount due Dorah A. Smith from last Return, see Book I, page 349

Recorded: 18 Aug 1875

Sale Bill of the Personal Property of R. C. Bridges, decd
Page 460

Purchasers: James Bridges, R. W. Lynch, James Messer, John Tillery, J. C. Williams, Miss Thuman, Lott Messer, J. M. Bridges, Barney Simmons, G. W. Borman, John Haistin, W. A. messer, Tom Edmondson, John Walker, Canady alker and W. W. Mathews.

Filed: 12 Apr 1875. Recorded: 7 Sept 1875

Inventory and Appraisement of Estate of R. C. Ellington, decd, as produced by J. H. and Z. T. Ellington, Admrs
Page 461

Appraisers: E. C. Buster and B. F. Hall
Recorded: 4 Sept 1875

Sale Bill of Real Estate of John Glass, decd, Sold for Cash by J. M. Austin, Admr, at Fayetteville, on first Tues. in Nov 1872
Page 462

One house and Lot in Fayetteville sold to LewisC Smith
Lot No. 124, 202 1/2 acres sold to L. A. Blalock
Lot No. 125, 202 1/2 acres sold to Susan Graves
E. 1/2 of Lot No. 100, 100 acres, sold to John D. Graves
Lot No. 172, 202 1/2 acres sold to J. P. Graves
Lot No. 162, 202 1/2 acres sold to W. P. Redwine

Recorded: 4 Sept 1875

Sale Bill of Part of Real Estate of Mary Fernander, Imbecile, by James M. Davis, Gdn, on the first Tues. in Jan 1875
Page 462

E. 1/2 of Lot No. 35 in 7th District of Fayetteville
100 acres sold to F. M. Davis
Recorded: 8 Sept 1875

Sale Bill of Personal Property of John Faver Sold by Paul Faver, Admr
Page 463-466

Among purchasers: C. H. Eastin, Simon Swanson, J. P. Graves, William Gilbert, A.J Shropshire, R. A. Rivers.

The following are the rents to be paid for the Mill and real estate -

W. C. Parker - merchant mill
James A. McEachern - 50 acres
C. H. Eastin - 50 acres, 75 acres, 50 acres, 60 acres, etc. and corn and cotton

Recorded: 8 Sept 1875

Return No. 6 of B. O. Jones 8 Jan 1874 to 8 Jan 1875 by John A. R. Richardson, Exr
Page 467-470

13 vouchers. Filed: 12 Jul 1875. Recorded: 20 Sept 1875

J. A. Chapman, Gdn of Mary A. E. Ballard, minor of William Ballard, from time of appointment to 2 Aug 1875
Page 470-471

3 vouchers.
Filed: 2 Aug 1875. Recorded: 2 Sept 1875

Estate of John Graves, decd, in Account Current with James M. Austin, Admr, from time of appointment o 8 Jul 1875
Page 472-479

To amount on hand at time of John Graves' death, see Appraise Bill Book I, page 149

To amount of sale of personal property, see Book I, page 152

to amount sale of real estate, see Sale Bill Book I, page 462

34 vouchers. Filed: 8 Jul 1875. Recorded: 2 Sept 1875

Heirs who received part shares:

J. L. Graves
Susan Graves (x, her mark)
J. P. Graves
Roxie A., Thomas L. and Hester A., minor children of Augustus Graves, decd, by C. A. Graves, Gdn
John L. Graves, Jr. and J. P. Graves, Gdn of ClementineGraves

Inventory and Appraisement of the Estate of Josiah H. Elder
Page 479-480

680 acres. Appraisers: M. J. Smith, W. P. Smith and A. M. Smith, sworn 30 Mar 1875
Recorded: 9 Aug 1875

James M. Davis, Gdn of Mary Fernandes, in Account Current with Estate of Mary Fernendes
Page 481-482

To amount received from sale of 1000 acres, being the E 1/2 of Lot No. 35 in the Town of Fayetteville - see Book I, page 462

5 vouchers. Recorded: 9 Oct 1875

Inventory and Appraisement of the Estate of Elizabeth Padgett
Page 483-484

Appraisers: C. S. Jones, Jemerson Alford, W. P. Jones, J. F. McLain, sworn 27 Oct 1875

Sale Bill of the Real Estate of John I. Whitaker, decd, Sold for Cash by C. B. Nipper on first Tues. in Nov 1875
Page 484

Lot No. 167, 4th District, Fayette Co. sold to Samuel Baily
300 acres, Lot No. 184, S 1/2 of Lot No. 185, 4th District, Fayette Co. sold to Samuel Baily

Recorded: 23 Nov 1875

Margaret J. Jones, Gdn of Emily J. Jones, minor child of Francis Jones, in Account Current with said ward from the time of appointment up to 4 Oct 1875 showing a Final Settlement with said ward
Page 484-485

Heir - E. J. Jones (voucher #1)
Filed: 4 Oct 1875. Recorded: 23 Nov 1875

Estate of John Faver, in Account Current with Paul Faver, Admr, from the time of appointment to 23 Sept 1875
Page 485-498

62 vouchers. Filed: 13 Oct 1875. Recorded: 8 Dec 1875

James J. Thomas, Gdn of the minor children of John T. Travis, decd, from 1 Dec 1869 to 25 Nov 1875, the same being a Final Settlement and Return Preparatory to Letters of Dismission
Page 499-500

To amount due Mary E. Thomas, see the last Return, Book N, page 868
To amount due John A. Thomas, see Book H, page 868
To amount due Cynthia Thomas, see Book H, page 868

Voucher #3. Received of James J. Thomas, my Gdn, the sum of $264.75 in full settlement with him as my Gdn this 26 Nov 1875. /s/Cynthia Dodd /s/John M. Dodd

Voucher #4. Received of James J. Thomas, my Gdn, the sum of $303.69 in full settlement with him as my Gdn, this 26 Nov 1875. /s/John H. Thomas

William Guice, Gdn of Linton and Elizabeth Guice, minors of Peter Guice, from 1 Mar 1874 to 1 Dec 1875 inclusive
Page 501

To amount on hand from last Return, see Book I, page 306
3 vouchers (tax collector)
Filed: 15 Nov 1875. Recorded: 8 Jan 1875

T. C. Speer, in Account Current with J. M. Speer, minor
Page 502

To amount on hand at time of last Return, see Book I, page 347
Filed: 6 Dec 1875

Sale Bill of Personal Property of J. P. Gay, Imbecile, for Cash, by W. J. Gay, Gdn, 16 Nov 1845
Page 503

Among purchasers: Love Gay, T. G. Gay, P. Gay

Return of land rented -

Farm, 40 acres, Coweta Co. to F. G. North
Farm on Flat Creek, 45 acres to R. W. Hardy
King Place, 55 acres, to J. M. Arnold
45 acres on White Water Creek to J. O. Stewart
Watt Place, 400 acres, to Love Gay
Bridge Field, 20 acres, to Jordan Price
Hillside, 30 acres, to J. M. Arnold
Camp Creek Place, 40 acres, to Jordan Price
Dike field, 25 acres, to Jordan Price
Home Place, 30 acres, to J. M. Arnold

Recorded: 24 Dec 1875

Inventory and Appraisement of the Estate of Francis Patterson, late of said county, decd
Page 505-506

101 1/4 acres E. 1/2 Lot No. 6, 6th District, Fayette Co.
101 1/4 acres N. 1/2 Lot No. 122, 4th District, Fayette Co.

Appraisers: T. W. Ballard, William Malone, W. L. Jones, N. Miller, sworn 30 Oct 1875
Tillman Patterson, Admr

Recorded: 20 Dec 1875

Sale Bill of the Real Estate of G. W. Stinchcomb made by Phillip Stinchcomb, Admr, Sold for Cash on the first Tues. in Nov 1873
Page 506

N. 1/2 of Lot No. 94, 100 acres, 7th District, Fayette Co. } Sold to J. O.Stinchcomb
N. 1/2 of Lot No. 99, 100 acres, 7th District, Fayette Co. }

Recorded: 18 Feb 1876

Sale Bill of Real Estate of John Faver, decd, Sold by P. Faver, Admr, on first Tues. in Jan 1876
Page 507

205 acres, Lot No. 15 and 201 acres, Lot No. 18, Fayette Co. sold to Henry Love Faver
183 acres, Lot No. 19 and 119 acres, Lot No. 46, Fayette Co. sold to Glenn Faver
25 acres, Lot No. 19, 81 acres, Lot No. 46, 15 acres,Lot No. 18 and 28 acres, Lot No. 47 (on mill) - sold to Glenn Faver.

Recorded: 18 Feb 1876

Inventory and Appraisement of the Estate of Mrs. J. D. Rogers
Page 507

Appraisers: J. J. Gilbert, J. H. Murphy, John C. Nash and J. M. Dickson, sworn 3 Feb 1876
W. L. Williams, Exr
Recorded: 18 Feb 1871

An Account Current with M. M. Collins, Gdn of Ida C. Collins, minor or Madison Collins, decd, from 1 Jan 1875 to 1 Jan 1876
Page 508

To amount on hand from last Return, see Book I, page 402
3 vouchers.
Filed: 3 Jan 1876. Recorded: 18 Feb 1876

L. M. Malone, minor of William Malone, in Account Current with T. C. Malone, from Jan 1875 to Jan 1876 inclusive
Page 508-510

To amount on hand from last Return, see Book I, page 397. 5 vouchers.
Filed: 1 Jan 1876. Recorded: 18 Feb 1876

Sale Bill of the Personal Property of the Estate of J. D. Rogers Sold 17 Feb 1876 by W. L. Williams for Cash
Page 511-513

Among purchasers: J. J. Gilbert, William Rogers, J. M. Rogers and W. P. Redwine
Recorded: 21 Feb 1876

Annual Return of William Shadrick, Admr of Estate of W. G. Norton, decd, showing a full amount of the receipts and disbursements by him as Admr since the last Return
Page 513-515

Voucher #13, Receipt from J. B. I. Norton (x, his mark), for part of "my father's estate", dated 8 Dec 1875

Herod Thornton, Admr of Haywood Thornton, decd, from 29 Apr 1874 to 1 Mar 1874 inclusive
Page 515-517

To amount on hand from last Return, see Book I, page 313
11 vouchers. To amount paid - Haywood Thornton, Herod Thornton, Admr, Isaac Stone, D. M. Franklin, P. Faver, J. O. Blalock, G. M. Davis, C. A. Thornton, John Davis, L. P. Griggs

Filed: 29 Feb 1876. Recorded: 5 Apr 1876

An Account Current with W. J. Russell, Gdn of his minor children from his appointment to date, 1 Apr 1876
Page 517-519

4 vouchers. Shares paid to heirs (each entitled to $137.37) - W. S. Russell, F. M. J. Russell, M. T. Russell, M. A. Russell

Filed: 3 Apr 1876. Recorded: 4 May 1876

Inventory and Appraisement of the Estate of Jordan Lord, decd
Page 520

Appraisers: G. W. Bottoms, Newton Orr, Henry Simpson, A. C. Cato.
Years support set apart for the widow of Jordan Lord
Recorded: 12 May 1876

Inventory and Appraisement of the Estate of Alford Dorman
Page 521-522

Lot No. 73, Fayette Co.
Appraisers: Hubbard Stubbs, Richmond Dorman and John C. Nash, sworn 15 Apr 1876
Recorded: 13 May 1876

Sale Bill of Personal Property and Land Belonging to the Estate of Elizabeth Padgett, decd, Sold 20 Oct 1875 by J. W. Padgett for Cash
Page 522-524

Among purchasers: J. W. Padgett, W. F. Padgett, H. B. Padgett, W. W. Padgett and J. T. Padgett

Recorded: 13 May 1876

Sale Bill of the Land Belonging to the Estate of Asa Martin, decd, Sold by R. W. Lynch, Admr, on the first Tues. in Dec 1875 for Cash
Page 524

50 acres in Lot No. 38, 6th District, Fayette Co. to A. Steenheimer
128 1/2 acres, Lot No. 37, 6th District, Fayette Co. to A. Steenheimer

Recorded: 13 May 1876

An Account Current with R. W. Lynch, Admr, on the Estate of Asa Martin, decd, from the time of appointment to 1 May 1876 Showing Final Settlement
Page 525-530

To amount of sale of person property, see Book I, page 394
To amount of sale of land, see Book I, page 524

30 vouchers

Heirs: A. C. Martin, J. W. Martin, J. G. Harper, M. G. Harper, S. J. Martin, J. P. Martin, M. H. Martin, J. J. Martin and Nancy Martin.

Rebecca C. Smith, Gdn of David W. and M. A. C. Speer, minors of Henry C. Speer, decd, in Account Current with said minors from 1 Jul 1871 to 1 May 1871 inclusive
Page 530-531

To amount on hand since last Return, see Book I, page 61
5 vouchers. To cash paid - W. P. Cochran, C. M. Davis, C. A. Thornton, L. P. Griggs and Rebecca C. Smith.

Filed: 25 Apr 1876. Recorded: 18 Aug 1876

Inventory and Appraisement of the Estate of Levicy Whitaker, late of said county, decd
Page 531-532

Appraisers: T. W. Ballard, I. G. Wansly, John Sneed, W. R. Whitaker, sworn 11 Feb 1876
C. P. Nipper, Admr

Recorded: 9 Jun 1876

Inventory and Appraisement of Estate of Martha King
Page 533

Includes 6 acres. Appraisers: M. T. Travis, C. P. Jones, W. J. Jones, sworn 3 May 1876
Willis Brassell, Temp. Admr

Recorded: 30 Jun 1876

Sale Bill of Personal Property of Martha King, decd, Sold 2 May 1876 for Cash by Willis Brassell, Admr
Page 534-535

Among purchasers - H. B. Padgett, W. K. Padgett, T. J. Padgett, Charles Jones and W. J. Jones.
Filed: 5 Jun 1876. Recorded: 30 Jun 1876

Estate of John I. Whitaker, decd, in Account Current with C. B. Nipper, Admr, from 8 Jul 1874 to present time
Page 536-540

To amount received from sale of personal property, see Book I, page ____
21 vouchers.
Filed: 2 Jun 1876. Recorded: 8 Jul 1876

Estate of J. P. Shropshire, decd, in Account Current with A. J. Shropshire, Admr, from 2 Feb 1875 to 1 May 1876, being the Final Settlement of the Estate
Page 541-543

To amount received as contained in 1st Return, see Book I, page 331
To amount received as contained in 2d Return, see Book I, page 403

Heirs - Fannie Shropshire, A. J. Shropshire, M. L. Shropshire, Aurelia S. Johnson, A. J. Shropshire, Gdn of Minnie and Johnie, minors of John W. Shropshire.

Filed: 5 Jun 1876. Recorded: 8 Jul 1876

Sale Bill of Personal Property Belonging to the Estate of R. C. Ellington, decd, Sold by J. H. and Z. T. Ellington
Page 544-545

Among purchasers: M. Yates, John Lester, Robert Peek, J. McEachin, Mrs. E. E. Ellington, J. A. Ellington
Includes 400 acres.
Recorded: 8 Jul 1876

An Account Current with J. N. and Z. T. Ellington, Admrs of R. C. Ellington, decd, from the time of appointment to date, 1 Mar 1876
Page 546-550

To amount received from sale of personal property, see Book I, page 544
17 vouchers.

Heirs - J. A. Ellington, Eliza E. Ellington (12 months' support), Z. T. Ellington, J. H. Ellington

Filed: 18 May 1876. Recorded: 8 Jul 1876

A. B. Tinsley, Gdn of Josephine and Marion and J. B. Smith, minor children of Malissa M. Smith, decd, from time of appointment to 5 Jul 1876
Page 551-552

To amount received from last Return of said minors in which elder sister of Z. B. Hewett had 1/4th interest, see Sale Bill Book I, page ____. 6 vouchers.

Filed: 5 Jun 1876. Recorded: 8 Jul 1876

Estate of G. W. Stinchcomb, in Account Current with Phillip Stinchcomb, Admr, from 1 Jul 1873 up to present time
Page 552-554

To amount received from sale of personal property, see Book I, page 223
To amount received from cotton, 1st Return, see Book I, page 285
To amount received from sale of land, see Book I, page 505
By amount paid out, see 1st Return, see Book I, page 285

19 vouchers. Includes an account from W. R. Spruell in St. Clair Co., Alabama.

Filed: 5 Jun 1871. Recorded: 8 Jul 1876

Estate of Francis Patterson, decd
Page 555

12 months' support ordered to be set aside to widow of Francis Patterson

Appraisers: T. W. Ballard, William Malone, W. L. Jones, N. Miller, sworn 30 Oct 1875

Filed: 30 Dec 1875. Recorded: 8 Jul 1876

W. J. Gay, Gdn of I. P. Gay, Imbecile, in Account Current with the said Ward, from 1 Jul 1875 to 1 Jul 1876 inclusive
Page 556-557

To amount on hand since last Return, see Book I, page 438
14 vouchers.
Filed: 3 Jul 1876. Recorded: 5 Aug 1876

Estate of William Head, in Account Current with S. F. Head, Admr, from 1 Jul 1872 to 1 Jul 1876
Page 559-560

To amount on hand from last Return, see Book I, page 162
4 vouchers.
Recorded: 8 Aug 1876

Inventory and Appraisement of the Estate of Leonard M. Johnson, late of said county, decd
Page 560-561

Appraisers: S. T. W. Minor, J. L. Graves, N. C. Walls, J. T. Brogdon, sworn 31 Dec 1875

Widow's support was set apart for widow and children.

Filed: 1 Jan 1876. Recorded: 8 Aug 1876

4th Annual Return of F. P. Swanson upon the Estate of Samuel Swanson, decd, from 12 Jun 1876 to 8 Aug 1876
Page 561

Recorded: 8 Aug 1876

Elizabeth Padgett, decd, in Account Current with J. W. Padgett, Admr, from the time of appointment to 3 Jul 1876
Page 562-563

To amount received from sale of personal property, see Book I, page 522
To cash paid - C. A. Thornton (tax collector), J. T. Padgett, W. F. Padgett, A. W. Gable, Frank Hand (x, his mark), and L. P. Griggs. 6 vouchers.

Filed: 4 Jul 1876. Recorded: 8 Aug 1876

An Account Current with H. C. Fisher, Gdn of Minnie G., Sallie A. and Norah H. Smith, minors of Isaac N. Smith, decd, from 7 Jul 1875 to 1 Jul 1876 inclusive
Page 564-566

To amount due Minnie G. Smith, see Book I, page 456
To amount due Sallie A. Smith, see Book I, page 456
To amount due Norah H. Smith, see Book I, page 456

Filed: 7 Aug 1876. Recorded: 6 Sept 1876

Gainy Westbrook, Gdn, in Account Current with Lousia J. Edmondson, minor of James W. Edmondson, decd, from 8 Aug 1871 to 1 Jul 1876 inclusive
Page 567-568

Also includes the period of 2 Jul 1876 to 6 Sept 1876
Recorded: 6 Sept 1876

An Account Current with Gainy Westbrook, Gdn of the minor children of John Loyd, decd, from 1 Jul 1874 to 1 Jul 1876 inclusive
Page 569

To amount on hand from last Return, see Book I, page 380
3 vouchers. Filed: 3 Jul 1876. Recorded: 8 Sept 1876

Annual Return of Tracy Shell, Exr of LWT of Daniel Shell,
Page 570

To the real estate and personal property, she is entitled to the possession and proceeds of during his life.

To the choses in action belonging to said estate which remained in the possession of N. G. Holcombe, the Exr, up to the time of his death, and has since been turned over to me by his Extrx, to-wit:

One Note against J. C. Grimes, dated 22 Dec 1875
One Note against James D. Messer dated 8 Feb 1874
One Note against N. W. Gable dated 1 May 1871
One Note against A. C. Martin
One Note against John Tillery
One mule which I sold to C. W. Biles /s/Teresa Shell (x, her mark)

J. A. Chapman, Gdn of Mary A. E. Ballard, minor of W. Ballard, decd, from 2 Aug 1875 to 1 Aug 1876
Page 571

To amount on hand since last Return, see Book I, page 470
Filed: 1 Aug 1876. Recorded: 9 Sept 1876

T. C. Speer, Gdn, in Account Current with J. M. Speer, from 6 Dec 1875 to 4 Sept 1876
Page 571-572

7 vouchers. To cash paid - W. L. Jackson, C. A. Thornton, L. O. Griggs, J. M. Speer (x, his mark

Received of T. C. Speer, my Gdn, $125 in full settlement of all demands as my Gdn. /s/J.M.Speer (x, his mark).

Filed: 4 Sept 1876. Recorded: 3 Oct 1876

An Account Current between James Boyd, Gdn. and his Ward, Ida V. Spence, from 1 Mar 1871 to 1 Jul 1876 inclusive
Page 572-573

4 vouchers. To cash paid - Ordinary, J. B. Avera, G. M. Davis (tax collector) and C. A. Thornton.

Filed: 31 Aug 1876. Recorded: 3 Oct 1876

Martha Elder, Exr of J. H. Elder, decd, from time of appointment to 1 Sept 1876
Page 573-579

33 vouchers. Filed: 21 Aug 1876. Recorded: 5 Oct 1876

An Account Current with W. S. and T. M. J. Russell, Admr of W. J. Russell, decd, from time of appointment to 1 Sept 1876
Page 579-585

To amount from sale of personal property, see Book I, page 390. 33 vouchers

Filed: 2 Sept 1876. Recorded: 5 Oct 1876

John A. Richardson, Exr of B. O. Jones, decd, giving the following Return of said Estate from 8 Jan 1875 to 8 Jan 1876
Page 585-588

8 vouchers. To cash paid - E. G. Moore, H. F. Messer, Sandy DeVaughn, C. A. Thornton, L. P. Griggs, J. A. Richardson, J. J.and S. P. Richardson and R. T. Dorsey.

To the Ordinary of Fayette County - My first report was made with the Ordinary, R. T. Dorsey. No interest was then calculated. For this reason, no interest has been calculated in any of my Returns. It was thought that in the final settlement with the heirs of the estate, interest could be calculated upon the whole and all be made satisfactory. /s/ J. A. Richardson

Filed: 22 Sept 1876. Recorded: 9 Nov 1876

Sale Bill of the Personal Property of Williamson Jenkins, sold by T. H. Jenkins and George Dodd, Exrs, for Cash, on 31 Oct 1876
Page 588

Recorded: 9 Dec 1876

Inventory and Appraisement of Estate of Edmond Jackson
Page 589

M. E. Jackson and G. W. Robinson, Exrs.

Appraisers: J. M. Murphy, John Eason, Reuben Jackson, G. W. Clarke, sworn 3 Oct 1876
Recorded: 9 Dec 1876

Sale Bill of Perishable Property of Alfred Dorman, decd, Sold by J. H. Murphy, 26 Apr 1876 for Cash
Page 590-591

Among purchasers: Emiline Pharr, J. C. Nash, Mrs. E. Fortson, M. B. Dorman, Mrs. Mary Dorman, Mrs. E. Pharr, Mrs. Susan Stell, J. J. Gilbert.

Recorded: 9 Dec 1876

Inventory and Appraisement of Estate of Robert N. Harris, late of said county, decd
Page 592-593

Appraisers: C. E. Austin, B. T. Harper, Robert A. Reeves, J. G. Lester, sworn 1 Oct 1876
Recorded: 9 Dec 1876

Inventory and Appraisement of Estate of Mrs. Sarah F. Shell
Page 593-594

Appraisers: W. F. Kelly, J.A. Haisten, John Tilly, H. H. Haisten, sworn 20 Dec 1875

Setaside for Willie D. and Mary C. Shell, minor children
I, John Rush, Gdn of the person and property of Willie O. and Mary L. Shell....swear .... 2 Mar 1876

Filed: 1 Mar 1876. Recorded: 9 Dec 1876

Widow's Support of Estate of Alfred Dorman
Page 595

Appraisers: John C.Clark, Richmond Dorman and Hubbard Stubbs, sworn 15 Apr 1876

Filed: 25 Apr 1876. Recorded: 1 Feb 1877

Estate of Alexander Reeves, decd
Page 595

Georgia, Fayette Co., We, the undersigned, appraisers, appointed H. S. McLane, J. O. Brown, J. H. Harvell and N. W. Gable, to make use of a schedule of property belonging to Alexander Reeves, decd, submit the following - 1 acre and dwelling, part of Lot No. 219, 6th District.

Recorded: 1 Feb 1877

An Account Current with J. M. Bridges, Gdn of Rachel, Ida and Thomas Bridges, minors of R. C. Bridges, decd, from the time of appointment to 20 Nov 1876
Page 596

Filed: 20 Nov 1876. Recorded: 1 Feb 1877

An Account Current with M. M. Collier, Gdn of Ida C. Collier, minor of Minton Collier, from 1 Jan 1876 to 1 Jan 1877
Page 596-597

3 vouchers. Filed: 1 Jan 1877. Recorded: 7 Jul 1877

An Account Current with Tillman Patterson, Admr of Francis Patterson, decd, from the time of appointment to 18 Dec 1876 showing a Final Settlement
Page 597-600

100 acres sold 2 Dec 1875
36 2/3 acres sold 7 Nov 1876

8 Heirs:

Emily Horton, Tillman Pattersn, Rebecca Fills' children, Francis Patterson's children, John L. Patterson's children, Mary A. Kimbrew, A. E. Ward, Martha F. Harris.

Voucher #12 - Temperance Patterson vs. L. Patterson - Received of Tillman Patterson, Admr, $5.75 /s/A. E. Stokes, Clerk, in the above case.
Recorded: 7 Feb 1877

Sale Bill of Estate of Wiel Chandler, decd, Sold by E. W. Leach for Cash, 21 Nov 1874
Page 601-603

Among purchasers - A. Speer, Robert Whitlock, John Whitlock, D. C. Stokes, Isaac Chandler, James Chandler and John Chandler.

Recorded: 7 Feb 1879

A Sale Bill of the Real Estate of Wiel Chandler Sold by E. W. Leach, Admr, for Cash 3 Nov 1874
Page 603

192 3/4 acres, Lot No. 7, 7th District, Fayette Co. to W. A. Leach
86 1/2 acres, Lot No. 6, Coweta Co. to G. W. Ware
Sold 5 Jan 1875. Recorded: 7 Jul 1877

Sale Bill of Property of Robert N. Harris, decd
Page 604-6

Among purchasers - John Lester, J. G. Lester, Martha Harris, B. F. Harper, Chelly Roberts.
Recorded: 7 Feb 1877

Inventory and Appraisement of Estate of Pheraby Harris, decd, Nov 1871
Page 607-608

101 1/4 acres, being part of Lot No. 255, Fayette Co.

Appraisers: John Coleman, Isaac Hartly, E. W. Boatright, J. T. Brogdon, sworn 4 Nov 1871
Sale Bill on 27 Dec 1871. Purchasers were: B. Thornton, J. Thornton, Needham Jenkins
Recorded: 7 Feb 1877

Sale Bill of Real Estate and other Property of the late Alfred Forman's Estate
Page 608

Land sold to J. M. Dickson and other items to - T. D. King, F. B. Pharr, Z. B. Blalock, L. F. Blalock, T. Byrne, M. B. Dorman.

Recorded: 7 Jul 1877

Sale Bill of Real Estate of Francis Patterson, decd, Sold by Tillman Patterson, Admr, First Tues. in Dec 1875
Page 609-614

36 2/3 acres to Temperance Patterson
100 acres to L. F. Blalock
Recorded: 7 Jul 1877

Herod Thornton, Admr of Estate of Pheriby Thornton, decd, in Account Current, from the time of appointment to 1 Jan 1877 Showing a Final Settlement with deceased's Estate
Page 614

17 vouchers. Voucher #4. Received of Herod Thornton, Admr of Pheriby Thornton, decd...$75.35 in full settlement of all the rights, claims and interest...or demand I might have upon the estate, real and personal...of my mother with said H. Thornton, Admr as aforesaid. Signed, sealed and delivered in the present of of Y. H. Thornton and John Coleman, J. P. /s/William McCleny, by his attorney in fact, James W. McCleny

Other receipts from children of Pheriby Thornton from - Blackman Uncy? (x, her mark), Eveline Jackson (and Needham Jackson, x his mark), David McCleny.

Receipts from grandchildren: Jordan Thornton, grandson of Pheriby Thornton, Herod Thornton (x, his mark), grandson of Pheriby Thornton and Haywood Thornton (x, his mark), grandson of Pheriby Thornton.

Mississippi, Panola Co. - S. A. Betterton, grandson of Pherbiy Thornton receipt
Mississippi, Tallahatchie Co. - Henry Birdson, Gdn of Mollie Betterton receipt
Mississippi, Panola Co. - R. K. Taylor, grandson
Mississippi, Panola Co. - Samuel D. Johns, grandson
Georgia, Fayette Co. - Elizabeth Thornton (x, her mark), granddaughter
Georgia, Fayette Co. - Herod Thornton, Jr., Gdn of May Thornton, granddaughter
Georgia, Fayette Co. - Herod Thornton, Jr., Gdn of Bennett Thornton, grandson

Filed: 8 Jan 1877. Recorded: 8 Mar 1877

Estate of Charles Clements, in Account Current with L. F. Blalock, Admr, from 7 May 1866 to 1 Jan 1877, the same being a Final Return and Settlement of said Estate
Pae 615-618

L. F. Blalock, see Book G, page 561
L. F. Glalock, Gdn of Rom. A. Clements, see Book G, page ___
F. M. Lester, Gdn of S. A. Clements, see Book G, page 561, Book H, page 424

Heirs Receipts - (7 heirs)
Martha A. Adams Clements, Gdn of Malissa E. Clements, see Book G, page 561 and Book H, page 424
L. F. Blalock, Gdn of Rosa A. Clements
Filed: 19 Jan 1877. Recorded: 8 Mar 1877

Estate of Catherine DeVaughn, in Account Current with John H. Farr, Exr, from 5 Jun 1875 to 29 Jan 1877
Page 618-634

To amount received from sale of personal property, see Book I, page 214
To amount received from sale of land, see Book I, page 206
Admrs. expenses, etc. in 1st Return, see Book I, page 324
Admrs expenses, etc. in 2d Return, see Book I, page 428

This final ($908.60) belongs under the Will of Catherine DeVaughn to her brothers and sisters of her deceased husband, M. DeVaughn.

Estate of Catherine DeVaughan contd.....

To total amount due the Gillam legatees, brother of testatrix ($517.90)
To amount due the DeVaughn children ($454.30)
By amount paid Eliza B. DeVaughn, Admx on Estate of Elijah DeVaughn per Voucher #6

Heirs Receipts (part shares) -

H. J. Gillam for distribution of share of H. J., W. J. and J. H. Gillam, Anna O' Brien and W. B. O' Brien, Exr of Estate of Jane Grammitt, decd and W. B. O' Brien who owns the interest of John Gillam, decd and Mary J. Gillam. /s/H. J. Gillam

Samuel H. Gillam, Gdn for Elizabeth M. Gillam

Samuel H. Gillman, Gdn of Ailsey D. Gillam

Eliza P. DeVaughn, Admr of Elijah DeVaughn, received from John H. Farr, Admr of Catherine DeVaughn.

Alabama, Tallapoosa Co.... Samuel H. Gillam represents to the court that Elizabeth M. Gillam is a minor aged 19 years on the 2d day of Dec 1876 and Ailsey D. Gillam, a minor, 16 years on 25th Sept. 1876, and that they have no father living or other legal guardian....petitions to be nominated as Gdn, this 3 Jan 1877. Certified by Harry J. Gillam, N. P.

Alabama, Tallapoosa Co. - Bond of Samuel H. Gillam, William B. O' Brien, William H. Shepherd, Thomas L. Johnson and John T. Shepherd, this 23 Jan 1877.

Alabama, Tallapoosa Co. - Order probating the LWT and granting Letters in the Probate Court, 14 Oct 1875, William B. O' Brien (Exr) to probate the LWT of Jane Greenwith of Tallapoosa Co., Alabama. That 14 Sept 1870 by notice duly sworn upon Samuel Gillam, Matilda Gillam, Ailsy Gillam, Anna O' Brien, H. J. Gillam, Mary J. Gillam, William J. Gillam and James I. Gillam by citation and presentation in a newspaper for 3 weeks. Submitted for probate 27 Oct 1875. LWT admitted to record: 27 Oct 1875.

Alabama, Tallapoosa Co., Claim of W. B. O' Brien, Gdn, in Estate of Catherine DeVaughn, acknowledged. Gillam children appointed said O' Brien attorney in fact to collect from Estate of Catherine DeVaughn.

Filed: 29 Jan 1877. Recorded: 9 Mar 1877

Estate of Mary Fernandes, Imbecile, in Account Current with James M. Davis, Gdn, from 6 Sept 1875 to the present time
Page 635-636

To amount on hand from last Return, see Book I, page 481

5 vouchers. Voucher #5...Received of James Davis, Gdn of Mary Fernandes, $29, in full of the money and proceeds of sale of property of said imbecile...this 5th Feb 1877. /s/W. R. McLewany (x, his mark), Gdn of Mary Fernandes.

Susannah and Mathew Harper, minor children of William Harper, decd, in Account Current with John J. Gilbert, Gdn, from 1 Jun 1868 to 1 Mar 1877 inclusive, the same being a Final Settlement of said Estate
Page 636-639

To amount on hand from last Return, see Book H, page 722
To amount received from B. F. Harper, Exr of Estate of Frederick Harper, 28 Dec 1869

Heirs receipts - M. G. Harper and Susannah G. Harper. 13 vouchers.

An Account Current with T. H. Jenkins and George Dodd, Exrs, on Estate of Williamson Jenkins, decd, from time of appointment to 1 Apr 1877 inclusive
Page 639-640

To amount received from sale, see Book I, page 588
Recorded: 8 May 1877

Estate of Louisa J. Edmondson, minor of James W. Edmondson, in Account Current with Gainy Westbrook, Gdn, from 1 Jul 1876 to 1 Feb 1877, the same being a Final Return and Settlement with Malissa O. Westbrook, Gdn of the said Louisa J. Edmondson
Page 641-642

To amount on hand from last Return, see Book I, page 517
6 vouchers. Voucher #6, Received of Gainy Westbrook, Gdn of James W. Edmondson, minor child of James W. Edmondson, d ecd, $700.92 in full payment with him as my Gdn, this 10 Feb 1877. /s/M. O. Westbrook

Estate of Alfred Dorman, decd, in Account Current with James H. Murphy, Admr, from the time of appointment to 2 Apr 1877, the same being a Final Settlement of said Estate
Page 642-651

To amount received from sale of personal property, see Book I, page 590
12 months' support (Mrs. Ann Dorman), see Book I, page 595
To amount received from sale of personal property, see Book I, page 609

9 vouchers. Heirs - Ann Dorman (widow), Morgan B. Dorman, Nancy E. Pharr, E. B. Fortson, Mary A. H. Chambers.

Alabama, Coosa Co...... A Gdn was appointed for Sallie C. Dorman, a minor heir of John H. Dorman, decd, i. e., John T. Miller.

Nancy Ann Miller and her husband, John T. Miller, Gdn of Sallie C. Dorman, appoint Thomas H. Dorman as atty to receive their portion, this 17 Feb 1877.

Filed: 31 Mar 1877. Recorded: 8 May 1877

T. B. Swanson, Admr of Samuel Swanson, decd. in Account Current with said Estate, from 12 Jun 1876 to 2 Apr 1877 Showing a Final Settlement with the Estate
Page 652-653

6 vouchers.

Voucher #1. Received of Turner B. Swanson the sum of $50 in full of my fee in a case in Campbell Superior Court being a Bill in Equity filed by Leach gardianship, said Swanson, admr and others, in which a decree was this day taken, this 21 Feb 1877. /s/George N. Lester

Voucher #2. Received of T. B. Swanson, Admr on the Estate of Samuel Swanson, decd, the sum of $3290.85 in full of a decree in Campbell Superior Court in favor of E. W. Leach, Gdn of M. E. M. and M. N. Swanson vs. T. B. Swanson, Admr of Samuel Swanson, decd, so far as only its decree remains with me to be paid, 21 Feb 1877. /s/R. T. Dorsey, atty at law for E. W. Leach, Gdn of M. E. M. and M. N. Swanson

Filed: 3 Apr 1877. Recorded: 9 May 1877

In Account with A. J. Shropshire, Gdn of Nannie and Johnie, minors of J. W. Shropshire, decd, from 1 Dec 1875 to 1 Jan 1877
Page 653-656

To amount received from A. J. Shropshire, Admr of J. P. Shropshire, decd, see Book I, page 541
15 vouchers.
Appraisers: A. L. Tally, P. A. Denham (tuition), Burk Hancock & Co., Hitchcock & Walden, Regenstell & Co., W. H. Brotherton, C. A. Thornton.

Filed: 5 Apr 1877. Recorded: 9 May 1877

An Account Current with M. L. Yates, Admr de bonis non of the Estate of J. W. Head, decd, from 4 Jul 1875 to 1 Jul 1877 inclusive
Page 656-657

To amount on hand from last Return, see Book I, page 402
3 vouchers. To amount paid - L. B. Griggs and C. A. Thornton
Filed: 26 May 1877. Recorded: 7 Jul 1877

An Account Current with M. L. Yates, Admr de bonis non of the Estate of R. N. Harris, decd, from time of appointment to 1 Jul 1877
Page 657-666

To amount of personal property, see Book I, page 604
27 vouchers. Paid J. G. Lester for tuition, and 12 months' support to Martha E. Harris.

Filed: 26 May 1877. Recorded: 7 Jul 1877

Martha Elder, Extrx of J. H. Elder, decd, from 1 Sept 1876 6o 1 Jun 1877
Page 667-674

To amount on hand from last Return, see Book I, page 573
46 vouchers.
Filed: 31 May 1877. Recorded: 9 Sept 1877

Return No. 8, B. O. Jones' Estate
Page 674-676

John A. Richardson, Exr of B. O. Jones, decd, makes the following annual return from 8 Jan 1876 to 8 Jan 1877

9 vouchers. To amount paid - R.T. Dorsey, W. A. Haynes, J. A. Taylor, H. F. Mosses, John H. Doan, Thomas Pullium & Co., L. G. Holland, J. A. Richardson.

Filed: 29 Jun 1877. Recorded: 8 Aug 1877

Estate of Elizabeth Padgett, decd, in Account Current with John W. Padgett, Admr, from 3 Jul 1876 to 1 May 1877
Page 677-681

To balance on hand 3 Jul 1876, see Book I, page 562
To amount received from rent of place for 1876, see Book I, page 522
23 vouchers. By amount paid out for expenses as follows: J. W. Brown, L. B. Griggs, Z. B. Blalock, C. A. Thornton, M. J. Goodman, Al B. Couch, W. W. Padgett.

Balance for distribution -
W. W. Padgett, in his own right as Gdn of J. L., M. F. and J. C. Padgett
M. J. and J. J. Riggins
W. F. Padgett
H. B. Padgett
S. E. and W. L. Kennedy
John W. Padgett

Voucher #7, Brooks Station, Ga., 28 Sept 1875, Tucker Padgett to make coffin & box for the decd, Mrs. Padgett, dated 2 Jun 1875.

Filed: 30 Jun 1877. Recorded: 8 Aug 1877

An Account Current with J. H. and Z. T. Ellington, Admrs of R. C. Ellington, decd, from 1 Jun 1876 to 1 Jul 1877 inclusive
Page 682-683, blank page, then 684

6 vouchers. Filed: 2 Jul 1877. Recorded: 8 Aug 1877

L. M. Malone, minor of William, in Account Current with T. C. Malone, Gdn, from 1 Jan 1876 to 6 Feb 1877
Page 685-686

To amount on hand from last Return, see Book I, page 509
5 vouchers. By amount paid - L. B. Griggs, C. A. Thornton, G. C. Lomey (tuition for Lola Malone), and C. W. Hodnett

Filed: 30 May 1877. Recorded: 8 Aug 1877

Estate of Haywood Thornton, decd, in Account Current with Herod Thornton, Admr cum Testamento annexed, it being a recapitulation of the entire estate and final settlement of the same showing amounts received and paid out and balance on hand for distribution
Page 686-689

To amount on hand from last Return (as corrected), see Book I, page 105
Heirs: Elizabeth, Haywood, Jordan and Herod Thornton
Filed: 19 Jul 1877. Recorded: 8 Sept 1877

Annual and Final Return of W. J. Gay, Gdn of J. P. Gay, Imbecile, preparatory for settlement with Exrs, said J. P. Gay, decd
Page 690-695

To amount on hand from last Return, see Book I, page 556.
16 vouchers.
Voucher #16. eceived of W. J. Gay, Gdn of J. P. Gay, imbecile, in full of all money, notes, a/c and personal property and in full to heirs as said Gdn, $3287.00, thisbeing for all money that came into the hands, the notes, sale, appraise bill on S. T. Gay and William J. Gay......... this 30 Jul 1877.
/s/W. J. Gay, Exr of J. P. Gay
/s/P. G. Gay
/s/Sandford Gay

The Estate of Edward Jackson, decd, in Account Current with G. W. Robinson and M. e. Jackson, Exrs, from the time of appointment to 6 Aug 1877
Page 695-696

To amount of Appraise Bill of personal property, see Book I, page 589
Sarah Jackson (x, her mark) receipt for personal property, rents from the farm of decd, etc.
Filed: 6 Aug 1877. Recorded: 8Sept 1877

J. A. Chapman, Gdn of Mary Ballard, in Account Current with said minor, 1 Aug 1876 6o 1 Aug 1877 inclusive
Page 696

To amount on hand from last Return, see Book I, page 591
Filed: 1 Sept 1877. Recorded: 1 Oct 1877

The Estate of John Faver, decd, in Account Current with Paul Faver, Admr, from 13 Oct 1875 to 7 Sept 1877 inclusive
Page 697-701

To amount on hand, see Book I, page 487
From the sale of land, see Book I, page 407
22 vouchers. Receipt from M. A. Faver, Gdn of J. Jewel Faver, for clothing, etc.

Heirs as follows -
Love Faver
Glenn Faver
M. F. Faver, Gdn of Jewel Faver
Sam Faver
Paul Faver
G. W. Ware
Sallie Ware
Filed: 1 Sept 1877. Recorded: 8 Oct 1877

An Account Current with Terresa Shell, Extrx of Daniel Shell, decd, from 20 Jul 1876 to 2 Jul 1877 inclusive
Page 701

To amount on hand from last Return, see Book I, page 570
By amount paid - C. A. Thornton (1 voucher).
Filed: 18 Jul 1877. Recorded: 8 Oct 1877

Georgia, Fayette Co., A sum set aside for the widow and children of R. N. Harris, late of said co., decd, 12 months' support
Page 701-702

Appraisers: J. F. Lester, R. A. Rivers, E. C. Bustin

Inventory and Appraisement of Estate of E. J. Hudson, late of said county, decd
Page 702-703

Appraisers: J. Hamply, Richmond Dorman, E. S. Hughes, G. W. Clark, sworn 9 Oct 1876

Inventory and Appraisement of Estate of T. B. Johnson, late of said county, to-wit:
Page 703-704

50 acres in the 7th District of Fayette Co., NW corner of Lot No. 44

Appraisers: R. F. Head, W. P. Head, M. J. Smith, Z. T. Ellington
Filed: 12 Jan 1877. Recorded: 24 Oct 1877

Georgia, Fayette Co., To the Honorable Court of Ordinary of said county...This is to certify that the foregoing is a true Return of all the property and effects in my hands as Gdn for John W. T. Speer, minor son of John T. Speer, decd, from 1 Jun 1872 to 1 Oct 1877
Page 105

In person appearing E. C. Bustin, Agent for Amanda J. Speer, Gdn of John W. T. Speer, minor of John T. Speer, decd, who, being sworn, says that the above is just and true as stated. /s/E. C. Bustin

Recorded: 1 Nov 1877

Estate of Wiet Chandler, decd, in Account Current with E. W. Leach, Admr, from the time of appointment until 1 May 1877
Page 705-714

To amount received from sale of personal property, see Book I, page 603
To amount received from sale of real estate, see Book I, page 603

11 vouchers. Filed: 21 Apr 1877. Recorded: 5 Jan 1878

E. N. Leach, Admr de bonis non of Estate of Larkin Landrum, decd
Page 715-720

(Also see Page 760-761 for receipts)

To amount received on Fi.Fas. in favor of J. W. Smith vs. F. Landrum, U. Slaton and W. J. Campbell Shares to be divided into five pats -

Washington Landrum's children, with E. W. Leach, Gdn
Jeptha Landrum's children, with E. W. Leach, Gdn
Willis Landrum's children, with Nancy J. Landrum, Gdn
Jefferson Landrum
Jasper Landrum
Franklin Landrum
John W. Smith
Isariah Slaton
Madison Landrum

Jasper and Jefferson Landrum's receipts were dated at Cherokee Co., Texas

Filed: 14 Dec 1874. Recorded: 9 Jan 1878

An Account Current with Mrs. Mary E. Rountree, Gdn of Young and Cynthia Ella, minor children of Ephraim Rountree, decd, from 7 Dec 1874 to 1 Dec 1877, putting a Final Settlement with said Wards
Page 721

To amount on hand from last Return, see Book I, page 398

By amount paid to heirs - Young Rountree and Cynthia E. Rountree (Adams)

Filed: 28 Nov 1877.
Recorded: Jan 1878

Estate of Sarah Baily, decd, in Account Current with D. D. Denham, Exr, from 4 Dec 1874 to 1 Dec 1877 inclusive
Page 721-723

To amount of sale of personal property, see Book H, page 2

6 vouchers. To cash paid - Ordinary, M.M. Collier, W. W. Walker, Henry Morgan, A. J. Davis and Sarah F. Youngblood.

Filed: 5 Dec 1877.
Recorded: 9 Jan 1878

Annual and Final Return of J. Madison Smith, Admr of the Estate of L. C. Smith, decde, showing condition of the entire estate from the time of appointment
Page 724-729

To amount received from sale of personal property, see Book I, page 410
11 vouchers.

Heirs as follows:

Aly H. Davis
Martha Doss
E. W. Phillipps
L. C. Smith
William Smith
D. M. Smith
J. M. Smith
J. L. Graves, Gdn of Willis, George and Daley Miles
M. M. Smith

Filed: 7 Jan 1878. Recorded: 11 Feb 1878

Account Current with S. B. Lewis, former Gdn of Mary, Exer, Helen, Eliza, Sallie, Samantha and Henry Wilkins, minor children of W. H. Wilkins, decd, from the time of his appointment to date showing a Final Settlement with Z. B. Blalock, present Gdn
Page 729

4 vouchers. By amount paid - 1876 taxes, L. B. Griggs and Z. B. Blalock
Filed: 26 Dec 1877. Recorded: 12 Feb 1878

E. W. Leach, Gdn, in Account Current with J. Q. and J. L. Landrum, minor heirs of Washington Landrum, decd, from 1 Jul 1870 to 1 May 1877
Page 730-736

To amount due, see Book I, page 247
To amount due J. L. Landrum, see Book I, page 247

Voucher #25, E. W. Leach, Gdn for Luther Landrum, to J. E. C. W. Smith, 1876, visiting doctor and medicine. 34 vouchers.

Filed: 29 Dec 1877. Recorded: 12 Feb 1878

An Account Current with M. M. Collier, Gdn of Ida C. Collier, from 1 Jan 1877 to 1 Jan 1878
Page 737

To amount on hand from last Return, Book I, page 597
2 vouchers.
Filed: 29 Dec 1877. Recorded: 12 Feb 1878

E. W. Leach, Gdn, in Account Current with Marshall and Lizzie Swanson, minor of Paul Swanson, decd, from time of appointment until present, to-wit: 20 Mar 1878
Page 738-740

10 vouchers.
Filed: 20 Mar 1878. Recorded: 8 May 1878

John Stinchcomb, Gdn of Talulah, minor of G. W. Stinchcomb, decd, in Account Current, from time of appointment to present time in full settlement of the same
Page 741-742

12 vouchers.
Filed: 15 Jan 1878. Recorded: 8 May 1878

W. R. McLewaney Gdn of Mary Fernandes, Imbecile, from the time of appointment to 1 Feb 1878
Page 742-743

To amount received from J. M. Davis, former Gdn, see Book I, page 635
3 vouchers.
Filed: 4 Feb 1878. Recorded: 8 May 1878

Martha A. Stinchcomb, Gdn of George Stinchcomb, in Account Current with said minor from the time of appointment to 1 Mar 1878
Page 743-744

3 vouchers. Filed: 1 Mar 1878. Recorded: 8 May 1878

P. M. Trimble, Gdn of Martha Ballard, minor child of William Ballard with said ward, from 21 Jul 1874 to 23 Jul 1878 inclusive
Page 744-745

To amount on hand from last Return, see Book I, page 381.
2 vouchers. Filed: 23 Feb 1878. Recorded: 8 May 1878

An Account Current with J. J. Gilbert, Gdn of Charles Rogers, minor of H. M. Rogers, decd, from the time of appointment to 1 Apr 1878
Page 745

To amount received from W. L. Williams, Exr of J. D. Rogers, decd.
Filed: 1 Apr 1878. Recorded: 8 May 1878

Return No. 9, B. O. Jones' Estate in Account Current with John H. Richardson, Exr, from 8 Jan 1877 to 20 Mar 1878
Page 746-750

21 vouchers. Filed: 1 Apr 1878. Recorded: 8 May 1878

Robert L. Rogers, Sec. for J. D. Rogers, Gdn for his minor children in a/c Current with said children from time of appointment to 1 Apr 1878
Page 750

2 vouchers. Filed: 1 Apr 1878. Recorded: 8 May 1878

Estate of John L. Mackey, decd, in Account Current with S. T. Bridges, Admr, from 1 Apr 1875 to 1 Apr 1878 inclusive
Page 751-754

By amount from last Return to Admr in 1875, see Book I, page 415
12 vouchers. Includes Misses Florence and Tommie Mackeys accounts with M. H. Couch.
Filed: 15 Apr 1878. Recorded: 14 Jun 1878

J. H. Murphy, Gdn of James B. Rogers, minor, in Account Current with said minor from time of appointment to 1 Apr 1878
Page 754-755

8 vouchers.
Filed: 19 Apr 1878.
Recorded: 14 Jun 1878

An Account Current with M. L. Yates, Admr de bonis non of James W. Head, decd, showing settlement with the Legatees:
Page 756-758

Heirs as follows -
W. T. Head (x, his mark)
M. L. Head
Robert Kerly and Nancy Kerly (x, their marks)
Emily E. Head (x, her mark)
J. R. and Mrs. W. H. Peppers.

Filed: 6 May 1878.
Recorded: 14 Jun 1878

Return of David McLucas, Admr of Estate of Andrew McLucas, decd, Jan 1878
Page 759-760

6 vouchers. By amount paid - Ordinary, D. A. McLucas (tuition of minor children, John H. McLucas (my share of estate), Mary J. McLucas (my share of estate), W. L. Cox (tax collector) and Martha E. Jackson (my share of estate).

Filed: 6 May 1878.
Recorded: 15 Jun 1878

END OF BOOK

Fayette County Ordinary Mixed Records
Inventories, Appraisements, Sales and Returns
Book J (1878-1885)

Return of David McLucas, Exr of Estate of Joseph Banks, decd from 26 Aug 1874 to 1 May 1878
Page 1-3

To account received for sale of land, see Sale Book page 9
To account received for perishable property, see Sale Book page 9

8 vouchers. To cash paid - Hinson Turner, W. F. Banks, W. L. Cox, W. B. Stewart, Ordinary, Z. B. Blalock, E. B. Weeden and L. B. Griggs.

Filed: 6 May 1878. Recorded: 15 Jun 1878

E. W. Leach, Gdn of Joseph, Jeptha T., Lara T., and Napoleon B. Landrum, minor children of Jeptha Landrum, Jr., decd, in Account with same from time of appointment until 1 May 1878
Page 4-7

17 vouchers. To cash paid - D. C. Minor, J. W. Brown, N. Shelnutt, J. F. Cochran, E. R. Sharp, L. B. Griggs, J. L. Veal, F. M. Ellison, R. R. Jones and J. M. Hamrick.

Filed: 23 Apr 1878. Recorded: 15 Jun 1878

An Account Current with M. L. Yates, Admr of R. N. Harris, decd, from 1 Jul 1877 to 1 Jul 1878
Page 8-10

8 vouchers. To cash paid - Wilkins and Franklin, W. L. Cox, E. C. Bustian, et al (commissioners for setting aside dower for Martha E. Harris, widow), C. B. Vickers, A. E. Stokes, L. B. Griggs, Z. B. Blalock.

Recorded: 8 Jul 1878

In Account with A. J. Shropshire, Gdn of Nannie and Johnnie Shropshire, minors of John W. Shropshire, decd, from Jan 1877 to 1 Jan 1878
Page 11-12

8 vouchers. To cash paid - L. B. Griggs, Chamberlain B. Co., C. H. Brotherton, James A. Watson, W. L. Jackson, James H. Watson, John Ryan, W. L. Cox.

Recorded: 8 Jul 1878

An Account Current with W. W. Bearden, Gdn of his minor children from 1 Jul 1874 to 1 Jul 1878
Page 13

2 vouchers. Voucher #2 - Received of W. W. Bearden as Gdn $17.02, it being my distributive share of said estate, Dec 29 1877. /s/ M. J. E. Bearden
Recorded: 7 Aug 1878

In Account Current with J. H. and Z. T. Ellington, Admrs of R. C. Ellington, decd, from 1 Jul 1877 to 1 Jul 1878
Page 13-16

11 vouchers. To cash paid - W. L. Cox, Speer and Stewart, L. B. Griggs, J. F. Hayes, Boynton & Dismuke, A. E. Stokes, A. F. Colledge, Speer Stewart.

Voucher #7. Received of Z. T. Ellington, one of the admrs of R. C. Ellington, decd, $5.75 cash for dower of widow of said decd, this 18 May 1878. /s/A. E. Stokes, Clerk
Recorded: 7 Aug 1878

Estate of Edmond Jackson, decd, in Account with G. W. Robinson and M. E. Jackson, Exrs of said Estate, from 6 Aug 1877 to 5 Aug 1878
Page 16-17

See Book I, page 695
Filed: 5 Aug 1878. Recorded: 3 Sept 1878

J. A. Chapman, Gdn of Mary A. E. Bullard in Account with said minor from 1 Aug 1877 to 1 Aug 1878
Page 17-18

2 vouchers. To cash paid - G. S. Trimble and L. R. Griggs.
Filed: 5 Aug 1878. Recorded: 3 Sept 1878

Anna F. Brassell, widow of Willis Brassell, decd, 12 months' support for herself and children
Page 18-19

Georgia, Fayette Co. In obedience to an Order passed by the Honorable the Ordinary of Fayette County directed to us as Commissioners and Appraisers to set apart and assign to Anna F. Brassell, widow of Willis Brassell, decd, her minor children - Jesse W. and Nellie E. Brassell. Also for Emma, Eliza, Mary, Alice and Rosamond Brassell, minors of said decd by a second wife, and also Napoleon B. and Delilah F. Brassell, children by a first wife, a sufficiency from the estate of said decd for the maintenance of said widow and
minors for one year from 1 Oct 1877..... /s/John W. Dunbar, N. M. Gable, Hillery Brooks, J. W. Tillery.
Note: cash, furniture, etc. set apart.

Filed: 26 Oct 1877. Recorded: 3 Aug 1878

Bennett Jackson, decd
Page 19-20

The undersigned were ordered by Fayette Court of Ordinary to set apart a sum necessary for the support and maintenance of the minor children of Bennett Jackson, decd, for 12 months from the date of Bennett Jackson.. also property, etc. /s/John W. Kitchens, W. P. Eason and J. N. McEachern

2.5 acres valued, Lot No. 22 of SE corner, bounded on E by W. P. Eason and on S by Thornton Brooks, on W by Marion Jackson, on N by Needham Jackson.

Filed: 15 Jan 1878. Recorded: 3 Sept 1878

Estate of I. R. Elder, decd, in Account Current with Mrs. Martha Elder, Extrx, from 31 May 1878 to 29 Aug 1878
Page 21-28

47 vouchers.
Recorded: 9 Oct 1878

In Account with H. C. Fisher, Gdn of Minnie G., Sallie and Nora Smith, minos of I. H. Smith, decd, from 1 Jul 1876 to 1 Jul 1878 inclusive
Page 28-32

9 vouchers. To cash paid - L. B. Griggs, J. J. May, F. E. Atkinson, J. R. Brantley, C. R. Finley, C. A. Green, H. C. Fisher, Oney Swanson (tuition for Alberta, F. M. Brantley, Jr. (tuition of Berta)

Filed: 2 Sept 1878. Recorded: 9 Oct 1878

Martha A. Butler, Gdn of George Murphy in Account with said ward from time of appintment to 1 May 1878
Page 33

6 vouchers. Recorded: 9 Oct 1878

The Estate of I. P. Gay, decd, in Account Current with T. G., W. J. and Sandford Gay, Exrs, from time of appointment until 18 Sept 1878
Page 34-37

16 vouchers. Heirs: C. H. North for B. T. North, C. H. North, Wilham Glass, Jr. and V. Glass, W. J. Gay, Sandford Gay, T. G. Gay.
Recorded: 7 Nov 1878

An Account with M. L. Yates, Admr of Estate of R. N. Harris, decd, from 1 Jul 1878 to date showing a Final Settlement with said Estate
Page 37-45

To amount on hand from last Return, see Book J, page 8
21 vouchers. To cash paid - L. B. Griggs, W. L. Cox, J. G. Lester, E. S. Strickland, T. G. Hinet, W.T. Roberts, J. T. Stephens, G. W. Torence, R. Baily, B. F. Harper, Parker and Hatchcock, S. A. Harris, O. F. Harris, G. L. Harris, Shropshire & Johnson, Paul Faver, Z. B. Blalock, B. F. Harper and W. F. Define.

Filed: 1 Jan 1879. Recorded: 7 Feb 1879

M. M. Collier, Gdn of Ida Collier in Account with said ward from 1 Jan 1878 to 1 Jan 1879
Page 45

1 voucher
Filed: 1 Jan 1879
Recorded: 7 Feb 1879

Estate of H. M. Rogers, decd in Account Current with W. L. Williams and John J. Gilbert, Admrs
Page 46-48

3 vouchers. Heirs -

J. K. Tarply, Gdn of Mattie A. Tarply, minor heir
R. L. Rogers, Gdn of R. L. and J. M. Rogers, minor heirs
R. L. Rogers, Gdn of John M. and R. L. Rogers, minors
J. H. Franklin?, Gdn of James Rogers, minor
W. M. Rogers
J. J. Gilbert, Gdn of Charley Rogers

Recorded: 4 Mar 1879

Estate of Sarah Baily, decd, in Account with D. D. Denham, Exr of Estate of Sarah Baily, from 4 Dec 1877 to 4 Dec 1878 inclusive
Page 48-50

13 vouchers. To cash paid - Martha Elder, William Elder, Sterling Russell, J. T. Askew, Bethena Baily
Recorded: 4 Mar 1879

Estate of Mary Bagwell in Account Current with Blakly Bagwell from 1 Jul 1874 to 18 Feb 1879
Page 51-53

To balance on hand, see Book I, page 353

9 vouchers. To cash paid - Stewart and Newton, L. B. Griggs, J. F. Gray, G. M. Davis, P. M. Bethune, C. A. Thornton, W. L. Cox.

Filed: 20 Feb 1879. Recorded: 8 Apr 1879

An Account with J. M. Bridges, Gdn of Rachel, Ida and Thomas Bridges, from 20 Nov 1876 to 1 Feb 1879
Page 54-55

To cash paid - Rachel Bridges (X, her mark).
Received of J. M. Bridges, former gdn of Ida Cobb, formerly Ida Bridges, $110.72 in full of his distributive share in Estate of R. C. Bridges, decd, this 1 Feb 1879. /s/L. T. Cobb

Filed: 2 Feb 1879. Recorded: 8 Apr 1879

Gainy Westbrook, Gdn in Account Current with minor children of John W. Loyd, decd, from 1 Jul 1876 to 1 May 1879
Page 55-56

3 vouchers. To cash paid- C. A. Thornton, W. L. Cox.
Filed: 31 Mar 1879. Recorded: 1 May 1879

W. R. McElwaney, Gdn of Mary Fernander, imbecile, in Account with Mary Fernander from 1 Feb 1878 to 1 Feb 1879
Page 56-57

3 vouchers. Filed: 8 Feb 1879. Recorded: 7 May 1879

Rebecca C. Smith, Gdn of David W. and M. A. L. Speir, minors of Henry C. Speir, decd, in Account Current with said minors from 1 May 1876 to 1 May 1879
Page 57-58

5 vouchers. To cash paid - C. A. Thornton, W. L. Cox, W. S. Russell and L. B. Griggs.
Recorded: 4 Jun 1879

Herod Thornton, Jr., Gdn of Bennett and Mary Thornton, minors of Haywood Thornton, decd, from time of appointment to 1 Apr 1879
Page 58-59

7 vouchers. To cash paid - Haywood Thornton, Jordan Thornton, etc.
Filed: 20 Apr 1879. Recorded: 4 Jun 1879

Jordan Thortnon and C. H. Eastin, Admrs of Herod Thornton, Jr., decd, from time of appointment to 1 Apr 1879
Page 60-65

19 vouchers.

Voucher #12. By the 25th of Dec 1877 we or either of us promise to pay W. P. Eason or bearer the sum of $200... It part of the purchase money for land Lot No. 229 in 709th District G. M. of Fayette Co., this 27 Jan 1877. /s/Herod Thornton, Jordan Thornton and Haywood Thornton (x, his mark)

Filed: 20 Apr 1879. Recorded: 4 Jun 1879

The Estate of Harlin Brown in Account Current with John L. Burdett from time of his appointment to 1 May 1879
Page 66-68

12 vouchers. Filed: 28 Apr 1879. Recorded: 4 Jun 1879

Estate of J. F. Mackey, decd, in Account Current with S. T. Bridges from 1 Apr 1878 to 1 Apr 1879
Page 68-69

To amount received from sale of wild land, Lot No. 1083 in 19th District, 2nd Section of Cobb Co. containing 40 acres sold to W. P. Anderson for $200.

3 vouchers. Filed: 28 Apr 1879. Recorded: 5 Jun 1879

In Account with A. J. Shropshire, Gdn of Nannie and Johnie Shropshire, minor children of John W. Shropshire, decd, from 1 Jan 1878 to 1 May 1879
Page 70-72

15 vouchers.
Recorded: 5 Jun 1879

An Account Current with J. H. and Z. T. Ellington, Admrs of R. C. Ellington, decd, from 1 Jul 1878 to 1 Jul 1879
Page 73-77

23 vouchers.

Heirs -

F. S. C. Yates, E. M. B. Cleckler, L. A. Veal, J. A. Ellington, Z. T. Ellington, George Latham, J. D. Stewart, W. L. Cox, L. B. Griggs, and J. S. Ellington.

Recorded: 8 Jul 1879

An Account Current with W. W. Beardin, Gdn of his minor children from 1 Jul 1878 to 1 Jul 1879
Page 77

2 vouchers. Paid distributive share - L. T. Bearden
Recorded: 5 Aug 1879

E. W. Leach, Gdn of Josephine, Jeptha T., Laura T. and Napoleon B. Landrum, minors of Jeptha Landrum, Jr., decd, from May 1878 to 1 May 1879
Page 78

Filed: 7 Jul 1879. Recorded: 5 Aug 1879

E. W. Leach, Gdn, in Account Current with Marshall and Lizzie Swanson, minor children of Samuel Swanson, decd, from 20 Mar 1878 to 1 Jul 1879
Page 79-80

7 vouchers. Paid Rhoda Handley, teacher, tuition for 1878.
Filed: 7 Jul 1879. Recorded: 5 Aug 1879

Estate of Edmond Jackson, decd, in Account Current with G. W. Robinson and M. E. Jackson, Exrs, from 6 Aug 1878 to 1 Jul 1879
Page 80-81

2 vouchers. To cash paid - Sarah Jackson (x, her mark)
Filed: 31 Jul 1879. Recorded: 7 Nov 1879

William Guice, Gdn of Linton and Elizabeth Guice in Account Current from 1 Dec 1875 to 1 Oct 1879
Page 81-82

7 vouchers.
Vou. #5. Received of William M. Guice, former Gdn of Margaret E. Vincent (formerly M. E. Guice), $86.44 in full of her share in the Estate of Peter Guice this 5 Jan 1880. /s/W. R. Vincent (x, his mark)

Vou. #6. Received of W. M. Guice, my Gdn, $84.28 in full of the money due me from him as my Gdn. this 8 Mar 1879. /s/L. S. Guice

Recorded: 7 Nov 1879

Estate of W. F. Kelly in Account Current with J. A. Carmichael, Admr from time of appointment o 1 Dec 1879
Page 83-93

44 vouchers. Receipts include - Thomas Kelly (x, his mark) for his part of the crop, George Kelly, Daniel Kelly, Hester Kelly (x, her mark), etc.

Recorded: 7 Jan 1880

Estate of J. H. Elder in Account with Martha Elder from 29 Aug 1878 to 17 Sept 1879 inclusive
Page 93-99

36 vouchers.
Recorded: 8 Jan 1880

Estate of Willis Brassell, decd in Account Current with J. W. and T. W. Brassell, Exrs of Willis Brassell, decd - Showing Disposition of Land and Proceeds of Estate
Page 100-110

37 vouchers. Includes dower of Fannie Brassell.
78 acres sold 1st Tues. in Oct of 1878 to B. F. McCollum (W side of LL 155 in 6th District)
60 acres W corner of LL 190 in 6th District known as King Place sold to R. T. Dorsey.

The following property situated in Brooks Station, Ga. was sold -

1/2 interest in stone house, vacant lot, house and lot in Brooks set apart for widow's dower.

Recorded: 8 Jul 1880

A. B. Tinsley, Gdn of the minor heirs of Melissa Smith in an Account from 5 Jul 1876 to 6 Oct 1879
Page 111

4 vouchers. Filed: 6 Oct 1879. Recorded: 8 Jan 1880

J. A. Chapman, Gdn of Mary A. E. Bullard in an Account Current from 1 Aug 1878 to 1 Aug 1879
Page 112

3 vouchers. Recorded: 8 Jan 1880

An Account Current with H. C. Fisher, Gdn of Minnie G., Sallie A. and Nora H. Smith, from 1 Jul 1878 to 1 Jul 1879
Page 113-116

15 vouchers.
Recorded: 8 Jan 1880

Estate of Sarah Baily, decd, in Account Current with D. D. Durham, Exr, from 4 Dec 1878 to 4 Dec 1879
Page 116

2 vouchers. To cash paid - Bethena Baily (x, her mark), L. B. Griggs, Ordinary
Recorded: 8 Jan 1880

An Account Current with Sarah McKee, Gdn of Joseph McKee from time of appointment to 1 Dec 1879
Page 117

5 vouchers. To cash paid - Sarah McKee, Paul Faver, L. B. Griggs.
Recorded: 8 Jan 1880

Martha A. Butler, Gdn of George Murphy in Account Current from 1 May 1878 to 1 Dec 1879
Page 118

Paid taxes. Recorded: 8 Jan 1880

An Account Current with M. A. Griffith, Temporary Admr of Estate of A. M. Griffith, decd, from time of appointment to 10 Dec 1879
Page 119-122

12 vouchers. To cash paid - W. J. Jacobs, Z. B. Blalock, L. F. Blalock, J. H. Ware, A. C. and J. E. Blalock & Co., W. T. Cleveland, Lewis Williams, W. B. Stewart and L. B. Griggs.

W. J. Jones, Gdn of W. J. Jones, Jr., is entitled to $108.90 (leaves nothing due)
Mrs. M. A. Griffith is entitled to $108.90 (leaves nothing due)

Filed: 10 Dec 1879. Recorded: 4 Feb 1880

M. M. Collier, Gdn of Ida Collier in Account Current from 9 Feb 1879 to 6 Jan 1880
Page 122

Paid Ordinary and tax collector
Filed: 6 Jan 1880. Recorded: 4 Feb 1880

Estate of G. C. King, decd, in Account Current with Larkin Harrison, Admr, from time of appointment to date, 15 Dec 1880
Page 123-125

8 vouchers. To cash paid - M. L. Parker, W. B. Stewart, J. L. Blalock & Co., J. S. Simmons, W. L. Cox, W. J. Jacobs and L. B. Griggs.

Heirs receiving distributive shares -

Mrs. Amelia Norris
Fannie Dorsey
B. H. Dorsey, Gdn of John King

Filed: 5 Jan 1880. Recorded: 4 Feb 1880

An Account Current with Elizabeth Rush, Extrx of Estate of John Rush, decd, from time of appointment to 5 Jan 1880
Page 126-128

13 vouchers.
Recorded: 4 Feb 1880

Margarett J. Jones, Gdn of J. H. and M. F. Jones, minors of Francis Jones, decd, in Account with said minors from time of appointment to 5 Jan 1880 showing a Final Settlement with said minors
Page 128-129

Filed: 5 Jan 1880. Recorded: 4 Feb 1880

Estate of L. M. Malone, minor of William Malone, in Account Current with T. C. Malone, Gdn, from 1 Feb 1877 to 1 Jul 1880
Page 129-130

7 vouchers. Recorded: 4 May 1880

In Account with A. J. Shropshire, Gdn of Nannie and Johnie Shropshire, minor childen of John W. Shropshire, decd, from 1 May 1879 to 1 May 1880
Page 131-133

14 vouchers
Filed: 1 Jun 1880. Recorded: 7 Jul 1880

Estate of W. L. Williams, decd, in Account Current with M. L. Redwine, Admr, from time of appointment to 1 Apr 1880
Page 134-141

Includes a long list of accounts collected.
Sale of 50 acres sold 1st Tues. in 1879, being the SE corner of Lot No. 224 in 6th District of Coweta Co.
Sale of 5 acres, fraction of land situate in Red Oak, Campbell Co., sold 1st Tues in 1879
25 accounts paid.
Filed: 1 Jun 1880. Recorded: 7 Jul 1880

See Page 364 for Receipts of Alice McKee and Mary Suduth, heirs of Samuel Johnson
Page 141

Only notation.

John Bagwell, minor of John Bagwell, decd, in Account Current with Blakely Bagwell, from time of appointment to 1 Aug 1880
Page 142

Receipt from W. W. Mitcham for tuition for John Bagwell for 1879.
Recorded: 4 Aug 1880

An Account Current with J. H. and Z. T. Ellington, Admrs of Estate of R. C. Ellington, decd, from 1 Jul 1879 to 1 Jul 1880
Page 143-145

10 vouchers.
W. S. Russell give his note for W. J. Russell's note which appears on Appraise Bill. See Book J, page 461
Receipts from J. H. and Z. T. Ellington for their distributive shares of estate, dated 12 Jun 1880.
Note on E. H. Cleckler, husband of Eliza M. B. Cleckler, daughter of said decd
Note on William W. Veal, husband of L. A. Veal, daughter of said decd
Note on John H. Ellington, son of decd
Note on J. H. Ellington, son of decd
Note of Z. T. Ellington, son of decd
Recorded: 8 Apr 1880

J. A. Chapman, Gdn of Mary H. E. Bullard, in Account Current with said minor from 1 Aug 1879 to 8 Aug 1880
Page 145-146

3 vouchers. Recorded: 4 Aug 1880

In Account Current with B. F. Head, Exr of Estate of William Head, decd, from 1 Jul 1876 to 1 Jul 1880
Page 146-147

7 vouchers. Filed: 2 Aug 1880. Recorded: 7 Sept 1880

J. A. Chapman, Gdn of Mary A. E. Bullard in Account Current with said minor from 1 Aug 187 to 1 Aug 1880
Page 148

3 vouchers. To amount paid - C. L. Bullard, L. B. Griggs.
Filed: 2 Aug 1880. Recorded: 7 Sept 1880

Miss Kitty C. Thornton, decd
Page 148-150

Georgia, Fayette Co. | To the Ordinary of said county - B. L. Thornton shows to the court of Ordinary that his sister, Miss Kitty C. Thornton, departed this life leaving a Will which has been probated and naming C. B. Brogdon her Exr, and he refusing to qualify as such Exr, and the said legatees agreeing to....appoint me (B. L. Thornton) to act as agent to carry out the Will....Therefore, I have turned over the property of said decd to the legatees as described in said Will and taken their receipts and turned over the land as bequeathed in the Will of Miss Kitty C. Thornton to M. J. H. Thornton and Fereby Teel, tenants for life, and taken their receipts....11 Aug 1880. /s/B. L. Thornton

Agreeing to the division of the estate, 2 Aug 1880, were: Fereby Teel, D. I. Thornton, Eveline Heath, M. J. H. Thornton, R. L. Thornton, Rebecca Hartley, Anna Stanley.

Heirs receipts - M. J. A. Thornton, Phereby Teel, Eveline Heath, D. L. Thornton, Rebecca Hartley, Anna Stanley, B. Thornton (x, his mark).

J. E. Spurlin, Gdn in Account Current with Estate of Mrs. M. A. Goodman from time of appointment to 6 Sept 1880
Page 150-151

5 vouchers. Filed: 6 Sept 1880. Recorded: 5 Oct 1880

An Account Current with James Boyd, Gdn of Ida V. Spencer, from 1 Jul 1876 to 1 Jul 1880
Page 151-152

9 vouchers. To cash paid - L. A. Spencer, C. A. Thornton, W. L. Cox, W. J. Jacobs, L. B. Griggs.
Recorded: 1 Nov 1880

Estate of J. H. Elder, decd, in Account Current with Martha Elder, Extrx, from 17 Sept 1879 to 1 Nov 1880
Page 153-159

40 vouchers.
Note: Apparently this was a large estate, as cotton bales, oats, fodder, farm labor, etc. are included in the accounts.
Recorded: 8 Dec 1879

An Account Current with W. W. Padgett, Gdn of M. F. Padgett, now M. F. Cox) from time of appointment to 1 Nov 1880
Page 160

3 vouchers. To cash paid - L. B. Griggs and M. F. Cox.
Voucher #2. Receipt of W. W. Padgett, Gdn, $244.24 as my distributive share of the Estate of Elizabeth Padgett and Martha King's. 8 Jan 1880. /s/M. F. Cox /s/W. H. Cox
Filed: 8 Nov 1880.

Rachel Eason, Admx of Estate of Richard I. Eason in Account Current with said Estate from Jan 1874 to Dec 1880 showing a Final Settlement with the heirs and creditors of said decd
Page 161-164

10 vouchers. To cash paid - G. M. Davis, C. A. Thornton, W. L. Cox, W. J. Jacobs, L. B. Griggs, J. N. Carlile and Robert Eason

There are six childre and this account to be divided equally....

Mrs. Rachael Eason is entitled to $76.54 (leaves nothing due)
John Eason is entitled to $51.03
James Eason is entitled to $51.03
Mary Eason is entitled to $51.03 (leaves nothing due)
Martha Eason is entitled to $51.03 (leaves nothing due)
Robert Eason is entitled to $51.03 (leaves nothing due)
E. P. Eason is entitled to $51.3 (leaves nothing due)

Filed: 4 Dec 1880
Recorded: 8 Feb 1881

An Account Current with W. J. Jones as Gdn of W. J. Jones from time of appointment to date 24 Dec 1880
Page 165

3 vouchers. Vou. #3. Received of W. J. Jones, Sr. my Gdn, $126.40 in full for the money he held as Gdn for me ...coming from the estate of G. W. Griffith, decd, by Will of said G. W. Griffith, 24 Dec 1880. /s/W. J. Jones, Jr.

Filed: 24 Dec 1880
Recorded: 8 Feb 1880

A Final Return of Daniel McLucas, Exr of Estate of Joseph Banks
Page 166-168

14 vouchers. To cash paid heir -

Malinda Turner (x, her mark)
B. T. Banks (x, his mark)
W. L. Banks (x, his mark)
Emily Stubbs by Drewry Farren, atty in fact
F. M. Banks (x, his mark)
I. N. Banks (x, his mark)
Permelia Farren (x, her mark)
A. D. Banks, Sarah E. Banks, Kinyon B. Banks, by Netty Banks, Gdn (x, her mark)
Permelia F. Shipp
Elvina William Cooper (x, his mark)
Louisa J. Belish
John G. Banks (x, his mark)

M. M. Collier, in Account Current with Ida Collier from 1 Jan 1880 to 1 Jan 1881
Page 168-169

2 vouchers. Filed: 3 Jan 1881. Recorded: 8 Feb 1881

An Account Current with S. C. Travis, Gdn of E. M. Travis and Miss N. E. Travis, minors of H. C. Travis, decd, from time of appointment to 1 Jan 1881 showing a Final Settlement
Page 169-170

E. M. Travis is entitled to $234.67
M. M. Travis has received $291.57
Miss N. E. Travis is entitled to $234.67

Filed: 10 Jan 1881. Recorded: 8 Feb 1881

Elizabeth Rush, Extrx on Estate of John Rush, decd, in Account with said Estate from 5 Jan 1880 to 5 Jan 1881
Page 171-173

8 vouchers. Filed: 7 Mar 1881. Recorded: 5 Apr 1881

E. W. Leach, Gdn of Marshall and Lizzie Swanson, minors of Paul Swanson, decd, in Account Current with said wards from 1 Jul 1879 to 14 Apr 1881
Page 173-174

6 vouchers. Filed: 29 Mar 1881. Recorded: 4 May 1881

Estate of William F. Kelley, decd, in Account Current with J. A. Carmichael, Admr, from 1 Dec 1879 to 1 Apr 1881 inclusive
Page 175-179

8 vouchers.
W. F. Kelly waives all rights or claims on all property of estate. (Brooks Station, Ga.), 16 Jan 1878
Tuition paid for - R. L. Kelley, J. H. Kelley.
Filed: 4 Apr 1881. Recorded: 3 May 1881

Estate of Catherine DeVaughn, decd in Account Current with John H. Farr, Exr, from 29 Jan 1877 (last Return) until 3 oct 1881
Page 180-181

Filed: 18 Apr 1881. Recorded: 3 May 1881

S. T. Bridget, Admr of Estate of J. F. Mackey, decd in Account Current from 1 Apr 1879 to 1 Apr 1881
Page 182-185

4 vouchers. Includes accounts in Senoia, Ga. for Miss Florence Mackey .Filed: 1 Apr 1881. Recorded: 3 May 1881

J. H. Murphy, Gdn of J. B. Rogers from 1 Apr 1878 to 1 Apr 1881
Page 186-187

8 vouchers. Recorded: 8 Jun 1881
Vou. #3. Received of J. H. Murphy, Gdn of James B. Rogers, minor child of H. M. Rogers, decd, $11.77 as interest on money of said minor child in his hands and for the support of said child, this 7 Mar 1879. /s/J. K. Tarpley. (also vou. #4)

In Account with A. J. Shropshire, Gdn of Nannie and Johnie Shropshire, minor children of John W. Shropshire, decd, from 1 May 1880 to 1 May 1881
Page 188-189

11 vouchers. Filed: 6 Jun 1881. Recorded: 7 Jul 1881

In Account with H. C. Fisher, Gdn of Minnie G., Sallie A. and Nora H. Smith from 1 Jul 1879 to 1 Jul 1881
Page 191-193

8 vouchers.
Filed: 13 Jul 1886. Recorded: 14 Oct 1881

An Account Current with Catherine Parrott, Extrx of Estate of John Parrott, decd, from 1 May 1868 to 1 Apr 1881
Page 194

3 vouchers. Recorded: 14 Oct 1881

An Account Current with R. A. Tilghman, Admr and S. T. C. Yates, Admx, on Estate of Mathew Yates, decd, from time of appointment to 1 Apr 1881
Page 195-199

24 vouchers. Recorded: 14 Oct 1881

James N. Kelley, Admr on Estate of J. W. Kelley, Sr., from time of appointment to 5 Sept 1881
Page 200-202

10 vouchers. Filed: 5 Sept 1881. Recorded: 14 Oct 1881

Estate of R. C. Ellington in Account Current with J. H. Ellington, the surviving Admr, from 1 Jul 1880 to 12 Jul 1881, the other Admr having died since the last Return was made
Page 202-204

5 vouchers. Filed: 5 Sept 1881. Recorded: 14 Oct 1881

J. H. Ellington, Temp. Admr on Estate of Z. T. Ellington, decd, in Account Current with said Estate from time of appointment to 5 Sept 1881
Page 204-206

8 vouchers. Filed: 5 Sept 1881. Recorded: 14 Oct 1881

Martha Elder, Extx Estate of Josiah H. Elder, in Account Current from 1 Nov 1880 to 3 Oct 1881
Page 207-213

Cash on hand from last Return, see Book J, page 153
43 vouchers. Receipts include names of J. L. Elder and Berry Elder
Filed: 29 Sept 1881, Recorded: 12 Nov 1881

R. H. Woods, Admr of Hillery Brooks, decd, from date of appointment to 1 Oct 1881
Page 214-217

To amount from sale of personal property, see Book A, page 26
15 vouchers. Recorded: 12 Nov 1881

Joe L. Graves, Gdn of the minor children of J. G. Miles, from date of appointment to 1 Oct 1881
Page 218

3 vouchers. Filed: 29 Sept 1881. Recorded: 12 Nov 1881

T. B. Tinsley, Gdn of minor Heirs of Melissa Smith, from 6 Oct 1879 to 12 Nov 1881
Page 219-220

Received of A. B. Tinsley, Gdn, $38.21, the same being the amount due me from him as such guardian, this 20 Oct 1879. /s/Josie Smith (x, her mark)
Full distribution paid to Wilson M. Smith (x, his mark)
Filed: 1 Nov 1881. Recorded: 8 Nov 1881

Martha A. Butler, Gdn of George Murphy, from 1 Dec 1871 to 1 Dec 1881
Page 224-225

Filed: 5 Dec 1881. Recorded: 14 Jan 1882

A. J. Shropshire, Gdn of Nannie, now Nannie Madaris, and Johnnie Shropshire, from 1 May 1881 to 29 Dec 1881, showing a Final Settlement
Page 225-226

To amount on hand from last Return, see Book J, page 188
Received $316.10 of A. J. Shropshire, former Gdn of Johnnie Shropshire...in full of monies and property that went into his hands as such Gdn, this 29 Dec 1882. /s/G. W. Madaris, Gdn for Johnnie Shropshire

Received $312.33 of A. J. Shropshire, former Gdn of Nannie Shropshire...in full of monies and property that went into his hands as such Gdn, this 29 Dec 1882. /s/G. W. Madaris for Nannie Madaris

W. W. Padgett, Gdn of Jimmie Padgett, from date of appointment to 2 Jan 1882
Page 227

3 vouchers. Filed: 2 Jan 1882. Recorded: 7 Feb 1882

W. W. Padgett, Gdn of J. T. Padgett, from date of appointment to 2 Jan 1882
Page 228

3 vouchers. Filed: 2 Jan 1882. Recorded: 7 Feb 1882

Estate of W. F. Kelley, decd, in Account Current with J. A. Carmichael, Admrs, from 1 Apr 1881 to 1 Feb 1882 inclusive
Page 229-231

To cash on hand from last Return, see Book J, page 175. 7 vouchers. Filed: 21 Jan 1882. Recorded: 7 Feb 1882

Blakely Bagwell, Gdn of John Bagwell, from 1 Aug 1880 to 1 Jan 1882 inclusive
Page 232-233

4 vouchers. Recorded: 7 Mar 1882

J. H. Ellington, Admr of Estate of Zack T. Ellington, decd, from 5 Jan 1881 to 17 Jan 1882
Page 233-246

34 vouchers consisting of cotton bills, etc. Some Fairburn, Ga. accounts
Filed: 17 Jan 1882. Recorded: 7 Mar 1882

Estate of Josiah H. Elder, decd, in Account Current with Martha Elder, Extrx, from 3 Oct 1881 to 1 Feb 1882 for Final Settlement of the Estate Except the Dower of the Wife
Page 247-251

To amount on hand from last Return, see Book J, page 207. 18 vouchers.

Mrs. Racheal E. Lanier under the Will and each of his four children at home to the time of his death was to get $800 first, with the remainder to be divided equally. See the Will.

Each of the following received $800.00 -
Martha A. Elder
Josiah L. Elder
Francis V. Lanier
C. C. Elder
A complete explanation of the settlement was given 25 Feb 1882 by Martha Elder (x, her mark), stating that 5 children were mentioned in the Will.

Heirs Receipts -
F. V. Lanier
C. C. Elder
M. A. Lanier
J. L. Elder
James A. Lanier, Gdn of Cora L., Sallie, William C., Alice, Robert L., James L. and Russie Lanier, the 7 minor children of Racheal E. Lanier, decd (heir of Josiah H. Elder, decd)
Filed: 25 Feb 1882. Recorded: 4 Apr 1882

M. M. Collier, Gdn of Ida Collier, now Ida Neely, in Account Current from 1 Jan 1881 to 1 Jan 1882
Page 251-252

To amount on hand from last Return, see Book J, page 168
2 vouchers. Filed: 28 Mar 1882. Recorded: 4 May 1882

Henry S. Rivers, Gdn of Nancy J. and Millie E. Milam, minors of John R. Milam, decd, from date of appointment to 1 Apr 1882
Page 252-253

3 vouchers. Recorded: 4 May 1882

Estate of Catherine DeVaughn, in Account Current with J. H. Farr, Exr, from 1 Apr 1881 to 1 Apr 1882
Page 253

Cash from last Return, See Book J, page 180. 2 vouchers. Recorded: 4 May 1882

Perry Hicks, Gdn of Emmett Pyron, in Account Current from date of his appointment to 1 Apr 1882
Page 254

1 vouchers. Filed: 3 Apr 1882. Recorded: 4 May 1882

Final Return of Mrs. Mary Jane Farr, Gdn for Mandy Rush
Page 255-256

Mary Jane Farr, in Account with her wards-Mary E., Eveline (formerly Rush) and Sarah F. Rush 1864. Stated that she has on hand worthless Confederate money. Filed: 21 Mar 1882. Recorded: 4 May 1882

Estate of John Welborn Kelley, decd, in Account Current with J. N. Kelley, Admr, from 5 Sept 1881 to 1 May 1882 inclusive
Page 257-263

Balance on hand, see Book J, page 200
From sale of real estate, see Book H, page 13
Rent of land in Spalding Co.
Rent from T. J. Vaughn for storehouse in Senoia, Ga.
Rent from Jeff Holland for Grant Place
Rent from John W. Kelley for Wright Place

Division of shares as follows -
E. R. Kelly entitled to receive $216.15
Camilla Hutchison entitled to receive $216.15
W. H. Hutchison entitled to receive $216.15
Lucy A. Edmondson entitled to receive $216.15
John W. Kelley entitled to receive $216.15
J. N. Kelley entitled to receive $216.15

Voucher #1. Estate of Welborn Kelley, decd, to Amanda Collins, for 1880 tuition of son
Martha E. Kelly received in lieu of dower interest in Spalding and Coweta Co property.
Filed: 1 May 1882. Recorded: 7 Jun 1882

Benjamin Hutchinson, Gdn of Bascomb Y., John H., Robert E. and Ida R. B. Kelley, in Account Current with said minors of W. F. Kelley, decd, from time of appointment to 21 Feb 1882
Page 263-264

4 vouchers. Recorded: 12 Jul 1882

Martha Elder, Admx of Miss Bethena Bailey, decd, from time of appointment to 1 Mar 1882
Page 265-267

From sale of personal property, see Book A, page (blank)
From sale of 99 acres, see Sale Book A, page (blank)
Received from Mary A. Hollingsworth on Fi.Fa.

11 vouchers. Filed: 25 Feb 1882. Recorded: 12 Jul 1884

Elizabeth Rush, Extrx of John Rush, from 5 Jan 1881 to 5 Jan 1882 inclusive
Page 268-269

9 vouchers. Filed: 6 Mar 1882

S. T. Bridges, Admr of J. T. Mackey, decd, in Account Current from 1 Apr 1881 to 1 Apr 1882
Page 269-272

4 vouchers. includes an account of Miss Florence Mackey (vou. #3)
Filed: 12 Apr 1882. Recorded: 12 Jul 1882

Estate of L. M. Malone (now L. M. Matthews), in Account Current with T. C. Malone, Gdn, from 1 Apr 1882 to 1 Apr 1882, showing a Final Settlement
Page 272-274

8 vouchers After the accounts are paid, a notation "leaving nothing to ward."
Filed: 2 Apr 1882. Recorded: 12 Jul 1882

E. W. Leach, Gdn of Jeptha T. Landrum, in Account Current from 1 May 1879 to 1 May 1882
Page 274-275

Cash on hand from last Return, see Book J, page 78
5 vouchers. Recorded: 12 Jul 1882

E. W. Leach, Gdn of Marshall Swanson and Lizzie Flowers (formerly Lizzie Swanson), from 1 Apr 1881 to 1 Apr 1882 inclusive
Page 276

Cash on hand from last Return, see Book J, page 173. 4 vouchers. Filed: 1 May 1882. Recorded: 12 Jul 1882

R. A. Tilghman, Admr, and S. F. C. Yates, Admx of Estate of Mathew Yates, decd, from 1 Apr 1881 to 1 Apr 1882 inclusive
Page 277-283

Cash received on various cotton bills. 22 vouchers. Filed: 12 May 1882. Recorded: 12 Jul 1882

Annual Return with R. H. Woods, Admr of Hillery Brooks, decd, from 1 Oct 1881 to 1 Jun 1882
Page 283-287

Cash on hand, see Book J, page 214
Sale of 48 acres to F. A. Woods
Sale of Town Lots in Brooks Station - Lots 2, 5, 9 and 22 sold to W. W. Mitcham; Lot 3 sold to F. A. Woods, Lots 10 and 23 to J. Spurlin; Lot 19 to J. W. Dunbar; Lots 20 and 21 to J. W. Padgett (acre lots)

13 vouchers. Filed: 12 Jun 1882. Recorded: 8 Aug 1882

Estate of J. P. Gay, decd, in Account Current with W. J. Sandford and T. G. Gay, Exrs, from 18 Sept 1878 to 1 Jul 1882
Page 287-290

To total amount of estate received, see Book J, page 34. 3 vouchers.

We now deduct the Special Legacy to Zora North (See Will). J. P. Gay.

Balance of estate to -

W. J. Sandford, T. G. Gay and the children named in the Will of said Gay of Zora North's 5 children
T. G. North, Gdn of John E. and Everett W. North
Viola Glass entitled to $995.84 (William G. Glass signed receipt for her)
B. F. North entitled to $995.84

Filed: 1 Jun 1882. Recorded: 8 Aug 1882

Annual Return of of C. J. Fall, Admr of Estate of Joseph Speer, decd, to 1 Jun 1872
Page 291-299

38 vouchers. Heirs as follows -

T. C. Speer
S. A. Loyd by Samuel Loyd
James J. Speer
J. M. Speer
Malissa T. Thompson by J. M. Speer (her father, Joseph Speer, decd)
William and Malvin A. Thompson by J. M. Speer (estate of my father)
James Young, in right of wife, Elizabeth
Mary Speer (her father, Joseph Speer, decd)
Patrick Carmichael for wife, Mary Ann, daughter of Joseph Speer, decd
Joseph F. Speer for wife, Nancy C.
W. R. Spruill/H. A. Spruill - Estate of my father, Joseph Speer, decd
R. A. Carter/J. W. Carter - Estate of my father, Joseph Speer, decd
James J. Speer
T. C. Speer
Joseph M. Speer
Sarah H. Loyd/Samuel Loyd
Matilda Thompson by James J. Speer
Malviny Thompson by James J. Speer
Mary Speer, Admx
Teresa A. Carter
M. K. W. Luck

Estate of Joseph Speer (Heirs) contd....

Sarah F. Vincent
J. C. Vincent
T. C. Speer
J. W. Speer (x, his mark)
J. M. Speer
James J. Speer, Exr of John W. Speer, decd, having been the son of Joseph Speer, decd, dated 29 Oct 1872

Martha A. Stinchcomb, Gdn of Georgia Stinchcomb from 1 Mar 1878 to 1 Mar 1881
Page 299

Cash from last Return, see Book I, page 743. 1 voucher. Recorded: 9 Nov 1882

In Account Current with William A. Messer, Exr of the LWT of Lot Messer, decd, from the time of appointment to 1 Sept 1882
Page 300-303

10 vouchers. Amanda Messer (x, her mark), account for Mandy and Missouri Messer
Al A. Messer acct. Receipt from Anna Messer (x, her mark) for support

Filed: 4 Sept 1882. Recorded: 9 Nov 1882

William J. Grant, Gdn of M. T. Grant (late Patterson) in full of all demands as such Gdn, 15 Dec 1881
Page 304

Receipt of E. F. and T. H. Chaffin in full for all demands, dated 15 Dec 1881.
Receipt of M. H. Patterson in full for all demands

State of Arkansas }
County of Columbia }

M. T. R. Grant, M. H. Patterson and E. P. Chaffin and T. H. Chaffin, acknowledged executing receipts in full satisfaction of all demands against William J. Grant, their late Gdn, this 15 Dec 1881. /s/Dave Dixon, Clerk
Recorded: 27 Nov 1882

Account Current with M. M. Collier, Gdn of Ida Collier, now Ida C. Neely, from 1 Jan 1882 to 1 Nov 1882 inclusive
Page 305

To cash on hand from last Return, see Book J, page 251
Paid Ida P. Neely in full for estate of her grandfather, William Johnson, decd.
Recorded: 7 Dec 1882

An Account Current with Hiram Turner, Exr of Moses T. Turner, decd, from date of appointment to 1 Nov 1882 inclusive
Page 306-309

From sale of personal property, see Book H, page 531
Rent of Quick Place 1880-1881. 23 vouchers. Filed: 10 Nov 1882. Recorded: 3 Jan 1883

Rebecca C. Smith, Gdn of David W. and M. A. L. Speer, minors of Henry C. Speer, from 1 May 1879 to 1 Nov 1882 inclusive
Page 309-310

David W. Speer having become of age, we now divide the $440.30 between him and M. A. L. Speer, she not being of age yet.
4 vouchers. Recorded: 3 Jan 1883

David McLucas, Admr of Andrew McLucas, from 1 May 1878 to 4 Dec 1878, Final Settlement
Page 311

Cash on hand from last Return, see Book I, page 759. 5 vouchers.
Heirs - Sarah C. Harrison and Hiram Youngblood
Filed: 4 Dec 1882. Recorded: 3 Jan 1883

In Account with W. A. Messer, Exr of Lot Messer from 1 Sept 1882 to 21 Dec 1882
Page 312-313

4 vouchers.
#1, Received of W. A. Messer, Exr of the Estate of Lot Messer, decd, $300.00, to-wit: one note.../s/ Amy Messer (x, her mark)

Received of W. A. Messer, Exr on Estate of Lot Messer, decd, all due stock and household and kitchen furniture.......21 Oct 1882. /s/Amy Messer (x, her mark)
Filed: 21 Dec 1882. Recorded: 7 Feb 1883

George W. Madaris in Account Current with Nannie Madaris and Johnnie Shropshire, now JohnnieMcEachern, from time of appointment to 1 Jan 1883 inclusive
Page 313-314

Filed: 10 Jan 1883. Recorded: 8 Mar 1883

John Sneed and W. P. Hemphill, Admrs of the Estate of John R. Smarr, decd in Account Current from time of appointment to 15 Jan 1883
Page 315-320

21 vouchers.
Each child is entitled to $53.85.
Martha E. Smarr, Gdn of her children, is entitled to $215.40 (Avery D., William F., Alonzo P. and James J. Smarr, minor children)
W. P. Hemphill, Gdn of five of the minor children is entitled to $269.25 (Robert R., Ella, Benson, Linnie and Mattie)

M. E. Smarr gave receipt acknowledging years' support 9 Nov 1882.
R. R. Smarr's account paid by Exr.
Filed: 15 Jan 1883. Recorded: 8 May 1883

J. H. Ellington, Admr of Z. T. Ellington, decd, in Account Current from 17 Jan 1882 to 17 Jan 1883
Page 320-321

7 vouchers.
To amount on hand from last Return, see Book J, page 235
Filed: 2 Feb 1883. Recorded: 8 May 1883

J. H. Ellington, Admr of R. C. Ellington, decd, in Account Current from 1 Jul 1881 to 1 Jul 1883
Page 322-325

To amount on hand from last Return, see Book J, page 202. 18 vouchers.
Distribution to Heirs - J. H. Ellington, L. A. Veal, E.M. C. Cleckler, S. T. C. Yates, Josiah A. Ellington, J. H. Ellington (received as Admr of Z. T. Ellington, for Z. T. Ellington's share).
Filed: 2 Feb 1883. Recorded: 8 May 1883

Estate of J. P. Shropshire, decd, in Account Current with A. J. Shropshire, Admr de bonis non, from time of appointment to 1 Mar 1883, the time of the Final Return
Page 326-329

10 vouchers. Heirs receiving $445.20 each:

Fannie Shropshire
Mrs. Aurelia S. Johnson
Mrs. Laura Crawford (receipt from M. L. Crawford)
G. W. Madaris, as Gdn of Nannie Madaris and Johnnie McEachern (formerly Nannie and Johnnie Shropshire, minor children of John Shropshire, decd)

Filed: 15 Feb 1883. Recorded: 8 May 1883

J. E. Spurlin, Gdn of Mrs. M. A. Goodman in Account Current with said ward from 1 Oct 1881 to 1 Feb 1883
Page 329-330

Filed: 9 Feb 1883.

W. A. Leach for E. W. Leach, decd, Gdn of Jeptha T. Landrum in Account Current with said J. T. Landrum from 1 May 1882 to 1 Feb 1883 Showing Final Settlement
Page 330

Receipt from Jeptha T. Landrum from his gdn, W. A. Leach, all money due him from decd's estate.
Recorded: 8 May 1883

B. H. Dorsey, Gdn of John King, minor of G. C. King, decd, in Account Current with his ward from time of appointment to 1 Apr 1883
Page 331-332

Received of B. H. Dorsey, my Gdn, $109.50, part of my money in his hands as my Gdn, 10 Jan 1883. /s/ J. L. King
Received of B. H. Dorsey, my Gdn, $70.11 in full of the money, interest and effects in his hands as my Gdn, this 21 Mar 1883. /s/ J. L. King
Filed: 21 Mar 1883. Recorded: 8 May 1883.

L. L. Handley, Admr of Estate of Jane Handley, decd, in Account Current from time of appointment to 1 Apr 1883
Page 332-333

Account of Jared Handley with L. L. Handley, for making coffin, etc.
Filed: 2 Apr 1883. Recorded: 8 May 1883

J. S. Thornton, Gdn of M. L. Thornton and H. S. W. Marshburn in Account with his said ward from time to appointment to 1 Apr 1883
Page 334

2 vouchers. Filed: 7 Apr 1883. Recorded: 8 May 1883

R. A. Tilghman, Admr and S. T. Yates, Admx of the Estate of Mathew Yates, in Account Current from 1 Apr 1882 to 1 Apr 1883
Page 335-338

18 vouchers. Filed: 1 May 1883. Recorded: 1 May 1883

John W. Kelley, Gdn of George C. Kelley in Account Current with his said ward from time of appointment to 7 May 1883
Page 339

2 vouchers. Filed: 7 May 1883. Recorded: 3 Jul 1883

Benjamin Hutchinson, Gdn of Bascomb Y., John H., Robert E. and Ida R. B. Kelley, minors of W. F. Kelley, decd, from 21 Feb 1882 to 1 May 1883
Page 339-341

4 vouchers. To cash paid - H. C. Reeves, J. M. North (tax collector), L. B. Griggs (Ordinary), and E. R. Kelley, as Gdn of Bascomb Y., John H., Robert E. and Ida R. B. Kelley.
Filed: 7 May 1883. Recorded: 3 Jul 1883

Joseph L. Graves, Gdn of George J. Miles & Dolcey Miles in Account Current with his said wards from 1 Oct 1881 to 8 Jun 1883
Page 342

To amount due Dolcey Miles from last Return, see Book J, page 218
To amount due George J. Miles from last Return, see Book J, page 18
Receipt from George J. Miles in full for his distribution.

In Account Current with H. C. Fisher, Gdn of Sallie A. and Nora H. Smith from 1 Jul 1881 to 1 Jul 1883
Page 343-347

13 vouchers. Recorded: 4 Sept 1883

Receipt from H. S. Jones for tuition 1880.
Receipt from Dora Brantley for boarding Sallie A. Smith.

In Account Current with R. H. Woods, Admr of Hillery Brooks, decd, from 1 Jun 1882 to 1 Jun 1883
Page 348-349

6 vouchers. Filed: 3 Sept 1883. Recorded: 3 Oct 1883

W. W. Padgett, Gdn of Jimmie Padgett in Account Current with his said ward from 2 Jan 1882 to 1 Sept 1883
Page 349

To amount on hand from last Return, see Book J, page 227
Filed: 11 Sept 1883. Recorded: 7 Nov 1883

Elizabeth Rush, Extrx of John Rush in Account Current from 5 Jan 1883 to 1 Sept 1883
Page 350-351

10 vouchers. Filed: 17 Sept 1883. Recorded: 7 Nov 1883

James Boyd, Gdn of Miss Ida V. Spence in Account Current with his said ward from 1 Jun 1880 to 1 Oct 1883
Page 351-353

To amount on hand from last Return see Book J, page 151
To cash paid - Lucy A. Spence, Ida V. Spence, H. C. Reeves (tax collector).
Received of H. S. Rivers, Exr of James Boyd, Gdn of Miss Ida V. Spence, $1.50 for this Return. /s/L. B. Griggs, Ordinary.
Filed: 1 Oct 1883. Recorded: 7 Nov 1883

J. T. McLean, Gdn in Account with A. R. Porter since last Return
Page 353-356

Vouchers pay Ordinary, taxes, etc.
Receipt from C.W. Richter for tuition for Ophelia J. Porter

Filed: 5 Nov 1883. Recorded: 5 Dec 1883

James T. Travis, Admr of C. E. Travis, decd, in Account Current from time of appointment to 8 Oct 1883
Page 356-358

6 vouchers. Filed: 5 Nov 1883. Recorded: 5 Dec 1883

W. W. Bearden, Gdn of W. A. and E. L. S. Bearden from 1 Jul 1879 to 1 Dec 1883
Page 358-359

Receipt from W. N. Bearden for his distributive share.
Receipt from E. L. S. Bearden for his distributive share

Filed: 1 Dec 1883. Recorded: 8 Jan 1884

Blakely Bagwell, Admr of Mary Bagwell, decd, in Account Current with said Estate
Page 359

To amount on hand from last Return, see Book J, page 51
Vou. #1. Receipted of B. Bagwell, Admr of Mary Bagwell, decd, $249.84 amount due me as Gdn of John Bagwell from the Estate of Mary Bagwell, decd, the same being in full this 29 Dec 1883. /s/B. Bagwell (x, his mark), Gdn of James Bagwell

Recorded: 8 Jan 1884

J. H. Ellington, Admr of Z. T. Ellington, decd, in Account Current from 17 Jan 1883 to 1 Jan 1884
Page 360-361

Received of J. H. Ellington, Admr of Z. T. Ellington, decd, $507.00 in part of the distributive share of Zachery P., Susan E., Richard F. and Josiah S. Ellington, minors of Z. T. Ellington, decd, this 17 Nov 1883. /s/R. A. Ellington, Gdn of said minors
5 vouchers. Recorded: 3 Feb 1884

Final Return of Lucy Morris, formerly Lucy Stephens, Gdn for George T. Stephens, Martha C. Milam, Alexander D. Stephens, Jefferson D. Stephens and Mary F. Milam, showing a Full Settlement with said wards
Page 361-363

Heirs receipts as follows -

G. T. Stephens
Martha C. Milam
H. D. Stephens
J. D. Stephens
M. F. Milam

Recorded: 5 Mar 1884

William J. Grant, Gdn of Drury Patterson
Page 363

Received, Magnolia, Columbia Co., Arkansas, 29 Jan 1883 of William J. Grant, Gdn of Drury Patterson, in full of all demands against him as such Gdn. /s/F. D. Patterson

M. L. Redwine, Admr of Estate of W. L. Williams, decd
Page 364

Georgia, Cobb Co. Personally appeared Mary Suderth and Alice McKee ...and say that they are the children of Samuel Johnson and only heirs of Samuel Johnson. /s/Alice McKee (x, her mark) /s/Mary Suduth
Sworn before me 8 Apr 1882. /s/H. M. Hammett, Ordinary

Received of M. L. Redwine, Admr on Estate of W. L. Williams, decd, $30.39, the sum being due from W. L. Williams as Admr on the Estate of William Johnson, this 8 Apr 1882. /s/Mary Suduth /s/Alice McKee (x, her mark)

Georgia, Cobb Co. Personally came before me, H. M. Hammett, Ordinary of said county, Alice McKee and Mary Suduth who, being duly sworn, depose and say that their mother's maiden name was Annie McKillian before her intermarriage with Samuel Johnson and that their mother has been dead about 12 years.....ced/s/Alice McKee (x, her mark) /s/Mary Suduth

Estate of John Phillips in Account Current with Louisa Phillips, Admx, from 1 Jul 1874 to 1 Nov 1883
Page 365-369

13 vouchers. Filed: 20 Nov 1883. Recorded: 3 Apr 1884
State of Georgia
Fayette Co..... To all and singular the Sheriffs of said State Greeting,... We Command you that of the goods and chattels, lands and tenements of George May, principal, T. J. Edmondson, John Huie, P. H. Brassell and John Phillipps, securities, you cause to be made the sum of $68.75.....to recover...William Bennett recovered against George May, etc. 29 May 1873.

Martha Elder, Extrx of Miss Bethena Baily, decd in Account Current from 1 Mar 1882 to 1 Mar 1884, Showing a Final Settlement with said Estate
Page 370-373

Distributive shares paid - S. D. Jackson, S. L. Weaver, H. O. Weaver, Mattie Weaver, S. L. Weaver, R. W. Pentecost (for his wife Harriett Pentecost, distributive share), Martha Elder, H. B. Weaver and M. B. Weaver.
Filed: 17 Mar 1884. Recorded: 2 Apr 1884

Receipt of Harriet L. Pentecost from Brown Co., Texas, 23 Jan 1884

Benjamin Hutchinson, Gdn of Bascomb Y., John H., Robert E. and Ida R. Kelley, minors of W. F. Kelley, decd, from 1 May 1883 to 1 May 1884
Page 374

3 vouchers. Recorded: 3 Apr 1884
Receipt from E. R. Kelley for boarding the minors.

G. W. Madaris, Gdn of Nannie Madaris and Johnnie McEachern in Account Current with said wards from 1 Jan 1883 to 1 Jan 1884
Page 375-376

4 vouchers.
Filed: 27 Mar 1884. Recorded: 7 May 1884

Amanda J. Boggs, Gdn of J. H. and A. G. Gardener in Account Current with her said wards from time of appointment to date, 7 Apr 1884
Page 376

2 vouchers. Recorded: 8 May 1884

A. J. Shropshire, Exr of Estate of M. L. Shropshire, decd in Account Current from qualification to 1 Mar 1884 inclusive
Page 377-380

12 vouchers
Balance for distribution (each heir due $42.67) as follows -

A. J. Shropshire
S. F. Shropshire
A. S. Johnson
M. L. Crawford
Filed: 20 May 1884. Recorded: 4 Jul 1884

R. A. Tilghman and S. T. Yates, Admrs of Matthew Yates in Account Current with said Estate from 1 Apr 1883 to 1 Jun 1884
Page 380-383

23 vouchers includes cotton bills, etc.
Recorded: 4 Jul 1884

F. D. Hewell, Gdn of E. H. Boggers in Account Current with said ward from time of appointment to date, 1 May 1884
Page 383

2 vouchers. Recorded: 4 Jul 1884

John W. Kelly, Gdn of George C. Kelly in Account Current from 7 May 1883 to 7 May 1884
Page 384

3 vouchers. Recorded: 4 Jul 1884

A. B. Tinsley, Gdn of Ira B. Smith, minor of Malissa Smith in Account Current with said ward from 6 Oct 1879 to 1 Jul 1884
Page 384-385

Received of A. B. Tinsley, my Gdn, $43.65 in full of all the money and effects he holds in his hands as such Gdn coming from my mother's estate, this 27 Jun 1884. /s/Ira B. Smith (x, his mark)
5 vouchers. Recorded: 8 Aug 1884

Account Current with J. E. and O. O. Blalock, Admrs of Z. B. Blalock, decd, from time of appointment to 1 Jul 1884
Page 386-400

22 vouchers. Numerous accounts, notes, etc. received int the estate.
Receipts from A. C. Blalock, S. T. Blalock, M. A. Blalock, and M. A. Blalock, Gdn for G. Z. Blalock, representing their distributive shares of estate.

W. S. Shell and H. L. Griffin, Admrs of Daniel Shell, decd, from time of appointment to 1 Jun 1884
Page 401-406

27 vouchers. Heirs as follows - F. L. Westbrook, R. B. Shell, J. S. Shell, Mary J. Shell, Mrs. L. N. Johnson.
Recorded: 3 Sept 1884

Amanda J. Speer, Gdn of J. W. T. Speer from 10 Feb 1877 to 1 Aug 1884
Page 406

Received of Amanda J. Speer, my Gdn, $440.00 in full of all the money and effects in her hands for me as such Gdn. /s/J. W. T. Speer
Recorded: 5 Sept 1884

An Account Current with H. C. Fisher, Gdn of Sallie A. Smith and Nora H. Smith, from 1 Jul 1883 to 1 Jul 1884 inclusive
Page 407-408

4 vouchers. Recorded: 6 Aug 1884

Annual Return of R. W. Hardy, Gdn of Annie W., William Spalding and Oliver McLendon, minors
Page 408

1 voucher. Recorded: 3 Sept 1884

George S. Banks, Exr of Wiseman Banks, decd
Page 409-414

Each child is entitled to receive $64.15 as follows -

G. S. Banks, J. M. Banks, Susan Morris, Joseph N. Banks, Julia T. Murphy, Sandford Banks, S. T. Richardson, Mary Turner, and Jacob W., George W., L. C. and Martha Barrentine
27 vouchers. Recorded: 3 Sept 1884

Estate of Larkin Harrison, decd. in Account Current with S. T. and A. O. Blalock, Temporary Admrs from time of appointment to 15 Nov 1884
Page 415-417

6 vouchers. Includes receipt from Sarah C. Harrison (widow) for years' support.
Recorded: 9 Jan 1884

Elizabeth Rush, Extrx of Estate of John Rush in Account Current from 1 Sept 1883 to 1 Sept 1884
Page 417-419

To amount received from rent of Coweta farm, 1883 - $63.50
To amount received from rent of Fayette farm, 1883 - $20.10
8 vouchers. Recorded: 9 Jan 1885

J. H. Ellington, Admr of Estate of R. C. Ellington, decd, from 1 Feb 1883 to 1 Dec 1884
Page 419-420

3 vouchers. Recorded: 9 Jan 1885

Mrs. R. A. Ellington, Gdn of her minor children, from time of appointment to 1 Dec 1884
Page 420-421

To amount received from J. H. Ellington, Admr of Z. T. Ellington, 17 Nov 1883 - $507.00
To amount received from J. H. Ellington, Admr of Z. T. Ellingtn, 22 Nov 1884 - $45.00

4 vouchers. Voucher #3. Fayetteville, Ga., 1 Dec 1884, Received of Mrs. R. A. Ellington, Gdn of Zachery P., Susan E., Richard F. and Josiah S. Ellington, minor children of Z. T. Ellington, decd, $450.00 for the purchase of land for said minors, the same was invested in land by Order of the Court of Ordinary of Fayette Co. allowing said Gdn to purchase land for said minors. /s/J. H. Ellington, Admr of Z. T. Ellington

An Account Current with J. W. Kitchens, Gdn of Rufus G., Charles W., John H. and Mary M. M. Kitchens, his minor children, from time of appointment to 1 Jan 1885
Page 421-422

To amount received from sale of personal property, see Sale Bill, Book A, page (blank)
4 vouchers. Recorded: 12 Feb 1885

Return No. 10 of Estate of B. O. Jones, decd, in Account Current with John A. Richardson, Exr
Page 422-425

6 vouchers. Vouchers #3 and 4 mention drugs and boarding for Bartee Jones. Recorded: 19 Feb 1885

J. H. Ellington, Admr of Estate of Z. T. Ellington, decd, from 1 Jan 1884 to 1 Jan 1885
Page 425-426

3 vouchers. Voucher #1. Received of J. H. Ellington, Admr, $45.00, being part of my distributive share of Z. T. and S. E. and R. F. and J. S. Ellington, minors of Z. T. Ellington, decd, this 22 Nov 1884. /s/R. A. Ellington, Gdn for said minors

Recorded: 11 Mar 1885

J. H. Murphy, Gdn of J. Bartow Rogers, from 1 Apr 1881 to 1 Jan 1885
Page 426-429

11 vouchers. To cash paid - R. E. Merrell, H. C. Reeves, H. D. Humphries, S. T. and A. C. Blalock, J. J. Hanes (clothes for Bartow Rogers), J. W. Denton and J. H. Murphy.
Recorded: 24 Mar 1885

Martha A. Butler, Gdn of George W. Murphy, in Account Current from 1 Dec 1881 to 2 Feb 1885
Page 429-431

Cash from last Return, see Book J, page 224. 5 vouchers. Recorded: 6 Apr 1885

Account Current with W. T. Glover, Gdn of Marshal N. Swanson and Mrs. Martha E. A. Flowers (formerly Swanson), minors of Samuel Swanson of Fayette Co., from time of appointment to 20 Jan 1885
Page 431-434

7 vouchers. Recorded: 6 Apr 1885

Benjamin Hutcherson, Gdn of Bascomb Y., John H., Robert E. and Ida R. Kelley, minors of W. F. Kelley, from 1 May 1884 to 1 May 1885
Page 434-435

3 vouchers. Recorded: 2 Jun 1885

John W. Speer, Admr of Estate of Harriett Smallwood, from time of appointment to 1 Jan 1885
Page 435-438

10 vouchers. To amount paid - W. P. Smith, I. E. W. Smith, J. E. H. Ware, S. B. Griggs, Parlie Davis, W. B. Edmonds, S. A. Brown and R. A. Denham.
Recorded: 10 Jun 1885

F. D. Hewell, Gdn of E. H. Boggus in Account Current from 1 May 1884 to 8 May 1885
Page 438-439

3 vouchers. Recorded: 9 Jul 1885

H. S. Rivers, Gdn of Nancy J. and Millie E. Milam, minors of J. R. Milam, from 1 Apr 1882 to 1 Apr 1885
Page 439-441

To amount on hand from last Return, see Book J, page 282
8 vouchers. Paid J.D. Smith (tuition for N. J.and M. E.Milam)
Recorded: 9 Jul 1885

John W. Kelly, Gdn of George C. Kelly, in Account Current from 7 May 1884 to 7 May 1885
Page 441-442

To amount on hand from last Return, see Book J, page 384
2 vouchers. Recorded: 9 Jul 1885

R. A. Tilghman and S. Francina C. Yates, Admrs of Matthew Yates from 1 Jun 1884 to 1 Jun 1885
Page 442-450

The many accounts include cotton bills. 52 vouchers. Distributive share paid to Annie H. Graves.
Recorded: 3 Aug 1885

Return made by M. E. Jackson as one of the Exrs of the Estate of Edmond Jackson, decd, late of Fayette Co., from 9 Nov 1882 to 3 Jul 1885
Page 450-453

12 vouchers. Includes distress warrant, viz: Mathew E. Jackson, Exr of Edmond Jackson vs. G. W. Robinson, defendant, J. S. Bennett, Claimant
Recorded: 8 Aug 1885

2nd Annual Return of Rufus W. Hardy as Gdn of Annie Wilson, Oliver McClendon and Spalding McClendon, from 5 Mar 1884 to 5 Mar 1885
Page 454-455

5 vouchers. Recorded: 26 Sept 1885

Estate of Larkin Harrison, decd, in Account Current with James M. Carlisle, Admr, from the time of appointment to 1 Jul 1885
Page 455-460

To amount received from sale of personal property and renting of real estate for 1885, see Sale Bill, Book A, page 55
To amount received of S. T. and A. O. Blalock, temp. Admrs, see Book J, page 415, 586, 91.
18 vouchers. Recorded: 26 Sept 1885

Daniel McLucas, J. C. Hightower and E. B. Weldon, securities of D. A. McLucas, Admr of Estate of Ephraim Sweat, from date of appointment (6 Oct 1879) to 1 Jul 1885
Page 460-480

50 vouchers. Includes notes given by decd to Elisa J. Armstrong, E. S. Sweat, Emily C. Cato, Sarah C. Sweat and P. C. Turner.

Estate of Ephraim Sweat contd.....

Heirs:

A. J. Baugh, receipt signed at Jonesboro 24 Oct 1882
Ephraim Baugh (x, his mark), receipt signed 29 May 1883
J. O. A. Turner (x, his mark), receipt signed 2 Mar 1883
E. J. Baugh (x, his mark), receipts signed 22 Mar 1883 and 14 Apr 1883
S. A. Duffie (x, his mark), receipt signed 30 Mar 1883
A. J. Turner, receipt signed 25 May 1883
E. E. Turner, receipt signed 25 May 1883
Sarah E. Turner
Charlotte Sweat
S. S. Turner
P. C. Turner
J. R. Turner (x, his mark), Gdn of James K., Lilla C., Cintha D. and Tabitha Jane Turner
Martha West (x, her mark)
Jane Hanner (x, her mark)

Taxes paid in Randolph Co., Alabama. Recorded: 28 Sept 1885

W. S. Shell and H. S. Griffin, Admrs of Estate of Daniel Shell, decd, from 1 Jun 1884 to 1 Jul 1885
Page 480-481

To amount on hand from last Return, see Book J, page 401
4 vouchers. Heirs receipt from Mary J. Shell by J. S. Shell, signed at Griffin
Recorded: 30 Sept 1885

A. O. Gay, Admr and Mary W. Malone, Admx, from time of appointment to 1 Apr 1885
Page 481-490

To amount received from sale of personal property, see Book A, page (blank)
29 vouchers. Receipts from O. T. Malone for 50 acres (2 tracts) in Fayette Co.
Recorded: 1 Oct 1885

Estate of Sarah Jackson, in Account Current with G. W. Clark, Admr, from time of appointment to 2 Nov 1885 showing a Final Settlement
Page 490-491

To sale of personal property, see Book A, page 59
For notes on hand see Appraise Bill, Book A, page 60
3 vouchers. Recorded: 21 Dec 1885

Rebecca C. Smith, Gdn of M. A. L. Speir, minor child of Henry C. Speir, from 1 Nov 1882 to 27 Oct 1885
Page 491-492

To cash on hand from last Return, see Book J, page 309.
3 vouchers.
M. A. Speir having become of age, she has received her portion of said estate, the same being $216.00, nothing having been reserved for dismissal. /s/Rebecca C. Smith, gdn

Margarett J. Jones, Gdn of W. F. and M. A. Jones (now M. A. Wesley), minors of Francis P. Jones, decd, from time of appointment to 16 Dec 1885 showing Final Settlement
Page 492-493

Receipts for receiving full shares of estate - W. F. Jones and M. A. Wesley, dated 4 Dec 1882
Recorded 12 Feb 1886

J. H. Ellington, Admr of Estate of Z. T. Ellington, decd, in Account Current from 1 Jan 1885 to 1 Jan 1886
Page 494-495

4 vouchers. Recorded: 22 Mar 1886

W. W. Padgett, Gdn of Jimmie Padgett in Account Current with said ward from 1 Sept 1883 to 20 Jan 1886
Page 495-496

To amount on hand from last Return, see Book J, page 349
Recorded: 22 Mar 1886

John W. Speer, Admr of Harriet A. Smallwood in Account with Estate from 1 Jan 1885 to 1 Apr 1886 being a Final Settlement of said Estate
Page 496-500

To amount on hand from last Return, see Book J, page 435
14 vouchers. Heirs receipts as fllows -

M. B. Edwards
W. R. Smallwood (x, his mark)
J. F. Smallwood
S. A. Brown of Lamar Co., Texas

Benjamin Hutcherson, Gdn of Bascomb Y., John H., Robert E. and Ida R. Kelley, minors of W. F. Kelley, decd, in Account Current from 1 May 1885 to 1 May 1886
Page 501-502

3 vouchers. To cash paid - P. A. Denham, D. M. Franklin and Mrs. E. R. Kelley.
Filed: 5 Apr 1886

John W. Kelly, Gdn of George C. Kelly in Account Current with said ward from 7 May 1885 to 7 May 1886
Page 503

2 vouchers. Filed: 5 Apr 1886

Amanda J. Boggs, Gdn of J. A. and A. G. Gardiner in Account Current with said wards from 7 Apr 1884 to 13 Apr 1886
Page 503

To amount on hand from last Return, see Book J, page 376
J. A. Gardiner's share
A. G. Gardiner's share
Recorded: 12 Apr 1886

F. D. Hewell, Gdn of Emmet H. Boggers from 8 May 1885 to 21 May 1886
Page 504

2 vouchers. Filed: 28 May 1886

Martha A. Weir, Gdn of Georgia A. Stinchcomb in Account Current with her said ward from 1 Mar 1882 to 1 Mar 1886
Page 505

1 voucher. Filed: 7 Jun 1886

S. F. C. Yates and R. A. Tilghman, Admx and Admr of Estate of Matthew Yates, decd, from 1 Jun 1885 to 7 Jun 1886
Page 506-515

37 vouchers. By amount paid - R. A. Tilghman, George W. Scott, M. Curry & Co., W. A. McCurry, Camp & Parker, Shropshire & Johnson, M. P. Harvey, J. T. Edmondson, C. B. Brogdon, Paul Faver, J. E. Harrison, J. W. Kitchens, W. H. Brotherton, J. W. Rivers, P. A. Denham, Needham Jackson, J. D. Smith, A. B. Johnson, E. M. Pollard, W. T. Roberts, Peter Lynch, Samuel Wilkins, and D. C. Loeb

Filed: 7 Jun 1886

Susan R. Stell, Admrx de bonis non of Tandy D. King, decd, in Account with said Estate from time of appointment, November Term 1884, to 15 May 1886, the same being a Final Settlement
Page 515-519

To amount of sale of personal property sold by Larkin Harrison, first admr of said decd, see Sale Book A, page 65

To amount received from sale of 101 1/4 acres of land, the W half of Lot 56 in 5th District of Fayette Co., sold first Tues. in Nov 1885 to Jesse Hubbard

To amount received from sale of 2 lots wild land in Cherokee Co., sold at private sale by Joshua Roberts under power of attorney

14 vouchers.
Received on the within note of Larkin Harrison, Admr of T. D. King, $217.00, the same being the amount of the value of property bought by me at the sale of said decd after the rent of the land in 1884. /s/S. R. Stell

Received of S. R. Stell, Admx de bonis non of T. D. King $93.83 in full of all demands on the within note against the estate of said decd, this 15 May 1886. /s/J. E. Matthews
Recorded: 11 Aug 1886

W. F. Jones, Admr de bonis non of John T. Mackey, decd, in Account with said estate from time of appointment Jan Term of this Court 1884 to Jul Term 1886, showing Final Settlement
Page 519-520

To cash paid Heirs - Florence L. Mackey, S. T. Jones and Mary L. Jones
Filed: 5 Jul 1886

A. O. Gay, Admr and Mary W. Malone, Admx of Estate of O. T. Malone, decd, from 1 Apr 1885 to 1 Apr 1886
Page 521-523

8 vouchers.
Filed: 5 Jul 1886. Recorded: 11 Sept 1886

Martha A. Butler, Gdn for George W. Murphy from 2 Feb 1885 to 1 Jul 1886
Page 524-525

6 vouchers. Filed: 5 Jul 1886. Recorded: 14 Sept 1886

Estate of Larkin Harrison, decd, in Account Current with James M. Carlile, Admr from 1 Jul 1885 including 1 Jul 1886
Page 526-561

To balance on hand see Book J, page 455
To amount received from sale of land of estate, see Sale Bill Book H, page 68
Amounts recd from notes of J. D. Perry, Susan R. Stell, Sam Hales and Al Glass, A. J. McBride.
59 vouchers. Receipt from S. C Harrison Mar 1886, for her dower for 1885.
Includes many deeds of Larkin Harrison, notes, and farm accounts in Fayetteville, Hampton, Lovejoy and Campbell Co.

G. A. Jones, Exr and Nancy Jones, Extrx to LWT of W. J. Jones in Account Current with said Estate from time of their appointment, Dec Term 1885, Fayette Court of Ordinary, to 15 Aug 1886
Page 561-565

Includes cotton bills, etc. 15 vouchers.
Filed: 16 Aug 1886

An Account Current with R. H. Woods, Admr of Hillery Brooks, decd, from 1 Jun 1883 to 4 Oct 1886
Page 565-567

10 vouchers

To cash paid Heirs - L. F. Woods, Mary E. Woods, F. M. Henderson, R. H. Henderson, N. L. Henderson, N. C. Rivers, W. M. Hand, J. T. Methvin, D. M. Franklin and A. A. Steinheimer

Recorded: 13 Dec 1886

F. M. Ellison, Admr of Nancy P. Landrum in Account with said Estate from time of appointment to 11 Oct 1886, the same being the Final Settlement
Page 568-571

8 vouchers
Recorded: 15 Dec 1886

F. M. Ellison, Exr of W. W. Landrum in Account Current with said Estate from time of appointment 11 Oct 1886 showing a Final Settlement
Page 572-586

To amount recived from sale of property of W. W. Landrum, see Sale Book A, page 65

Rents recd - J. M. Davis, 1881-1882, Ira Slaton, 1882, from Estate of Nancy J. Landrum, Rachael Davis, 1882.

40 vouchers. Account of Billie Landrum to W. S. Russell (doctor). Receipt of M. A. Landrum for years' support, dated 22 Nov 1883.

Filed: 11 Oct 1886
Recorded: 16 Dec 1886

Annual Return of R. W. Hardy Gdn of Ann Wilson, Spalding McLendon and Oliver McClendon, minors, 5 Mar 1885 to 5 Mar 1886
Page 586-588

9 vouchers. To cash paid - Annie Wilson, Spalding McClendon, S. M. McClendon.

Filed: 10 Nov 1886
Recorded: 5 Jan 1887

END OF BOOK J

Fayette County Ordinary Mixed Records
Inventories, Appraisements, Sales and Returns
Book K (1886-1889)

J. H. Ellington, Admr of Z. T. Ellington in Account Current with said Estate from 1 Jan 1886 to 1 Jan 1887
Page 1-2

3 vouchers. To cash paid - R. A. Ellington in part payment of the distributive share of Zachry P. Ellington, Elizabeth Ellington, Richard Ellington, Joseph Ellington, minors of decd, this 15 Jan 1887. Filed: 17 Jan 1887. Recorded: 10 Mar 1887

W. T. Glower, Gdn of Marshal N. Swanson and Mrs. M. E. A. Flowers in Account with said wards from 20 Jan 1885 to17 Jan 1886 being a Final Settlement with said wards
Page 1-5

The Return of Gdn made 20 Jan 1885, see Book J, page 431 was made to show a final settlement with Mrs. M. E. A. Flowers, formerly M. E. A. Swanson

To amount on hand from last Return, see Book J, page 431
8 vouchers.

Property in kind turned over to M. N. Swanson and Mrs. Martha E. A. Flowers in Vou. No. 9....
Filed: 17 Jan 1887. Recorded: 10 Mar 1887

Susan Long, Gdn of H. A. N. Long in Account
Page 5-6

To amount cash on hand from last Return, 1 Dec 1881
Filed: 22 Feb 1887. Recorded: 7 Apr 1887

Perry Hicks, Gdn of Willie A. Brown from time of appointment to 4 Apr 1887
Page 6-7

By amount paid Willie A. Brown as per voucher No. 1- $434.30. The tax receipts are not in the hands of Gdn, but he says that he paid out the above amount named in voucher 1, including taxes. He further states that he makes no charges for his services as said ward is his granddaughter.
Filed: 5 Apr 1887. Recorded: 9 Jun 1887

Voucher #1 - Georgia, Fayette Co., Received of Perry Hicks, my Gdn, $200 in land, the same being 25 acres, also $100 supplies furnished me at sundry times, also $129.50, the same arising from rent of above land. Also $4.80 tax he paid for 4 years, the same being in full of all demands against him as Gdn as above, this 4 Apr 1887. /s/Willie A. Brown /s/T. L. Brown

John W. Kelley, Gdn of George C. Kelley in Account Current with said ward from 1 May 1886 to 7 May 1887
Page 7

2 vouchers. Filed: 4 Apr 1887. Recorded: 9 Jun 1887

Benjamin Hutchinson, Gdn of Bascomb Y., John H., Robert E. and Ida R. Kelley, minors of W. F. Kelley, decd, in Account Current with said wards from 1 May 1886 to 1 May 1887
Page 8-9

3 vouchers.Filed: 4 Apr 1887. Recorded: 10 Jun 1887

A. O. Gay, one of Admrs of Estate of O. T. Malone, decd, from 19 Apr 1885 to 11 Mar 1887
Page 9

For this Return for expense of being dismissed, I have not kept back any money. I having this day made application to be released from said trust and Mary W. Malone, The Extrx, associated with me and who accepts the whole trust, having agreed to pay the expenses of the same. (By amount paid Mary W. Malone, $616.65, vou. #1)

Recorded: 10 Jun 1887

W. J. Gay, Temp. Admr of Estate of Martha McLeroy, decd, from time of appointment to 20 Dec 1886
Page 10-12

8 vouchers. To cash paid - M. F. Allen, J. T. Spence, R. H. McLeroy, J. H. DeVaughn, J. W. McLeroy, D. H. Franklin, W. J. Gay.
Heirs receipts for partial distribution - J. W. McLeroy, J. H. DeVaughn, P. W. McLeroy for Annie and Earl McLeroy, children of E. T. McLeroy, decd.
Recorded: 10 Jun 1887.

B. L. Johnson, Admr of D. A. Brown, decd, in Account Current from time of appointment to 3 May 1887, the same being a Final Settlement of said estate
Page 12-17

17 vouchers.
To amount received from sale of personal property, see Book A, page 60
To amount received from sale of land, see Book A, page 61

Receipt from Lucy J. Brown for 12 months' support, 15 Dec 1885 for herself and 4 minor children
Filed: 3 May 1887. Recorded: 10 Jun 1887

H. S. Rivers, Gdn of N. J. and M. E. Milam, minors of J. R. Milam, decd, from 1 May 1885 to 1 May 1887
Page 17-19

8 vouchers. To cash paid-A. M. Patterson, J. H. Luck, S. C. Milam, J. W. T. Spier, C. T. Landrum, D. M. Franklin. To amount on hand from last Return, see Book J, page 439
Recorded: 6 Jul 1887

Annual Return of W. S. Shell and H. S. Griffin, Admrs of Daniel Shell, decd, of Fayette Co., Ga. for the year 1887
Page 19-21

Notes of Terracy Shell, W. O. Shell, C. T. Shell and J. S. Shell
Georgia, Henry Co. Personally before me, comes W. S. Shell, one of the Admrs of Daniel Shell, who, on oath, says that the above and foregoing Return is just and true......./s/W. S. Shell

Estate of Daniel Shell contd.....

Heirs receiving distributive shares -

W. O. Shell, receipt signed at Hampton, Ga., 7 Aug 1885
J. S. Shell, receipt dated 19 May 1887
Filed: 10 Jun 1887. Recorded: 16 Aug 1887

Annual Return of R. W. Hardy as Gdn of Annie Wilson, Oliver McClendon and Spalding McClendon for year ending 5 Mar 1887
Page 21-22

Georgia, Coweta Co. In person before me came R. W. Hardy who swore that the above Annual Return in matter of himself as Gdn for Annie Wilson, Oliver and Spalding McClendon for year ending 5 Mar 1887 is true and correct. /s/Rufus W. Hardy

G. W. Clark, Admr of Sarah Jackson, decd, late of Fayette Co., from time of appointment to 1 Jul 1887
Page 22-26

To one Fi Fa. received of J. T. Brogdon, J. P. of 709th District
To amount received of G. W. Robinson surviving Exr of the LWT of Edmond Jackson
6 vouchers. Filed: 27 Jun 1887. Recorded: 17 Aug 1887

Robert Matthews, Admr of T. C. Matthews of Fayette Co., decd, from time of appointment to 1 Jun 1887
Page 26-27

4 vouchers. Filed: 23 Jun 1887. Recorded: 19 Aug 1887

B. L. Johnson, Exr of W. M. Rivers, decd, from time of qualification as such Exr to 1 Jun 1887
Page 27-34

Cotton bills, etc. 15 vouchers.
Recorded: 22 Aug 1887

J. M. Palmer, Exr of LWT of Margaret J. White in Account Current with said estate from time to appointment to 31 May 1887
Page 34-45

To amount received from sale of personal property see Sale Bill, Book A, page (blank)
18 vouchers. Filed: 25 Jun 1887. Recorded: 25 Aug 1887

Mrs. S. F. C. Yates, Admx of Matthew Yates, decd, from 1 Jun 1886 to 1 Jun 1887
Page 45-56

Incudes sales of cotton, oats, etc. 14 vouchers. Filed: 16 Jun 1887. Recorded: 26 Aug 1887

Return of Daniel McLucas, Gdn of A. C., D. M., G. I. and E. C. Harrison from 5 Jul 1887 to 8 Sept 1887
Page 57

23 Mar 1887. Received of J. M. Carlisle, Admr. his distributive share of Estate of Larkin Harrison. /s/A. C. Harrison

W. P. T. Harp, Gdn of A. F., B. M., R. H. and J. G. Harrison in Account Current from time of appointment to 1 Jul 1887
Page 58

1 voucher.
Filed: 5 Nov 1887
Recorded: 8 Aug 1887

Mary W. Malone, Admx of O. T. Malone, decd, from 1 Apr 1886 to 1 Apr 1887
Page 59-60

To amount of last Return, see Book J, page 52
5 vouchers. Includes cotton bills. 12 months' support to Mary W. Malone.

Filed: 4 Jul 1887. Recorded: 9 Sept 1887

G. A. Jones, Exr, and Nancy Jones, Extrx, of W. J. Jones, decd, in Account Current from 15 Aug 1886 to 1 Jul 1887
Page 61-66

Filed: 9 Jul 1887. Recorded: 9 Sept 1887

J. L. Graves, Gdn for Dolsey Miles, now Dolsey Rutledge, in Account Current from 8 Jun 1883 to 18 Jul 1887
Page 66-67

She now being of age, this Return being a Final Settlement with her.
To amount from last Return, see Book J, page 342. 2 vouchers.

Voucher #1. Received of J. L. Graves, my Gdn, $28.03, my full distributive share of the money received by my Gdn from J. M. Smith who was the Admr of my grandfather, L. C. Smith of Fayette Co., decd, this 18th Jul 1887 /s/Dolsey Rutledge

Filed: 27 Jul 1887. Recorded: 10 Sept 1887

B. L. Johnson, Gdn for J. R., C. M. and Eugene A. Whitlock, minor children of John A. Whitlock, from the time of his appointment to 25 Jul 1887
Page 68-70

To amount received from sale of personal property, see Bill Sale Book A, page 72. 9 vouchers.

Recorded: 12 Sept 1887

Annual Return of M. D. Sams, Admr of T. B. Gay, decd, on 4 Jul 1887
Page 70-78

12 vouchers.
Filed: 4 Jul 1887
Recorded: 14 Sept 1887

Estate of Larkin Harrison in Account Current with J. M. Carlisle, decd, Admr, in Account Current sworn to by George W. Clark, Admr on Estate of James M. Carlisle, decd, from 1 Jul 1886 to 1 Sept 1887
Page 78-88

To amount on hand 1 Jul 1886 see Book J, page 526
To amount of mistake in last Return as to amount received by Susan R. Stell, the former Return showing $570.20 collected when he really collected $580.60. See Return of Susan R. Stell, as Admx of T. D. King, Book J, page 515.

22 vouchers. Heirs:
T. B. Harrison
Daniel McLucas for A. C. Harrison and D. M., G. L.and E. E. Harrison and A. C.
W. N. T. Harp, Gdn of A. F., B. M., R. H. and J. G. Harrison
Filed: 7 Sept 1887. Recorded: 10 Nov 1887

Final Return of R. H. Woods, Admr of Estate of Hillery Brooks, late of said county, decd
Page 89-90

Filed: 19 Sept 1887. Recorded: 18 Nov 1887

Jurden Thornton, Admr of Miss Elizabeth Jackson, from time of appointment to 19 Sept 1887, the same being Final Settlement
Page 90-92

To amount received from sale of 25 acres belonging to the estate of the decd, the SW corner of Land Lot 252 in 13th District sold to Marion Eason the first Tues. in 1886.
3 vouchers. Filed: 1 Oct 1887. Recorded: 22 Nov 1887

M. M. Collier, Admr of C. P. Collier, from time of his appointment on 3 Nov 1884 to 21 Nov 1887
Page 92-92

16 vouchers. Divison to heirs as follows -
M. M. Collier
Emily Ellison
Martha Hix
Sisley A. Bearden
F. M. Collier
Ida C. Neeley
Thomas Landrum, receipt given at Cherokee Co., Texas

Return of G. W. Robinson Showing Exr of LWT of Edmond Jackson of Fayette Co., decd, from 3 Jul 1885 to 24 Nov 1887
Page 97-114

To amount received from sale of land, see Sale Bill Book A, page (blank)
To amount received from sale of personal property, see Book A, page (blank)

Estate of Edmond Jackson contd....

Heirs as follows -

Miller Co., Arkansas, paid W. R. Graves, atty in fact for W. J. Miars, Mary J. Dodd, Prudence D. Spence, Martha B. Graves, J. E., W. E. and D. T. Jackson (leaving nothing due them)

Brown Co., Texas, paid A. O. Blalock, atty in fact for Sarah Ann Selena Jackson (leaving nothing due her)

Greene Co., Georgia, paid A. O. Blalock, atty in fact for Sarah A. Dennis (leaving nothing due her)

Chambers Co., Alabama, paid Hiram E. Jordan, atty for Martha F. Jordan

Jackson Co.,Alabama, paid T. J. Holman, James Holman, N. A. Holman, Theophilus Cobb, Sarah J. Cobb, S. R. Holman, Mary Cobb and Henry Cobb (leaving nothing due them)

Fayette Co., Georgia, paid G. W. Clark of which all of 1 1/2 shares of Estate of Edmond Jackson

Fayette Co., Georgia, paid G. W. Clark, Admr Estate of Sarah Jackson, 1 share in Edmond Jackson's est.

Fayette Co., Georgia, paid L. S. Roan, atty for Mrs. A. M. Jackson, Extrx of LWT of M. E. Jackson

Montgomery Co., Mississippi, Paid W. N. Jordan, Gdn for Charles N. Jordan (leaving nothing due him)

W. R. Smallwood, Gdn for Mary B. Edmunds, from 3 Jan 1881 to 12 Dec 1887
Page 115-117

5 vouchers. Voucher #1.................for conveying Mary B. Edmunds from Senoia to asylum in Milledgeville, 22 Nov 1886. /s/W. R. Smallwood
Recorded: 15 Feb 1888

G. W. Madaris, Gdn of Johnnie McEachern in Account Current from 1 Jan 1884 to 2 Feb 1888
Page 117

Admitted to record March term 1888 and recorded in Book K, page 117 on 7 Mar 1888
Receipt from Johnie McEachern acknowledging receiving all monies from his Gdn, dated 2 Feb 1888

J. H. Ellington, Admr of Z. T. Ellington, in Account Current with 1 Jan 1887 to 1 Jan 1888
Page 118-119

To amount of last Return, see Book K, page 1. 4 vouchers.

Distributive shares paid to -

R. A. Ellington, Gdn for Zachery P., Susan E., Richard F. and Josiah S. Ellington, minors of Z. T. Ellington, decd.

Filed: 24 Jan 1888. Recorded: 7 Mar 1888

Mrs. R. A. Ellington, Gdn for Zachery P., Susan E., Richard F. and Josiah S., minors of Z. T. Ellington, decd, from 5 Nov 1883 to 25 Jan 1888
Page 119-124

21 vouchers. Recorded: 7 Mar 1888

J. S. Thornton, Gdn of M. L. Thornton and H. S. W. Marshburn, from 1 Apr 1883 to 23 Mar 1888
Showing Full Disposition of Estate
Page 124-126

To amount of last Return, see Book J, page 334. 4 vouchers.

Received from J. S. Thornton, Gdn of Hesper S. W. Marshburn, decd and as agent of heirs at law of same, monies for all claims, etc. /s/Hesper S. W. Marshburn, 20 Mar 1885

Received from J. S. Thornton, Gdn of Hesper S. W. Mashburn, decd and as agent of heirs at law of same, monies for all claims, etc. /s/G. M. Dorman and Alice O. Dorman

Benjamin Hutchinson, Gdn of Bascomb Y., John H., Robert E. and Ida R. Kelley, in Account Current from 1 May 1887 to 5 Jul 1888
Page 126-128

7 vouchers. Receipts for full shares given by Bascomb T. Kelley (x, his mark) and E. R. Kelley.

Clarissa Drennan, Admx of LWT of Hugh Drennan, from 2 Aug 1886 to 5 Apr 1888
Page 129-133

To amount received from sale of personal property, see Sale Bill Book A, page 71
17 vouchers

Voucher #10. Received of Clarissa Drennan, Admx, 30 acres in Land Lot 87 and 50 acres in Land Lot 88, 5th District of Fayette Co., and all farming equipment as devised by the LWT of decd, which is in full and entire satisfaction of all my right and interest as Gdn for John H., William B. and Martha E. Drennan (now Martha E. Newton), said children being disributees of said Estate, 2 Apr 1888. /s/Susan A. Drennan
Recorded: 9 May 1888

W. N. T. Harp, Gdn of A. F., B. M., R. H. and J. G. Harrison, in Account Current from 1 Jul 1887 to 1 Jul 1888
Page 134-135

To amount on hand from last Return, see Book K, page 58. 7 vouchers
Receipt from A. C. Harrison (tuition for A. F., B. M. and R. H. Harrison)
Receipt from Ida Bull (tuition for Ben and Ada Harrison)
Receipt from Sarah C. Harrison (funds for benefit of children)
Filed: 1 Jul 1887. Recorded: 1 Jul 1888

John W. Kelley, Gdn for George C. Kelley, from 7 May 1887 to 7 May 1888
Page 136-137

3 vouchers. Filed: 30 May 1888. Reocrded: 10 Jul 1888

B. L. Johnson, Exr of Estate of W. M. Rivers, decd, from 1 Jun 1887 to 11 May 1888
Page 137-144

32 vouchers. Filed: 11 May 1888. Recorded: 10 Jul 1888

Return of J. L. Whitlock, Admr of J. A. Whitlock, decd, Showing Full Settlement
Page 144-148

To amount received from sale of 195 1/2 acres, Land Lot No. 76 in 7th District of Fayette Co., sold to K. V. Adams, the first Tues. in Nov 1887, the remainder sold to Marietta Smith

Division among heirs -

J. L. Whitlock
J. R. Whitlock
Marietta Smith
N. C. Adams
B. L. Johnson, Gdn for C. M. and Eugenia A. Whitlock
(leaves nothing due estate)

Filed: 11 May 1888. Recorded: 11 Jul 1888

Estate of Daniel Shell
Page 149

Georgia, Henry Co...Personally appeared before me, W. S. Shell, who, on oath, says the attached receipt is the only disbursement made by him as Admr of the Estate of Daniel Shell for last 12 months and received nothing..../s/W. S. Shell

Share distributed to J. S. Shell, Hampton, Ga., on 31 Jan 1888
Filed: 5 Jun 1888. Recorded: 8 Aug 1888

Annual Return of M. D. Sams, Admr of T. B. Gay, decd, 30 Jun 1888
Page 149-170

7 vouchers. Notes, accounts. Recorded: 8 Aug 1888

J. Q. Landrum, Gdn for Courtney A. Edmondson, from 12 Dec 1887 to 1 Jul 1888
Page 171

To amount of last Return, see Return of W. R. Smallwood, Book K, page 115. 1 voucher.
Filed: 2 Jul 1888. Recorded: 10 Aug 1888

A. M. Jackson, Exr of LWT of Matthew E. Jackson, decd
Page 172-177

7 vouchers.
Georgia, Campbell Co...L. S. Roan.. his account is just and true as was due to Roan and Rosser from the Estate of Sarah Jackson...that Mrs. A. M. Jackson, as Extrx of the Estate of M. E. Jackson, the Admr of Sarah Jackson, paid said account to me., 28 Aug 1886. /s/L. S. Roan

Mary W. Malone, Admr of Estate of O. T. Malone, from 1 Jul 1887 to 1 Jul 1888
Page 178-180

To amount from last Return, see Book J, page 59. 6 vouchers.
To amount received of Atlanta and Florida Railroad for right of way, etc.

Mary W. Malone, for 3rd and 4th years' support for herself and children, gives receipt, at Fayetteville, on 5 Mar 1888.

Filed: 2 Jul 1888. Recorded: 11 Aug 1888

D. H. McLucas, Admr de bonis non of Larkin Harrison, decd, in Account Current from 3 Jul 1888 to 11 Aug 1888 inclusive
Page 180-182

5 vouchers. Filed: 3 Jul 1888. Recorded: 14 Aug 1888

Daniel McLucas, Gdn for A. C., D. M., G. E. and E. E. Harrison, in an Account Current from 1 Jul 1887 to 1 Jul 1888 inclusive
Page 183-184

To amount of last Return, see Book K, page 57
Heirs receipts given by - A. C. Harrison and D. M. Harrison
Filed: 3 Jul 1888. Recorded: 14 Aug 1888

Mrs. S. F. C. Yates, Admx and R. A. Tilghman, Admr of Matthew Yates, decd, from 1 Jun 1887 to 1 Jun 1888 inclusive
Page 184-194

35 vouches. Includes cotton sales, etc.
Filed: 12 Jul 1888. Recorded: 3 Sept 1888

Annual Return of R. W. Hardy, Gdn of Annie Wilson, Spalding and Oliver McClendon, from date of last Return to 5 Mar 1888
Paage 194-196

29 Aug 1887 distribution made to Oliver McClendon (x, his mark) from Estate of his mother, Mrs. Lue McClendon, decd, of Meriwether Co., Ga.

Distribution made to M. E. Hill, atty for Annie Wilson (formerly Annie McClendon)
Filed: 13 Oct 1887. Recorded: 6 Sept 1888

B. L. Johnson, Gdn for J. R., C. M. and Eugenia A. Whitlock, minor children of John A. Whitlock, decd, from 25 Jul 1887 to 1 Jul 1888
Page 197-199

To amount of last Return, see Book K, page 68. 4 vouchers. Includes receipt of J. R. Whitlock (tuition for Charles Whitlock).

Filed: 9 Aug 1888. Recorded: 15 Oct 1888

W. M. and J. A. Brown, Exrs of LWT of Demcy Brown, in Account Current from 30 Oct 1873 to 17 Oct 1888 inclusive
Page 199-206

See Book I, page 291 for First Return
To amount received from sale of perishable property, see Book A, page 82
To amount received from sale of land, see Book A, page 86
9 vouchers. Heirs - W. M. Brown, J. A. Brown, and 5 heirs of Sarah A. Stinchcomb

Power of Atty of G. W. Stinchcomb of Kingston, Sierra Co., New Mexico to John O. Stinchcomb of Flat Creek, Fayette Co., Ga. to collect from Estate "of my grandfather, Demsey Brown, late of Fayette Co., Georgia"...

Power of Atty from W. P. Stinchcomb and J. F. Stinchcomb, Denton Co., Texas, to P. T. Johnston to collect from Estate of Demcy Brown of Fayette Co., Ga., dated 19 Dec 1887

N. D. Stinchcomb received his share 8 Feb 1888, and Mrs. E. A. Mosley of Denison, Texas.

D. A. McLucas, Admr of Estate of Ephraim Sweat, decd, in Account Current from 1 Jul 1885 to 12 Dec 1885, the same being a Final Return
Page 206-212

In the division of the Estate, the distributive share of each heir was estimated at $192.72. The share of Emily C. Cato, an heir of said estate, at the estimated share of each heir, liked $6.72 of amount to the demands the estate held against her. (Other heirs gave $6.72 to Emily).

The amount receipted for James W. Sweat was for advancements made in the life of his father, therefore, his share was not estimated in the division of the estate.

To amount due Estate as shown by the Return made to 1 Jul 1885, see Book J, page 460
By amount of Cato note which was given by heirs at division, 12 Dec 1885, see Appraisal Bill Book A, page 22

12 heirs....which was paid out as shown by the following vouchers and Return of 1 Jul 1885. See Book J, page 460. Heirs as follows -

Joseph R. Turner (x, his mark)
Emily C. Cato
A. J. Turner
E. J. Armstrong
E. S. Sweat by W. S. Sweat
Mary Jane Hanner (x, her mark)
James W. Sweat
Sarah A. Duffey (x, her mark)
J. O. A. Turner (x, his mark)
S. S. Turner
S. C. Turner
E. E. Turner
Receipt for their several interests, in full settlement, Benjamin F. Sweat, S. C. Sweat, F. D. Sweat, Martha Sweat (x, her mark), and Amanda A. Sweat (x, her mark)

John L. Graves, Exr of LWT of Susan Graves, in Account Current with said Estate from time of appointment to 19 Oct 1888, the same being a Final Settlement
Page 212-214

5 vouchers. Filed: 19 Oct 1888. Recorded: 13 Dec 1888

J. H. Murphy, Gdn of J. B. Rogers, minor child of H. M. Rogers, decd, from 1 Jan 1885 to 1 Jan 1887
Page 215-218

10 vouchers. Filed: 26 Dec 1888

J. H. Ellington, Admr of Z. T. Ellington in Account Current with said Estate from 1 Jan 1888 to 1 Jan 1889
Page 218-219

Vou. #2. Received of J. H. Ellington, Admr of Z. T. Ellington, decd, $25.00 in part payment of the distributive share of Zachry P. and Elizabeth and Richard F. and Josiah S. Ellington, minors of said decd. /s/R. A. Ellington, Gdn for said minors
Filed: 14 Jan 1889. Recorded: 5 Mar 1889

An Account Current against William Whatley, Admr of Jurden Price, decd
Page 220-224

Receipt from Sarah Price for 12 months' support for herself and her children. Recorded: 6 Mar 1889

First Final Return of James E. Thompson, Temporary Admr of Mathew Reade, decd
Page 224-229

12 vouchers. To cash paid - Henry Lane, John F. Mims, S. J. Hillman, J. C. Landrum, J. A. Vickery, A. W. McCurry, M. H. Woodall, S. H. Brantley, W. T. Roberts.
Recorded: 3 Apr 1889

Mrs. R. A. Ellington, Gdn of her children and minors of Z. T. Ellington, decd, in Account Current with her said wards from 25 Jan 1888 to 25 Jan 1889
Page 229-231

To amount on hand from last Return, see Book K, page 119. Recorded: 4 Apr 1889

W. S. Milner, Admr of Estate of Jennie L. Hilsman in Account Current with said Estate from 28 Apr 1874 to 7 Jan 1889
Page 231-234

To amount on hand from last Return, see Book I, page 316
Filed: 11 Mar 1889. Recorded: 11 May 1889
14 receipts given by J. W. Hilsman for tuition of Lula Hilsman, minor of Jennie L. Hilsman

Benjamin Hutchinson, Gdn of John H., Robert E. and Ida R. Kelley, in Account Current with said wards from 1 May 1888 to 1 May 1889
Page 235-236

To amount on hand from last Return, see Book K, page 126
3 vouchers. To amount paid - I. N. Farmer, E. R. Kelley and D. M. Franklin
Recorded: 12 Jun 1889

Supplemental Return of Mrs. R. A. Ellington, Gdn of her own children, minors of Z. T. Ellington, decd, made for her wards 1 Dec 1884 covering the time of her appointment to that date.
Page 236-237

The Return made 25 Jan 1888 was made without any reference to the former Return. This Return is now made to correct the errors in the two last Returns.

For amount on hand 1 Dec 1884, see Book J, page 420
Filed: 10 May 1889 Recorded: 6 Jul 1889

H. S. Rivers, Gdn of N. J. and M. E. Milam, minors of J. R. Milam, decd. from 1 May 1887 to 1 May 1889
Page 238-240

10 vouchers. Receipt of S. C. Milam as tuition for Nannie and Emma Milam, minor children of John R. Milam for 1888. Receipt from E. B. Chapman, Treas. of School Board, tuition for 1889 for Emma and Nannie Milam.
Recorded: 6 Jul 1889

Mrs. S. F. Yates, Admx and R. A. Tilghman, Admr of Matthew Yates, in Account Current with said estate from 1 Jun 1888 to 1 Jun 1889
Page 241-253

To amount on hand from last Return, see Book K, page 184
Includes receipts from cotton sales, farm merchandise, etc. 54 vouchers.
Filed: 5 Jun 1889. Recorded: 9 Aug 1889

J. W. Kitchens, Gdn of Rufus G., Charles W., John and Mary M. M. Kitchens, his own minor children from 1 Jan 1885 to 1 Jul 1889
Page 254

To amount on hand from last Return, See Book J, page 421
Recorded: 12 Aug 1889

Mary W. Malone, Admx of Estate of O. T. Malone from 1 Jul 1888 to 1 Jul 1889
Page 254-256

To amount on hand from last Return, see Book K, page 178
4 vouchers. Received monies from cotton sales. Receipt of Mary W. Malone for 5th year of support.
Recorded: 12 Aug 1889

J. W. Dunbar, Jr., Admr of J. W. Dunbar, Sr., from time of appointment Jan. Term of 1885 to 1 Jul 1889
Page 256-269

To amount received from sale of perishable property, see Book A of Sale Bills, page 49
To amount received from sale of land sold 1st Tues. in Dec 1885 to Mrs. M. W. Malone for cash. Town property. One store house and lot in Brooks Station sold the same time to A. C. Dunbar. Another small lot in Brooks Station sold at the same time to W. G. Bishop. The lands in Spalding Co. sold the 1st Tues. in Nov. 1885 to J. H. Crowder for cash.

59 vouchers. Filed: 1 Jul 1889. Recorded: 12 Aug 1889

Final Return of L. F. Blalock, Admr of H. H. Pope, decd
Page 270-283

34 vouchers. Heirs paid distributive shares - J. D. Pope, Stephen T. Pope, Alex S. Pope
Recorded: 15 Aug 1889

Daniel McLucas, Gdn of A. C., D. M., G. I. and E. E. Harrison, from 1 Jul 1888 to 1 Jul 1889
Page 283-286

To amount on hand from last Return, see Book K, page 183
8 vouchers.

Receipt from D. M. Harrison dated 6 May 1889, Inman, Ga. for his distributive share of estate of Larkin Harrison. By A. C. Harrison, Atty in fact

Power of Atty from D. M. Harrison dated 2 May 1889, Tallahatchie Co., Mississippi, appointing A. C. Harrison of Fayetteville, Fayette Co., Ga. as his atty to collect his share on estate of Larkin Harrison.

Daniel McLucas, Admr de bonis non on Estate of Larkin Harrison, decd, from 1 Jul 1888 to 1 Jul 1889
Page 286-287

To amount on hand from last Return, see Book K, page 180
4 vouchers. Recorded: 17 Aug 1889

W. N. T. Harp, Gdn for A. F., B. M., . H. and J. G. Harrison, minor children of Larkin Harrison, from 1 Jul 1888 to 1 Jul 1889
Page 287-289

To amount on hand from last Return, see Book K, page 134
6 vouchers Recorded: 17 Aug 1889

B. L. Johnson, Gdn for minor heirs of J. A. Whitlock from 1 Jul 1888 to 1 Jul 1889
Page 289-290

To amount on hand from last Return, see Book K, page 197
6 vouchers. To cash paid - K. V. Adams, D. M. Franklin, Charlie Whitlock, Eugenia A. Whitlock, J. H. Williford. Recorded: 17 Aug 1889

J. Q. Landrum, Gdn for Courtney A. Edmondson from 1 Jul 1888 to 1 Jul 1889
Page 291

2 vouchers. Recorded: 17 Aug 1889

John W. Kelley, Gdn for George C. Kelley from 7 May 1888 to 27 May 1889
Page 292

To amount on hand from last Return, see Book K, page 136. 2 vouchers.
Recorded: 8 Jan 1890

Return of E. Zorn of the Sale of 120 acres of land of William Zorn, decd, by an Agreement of the Heirs....
Page 293

3 vouchers. To cash paid - William Zorn (x, his mark) and J. C. Zorn.
Filed: 28 Dec 1889. Recorded: 10 Feb 1890

Amanda Boggs, Gdn of J. A. and A. G. Gardiner from 13 Apr 1886 to 24 Jan 1890
Page 294-305

To amount due J. A. Gardiner last Return, see Book J, page 503
Heirs receiving equal share - Mary Griffin, Martha M. White, Lottie E. Davis, C. Mills

Heirs - Sallie R. Gibson and H. H. Gibson, S. N. Murphy, Ms. Fannie Gare, Masters Gare, Jane Loyd, Laura S. Carden, Martha A. Turner, Thomas M. Loyd, Mary B. Loyd

Heirs from Duval Co., Florida - Maria C. Murphy, H. Earnest Murphy, R. E. L. Murphy, Eva R. Murphy, Florence Murphy Cooly, R. Clifton Cooley, husband of Florence Murphy Cooley.

Heirs - N. W. Murphy, Martha E. Duffey.
Note: Please read these receipts to get full details.

J. H. Ellington, Admr of Z. T. Ellington, decd, from 1 Jan 1889 to 1 Jan 1890
Page 306

3 vouchers. Recorded: 24 Mar 1890

Robert Matthews, Admr of Estate of T. C. Matthews, decd, from 1 Jun 1887 to 28 Jan 1890
Page 307-310

To whole amount received, see Book K, page 26
Paid Nancy Matthews for 12 months' support. Paid Ida M. Bennett to make her equal with ther heirs.
Heirs as follows -

Mrs. Ida Matthews Bennett
Clestia A. Barnes
Lizzie E. Edge of Douglas Co., Ga.
J. J. May, Gdn of Eunice S., Robert Z., Lucy A. and Mary M. May of Haralson Co., Ga.
Louis B. McElreath of Douglas Co., Ga.
Mary A. Underwood of Dallas, Texas
J. J. May of Fayette Co., Ga.
W. H. Persons, Gdn of William Thomas Matthews

Annual Return of M. D. Sams, Admr of T. B. Gay, decd up to 31 Jan 1890
Page 310

To balance on hand at Return of 30 Jun 1888, see Book K, page 149
Filed: 31 Jan 1890. Recorded: 31 Mar 1890.

Return of Mrs. R. A. Ellington, Gdn for her own children, minors of Z. T. Ellington, decd, from 25 Jan 1889 to 25 Jan 1890
Page 311-313

8 vouchers. To amount on hand from last Return, see Book K, page 236
Filed: 10 Mar 1890. Recorded: 8 May 1890

G. A. Davis, Exr of LWT of G. M. Davis from time of appointment 3 Jun 1889 to 4 Apr 1890
Page 313-316

8 vouchers. By amount turned over to Emily W. Davis as devised by said will (vou. #1)
Filed: 4 Apr 1890. Recorded: 8 May 1890

Benjamin Hutchinson Gdn of John H., Robert E. and Ida R. Kelley from 1 May 1889 to 1 May 1890
Page 316-317

3 vouchers. Filed: 21 Apr 1890. Recorded: 11 Jun 1890
Receipt from E. R. Kelley for his interest in money due him, etc., dated 29 Mar 1890

Estate of W. E. Posten in Account Current with George W. Posten, Admr from time of appointment to Apr Term 1890 of Fayette
Page 317-324

To sale of land, see Sale Book, sold first Tues. in Apr 1889 to R. H. Bennett. 13 vouchers.
Recorded: 11 Jun 1890

Burrell B. Posten of Walker Co., Ala. appointed O. Wynn of Coweta Co., Ga. as his atty in fact to deliver receipts from Estate of George W. Posten, decd., /s/Dec 1889.

John W. E. Posten of Jefferson Co., Ala. gives power of atty to O. Wynn of Coweta Co., collect his interest in Estate of George W. Posten, decd. signed 16 Dec 1889.

Susannah Messer of Cleburn Co., Ala. appointed J. H. Wynn as atty in fact to collect from estate of G. W. Posten of Coweta Co., Ga. Nov 1889.

Receipt from Emily Parrott for her share of the estate.
Receipt from T. P. Lester, atty for Mrs. Elvira Speight for her share of estate.
M. A. B. Griggs' receipt for his part o estate
Rebecca Davis (x, her mark) for her share of estate
Elma Posten for his part of estate.
G. W. Posten for his share of estate.

Return of Mrs. P. Lindsey, Temporary Admx in Estate of F. P. Lindsey, decd
Page 325-374

Includes accounts, merchantile business of F. P. Lindsey, list of debtors of estate.
Note: An extensive estate. One should read the contents to understand interests of the decd.
Recorded: 11 Jul 1890

W. N. T. Harp, Gdn of A. F., B. M., R. H. and J. G. Harrison, minor children of Larkin Harrison, from 1 Jul 1889 to 1 Jul 1890
Page 375-376

To amount on hand from last Return see Book K, page 287
To amount received of D. McLucas, Admr of Larkin Harrison
Recorded: 15 Aug 1890

Martha A. Weir, Gdn of Georgia A. Stinchcomb in Account Current with her said ward from 1 Mar 1886 to 1 Mar 1890
Page 376-377

To amount on hand from last Return, see Book J, page 505
Recorded: 15 Aug 1890

Mrs. S. F. C. Yates, Admx and R. A. Tilghman, Admr of Matthew Yates from 1 Jun 1889 to 1 Jun 1890
Page 377-388

Includes numerous cotton bills and farm accounts. 39 vouchers.
Recorded: 16 Aug 1890

First Annual Return of Lavender R. Ray as Admr of Estate of Matthew Read, decd, from date of Letters (4 Feb 1889) to 4 Feb 1890
Page 389-396

Paid State and County taxes in Wilcox, Haralson, Douglas, Campbell, Gilmer, Fayette and Fannin Counties.
Recorded: 23 Aug 1890

Daniel McLucas, Admr de bonis non of Larkin Harrison, decd, in Account with said Estate from 1 Jul 1889 to 1 Jul 1890, being a Final Return
Page 396-398

To amount on hand last Return, see Book K, page 286
Received from W. N. T. Harp from sale of 14 acres of land, sold 1st Tues. in Jan 1890
8 vouchers. Recorded: 25 Aug 1890

Daniel McLucas, Gdn of A. C., D. M., G. L and E. E. Harrison from 1 Jul 1889 to 1 Jul 1890
Page 399-400

Receipt from A. C. Harrison and D. M. Harrison for their demands, rights and credits to which they are entitled to received from estate of their father.
Recorded: 25 Aug 1890

B. L. Johnson, Gdn for minor heirs of J. A. Whitlock from 1 Jul 1889 to 12 Jul 1890
Page 400-401

To amount on hand from last Return, see Book K, page 289
2 vouchers. Recorded: 26 Aug 1890

W. W. Malone, Mary W. Malone, Admx of Estate of O. T. Malone from 1 Jul 1889 to 1 Jul 1890
Page 401-402

To amount on hand from last Return, see Book K, page 254
Receipt of Mary W. Malone for the 6th year support from estate.
Recorded: 26 Aug 1890

B. M. Sprayberry, Admr of Estate of M. J. Smith, decd, in Account Current with said estate from 3 Jun 1889 to 3 Jun 1890
Page 403-404

To cash paid - Clinton & Beadles, D. M. Franklin, F. M. Davis, G. L. Harris and Harriett Smith
By amount paid W. H. Clark to be used for the support of I. B. and Valley Smith, two of the minor children
By amount paid B. M. Sprayberry for years' support of C. N., I. B. and V. S. and W. H. Smith
Recorded: 3 Sept 1890

J. O. Landrum, Gdn for Courtney A. Edmonds in Account Current with his swaid ward from 1 Jul 1889 to 1 Jul 1890
Page 405-406

To amount on hand from last Return, see Book K, page 291
Recorded: 5 Sept 1890

George W. Clark, Admr of Estate of J. M. Carlisle, decd, from time of his appointment to 1 Dec 1889
Page 406-415

To amount received from sale of personal property, see Book A, page 84
To amount received from sale of town lots in town of Fayetteville
To amount received from sale of plantation, LL No. 37 in 5th District, Fayette Co., sold first Tues. in Dec 1887
Includes receipts for cotton bill accounts, etc.
Recorded: 5 Sept 1890

George Clark, Admr to E. H. Frazer DR Sept 1888 to legal services rendered in arbitration of matters between Estate of James Carlisle and Mrs. Carlisle and Martin, claimants. Atlanta, Ga.

Voucher #6. Received of G. W. Clark, Admr of J. M. Carlisle, who was the Admr of Larkin Harrison, the sum of $1157.00, the same being due from the estate of J. M. Carlile to the estate of Larkin Harrison, this 14th day of Jan 1888. /s/Daniel McLucas

Receipt of B. J. Carlisle for 12 months' support

Martha A. Butler, Gdn of George W. Murphy, in Account Current with her said ward from 1 Jul 1886 to 1 Jul 1890
Page 416-419

To amount on hand from last Return, see Book J, page 524

16 vouchers.
Recorded: 11 Nov 1890

Hinson Turner, Exr of Moses T. Turner, decd, from 1 Nov 1882 to 1 Nov 1886
Page 420-425

To amount on hand from last Return, see Book J, page 306
Heirs paid -
Lucrecia Turner (x, her mark)
Mary English (x, her mark)
John W. Turner (x, his mark)
Thomas Ogborn (x, his mark) Elizabeth Ogborn (x, her mark)
N. S. Turner
Jane Stubbs (x, her mark)
Druzilla Quick (x, her mark)
Serena Jane Quick (x, her mark)
J. B. Turner (x, his mark)
Sarah Turner (x, her mark)
Kenion Turner (x, his mark)
Moses Turner (x, his mark)
Eliza Turner (x, her mark)
Miss Ellen English (x, her mark)
Mary Lickler (x, her mark)
Mrs. M. J. Henly
Lucinda Turner (x, her mark), signed at Randolph Co., Alabama
T. M. Turner
Henson Turner (x, his mark)
26 vouchers. Filed: 4 Nov 1890. Recorded: 17 Jan 1891

Estate of M. J. Smith, decd, in Account Current with B. M. Sprayberry, Admr, from 1 Jul 1890 to 1 Dec 1890 inclusive, the same being a Final Return
Page 426-431

To amount received from sale of 500 acres of land being all the estate of said decd, sold for cash on first Tues. in Nov 1890 to L. F. Blalock, he being the highest bidder.

In my Return made 5 Jun 1890 and filed in Ordinary's Office 1 Jul 1890 there is a mistake in said Return and the amount shown in years support of the widow and minor children of M. J. Smith...

14 vouchers. Recorded: 19 Jan 1891

Paul Faver, Admr of Estate of John Faver in Account Current with said Estate from 7 Sept 1877 to 18 Dec 1890 the same being a Final Settlement
Page 431-442

To amount on hand from last Return, see Book I, page 697
Coweta Co. land rented in 1886-1888
28 vouchers.

We, the legatees of John Faver, late of Fayette Co., decd, hereby receipt Paul Faver Admr as to all insolvent papers which have been charged......(fi.fas. of J. C. Lumpkin, James Hobgood, W. G. Hill) This 5 Nov 1890. /s/S. L. Faver, Glenn Faver and Love Eastin

28 vouchers (many of which include expenses for Admr attending court on various Fi.Fas.)
Recorded: 10 Feb 1891

R. F. Dorsey, permanent Admr of F. P. Lindsey, decd
Page 443-444

Georgia, Fayette Co....The temporary Admx wishes to submit to you the following statement in reference to several claims of the estate you represent. In reference to the note of T. J. Durrengh which was charged up in the appraisement as a part of the assets of the estate although payable to hand and Lindsy the note was for $10.44 when only $5.22 belong to the estate. The same may be said of a note of G. H. Sansom for $12.50 only due the estate.....

/s/Mrs. P. Lindsey. 27 Jan 1891

Filed: 4 Feb 1891 . Recorded: 6 Mar 1891

The Estate of Frank P. Lindsey, decd, in account Current with R. T. Dorsey, Admr from time of his appointment to 1 Feb 1891
Page 445-514

To amount received from Mrs. P. Lindsey, temp. Admx, 2 Dec 1889 - $7963.66
Includes many notes collected on estate and extensive purchases for estate.
Filed: 21 Jan 1891

J. H. Murphy, Gdn of Bartow rogers, minor child of H. M. Rogers, decd, from 1 Jan 1889 to 5 Feb 1891
Page 515

2 vouchers. To cash paid J. B. Rogers, receipt dated 7 Feb 1891, in full for his interests in said estate
Recorded: 5 Apr 1891

J. H. Ellington, Admr of Z. T. Ellington from 1 Jan 1890 to 1 Jan 1891
Page 516-517

To amount on hand from last Return, see Book K, page 306

To amount paid - R. A. Ellington for his distributive share of estate.
Recorded: 16 Apr 1891

Martha A. Weir, Gdn of Georgia S. Stinchcomb by her security, B. F. Harper, from 1 Mar 1890 to 1 Mar 1891
Page 517

To amount on hand from last Return, see Book K, page 376
Recorded: 8 May 1891

M. M. Collier, Admr of C. P. Collier from 21 Nov 1887 to 6 Apr 1891
Page 518-519

5 vouchers.
Recorded: 3 Jun 1891.

Rufus M. Owen, Admr in Account Current with Estate of Mrs. Louisa Fowler from time of his appointment (2 Feb 1885) to 29 Apr 1891
Page 519-531

42 vouchers. Recorded: 15 Jul 1891
Heirs as follows -
D. A. Nickols of Senoia, Ga.
Thomas J. Nickols of Clay Co., Ala.
William Nickols of Chambers Co., Ala.
M. H. Couch of Senoia, Ga.
Susan Lively by G. F. Lively, of Fayette Co., Ga., being a dau. of Rina Cook who is dead, a sister of Louisa Fowler, decd.
Carrie E. Kent of Meriwether Co., Ga., dau. of Rina Cook who is dead, a sister of Louisa Fowler, decd.
Sarah E. Jacobs of Fayette Co., Ga., share of est. of Louisa Fowler, being a dau. of Rina Cook who is now dead who was a sister of Louisa Fowler, decd.
E. C. Cook of Coweta Co., Ga., share of Rina Cook (being a dau. of) who is now dead who was a sister of Louisa Fowler, decd.
W. T. Cook of Haralson Co., Ga., 1/6th share of estate of Louisa Fowler, being a son of Rina Cook who is now dead who was a sister of Louisa Fowler, decd.
Lucy Butts of Carroll Co., Ga. for 1/3 share of 1/6 share of grandmother Rina Cook, who is now dead, who was a sister of Louisa Fowler, decd, she being a granddau of said Rina Cook.
Mary Spurlin of Fulton Co., Ga. 1/2 share of grandmother, Rina Cook, who is now dead who was sister of Louisa Fowler, decd.
C. L. Jacobs of Cobb Co., Ga. being 1/3rd share of 1/6th share of her grandmother, Rina Cook who is now dead, who was a sister of said Louisa Fowler, decd, he being a grandson of Rina Cook who is now dead.
Ailey A. Cook of Harris Co., Ga., 1/2 share of a 1/6 share in estate of Louisa Fowler, decd, being a dau. of Eliza Smith who was a sister of said Louisa Fowler, decd.
James T. Smith of Harris Co., Ga., 1/4th share of grandmother, Eliza Smith who was a sister of said Louisa Fowler, decd, being a son of W. B Smith who was a son of said Eliza Smith, decd.
J. T. Smith of Harris Co., Ga. 1/4th share of grandmother, Eliza Smith, who was a sister of Louisa Fowler, decd, she being a dau. of W. B. Smith, who was a son of said Eliza Smith, decd.
Emma Smith of Harris Co., Ga. 1/4th share of grandmother, Eliza Smith, who was a sister of Louisa Fowler, decd, she being a dau. of W. B. Smith, who was a son of said Eliza Smith, decd.
Matilda Wyche of Harris Co., Ga. 1/4th share of grandmother, Eliza Smith, who was a sister of Louisa Fowler, decd, she being a dau. of W. B. Smith who was a son of said Eliza Smith, decd.
J. R. Owen of Meriwether Co., Ga., being a son of Harriet Owen who is dead who was a sister of Louisa Fowler, decd.
E. P. Owen of Meriwether Co., Ga., being a son of Harriet Owen who is dead who was a sister of Louisa Fowler, decd.
Rufus M. Owen of Meriwether Co., Ga., being a son of Harriet Owen who is dead who was a sister of Louisa Fowler, decd.
R. S. Owen of Polk Co., Arkansas, being a son of Harriet Owen who is dead who was a sister of Louisa Fowler, decd.
S. A. Bishop of Limestone Co., Texas, being a dau. of Harriet Owen who is dead who was a sister of Louisa Fowler, decd.
Nancy M. L. Taylor of Polk Co., Arkansas, being dau. of Harriet Owen who is dead who was a sister of Louisa Fowler, decd.
Mary E. Williams of Hempstead Co., Arkansas, for payment of 1/7th distributive share in estate of Louisa Fowler, decd, being a dau. of Harriet Owen who is now dead, who was a sister of said Louisa Fowler.

Benjamin Hutchison, Gdn of John H., Robert E. and Ida R. Kelley from 1 May 1890 to 1 May 1891
Page 532-533

3 vouchers. Recorded: 2 Jul 1891

H. S. Rivers, Gdn of N. J. and M. E. Milam, minors of J. R. Milam, decd, from 1 May 1889 to 1 May 1891
Page 533-535

To amount on hand from last Return, see Book K, page 238
13 vouchers. Recorded: 20 Jul 1891

R. A. Ellington, Gdn of Z. P. Ellington, S. E. Ellington, R. F. Ellington and J. S. Ellington, minor children of Z. T. Ellington from 25 Jan 1890 to 25 Jan 1891
Page 535-540

To amount on hand from last Return, see Book 79, page 311
20 vouchers. There is now due ($126.071/2 each) to: Z. P. Ellington, S. E. Ellington, R. F. Ellington, and J. S. Ellington.
Recorded: 13 Aug 1891

Second Annual Return of Lavender R. Ray as Admr of Estate of Matthew Read, decd, from 4 Feb 1890 to 4 Feb 1891
Page 540-561

Sale Bill incoudes land in Fulton Co., land in Wilcox Co., and settlement of Roan case in Campbell Superior Court. 67 vouchers.
Recorded: 14 Aug 1891

J. E. Spurlin, Admr de bonis non with LWT of Sarah Jones from time of appointment (2 Jun 1890) to 1 May 1891
Page 562-563

4 vouchers. Recorded: 18 Aug 1891

J. Q. Landrum, Gdn for Courtney A. Edmonds from 1 Jul 1890 to 1 Jul 1891
Page 563-564

Filed: 6 Jul 1891. Recorded: 11 Sept 1891

J. M. Spurlin to Estate of Thomas Jones, as Admr, for 1890
Page 564-568

To said Jones, widow, for years' support.
To Mrs. Permelia Spurlin, etc. Recorded: 28 Sept 1891

Mrs. M. W. Dickerson, Admx on Estate of O. T. Malone
Page 569-570

Recorded: 29 Sept 1891

B. F. Johnson, Gdn of minor heirs of J. A. Whitlock, decd, from 1 Jul 1890 to 1 Jul 1891
Page 570-571

To amount on hand from last Return, see Book K, page 400
2 vouchers. Recorded: 29 Sept 1891

Martha A. Butler, Gdn of George W. Murphy from 1 Jul 1890 to 3 Aug 1891
Page 571-573

4 vouchers. Recorded: 30 Sept 1891

Estate of Miss M. J. Harris in Account Current with C. A. Eason, Admr from time of appointment 5 May 1890 to 18 Jul 1891, the same being a Final Settlement
Page 574-581

23 vouchers. Recorded: 30 Sept 1891
Receipt for shares of estate - W.F. Harris per A. C. Harris, Jesie Graves, J. S. Harris of Wood Co., Tx., Mag Wyatt of Fulton Co., Ga., L. T. Harris of Wood Co., Tx. ,Telitha Harris of Brown Co., Tx., M. E. Beard of Brown Co., Tx., W. B. Stewart of Jonesboro, Ga. on Estate of Seaborn Harris.

Daniel McLucas, Gdn of G. I. and E. E. Harrison in Account with said wards from 1 Jul 1890 to 1 Jul 1891
Page 581

Filed: 7 Sept 1891. Recorded: 9 Nov 1891

Annual Return of D. J. Price, Exr of Q. S. Price from time of appointment to 21 Oct 1891
Page 582-585

9 vouchers. Filed: 21 Oct 1891. Recorded: 15 Dec 1891

END OF BOOK K

Fayette Co., Georgia
Annual Returns, Book L
(1890-1894)

W. N. T. Harp, Gdn for minor children of L. Harrison in Account Current from 1 Jul 1890 to 1 Jul 1891
Page 1-2

4 vouchers. To cash paid - John W. Denton, Agent (tuition at Inman High School)
Filed: 28 Oct 1891. Recorded: 29 Dec 1891

John Dunbar, Admr of Estate of J. W. Dunbar, Sr., from 1 Jul 1889 to 2 Nov 1891
Page 2-6

To amount on hand from last Return, Book K, page 256. 15 vouchers.
To cash paid heirs as follows -

B. H. Dunbar
A. C. Dunbar
D. E. Dunbar
R. G. Prince
J. K. Prince

Filed: 2 Nov 1891. Recorded: 29 Dec 1891

Money Received from Estate of J. W. Lynch, R. W. Lynch, Exr
Page 7-13

15 vouchers.
Filed: 1 Feb 1892. Recorded: 28 Mar 1892

R. A. Rivers, Admr of Robert Rivers, from August Term 1891 (date of appointment) to 1 Jul 1892
Page 15-18

Sale Bill, Book A, page 104. 11 vouchers.
Filed: 11 May 1892. Recorded: 7 Jul 1892

Benjamin Hutchinson, Gdn of John H., Robert H. and Ida R. Kelley, from 1 May 1891 to 1 May 1892
Page 19-20

For last Return, Book K, page 532
4 vouchers. Recorded: 9 Jul 1892

R. A. Ellington, Gdn for Z. P., S. E., R. F. and J. S. Ellington minor children of L. T. Ellington, from 25 Jan 1891 to 25 Jan 1892
Page 20-27

To amount of last Return see Book K, page 535 when a division was made with said wards.
37 vouchers.

Annual Return of Francis C. Speer and S. E. Speer, Admrs of James J. Speer, decd, from 20 Mar 1891 to 1 Jun 1892
Page 28-39

46 vouchers which include plantation business, such as picking cotton, repairs, grinding, etc.
Filed: 17 Jun 1892. Recorded: 11 Aug 1892

J. E. Spurlin in Account with Estate of Sarah Jones for 1891
Page 40

1 voucher. Recorded: 17 Aug 1892

L. C. Ellison, Admr of Estate of Simon Swanson from 6 Apr 1891 to 1 Jul 1892
Page 41-45

To amount received from sale of land, 258 acres sold 1st Tues. in Nov 1890 to W. A. McCurry
9 vouchers.
Recorded: 17 Aug 1892

J. R. Murphy, Gdn for G. W. Murphy from time of appointment 2 Aug 1891 to 1 Jul 1892
Page 46-57

19 vouchers. To cash paid - J. T. Guy, J. W. Kitchens, J. C. Morgan, A. W. Cousins, F. M. Davis, Cannon & Evans, T. C. Cannon, T. F. Blalock, S. C. and J. E. Blalock (for George W. Murphy), J. L. Blalock, J. H. Blalock, Fayetteville News, and J. R. Murphy.
Recorded: 23 Aug 1892

Third Annual Return of Lavender R. Ray as Admr of Estate of Matthew Read, decd, from 4 Feb 1891 to 4 Feb 1892
Page 57-62

1891 June 18, Thomas W. Ezzard in full of the decree in Douglas Superior Court fixing the title to lot of land No. 58 in 2nd District of Douglas in said Ezzard

Dec. 7, William Ragan for rent of 1/2 interest in Lot No. 9, Fannin Co., for 1890
Vouchers numbered 68-80.
Filed: 25 Jun 1892. Recorded: 25 Aug 1892

Mrs. S. F. C. Yates, Admx, and R. A. Tilghman, Admr of Estate of Martha Yates in Account Current with said Estate from 1 Jun 1890 to 1 Jun 1892
Page 63-81

To amount on hand from last Return, see Book K, page 377
Includes sums of money received for cotton bales. 80 vouchers pertaining to plantation business.
Recorded: 29 Aug 1892

Annual Return of Mrs. Mary Dickenson, Admx on Estate of O. T. Malone
Page 82-83

7 vouchers. Voucher #7, Received from Mrs. Mary Dickenson, Admx on Estate of O. T. Malone, decd, $250, the same being for the ward and support of Sallie Malone one year $200.00 and Annie Malone, $150. 30 Jun 1892. /s/Mary W. Dickenson
Filed: 1 Jul 1892. Recorded: 31 Aug 1892

J. M. Spurlin, Admr of Estate of Thomas Jones, decd, Annual Return
Page 84-85

5 vouchers. Voucher #5. Lewis, Ga., 21 Nov 1891. Received of J. M. Spurlin $39.00 for my part of rent in full for the year 1890 and 1891 and this rent shall show that the said Sarah Jones has paid to the said J. M. Spurlin $4.00 in court costs of said receipt... /s/Sarah E. Jones by W. T. Jones
Filed: 6 Jul 1892. Recorded: 14 Sept 1892

First Annual Return of W. W. Dickson, Admr of the Estate of J. M. Dickson, decd, up to 1 Jul 1892
Page 86-96

Includes sales from estate of numberous cotton bales. 26 vouchers.
Filed: 6 Jul 1892. Recorded: 15 Sept 1892

J. Q. Landrum, Gdn, for Courtney A. Edmondson in Account Current with his said ward from 1 Jul 1891 to 1 Jul 1892
Page 97-98

1 voucher. Filed: 8 Jul 1892. Recorded: 17 Sept 1892

B. F. Johnson, Gdn of Miss Eugenia A. Whitlock, minor child of J. A. Whitlock in Account Current with his said ward from 1 Jul 1891 to 1 Aug 1892, the same being a Final Settlement
Page 98-99

Amount of principal last Return, see Book K, page 570
Amount of interest due said ward at last Return, see Book F, page 570

Voucher #2, Fayetteville, Ga. 1 Aug 1892. Received of B. L. Johnson, former Gdn for Miss E. A. Whitlock $219.05 in full of all the money in his hands as such guardian. Also $5.40 as the share of J. R. and C. M. Whitlock for dismissal held by the said guardian when he settled with item as his wards. /s/N. C. Adams

Filed: 1 Aug 1892. Recorded: 17 Sept 1892

R. W. Lynch and W. L. Bowers, Exrs of the LWT of James W. Lynch in Account Current with said Estate from 1 Jul 1781 to 1 Jul 1892
Page 100-103

5 vouchers. Filed: 10 Sept 1892. Recorded: 21 Nov 1892

Daniel McLucas, Gdn for A. C., D. M., G. C. and E. E. Harrison. Return with his said wards from 1 Jul 1891 to 1 Jul 1892
Page 103-104

Voucher #4. 30 Jan 1892. Received of Daniel McLucas, my Gdn, $438.50, being the full amount of my distributive share of my father's estate. /s/G. C. Harrison
Filed: 12 Sept 1892. Recorded: 21 Nov 1892

Estate of F. P. Lindsey in Account Current with R. T. Dorsey, Admr, from 1 Feb 1891 to 1 Sept 1892
Page 105-167

To amount on hand from last Return, See Book K, page 446
(collected various notes). 71 vouchers (accounts of the plantation including some dated at Brooks Station, Ga. and Chattanooga, Tn.). Filed: 19 Sept 1892.

Annual Return of V. T. Davis, Admr de bonis non with LWT annexed of Estate of John Rush, decd, in Account Current with said estate from time of appointment Jan term 1891 to 13 Dec 1892
Page 167-169

13 vouchers. Filed: 13 Dec 1892. Recorded: 20 Feb 1893

Annual Return of V. T. Davis, Admr of Elizabeth Rush, decd, in Account Current with said estate from time of appointment, Feb term 1891 up to 13 Dec 1892
Page 170-175

13 vouchers. Filed: 13 Dec 1892. Recorded: 23 Feb 1893

G. A. Davis, Exr of LWT of G. M. Davis in Account Current with said Estate from 4 Apr 1890 to 13 Dec 1892
Page 175-180

To amount received from sale of personal property, see Book D, page 114
This property belongs to J. J. Davis by Will of G. M. Davis
11 vouchers and 13 vouchers.
Recorded: 2 Feb 1893

G. W. Clark as Admr de bonis non of Estate of Sarah Jackson, decd, in Account Current with said estate from 1 Jul 1887 to present time, 25 Dec 1892
Page 180-187

11 vouchers.
Vou. #1. Received of G. W. Clark, Admr de bonis non of Sarah Jackson, decd, the sum of $50 and one Fi.Fa issued from the 709th District G. M. Justice Court in favor of M. E. Jackson vs. J. E. Jackson for the sum of $50.00 principal. In settlement of all claims against the estate of Sarah Jackson, decd. This 3 Oct 1887. /s/M. E. Hill, atty for J. E. Jackson

Vou. #9. Estate of Edmond and Sarah Jackson to Thomas Speight dated 13 Feb 1888.
Filed: 23 Dec 1892. Recorded: 28 Feb 1893

J. R. Brooks, Admr de bonis non of Hillery Brooks from time of his appointment up to 11 Jan 1893
Page 187-189

3 vouchers.
Distributees: M. E. Woods and L. F. Woods
Filed: 11 Jan 1893. Recorded: 27 Mar 1893

K. V. Adams, Admr of J. W. (Westley) Watson in Account Current with said Estate from time of appointment, Dec 7 1891 up to and including Feb 16 1893
Page 189-193

13 vouchers. Voucher #13 from Miss E. Watson and Miss E. E. Watson for nursing of J. W. Watson, decd for the year of 1887.
Filed: 20 Feb 1893. Recorded: 14 Apr 1893

Mrs. R. A. Ellington, Gdn for Z. P. Ellington, S. E. Ellington, R. F. Ellington and J. S. Ellington, minor children of Z. T. Ellington in Account with her said wards from 25 Jan 1892 to 25 Jan 1893
Page 194-198

To amount on hand from last Return, see Book T, page 20
15 vouchers.
Recorded: 8 Jun 1893

Annual Return of Joseph T. Graves, Admr with LWT annexed of Oliver Faver of Fayette Co., decd, from time of appoint at Dec Term 1890 to 16 May 1893 inclusive
Page 199-203

12 vouchers.

Vou. #6. Fayetteville, Ga. Dec 8, 1891. Received of Joseph L. Graves, Admr with the LWT annexed of Oliver Faver of said county, decd, who was my father, $160.23 in full of all my interest, rights and credits in the estate of said decd as devised by his LWT. /s/Jane Baker (x, her mark)

Vou. #7. Fayetteville, Ga., Dec 8, 1891. Received of Joseph L. Graves, Admr with LWT annexed of Oliver Faver, who was my father, $161.22 in full of all my interest rights and credits in the estate of the said decd, as devised by his LWT. /s/Mary Bird (x, her mark)

Vous. #8-12. Fayetteville, Ga., Dec 8, 1891. Received of Joseph L. Graves, Admr with LWT annexed of Oliver Faver of said county, decd, who was my grandfather, $32.24 in full of all my interests, rights and credits in the estate of the said decd as devised by his LWT. I being a daughter of Emily Hudson named as one of the heirs in the said LWT and receiving 1/5th of one share.
/s/Kittie Askew (x, her mark)
/s/John Hudson (x, his mark)
/s/Stonewall J. Faver
/s/Nova Hudson (x, her mark)
/s/Ella Hudson (x, her mark) of Clayton Co., Ga. who authorized J. R. Nisbet of Clayton Co. to collect for her
Recorded: 13 Jul 1893

Benjamin Hutchinson, Gdn of Robert E. and Ida R. Kelley in Account Current with said wards from 1 May 1892 to 1 May 1893
Page 204-205

4 vouchers. Filed: 32 May 1893. Recorded: 14 Jul 1893

R. A. Rivers, Admr of Robert Rivers in Account Current with said Estate from 1 Jul 1892 to 1 Jul 1893
Page 205-209

To amount of administration from last Return, see Book L, page 15
To amount received from sale of land sold 1st Tues. in Nov 1892 sold to N. Rivers

7 vouchers. $837.81 is to be divded into 5 parts for each heir, less $167.56 which is the share of the administrator.... and he receiving no commission on it leaves $670.24 which is to be divided into four parts....

Estate of Robert Rivers contd.....

Vou. #5. Jane C. Rivers } Dower
vs.
Robert A. Rivers, Admr of Robert Rivers
Filed: 7 Jun 1893. Recorded: 11 Aug 1893

Received of Robert A. Rivers $5.00 in full cost of above state case. /s/A. E. Stokes, Clerk
Distributees Receipts as follows -

J. N. Rivers
T. A. Thornton
S. E. Lester
R. A. Rivers
R. J. Speir
Henry Speir

Annual Return of Mrs. F. C. Speer, Admx and S. E. Speer, Admr of J. Speer made from 1 Jun 1892 to 1 Jun 1893
Page 210-212

To amount collected on rent of 35 acres of land in 1892 (of J. N. Davis)
5 vouchers. Vou. #3. Fayetteville, Ga., Mar 23 1893. Received from Ed Speer $10.00 part fee for service in settling up estate of J. J. Speer, decd. /s/J. M. Shell, atty for estate

Filed: 14 Jun 1893. Recorded: 12 Aug 1893

Estate of Robert Matthews, decd, in Account with S. C. Travis, Admr, from time of his appointment up to the present
Page 213-219

Includes cotton sales of estate and other plantation business.
Vou. #1 for advertising in Fayetteville News, 22 May 1892 (date of receipt)

Vou. #7. Received of S. C. Travis, Admr of Robert Matthews of said county, decd, $70.65 in full of all demans against him for my share in the years support from said estate to the widow and minor children.
/s/N. S. Matthews
/s/J. E. Matthews

Vou. #8, Fayetteville, Ga. Oct. 1892. Received of S. C. Travis, Admr of Robert Matthews of said county, decd, $70.65 in full of all demands against him for myshare in the years support from said estate to the widow and minor children.
/s/J. E. Mathews

Vou. #9, Fayetteville, Ga., Oct 1892. Received of S. C. Travis, Admr of Robert Matthews of said county, decd, $70.65 in full of all demands against him for my share in the years support from said estate to the widow and minor children.
/s/S. F. Matthews
/s/J. E. Matthews

Estate of Robert Matthews contd....

Vou. #10. Fayetteville, Ga. Oct 1892. Received of S. C. Travis, Admr of Robert Matthews of said county, decd, $70.65 in full of all demands against him for my share in the years support from said estate to the widow and minor children.
/s/M. E. Matthews
/s/J. E. Matthews

Vou. #11. Fayetteville, Ga. Oct 1892. Received of S. C. Travis, Admr of Robert Matthews of said county, decd, #70.65 in full of all demands against him for my share in the years support from said estate to the widow and minor children.
/s/F.C. Matthews
/s/J. E. Matthews

Vou. #14. Fayetteville, Ga., Nov. 15 1892. Received of S. C. Travis, Admr of Robert Matthews of said county, decd, $70.65 in full of all demands against him for my share in the years support from said estate to the widow and minor children.
/s/J. E. Matthews
/s/Robert Matthews, Jr.
/s/H. T. Matthews

Vou. #15. Fayetteville, Ga., nov 16, 1892. Received of S. C. Travis, Admr of Robert Matthews of said county, decd, $70.65 in full of all demands against him for my share in the years support from said estate to the widow and minor children.
/s/H. T. Matthews

Filed: 14 Jun 1893. Recorded: 14 Aug 1893

Fourth Annual Return of Lavender R. Ray as Admr of Estate of Mathew Read, decd, from 4 Feb 1892 to 4 Feb 1893
Page 219-224

Rent of cabin in Fairburn for 1892
Sale of land in Fannin and Gilmer counties
Vouchers 81-95. (includes advertising in the Banner Messenger)

Filed: 14 June 1893. Recorded: 18 Aug 1893

J. P. Starr, Gdn for R. L. Matthews, H. T. Matthews, M. C. Matthews, J. C. Matthews, S. F. Matthews and Minnie Matthews, minor children of Robert Matthews from time of his appointment, 7 Nov 1892 to 1 Jul 1893
Page 224-225

3 vouchers. Filed: 20 Jun 1893. Recorded: 21 Aug 1893

J. E. Spurlin, Admr of Sarah Jones up to 21 Jun 1893
Page 226

Vou. #2, Received of J. E. Spurlin as Admr of Sarah Jones, $60 to us applied to commission in Jones will case, this 13 May 1893. /s/J. M. Spurlin, Admr of Thomas Jones
Filed: 29 Jun 1893. Recorded: 21 Aug 1893

J. E. Spurlin, Exr of J. M. Spurlin
Page 227-233

To cash paid Nov. 16, 1887 for coffin of Reuben Spurlin
28 vouchers.

Receipts from heirs -

J. J. Spurlin
T. J. Spurlin
Anna Goodman
J. P. Spurlin
E. J. Spurlin, Gdn for J. A. Spurlin
David Samuel Spurlin (x, his mark)
A. J. Spurlin
J. Crumbie (for Emma J. Grady, Sallie Crumbie, Mollie Crumbie, J. R. Crumbie, W. J. Crumbie, G. N. Crumbie, M. J. Veasy, M. C. Peavey, H. G. Crumbie and J. F. Crumbie of the Estate of J. M. Spurlin, decd, being the heirs of of C. C. Crumbie, decd. this 23 Jan 1893

Bulah L. Hairston

Filed: 29 Jun 1893. Recorded: 21 Aug 1893

R. W. Lynch and W. L. Bowers, Exrs of J. W. Lynch in Account Current with said Estate from 1 Jul 1892 to 12 Jul 1893
Page 234-238

4 vouchers. Filed: 29 Jun 1893. Recorded: 22 Aug 1893

Mrs. C. S. McLucas, Admx of the Estate of J. C. Hightower in Account Current with said Estate from time of her appointment to 1 Jul 1893
Page 239-240

5 vouchers. Filed: 3 Jul 1893. Recorded: 23 Aug 1893

3 Jul 1893, the Final Return of the Estate of Thomas Jones, decd
Page 241-243

17 Nov 1892 - Paid Mrs. Mattie Rentfrow in full of her share of the Estate of Thomas Jones (Vou.#2)

26 Oct 1892 - Paid Luina Ogletree by W. Ogletree for her claim on Estate of Thomas Jones (Vou. #3)

Lowry, Ga., 17 Nov 1892 - Paid George M. Martin, Gdn of M. W. Jones, for his claim as Gdn on Estate of Thomas Jones, Jr., decd (Vou.#5)

Receipt of J. D. Jones (Vou. #6) as Gdn of H. H. Jones' grandchildren, that is, two of them, Henry and Susan...for their share of estate of Thomas Jones, decd. ...24 Oct 1892.

Receipt of Rebecca J. Akins, dated 24 Sept 1892 at Lowry, Ga. for her share of estate of Thomas Jones, decd.
(Vou. #7)

Estate of Thomas Jones contd.....

Lowry, Ga., 27 Sept 1892, receipt of Pauline A. Spurlin for her share of estate of Thomas Jones, decd. (Vou. #8)

Lowry, Ga., 24 Nov 1892, receipt of Permelia A. Spurlin for her share of estate of Thomas Jones, decd (Vou. #9)

Lowry, Ga., 13 Oct 1891. Receipt of William L. Jones for receiving all of said Jones' clothes, bedclothes, kitchen furniture, etc.

Final Return of Joseph L. Graves, Admr with LWT annexed of Oliver Faver, decd, of Fayette Co., Ga. in Account Current with said Estate from time of last Return up to and including 5 Jun 1893
Page 243-

3 vouchers. Filed: 5 Jun 1893. Recorded: 23 Aug 1893

W. W. Dickson, Admr of J. M. Dickson in Account Current with said Estate from 1 Jul 1892 to 1 Jul 1893
Page 245-286

To amount on hand since last Return, see Book L, page (blank)
To sale of land, N.T. Dickson, Beauregard Russell and J. J. Gilbert
56 vouchers consists of plantation sales and purchases.
Filed: 5 Jul 1893. Recorded: 23 Aug 1893

J. L. McLucas, Gdn for minor children of J. L. Harrison in Account Current with said wards from 22 Oct 1892 that being the time of settlement with W. N. T. Harp, their former Gdn, to 1 Jul 1893
Page 286-289

8 vouchers.
Vou. #2. Received of W. N. T. Harp, Gdn for A. F. B., M. R. H. and J. G. Harrison. $30. /s/S. C. Harrison
Vou. #3, receipt of W. H. Wooding for tuition for Ben, Robert and Glenn Harrison

Filed: 10 Jul 1893. Recorded: 27 Sept 1893

H. S. Rivers, Gdn for Nannie J. Milam, now Nannie J. Landrum, and Millie E. Milam, minors of John R. Milam, in Account with said wards from 12 May 1892 to 1 May 1893
Page 290-294

Said Return shows a recapitalization of the whole of the transactions of said Gdn.
To amount on hand at first Return, see Book J, page 252.
Recorded: 28 Sept 1893

Mrs. N. C. Adams, Gdn for Miss E. A. Whitlock, in Account Current with her said ward from time of appointment to 1 Jul 1893
Page 294

To amount received of B. L. Johnson, former Gdn, see Book L, page 89
Filed: 2 Aug 1893. Recorded: 29 Sept 1893

W. T. Williams, Admr de bonis non with LWT annexed of Danville Mitchell from the time of his appointment as such Admr, Jan Term 1892, to 7 Aug 1893
Page 295-305

To amount received from sale of personal property, see Sale Bill Book A, page 112 and for the rent of said land in 1892. 25 vouchers.

Heirs receipts, as follows:

{Brooks Station, Ga., M. F. Thornton by Rev. J. T. Mitchell, atty in fact
{Cass Co., Texas, M. F. Thornton (gives her power of atty to Rev. J. T. Mitchell, x, her mark)

Brooks Station, Ga., L. A. Mitchell per J. T. Mitchell

Georgia, Bibb Co., Know all men by these presents that I, Lewis A. Mitchell of Bibb Co., Ga., heir and next of kin entitled to a distributive share in the estate of my deceased grandmother, Fannie Mitchell, late of Fayette Co....have constituted J. T. Mitchell of Spalding Co., Ga. my true and lawful atty....to collect....this 10th day of Jul 1893. /s/L. A. Mitchell

Fayette Co., Ga., K. D. Banks

Fayette Co., Ga., Allie Williams (x, her mark)

Fayette Co., Ga., Rachel Chapel (x, her mark)

Fayette Co., Ga., E. Pherl Coper (x, her mark)

Fayette Co., J. G. Banks

Fayette Co., A. D. Banks

Brooks Station, Ga., L. J. Bellisle

Fayette Co., Ga., J.T. Mitchell

Fayette Co., Ga., Lucinda Hubbard (x, her mark)

Brooks Station, Ga., Kizzie Williams (x, her mark)

Brooks Station, Ga., Belzie Banks (x, hermark)

Brooks Station, Ga., Saley Banks

Filed: 7 Aug 1893. Recorded: 12 Oct 1893

Estate of F. P. Lindsey, decd, in Account Current with R. T. Dorsey, Admr, from 19 Sept 1892 up to and inclusive of 1 Sept 1893
Page 304-305

2 vouchers. Filed: 24 Aug 1893. Recorded: 24 Oct 1893

Return of Daniel McLucas, Gdn for Miss Effie E. Harrison from 1 Jul 1892 to 1 Jul 1893
Page 306-307

To cash paid - E. E. Harrison, F. M. Davis and E. B. Weldon. 9 vouchers.

Recorded: 22 Sept 1893

B. F. Harper, security for Martha A. Weir of Alabama, Gdn for Georgia A. Stinchcomb in Account Current with said ward...from 16 Mar 1891 to 20 Dec 1893, the same showing a Final Settlement
Page 308-309

To amount on hand from last Return, see Book K, page 517

Vou. #3. Received of Georgia Stinchcomb $3.60, the same having been advanced by me as curt cost as security for her mother, Martha A. Weir in making settlement for Gdn, she being a non-resident of this county. 20 Dec 1893. /s/B. F. Harper

Filed: 20 Dec 1893. Recorded: 20 Feb 1894

Annual Return of J. B. Hewell, Gdn of the property of Stark B., Fred C., Jesse R. and Walter S. Cargile, from time of appointment to 29 Jan 1894
Page 309-312

To money received from C. A. Pitman, Exr of John W. Cargile, decd, on account of wards as follows:

Amount recd for Stark B. Cargile $21.44

Amount recd for Fred C. Cargile $21.44

Amount recd for Jesse R. Cargile $21.44

Amount recd for Walter S. Cargile. $21.44

7 vouchers. Recorded: 24 Mar 1894

Apprenticeship of Clarence Washington and Herbert Washington
Page 312-313

Georgia, Fayette Co. This indenture made and entered int this 26 day of Apr 1894 between A. B. Connally of said county and state of the one part and Lizzie Washington, the mother of Clarence Washington, age 9 years, 11 months and 23 days, and Herbert Washington, aged 6 years and 3 months, all of Spalding Co. Witnesseth that the said Lizzie Washington hereby binds and apprentices to the said A. B. Connally the said Clarence Washington and Herbert Washington until they.....are twenty-one years old....

/s/A. B. Connally
/s/Lizzie Washington (x, her mark)

The Last and Final Return of I. E. C. W. Smith, Gdn for S. F. Vincent nee S. F. Speer and T. C. Speer in Account Current with the said wards from 1 Jul 1873 up to and including the 5th day of Mar 1894
Page 313-315

To amount due S. F. Vincent nee S. F. Speer at last Return, see Book I, page 263
5 vouchers.

Voucher #1. Received of Mary A. Leach, Admx of the Estate of E. W. Leach and T. C. Speer the sum of $53.69 in which is included a receipt for $10 given by T. C. Speer on Oct 9, 1890 to E. C. W. Smith, Gdn, leaving a balance of $43.69 as a settlement in compromise of my claim against him from my grandmother Loyd's estate, and also of a judgment in my favor in the Court of Ordinary of Fayette Co. against I. E. C. W. Smith,Gdn. for the sum of $19.69.....21 Nov 1890. /s/T. C. Speer by his Atty, T. P. Lester

Voucher #2. State of Alabama, County of Calhoun. Received of I. E. C. W. Smith of Campbell Co., Ga., my Gdn, paid by T. C. Speer and W. A. Leach, $46.25 in fulll of all balances, rights and credits due me from the estate of my father, John W. Speer and estate of my grandfather and grandmother Loyd, all late of Fayette Co., Ga., decd. This the 4th day of Jan 1894. /s/S. F. Vincent

Filed: 5 Mar 1894. Recorded: 10 May 1894

Final Return of G. A. D. Davis, Exr of G. M. Davis, decd, in Account Current with said estate from 13 Dec 1892 to 27 Jan 1894
Page 315-325

By amount balance due John J. Davis, final settlement from estate of his father, Vou. #29

Vou. #30, receipt of John J. Davis for furniture, 101 1/4 acres of land, being the S half of Lot No. 81 and 101 1/4 acres of Lot No. 32, the same being W half of said Lot 32, all of said two parcels being in 7th District of Fayette Co., Ga., as contemplated in the LWT of my father, which is recorded on page 529, Will Book, Ordinary's Office. this 24 Jan 1894. /s/John J. Davis

Vou.#5. Received of G. A. Davis, Exr of G. M. Davis, decd, 101 1/4 acres of land in Lot No. 3, being the S half of said lot and 101 1/4 acres of Lot No. 30, being the N half of said lot, all of said two parcels being in 7th District of Fayette Co. and as contemplated in my father's LWT, recorded page 529 in Will Book, Ordinary's Office. This 24 Jan 1894. /s/E. B. Brown

30 vouchers.
Recorded: 15 May 1894

J. R. Murphy, Gdn for G. W. Murphy in Account Current with his said ward from 1 Jul 1892 to 31 Mar 1894
Page 325-330

7 vouchers.
Filed: 2 Apr 1892
Recorded: 18 May 1894

A. Steinheimer, Admr of Estate of B. F. Posey in Account Current with said estate from the time of his appointment on 3 Oct 1892 to 3 Apr 1894
Page 330-339

To amount received from sale of personal property sold 17 Nov 1892 for cash, see Sale Bill, Book A, page 132.

To amount received from James Posey realized from the sale of horse cropper, traction engine, B. F. Posey owning half interest in said engine.

To amount received from sale of personal property sold 15 Nov 1893, see Sale Bill, Book A, page 129.

To amount received from sale of land sold on the 1st Tues. in Feb 1894 sold to L. F. Blalock, to-wit: 39 acres of land Lot No. 99 and 100 acres off Lot No. 94, all in Brooks Station, Ga., and sold subject to dower.

38 vouchers
Filed: 3 Apr 1894
Recorded: 19 May 1894

W. W. Dickson, Admr on Estate of J. M. Dickson in Account Current with said estate from 1 Jul 1893 to 3 Apr 1894, the same being a Final Settlement of said Estate
Page 340-345

13 vouchers.

Vou. #11. Received of W. W. Dickson, Admr of the Estate of J. M. Dickson, $347.68 in full of all the interests, rights and credits of Oscar L., Lester C., Lela M., Willie A. and Johnie O. Dickson in estate of J. M. Dickson...this Apr 3rd 1894 /s/N. T. Dickson

Filed: 3 Apr 1894. Recorded: 21 May 1894

J. Q. Landrum, Gdn for Courtney A. Edmondson in Account Current with said ward from 1 Jul 1892 to 9 Apr 1894
Page 346

To amount on hand from last Return, see Book L, page 97.

To amount of interest on $155.30 from 1 Jul 1892 to 8 Mar 1894 at 7%, that being the day that Courtney A. Edmondson, my ward, arrived at 21 years of age.

Vou. #1. Evansville, Indiana, 8 Mar 1894. Received of J. Q. Landrum, my Gdn of Fayette Co., in the State of Ga., $157.90 in full of my interests....the money that was left after burial expenses and doctors bill of my mother, Mary A. Edmondson of Fayette Co., decd /s/Courynry A. Edmondson.

Recorded: 5 Jun 1894

J. H. Ellington, Admr of the Estate of Z. T. Ellington in Account Current with said estate from 1 Jun 1891 including 20 Apr 1894
Page 347-348

To amount on hand from last Return, see Book K, page 516
5 vouchers.

Vou.#3, Received of J. H. Ellington, Admr of estate of Z. T. Ellington....in full of all balances due me as Gdn for Paul, Richard and Ellington, minors of Z. T. Ellington,decd. This 3 Apr 1894. /s/R. A. Ellington,Gdn.

Vou.#4, Received of J. H.Ellington, Admr of estate of Z. T. Ellington....in full of all money due me as Gdn of S. E. Tarpley nee S. E. Ellington from his administration of Z. T. Ellington's estate. Apr 20, 1894. /s/R. O. Tarpley, Gdn.
Filed: 20 Apr 1894. Recorded: 5 Jun 1894.

Final Return of J. E. Spurlin, Exr of J. M.Spurlin, decd, 7 May 1894
Page 349-353

Heirs receipts, as follows -
J. P. Spurlin
E. J. Spurlin, Gdn of John A. Spurlin
D. S. Spurlin (x, his mark)
A. J. Spurlin
T. J. Spurlin
H. G. Crumbie
G. W. Crumbie
J. T. Crumbie
N. J. Veaysey
Sallie Crumbie
M. A. Crumbie
Emma J. Grady
Mrs. B. L.Hairston of Falls Co.,Texas
J. R. Crumbie
W. J. Crumbie
M. C. Veazey
J. M.Spurlin
A. A.Goodman
Mrs. Lou Spurlin,Gdn of Wilbe, Otla and Crattie Spurlin of Leander, Texas
Beulah Bragg and M. A. Spurlin of Ellis Co.,Texas
J. E. Spurlin

Filed: 7 May 1894. Recorded: 6 Jul 1894

Benjamin Hutchinson, Gdn of Robert E. and Ida R. Kelley, in Account Current with said wards from 1 May 1893 to 1 May 1894
Page 353

To amount on hand at last Return, see Book L, page 204

Filed: 7 May 1894. Recorded: 6 Jul 1894

S. F. C. Yates, Admx and R. A. Tilghman, Admr of Estate of Matthew Yates with LWT annexed in Account Current with the Estate from 1 Jun 1892 to 1 Jun 1894
Page 354-367

43 vouchers. Filed: 16 May 1894. Recorded: 6 Jul 1894

Mrs. R. A. Ellington, Gdn for Paul Ellington, R. F. Ellington and J. S. Ellington in Account with said wards from 25 Jan 1893 to 25 Jan 1894
Page 367-370

To amount on hand from last Return, see Book L, page 194
To amount paid - R. O. Tarpley, Gdn for S. E. Tarpley, nee S. E. Ellington, etc. 9 vouchers.
Recorded: 18 Jul 1894

H. S. Rivers, Gdn for M. E. Milam in Account Current with said ward from 1 May 1893 to 1 May 1894
Page 370-371

To amount on hand from last Return, see Book L, page 290
3 vouchers. To cash paid - W. T. Roberts, J. D. Smith and S. C. Milam
Recorded: 19 Jul 1894

Final Return of J. B. Hewell, Gdn of property of Walter S. Cargile, Jesse R. Cargile, Fred C. Cargile and Stark B. Cargile from time of last Return, 29 Jan 1894 and including 13 Mar 1894
Page 371-372

To amount on hand from last Return, Book L, page 309

Vou. #2. Received of J. B. Hewell, Gdn of the property of Walter S. Cargile, $10.65, the balance due said ward on final settlement....this 13 Mar 1894. /s/F. W. Cargile
Filed: 1 Jun 1894. Recorded: 15 Aug 1894

Mrs. N. C. Adams, Gdn for Miss E. A. Cook, now Miss E. A. Whitlock, in Account Current with her said ward from 1 Jul 1893 to 1 Jul 1894
Page 372-373

To amount received of J. O. Wynn from sale of land of Samuel Lively. 3 vouchers
Recorded: 15 Aug 1894.

Estate of Robert Matthews, decd, in Account Current with S. C. Travis, Admr, from 14 Jun 1893 to 22 May 1894
Page 373-382

To amount received from sale of land, see Sale Bill in Book A page (blank)
To amount on hand from last Return, see Book L, page 213

19 vouchers. Vou. #2 from News Publishing Co. for advertising lease to sell lands of estate
Filed: 13 Jun 1894. Recorded: 15 Aug 1894

Annual Return of Mary W. Dickenson, Gdn of Miss Sallie and Annie Malone
Page 383-394

3 vouchers. Filed: 28 Jun 1894. Recorded: 24 Aug 1894

Mrs. N. T. Dickson, Gdn for Oscar L., Lester C., Lela M., Willie A. and Johnie M. Dickson, orphans of J. M. Dickson in Account Current with her said wards from the time of her appointment to 1 Jul 1894
Page 384-387

9 vouchers. Filed: 2 Jul 1894. Recorded: 24 Aug 1894

Mrs. S. A. Gable and N. W. Gable, Admrs of Estate of N. W. Gable from time of their appointment to 1 Jul 1894
Page 388-413

To amount received from sale of personal property, see Sale Bill Book A page 127
31 vouchers, includes numerous collections. Recorded: 25 Aug 1894

J. P. Starr, Gdn for R. L. Matthews, N. T. Matthews, M. C. Matthews, J. C. Matthews, S. F. Matthews and Ninnie Matthews, minor children of Robert Matthews in Account Current with his said wards from 1 Jul 1893 to 1 Jul 1894
Page 414-415

To amount due all of wards 1 Jul 1893, see Book L, page 224
Receipt from C. W. Richter for tuition.
Filed: 3 Jul 1894. Recorded: 31 Aug 1894

R. W. Lynch and W. L. Bowers, Exrs to LWT of J. W. Lynch in Account with said Estate from 1 Jul 1893 to 1 Jul 1894
Page 416-418

To amount on hand from last Return, see Book L, page 234
2 vouchers. Filed: 12 Jul 1894. Recorded: 12 Sept 1894

Estate of J. E. Spurlin as Admr in Account Current with the Estate of Sarah Jones, decd
Page 419-420

4 vouchers. Filed: 28 Jul 1894. Recorded: 13 Sept 1894

Fifth Annual Return of Lavender R. Ray as Admr of Estate of Matthew Read, decd...from 4 Feb 1893 to 4 Feb 1894
Page 421-433

Amount of Sale Bill, land sold in Campbell Co., Nov 1883.
Vouchers 96-116.
Heirs receipts, as follows -
Mary Stern of New York City by Thomas W. Latham, her Agt and atty in fact

Michael Keegan of Great Britain, Ireland, County Meath, by his Agt and atty in fact, Thomas W. Latham

Matthew S. Reade of New York City by his Agt and atty in fact, Thomas W. Latham

James Hughes of New York City, by his Agent and Atty in fact, Thomas W. Latham

Rose Mary Hughes of New York City by Thomas W. Latham, her Agt and atty in fact

James Keegan, Admr of Estate of Ann Keegan of New York City
Filed: 1 Aug 1894. Recorded: 18 Sept 1894

J. L. McLucas, Gdn for Ada, Ben, Robert and Glenn Harrison...from 1 Jul 1893 to 1 Jul 1894
Page 434-436

To amount of principal on hand from last Return, see Book L, page 286
6 vouchers. Recorded: 17 Oct 1894

Mrs. B. J. Carlisle, Gdn for Paul Carlisle, Hester B. Carlisle and Lizzie J. Carlisle from time of her appointment as Gdn Jul Term 1887 to 1 Jul 1894
Page 436-438

7 vouchers. Recorded: 16 Nov 1894

H. P. Landrum, Gdn for Mrs. Nannie J. Landrum nee Nannie J. Milam....from time of his appointment as such Gdn to 21 Sept 1894, the same being a Final Return with said ward
Page 439

Vou. #1, Received of H. P. Landrum, Gdn, $404.52 in full of all my interest in the estate of my father, J. R. Milam,decd. /s/Nannie J.Landrum
Recorded: 19 Nov 1894

Supplementary of J. E. Spurlin Exr of J. M. Spurlin, decd, to Return of 7 May 1894, this 1 Oct 1894
Page 440-441

2 vouchers. Recorded: 19 Nov 1894

Final Return of Daniel McLucas, Gdn for A. C., D. M., G. D. and Effie C. Harrison
Page 441-442

Receipt for distributive shares on estate of (herr father) - Effie Harrison
Recorded: Jan Term 1895

Mrs. F. C. Speer, Admx, and S. E. Speer, Admr of Estate of J. J. Speer, from 1 Jun 1893 to 24 Dec 1894
Page 442-449

Heirs receipts, as follows -

S. A. F. Brown
Tallulah Harrell
M. E. Speer (from estate of my father, J. J. Speer)
S. E. Speer
Bertha Davis
E. M. Tinsley
J. J. Speer
25 vouchers. Filed: 24 Dec 1895. Recorded: 11 Feb 1895

J. W. Dixon, Gdn for A. E. Burge, an Account from the time of his appointment as Gdn to 21 Jan 1895
Page 449-450

6 vouchers. Filed: 22 Jan 1895. Recorded: 14 Mar 1895

Return of W. P. Lanier, surviving security of James H. Lanier who was Gdn for his own children
Page 450-452

Vou. #1. This is to show that I received from my father, J. A. Lanier, in his lifetime, all that was due from him as my Gdn.../s/W. C. Lanier

Vou. #2. This is to show that I received from my father, J. A. Lanier, in his lifetime, all that was due me from him as my Gdn..../s/Sallie Slaton

Vou. #3. This is to show that I received from my father, J. A. Lanier, in his lifetime, all that was due me from him as my Gdn..../s/Alice Smith

Vou. #4. This is to show that I received from my father, J. A. Lanier, in his lifetime, all that was due me from him as my Gdn...../s/Cora L. Smith

Recorded: 16 Mar 1895

Mary A. Leach, Admx of Estate of E. W. Leach, late of Fayette Co., decd, from time of her appointment, Jul Term of 1893 including 18 Mar 1895, same being a Final Settlement of said estate
Page 453-455

Vou. #3, Received of Mrs. Mary A. Leach, Admx of Estate of E. W. Leach, decd, who was the former Gdn of Elizabeth Flowers, formerly Swanson, and M. W. Swanson, minor children of Samuel Swanson, decd..../s/W.T. Glower, Gdn, dated 16 Sept 1894

Heirs receipt of - W. A. Leach and N. C. Smith
7 vouchers. Filed: 26 Mar 1895. Recorded: 11 May 1895

J. W. Kitchens, Gdn of his children - R. G., C.W., J. H. and M. M. M. Kitchens, from 1 Jul 1889 including 12 Apr 1895 the same showing a Settlement with R. G. Kitchens, he being 21 years of age
Page 456-457

To amount on hand from last Return, see Book K, page 254

Receipt of R. G. Kitchens for full settlement of estate of his mother, Roxa E. Kitchens, dated 12 Apr 1895. Filed: 13 Apr 1895. Recorded: 13 Jun 1895

Benjamin Hutchinson, Gdn of Robert E. and Ida R. Kelley from 1 May 1894 to 1 May 1895
Page 457-458

To amount on hand from last Return, see Book L, page 353. 4 vouchers.
Filed: 3 May 1895. Recrded: 20 Jun 1895

Mrs. S. A. Gable, Admx, and N. W. Gable, Admr of N. W. Gable from 1 Jul 1894 to dismissal of administration of said estate
Page 459-469

To amount on hand from last Return, see Book L, page 388
Part of land indower and 1/3rd of rent was kept by the widow
21 vouchers.

Filed: 17 May 1895. Recorded: 9 Jul 1895

J. P. Starr, Gdn for H. T. Matthews, M. C. Matthews, J. C. Matthews, S. Matthews and Nannie Matthews, minor children of Robert Matthews...from 1 Jul 1894 to 1 Jul 1895
Page 470-471

To amount on hand from last Return, see Book L, page 414
Recorded: 8 Aug 1895

Mrs. N. C. Adams, Gdn for Mrs. E. A. Cook, nee Miss E. A. Whitlock...from 1 Jul 1894 to 1 Jul 1895
Page 471-472

To amount on hand from last Return, see Book L, page 372
Recorded: 8 Aug 1895

Mrs. B. J. Carlisle, Gdn for Paul, Hester B. and Lizzie Carlisle in Account Current with said wards (they being her own children), from 1 Jul 1894 to 1 Jul 1895
Page 472-474

To amount on hand from last Return, see Book L, page 436
Recorded: 13 Aug 1895

Annual Return of Mrs. M. W. Dickenson, Admr of O. T. Malone, decd
Page 474

1 voucher. Recorded: 15 Aug 1895

J. E. Spurlin, in Account Current with the Estate of Sarah Jones, decd
Page 475

3 vouchers. Recorded: 13 Aug 1895

Mrs. R. A. Ellington, Gdn for Z. P. Ellington, R. F. Ellington and J. S. Ellington from 25 Jan 1894 to 25 Jan 1895
Page 476-478

To amount on hand from last Return, see Book L, page 364
4 vouchers. Recorded: 15 Aug 1895

Real Estate, Sixth Annual Return of Lavender R. Ray as Admr of Estate of Matthew Read, decd, from 4 Feb 1894 to 4 Feb 1895
Page 478-481

Vouchers 117-124
Recorded: 24 Sept 1895

R. W. Lynch, one of the Exrs of the LWT of J. W. Lynch from 1 Jul 1894 to 1 Jul 1895
Page 482-483

To amount on hand from last Return, see Book L, page 416
5 vouchers.
Recorded: 27 Sept 1895

A. Steinheimer, Admr of Estate of B. F. Posey from 3 Apr 1894 to 3 Sept 1895
Page 484-485

6 vouchers. Recorded: 11 Oct 1895

Mrs. N. T. Dickson, Gdn for Oscar L., Lester C., Lela M., Willie A. and Johnie M. Dickson, orphans of J. M. Dickson, from 1 Jul 1894 to 1 Jul 1895
Page 486-490

To amount of wards money on hand last Return, see Book L, page 384
10 vouchers. Recorded: 11 Nov 1895

Estate of William B. Jones, decd
Page 490-491

Recorded: 14 Nov 1895

Return of J. L. McLucas, Gdn for Ada, Ben, Robert and Glen Harrison, minor children of Larkin Harrison, decd, from 1 Jul 1894 to 1 Jul 1895
Page 492-493

4 vouchers. ecorded: 12 Nov 1895

J. H. Jones, Admr of Estate of W. C. Reeves from time of his appointment to 21 Oct 1895
Page 493-494

I was appointed Admr of said estate to defend the title of land of said estate. The whole of said estate having been set aside as a years support for the widow and children of W. C. Reeves before I was appointed....

5 vouchers. Recorded: 6 Dec 1895

H. S. Rivers, Gdn of Miss M. W. Milam from 1 May 1894 to 1 May 1895
Page 495-497

To amount on hand from last Return, see Book L, page 270. 6 vouchers.
Recorded: 23 Jan 1896

Nancy M. Snead, Gdn for John W. and Mamie Snead
Page 497

Woolsy, Ga., Feb 25, 1896

This is to certify that I, Nancy M. Snead, Gdn for John W. and Mamie Snead, now have on hand the following property belonging to my words ($1100.00) /s/N. W. Snead, Gdn
Recorded: 16 Apr 1896

A. Steinheimer, Admr of Estate of B. F. Posey from 3 Apr 1894 to 30 Apr 1896, bgeing a Final Return
Page 498-499

To amount on hand from last Return, see Book L, page 484
3 vouchers. Recorded: 3 Jun 1896

Benjamin Hutchinson, Gdn of Ida R. Kelley from 1 May 1895 to 1 May 1896
Page 499-500

To amount on hand from last Return, see Book L, page 353
2 vouchers. Recorded: 1 Jul 1896

Mrs. R. A. Rivers nee R. A. Ellington, Gdn of Z. P., R. F. and J. S. Ellington, from 25 Jan 1895 to 25 May 1896
Page 500-502

To amount on hand from last Return, see Book L, page 476
7 vouchers. To cash paid - J. W. A. Speir, W. H. Redwine, Z. P. Ellington, J. S. Ellington, Z. P. Ellington and R. F. Ellington

Heir receipts (for his father, Z. T. Ellington), as follows - Z. P. Ellington
Recorded: 7 Aug 1896

Mrs. N. C. Adams, Gdn for Mrs. E. A. Cook nee Miss E. A. Whitlock from 1 Jul 1895 to 1 Jul 1896
Page 502

To amount on hand from last return see Book L, page 471
2 vouchers. Recorded: 8 Aug 1896

W. O. Graves, Admr of Estate of Jasper L. Graves, decd, from time of appointment to 2 Jan 1896
Page 503-504

6 vouchers.
Recorded: 18 Aug 1896

Annual Return of Mrs. M. W. Dickenson as Admx of O. T. Malone, decd
Page 505

1 voucher. Paid tuition of Sallie T. and Annie M. Malone.
Recorded: 18 Aug 1896

J. E. Spurlin in Account Current with Estate of Sarah Jones, 30 Jun 1896
Page 506-507

2 vouchers. Recorded: 10 Sept 1896

J. P. Starr, Gdn of minor heirs of Robert Matthews of Fayette Co., decd: M. C., J. C., S. F. and Nannie Matthews, from 1 Jul 1895 to 1 Jul 1896
Page 507-509

7 vouchers. To cash paid - R. L. Matthews for J. C. and S. F. Matthews, Clyde Matthews, Sarah Matthews, and D. M. Franklin.
Recorded: 17 Sept 1896

Estate of Robert Rivers in Account Current with R. A. Rivers, Admr from 1 Jul 1893 to 15 Jul 1896
Page 509-511

4 vouchers. Recorded: 19 Sept 1896

R. W. Lynch Exr of LWT of James W. Lynch from 1 Jul 1895 to 1 Jul 1896
Page 511-513

To amount on hand from last Return, see Book L, page 482
5 vouchers. Recorded: 22 Sept 1896

Mrs. N. T. Dickson, Gdn for Oscar T., Lester C., Lela M., Willie A. and Johnie M. Dickson, orphans of J. M. Dickson, and being her own children, from 1 Jul 1895 to 1 Jul 1896
Page 514-517

9 vouchers. To amount on hand from last Return, see Book L, page 486
Recorded: 16 Oct 1896

S. C. Travis, Admr of Estate of Robert Matthews, decd, from 22 May 1894 to 5 Nov 1896, the same being a Final Return
Page 518-519

3 vouchers. Recorded: 5 Nov 1896

W. D. Wallis in Account with Estate of James Graves, decd
Page 520-522

14 vouchers.
Heirs receipts, as follows -

W. C. Graves, Admr of Jasper L. Graves, decd
Permelia A. Franklin
Eliza E. Wallis
E. Neely

Recorded: 29 Feb 1897

R. F. Harper, Gdn fr his own children, John F., Nancy A., James E., Hattie E. and Martha A. Harper, in Account from the time of his appointment and qualification as such Gdn to and including 3 Feb 1897
Page 523

To amount received from Emanual Huffman of Macon Co., Alabama, Exr to the LWT of James Hoffman, decd, 28 Feb 1897.
2 vouchers. Recorded: 8 Mar 1897

J. W. Dixon, Gdn of Andrew E. Barge's Property in Account Current with said ward from 21 Jan 1895 to and including 21 Jan 1897
Page 524

Amount on hand from last Return, see Book L, page 449
3 vouchers. Recorded: 7 Apr 1897

J. A. J. Tidwell, Gdn of E. M. Milam whose name has previously been recorded as M. E. Milam in Account Current with his said ward from the time of his appointment as such Gdn and Settlement with H. S. Rivers, former Gdn, 3 Feb 1897 up to and including 13 Feb 1897
Page 525

To amount received of H. S. Rivers, former Gdn, see Book L, page 496
3 vouchers.
Recorded: 7 Apr 1897

Mrs. N. M. Snead, Gdn for her children, J. W. Snead and Mamie L. Snead, in Account Current with said wards and children from the time of her appointment as Gdn, Jan. Term 1894
Page 526-527

The reason for making this Return from time of my appointment as such Gdn is to correct the errors that are in former Returns which were made out by my uncle...recorded in Book L, page 452 and 497 of Annual Returns.

3 vouchers. Recorded: 7 Apr 1897

R. A. Rivers, Admr of Robert Rivers of Fayette Co., decd, in Account Current with said Estate from 1 Jul 1893 and including 10 Mar 1897
Page 527-534

The Returns made from 1 Jul 1893 to and including 15 Jul 1896 only showed a disposition of the share of J. C. Speir in said estate, he being a child of Mrs. Eliza A. Speir, daughter of Robert Rivers.

To amount received from sale of 28 acres of land, the same being the dower of Jane C. Rivers in the estate of Robert Rivers sold the 1st Tues. in Nv 1896 to L. J. Jones.

To amount on hand and due to minor heirs of Mrs. Eliza A. Speir 9 Jul 1893, see Book L, page 205

15 vouchers. Recorded: 6 May 1897

Vou. #4. Received of R.A. Rivers $19.00 in full for burial expenses of Mrs. Jane E. Rivers, decd, 28 Oct 1896. /s/W. T. Roberts

Vou. #11. Campbell Co., Ga., 11 Dec 1896. Received of R. A. Rivers, Admr of the Estate of Robert Rivers of Fayette Co., Ga., decd, $98.76 in full of all balance of my interests, rights and credits....../s/S. E. Lester

Vou. #12. Fayette Co., Ga., 11 Dec 1896. Received of R. A. Rivers, Admr of the Estate of Robert Rivers of Fayette Co., Ga., $98.16 1/2 in full of all balance of my interest, rights and credits in said estate............/s/J. N. Rivers

Vou. #13. Fayette Co., Ga., 11 Dec 1896. Received of R. A. Rivers, Admr of Estate of Robert Rivers of said county, decd, $98.16 1/2 in full of all balance of my interest, rights and credits in said estate............ /s/T. A. Thornton

Vou. #14. Campbell Co., Ga., 11 Dec 1896. Received of R. A. Rivers, Admr of Estate of Robert Rivers of said county, decd, $19.75 in full of all balance of my interest, rights and credits in said estate. /s/Jennie Banks

Vou. #15. Spalding Co., Ga., 5 Mar 1897. Received of R. A. Rivers, Admr of Estate of Robert Rivers of said county, decd, $19.75 in full of all balance of my interest, rights and credits in said estate. /s/R. R. Speir.

Benjamin Hutchinson, Gdn of Ada R. Kelley, in Account Current with said ward from 1 May 1896 to 1 May 1897
Page 534-535

To amount on hand at last Return, see Book L, page 499

3 vouchers. Recorded: 15 Jun 1897

J. P. Starr, Gdn for his minor Heirs of Robert Matthews of Fayette Co., Ga., decd, to-wit: M. C. Matthews, J. C. Matthews, S. F. Matthews and Nannie Matthews in Account Current with his said wards from 1 Jul 1896 to 1 Jul 1897
Page 535-536

To amount due wards at last Return, see Book L, page 507. By last Return there was due each ward as principal - $216.41 5/6

2 vouchers. Recorded: 6 Aug 1897

Mrs. R. A. Rivers nee R. A. Ellington, Gdn for her children - Paul Ellington, R. F. Ellington and J. S. Ellington in Account Current with her said wards from 25 Jan 1896 to 25 Jan 1897
Page 537-538

To amount due Paul Ellington at last Return, see Book L, page 500 - $142.77
To amount due R. F. and J. S. Ellington at last Return - $448.94 1/2

3 vouchers. Recorded: 7 Aug 1897

Mrs. N. C. Adams, Gdn for Mrs. E. A. Cook, nee Miss E. A. Whitlock, in Account Current with her said ward from 1 Jul 1896 to 1 Jul 1897
Page 539

To amount on hand from last Return, see Book L, page 502
1 voucher. Recorded: 25 Jun 1897

Return of John L. McLucas, Gdn for Ada, Ben, Robert and Glenn Harrison Showing Amount Received and Paid out in Account of said wards from 1 Jul 1895 to 1 Jul 1897
Page 540-544

No Return having been made for year 1896
18 vouchers. Recorded: 10 Aug 1897
Paid tuition at Fayetteville Institute in 1895 for Ben Harrison, Robert Harrison, Glenn Harrison
Ada Harrison received tuition for 1896-1897 from her guardian

W. O. Graves, Admr of Estate of Jasper L. Graves of Fayette Co., decd, in Account Current with said estate from 1 Jul 1896 to 1 Jul 1897
Page 544-546

To amount on hand from last Return, see Book L, page 503
To amount received of W. D. Wallis, Admr of Estate of James Graves, 25 Nov 1896
4000 lbs of cotton, which was set aside as a second years' support for widow and children
Rent of farm for second years' support for widow and children

7 vouchers.

Jasper L. Graves contd....

Heirs (children of Jasper L. Graves) receipts -

J. W. Graves
Naomi Graves
J. R. Graves
W. O. Graves

Receipt frm Pellie A. Graves, 30 Nov 1896, for second years' support for her and minor children.
Recorded: 16 Aug 1897

R. W. Lynch, one of the Exrs to the LWT of J. W. Lynch, late of Fayette Co., decd, in Account Current with said Estate from 1 Jul 1896 to 1 Jul 1897
Page 546-548

To amount on hand at last Return, see Book L, page 511.
4 vouchers. Vou. #3 addressed to Mrs. Lydia Lynch (for groceries)
Recorded: 20 Aug 1897

J. E. Spurlin, in Account Current with Estate of Sarah Jones, decd, 30 Jun 1897
Page 548

Paid taxes. 1 voucher. Recorded: 5 Jul 1897

James A. Chambers, Admr of Estate of W. B. Jones of Fayette Co., decd, in Account Current with said Estate from 11 Sept 1896 (see Book L, page 489) to 1 Jul 1897
Page 549-554

13 vouchers.
Vou. #5. Catharine Jones recovered against James A. Chambers, Admr of Burton Jones, decd, in Clayton Co., Ga. Superior Court, $175 plus interest, 9 Dec 1896.

Paid distributive shares to -
R. A. Jones (x, his mark) of Inman, Ga.
John B. Jones (x, his mark) of Inman, Ga.
W. F. Jones (x, his mark) of Inman, Ga.
Susan Aminda Turner (x, her mark) of Inman, Ga.
W. P. Jones (x, his mark) of Inman, Ga.
America E. Crawley (x, her mark) of Inman, Ga.
Tilder C. Jones (x, her mark) of Inman, Ga.
Recorded: 28 Sept 1897

Annual Return of L. J. McLane, Admr of the Estate of Charley Arnold, late of Fayette Co., 26 Jul 1897
Page 554-560

Return Sale Bill Perishable Property Book A, page 141
Real Estate sold to Baggerly Bros. 101 1/4 acres of land, No. 41
Real Estate sold to J. O. Towns 67 acres, No. 42

Dower laid off for Sallie Arnold, widow of Charley Arnold by J. M. Couch (x, his mark), James P. Chappell, Sandford Gay and J. M. Arnold
18 vouchers. Recorded: 26 Jul 1897

Mrs. C. S. McLucas, Admx of Estate of J. C. Hightower in Account Current with said Estate from 1 Jul 1893 to 30 Jul 1897, the same Showing a Final Settlement
Page 560-563

To balance on hand 1 Jul 1893, see Book L, page 239

Collected notes of - Q. C. Grice, S. C. Grice, J. W. Chambers, John McLucas, T. W. Tarpley, D. A. McLucas and J. B. Hightower
13 vouchers.

Distributive Shares paid to Heirs -

Fannie H. Elder
J. O. Hightower
M. C. Hill
Julia A. Mitchell (x, her mark)
Etta S. Tarpley
J. B. Hightower
C. S. McLucas

Recorded: 30 Sept 1897

J. Q. Landrum, Admr de bonis non of Estate of Edward Bearden, decd, from time of his appointment, Feb Term of 1892, to and including 31 Dec 1897
Page 564-569

17 vouchers.

Distributive Shares paid to -

M. J. Bearden (x, his mark)
S. D. Lambert
Susan Campbell (x, her mark)
Parthena Posten (x, her mark)
Alice Coln
Martha Head (x, her mark)
Wilson Pate
W. W. Bearden (x, his mark)
Island Bearden (x, his mark)
Lovice Bradley (x, her mark)
Sarah Bearden (x, her mark)
James Bearden (x, his mark)
Susan Campbell by B. J. Campbell
Aaron Campbell (x, his mark)
J. H. Campbell of Autauga Co., Alabama

Recorded: 30 Sept 1897

W. T. Murphy, Gdn of the Property of his children - Lula W. Fitzgerald (now Lula W. Murphy), Lee Dora McBride (now Lee Dora W. Murphy), John W. Murphy, Sarah L. Murphy, Mary Murphy, Nancy Murphy, Eva E. Murphy and Ida Murphy in Account Current from time of his appointment 16 Nov 1888 to and including 23 Aug 1897
Page 569-572

The property or money was received from the sale of their undivided interest in the land of their grandfather, Jonathan Mitchell of Fayette Co., Ga., decd. Their mother Charlotte Murphy being a daughter of said Jonathan Mitchell. This Return shows a final settlement with his children.

6 vouchers.
Distributees as follows -

Lula W. Fitzgerald (having become 21 years of age), of Fayette Co., Ga.
Lee Dora W. McBride (having become 21 years of age) of Fayette Co., Ga.
J. W. Murphy (having become 21 years of age) of Fayette Co.
Recorded: 8 Oct 1897

H. L. Hicks, Admr of Perry Hicks of Fayette Co. in Account Current from time of his appointment, 2 Sept. 1889 to 1 Jul 1897
Page 572-587

To amount received from sale of perishable property, see Sale Bill Book A, page 88
39 vouchers. Includes some Fi.Fas. and notes in Coweta Co. and Senoia, Ga. and Brooks Station, Ga.

Distribution to Heirs as follows -

J. E. Humphrey (x, his mark)
M. J. Reeves (x, her mark)
H. M. Hicks
D. Hicks of Waldo, Alechua Co., Florida
W. I. Hicks of Morgan Co., Alabama
H. L. Hicks
M. C. Pyron
M. C. Pyron as Gdn of Oscar Pyron, Jess Pyron, Lois Pyron and Zella Pyron
W. R. Harris
Susie E. Pounds
F. M. Swann of DeKalb Co., Alabama
J. A. Swann (x, his mark)
Willie Brown of Cass Co., Texas
Mattie Yancey of Cass Co., Texas
S. E. Pyron
Recorded: 5 Nov 1897

J. W. Kitchens, Gdn for his children, C. W., J. H. and M. M. M. Kitchens in Account Current with said wards from 12 Apr 1895 to 18 Sept 1897
Page 588-596

To amount on hand at last Return, see Book L, page 456
1 voucher
Recorded: 8 Nov 1897

T. J. McLane, Admr of Estate of Charley Arnold in Account Current with said Estate from 26 Jul 1897 to 4 Oct 1897, the same being a Final Return
Page 589

See Minutes of the Court and Book L of Annual Returns, page 554
11 vouchers includes notes given by Charley Arnold

Received from Estate of Charles Arnold $57.51 in full settlement against said estate. 23 Sept 1897. /s/T. J. McLane.

Recorded: 10 Dec 1897

END OF BOOK L

INDEX

-A-

A. GRAY & HARRIS, 237
A. S. FOSTER & CO., 238
ABERCROMBIE,
  W. J., 141
ACHORD,
  John F., 3
ADAMS,
  Amy, 170
  B., 316
  Benjamin, 235
  Bennett, 170, 183, 300, 315, 316
  D., 314
  Elias, 170
  Hiram, 219
  K. V., 401, 406, 419
  N. C., 401, 418, 439
  N. C., Mrs., 424, 430, 433, 436
  S., 283
  Sandford, 102, 333
  Sanford, 149, 170
  Thomas A., 166(2), 308
AKINS,
  John M., 46
  Rebecca J., 423
ALDINGS,
  E. R., 226
ALDRIDGE,
  P. H., 287
ALEXANDER,
  William, 98, 259
ALFORD,
  James W., 13
  Jemerson, 129, 337
ALLEN,
  Bryan, 25, 72
  Coleman A., 101
  E. P., 10, 12, 13, 25(2)
  Elijah P., 13, 18, 25(2)
  George, 13
  J. B., 217
  James M., 270

John, 30
John B., 30, 65, 93, 207, 221, 236, 257, 288
M. P., 395
Morris H., 101, 270
P. E., 43
P. H., 59, 108, 253, 255, 270
Patrick H., 19, 92(4), 113, 124, 231, 267
Stephen W., 216
W. P., 5, 21, 26, 107, 200
W. S., 270
Whitmel P., 91, 92(2), 108, 113
Whitmell P., 92(2)
Whitmill, 270
William L., 295
William S., 115, 241
Y. L., 226
Y. S., 219
ALLISON,
  P. H., 111
ANDERSON,
  W. P., 364
ANDREWS,
  Rufus W., 313
ANSLEY,
  Emma J., 132
  John, 132
ANTHONY,
  Barr B., 25
  Bob, 25
  Harriet Ann, 235
  I. M., 25
  I. T., 17
  J., 54
  James M., 226
  Jesse T., 32, 109(2), 111, 226, 239
  John D., 44, 226, 235
  Joseph, 22, 25, 34, 226, 235
  Middleton M., 235
  Poll, 239
  Polley, 235

S. M., 25
ANTONY,
  James, 259
ARCHER,
  William E., 135
ARMSTRONG,
  E. J., 403
  W., 324
ARNOLD,
  Barny, 325
  C. M., 242, 256, 277
  Charles, 443
  Charley, 440, 443
  J. M., 339(2), 440
  J. W., 310
  P. E., 276
  Sallie, 440
ASKEW,
  D. R., 39
  J. T., 363
  Kittie, 420
  T. J., 314, 315, 316, 331
ATKINSON,
  B., 226
  F. E., 362
  Jesse, 31
  Sarah, 55
  William, 31, 55
  William A., 65
ATTAWAY,
  John W., 232
ATTKINSON,
  Jesse, 65(2)
  John D., 65
  Joseph, 65
  Sarah, 65
  William, 65(2)
ATTKISSON,
  J., 20
  Jesse, 20
  Sarah, 20
  William, 20(2)
AUSTELL,
  Alfred, 104(2), 112
AUSTELL & CAMP, 71
AUSTIN,

444

INDEX

AUSTIN (continued)
  Alfred, 203
  C. E., 346
  Charles, 262, 327, 329
  I. M., 111, 222
  J. M., 182, 275, 329, 336
  James, 39, 275
  James M., 132, 139,
    141(2), 181, 182, 309, 337

  M., 326
  N., 329
AVERA,
  A. B., 178
  Barbary, 77
  Elizabeth Anne, 77
  I. B., 254, 278, 323, 345
  Isaac B., 19, 77, 274,
    276, 290
  J. B., 69, 303
  Mary Jane, 77(2)
  R. M., 19
  R., Mrs., 19
  William H., 19, 77

-B-

BABB,
  Kellet, 321
BAGGETT,
  William, 94
BAGLEY,
  William, 320
BAGWELL,
  B., 382
  Blakely, 189(2), 329, 368,
    374, 382
  Blakly, 363
  J. S., 304
  J. W., 304
  John, 189(2), 368, 374,
    382
  John T., 138, 155
  John W., 155
  Mary, 189, 321, 329, 363,
    382
  Mary S., 155(2), 322
BAILEY,

Bethena, 376
Charles, 141, 200, 218(2),
  309(2)
Charlie, 309
Dover, 309
J. R., 312
James R., 145, 304(2),
  312(2)
Jefferson, 309
Loisa, 312
Mary C., 309
BAILY,
  Bethena, 363, 366, 384
  Charles, 153, 155, 158(3),
    167(4), 172(2)
  Charles Jefferson, 173
  Dorah, 158, 167
  James R., 326(2)
  Jefferson, 158, 167
  John C., 158, 167, 172
  Madora, 173
  Mary C., 158, 172
  R., 362(2)
  Samuel, 338
  Sarah, 73, 356, 363, 366
BAKER,
  Elisha, 35, 295
  J. W., 295
  James, 132, 319
  Jane, 420
  Mathew, 132, 319
  O. O., 314
BAKS,
  William T., 18
BALLARD,
  Elijah, 35, 56
  Indiana, 304
  Lorenza, 304
  Margaret A., 304, 313
  Martha, 358
  Martha L., 312, 313, 319,
    330
  Mary, 354
  Mary A. E., 337, 345
  Mary Indian E., 179
  Sarah, 304(2)
  Sarah C., 177, 312, 313,
    319, 323(2)

T. W., 315, 322, 339, 342,
  343
Thomas W., 221
W., 345
Walter, 312(2)
William, 119, 176(2), 177,
  179, 248, 262, 304,
  312(3), 313(2), 319, 330,
  337, 358
William B., 176(2)
William M., 313
BANISTER,
  Guy, 306, 315(2)
  Guy Anna, 304
  Cuyanna, 306, 315
  Jesse, 265
  John, 306
  John L., 304, 315
  Louanna, 306
  Louisa, 304(2), 315
  O. F., 315
  O. T., 304, 306
BANKS,
  A. D., 371, 425
  B. T., 371
  Belzie, 425
  Bradford, 157
  F. M., 371
  G. S., 386
  George S., 386
  H., 231
  Henry, 230, 280(2)
  I. N., 371
  J. A., 238
  J. C., 238
  J. G., 425
  J. M., 386
  J. W., 314
  Jennie, 438
  John G., 371
  Joseph, 310, 314(2), 331,
    360, 371
  Joseph N., 386
  K. D., 425(2)
  Kinnan, 144
  Kinyon B., 371
  Nancy, 331
  Nettie Ann, 144

INDEX

Netty, 371
S. F., 38, 63
Saley, 425
Sandford, 386
Sarah E., 371
W. P., 360
W. L., 371
William, 231
Wiseman, 71, 386
BANNISTER,
 Guy, 304
BARENTINE,
 Jesse, 173
BARFIELD,
 J. N., 9
 James M., 9
BARGE,
 Andrew E., 437
 E. M., 303, 330, 334
 Emily A., 325
 Z. T., 331
BARINTINE,
 Daniel, 127
 David, 128, 238, 278, 287
 Jesse, 94, 127, 128, 209,
  216, 232, 242, 287
 Jesse, Jr., 84
 Mary, 278
 Nancy, 209
 Sarah Elizabeth, 209
BARNES,
 Clestia A., 407
 J. I. I., 9
 Michael, 9
 William J., 26
BARNS,
 W. D., 9
BARR,
 J., 232
BARRENTINE,
 David, 299
 Elizabeth, 254
 George W., 386
 Jacob W., 386
 Jesse, 192, 206, 299
 L. C., 386
 Martha, 386
 Mary, 299

BARRINGTON,
 Jesse, 261
BARRINTINE,
 Jesse, 131, 257, 261
 Sarah E., 261
BARRON,
 John, 210
BARROW,
 John, 290
BATEMAN,
 David R., 271
 Eliza, 271
 Howel T., 271
 William, 271(2)
BATES,
 William T., 15, 32
BAUGH,
 A. J., 389
 E. J., 389
 Ephraim, 389
 Robert, 311
BEADSIL,
 G., 1
 Sarah, 1
 Turner, 1
BEALL,
 Augustus R., 2, 14
 M. A. H., Mrs., 13
 P. O., 2, 13, 14
 R., 13
 Thadeus, 13
BEARD,
 M. E., 415
BEARDEN,
 Aaron, 36
 Agnes, 54
 Asa I., 275, 283
 Asa J., 84, 198, 211, 251
 E. L. S., 382
 Edward, 24, 28, 36, 54,
  179, 198(4), 199, 211,
  212, 223, 251, 275,
  283(2), 441
 Edwin, 201
 Evaline S., 179
 Frances, 283
 Frances, Mrs., 54
 Francis, 62

 G., 314
 G. W., 311
 Island, 441
 J. A., 311
 James, 441
 Jefferson, 84, 199, 211
 Larkin, 84, 198, 212, 251,
  275, 283
 M. A. E., 318
 M. J., 441
 M. J. E., 360
 Martha A. E., 179
 Mary J. E., 179
 Parthena, 84, 251
 Partheny, 211
 Perthena, 198
 Quiller, 84, 199, 211, 251
 Sarah, 441
 Sarah A., 198, 211
 Sarah Ann, 84(2), 251,
  275, 283
 Sisley A., 398
 Solomon, 54
 Susan F., 179
 Vicy, 54(2), 62, 201, 223
 W. A., 382
 W. P., 311
 W. M., 382
 W. T., 311
 W. W., 179(2), 201,
  311(3), 318, 328, 360,
  382, 441
 Washington, 59
 William W., 54(3), 62, 223
 Willis N., 179
 Y. H., 179
BEARDIN,
 L. T., 365
 W. W., 365
BEAVERS,
 Cornelius, 26
 Martha, 222
 W., 219
 Willis, 109, 111, 219,
  222, 227, 228, 238, 239,
  248, 268, 286, 296
 Willis C., 108
BECKMON,

INDEX

BECKMON (continued)
  J. F., 313
BEDSIL,
  Sarah, 8, 31
  Turner, 8
BEEKS,
  J. A., 249
BELISH,
  Louisa J., 371
BELLILE,
  Martin, 128
BELLISLE,
  L. J., 425
BENNETT,
  C. E., 27, 101, 114, 124,
    127, 139, 187, 205, 219,
    225, 238, 240(2), 241(2),
    263, 271, 275(2), 281,
    291, 334
  Chambers E., 105
  Cornelius, 99
  E. E., 237
  Ida M., 407
  Ida Matthews, 407
  J. S., 388
  R. H., 187, 408
  T. C., 228
  Thomas, 4
  William, 4(2), 51, 65,
    105, 114, 121, 127, 256,
    297
BENTLY,
  Jacob, 23
BEORNY,
  W. A., 22
BERRY,
  David J., 10
  George M., 77
  Wiley, 235
BETHUNE,
  P. M., 363
BETSILL,
  Godfrey J., 63
BETTERTON,
  Mollie, 349
BETTS,
  William O., 226
BILES,

  C. W., 331, 345
  Charles W., 327, 334
BIRD,
  Mary, 420
BIRDSON,
  Henry, 349
BISHOP,
  Amanda, 7
  Amandy Caroline, 126
  Elbert, 71, 82, 83, 201,
    222, 259, 279, 287
  Elisa, 16
  Eliza, 21, 30
  Francis, 126
  Henry, 138
  Joseph, 138
  Lavonia, 126
  M. T., 7, 17
  Martha T., 31
  Mathew T., 22, 61
  Matthew T., 16, 21, 30
  Moses T., 287
  Nancy, 31, 61
  Nancy T., 17
  Prometia Thomas, 126
  S. A., 413
  Sarah P., 126
  T. H., 274
  W., 227
  W. G., 327, 405(2)
  William C., 287
  William G., 158, 161
  William M., 126
  William S., 287
  Willis M., 137, 138, 238
BITTERTON,
  Joseph R., 239
BIVINS,
  W. J., 219
BLACK,
  D. A. J., 311(2)
  James, 147, 165
BLACKMAN,
  William, 21
BLACKWELL,
  Ambrose, 9
  William R., 32
BLALOCK,

  A. C., 367, 385, 387
  A. O., 386, 388, 399
  A. W., 258
  G. Z., 385
  I. L., 55
  J. E., 367, 385, 417
  J. F., 115
  J. H., 417
  J. L., 19, 65, 126, 128,
    169, 180, 187, 188, 191,
    193(2), 217, 223(2), 229,
    237, 238, 252, 270, 417
  J. M., 271
  J. O., 340(2)
  J. S., 189, 235
  Jesse, 188
  Jesse L., 47, 78(2), 79,
    127, 129(2), 164, 195
  Jessie L., 210
  John L., 164
  L., 71
  L. A., 336
  L. B., 177, 309
  L. F., 99, 105, 110, 112,
    114, 122, 123(2), 130,
    131, 133, 134, 135,
    137(2), 138, 139, 140,
    142, 145, 146, 147, 148,
    162, 173, 180, 217, 219,
    238, 250, 254(2), 256,
    273(2), 279, 293(3), 297,
    314, 348(2), 349, 367,
    406(2), 411(2), 428
  Lewis F., 122, 125(3),
    155, 164, 270
  M. A., 385
  O. O., 385
  S. C., 417
  S. F., 228
  S. T., 385, 386, 387, 388
  T. F., 417
  W. H., 10, 19, 32, 69, 71,
    217, 290, 314
  W. N., 19
  William B., 55
  William H., 32, 78, 80,
    81(2), 84, 94, 109, 117,
    118, 120, 122(2), 137,

INDEX

138, 139, 140, 151, 167,
168, 198(2), 199, 211,
212, 238, 251, 275,
283(2), 287, 298
Y. B., 310
Z., 120, 222
Z. B., 169, 183, 184, 219,
233, 238, 284, 314, 321,
322, 324, 348, 353, 357,
360(2), 362, 367, 385
Zadock, 77, 84, 109, 228,
283
Zadok, 77, 80, 112, 168,
247, 270
BLALOCK & BROS., 224, 238,
248, 271
BLALOCK & CAMP, 293
BLALOCK & CO., 228
BLAND,
  Simeon, 3
BLANKENSHIP,
  John T., 271(2)
  Tempy, 271
BLAYLOCK,
  Z., 25(2), 27, 33
BLOODWORTH,
  S. W., 18
BOATRIGHT,
  C. U., 147
  E. W., 348
BOGGERS,
  E. H., 385
  Emmet H., 391
BOGGS,
  Amanda, 407
  Amanda J., 384, 390
BOGGUS,
  E. H., 387
BOLTON,
  Elisha P., 67
BOOTHE,
  Archibald, 3
BORMAN,
  G. W., 336
BOSWORTH,
  I., 18
  J. R., 31(2)
  James, 31(2)

Josiah R., 18(2), 31(2)
Phillip H., 116
Thomas C., 18, 31
W. W., 110, 112, 116, 181,
219, 238, 254
Wiley W., 112, 162
Wyley, 181
BOTTOMS,
  A. L., 274
  Aaron L., 261
  G. W., 334, 341
  James, 137(2), 248
  Martha, 261
BOWEN,
  C. C., 71
  Christopher C., 52, 53,
    76, 81, 83
  Chrit, 73
  John, 83
BOWERS,
  Jacob, 200(2), 332
  John, 240(2), 271(2)
  L. J., 200
  Levi B., 264
  Lovick, 227
  W. L., 418, 423, 431
BOWLIN,
  C., 21
BOWLS,
  W., 238
BOYD,
  Caroline M., 144
  James, 133, 134, 139, 143,
    144, 208, 302, 345, 369,
    382
  M. H., 143
  William H., 144
BOYNTON & DISMUKE, 361
BOZEE,
  M., 13
BOZEMAN,
  James W., 123
  R. L. G., 121
BRADBERRY,
  James, 168
BRADLEY,
  J. P., 223
  Lovice, 441

Vicy, 223
William, 217, 237, 275,
297
BRADLY,
  William, 242
BRAGG,
  Beulah, 429(2)
BRANTLEY,
  Dora, 381
  F. M., 362
  F. M., Jr., 362
BRASENTINE,
  Daniel, 274
BRASLEY,
  William, 18
BRASSELL,
  Alice, 361
  Anna F., 361
  B. W., 237
  C. E., 224
  Delilah F., 361
  Eliza, 361
  Emma, 361
  Fannie, 366
  J. C., 72
  J. L., 238
  J. W., 366
  Jabez, 252
  Jabez M., 61, 79
  James, 72(2), 83, 203, 206
  James T., 83, 203, 206
  Jesse W., 361
  John, 32, 219
  John C., 9, 14, 31, 45(2),
    61, 72, 91, 92(2), 94(2),
    95, 100, 107, 136, 137,
    138, 140, 143, 152, 156,
    157(2), 220
  John O., 22
  Mary, 361
  Napoleon B., 361
  Nellie E., 361
  P. H., 22, 31, 35, 72(2),
    171, 224, 225, 233, 240,
    271, 384
  P. H., Dr., 194
  Philip H., 44, 129, 153
  Phillip H., 92(2), 100,

INDEX

BRASSELL (continued)
106, 107, 116, 129,
156(2), 204, 233, 234,
252(2), 253, 266, 269,
284(2), 285
Phillip S., 62
Rosamond, 361
T. W., 366
William, 9, 129(2), 206,
285
William H., 234
Willis, 94(2), 95, 107,
129(3), 135, 203, 206(2),
361, 366
BRASSELL & MAY, 193, 194
BRASSELL & RODGERS, 224
BRASSELL & ROGERS, 226
BRAY,
Cynthia, 263
Syntha, 236
William, 105, 106, 199(2),
216, 236, 238, 263(2)
BRIDGES,
B. C., 200
Ida, 347, 363
J. M., 336, 347, 363
James, 322, 336
James H., 188
P. C., 324
R. B., 22
R. C., 200, 237, 321, 336,
347, 363
R. E., 188, 237
Rachel, 347, 363
Robert C., 140, 141,
143(2), 145
S. T., 189, 314(2), 322,
333, 358, 364, 376
Solomon, 117
Solomon T., 121, 165, 258,
263, 309
Thomas, 347, 363(2)
BRIDGET,
S. T., 372
BRIGGS,
L. B., 369
BROGDEN,
John, 7, 9

Rebecca, 220
BROGDON,
C. B., 391
J. T., 320, 348, 396
J.T., 344
Rebecca, 199, 214
BROOKS,
A. G., 193, 232, 288
Albert G., 90(2)
George, 247
George W., 90, 167(2),
196, 208, 229, 269, 287
Harriet T., 90, 193, 232
Harriett T., 129, 288
Hillery, 140, 141, 143(2),
145, 361, 373, 377, 381,
392, 398, 419
Ivey, 90, 208(3), 232(2),
269(2), 288
Ivy, 229
J. M., 245(2)
J. R., 309, 419
Jacob, 212
Jacob M., 212
Jesse, 226
John N., 90, 196, 208,
232, 247, 269, 287
John R., 167(2), 172(2),
173
Lewis, 258
Rachael L., 212
Rachel L., 212, 245
Thornton, 361
William A., 158
William J., 163
BROTHERTON,
C. H., 360
W. H., 352, 391
BROWN,
A. J., 13, 22, 235
Alford, 283
Alfred, 7, 9, 15, 83, 91,
99, 205, 224
Benjamin, 115
Burrell, 3, 205(2), 226
D. A., 395
Demcy, 258, 403
Dempsey, 115(2), 226, 321,

322
E., 34
E. B., 427
Early, 262
Epps, 37, 70
Harlin, 364
J. A., 314, 328, 403
J. O., 347
J. W., 333, 353, 360
James, 226
James A., 306
James H., 322
John O., 99, 104, 154,
205, 224, 254, 283
Killis, 102, 104, 214,
226, 246, 298
Lenah W., 70
Lucy J., 395
M., 200
Martin, 322
Murphy, 39
R. A., 274
S. A., 387, 390
S. A. F., 432
Samuel, 258
Silas, Mia.
T. L., 394(2)
Thomas, 32
Thomas F., 17
W. M., 403
W. S., 173
Washington, 57
William G., 12
Willie, 442
Willie A., 394
Willis, 226, 268, 281
BUCKS,
J. A., 238
BUFFINGTON,
H., 20, 61
Henderson, 292
BULL,
Ida, 400
BULLARD,
C. L., 369
Mary A. E., 361, 366, 369
Mary H. E., 369
BUNE,

I N D E X

J., 228
BURCH,
  Martin N., 5
BURDETT,
  John L., 364
BURGAMY,
  Eli, 140, 141
  Emory G., 160
  Frances Jane, 141(2)
  John, 160, 286
  Pearch O., 142
BURGE,
  A. E., 432
  Edward H., 165
  Edwin W., 165
BURK,
  John, 114, 287
BURK HANCOCK & CO., 352
BURKE,
  Sarah Ann, 188
BURKS,
  Emily, 285
  Tilman, 218, 285
BURNS,
  James W., 285
  Mary, 285
BURNSIDE,
  A., 108
  Jackson, 235
  Julia, 108
  T., Mrs., 235
  Thomas, 108, 235
BURRELL,
  William, 187
BUSE,
  John, 44, 73
  William, 44, 73
BUSH,
  Mary, 246
  Mary E., 246
  Sarah F., 246
  William T., 246
BUSKIN,
  W. D., 330
BUSTER,
  E. C., 336
BUSTIAN,
  E. C., 360

BUSTIN,
  B. C., 274
  C. C., 319(2)
  E. C., 208, 274, 328, 334,
    355(2)
  E. W., 324
  Edward C., 171
BUTLER,
  George, 367
  George W., 387
  J. L., 312
  Martha A., 362, 367, 373,
    387, 392, 410, 415
  S. A. Emma, 312
BUTTS,
  Lucy, 413
BYINGTON,
  M. P., 58, 59(2)
BYNES,
  James, 265
BYRNE,
  T., 11, 21(2), 348
  Thomas, 9, 55, 66
BYROM,
  T., 10, 21
  Thomas, 18
BYROM & MYERS, 240
BYRUM,
  T., 19

-C-

C. H. JOHNSON & CO., 71
CALHOUN,
  James M., 258
CALLAWAY,
  E. M., 70
  Joshua, 238
  Joshua S., 225
CALLOWAY,
  Joshua S., 91
  JoshuaS., 205
CALVERSON,
  I., 219
CALWELL,
  John J., 32
CAMP,
  Abner, 32, 57, 79, 195,

    235
  Benjamin, 104(2), 112
  Caroline D., 124
  James M., 124, 128, 139,
    277
  John, 57, 79
  Joseph, 226
  M., 203, 219
  Nathan, 82, 97, 102,
    104(2), 112, 203, 219, 233

  Seaborn, 57
  Thomas J., 104(2), 219
  William, 256
CAMP & BLALOCK, 314(3)
CAMP & CHRISTIAN, 238(2)
CAMP & PARKER, 391
CAMPBELL,
  Aaron, 441
  B. J., 441
  E. D., 301
  J. H., 441
  Louisa E., Miss, 54
  Susan, 441(2)
  Thomas E., 54
  W. J., 314, 321, 328, 356
  Walter J., 54, 76
  William J., 57
CANES,
  David, 235
CANNON,
  Joshua, 120, 225, 270,
    282, 288, 289
  T. C., 417
CANNON & EVANS, 417
CARDEN,
  Laura S., 407
CAREW,
  Rody, 198
CARGILE,
  F. W., 430
  Fred C., 426, 430
  Jesse R., 426, 430
  John W., 426
  Stark B., 426, 430
  Walter S., 426, 430(2)
CARISON,
  J. J., 274

INDEX

CARLILE,
 J. N., 370
 James M., 392
CARLISLE,
 B. J., 410
 B. J., Mrs., 432, 434
 Hester B., 432, 434
 J. M., 396, 398, 410(2)
 James, 410
 James M., 388, 398
 Lizzie, 434
 Lizzie J., 432
 Paul, 432, 434
CARMICHAEL,
 J. A., 321(2), 324, 366,
  371, 374
 Patrick, 377
CARROLL,
 E. I., 4
 Elizabeth, 5
 Emily J., 23(2)
 Emily Jane, 4
 Emily L., 11
 Francis, 30
 Francis A., 24
 Francis M., 2, 4, 12, 17,
  41
 H. H., 71
 James, 5, 30
 John, 5, 30
 Levi, 3
 M. L., 4
 Narcus L., 4, 30
 Martha, 303
 Thomas, 2(3), 3, 4, 5(5),
  11, 12, 23(2), 24(3), 30,
  41
CARSON,
 Brassell, 125(2)
 Frances A. E., 289
 Francis, 166
 Francis E., 149
 J. J., 215, 230
 James J., 125, 136, 138,
  149, 289(2)
CARTER,
 J. W., 377
 Jesse, 133

Jesse H., 133
John W., 163
Mary E., 163
R. A., 377
Teresa A., 377
CASTLEBERRY,
 Jason, 239
CATO,
 A. C., 341
 Emily C., 403
 N. C., 334
 William, 316
CAVENDER,
 Delilah, 14, 22
 John, 61
 John H., 92(2), 204
 Joseph H., 35, 62, 204,
  252, 266, 284
 Joseph W., 44
 Martha A., 267
 Martha M., 45, 61, 91,
  204, 224, 280, 296
 Mary M., 241
 W. H., 13, 14
 Wade H., 14, 22, 31, 44,
  45(2), 61(2), 62, 91,
  92(2), 204, 224, 233, 241,
  252, 266, 267, 280, 284,
  296
 William A., 61
CEGGANS,
 Silas, 238
CHAFFIN,
 E. F., 378
 T. H., 378
CHAMBERS,
 J. P. R., 235
 J. W., 441
 James A., 185, 186, 440(2)
 M. S. P., 235
 Mary A., 351
 William S., 100, 220, 235
CHAMPION,
 Abner, 14(2), 15(2),
  20(4), 32(2), 33(2), 42,
  43, 58(2)
 Abner G., 10, 11, 15, 20,
  33, 43, 58

Abner M., 10(4), 11(4)
Adison, 10, 20
Adison C., 11
Adison J., 33
Adison L., 15
Allison, 58
Allison J., 42
Cintha P., 32
Cynthia A., 14, 42
Elizabeth A., 42
Meriman P., 10, 11, 14,
 20, 32
Synthia, 11
Synthia A., 10, 20
William, 20(4)
William C., 10(4), 11(4),
 14(2), 15(2), 32(2),
 33(2), 42(2), 43, 58
Willis, 16, 32
CHANDLER,
 A., 57
 Anna, 263, 333
 F. M., 333
 Isaac, 348
 J., 333
 J. W., 333
 James, 348
 John, 333, 348
 W. P., 277, 303, 320, 324,
  333, 334
 W. T., 187
 Wiel, 348
 Wiet, 355
 William P., 120(2), 121,
  266, 277, 293, 335
 Wit, 324
 Witt, 316, 320, 328, 348
 Wyat, 120
 Wyatt, 306
CHAPEL,
 Rachel, 425
CHAPMAN,
 E. B., 405
 J. A., 179, 313, 337, 345,
  354, 361, 366, 369(2)
 J. A>, 369
 John M., 37
 William H., 231

INDEX

CHAPMAN HILL & COX, 21
CHAPPELL,
  James P., 440
  R. J., 274
CHASE,
  Oliver, 18
CHECK,
  Elisha, 6
CHRISTIAN,
  Claborn A., 50, 59, 68,
    216, 243, 265(2), 282
  H., 242
  H. C., 221, 243, 264
  Harriett, 50
  J. A., 68
  J. G., 68
  James C., 59, 60
  James G., 50, 51, 215,
    216, 221(2), 242, 243,
    264, 265(2), 282(2), 283,
    294
  James I., 50
  James J., 60, 274
  John A., 50, 59, 216
  Lucy J., 50, 59, 68, 215,
    265(3)
  Lucy K., 68
  Morgan (Mary) F., 264
  Morgan F., 50, 59, 68,
    282, 294
  Morgan H., 242
  Sarah Ann, 51, 60, 243,
    283, 294
  W. H., 219
  William M., 50
CHRISTOPHER,
  J., 315
  S. E., 330, 334
  Samuel E., 168
CLARDAY,
  A., Mrs., 275
CLARDY,
  A. N., 18
  C. S., 303
CLARK,
  F. J., 312
  G. W., 189, 355, 389, 396,
    399, 419

  George, 410
  George W., 312, 410
  H., 278
  H. B., 312
  John C., 347
  L. B., 149, 242, 286, 304,
    312
  Mary, 149
  Mary M., 312
  Rilia, 312
  W. H., 410
CLARKE,
  G. W., 346
  L. B., 326(2)
  W. F., 326(2)
CLECKLER,
  Catherine E., 315
  E. E., 19
  E. H., 368
  E. M. B., 365
  E. M. C., 380
  Elijah, 56, 62, 273
  Eliza M. B., 368
  Francis, 311
  Hilery, 83
  Hillery, 72, 315, 330
  Jacob W., 311
  Joseph, 311
  Julia A., 311
  Minerva Ann, 331
CLEMENTS,
  Adam, 125, 273, 290
  Charles, 19(2), 80, 102,
    122, 224, 257(2), 273,
    275, 279, 290, 291, 293,
    349
  M. A., 275(2)
  M. A. D., 275
  M. E., 275, 290
  Malissa E., 125, 273(2),
    349
  Margaret, 273
  Martha A., 273(2)
  Martha A. Adams, 349
  Mary, Miss, 275
  Roxey, 125, 273
  Roxey A., 273
  Sarah A., 291

  Sarah Ann, 125
  Sarah Ann, Miss, 273
  W. J., 273
  William, 125
  William J., 273, 290
CLEVELAND,
  W. T., 367
CLINE,
  Christopher, 105, 200,
    216, 226, 237
  Mrs., 200
  William, 21, 55
CLINTON & BRADLES, 410
CLIZBE,
  Mary, 71
COACH,
  Drury, 219
COBB,
  Henry, 399
  Ida, 363
  L. M., 322
  L. T., 322, 363
  Leroy M., 138, 152, 155,
    166
  Mary, 399
  Sallie, Mrs., 320
  Sarah J., 399
  Theophilus, 399
  Thomas, 322
COBBS,
  Leroy M., 286
COCHRAN,
  Caroline, 307
  J. F., 360
  Jones, 139
  Thomas, 228
  Thomas J., 283
  W. P., 341
  W. W., 331
COCKRELL,
  Mary, 91
COFFEE,
  Emily, 311
COFIELD,
  Annah, 151
  Anneleza, 142
  Exor, 142, 151
  Joseph A., 139

INDEX

COFIELD (continued)
  Martha, 151
  Martha Ann, 142
  Uriah, 142, 151
  Uriah P., 139
  Warner, 139
COKER,
  Abner, 37
COLE,
  Robert, 222
  S., 219
COLE & MALONE, 280
COLEMAN,
  John, 348
  W., 314
COLLEDGE,
  A. P., 361
COLLIER,
  . M., 332
  C. P., 398, 412
  F. M., 398
  Ida, 362, 367, 371, 375, 378
  Ida C., 332, 347, 357
  M. N., 190, 347, 356, 357, 362, 367, 371, 375, 378, 398, 412
  Madison, 332
  Minton, 347
  Sarah, Mrs., 320
COLLIN,
  Ezzard Y., 226
COLLINS,
  Amanda, 375
  E., 260
  E., Mrs., 69
  Elizabeth A., 235
  Elizabeth M., 89
  Emelina, 278, 293
  Emelina V., 278, 293
  Emeline, 76, 235
  Emiline, 260
  Emiline, Mrs., 69
  Emily, 118, 154, 235, 236
  Emily A., 236
  Emily C., 89
  F. M., 312
  F. W., 312

  Ida C., 190, 340
  J. A. H., 236
  James, 260, 278, 293
  James A., 89, 118, 235, 236(2)
  M. A., 293
  M. A. E., 118, 235, 236(2)
  M. H., 259(3)
  M. M., 340
  Madison, 190, 340
  Martha, 236
  Martha H., 235
  Martin, 89, 134, 136
  Martin H., 118, 236
  Michael A., 260, 278
  Michael A. E., 89
  Nathaniel L., 170
  P. E., 301
  P. Romulus, 154
  Paschal, 76, 89, 118, 154, 235(2), 236, 260, 293, 301
  Paschal E., 9, 16, 39, 69, 71, 81, 83, 236(2), 259, 260, 278(2), 292, 293(2), 301
  R. D., 118, 235(2), 236
  R. E., 301
  R. S., 236
  Romalis E., 301
  Romalous, 278
  Romalus, 292
  Romulus D., 89
COLN,
  Alice, 441
COMPTON,
  Gaskey, 237
COMINE,
  W. Y., 200
  William Y., 82
CONNALLY,
  A. B., 426
CONNELL,
  William M., 259
CONNER,
  Edward, 115
CONNER & STONE, 66, 71
CONNOR,

  E., 318
  Edward, 98, 100(2), 101, 116(2), 145, 254
  edward, 173
  Sadock, 98
COOK,
  Ailey A., 413
  Becky Ann, 117
  C. M., 210
  Calbe M., 210
  Caleb, 268
  Caleb M., 210(2), 248
  E. A., Miss, 430
  E. A., Mrs., 433, 439
  E. A.,Mrs., 436
  E. C., 413
  Elizabeth, 268
  George, 109
  George M., 117, 268, 299
  George M. C., 248, 262(2)
  H., 315
  Harbard, 117, 262(2), 275
  Harbert, 109, 193, 207, 210, 229, 248, 268, 286, 295, 299(2)
  J. A., 268
  J. B., 35, 173, 238
  J. O., 268
  J. P., 210
  James A., 268
  James O., 248
  James P., 210
  Jesse, 119
  Joshua, 117, 193, 210, 248, 262, 275
  Joshua A., 109, 248, 262, 268, 299
  L. A. E., 248(2)
  Rebecca A. D., 248
  Rebecca A. P., 262
  Rebecca P., 109, 119, 210
  Rina, 413
  S. C., 248
  Seaborn C., 210
  Temperance E., 268
  Thomas E., 109, 248, 299
  Thomas Elbert, 117
  W. M., 168, 180, 268(2)

INDEX

W. T., 413
William N., 193, 207, 229,
  248(2), 268(2), 286, 295
COOLY,
  Florence Murphy, 407
  R. Clifton, 407(2)
COOPER,
  Elvina William, 371
  John T., 129
  M. W., 258
COPELAND,
  D. P., 259
  David T., 259
  Eli, 259
  James M., 259(2)
  James W., 98
  John P., 98, 259
  William, 259(2)
  Willis M., 259
COPER,
  E. Pherl, 425
COPPEDGE,
  Thomas, 19
COTER,
  Eveline, 308
  William, 308
COUCH,
  Al B., 353
  J. M., 440
  James M., 71
  M. H., 358, 413
  W. B., 227(2)
COUSINS,
  A. W., 417
COWAN,
  Adaline, 195, 256
  Adaline M., 6, 253
COWEN,
  Joseph S., 6
COX,
  Helen M., 7, 10, 16
  I. T., 313
  John C., 7, 10, 16, 22
  John H., 70
  M. P., 370(3)
  Martha C., 21
  P. B., 73
  P.B., 73

Samuel, 149, 256
Samuel W., 7, 10, 16, 22,
  70
W. H., 370
W. L., 359, 360(3), 361,
  363, 365, 367, 369, 370
CRAFIELD,
  Lewis, 310
CRAIG,
  Judy Ann, 39
  Mrs., 239
  Robert, 45
  William, 3, 239
  William M., 39, 196
CRAWFORD,
  Laura, Mrs., 380
  M. L., 380, 384
CRAWLEY,
  America E., 440
CREAL,
  George, 105, 106, 219, 263
  H. T. D., 219
  William, 105, 219
CREEL,
  George, 238
  William, 199
CRITTENDON,
  I. H., 15
CROMBIE,
  William A., 210, 248
CROW,
  S. T. W., 264
  Townsen, 195
CROWDER,
  George M., 256
  J. H., 405
CRUMBIE,
  G. N., 423
  G. W., 429
  H. G., 423, 429
  J., 423
  J. F., 423
  J. R., 423, 429
  J. T., 429
  M. A., 429(2)
  Mollie, 423
  Sallie, 423, 429
  W. E., 9

W. J., 423, 429
CRUMBLEY,
  J. H., 309
CRUTCH,
  A. G., 193
CULPEPPER,
  John W., 276

-D-

DAHALL,
  Thomas M., 226
DANFORTHAND,
  William, 219
DANIEL,
  Martha E., 215
  Moses, 116
  Thomas R., 215
  W. R., 175(2)
  William, 226
DAVIS,
  A. E., 180
  A. J., 356
  Aly H., 357
  Andrew J., 203
  B. L., 180
  B. W., 180
  Bertha, 432
  C. G., 303, 317
  C. M., 341
  E. W., 180
  Emily H., 304
  Emily W., 408
  F. M., 331, 410, 417, 426
  G. A., 180, 408, 419
  G. A. D., 427
  G. M., 304, 318, 340, 345,
    363, 370, 408, 419(2), 427

  Gary, 255
  George M., 150, 304, 312
  George N., 180
  J. J., 236, 419
  J. M., 300, 333, 358, 393
  J. W., 318
  J. W., Jr., 312
  James, 9, 37, 316, 350
  James M., 336, 337, 350

454

INDEX

DAVIS (continued)
  Jesse H., 258
  John, 340
  John J., 427
  John W., 150, 180, 300, 304, 312
  Lottie E., 407
  M. C., 180
  N. L., 180
  M. M., 333
  Parlie, 387
  Rachel, 275, 331
  Rebecca, 408
  V. T., 419(2)
  Wesly M., 150
  Zadock, 160
DAVOR,
  John, 169
DAY,
  J. L., 268
DEASON,
  J. C., 208
DEAUGHAN,
  Milligan B., 93
DEFINE,
  W. F., 362
DELILE,
  Martin, 298
DENHAM,
  D. A., 301
  D. D., 13, 27, 33, 78, 79, 290, 298, 324, 356, 363
  Daniel D., 123(2), 145(2), 146, 298
  P. A., 332, 352, 390, 391
  R., 238
  R. H., 332
DENHANN,
  R. A., 387
DENNIS,
  Sarah A., 399
DENSON,
  C. Y., 248
  E. Y., 268
  H. C., 248
  W. A. J., 268
  W. H. E., 226
  William, 210

DENTON,
  J. W., 387
  John, 157
  John W., 416
DEVAUGHAN,
  A. B., 222(2)
  John, 132, 218
  Jonathan, 235
  M. B., 92(4), 213, 222
  Milligan B., 132
  William B., 213
DEVAUGHN,
  C., 314
  Catharine, 335
  Catherine, 315, 326(2), 349, 350, 372, 375(2)
  Elijah, 350
  Eliza B., 350
  Eliza P., 350
  J. H., 395
  John, 41, 298
  M., 349
  N. B., 305
  Rose, 314
  Sandy, 333, 346
  W. B., 182
DEWBERRY,
  Thomas, 118
DICKENSON,
  M. W., Mrs., 434, 436
  Mary W., 430
  Mary, Mrs., 417(2)
DICKERSON,
  M. W., Mrs., 414
DICKSON,
  J. M., 340, 348, 418, 424, 428(3), 431, 437
  John O., 1, 8, 19, 31, 34, 80, 82, 83, 84, 85(2), 95, 99, 207, 229(2), 230, 248, 249, 251, 277, 290
  Johnie M., 431, 435, 437
  Johnie O., 428
  Lela M., 428, 431, 435, 437
  Lester C., 428, 431, 435
  N. T., 424
  N. T., Mrs., 431, 435, 437

  Oscar L., 428, 431, 435
  Oscar T., 437
  Robert D., 48, 95
  W. W., 418, 424, 428(2)
  Willie A., 428, 431, 435, 437
DIETY,
  Elizabeth, 192
DIETZ,
  Paul, 192
DIXON,
  J. W., 432, 437
DOAN,
  John A., 226
  John H., 353
DOBBINS,
  N. G., 306
DOBBINS & BRASSELL, 304
DODD,
  Cynthia, 338
  Edward, 247
  George, 346, 351
  John M., 338
  Mary J., 399
DODSON,
  Joshua, 266
  W. H. C., 220
DOO,
  B. W., 21
DORAY,
  R. T., 335
DORIS,
  Catherine, 326
DORMAN,
  Alford, 38, 63, 341
  Alfred, 38, 40, 74(2), 346, 347, 351
  Alice O., 400
  Ann, Mrs., 351
  David, 274
  G. M., 400(2)
  Hiram, 63
  John, 38, 40, 63(2), 74(2)
  John H., 351(2)
  M. B., 346, 348
  Mary, Mrs., 346
  Morgan B., 351
  R., 217, 309

INDEX

Richmond, 38, 63, 153,
    162, 171, 250, 286, 298,
    310, 322
Sallie C., 351
Thomas H., 351
DORRISS,
    J. G., 303
DORSEY,
    B. H., 367, 380
    Fannie, 367
    James, 200
    R. F., 412(2)
    R. J., 303
    R. T., 187, 314, 318, 346,
        352, 353, 412, 418(2), 425

    S. D., 21, 122, 137, 250
    Solomon D., 122, 123, 142,
        143, 265
    Stephen G., 101
DORSEY & HUMPHREY, 238, 271
DOSS,
    Martha, 357
DOYAL,
    L. T., 206, 259
DRAKE,
    Thomas, 200
DRENNAN,
    Clarissa, 400
    Hugh, 400
    John H., 400
    Martha E., 400
    Susan A., 400
    William B., 400
DREWRY,
    F. O., 228
    P. O., 228
DRURY,
    D. E., 193(2)
DUFFEL,
    Andrew, 30
    M. A., 317
    Martha A., 304
    Mrs., 244
    O. W., 212
    Patience, 304, 317
    Sarah, 212
    Susan, 317

T. D., 229
T. L., 194, 229, 257
DUFFELL,
    Columbus W., 182
    F. L., 212
    L., 149
    Martha A., 152, 182, 305,
        309
    Martha Ann, 149
    Misouri, 147
    Mrs., 245
    Patience, 305, 309
    Rachael L., 212
    Rachel L., 212, 245
    Susan S. T., 154
    T. L., 240, 245, 257
    Thomas E., 182
    Thomas H., 18
    Thomas L., 152, 154, 182,
        220
    W. O., 212, 240, 245(2)
    Washington, 131, 288, 298
    Washington D., 147
    Washington O., 288
DUFFEY,
    David L., 206
    Martha E., 407
    Sarah A., 403
DUFFIE,
    S. A., 389
DUKES,
    B. B., 238
DUNBAR,
    A. C., 405, 416
    B. B., 416
    D. E., 416
    J. W., 377
    J. W., Jrs., 405
    J. W., Sr., 405, 416
    John, 416
    John W., 327, 361
DUNN,
    Ishmael, 16, 37(2), 52(2),
        53(2), 71, 73, 201, 227
    Martha W., Mrs., 36
DURHAM,
    D. D., 35, 319(2), 366
    Daniel D., 287

DURRENCE,
    T. J., 412
DYKES,
    B. B., 105, 225, 258,
        276(2), 289
    Benjamin, 240
    Benjamin B., 105, 112, 117

-E-

EARNEST,
    L. M., 261
EASON,
    Abraham, 215, 267
    Aley, 189
    C. A., 415
    E. P., 370
    James, 323, 370
    John, 301, 346, 370
    Marion, 398
    Martha, 370
    Mary, 323, 370
    Nathan, 39, 75, 141(2),
        147(2), 148, 159, 161,
        188, 206(2), 262
    P., 21
    Parker, 12, 32, 41, 42,
        58, 80, 214, 236, 271(2)
    R. B., 305
    Rachael, 215, 232
    Rachael, Mrs., 370
    Rachel, 97, 305, 323, 370
    Rasbury, 108, 216
    Rhoda A., 237
    Rice, 95(2), 144, 157,
        188, 189
    Richard B., 97, 215, 232,
        323
    Richard I., 370
    Robert, 370(2)
    Sarah Ann, 267
    W. F., 270(2)
    W. P., 361(2), 364
    William, 157
    William F., 108, 216, 238
    William P., 135, 186, 188
EASTIN,
    C. H., 301(2), 323(2),

INDEX

EASTIN (continued)
  328, 334, 336(2), 364
  Cicero, 289, 293
  Cicero H., 175
  E. P., 262, 293
  Eilas G., 236
  Elijah P., 137, 290
  Louisa D., 311
  Margaret, 257, 288, 289, 293
  Margaret, Miss, 293
  P. G., Miss, 293
  Permelia, 289, 301
  Permelia C., 175, 293, 301
  S. G., 56, 175
  Silas, 289
  Silas G., 55, 62, 130, 207, 221, 257, 289, 290, 293
EDGE,
  Lizzie E., 407
EDMONDS,
  Courtney A., 414
  W. B., 387
EDMONDSON,
  Courtney A., 401, 406, 410, 418, 428
  Eli, 3(2), 13, 25, 30(2), 40, 41, 58, 78, 87, 118, 124, 139, 140(2), 142(2), 144, 150, 154, 265, 280, 285(2), 296, 303
  G. W., 182
  George W., 154, 303
  J., 274(2)
  J. A., 303
  J. T., 391
  James, 306
  James W., 132, 133, 154, 344, 351(2)
  Jane, 150
  John, 150, 151, 154, 170, Mia.
  Louisa J., 154, 344, 351
  Lucy A., 375
  Luisa Jane, 306
  Mary A., 428
  Peter E., 303

S. Elizabeth, 170
T. J., 384
Thomas, 274
Thomas J., 151, 156, 170
Tom, 336
EDMUNDS,
  Mary B., 399
EDWARD,
  M. B., 390
EDWARDS,
  William G., 21
ELBERT,
  J. J., 216
  Thomas, 262, 275
ELDER,
  Berry, 373
  C. C., 374
  David P., 35, 48(2), 74(3)
  Fannie H., 441
  H. D. L., 102
  Howell, 102
  Howell L., 34
  I. R., 362
  J. H., 333, 345, 352, 366, 370
  J. L., 332, 373, 374
  John, 26, 41
  John L., 24
  Josh, 287
  Joshua, 19, 30, 31, 35, 44, 74, 102(2)
  Josiah H., 19, 125, 257, 337, 373, 374(2)
  Josiah L., 374
  M. M., 44
  Martha, 345, 363, 366, 370, 373, 374, 376, 384(2)
  Martha A., 19, 374
  Martha, Mrs., 362
  S. P., 228
  Sterling, 5, 102
  Sterling J., 40, 50, 67, 197, 208, 250, 267, 289
  William, 363
  William F., 31
  William F. M., 19
ELDERS,

Sterling J., 228
ELINGTON,
  David W., 149
  Robert C., 149
ELISON,
  Samuel H., 207
  W. L., 184
ELKINS,
  Ann, 240
  B. G., 224
  Eliza F., 225
  Eliza T., 263
  Elizabeth, 240
  Elizabeth P., 105, 291
  Emeline, 105, 225, 240, 241(3), 263, 291
  Emmah, 162
  James, 105, 162, 216(2), 225(2), 240(2)
  Mary E., 105, 225, 241(2)
  Sarah, 240, 241
  Sarah J., 105, 114, 240(2), 241
  Susan A., 240(2)
  Thomas, 240
  Thomas W., 105, 225, 241, 263, 281, 291
  William S., 131
  William T., 240(2)
ELLIINGTON,
  J. A., 343
  J. H., 343, 386(2)
  J. S., 416
  Josiah S., 386
  L. T., 416
  R. A., 416
  R. A., Mrs., 386(3)
  R. C., 386
  R. F., 416
  Richard F., 386
  S. E., 416
  Susan E., 386
  Z. P., 416
  Z. T., 386(2)
  Zachery P., 386
ELLINGTON,
  E. E., Mrs., 342
  Elizabeth, 394, 404

INDEX

Ellington, 429
J. A., 342
J. H., 336, 342, 353, 361,
  365, 368(2), 373, 374,
  379, 380(2), 383, 387,
  390, 394, 399, 404, 407,
  412, 429
J. N., 343(2)
J. S., 365, 387, 414, 420,
  430(2), 434, 436(2), 439
John H., 368
Joseph, 394
Josiah S., 383, 399(2),
  400, 404
Paul, 429, 430, 439
R. A., 394, 399, 412, 414,
  436, 439
R. A., Mrs., 400, 404,
  405, 408, 420, 430, 434
R. C., 13, 275, 336,
  342(2), 343, 353, 361,
  365, 368, 373, 380
R. F., 387, 414, 420, 430,
  434, 436(2), 439
Richard, 394, 429
Richard F., 383, 399, 400,
  404
S. E., 387, 414, 420, 429,
  430
Susan E., 399, 400
Susan E>, 383
Z. P., 414, 420, 434,
  436(2)
Z. T., 336, 342, 343, 353,
  355, 361, 365, 368(2),
  373, 379, 380, 383, 387,
  390, 394, 399, 400,
  404(2), 405, 407, 408,
  412, 414, 420, 429(2)
Zachery P., 383, 399, 400
Zachry P., 394, 404
Zack T., 374
ELLINGTOON,
  Josiah A., 380
ELLIS,
  Thomas, 126
  William L., 324
ELLISON,

Emily, 316(2), 398
F. M., 321, 328, 360, 392,
  393
L. C., 417
L. H., 57
Samuel, 158
Samuel H., 35, 79, 164(2),
  198, 316, 321, 328(2)
Sarah H., 24
W. L., 169, 316, 321, 328,
  333
William, 184
William C., 184
William L., 328
ELMORE,
  Jacob, 252
ENGLISH,
  Ellen, 411
  Mary, 411
ESTES,
  Allen, 235
EVANS,
  B. Y., 39
  Daniel, 63, 65
  David, 235
  Hugh, 219, 220, 235
  Matilda, 143
  Nelley G., 123
  Nelly G., 109, 219
EVERETT,
  Richard M., 288, 294(3)
EVERITT,
  Richard M., 126(2), 127(2)
EWEN,
  Thomas, 214
EZZARD,
  Thomas W., 417(2)

-F-

FALKNER,
  John M., 32
FALL,
  C. F., 183, 189
  C. J., 300, 307, 377
  Calvin J., 165(2), 170
FARBER,
  Nathan, 322

FARMER,
  I. N., 404
FARR,
  Elizabeth, 275
  J. H., 375
  John, 314
  John H., 171, 326, 335,
    349, 350
  Joseph H., 171
  Mary Jane, Mrs., 375
  Thomas, 314
FARREN,
  Drewry, 371
  Permelia, 371
FAULKNER,
  Eliza C., 210
  John, 52
  John M., 18, 56
  Thomas, 210(2)
FAVER,
  Glenn, 339, 354
  Henry Love, 339
  Jewel, 354(2)
  John, 172, 175, 257, 328,
    334, 338, 339, 354, 411
  Love, 354
  M. F., 354(2)
  Oliver, 420, 424
  P., 340
  Paul, 328, 336, 338, 354,
    362, 367, 391, 411
  S. L., 411
  Sam, 354
  Stonewall J., 420
FAVOR,
  John, 199, 323(2)
FAVOR & RUD, 229
FEARS,
  A. B., 304
FEMER,
  Westley, 270
FERNADES,
  Mary, 358
FERNANDER,
  Mary, 75, 331, 336, 363
FERNANDES,
  Mary, 337, 350
FIELD,

INDEX

FIELD (continued)
  E. F., 228
  Emma, 145
  Isaac, 122
  Isaiah M., 145
FILES,
  Sebon J., 65
FILLAS,
  Phineus, 259
FILLS,
  Rebecca, 347
FINLEY,
  C. R., 362(2)
FISHER,
  H. C., 179, 181, 310, 313(2), 318, 328, 335, 344, 362, 366, 381, 385
  H. C>, 362
  H. W., 306
FISHER & SHEPHARD, 314
FISSHER,
  H. C., 372
PITTS,
  John B., 150, 264
  N. M., 193
  N. V., 193
  Newton M., 90, 193(2), 218
  Sarah S., 150
  Walker, 90, 193
FITZGARRELL,
  L., 2
  Mary A., 2
  P., 2(2)
FITZGERALD,
  Ann, 234
  Henry P., 40
  James, 6(2), 10, 11, 21(2), 40(2)
  James D., 6
  James P., 11, 21, 28, 197, 198, 234
  Lula W., 442
  Mary A., 28, 40
  Mary Ann, 6, 10, 21
  Nancy, 21
  P., 10(2), 11, 13
  Philip, 5, 6(3), 28(2), 40
  Phillip, 235(2)

  Phillip P., 21(2)
FITZGERROLD,
  Phillip, 4
FLETCHER,
  James, 235
  James M., 219, 220
  William L., 315, 322
FLOWERS,
  B., 9
  Elizabeth, 433
  Lizzie, 376
  H. E. A., Mrs., 394
  M. H., 9
  Martha E. A., Mrs., 387, 394
  W. H., 5
  William H., 77, 86
FLOYD,
  James, 32, 240
FOLSOM,
  Benjamin, 52, 62
FORMAN,
  Alfred, 348
FORNEY,
  James F., 72
FORSTON,
  Jane, 52
FORTSON,
  B. F., 237
  B. H., 213
  Ben, 276
  Benjamin G., 8
  E. B., 351
  E. H., 186
  E. K., 185
  E., Mrs., 346
FOSTER,
  J., 234
  T. J., 234
  Thomas J., 61
FOWLER,
  Louisa, 413
  Louisa, Mrs., 413
FRANCES & REDD, 232
FRANKLIN,
  D. H., 395
  D. M., 332, 340, 390, 392, 395, 404, 406, 410, 436

  J. H., 262, 363
  Permelia A., 437
  W. F., 323
  W.G., 323
  William F., 262
FRAZER,
  E. H., 410
FRAZIER & MOON, 9
FREEMAN,
  Robert R., 9
FREMAN,
  Henry, 232
FULLER,
  S., 13(2)
  Tilmon, 134, 189
  W. B., 18(2), 19, 223, 261
  William A., 92(2)
  William B., 37, 85(2), 91, 193(2), 224

-G-

G. H. HOLIDAY & CO., 312
G. M. DAVIS & CO., 323
GABLE,
  A. W., 344
  H. M., 361
  N. N., 324
  N. W., 302, 321, 327, 331, 334, 345, 347, 431, 433
  S. A., Mrs., 431, 433
GAMAGE,
  Floyd, 72
  Thomas M., 72
  William, 72
GAMMAGE,
  Floyd, 78
  Thomas M., 78
  William, 78(2)
GANT,
  Johnson W., 216
GARDENER,
  A. G., 384
  J. N., 384
GARDINER,
  A. G., 390, 407
  J. A., 390, 407
GARDNER,

INDEX

Ezekiel, 179
GARE,
  Fannie, 407
  Masters, 407(2)
GASDEN,
  Cornilla J., 180
  Jackson, 180
  Nancy J., 180
  William H., 180
GASKIL,
  V. A., 232
GASKILL,
  V. A., 119, 231
  Varney A., 99
GATES,
  Mathew, 52
GAY,
  A. O., 186, 389, 392, 395
  Gilbert, 56
  Gilbert, Jr., 68
  I. P., 218, 229, 258, 362
  I. T., 226
  Isaac P., 52, 101, 142,
    165, 189, 322, 329
  J. P., 335, 339, 354,
    377(2)
  John T., 119
  L. P., 343
  Love, 325, 339(2)
  P., 339
  P. G., 354
  S. T., 354
  Sandford, 354, 362(2),
    377, 440
  Sherod H., 104, 222, 284
  T. B., 199, 397, 401
  T. G., 339, 362(2), 377
  Thomas B., 4, 9, 56, 71,
    121, 165, 256
  Thomas G., 196
  W. J., 300, 329, 335, 339,
    343, 354, 362(2), 377,
    395(2)
  Wiley J., 107, 165, 222
  William J., 189, 354
GAY & HARRIS, 238
GAYDEN,
  P. T., 226

GENTRY,
  Emily, 110
  Mary, 110
  Mason, 102, 104, 110, 195,
    200, 214, 226, 246, 268,
    298(2)
  Moses, 281
GEORGE,
  J. D., 300
GIBSON,
  H. H., 407
  Sallie R., 407
  Shockley, 49
GILBERT,
  I.I., 210
  J., 291
  J. J., 177, 290(2), 308,
    327, 335, 340(2), 358, 363
  John I., 210
  John J., 126, 130, 131,
    134, 135, 137, 142, 145,
    178, 188, 216, 297, 298,
    308, 316, 363
  William, 70, 336
GILES,
  J. C., 205(2)
GILHAM,
  Harry J., Jrr., 326
  Harry, Sr., 326
  Robert, 326(2)
GILLAM,
  Ailsey D., 350
  Ailsy, 350
  Elizabeth M., 350
  H. J., 350(3)
  Harry J., 350
  J. H., 350
  James I., 350
  John, 350
  Mary J., 350(2)
  Matilda, 350
  Robert, 335
  Samuel H., 350
  W. J., 350
  William J., 350
GILMER,
  Daniel, 266

Daniel K., 119, 199
Elizabeth A., 266
Helena M., 266
Leah S. C., 266
Rebecca J., 266
Samuel K., 266
William E., 266
GLASS,
  Al, 392
  Andrew J., 259
  Elijah, 34, 38(2), 48,
    56(2), 66, 68, 78, 81,
    85(2), 93, 100, 107, 108,
    127, 133(2), 136(2), 145,
    146, 150, 209, 210, 224,
    229
  Frederick, 262
  James D., 146
  John, 336
  L., 8
  Lovzinski, 8
  M., 21
  Uriah, 77
  V., 362
  Viola, 377
  Warren N., 77
  Wiley W., 77
  William, 56, 69, 110, 120,
    121, 129, 130, 196, 210,
    217, 238, 254, 256, 264,
    276, 277(2), 289
  William G., 377
  William, Jr., 362
GLOVER,
  W. T., 387
GLOWER,
  W. F., 314
  W. T., 183, 186, 187,
    191(2), 300, 333, 394
  William T., 183
GLOWERS,
  W. T., 316
GODSIN,
  J. C. W., 82
GODWIN,
  Aaron, 65(2)
  Joel G., 323(3)
GOODMAN,

INDEX

GOODMAN (continued)
A. A., 429
Anna, 423
M. A., Mrs., 380
M. A>, Mrs., 369
M. J., 353
Margaret, 326
T. L., 326
GOODSON,
Fanny, 256
Jordan, 39
GOOSLEY,
Marion, 320
GORMAN,
C., 238
GOSDEN,
J. C. W., 82
Kemler Guinett, 115
Nancy Jane, 115
W. B., 56
William Henry, 115
GRACE,
Joshua, 22
GRADY,
Emma J., 423, 429
GRANT,
Exy, 302
Filmore, 302
G. G., 174
M. T., 378
M. T. R., 378
Martha, 322
Patterson, 302
Ressie, 302
Roxana, 302
Serena, 302
W. J., 69, 302, 312(2)
William J., 161, 256, 378, 383
GRAVES,
A. R., 139, 141, 262
Annie H., 388
Augustus, 337
Charles, 55, 56
Charley, 175
Clementine, 337
David, 72, 83, 214(2)
E. M., 320

Elizabeth, 175, 320
Elizabeth, Mrs., 320
F., 265
Francis W., 214
George W., 175
Hardy, 320
Hester A., 337
J. H., 310
J. L., 320, 323, 333, 337, 344, 357, 397
J. P., 191, 336(2), 337(2)
J. R., 440
J. T., 310
J. W., 440
James, 7, 17, 172(2), 320(2), 437, 439
James P., 320
Jasper, 172
Jasper L., 323, 436, 437, 439, 440
Jesie, 415
Joe L., 373
John, 4, 30, 72, 83, 172, 182(2), 191, 310, 320, 322, 337
John D., 336
John L., 191, 404
John L., Jr., 337
Joseph L., 381, 420, 424
Joseph T., 420
Kitey Ann, 214
Leah Oliva, 214
Lear, 107
Martha, 141, 144, 275, 320
Martha B., 399
Matilda, 72, 83, 107, 123, 214(2), 265, 279, 297
Minton, 72, 83, 172(2), 287, 320
Minton, Jr., 127
Minton, Sr., 265
Naomi, 440
Pellie A., 440
R., 265
Roxey, 146
Roxie A., 337
Rufus, 146
S. C., 191

Salena, 107, 214, 265
Sally, 320
Susan, 336, 337, 404
Thomas L., 337
Vines, 123, 141, 144, 214, 265, 279
W. C., 437
W. O., 436, 439, 440
W. R., 399
Wiley, 72, 124, 146, 147, 214, 297
Wiley V., 144
GRAY,
A., 19, 22
A. W., 199
Benjamin, 237
J. F., 363
John T., 119
T. P., 327
GREEN,
C. A., 362
Joseph, 203
GREENWITH,
Jane, 350
GRICE,
Q. C., 217, 219, 237, 441
S. C., 441
GRIFFIN,
H. L., 385
H. S., 389, 395
L. H., 81, 217
Mary, 407
William T., 80
GRIFFITH,
A. M., 367
G. W., 256, 370
George W., 242
M. A., 367
M. A., Mrs., 367
GRIGGS,
Benjamin J., 159
Bryan, 3, 6, 11, 18, 23, 37, 41, 45(2), 197
Bryant, 70, 131, 192, Mia.
Green, 93, 192, 202, Mia.
Gryan, 36
Jane E., Miss, 36, 45, 63
John W., 37, 131, 157

INDEX

L. B., 181, 187, 318, 323, 325, 352, 353(2), 357, 360(4), 361, 363, 365, 366, 367(2), 370(2), 381, 382
L. O., 345
L. P., 340, 341, 344, 346
L. R., 361
Lewis B., 162(2)
M. A. B., 408
Mary H., Miss, 36
Rocella, 3, 11
S. B., 387
Sarah W., 45
Susan A., 164
T. B., 316
William G., 37
GRIMES,
J. C., 327, 330, 345
GUICE,
A. F., 176
Alvin F., 167
Billie, 323
Elizabeth, 314, 323, 338, 365
John, 167
Linton, 314, 323, 338, 365
Linton S., 176
M. E., 365
Margaret E., 176
Peter, 167, 176, 303, 314, 323, 338, 365
Q. C., 169
William, 176, 303, 314, 323, 365
William M., 365
GUY,
J. T., 417
William J., 321

-H-

H. RENTFROW & CO., 21
HABLETT,
S. D., 71
HADDEN,
William, 18
HAGGES,
Jesse, 304(2)
HAIL,
Robert, 118
Thomas J., 108
HAINES,
E., 9
James, 45
HAINS,
David, 22
HAIRSTON,
B. L., Mrs., 429
HAISTEN,
H. H., 300, 347
I. A., 309
Isaac, 219
Isaac A., 138(2), 153, 155, 158, 160, 300
J. A., 274, 321, 347
James E., 167, 219(2)
John, 336
John A., 300
L. D., 236
HALE,
Joseph, 218, 285
Robert, 280, 285
Thomas, 226, 265, 285
HALES,
Joseph, 247
Sam, 392
Susan G., 247
Thomas, 218, 247(2)
HALL,
B. F., 336
Joseph, 218
Robert, 260
William, 3
HAMMOCK,
Mary, 4(2), 5
HAMPLY,
J., 355
HAMRICK,
J. M., 360
HANCOCK,
A. G., 12, 36, 70
Albert G., 12, 16, 21
C. T., 21
Mary, 21
HAND,
A. J., 167, 172(2), 173, 309
Frank, 344
W. H., 392
HANDLEY,
J., 217
Jane, 380
Jared, 380(2)
Jarod, 116
Jarot, 135
L. L., 380
L. T., 331
Larkin L., 116
Rhoda, 365
Rhoda F., 135(2)
T. H., 217
Thomas J., 135
HANDLY,
Jarrot, 79
John J., 159
L. L., 330
Thomas J., 159
HANES,
Daniel, 117, 226
David, 92(2), 235, 238
J. J., 387
James, 29, 62, 88, 93, 142, 227
James, Jr., 200(4), 246, 250, 281
W. C., 253
HANEY,
David, 8
HANNER,
Jane, 389
Mary Jane, 403
HARDEMAN,
William B., 9
HARDEN,
Augustin, 120
Augustin C., 270
Augustine E., 282
C. A., 120, 270, 282
John, 270, 282
John H., 120
HARDIN,
Augustine E., 296
C. A., 120, 296

INDEX

HARDIN (continued)
  John, 296
HARDY,
  Isaac, 328
  R. W., 339, 386, 393, 396,
    402
  Rufus W., 388, 396
  William R., 229, 232
HARDY & MITCHUM, 225
HARINGTON,
  H., 67
HARKEN,
  B. T., 188
HARP,
  Moze, 217
  Mozee, 111(2), 169, Mia.
  W. N. T., 398, 400, 406,
    409(2), 416, 424
  W. P. T., 397
HARPER,
  B. F., 274, 348, 351,
    362(3), 412, 426(3)
  B. T., 346
  Charley P., 175
  Elizabeth J., 126
  Frederick, 351
  Hattie E., 437
  J. E., 175
  J. G., 341
  J. W., 175
  James E., 437
  John F., 437
  Luisa M., 175(2)
  M. G., 351
  Martha A., 437
  Mathew, 351
  Mathew G., 126, 135
  Nancy A., 437
  Nancy L., 175
  Q. A., 175
  R. F., 437(2)
  Susan, 175
  Susan G., 135
  Susanah G., 126
  Susannah G., 351
  W. A., 175
  W. E., 175
  William, 135, 351

  Wyatt A., 175
HARRELL,
  E. J., 321, 328
  F. M., 66, 271, 321
  J. H., 240
  John H., 245
  M. M., 205(2)
  Rachel, 245
  T. M., 226
  Tallulah, 432
HARRIS,
  A. C., 415
  David, 226
  Elbert, 90, 194, 207, 221
  G. L., 362, 410
  J. S., 415
  James, Jr., 30, 227
  L. T., 415
  M. J., Miss, 415
  Martha, 348
  Martha E., 352, 360
  Martha F., 347
  Morris, 57(2), 79, 195
  Pheraby, 348
  R. M., 201, 352, 355, 360,
    362
  Robert N., 346, 348
  S. A., 362
  Seaborn, 57, 316(2), 327,
    415
  Telitha, 415
  W. F., 415
  W. R., 442
HARRISON,
  A. C., 396(2), 398(2),
    400, 402(2), 406, 409,
    418, 432
  A. F., 397, 398, 400(2),
    406, 409
  A. F. B., 424
  Ada, 400, 432, 435, 439
  B. M., 397, 398, 400(2),
    406, 409
  Ben, 400, 424, 432, 435,
    439
  D. M., 396, 398, 402(2),
    406, 409, 418, 432
  E. C., 396

  E. E., 398, 402, 406, 409,
    415, 418, 426
  Effie C., 432(2)
  Effie E., 426
  G. C., 418
  G. D., 432
  G. E., 402
  G. I., 396, 398, 406, 409,
    415
  Glenn, 424, 432, 435, 439
  H., 406
  J. E., 391
  J. G., 397, 398, 400, 406,
    409, 424
  J. L., 424
  John, 95, 226
  L., 168, 303, 309, 314,
    416
  Larkin, 323, 367, 386,
    388, 391(2), 392(2), 396,
    398(2), 402, 406(2),
    409(2), 435
  M. R. H., 424
  R. H., 397, 398, 400(2),
    409
  Robert, 424, 432, 435, 439
  S. C., 392, 424
  Sarah C., 379, 386, 400
  T. B., 398
HART,
  Moses, 250
  Mose, 250
HARTLEY,
  Coleman, 214
  Isaac, 56, 132, 303
  J. J., 201
  Rebecca, 369
HARTLY,
  Isaac, 323, 334, 348
  J. J., 208
HARTSFIELD,
  William, 162
HARVELL,
  J. H., 347
HARVEY,
  C. A., 168
  M. P., 391
  Mary Ann, 284

INDEX

S., 305, 313
Spencer, 168
HATHCOCK,
 W. M., 313
HAWKINS,
 J. A. F., 236
 J. F., 235
 John A. F., 89, 235
HAYES,
 Archibald J., 43
 David, 9
 J. F., 361
 John, 9, 64
 Lewis, 43
 Martha Ann, 9
 Martha E., 53, 64
HAYNES,
 David, 19
 E. L., 305
 James, 45
 W. A., 353
HAYS,
 Archibald J., 59
 Cynthia, 9
 John, 8, 31, 215
 Lemuel M., 215
 Martha E., 8, 19, 31, 215
HAZE,
 John M., 22
 Martha E., 22
HEAD,
 A. L. F., 48
 Americus L., 125
 Americus Lafayette, 272, 277
 B., 319(2)
 B. F., 179, 303, 311, 324, 369
 Benjamin F., 311
 Edna Ann Francina, 272, 277(2)
 Edney Ann Francina, 125
 Emily, 311
 Emily E., 182, 359
 Frank, 38
 J. J., 226
 J. W., 311(2), 352
 James, 38, 253

James M., 48
James N., 311
James W., 124, 125(2), 179, 182, 195, 225, 272(2), 277, 311, 332, 359
Jane, 48
John G., 226
Louticia, 311
M. L., 182, 359
Martha, 311, 441
Meredith W., 311
Nancy, 311
Nancy Ann Laticia, 272, 277
Nancy Ann Luticia, 125
O. G., 38
O. I., 74
O. J., 48, 80
O. L., 74
Oliver J., 48, 79, 89
R. F., 355
Robert A., 48
S. F., 344
Sarah Jane, 125, 272, 277
T. J., 258, 274, 298, 311
Thomas Hammond, 272
Thomas J., 54
W. P., 355
W. R., 48
W. T., 359
William, 124, 125, 257, 277, 303, 311(3), 344, 369
William P., 167
William R., 38, 74(2)
William T., 182
William Thomas Hammond, 272
William Thomas T., 125
William Thomas Thurmond, 277
HEALTH,
 M. L., 301
HEARD,
 Elias W., 335
 Page W., 228
 Thomas, 228

Thomas J., 160
HEART,
 John J., 226
HEATH,
 Eveline, 369
 M. L., 71, 301
HEMPERLY,
 Edward, 141, 142
HEMPHILL,
 W. P., 379
HENDERSON,
 A. J., 250
 Andrew, 35
 Andrew M., 67, 73
 F. M., 392
 Mitchel, 32, 35, 52, 67(2), 73
 N. L., 392
 R. H., 392
 R. M., 310
 Robert, 226
 Rutha, 35, 52
 Thomas, 35, 52(2)
 Thomas J., 141, 143
 W. H., 226
HENDIX,
 R. W., 309
HENDLY,
 L. L., 334
HENING,
 Will I., 258
HENLY,
 M., Mrs., 411
HENON,
 John H., 192
 Martha F., 192
HENRY,
 Thomas E. B., 229
HENSON,
 James, 31
HERINGTON,
 William S., 71
HERNANDEZ,
 William S., 238
HERRING,
 Frances, 80
 Francis, 60(2), 66, 210, 255, 273, 292

INDEX

HERRING (continued)
  John, 80
  Johnathan, 209, 210, 233, 255, 272
  Jonathan, 60(2)
  Marcus, 60, 80, 208, 233, 273, 292
  Mary A., 33, 66, 210, 233
  Mary Ann, 27, 28, 46
  Thomas, 27, 28, 33, 46, 52, 60(2), 65, 66(2), 208, 209, 210, 233, 255, 272, 273, 292
  W. F., 10
  William, 3, 12
HERRONDALE,
  William S., 32
HEWELL,
  F. D., 385, 387, 391
  J. B., 426, 430
  Jeanett, 323
  John T., 148, 149(2), 156, 161, 321
HEWETT,
  Z. B., 343
HICKS,
  D., 227(2), 237, 442
  Delila, 226
  Dillard, 227(2)
  H. L., 442(2)
  H. M., 442
  Isham, 133
  James T. W., 133
  M. G., 228
  Parry, 19
  Perry, 105, 133, 200, 216, 226, 227, 237, 264, 274, 375, 394, 442
  W. I., 442
HIGHTOWER,
  George C., 25, 58
  Hilliard, 4
  Isaac, 4
  J. B., 441(2)
  J. C., 235, 388, 423, 441
  J. O., 441
  James C., 169
HILL,
  B. J., 13
  Elisabeth, 15
  Elisha, 8, 15, 199, 213, 250
  Elisha G., 8
  Elizabeth, 8
  Henry, 31, 55
  J. F., 220
  John W., 111(2), 220, 250, 254
  Lucy, 110
  Lucy A., 113, 220, 247
  M. C., 441
  M. E., 402, 419
  Martha, 8
  Mary, 220
  Sophronia P., 93
  Tidwell, Mia.
  W. G., 411
  W. N., 17, 19(2), 70, 111
  William H., 81
  William N., 22, 32(2), 34, 41(2), 42, 49, 55(2), 64, 69, 78, 81, 93, 103, 195(3), 217, 235, 254, 255(2), 271
  William NH., 61
HILLMAN,
  S. J., 404
HILLSMAN,
  Ellah G., 161
  J. L., 164
  James, 161
  James L., 161
  Jeffrey, 99
  Jeffrey E., 161
  Jeremiah, 161
  Junia L., 186
  Lucy T., 161
HILSMAN,
  A. J., 232
  Amanda, 119, 231
  Araminta, 231
  Araminta, 231
  Bennett, 231
  Bennett E., 232
  Ella, 119
  Ellen G., 325
  Irene, 232
  J. E., 325
  J. L., 324, 325
  J. W., 325, 404
  James, 119, 231, 232, 325(2)
  Jeff, 325
  Jeffrey, 119
  Jennie L., 325, 404(2)
  Jeremiah, 119
  John R., 232
  Josiah, 119(3), 325
  Lucy, 119
  Lula, 404
HINDMAN,
  William H., 295
HINET,
  T. G., 362
HITCHCOCK & WALDEN, 352
HIX,
  Martha, 398
HOBGOOD,
  J. I., 274(2)
  J. L., 91, 275
  James, 47, 411
  James L., 71, 78, 79, 82(2), 91, 97, 115, 126, 195, 198, 255, 270, 271, 281, 282
  Jane L., 126
  John L., 180
  Lewis, 2, 78, 82(2), 91
  Nancy, 271
  Priscilla Jannett, 126
  Salina J., 191
  Samuel E., 271(2)
  Samuel R., 91, 97, 113, 191, 255
  Selina, 113
  W. W., 71
  Willis W., 113, 191
HODGE,
  Jesse, 228
HODGES,
  Fleming J., 135
  George, 3
  Jesse, 32
  John, 3

INDEX

HODNETT,
  C. W., 353
HOFFMAN,
  Emanuel, 437
  James, 437
  Martha, 250
HOLCOMB,
  D., 55
HOLCOMBE,
  N. G., 345
HOLLAND,
  Jeff, 375
  L. G., 353
  Susan, 77
  Talton, 77
HOLLIDAY,
  Henry B., 134
  J. S., 217
  John, 63, 64, 111, 248, 269
  John L., 66, 209, 261, 290
  John S., 30, 49, 53, 54, 66, 75, 76(2), 77, 79, 85, 99, 102, 115, 117, 120(2), 132, 134, 136, 197(2), 209, 213, 215, 220, 237, 271, 282, Mia.
  K., 69
  R. K., 217, 238
  Robert, 4, 9, 134(2), 136, 237
  Robert H., 259(2)
  Robert K., 76, 80
  Robert, Sr., 13, 17
HOLLIDAY & WARE, 192, 194, 221, 223, 224, 228, 237, 238, 248, 271, 293
HOLLINGSWORTH,
  Isaiah, 335
  Mary A., 376
HOLMAN,
  James, 399
  N. A., 399
  S. R., 399
  T. J., 399
HORN,
  H. T., 229
  Mary A. R., 157

  T. H., 229, 240
  Thomas H., 157
HORNE,
  T. H., 218, 220
HORTON,
  Calvin, 274
  Emily, 347
  John C., 170
  Robert K., 170
  Stephen, 302
HOUGH & FAMBROUS, 219
HOUSE,
  James, 274
HOWARD,
  Mary A., 320
HOWELL,
  John T., 150, 171
HUBBARD,
  H., 2(2)
  Henry, 71
  Howell, 237, 276, 332
  Jesse, 71, 82, 83, 201, 222, 259, 279, 287(2), 391

  John, 274
  Lucinda, 425
HUDSON,
  A. G., 231
  E. J., 355
  Ella, 420
  Emily, 420
  John, 420
  Nova, 420
HUFF,
  Isaac B., 225
HUGHES,
  E. S., 355
  James, 431
  Mary, 431
HUGHIE,
  Henry J., 149, 286
HUGHS,
  Isaac, 13, 208
HUIE,
  A. L., 16, 36, 70, 253
  Alex L., 69
  Alexander, 70
  Alexander L., 21, 71

  Allen, 113
  J. M., 235, 239
  J. T., 256
  James, 253
  John, 100, 110, 124, 208, 275, 384
  John M., 106, 107, 110, 113(2), 220, 235(2), 247, 253
  John T., 271
  Joseph, 253
  Mary, 220, 253
  R. C., 21, 71, 222, 253
  R. J., 235
  Robert, 106, 107, 200, 253
  Robert C., 69, 106, 107, 253
  William M., 253
HUIE & CONNER, 193
HUIE & CONNOR, 239
HUMPERLY,
  E. T., 141
HUMPHEY,
  Thomas, 200
HUMPHREY,
  B. B., 290
  J. E., 442
  John, 206(2)
  R. B., 206
  R. D., 217
  R. R., 290
  Rachel B., 247
  Richard, 73
  Richard B., 115, 122, 128, 268, 279, 297(2)
  Sarah, 297
  T., 227
  Thomas, 73, 227
  William, 73
HUMPHRIES,
  H. D., 387
HUMPHRIS,
  Martha, Mrs., 305
HUNNICUTT,
  James B., 189
HUNT,
  John, 222
HUNTER,

INDEX

HUNTER (continued)
  F. F., 258
  James, 38, 73
HUTCHERSON,
  Benjamin, 387, 390
  Fanny, 1, 226
  L. C., 109, 226
  Ladson, 239
  Leander, 111
  M. A., 239
  M. M., 235
  Mary M., 239
  Mary W., 109(2), 111
  Milton, 219
  Polly, 239
  Rowland, 109, 111, 219, 239
  Rowland M., 239
  T., 226
HUTCHESON,
  Feiney, 57
  Rowland, 44
HUTCHINSON,
  Benjamin, 376(2), 381, 384, 395, 400, 404, 408, 414(2), 416, 420, 429(2), 433(2), 436(2), 439(2)
HUTCHISON,
  Arthur, 313
  Camilla, 375
  W. H., 375

-I-

IKENER,
  Michael, 3(2), 6, 30, 43, 64
IKENOR,
  Michael, 12, 18
IRVINGS,
  William, 1
IVERA,
  J. B., 332
IVERSON,
  R., 200, 227, 229
  Robert, 90(2), 129, 196, 200, 229, 232(2), 247, 269, 287(2)

IVESON,
  R., 274
IVEY,
  John L., 248

-J-

J. B. SARGENT & CO., 18
J. L. BLALOCK & CO., 367
JACKSN,
  Huie, 15
JACKSON,
  A. J., 308, 316
  A. M., 401
  B. M., 308
  Benjamin M., 131
  Bennett, 307, 361
  Bird, 210, 316
  Bird M., 177, 178(2), 216, 306, 316
  Birde, 5
  Blake, 56, 208
  D. T., 399
  E. B., 308(3), 316
  Edmond, 128, 262, 266, 301, 346, 361, 365, 388, 396, 398, 399(2), 419
  Edward, 354
  Elisha, 290, 308
  Elisha F., 137(2)
  Elizabeth, 308, 398
  Eveline, 349
  Francis, 286(2)
  Francis Marion, 137
  George H., 130, 262, 266, 286, 298
  George N., 286
  H. J., 286(2)
  J. E., 399, 419(2)
  J. J., 308
  James I. B., 137
  Jefferson F., 131, 290(2)
  Jesse, 316
  Jesse J., 308(2)
  John, 5
  John G., 223
  Jordan, 153, 152, 307(2), 308

L. B., 32
Littie Berry, 4
Lucinda C., 137
M. E., 22, 346, 354, 361, 365, 388, 399, 401, 419
Margaret F., 298
Marion, 316, 361
Martha, 306
Martha A., 305, 308
Martha Ann, 178
Martha E., 359
Martha Eliza, 137
Mathew E., 388
Matilda C., 312
Matthew E., 401
Mr., 3
Needham, 152, 153, 180, 199, 214, 220, 349, 361, 391
Needom, 307
R., 286(2)
Ralph, 38, 312
Rebecca, 308
Reuben, 346, 286
Reubin, 327
S. D., 384(2)
Samuel, 56
Sarah, 354, 365, 389, 396, 399, 401, 419(2)
Sarah Ann Selena, 399
Terrell A., 239
W. E., 399
W. L., 345, 360
William, 1, 7, 45, 134, 136, 219, 227, 286
JACOB,
  Thompson, 193
JACOBS,
  C. L., 413
  Sarah E., 413
  W. J., 367(2), 369, 370
  William, 9
JACOS,
  Morris, 257
JARROTT,
  Atha, 16
JASKEW,
  T., 190

INDEX

JENKINS,
  Needham, 348
  T. H., 346, 351
  Thomas L., 320
  Williamson, 7, 13, 30, 56,
    65, 124, 143, 145, 146,
    147, 265, 290, 346, 351
JENNINGS,
  A., 3
  Allen, 27, 28, 29, 39, 42,
    64, 76
  Cynthia, 64
  David, 320
  Elizabeth, 76, 232
  Elizabeth Jane, 39
  Elizabeth, Miss, 62
  James, 83
  James A., 27
  James B., 205(2)
  James R., 52, 86, 284
  James T., 97, 107, 156,
    233, 252, 269, 285
  John, 205
  John A., 27, 97, 205, 233,
    252(3), 253, 269(2), 284,
    285
  Mary Ann, 107, 252, 269,
    284
  Morgan, 97
  R. H., 226
  Rhoda E., 97, 285
  Roda, 107, 269
  Roda E., 253
  Sarah, 86
  Simon, 331(2)
  T. W., 224
  Thomas, 34(2), 39
  William, 27, 34, 39, 42,
    52, 56, 62, 64, 83, 101,
    107, 192, 196, 205, 215,
    226(2), 232, 234, 285
  William J., 97, 252, 269
  William, Jr., 76
JEWEL,
  N. F., 354
JINKINS,
  Williamson, 123
JINNINGS,

  Allen, 196, 239
  Allen A., 234
  John A., 126, 233, 234(3)
  Mary Ann, 234
  Robert M., 126(2)
  Roda E., 234
  Thomas, 196, 239
  William, 196(3), 234(2),
    239
  William J., 233
JOHNS,
  Samel D., 349
JOHNSON,
  A. B., 391
  A. P., 201
  A. S., 384
  Amanda M., 191, 334
  Arthur, 3
  Aurelia S., 342
  Aurelia S., Mrs., 380
  B. F., 415(2), 418(2)
  B. L., 186, 187, 190, 226,
    298, 319(2), 324, 332,
    395, 396, 397, 401(2),
    402, 406, 409, 418(2), 424

  Berry L., 195, 258, 279,
    294
  Bery L., 266
  Charles, 38, 56
  Curie, 241
  I., 19
  I. H., 10, 18, 19
  J. F., 11, 113
  J. H., 21(3), 31, 55
  J. W., 183, 187, 258,
    314(2)
  James, 235
  James F., 16, 27, 32, 35,
    37, 70(3), 84, 93, 104,
    192, 197, 224
  James H., 53
  James M., 191, 334
  James W., 154, 157
  John, 326
  John H., 191, 334
  John J., 191
  John N., 334

  L. N., Mrs., 385
  Landford, 259
  Lee K., 217
  Leonard H., 344
  Nancy, 317
  R. E., 258, 300, 331
  Samuel, 383(2)
  Susan S., 317
  T. B., 355
  T. L., 326
  Thomas, 1, 257, 258, 266,
    279, 294
  Thomas I., 350
  Thomas L., 326
  Thomas P., 195
  William, 317, 378
  William J., 191, 334
  William, Sr., 187
JOHNSTON,
  P. T., 403
JONES,
  A. J., 314
  B. C., 310, 311
  B. O., 12, 26, 29, 36, 45,
    63, 64, 300, 319, 327,
    337(2), 346, 353, 358, 387

  B. W., 319
  Bartee W., 310, 327
  Blalock &, 282
  Burton, 440
  C. O., 39
  C. P., 342
  C. S., 178, 337
  Cason, 271(2)
  Catharine, 440
  Charles, 146, 240, 342
  Charlotta T., 136
  E. J., 274(3), 338
  Eason, 226
  Elizabeth A., 289
  Ella, 300
  Ella, Miss, 311
  Emily J., 136, 166, 338
  Enock G., 127
  F. M., 9, 213
  F. P., 266
  Francis, 87, 338, 368

INDEX

JONES (continued)
  Francis H., 136
  Francis M., 87, 104, 224, 234
  Francis P., 119, 121, 159, 166, 218, 390
  Franklin B., 104, 113
  G. A., 392, 397
  Gaskey C., 136
  H. H., 423
  H. S., 381
  Henry, 289, 320, 423
  J. D., 300, 423
  J. H., 368, 435
  J. J., 226
  J. M., 218(2)
  J. S., 75
  James, 73
  James H., 166
  Jane, 159(2)
  Jeremiah S., 75(2)
  Jesse, 9, 34
  John, 121
  John B., 440
  John L., 119, 121, 199
  John R., 23
  L. W., 254
  M. A., 390
  M. F., 368
  M. Jane, 166
  M. W., 423
  Margaret J., 338
  Margarett J., 368, 390
  Mary L., 391
  Mathew, 87, 91, 136, 206, 231, 261, 276
  Matthew, 261, 309
  Matthew F., 166
  Missouri A., 166
  Nancy, 392, 397
  Nancy R., 136
  R. A., 440
  R. R., 360
  Richmond, 88
  Robert, 320, 324
  S. T., 391
  Samuel G., 9
  Samuel R., 146
  Sarah, 414, 417, 418, 422, 431, 434, 436, 440
  Sarah Francis, 224
  Seaborn, 5
  Susan, 423
  T. H., 9, 69, 238
  T. R., 256
  T. W., 300, 311
  Tabitha E., 225
  Thomas, 414, 418, 422, 423(2), 424
  Thomas A., 311
  Thomas M., 35, 114, 118, 126(2), 127, 288, 294
  Thomas P., 37
  Thomas, Jr., 423
  Tilder C., 440
  W. B., 190, 276, 277, 324, 440
  W. E. C., 239
  W. F., 390, 391, 440
  W. G. C., 181
  W. J., 240, 342(2), 367, 370, 392, 397
  W. J., Jr., 367, 370
  W. J., Sr., 370
  W. L., 339, 343
  W. P., 337, 440
  W. T., 418
  William, 34, 271
  William A., 56
  William B., 435
  William F., 166
  William L., 424
  Wynn F., 224
JORDAN,
  Charles M., 399
  Hiram E., 399
  L. H., 39
  Martha F., 399
  Willis A., 16
JORDAN & GOODSON, 9
JOSEPH M.,
  J. W. T., 318

-K-

KEEGAN,
  Ann, 431
  James, 431
  Michael, 431
KEILSMAN,
  James L., 321
KEITH,
  M. L., 252
KELLEY,
  Ada E., 439
  Bascom Y., 387
  Bascomb Y., 376, 381, 384, 390, 395, 400
  E. R., 381, 384, 400, 404, 408
  E. R., Mrs., 390
  George C., 381, 400, 406
  Ida R., 384, 387, 390, 395, 400, 404, 408, 414, 416, 420, 429, 433, 436
  Ida R. B., 376, 381
  J. H., 371(2)
  J. N., 375(2)
  J. W., Sr., 372
  James N., 372
  John H., 376, 381, 384, 387, 390, 395, 400, 404, 408, 414, 416
  John W., 375(3), 381, 400, 406
  John Welborn, 375
  R. L., 371
  Robert E., 376, 381, 384, 387, 390, 395, 400, 404, 408, 414, 420, 429, 433
  Robert H., 416
  W. F., 374, 376, 381, 384, 387, 390, 395
  Welborn, 375
  William F., 371
KELLOGG,
  H. P., 31
KELLY,
  D., 35
  Daniel, 366
  E. R., 375
  George, 366
  George C., 385, 388, 390
  Hester, 366

INDEX

J. W., 301
John W., 151, 154, 301,
  385, 388, 390
Martha E., 375
Thomas, 366
W. F., 321, 324, 347, 366,
  371
KENADY,
  Thomas, 331
KENDALL,
  Elizabeth T., 160
KENEDY,
  James L., 174
  Mildred Ann, 174
KENNEDY,
  E., 71
  George R., 71, 82
  John, 71
  John B., 82, 206
  S. E., 353
  Thomas, 334
  W. L., 353
  William W., 69, 71, 206
KENT,
  Carrie E., 413
KERKLIN,
  E. A., 311
KERKSEY,
  E. H., 270(2)
  Mary, 270
KERLEN,
  Samuel, 85, 86, 90
KERLIN,
  Samuel, 211
KERLY,
  Nancy, 359
  Robert, 359
KEY,
  Hanes, 253(2)
  Tandy, 333
KIELLEY,
  George C., 394
  John W., 394
KILLUM,
  Elizabeth, 194
KIMBALL,
  Isaac S., 42
  William D., 42

KIMBERLY,
  Charles, 268
  Charles E., 112, 193
  E., 28
  Edward, 28
  Isaac S., 24, 28
  J. M., 226
  James M., 112
  Mrs., 28
  Sarah E., 112
  Widow, 28
  William, 28
KIMBEW,
  Mary A., 347
KIMBLE,
  S. S., 323
KING,
  A. G., 223
  Emily, 229
  G. C., 367, 380
  George C., 117, 120,
    193(2), 195, 216, 217,
    223(4), 224(3), 226, 227,
    229(3), 258, 262, 270,
    271, 276, 284, 290, 293,
    298
  George D., 272
  George E., 295
  Henderson, 69
  J. L., 380
  John, 367, 380
  Madison, 143, 145
  Martha, 342(2), 370
  Martha P., 223
  R. R., 218, 285(2)
  Robert R., 38, 108
  Sephen H., 137
  Stephen H., 135
  Susannah, 285
  T., 218
  T. D., 56, 74(2), 168,
    181, 199, 348, 391
  Tandy D., 74, 391
  Thomas, 5
  Thomas I., 114
  Thomas J., 108, 218, 220,
    257, 285
  Thomas W., 38, 257

William P., 38, 63, 114,
    220, 229, 257
KIRKSEY,
  E. H., 111
  Mary, 180
KIRLIN,
  Robert, 182
KITCHENS,
  C. W., 433, 442
  Charles W., 386, 405
  J. H., 433, 442
  J. W., 386, 391, 405, 417,
    433, 442
  John, 405
  John H., 386
  John W., 361(2)
  M. M. M., 433, 442
  Mary M. M., 386, 405
  R. G., 433
  Roxa E., 433
  Rufus G., 386, 405
KITE,
  Carswell, 24
  Major, 147, 148
KNIGHT,
  Peter, 237
KNOLES,
  Benjamin E., 81
  Edmond, 81
  James M., 81
KNOWLES,
  C. H., 317, 332
  S. N., 316
KNOWLS,
  Benjamin E., 78
  Benjamin F., 78
  C. H., 300
  Edmond, 78

-L-

L. GLASS & BOHANNON, 335
LAINER,
  W. P., 258
LAMB,
  Barnard, 19
  J. J., 235
LAMBERT,

INDEX

LAMBERT (continued)
S. D., 441
LANDRUM,
A. P., 321
Anna A., 164
Billie, 393
Bosworth, 19
C. J., 317
C. T., 395
Columbus, 306
Edelia L., 158
F., 356
F. L., 193
Franklin, 193, 252, 257, 356
Frankln, 281
H. P., 432
J., 21, 58, 306
J. C., 404
J. D., 181
J. L., 181, 317(2), 357(2)
J. O., 410
J. Q., 181, 317, 357, 401, 406, 414, 418, 428(2), 441
J. T., 380
J., Sr., 287
Jane, 155, 156, 171, 281
Jasper, 198, 356(2)
Jefferson, 356(2)
Jefferson D., 317(2)
Jeptha, 7, 25, 28(2), 35(3), 36, 39, 51(2), 54(2), 57, 59(2), 88, 163, 164(2), 171(2), 184, 226, 258, 306, 315(2), 328, 356, 360
Jeptha T., 360, 365, 376, 380
Jeptha Tidwell, 164
Jeptha, Jr., 57, 94, 164, 184, 365
Jeptha, Sr., 27, 29, 88, 101, 102, 258
Joseph, 360
Joseph B., 164
Joseph Stolon, 184
Josephine, 365

L. A., 321, 328
Lara T., 184, 360
Larkin, 156, 171, 184, 356(3)
Laura, 164
Laura T., 365
Luther, 357
M. A., 393
Madison, 356
Mary E., 164
N. P., 328
Nancy, 158
Nancy J., 356, 393
Nancy P., 392
Nannie J., 424(2)
Nannie J., Mrs., 432
Napoleon B., 164, 184, 360, 365
Q. M., 306
Theoher, 164
Thomas, 306, 398
Ulissa A. F., 158
W. F., 193(2), 306
W. W., 393
Washington, 35, 163, 164, 181, 356, 357
William W., 158
Willis, 57, 158, 356
Willis F., 88
LANE,
Henry, 404
LANGSTON,
E. B., 228
LANIER,
Alice, 374
Cora L., 374
F. V., 374
Francis V., 374
J. A., 433
James A., 374
James H., 433
James L., 374
M. A., 374
Rachael E., Mrs., 374
Racheal E., 374
Robert L., 374
Russie, 374
Sallie, 374

W. C., 433
W. P., 433
William C., 374
LASSETER,
E. M., 200
Eleanor, 227, 248, 286
Elenor, 296
Elisha, 88, 200, 227, 246, 250, 281
Elizabeth, 88, 200(2)
Elleanor, 108, 268
Ellen, 222
J., 51
J. W., 235
Jacob, 30
Jacob F., 29
James T., 108, 228, 248, 268, 286, 296
Jesse, 9, 20, 29, 45(2), 62, 70, 77, 84(2), 197, 227(2), 228(2), 268, 286
Jesse, Jr., 222, 296
Mahala, 228
Malinda, 108, 222, 248, 268, 286, 296
Martha, 222
Reuben, 222, 296
Reuben M., 108, 228, 248, 286
Reubin M., 268
Sarah, 222
Sarah J., 108, 248, 268, 286, 296
Sarah Jane, 227
Seppa, 108
Seppers, 62
Seppy, 30, 222(2), 227, 248, 268, 286
Sophia, 93, 200, 246
Sophia F., 281
Taylor, 222
Thomas J., 45
Willis, 227
LATHAM,
George, 365
Thomas A., 55, 65
Thomas W., 431
LEACH,

471

INDEX

C. W., 324(2)
E. N., 310, 356(2)
E. W., 169, 173, 177, 179(2), 181, 182, 183(2), 184(3), 186(2), 187(2), 191, 258, 314(2), 316, 317, 319(2), 320, 321, 348(2), 355, 356, 357(3), 360, 365, 371, 376(2), 380, 427, 433(2), 352
E. W>, 365
Edward, 120
Edward W., 56, 313(2)
Mary A., 427, 433
W. A., 177, 181, 306, 328, 380
LEANDER C.,
George M.C., 239
Rowland M., 239
LEE,
Isam L., 261
Joel, 256
John, 33
Robert W., 250
W. G., 261
William G., 261
LEOPARD,
Holland, 25, 28, 35, 54, 59, 258
LESTER,
F. M., 258, 273(2), 349
Francis M., 125
George M., 352
J. F., 355
J. G., 346, 348, 352, 362
John, 132, 143(2), 151, 242, 256, 277, 317, 342, 348, 180
S. E., 421, 438
T. P., 408, 427
LEWIS,
E. C., 324
L. B., 321
S. B., 357
LEYLE,
Mathew, 1
LICKLER,
Hary, 411

LINCH,
James W., 158(2)
LINDSEV,
F. P., 408, 418, 425
Frank P., 412
P., Mrs., 408, 412
LISTER,
J. G., 332
Permelia G., 301
LITTER,
R. D., 228
LITTLE,
K. D., 272
Kindrick D., 89
R. D., 202
Talley, 202
Zabud, 89(2)
LIVELY,
G. F., 413
Samuel, 430
Susan, 413
LOBLIN,
M. J., 311
LOEB,
D. C., 391
LOGAN,
B. P., 223
J. B., 245
J. B. F., 245
John B. F., 223
Mary, 23
Mary E., 223
LOHEY,
G. C., 353
LONG,
Daniel, 21, 112, 217
F. L., 226
Francis, 226
George D., 162, 170, 309
H. A. N., 309, 394
Henry, 226
Henry A. U., 162
Isham, 94, 201, 224
Isham T., 106, 246
J. B., 246(2)
J. C., 226
John B., 116, 291
John W., 226

Marcus, 24, 94, 201, 224, 246, 291
Marcus H., 246
Martha, 107, 246
Martha Jane, 116, 291
Nancy C., 246
Penelope, 226
Susan, 162, 170, 246, 309, 394
T. Y., 246
Thomas, 201, 224, 246(2)
Thomas L., 94, 226
William H., 246
LONG WILLIAM,
James M., 226
LONGINO,
H. F., 143, 145
LOONEY,
M. H., 223, 228, 233
LOORD,
L. C. J., 308
Louisa C. J., 308
W. C., 308
LORD,
F. L., 226
Francis L., 95(2), 197
Henry, 95(2), 197
Jordan, 75, 290, 334, 341
Joshua, 56
W. C., 316
LOVEJOY,
A. B., 197, 233
Elizabeth, 197, 233
James, 235
James L., 89, 235
LOWRY,
M. H., 224
LOYD,
Ann, 187
Anna, 329
Eliza, 187, 329
Emily, 67
Emma, 191
F. M., 67
Frances, 75
James, 24, 27(2), 29(2), 34, 35(3), 38, 42, 44(2), 45, 46(2), 51, 58(2), 59,

INDEX

LOYD (continued)
  65, 67(2), 75(4), 76, 163,
  184, 185, 204, 206, 214,
  227, 229, 262, 316
Jane, 407
Jasper, 42, 65, 67, 75,
  275
John, 29, 44(2), 46(2),
  58, 67, 75(2), 76, 151,
  161, 187(2), 214(2), 227,
  249, 262, 329, 345
John W., 363
Marion, 29, 35
Mary B., 407
Mary E., 151
Milton, 29, 35, 46, 51,
  67, 191
N., 316
Newton, 42, 65, 67, 75,
  303
S. A., 377
Samuel, 45, 183(3),
  184(3), 185, 206, 229(2),
  258, 318, 377(2)
Sarah, 46, 58, 75, 76,
  151, 183(2), 316, 318
Sarah F., 204, 214
Sarah Frances, 44, 58, 67,
  75
Sarah H., 377
Thomas E., 44, 249, 262
Thomas Embry, 75(2)
Thomas Emery, 58
Thomas Emory, 67, 227
Thomas M., 407
Widow, 29
LUCK,
  J. H., 395
  James P., 208
  M. K. W., 377
LUCKIE,
  William E., 92(4)
LUMPKIN,
  J. C., 411
LUNSFORD,
  Martha, 250
LUPTOT,
  Bolin, 3

LUSTER,
  F. M., 291
LYLE,
  John, 222
  Joshua, 222(2)
  Joshua W., 140
LYNCH,
  C. P., 327
  J. W., 416, 423, 431, 434,
    440
  James N., 170
  James W., 327, 418, 437
  Lydia, Mrs., 440
  Peter, 391
  R. W., 336, 341(2), 416,
    418, 423, 431, 434, 437,
    440

-M-

M. CURRY & CO., 391
MCBRIDE,
  A., 2(3), 3, 4(2), 5(3),
    11(2), 12, 22, 23, 24(2),
    30, 256(2)
  A. J., 392
  Andrew, 4, 13, 30, 40, 78,
    79, 82, 100, 101, 112,
    118, 121, 125, 127, 129,
    130, 139, 268, 286, 289,
    298
  Andrew J., 84, 86, 88
  B., 256
  Benjamin, 256
  James, 129, 277(2)
  John A., 118, 256, 268,
    289, 298
  Lachland, 84, 86
  Lee Dora, 442(2)
  Mary, 256
  Solomon T., 277
  William, 84, 86
MCCLENDON,
  Annie, 402
  Lue, Mrs., 402
  Oliver, 393(2), 388, 396,
    402
  S. H., 393

Spalding, 388, 393, 396,
  402
MCCLENY,
  David, 349
  James W., 349
  William, 349
MCCONNEL,
  James, 37
  William M., 226
MCCONNELL,
  James, 93, 115, 217, 235
  James M., 101
  W. M., 270
  William, 226, 235(2), 239
  William N., 115, 241, 270,
    295
  William W., 217
MCCOY,
  Daniel, 3
MCCURRY,
  A. W., 404
  W. A., 417
MCDONALD,
  Barbary, 80
  John, 237
MCEACHERN,
  A., 170
  Daniel, 133, 174, 275
  Elijah M., 174
  J., 342
  J. N., 185, 361
  James, 174
  James A., 336
  James N., 189, 331(2)
  Johnnie, 379, 380, 384,
    399
  M., 275
  Malinda, 119, 122
  Martin, 119
  Martin P., 122, 242
  N., 301
MCEACHIN,
  A., 317
  J. M., 320
MCELREATH,
  Louis B., 407
MCELWANEY,
  W. R., 363

INDEX

MACEY,
  John T., 121
MCGAHAN,
  Thomas, 287
MCGEE,
  James A., 32
MCGINNIS,
  C. W., 226
MCGUIRT,
  Wyatt, 55
MCINTOSH,
  A. C., 84
  C., 86
  C. C., 108
  M., 222
  Marcellus E., 86
  Marcus E., 84
MACK,
  John, 320
MCKEAN,
  James, 200
MCKEE,
  Alice, 368, 383
  Sarah, 367
MACKEY,
  Florence, 358, 372, 376
  Florence L., 391
  J. F., 364, 372
  J. T., 376
  John L., 358
  John T., 258, 277, 309, 391
MCKEY,
  John T., 309, 314, 322, 333
MACKEY,
  M. C., 309
MCKEY,
  M. C., 309
MACKEY,
  M. O., 322
MCKEY,
  M. O., 314
MACKEY,
  Tommie, 358
MCKINNEY,
  M., 275
MCKINNY,

Jemina L., 206
MCKOWN,
  James, 69
  Robert, 69
  William, 18
MCKOWN & STRICKLAND, 238
MACKY,
  John T., 258, 333(2)
  John W., 263
  M. L., 333
  M. O., 333
  S. T., 333
MCLAIN,
  J. F., 337
  Mary, 259
  May, 223
  Oliver, 223, 259
MCLANE,
  H. N., 212
  H. S., 150, 347
  J. F., 185, 186, 315, 319
  James, 174
  Jason F., 322
  John, 140, 203
  John M., 157, 177, 296
  Joseph, 143, 203, 212
  Joseph F., 176, 177, 178
  Juan F., 140, 150
  L. J., 440
  Malinda M., 296
  Martha M., 296
  Mary, 94, 95, 194(2), 212
  Miram L., 245
  Olive, 94
  Oliver, 194, 212
  Oliver P., 150, 212
  Sarah, 212
  T. J., 443
  Theodolia, 174
  William F., 146
MCLEAN,
  Alison, 106
  Allison, 244, 245
  C. P., 245
  Elizabeth, 244
  Hamden Sidney, 104, 245
  J. M., 245
  J. T., 382

John, 14, 18(3), 40, 244(2), 245(2)
John M., 104
Joseph, 104, 106
Joseph M., 104, 106
Juan Fernander, 104
Juan Francis, 244, 245
Mary, 14, 18, 113
O. P., 244, 245
Oliver, 9, 14(2), 18, 113, 194, 245(2), 249
Oliver P., 130, 244(2)
Oliver R., 245
Rebecca, 106
Sidney, 244
U. U., 245
William, 106, 244, 245
MCLENDON,
  Annie W., 386
  Oliver, 386
  William Spalding, 386
MCLEROY,
  Annie, 395
  E. T., 395(2)
  Earl, 395
  Emily, 93, 217, 229
  Emily H., 92(2), 222
  Emily H. D., 253
  Emily U., 213
  Fred, 142
  H. D., 229
  Henry, 12, 38, 213(2), 222, 253, 272, 285
  itt L., 213
  J. W., 395
  James, 107, 222, 237
  James W., 302
  John, 5, 16, 31
  Martha, 5, 16, 31, 92(4), 213, 222(2), 229, 253, 272, 285, 395
  Martha F., 213, 253
  Martha H., 222, 229
  Mary, 237
  P. W., 395
  Peter, 69, 210, 308
  Peter E., 107, 136, 178, 210(2), 237, 290

INDEX

MCLEROY (continued)
  Peter L., 253
  Pitt L., 229
  Pitt M., 92
  Pitt N., 222
  R. H., 395
  Thomas, 222, 253
  Thomas E., 92
  Thomas E. B., 92, 213, 229
  Thomas W., 217(2)
  Wiley, 222
  Wiley H., 92(2), 213
MCLEWANEY,
  W. R., 358
MCLUCAS,
  Andrew, 161, 276, 301,
    359, 379
  C. S., 441
  C. S., Mrs., 423, 441
  D., 409
  D. A., 178, 359, 388, 403,
    441
  D. M., 402
  Daniel, 100, 161, 263,
    301, 314, 331, 371, 388,
    396, 398, 402, 406(2),
    409(2), 415, 418, 426, 432

  Daniel A., 162, 168, 178
  David, 161, 359, 360, 379
  J. L., 424, 432, 435
  John, 441
  John H., 359
  John L., 439
  Mary, 235
  Mary J., 359
MCMAHON,
  Thomas, 272
MCMICHAEL,
  William, 22
MCPEAK,
  William, 200
MCPHERSON,
  William, 58
MCQUIRT,
  Wyatt, 25
MADARIS,
  G. W., 373, 380, 384, 399

  G. W., 384
  George W., 379
  Nannie, 373, 379, 380, 384
MAHONEY,
  M. V., 21
  M. Vincent, 10
MALEER,
  M. P., 71
MALENO,
  William, 256
MALONE,
  Annie, 417, 430
  Joshua, 222
  L. M., 180, 340, 353, 368,
    376
  Lola, 323, 353
  Lula M., 310, 332
  M. W., Mrs., 405
  Mary W., 389, 392, 395,
    397, 402(2), 405(2), 410
  O. T., 389, 392, 395, 397,
    402, 405, 410, 414, 417,
    434, 436(2)
  Sallie, 417, 430
  Sarah, 332
  Sarah J., 310
  T. C., 180, 332, 340, 353,
    368, 376
  Thomas C., 310, 323
  W. W., 410
  William, 81, 180, 310,
    323, 339, 343, 353
MANDY,
  Thomas, 226
MANGUM,
  L. A., 235
MANN,
  G. F., 51, 216, 221, 242,
    243, 264, 282
  George, 18
  Gideon F., 50, 51, 59, 60,
    68, 215, 216, 282, 283,
    294
  Jesse, 287
  Jonathan, 4
  Martha, 4
  Peter, 89
  Sidney D., 89

  Zachariah, 4(2), 17, 57,
    235
MANSFIELD,
  George, 180
MANSON,
  R., 58
MARCUS,
  Johnathan, 66
MARRY & LOGAN, 32
MARSHBURN,
  H. S. W., 381, 400
  Hesper S. W., 400
  Mrs., 323
MARSHMAN,
  Samuel, 275
  Samuel W., 130
MARTIN,
  A. C., 331, 341, 345
  A. J., 82(2)
  Asa, 331, 334, 341(2)
  George M., 423
  J., 48
  J. L., 320
  J. W., 331, 341
  Jack, 48
  Jackson, 48, 78, 91, 97,
    110, 115, 125(2), 126,
    128, 148, 291
  James, 44
  M. H., 322, 331
  Mary, 148
  N. J., 341
  Nancy, 7, 331, 341
  S. J., 341(3)
  Samuel, 88
  William, 48, 82(2)
  Wright, 7, 47, 48, 71, 78,
    82, 91, 113, 115, 198,
    270, 271, 281
MASK,
  Bogan, 71
  Bogin, 310
MASON,
  John W., 162
MATHEWS,
  Doctor N., 85, 211
  Henry C., 47
  J. E., 391

INDEX

J. H. B., 233
John H., 85, 211
John T., 154
M. W., 317
Mel M., 90
N. W., 218
R. M., 317
T., 5(2)
T. C., 46, 142, 194, 219,
    220, 232, 233, 237, 271,
    285
Thomas C., 23, 46, 68(3),
    101, 109(2), 121, 129(2),
    142, 197, 249
W. W., 72(2), 150(2), 188,
    315, 316, 317(2), 320,
    322, 324, 336
William, 46, 219
William W., 105, 106,
    109(2), 123, 139, 142(2)
MATHEWS & EDMONDSON, 237
MATHIS,
    T. C., 17(2)
MATTHEWS,
    Clyde, 436
    F. C., 422
    F. F., 305
    H. T., 422(2), 433
    J. C., 422, 431, 433, 436,
        439
    J. E., 421, 422
    L. M., 376
    M. C., 422, 431, 433, 436,
        439
    M. E., 422
    M. W., 305
    Minnie, 422
    N. S., 421
    N. T., 431
    Nancy, 407
    Nannie, 433, 436, 439
    Ninnie, 431
    R. L., 422, 431, 436
    Rachael, 198
    Rachael A., 90
    Robert, 396, 407, 421,
        422(3), 430, 431, 433,
        436, 437, 439

Robert, Jr., 422
S., 433
S. P., 422, 431, 436, 439
Sarah, 436
T. C., 33, 218, 396, 407
Thomas C., 48, 63, 94(2),
    153
Thomas O., 95
W. M., 198
W. W., 305
William W., 151, 305
MAY,
    Drury, 8
    Drury B., 82
    Eunice S., 407
    Francis, 257
    George, 384(2)
    Ichabod R., 257
    J. J., 362, 407(2)
    J. V., 8
    James E., 8, 17, 22
    Jeptha V., 82
    Levi, 257
    Levi L., 257
    Lucy A., 407
    Mary, 257
    Mary M., 407
    Robert Z., 407
    William, 52, 99, 101, 196,
        205(3), 234(2)
MAYNARD,
    B. M., 327
    Barto, 327
    Christian, 327
    Ella, 327
    Larkin, 327
    M., 327
    P. M., 327(2)
    Permelia M., 189
    W. P., 327
MAYS,
    Drewry B., 5
MEADORS,
    A., 12, 13, 18
    Abraham, 13
    I. T., 13(2)
    Ira B., 12, 18
MEADOWS,

A., 25
Ira B., 25
Ira P., 25
John, 58
M., 25(2)
Margaret, 25
MEEKS,
    J. W., 163(2), 164
MEMOR,
    E. P., 13
MERRELL,
    R. E., 387
MESSER,
    Al A., 378
    Amanda, 378
    Anna, 378
    H. F., 346
    James, 336
    James D., 345
    Lot, 378, 379
    Lott, 336
    Mandy, 378
    Missouri, 378
    Susannah, 408
    W. A., 336, 379
    William A., 378
MESSES,
    H. F., 353
METHVIN,
    J. T., 392
MIARS,
    W. J., 399
MIERS,
    Andrew J., 127, 128, 135
    Harriet H., 127, 128, 135
    John E., 135
    Lucinda E., 135
    Mary Jane, 135
    Permelia, 135
    Sarah Ann, 135
    William, 135
MILAM,
    Emma, 405
    J. R., 388, 395, 405, 414
    John R., 375, 405, 424
    M. E., 388, 395, 405, 414,
        430, 438
    M. F., 383

INDEX

MILAM (continued)
  M. W., Miss, 435
  Martha C., 383(2)
  Mary F., 383
  Millie E., 375, 388, 424
  N. J., 388, 395, 405, 414
  Nancy J., 375, 388
  Nannie, 405
  Nannie J., 424, 432
  S. C., 395, 405, 430
  William, 144
MILES,
  Agnes, 152, 263
  Agness, 153
  Cressa, 277
  Crissa, 120
  Crissa B., 282
  Dalcy, 357
  Dolcey, 381
  Dolsey, 397
  E. J., 263
  G. F., 263
  G. J., 256
  George, 357
  George J., 90, 277, 293, 381
  J. G., 373
  John D., 282
  John L., 120
  John S., 152, 153, 277
  Levonia, 311
  Sarah, 277
  Thura Z., 90
  William, 4, 7, 9, 21, 30(2), 54, 65, 90, 120(3), 242, 256, 263, 266, 276, 277(2), 282(2), 293

  Willis, 220, 357
MILLAN,
  G. M., 253
MILLER,
  Francis, 159
  John T., 351
  M., 321, 339, 343
  Nancy Ann, 351
  Nathan, 256
  Nathaniel, 159, 218

  Robert, 9, 15
  William B., 239
MILLS,
  C., 407
MILLSAPS,
  H., 10
  Hiram, 1, 23
  L., 10, 300
  Larkin, 17, 23, 34
  O., 10
  Olive, 23
  P., 10, 23
  Partheny, 1
  Perthena, 6
  R., 205(2)
  Reuben, 1(2), 6, 10, 23, 39, 57, 196, 197, 239
  Rhoda Sophrona, 39
  Sophrody, 196
  T. M., 6, 19, 36
  Thomas M., 55, 64
  William, 23
MILNER,
  Elisabeth, 16
  J. H., 217
  J. P., 276
  James, 16
  James M., 42, 55, 70, 195, Mia.
  James W., 61, 111, 124, 128, 217, 246, 255(2), 267

  John, 16
  John H., 12, 55, 61(2)
  John W., 41
  Joshua A., 127, 140
  Mary Elisabeth, 14, 21
  May E., 41
  N., 256
  P. W., 217
  Peter W., 42, 195
  Pitt, 16
  Pitt W., 6(2), 12, 14, 16, 22, 27, 32(2), 35, 41(3), 42, 53, 55(2), 58, 61(2), 70, 80, 195(2), 214, 231, 236, 253, 255(2), 271, Mia.

  Pitt W. L., 70
  Pitt, Sr., 255
  Sarah A., 55, 231
  Sophronia, 16
  Susan, 108
  Susan A., 61, 70, 253, 255(2), 267, Mia.
  Susan Adaline, 14, 22, 41
  T. J., 71
  Thomas J., 127, 138, 140, 276
  W. J., 316
  W. S., 186, 325(2), 404
  William, 21, 143
  William L., 42, 58
  William S., 80, 159, 161(2), 164, 214, 233, 236, 271
MIMMS,
  A. Y., 210
MIMS,
  Andrew J., 275
  Azariah, 176(2), 304, 313
  David D., 248, 268
  Harriet, 275
  John F., 404
  Z. A., 312
MINER,
  S. T. W., 286
  T. W., 95
MINICK,
  James Wesly, 163
  Simeon A., 163
MINN,
  S. T. W., 209
MINNICK,
  Arthur, 145
  James R., 164
MINOR,
  Charlton, 262
  Charlton S., 148
  D. C., 301, 304, 305, 309, 314, 318, 332, 360
  Olive M., 331
  S. T. W., 102, 121, 147, 148(2), 168, 181, 182, 190(2), 229, 265, 271, 344

INDEX

S. T. W., Jr., 173
S. W., 13, 19
Samuel S. W., 91
Samuel T. W., 88, 99, 122,
 123, 127, 128, 153, 160,
 197, 262
W. B., 331
MITCHAM,
 P. W., 234
 W. W., 368, 377
MITCHEL,
 Danville, 274, 276
 Frances, 276
 Henry, 276
 Johnathan, 71, 276
MITCHELL,
 A. B., 226
 Asa B., 300
 Daniel, 200, 226, 264
 Danville, 425
 Henry, 274
 J. T., 425
 Jonathan, 442
 Julia A., 441
 W. D., 291
MOLDER,
 Catherine, 73
MOON,
 E., 7
 Edward, 149
 James P., 132
MOONEY BOYD & CO., 305
MOOR,
 Edward, 33
MOORE,
 A. R., 237
 Andrew R., 236
 E., 5
 E. G., 346
 E. Y., 25
 Edward, 1, 149, 152, 169,
 177, 178, 271, 304, 309
MORGAN,
 Francis, 237
 Henry, 356
 J. C., 417
 Joshua W., 160
 Josiah J., 160

Lorenzo, 144, 218, 264
MORRIS,
 Henry, 274
 J. H., 282
 James G., 154, 156
 James M., 71
 John B., 226
 Lucy, 383
 Susan, 386
 Thomas, 226
MORROW,
 P. J., 13
 R., 215
MOSBY,
 William R., 236
MOSELEY,
 Lewis E., 46
 R., 48
 W. R., 48
 William R., 46
MOSELY,
 May, 226
MOSES,
 A., 288
 Ann M., 245
 Ansley, 229, 232
 Delila, 91, 100, 224(2),
 267, 280(2)
 Delilah, 204, 241, 242,
 296, 297
 Hiram, 18, 82, 202(2),
 204, 212, 223, 224, 242,
 267(2), 280, 297
 Hiram D., 100, 204, 224,
 267, 280, 297
 John L., 100, 202, 212(2),
 245(2)
 Martha, 244(2), 245(2)
 Mary, 204, 223
 Mary E., 99, 212
 Moses E., 212
 Philip B., 267
 Phillip B., 100, 280, 297
 Phillip H., 242
 Rachel M., 245
 William N., 99, 204,
 212(2), 245, 253
MOSLEY,

E. A., Mrs., 403
 Lewis E., 63
MUCKY,
 Babe, 332
MULKEY,
 Elisabeth, 98
MUNDAY,
 A. J., 27, 45(2)
 Andrew J., 32, 62
 George W., 199
MUNDY,
 A. G., 222
 A. I., 17
 A. J., 87, 100, 197, 234,
 274
 Amanda A., 100
 Andrew J., 84, 87(2), 213,
 228
 George, 105
 Julia Ann, 100
 Reuben T., 84, 87, 100
 Roxanna J., 100
MURPHY,
 Andrew, 39, 43, 49, 67
 C. P., 206(2), 291
 Charles, 210
 Charlotte, 206, 442
 E. M., 38(2)
 Elizabeth, 39, 43, 49, 67,
 297
 Emanuel, 75
 Eva E., 442
 Eva R., 407
 G. W., 417, 427
 George, 362, 373
 George N., 146
 George W., 392, 410, 415,
 417(2)
 H. Erarnest, 407
 I. H., 49
 Ida, 442
 J. H., 39, 206, 321, 324,
 340, 346, 359(2), 372,
 387(2), 404, 412
 J. N., 49, 206, 346
 J. R., 417, 427(2)
 James, 34, 39, 43, 49(2),
 67, 78

INDEX

MURPHY (continued)
  James D., 139, 145, 286, 291
  James H., 351
  James P., 39, 43, 49(2), 67
  Jane, 297
  Jeptha, 75
  Jeptha M., 132(2), 206
  John, 39, 43, 49, 67(2), 78, 250
  John H., 49
  John M., 5(2), 38, 146, 210
  John M., Jr., 134, 139
  John M., Sr., 134
  John W., 442
  Joseph, 39
  Joseph A., 42
  Joseph H., 43, 49, 63, 75, 107, 206(2), 210, 286, 297
  Joseph R., 146
  Josiah H., 115
  Julia T., 386
  L. M., 34, 39, 53
  Lee Dora W., 442
  Lemuel E., 64
  Lemuel M., 31
  Lucinda, 206
  Lula W., 442
  M. J., 206(2)
  Maria C., 407
  Martha A., 146
  Mary, 442
  N. W., 407
  Nancy, 442
  Nancy M., 206
  R. E. L., 407
  Rebecca, 63, 75, 206
  S. N., 407
  Sarah E., 132
  Sarah L., 442
  Simon P., 38, 39, 42, 63, 206(3)
  Thomas E., 75, 206
  W. P., 297(2)
  W. T., 442(2)

  William P., 132
MURRAY & LOGAN, 18, 21
MURRY & LOGAN, 64

-N-

NASH,
  J. C., 216, 290, 321, 324, 346
  John, 39, 108, 254
  John C., 188, 238, 340, 341
NEAL,
  B. F., 158, 215(2), 231, 249, 280
  B. P., 231
  Benjamin, 8
  Benjamin F., 124, 158, 166, 230
  Emily J., 124, 215, 231, 280
  George F., 158, 215, 231
  George W., 124
  Harriett, 231
  J. F., 215
  James F., 158
  James T., 124, 231
  John P., 125, 215, 231
  Joseph, 231
  Lucretia, 230
  R. P., 158, 215
  Rachael, 231
  Rachel, 166
  Richard, 231(2)
NEALY,
  B., 203
NEEL,
  Amelia H., 89
  B. P., 280
  Benjamin F., 89
  Emily J., 289, 296
  Francis A. E., 89
  George F., 280
  George H., 296
  George W., 289
  J. F., 296
  James, 89
  John, 89

  John P., 289
  Pocahonta, 89
  R. P., 296
  Rachael, 280(2)
  Racheal, 289
  Robert, 149
  Sarah Jane, 89
NEELEY,
  Ida C., 398
NEELY,
  E., 437
  Ida, 375
  Ida C., 378
NEWTON,
  James A., 19, 65, 69, 81, 195(3)
  James J., 102, 115, 116(2), 254, 261
  Liles, 55
  Martha E., 400
  Miles, 254
  Nancy, 261
  Nancy J., 254
  Sarah, 69
NIBLET,
  I. H., 18
NICHOLAS & WARE, 232
NICHOLLS,
  Drury, 18
NICHOLS,
  John, 8
  Travis, 117
NICKOLS,
  D. A., 413
  Thomas J., 413
  William, 413
NIPPER,
  C. B., 185, 186(2), 318, 329, 338
  C. P., 342
  John, 186
  N. B., 342
NISBET,
  J. R., 420
NIX,
  Francis M., 78
NOLAN,
  George H., 259

INDEX

NORAS,
  A. C., 317
NORMAN,
  D., 200
  Daniel, 200
  G. W., 71
NORRIS,
  Amelia, Mrs., 367
  Furman, 300
NORTH,
  B. F., 377
  B. T., 362
  C. H., 362
  Everett W., 377
  F. G., 339
  J. M., 381
  John E., 377
  R. W., 228
  Zora, 377
NORTON,
  A. J., 190, 331
  Benjamin, 238
  Berry, 123, 262, 266, 301
  C. F., 190
  Eardley, 270
  Eardly, 110, 254(2), Mia.
  G. W., 190
  George W., 331
  Green, 181
  J. B. I., 340
  J. D., 193
  J. H., 190
  John G., 180
  John H., 331
  Lenora C., 331
  Manirva, 181
  Miles, 93, 108, 216,
    238(2), 254, Mia.
  N., 190(2), 331
  Nazareth, 185, 190(2),
    316, 331
  Sarah A., 159
  Stanley, 181
  Tinnytine, Mia.
  Turentine, 238, 270
  W. G., 181(2), 340
  Windsor G., 110
  Winslow, 159
  Winslow G., 93, 301
MUNCEY,
  Hugh D., 38

-O-

OAKELY,
  James M., 37
OAKLY,
  James M., 151
O'BRIEN,
  Anna, 326, 350
  W. B., 326, 350
  William, 350
  William B., 350
OGBORN,
  Elizabeth, 411
  Thomas, 411
OGILBY,
  Martha, 58
OGLETREE,
  H. H., 38
  Luina, 423
  W., 423
O'GLILM,
  Hope H., 35
OLIVER,
  Sanford C., 176(2)
OMAN,
  H. E., 228
ORR,
  H., 334
  Mathew, 321, 324
  Newton, 341
OSBORN,
  Benjamin F., 162
  I., 5
  James, 5
  James R. D., 15
  John, 162
  John M., 12
  Martha, 5
  Mary, 5
  William, 5, 9, 15, 22
  William G., 15
OSBURN,
  Randel T., 136
OWEN,
  E. P., 413
  Harriet, 413
  J. R., 413
  R. S., 413
  Rufus M., 413(2)
OWENS,
  Lucinda Caroline, 88
  Martha, 88, 140
  Martha Amanda, 88
  Matilda C., 88
  Robert Martin, 88
  Sarah Elizabeth, 88
  William, 88
OZBURN,
  Haywood, 88
  William K., 88

-P-

PADGETT,
  Elizabeth, 206, 337, 341,
    344, 353, 370
  H. B., 341, 342, 353
  J. C., 353
  J. L., 353
  J. T., 341, 374
  J. W., 341, 344, 377
  J.T., 344
  James M., 157(2)
  Jimmie, 374, 382, 390
  John W., 353
  L. D., 72, 203, 206, 285,
    237
  Lorenzo D., 83, 107, 135,
    136, 137, 143, 144, 157,
    171
  M. F., 353, 370
  Martha M., 177
  Moses, 38
  T. J., 342
  Tucker, 353
  W. F., 341, 344, 353
  W. K., 342
  W. W., 341, 353, 370(2),
    374(2), 382, 390
  William R., 217
PAGE,
  G. H., 22

INDEX

PAGE (continued)
  G. M., 258
  George H., 18
  Green, 18
  Seaborn, 69
PALLER,
  E., 18
PALMER,
  Barbary, 101, 165, 292
  Barbery, 165
  H. D., 110, 111, 159, 174,
    218, 224, 251(2), 268(2),
    279, 283, 291(2), 301, 308

  H. Q., 202
  H.D., 295
  Hansford D., 95, 122
  J. H., 292
  J. L., 291
  J. M., 239, 291, 292, 334,
    396
  J. S., 167, 307
  James M., 101, 159,
    165(2), 168, 301, 330
  John, 2, 47, 95, 101, 122,
    168, 202, 224, 239, 251,
    268, 292(2)
  John S., 174
  Joseph S., 101
  Laura E., 167
  Lula H., 174
  M. A., 174, 308
  N. J. E., 307
  Mary, 2
  Mary Jane Elizabeth, 167
  Mary S., 167
  S. E., 291
  Sarah E., 101, 292
  Thomas A., 167
PARHAM,
  S. W., 9
PARKER,
  A. M., 32, 34(2), 196(2),
    239
  Anderson, 39
  John A., 168
  Lucy Ann, 39
  M. L., 367

  Martha Jane A., 331
  Oney, 196
  W. C., 336
PARKER AND HATCHCOCK, 362
PARNELL,
  James D., 66
  Mary, 66
PARROT,
  A., 217
PARROTT,
  Catherine, 372
  Emily, 408
  John, 372
PARSON,
  Thomas R., 40
PARSONS,
  William H., 147(2)
PARTLOW,
  David, 23
PATE,
  Emily J., 160
  H., 7
  H. M., 219
  Henry M., 152, 155, 160
  Herod, 253
  Herrod, 2
  James M., 106, 199, 244,
    245, 263
  John W., 106, 245, 263
  Miram L., 245
  S., 237
  Seaborn, 134, 136, 152,
    189(2), 219(2)
  Stephen J., 160
  Wiley A., 7, 253
  Wilie A., 2
  Wilson, 441
PATTERSON,
  A. M., 395
  Drewry, 312
  Drury, 302, 383
  Exer Ann, 148
  F. D., 383
  F. M., 312
  Frances M., 193
  Francis, 90, 161, 339,
    343, 347(2), 348
  Francis Drury, 148

  Francis M., 148
  H. F., 300
  James Y., 305
  John J., 195
  John L., 216, 347
  L., 347
  M. H., 378
  M. T., 378
  Mary Terisa, 148
  Millard Hill, 148
  Pallestine, 148
  Rebecca, 148
  Roxanna, 312
  Serena, 312
  Temperance, 347, 348
  Tillman, 339, 347(2), 348
PEARCE,
  John, 199
PEARSON,
  Ann, 194, 212, 245
  Anne, 244
  O. M., 194, 218, 233,
    244(2), 249
  O. W., 212, 272
  Oliver M., M, 22, 94, 95,
    105, 212, 223, 224, 272
  Thomas R., 25, 250
PEARSONS,
  Oliver M., 194
  T. R., 197
PEEK,
  Robert, 342
PEGG,
  Samuel G., 9, 20, 22, 31,
    32, 226
PELDON,
  A. C., 225
  Tabitha E., Mrs., 225
PENTECOST,
  Harriet L., 384
  Harriett, 384
  R. W., 384
PEPPERS,
  J. R., 359
  Jane, 311
  W. M., Mrs., 359
PERDUE,
  G. W., 232

INDEX

George, 229
PERRY,
  J. D., 392
PERSONS,
  Oliver M., Jr., 193
  T. R., 27, 228
  Thomas R., 50, 67, 208, 267, 289
  W. H., 149, 407
  William H., 148
PETERS,
  George, 65(2), 302
  Kelly, 208
PETILLS,
  L., 13
PETTY,
  Zacariah, 3
PHARR,
  E., Mrs., 346
  Emiline, 346
  F. B., 348
  Nancy E., 351
PHILIPS,
  Piety, 65
PHILLIPPS,
  E. W., 357
PHILLIPS,
  Berry, 71(2)
  James R., 273
  John, 39, 146, 163, 170, 329, 332, 384(3)
  Louisa, 170, 332, 384
  Seaborn, 21
  William R., 232
PHILLIS,
  William R., 229
PINSON,
  Sam, 310
  Tuck, 310
PITMAN,
  A. J., 261
  M. H., 261
  William M., 261
PLEDGER,
  Counsel, 223
  John W., 61, 69, 81, 98, 203, 223
  Joseph P., 98, 223(2)

POE,
  W., 239
POLLARD,
  A. J., 204, 212(2), 229, 244, 245, 253
  Andrew J., 99, 100, 202, 223(2)
  C. F., 173
  E. M., 391
  Marietta, 304
  Mary, 315
  Mary E., 173
  Rachel, 212
  Rachel M., 245
  William, 21
POOL,
  Ephraim M., 86
POOLE,
  A., 9
  A. J., 200
POPE,
  Alex S., 406
  H., 305
  H. H., 305, 406
  Hardy H., 317
  J. D., 406
  Jesse, 13
  May, 203
  Norris, 203
  R. H., 316
  Ritter, 316
  Stephen T., 406
PORTER,
  A. R., 319, 382
  Archabal R., 176
  Archibald R., 134
  Haney, 129, 130
  Hany, 295
  Hugh, 73, 87(2), 88, 89, 129, 134, 176, 194, 201, 202, 230, 264(2), 286, 289, 295, 305, 319
  J. H., 319
  John, 305, 306
  John H., 134, 178
  John J., 308
  John M., 129(2), 178, 295, 305(2)

Nancy, 194
Ophelia, 319
Ophelia J., 134, 178, 382
R. C., 67
Robert C., 67(2), 73
POSEY,
  B. F., 428, 435(2)
  James, 428
POST,
  Susan, 311
POSTEN,
  Burrell B., 408
  Elma, 408
  G. W., 408(2)
  George W., 408(2)
  John W. E., 408
  Parthena, 441
  W. E., 408
POUNDER,
  Daniel M., 52
POUNDS,
  Susie E., 442
POWELL,
  James, 218
POWER,
  W., 216
POWERS,
  George, 84
  Nicholas F., 84
  Thomas M. G., 84
PRANSON,
  Anny, 18
PRESLEY,
  L. W., 212, 244
  Rachael, 244
  Rachael M., 212
  Rachel, 244
  Rachel M., 244
PRESSLEY,
  Nancy, 305
PRESTLEY,
  Nancy, 317
PRESTLY,
  L. W., 245
PRICE,
  D. J., 415
  Elizabeth, 40(2), 55
  Francis, 17, 25, 40(2), 55

INDEX

PRICE (continued)
  Jordan, 339
  Jurden, 404
  Q. L., 69
  Q. S., 25, 415
  Samuel, 25
  Sarah, 404
PRINCE,
  J. K., 416
  R. G., 416
PRUITT,
  Mary, 206
  Samuel, 206
PYRON,
  Emmett, 375
  Jess, 442
  John M., 308, 316
  Josiah, 143, 145, 238
  Lois, 442
  M. C., 442
  M. W., 286
  Oscar, 442
  Rebecca, 308(2)
  S. E., 442
  William M., 149
  Zella, 442

-Q-

QUICK,
  Druzilla, 411
  Eli, 235
  Serena Jane, 411
QUIN,
  Obe, 333

-R-

R. K. HOLLIDAY & CO., 65
R. W. HOLLIDAY & CO., 71
RAGAN,
  William, 417
RAINEY,
  H. A., 58
RAMSEY,
  Charity A., 114
  Eli W., 114
  James E., 114
  Julia F., 114
  Nancy I. C., 114
RANEY,
  M. A., 63
RAY,
  G. W., 238
  I. J., 239
  Lavender R., 409, 414,
    417, 422, 431, 434
READ,
  Mathew, 105, 114, 117,
    287, 422
  Matthew, 409, 414, 417,
    431, 434
  W. T., 314
READE,
  Mathew, 404
REDWINE,
  M. L., 368, 383
  W. D., 310
  W. H., 436
  W. P., 148, 185, 322, 328,
    334, 336, 340
  William P., 152, 210
  Williamson P., 155
REED,
  Henrietta Amelia, 289
  H., 23
REESE,
  Sarah, 18
REEVES,
  A. B., 32
  A. M., 15, 32, 237
  A. W., 56, 289
  Alexander, 317, 347(2)
  Allen, 9, 15, 35, 38, 56,
    71(2), 79(3), 85(2), 86,
    105, 106(3), 135, 185,
    194(3), 214, 239(2), 240,
    244, 245, 259, 278, 289,
    317(3)
  Amos W., 86, 221, 252, 294
  Dempsey A., 14, 15, 23,
    32, 44, 57
  E., 15
  Elizabeth, 244(2), 245(2),
    278
  Elizabeth A., 105, 259,
    289
  Elizabeth Ann, 245
  Elizabeth S., 245
  H. C., 381, 382, 387
  Henry C., 86, 221, 266,
    294
  J. H., 227
  J. M., 56
  J. Y., 18
  John H., 21
  John W., 32, 44, 57
  L. A., Miss, 56
  M. A., 239
  M. C., Miss, 56
  M. J., 442
  Martha A., 86(2), 114,
    221(3), 239, 252, 266(2),
    281, 294
  Martha W., 86, 114, 221,
    252
  Mary Ann, 57
  Mary Jane, 212(2)
  Nancy, 185, 317(2)
  O. A., 245
  Oliver A., 106, 244
  P. A., 15
  Piety, 317
  Robert A., 346
  Robert H., 86
  Robert W., 221, 252, 294
  Sarah Ann, 86, 114, 266,
    281, 294
  W. B., 56
  W. C., 435
  W. D., 15, 32
  W. J., 226
  W. L., 289
  W. S., 32, 56
  Widow, 56
  William, 15(2), 18, 52,
    56, 71, 79, 85, 86, 194,
    214, 221(2), 239, 252,
    266, 281, 294
  William A., 9
  William B., 15
  William C., 166
  William F., 86
  William P., 114, 221, 252

INDEX

William S., 193
Wyatt D., 15
Wyatt S., 23, 44, 85, 86
REGENSTELL & CO., 352
RENFRO,
  Henry, 42
RENTFRO,
  B., 178
  Henry, 24
RENTFROW,
  B., 285
  Burket, 150, 154, 186,
    191, 263, 271, 277
  Charley D., 173
  Council, 81
  Counsel, 20, 98(2), 99,
    105, 203, 223(3)
  Emily J., 162
  Henry, 23, 31, 54, 88, 162
  Mattie, Mrs., 423
  Stephen, 154, 173
REUBEN,
  D., 230
RHODES,
  Benjamin F., 71
  Jabez M., 35, 37
RIAL,
  J. M., 240
RICHARDS,
  J., 230
RICHARDSON,
  I., 221
  J. A., 310, 346(2), 353
  J. J., 346
  J. L., 316
  John A., 300, 310, 311,
    319, 346, 353, 387
  John A. R., 337
  John H., 358
  S. P., 346
  S. T., 386
RICHARDSON & MERRIT, 21
RICHMOND,
  J., 355
RICHTER,
  C. W., 323, 382, 431
RIGGINS,
  J. J., 353

M. J., 353
RIVERS,
  H. S., 382, 388, 395, 405,
    414, 424, 430, 435
  H. S>, 382
  Henry S., 375
  J. N., 421, 438
  J. W., 391
  Jane C., 421
  Jane E., Mrs., 438
  N. C., 392
  R. A., 336, 355, 416, 420,
    421, 436, 438(2)
  R. A., Mrs., 436, 439
  Robert, 416, 420, 421, 436
  Robert A., 421
  W. M., 396, 401
ROAN,
  L. S., 399, 401
ROBERTS,
  Chelly, 348
  D., 231
  E. H., 202, 230, 264(2)
  E. H. G., 194
  Francis M., 92(2)
  Griffin, 202, 230, 264(2),
    295
  Griffin A., 130, 194
  James G., 130
  James L., 264, 295
  James S., 89, 194, 202,
    230
  Joshua, 391
  Lawson W., 295
  Lewis E. H., 89
  Mary A., 88
  Nancy, 194
  O. F., 362
  R., 21
  S. T., 240
  Sampson W., 130, 201
  Sansom, 202
  Sansom W., 87(2), 194,
    230(2)
  Sarah F., 201
  Sarah T., 89, 130, 194,
    230, 264, 295
  W. T., 362, 391, 430, 438

William, 88
William H., 194
ROBERTSON,
  Arthur, 39
ROBINSON,
  Anna, 174
  Arthur, 43, 138, 166(2),
    286
  Charles J., 27, 160, 171,
    173, 242, 265, 266
  Charles J., Sr., 262
  E. W. F., 174
  G. W., 322, 346, 354, 361,
    365, 388, 396, 398
  George W., 310
  H. T., 235
  J., 327
  James, 319
  Jane, 300
  John B., 175
  John R., 171, 178(2), 304
  Luisa, 174
  Margaret S., 174
  Mary, 178
  Mollie, Miss, 300
  N. B., 178(2)
  Sallie, 300
  Samuel, 166, 216, 300, 308
  Samuel J., 174
  W. J., 174
ROE,
  Richard, 258
ROERS,
  H. M., 324
ROGERS,
  Abner D., 271
  Bartow, 387
  Charles, 358
  Charley, 363
  H. M., 321, 323, 324, 335,
    358, 363, 372, 412
  J. B., 372, 404, 412
  J. D., 340, 358(2)
  J. D., Mrs., 323, 335
  J. D.,Mrs., 340
  J. M., 363
  James, 363
  James B., 359, 372

INDEX

ROGERS (continued)
 John M., 363
 R., 53(2)
 R. L., 363
 R. R., 138, 285, 288
 Raman R., 136
 Robert L., 358
 W. M., 363
 William, 340
ROGGERS,
 H. M., 177, 178
ROUNTREE,
 C. E., 332
 Cynthia Ella, 332, 356
 E., 222
 Ephraim, 173, 332, 356
 M. F., Mrs., 332
 Mary E., Mrs., 356
 Synthia E., 173
 Wiley, 92(2)
 Younc, 332
 Young, 173, 332, 356
RPGERS,
 H. M., 188
RUNNELLS,
 Terry, 143
RUNNELS,
 Terry, 140
RUSH,
 Elisabeth, 265
 Elizabeth, 279, 367, 371, 376, 382, 386, 419
 Ellison, 111, 173, 174, 218, 251, 268, 283, 295
 Eveline, 375
 John, 110, 112(2), 217, 347, 367, 376, 382, 386, 419
 Mary, 265
 Mary E., 116, 375
 Mary Elizabeth, 291
 Mary Jane, 116, 291
 Sarah F., 116, 375
 Sarah Frances, 265
 Sarah Frances Smith, 291
 William, 112
 William T., 110, 217, 265, 291

Willie O., 347
RUSSELL,
 Charles C., 334
 F. M. J., 340
 Frank B., 334
 G. T., 334
 Gen. Beauregard, 173
 Gen. William R. L., 173
 Hester Ann Medorah, 173
 J. J., 228
 Len, 331
 M. A., 340
 M. T., 340
 Margaret A. D., 66
 Margaret H., 334
 Mary C., 173
 P. H., 55
 Pamelia, 287
 Parmelia, 123
 Permelia, 123, 298
 Sterling, 363
 T. M. J., 346
 W. J., 19, 60, 334, 340, 346, 368
 W. S., 340, 346, 364, 368, 393
 Wesley S. Thomas M. J., 173
 William, 33, 66, 123(2), 262, 287, 298
 William I., 46, 53, 55
 William J., 34, 35, 38, 46, 51, 52, 63, 66, 67(2), 70, 71, 80, 81, 84(2), 87, 94(2), 122, 125(2), 130, 139, 168, 173(2), 196, 208, 209, 210, 233(2), 255, 257, 272, 273, 292, 330, 331
 William R., 334
RUTLEDGE,
 Dolsey, 397
RYAN,
 John, 360

-S-

SAMS,

C. C., 133
 M. D., 397, 401, 407
 William J., 133
 William S., 256
SANDERS,
 Flora, 109, 112, 222, 228, 247, 270, 283
 Florda, 283
SANSOM,
 G. H., 412
SANSON,
 Samuel, 334
SARGENT & CO., 71
SCALES,
 Joseph, 117, 235, 247, 256, 268, 282
 Josephine, 282
 Martha, 256(4), 282(2)
 Martha M., 247
 May, 282
 S. M., 282
 W., 239
 Westley, 238
SCOTT,
 George W., 391
 Miles, 86
 Miles L., 70, 77
SEGRAVES,
 Edmond, 134
 Haney, 134, 176
SELLERS,
 John, 9, 16, 36, 37, 52, 53, 71, 227
 Louisa W., 53
 Martha W., Mrs., 36
 Widow, 16
SERLLS,
 Louisa W., 37
SHADDICK,
 William, 37
SHADRYCK,
 William, 12(2), 140, 159, 181, 220, 301, 340
SHARP,
 E. R., 360
SHELL,
 C. C., 69, 131, 290(2), 291, 293

INDEX

C. T., 395
Charles, 210
Charles C., 153, 156
D., 69
Daniel, 327, 345, 355,
 385, 389, 395, 396, 401
G. R., 291
J. M., 421
J. S., 385, 389, 395, 396,
 401
M. L., 291
Mary J., 385, 389
Mary L., 347
Mary C., 347
R. B., 166(2), 308, 385
Sarah A., 290
Sarah F., Mrs., 347(2)
Teresa, 345
Terracy, 395
Terresa, 355
Tracy, 345
W. O., 395, 396
W. S., 385, 389, 395(2),
 401
Widow, 291
William N., 12
Willie D., 347
Willie O., 347
SHELNUT,
 Andrew, 37, 43
 John, 37, 43, 74
SHELNUTT,
 N., 360
SHEPARD,
 Edmick, 228
SHEPHARD,
 Edward, 258
SHEPHERD,
 E., 226
 John T., 350
 Moab, 226
 Molen, 325
 William H., 350
SHERLING,
 Marion H., 238
SHIELDS,
 Robert O., 311
SHIPP,

Lemuel G., 52
Mark, 255
Permelia F., 371
SHROPSHIRE,
 A. J., 187, 190, 322,
  327(2), 332, 333, 336,
  342(2), 352, 360, 364,
  368, 372, 373, 380, 384
 Aurelia, 327
 Fannie, 342
 J. B., 342
 J. P., 110, 169, 187, 210,
  256, 257(2), 258, 290,
  298, 319, 322, 327, 332,
  333, 352, 380
 J. W., 190, 352
 John, 380
 John W., 364, 368, 372
 Johnie, 190, 342, 352,
  364, 368, 372
 Johnnie, 360, 373, 379,
  380
 Joshua, 324
 Joshua P., 133
 L. M., 327
 M. L., 322, 327, 342, 384
 M. L., Mrs., 324
 Minnie, 342
 Nannie, 368, 372, 373, 380
 Newman, 190
 S. F., 384
 S. Fanin, 327
 S. J., 322
 Seaborn, 57
SHROPSHIRE & JOHNSON, 362,
 391
SIBBY,
 W. W., 265
SIBLEY,
 W. W., 226, 260(2), 264,
  280, 285
 William, 247
 William W., 118
SIBLY,
 W. W., 200
SILLERS,
 John, 201
 Louisa W., 201

SILMAN,
 W. R., 175(2)
SILVEY,
 G. W., 238
 J. B., 203
SIMMONS,
 Barney, 336
 Caleb, 20, 195
 J. S., 367
 Julia Ann, 195
SIMPSON,
 Cane, 215
 R. H., 321
 R. W., 324, 334
 Henry, 38, 75, 341
 M. W., 333
 Mary, 43
 Thomas, 17, 97, 256
SIMS,
 Joanah, 116
SIMS & THRELKELD, 21
SLATON,
 Eusebeus, 164
 G. W., 187(2), 321, 333,
  334
 George H., 335
 George W., 320
 Isaiah, 356(2)
 Sallie, 433
 U., 356
 Usibious, 187
SLAYTON,
 A., 217
 Ucebius, 163
 Ucibious, 102
SMALLWOOD,
 Harriet, 57
 Harriet A., 390
 Harriet Ann, 198
 Harriett, 387
 J. F., 390
 M. P., 57
 Mark, 57(2), 79, 198, 207
 Martin C., 198
 Milligan, 57
 Riley, 57
 Tolbert, 198
 W. R., 390, 399(2), 401

INDEX

SHARR,
  Alonzo P., 379
  Avery D., 379
  Benson, 379
  Ella, 379
  James J., 379
  John R., 379
  Linnie, 379
  H. E., 379
  H.C., 71
  Martha C., 21, 43
  Martha C., Mrs., 36
  Martha E., 379
  Martin C., 23
  Mattie, 379
  R. R., 379
  Robert R., 15, 21, 36, 43, 379
  William F., 379
SMITH,
  A. M., 337
  A. R., 151, 172, 175, 303(2), 330
  A. T., 274
  A.R., 175
  Alexander, 33, 305, 316, 317
  Alice, 433
  Archabal, 282
  Archabald, 247
  Archabel, 282
  Archibald, 117(2), 226, 235, 268
  B. M., 303
  C. C., 310
  C. G., 310(2), 313
  C. N., 410
  C. W., 172, 217, 257
  Charles W., 95, 122, 125(2)
  Cora L., 433
  D. M., 333, 357
  Daniel, 208
  Dick, 310
  E. C. W., 182, 427
  Eliza, 413
  Elizabeth, 32, 37
  Emma, 313, 413
  Emma. Miss, 313
  Emmett, 334
  Gincy E., 109
  H. C., 303
  Hardaway, 122, 257
  Harriett, 410
  I., 37
  I. B., 410(2)
  I. E. C. W., 427
  I. E. W., 387
  I. H., 310(3), 313, 362
  Ira B., 385
  Isaac H., 177, 313(2), 328, 335
  Isaiah, 26, 40, 51
  J. A., 5
  J. B., 274(3), 343
  J. C., 270
  J. D., 388, 391, 430
  J. E. C., 303
  J. E. C. W., 319, 357
  J. M., 333, 357
  J. T., 310(2)
  J. W., 217, 235, 238(2), 310, 356
  James, 20
  James A., 32
  James G., 116, 264
  James M., 72
  James T., 413
  Jane E., 121, 219
  Jesse G., 71
  John, 8
  John A., 112
  John B., 288
  John H., 156
  John N., 54
  John W., 118, 155, 156, 182, 238, 356
  Johnathan, 216(2), 238
  Josephine, 343
  Josie, 373
  L. C., 17, 182, 275, 333(2), 357(2), 397
  L. H., 300
  Lewis C., 77, 97, 133, 145, 149, 171, 172, 275, 336
  Lewis W., 164
  Lucy Ann, 118, 238
  M. J., 218, 337, 355, 410, 411(2)
  M. M., 357
  M. P., 40
  Madison, 357
  Malissa, 385
  Malissa M., 343
  Margaret M. J., 118
  Marietta, 401
  Marion, 343
  Mary A., 245(2)
  Mary Jane, 212(2)
  Melissa, 366, 373
  Minia G., 179(3)
  Minnie, 328
  Minnie G., 313(2), 318(2), 335, 344, 362, 366, 372
  N. C., 222, 433
  Noah, 114, 126, 127, 274(2)
  Nora, 362
  Nora H., 313, 318, 366, 372, 381, 385
  Norah H., 179, 313, 328, 335, 344
  P. H., 258
  Patience, 317
  Patsey S., 219
  Patsey T., 121
  Patsy S., 219
  Patsy T., 109(2)
  R. N., 175(2), 303, 330
  Rebecca C., 179, 305, 325, 341(2), 364, 379, 389
  Rebecca W., 303(2)
  S. S., Mrs., 313(2)
  Sallie, 362
  Sallie A., 179, 313(2), 318, 328, 344, 366, 372, 381, 385
  Sally A., 335
  Sarah Ann, 32
  Sarah F., 182
  Seaborn, 9, 20, 37, 117, 200, 235, 247, 268, 282
  Stephen, 1, 25

INDEX

Thomas C. Speer, 182
Valley, 410
W. A., 245
W. B., 413
W. H., 410
W. N., 333
W. P., 15, 337, 387
Warren, 310
William, 34, 37, 310(3), 357
William A., 212(2), 244(2), 245
William G., 16, 21, 30
William L., 65
William P., 51
Wilson M., 373
Z. H., 179
SMITH & SILVEY, 238
SNEAD,
  J. W., 438
  John W., 435
  Mamie, 435
  Mamie L., 438
  N. N., Mrs., 438
  N. W., 435
  Nancy M., 435
SNEED,
  G. W., 300
  J., 300
  John, 300(2), 342, 379
SOUTEE,
  G. W., 213
SOUTER,
  G. W., 132, 199
SPARKMAN,
  William, 54(2)
SPARKS,
  Marberry, 19
SPEAR,
  Emily, 67
  J. F., 218
  John, Nia.
  John W., 35, 67, 258
  Joseph, 165, Nia.
  Joseph F., 258
  T. C., 191
  Thomas C., 165
  William, 202

William, 192
William M., 29, Nia.
SPEARR,
  Joseph, 93
  William F., 93
SPEER,
  A., 348
  A. C., 179, 325(2)
  Abe, 300
  Allison C., 172
  Amanda J., 313, 385
  Autney, 300
  David C., 179
  David W., 172, 341, 379
  Ed, 421
  Emily A., 325
  Emily Ann, 172
  F. C., Mrs., 421, 432
  Francis C., 417
  George, 300
  George W., 172
  H. C., 305, 325
  Henry, 303, 305
  Henry C., 172(2), 208, 341
  Henry W., 179
  J., 421
  J. J., 300(2), 303, 421, 432(2)
  J. L., 300, 303
  J. M., 328, 338, 345(3), 377, 378
  J. W., 300, 330, 378
  J. W. F., 176
  J. W. T., 318, 385
  James J., 303(2), 377(2), 417
  James M., 378
  John R., 328
  John T., 313, 355(7)
  John W., 176, 300, 303(2), 318, 319, 378, 387, 390
  John W. T., 355
  Joseph, 52, 97(2), 131, 204, 307, 377(2), 378
  Joseph F., 377
  Joseph M., 183, 377
  Joseph, Sr., 136
  M., 300

M. A. C., 341
M. A. L., 379(2)
M. E., 432
Martha A. L., 172
Mary, 377(2)
Mary A. S., 179
Mary Ann, 300, 303, 377
Nancy C., 377
S. E., 417, 421, 432(2)
S. F., 427
Sarah F., 204, 319
T. C., 176, 182, 183, 185, 300, 316, 318, 319, 321, 330, 338, 345, 377(2), 378, 427(3)
T. E., 300
Thomas C., 97, 204(2)
W. T., 330
William, 97, 318
William M., 131, 157, 162(2)
SPEER AND STEWART, 361
SPEIGHT,
  Elvira, Mrs., 408
  Thomas, 419
SPEIR,
  Allison, 174
  B. F., 174
  David W., 364
  Eliza A., Mrs., 438
  Henry, 421
  Henry C., 389
  J. C., 438
  J. W. A., 436
  James J., 166
  Lela V., 174
  M. A., 389(2)
  Martin V., 174
  Mary, 166
  Mary E., 173, 174
  R. J., 421
  R. R., 438
  William M., 166
SPENCE,
  Elizabeth, 139
  Ida, 139
  Ida V., 302, 382
  Iva V., 345

488

INDEX

SPENCE (continued)
  J. T., 395
  James, 9
  Lucy A., 382
  Prudence D., 399
  Victoria, 139
  Wilson, 133, 134, 302
SPENCER,
  Ida V., 369
  L. A., 369
SPIER,
  Allison, 153(2)
  Allison, Jr., 155
  Allison, Sr., 155
  Amanda J., 171
  Benjamin F., 153
  H. C., 146
  Henry C., 151
  J. W. T., 395
  James J., 51, 165
  John W. T., 171
  Joseph, 165
  Mary, 165
  Thomas C., 165
  William N., 165
SPRADLIN,
  Joseph W., 203
SPRAGGINS,
  William, 56, 208, 235
SPRATLIN,
  Elizabeth L., 130
  G. W., 300
  Jesse M., 130, 288
  Joshua, 333
SPRAYBERRY,
  B. M., 410, 411
SPRUELL,
  W. R., 343
SPRUILL,
  H. A., 377
  W. R., 377
SPURLIN,
  A. J., 423, 429
  Crattie, 429
  D. S., 429
  David Samuel, 423
  E. J., 423, 429
  I. P., 423

J. E., 369, 380, 414, 417, 422, 423, 429(2), 431, 432, 434, 436, 440
J. J., 423
J. M., 414, 418(2), 423, 429, 432
J. P., 429
James, 18
James M., 194, 218
John A., 429
Lou, Mrs., 429
M. A., 429
Mary, 413
Otta, 429
Pauline A., 424
Permelia, 414
Permelia A., 424
T. J., 423, 429
Willie, 429
STAINHEIMER,
  Abraham, 327
STALLINGS & VAUGHN, 309
STANDFIELD,
  William B., 128
STANFIELD,
  William B., 298
STANLEY,
  Anna, 369
STARNES,
  S. E., 311(2)
STARR,
  Benjamin, 7, 16
  J. H., 216, 239
  J. P., 422, 431, 433, 436, 439
  John H., 52, 213
  Joshua H., 86
STEENHEIMER,
  A., 341
STEINHEIMER,
  A., 428, 435(2)
  A. A., 392(2)
STELL,
  E. R., Mrs., 58
  Elizabeth, 58
  J. J., 58
  J. W., 270
  James I., 18

James J., 37, 46, 58
John D., 4, 7, 10, 16, 17, 18, 22, 27, 47, 55, 70, 74, 80
R. H., 46
R. Manson, 58, 74
Robert M., 37
S. R., 391
Susan R., 391, 392, 398
STEPHENS,
  Alexander, 163
  Alexander D., 383
  Elizabeth, 267
  F. M., 267
  G. T., 383
  George T., 163(2), 383
  H. D., 383
  J. D., 383
  J. T., 362(2)
  Jefferson, 163
  Jefferson D., 383
  John, 116, 158
  John L., 330(2)
  John T., 158(2)
  John W., 163, 330
  Lucy, 163, 383
  Martha C., 163
  Mary, 163
  Nancy, 116, 264
  T. H., 276
  Thomas H., 100, 101, 116, 145
STERN,
  Mary, 431
STEWART,
  Ephraim, 224
  F. G., 5
  George, 17
  J. D., 365
  J. O., 339
  John D., 305
  Speer, 361
  W. B., 360, 367(2), 415
STEWART & NEWTON, 323
STEWART AND NEWTON, 363
STINCHCOMB,
  A., 226
  G. P., 184

INDEX

G. W., 183, 184, 185, 314, 316, 339, 343, 358, 403
George, 358
George W., 188, 321
Georgia, 188, 378
Georgia A., 391, 409, 426
Georgia S., 412
J. F., 403
J. O., 183, 185, 339
John, 358
John O., 403
Lizzie, 184
M. A., Mrs., 316
Marietta, 185
Martha A., 188, 358, 378
N., 3, 304, 316
N. D., 403
Nathaniel, 24, 26, 27(3), 29, 35, 39, 57, 76, 77, 93, 132, 133, 154, 161, 176, 177, 179, 184, 185, 304, 315
P., 316
Philip, 187
Phillip, 183, 184, 321, 339, 343
Sarah A., 403
Tululah, 185
Victor, 161, 304
W. P., 403
STOKES,
A. E., 169, 326, 360, 361, 421
D. C., 164, 184, 321, 348
David E., 328
Davis C., 169
E., 347
L., 34
Littletn, 79
Littleton, 57, 79
S. T., 321
Sarah T., 328
STONE,
A. W., 195, 224, 258
Amherst W., 64, 66, 75
Isaac, 340
STOREY,
John T., 19(2)

STORY,
Calvin, 250(2)
E. W., 250
Elias, 250
Elias W., 250
Lucinda, 250
Mary, 250
STRATTON,
Almond, 13, 17, 19, 73
P., 21
P. N., 293
T., 21
STRICKLAND,
B. F., 276
B. C., 224, 263
Barney, 102
Cainey, 4
Caney, 20, 32, 34
Catharine, 62
E. S>, 362
Elizabeth, 62
Francis, 62
Harry, 20
Isaac, 32
Kinchen, 17, 20, 27, 32, 45, 62
M. P., 224
Martha, 62
Mary F. P., 102
R. G., 124, 263, 335
Russell C., 101
Russell G., 205, 224, 242, 263
Simeon, 101
Simon, 205, 224(2), 242
Susan, 62
Widow, 20
STRICKSTROM,
Dennis N., 286
STRIPLING,
Maria, 319
STUBBS,
Dennis, 3, 8, 80, 98, 128, 238, 261
Emily, 371
H., 56, 278
Hubbard, 1, 48, 56, 209, 261, 341, 347

Jane, 411
Nancy, 100, 261
Nancy J., 254
R., 213
Roland, 6, 12, 18
Rowland, 30, 43, 64, 68, 72, 80(2), 102, 115, 129, 136, 235, 261, 286, Mia.
Sarah, 18, 30, 56(2), 68, 72, 193, 209, 261
William, 1, 68, 72, 98, 100, 101, 116, 193(2), 235, 254, 261, Mia.
William Jr., 254
STURDIVANT,
Allen D., 335
SUDERTH,
Mary, 383
SUDOTH,
Mary, 368
SUMMERS,
Q. L., 237
SWAINY,
Emiline, 2
Francis, 2
Joseph, 2
Josiah, 2
Margaret, 2
Nancy, 2
Rebecca, 2
Susan, 2
William D., 2
SWAN,
A. J., 227(2)
H., 227
Henry, 227
John, 229, 232
Thomas, 274
W. H., 226
SWANN,
F. M., 442
J. A., 442
William B., 112
SWANSON,
A. V., 298
Albert, 315
Andrew P., 148
Andrew V., 151

INDEX

SWANSON (continued)
  Berta, 362
  Cordelian C., 151
  Elizabeth, 232, 433
  F. P., 344
  Kerdeliau C., 148
  Lizzie, 357, 371, 376
  Louis, 315
  M. A. P., 326
  M. A. P., Hrs., 314
  M. E. A., 394
  M. E. M., 352
  M. N., 352, 394
  M. R., 334
  M. W., 148, 169, 186(2), 191, 232, 239, 315(2), 316(2), 325(2), 433
  Marcus W., 126
  Marshal M., 191, 387, 394
  Marshall, 357, 371, 376
  Martha E. A., 387
  Martha E. M., 191
  N. W., 325
  Oney, 362
  Paul, 357, 371
  S., 326
  Samuel, 24, 26, 183, 191(2), 314, 315(2), 326, 344, 352(3), 433
  Simon, 315, 316, 336, 417
  T. B., 183(2), 315, 326, 352(3)
  Thomas B., 334
  Thomas P., 315, 326
  Turner B., 352
  W. W., 186, 315
  Widow, 315
SWEAT,
  Amanda A., 403
  Andrew J., 38, 39, 44, 73
  Benjamin F., 403
  Charlotte, 389
  E., 169, 274
  Ephraim, 38, 48(2), 73, 216, 388, 389, 403
  F. D., 403
  J., 73
  James W., 403

  Martha, 403
  S. C., 403
  S. S., 216
  Solomn, 276
SWINNY,
  W. E., 322

-T-

TALIAFERRO,
  Edward M., 238
TALLEY,
  James W., 202, 228, 272
TALLY,
  A. L., 352
  James W., 89
TANKERSLEY,
  A. M., 189
  Mary E., 241
TANKERSLY,
  A. M., 189
  George, 241
  Mary E., 241
TANNER,
  C. G., 130
TARPLEY,
  B. W., 308
  Etta S., 441
  H. B., 323
  J. R., 323
  J. W., 441
  R. O., 429
  R. W., 316
  S. E., 429, 430
TARPLY,
  J. K., 363
  Mattie A., 363
  R. W., 274
TAYLOR,
  J. A., 353
  Nancy M. L., 413
  R. K., 349
TEEL,
  Pereby, 369
TEMPLES & STEWART, 304
THAMES,
  Charles O., 171
  Cintha C., 118

  Cynthia, 168
  James, 118, 168
  James T., 118, 127
  John, 118(2), 168(2)
  Mary, 118, 168
  William, 102, 104, 118
THOMAS,
  C. O., 258
  Cynthia, 260, 338
  Daniel R., 13, 197, 209
  J. F., 295
  James, 260
  James J., 338(2)
  James T., 260
  John, 260(2)
  John A., 338
  John M., 333(2)
  M.L., 333
  Mary, 260
  Mary E., 338
  William, 195
THOMAS PULLIUM & CO., 353
THOMPSON,
  Allen, 17, 85, 91, 99, 193, 206, 209, 231, 237, 248, 261, 276
  Elisabeth, 17
  Ellen, 11
  George C. K., 167
  James, 84, 192, 206, 209, 232, 242, 257, 261(2)
  James E., 404
  James S., 151, 167
  Jeremiah, 17
  L. T., 11, 17, 27, 226
  Lewis, 11
  Lewis H., 17
  Lewis T., 99, 100, 147, 300
  Malissa T., 377
  Malvin A., 377
  Malviny, 377
  Martha, 85, 99, 193(2), 213, 237(2)
  Mary, 85, 99, 193, 215, 220, 248, 269
  Matilda, 377
  May, 261

INDEX

Oliver, 151, 167
Robert H., 167
S. A., 311
Samuel, 8, 11, 17(2), 35, 224
Samuel, Sr., 5
Sarah, 297
Sarah E., 261
W., 261
William, 91, 206, 231, 276, 309, 377
THOMSON,
M. H., 297
William, 261
THORNTON,
B., 169, 303, 348, 369
B. L., 369
Bennett, 349
Blackman, 97, 137, 138, 146, 160, 172, 179, 199, 214, 262(2)
C. A., 340, 341, 344, 345(2), 346, 352(2), 353(2), 355, 363(2), 369, 370
D. L., 369
David L., 146
Elizabeth, 146, 349, 354
Felix, 169, 214, 220
H., 71, 349
Haywood, 97, 160, 199, 214, 220, 307, 325, 340, 354(2), 364
Henry, 220
Herod, 97, 137, 138, 160, 169, 180, 214, 220(2), 340, 349, 354(2)
Herod, Jr., 349, 364(2)
Herod, Sr., 97, 199
Herrod, 307
Hiram H., 137, 138
J., 348
J. S., 381, 400(2)
J. T., 425
J. T., Rev., 425
John B., 199, 214
Jordan, 349, 354, 364
Jurden, 398

Kitty C., Miss, 369
L. A., 425
L. B., 352
M. F., 425(2)
M. J. H., 369
M. L., 381, 400
Mary, 364
May, 349
Pheraby, 180
Pheriby, 199, 349
Pherily, 214
Rebecca, 214
T. A., 421, 438
TRUMAN,
Miss, 336
THURMAN,
William T., 120, 225, 253, 272
THURMOND,
William S., 111
THREAT,
John, 161
TIDWELL,
C. M., 313
J. A. J., 438
H. M., 11, 12, 19(3), 35, 37, 71, 111, 120(2), 121, 139, 140, 142, 153, 170, 181, 217(3), 254, 255, 256(2), 263, 271, 282, 303(2)
M.M., 169, 303
Mial, 97, 109
Mial M., 85, 91, 99, Mia.
O. M., 270
P. M., 208
TIDWELL & FULLER, 226
TIDWELL & WOOTEN, 237, 238
TIDWELL & WOOTON, 238
TILGHMAN,
A. H., 65
Aaron, 4(2), 7, 9, 21, 30(2), 54, 65
Asbury Hull, 4
R. A., 372, 376, 381, 385, 388, 391, 402, 405, 409, 430
TILLERY,

J. W., 361
John, 336, 345
TILLY,
John, 347
TINSLEY,
A. B., 331, 343, 366, 373, 385
E. M., 432
L. G., 173
T. B., 373
TOBEY,
John, 227
TODD,
William, 262
TOMPSON,
Allen, 87
William, 87
TORENCE,
G. W., 362(2)
TOWNS,
J. O., 440
TOWSON,
James S., 25
TRANTHAM,
William, 121
TRAVIS,
B. M., 272
Benjamin, 272
C. E., 330, 382
E. M., 371
Elizabeth, 305
Fred, 330
H. C., 330, 371
Harbert, 25
Hiram, 17, 19, 73
Howard C., 149, 150
J. F., 309
J. T., 168, 304, 330
James T., 31, 131, 152, 177, 178, 298, 305, 309, 317, 320, 324, 382
John T., 338
M. T., 218, 342
Martha, 272
Martin, 330
Mary, 149, 150, 304, 305, 309, 316, 317, 330
N. E., Miss, 371

492

INDEX

TRAVIS (continued)
  S. C., 330, 371, 421, 422,
    430, 437
TRIMBLE,
  G. S., 361
  J. M., 117
  P. M., 177, 179, 312(2),
    313, 319, 330, 358
  S. S., 177, 179, 312(3),
    313(2), 319
TRUETT,
  John W., 128
TUCKER,
  D. R., 3(2)
  Daniel R., 3
  W. E., 20(2), 225
  William E., 34, 91, 205,
    216, 235, 238
TULLY,
  I. W., 221
TURNER,
  A. A., 190(2), 324
  A. J., 389, 403
  Ann, 207(3), 277(2), 278
  Anna, 66
  Cintha D., 389
  E. E., 389, 403
  Eliza, 411
  Emily, 83, 192, 215, 234
  Fdrick, 85
  Frederick, 95, 207,
    230(2), 248, 277
  Henson, 310, 411
  Hinson, 190, 235, 324,
    360, 411
  Hiram, 378
  J. B., 411
  J. O. A., 389, 403
  J. R., 389
  J. V., 330
  James, 38, 48, 78(2), 83,
    85, 192, 207(2), 209, 215,
    229(3), 248(2), 249,
    277(2)
  James K., 389
  James, Jr., 48
  James, Sr., 50, 66
  John W., 411
  Joseph R., 403
  Kenion, 411
  Levi, 3
  Lilla C., 389
  Loduska, 324
  Lucinda, 411
  Lucrecia, 411
  Luduska, 190
  Malinda, 371
  Martha A., 407
  Martha Ann, 144(2)
  Mary, 386
  Moses, 235, 256, 276, 411
  Moses T., 378, 411
  Moses, Jr., 71
  Moses, Jr., 289
  N. S., 411
  Nathan, 95, 121, 207, 229,
    248
  P. C., 389
  Peter, 193, 238
  S. C., 403
  S. S., 389, 403
  Sampson, 85, 95, 207, 249,
    278(2)
  Sarah, 411
  Sarah E., 389
  Susan Aminda, 440
  T. M., 411
  Tabitha Jane, 389
  Thomas, 48, 235
  Trustin, 142, 144
  Westley, 136
  Westly, 250
  William B., 144
  Zachariah, 85, 95, 207,
    229, 249(2)

-U-

UNDERWOOD,
  H. F., 87, 88, 89, 219,
    254
  Mary A., 407
UPCHURCH,
  Ga, 9
  Gay, 12, 15, 22
  Guy, 9

USH,
  Ellison, 110

-V-

VARNER,
  Marcus, 27, 34, 186, 240,
    271, 320, 324, 325
  Mary, 325
  Moses, 325
VAUGHAN,
  Benjamin, 271(3)
  Howel, 117(2), 271
  John, 271(2)
VAUGHN,
  Benjamin, 240
  Elizabeth, 240, 271
  Howell, 120, 240
  T. J., 375
VEAL,
  J. L., 360
  L. A., 365, 368, 380
  William W., 368
VEASEY,
  N. J., 429(2)
VEASY,
  M. J., 423
VEAZEY,
  M. C., 429
VENABLE,
  W. R., 311
VERNON,
  James, 27
  Rocella, 27, 37, 41, 70
  William, 194
VICKERS,
  A. J., 163(2)
  C. B., 360
  James R., 163(2)
VICKERY,
  A. J., 164
  J. A., 404
  James R., 164
VINCENT,
  Margaret E., 365
  S. F., 427
  Sarah F., 378
  W. R., 365

INDEX

-W-

WADE,
  Jesse L., 158
WAGLERS,
  Ben, 325
WAKEFIELD,
  F. M., 20
  William, 65
WALDEN,
  Elisha, 199
WALDROP,
  J. H., 33
  J. L. H., 180
WALDROUP,
  James H., 284
  John R., 20, 57
  John T., 274
  M., 56
  Mary, 38, 43, 75, 205
  May, 238
  T., 284
  Thomas, 111
  Thomas D., 205, 265, 267, 284
WALDRUP,
  James H., 87
  Mary, 93
  Thomas D., 93
WALKER,
  Canady, 336
  D. F. H., 261
  Daniel, 314
  Harrison, 65
  James, 210, 248
  John, 336
  Samuel, 258
  Thomas, 332
  W. W., 314, 356
WALLIS,
  Eliza E., 437
  J. N., 333
  N. G., 320, 323(2)
  Reuben, 1, 5, 38, 85, 87, 89, 144, 219
  Reubin, 33, 75
  Richard, 229

  W. D., 437, 439
WALLS,
  Ann W., 245
  Callaway, 244, 245
  N.C., 344
  William B., 245
WANSLY,
  I. G., 342
WARD,
  A. E., 347
  J., 20
  James, 144
  Jesse, 17, 22, 33, 53(2), 57, 61, 83, 107, 140, 144, 274
  John, 37, 65, 74, 235
  John M., 154, 156
  Leny, 244
  Leny M., 244
  Linny, 245
  Liny M., 212
  Miles, 18, 154, 156, 212, 216, 244, 245
WARE,
  Amanda C., 63
  Amanda Catherine, 63
  Ann, 49
  Ann C., 223
  Ann E., 192, 205, 240, 270, 288
  Ann Eliza, 49, 60
  B. A., 48, 121
  Burrel, 192
  Burrell, 64, 66, 75, 249
  Burrell A., 49, 63, 76(2), 77, 120, 194, 213, 224, 269, 287
  Catherine, 49(2), 63, 77
  Emily F., 49, 66
  F., 314
  G. W., 48, 111, 181, 182, 334, 354
  George, 4, 6, 11, 23, 26, 30(2), 48, 49, 54, 60(3), 63, 64, 66(2), 76, 192, 194, 197, 205, 209, 213, 223(2), 224, 240, 269(2), 270, 287, 288

  George S., 117, 271
  George W., 48, 49, 111, 120(2), 136, 153, 156, 237, 267, 284
  J. E. H., 181, 314, 387
  J. H., 367
  James, 49, 66, 77, 192, 333
  James C. H., 269
  James E., 60
  James E. C., 194
  James E. H., 213, 224, 249, 287
  Jesse, 17
  Letty, 192
  Louisa L., 49, 66
  Mary Almannia, 192
  Mildred, 48, 49, 54, 60(2), 64, 66, 76, 192, 197, 205, 209, 223(2), 240, 269, 270, 288
  R. D., 181
  Richard, 49, 60, 192, 205
  Richard F., 269
  Richard P., 223, 240, 288
  Sallie, 354
WARNER,
  G. L., 228
WARREN,
  Abram, 23
  G. L., 235
  Isaiah, 8, 16
  Josiah, 13, 23
  Lovett, 258
WASHINGTON,
  Clarence, 426
  Herbert, 426
  Lizzie, 426
WATERS,
  Johnson, 57
WATERSON,
  D. S., 51
  Daniel S., 33
  Kisiah, 51
  W. L., 304
WATSON,
  E. E., 311
  E. E., Miss, 419

INDEX

WATSON (continued)
 J. W., 311, 419
 J. Westley, 419
 James A., 360
 James H., 360
 John, 25, 41, 101, 110,
  111, 218, 251(2), 268,
  279, 283, 295
 Mary, 36
 May, 41
 Nancy, 147, 295
 R. N., 311
 Robert, 41
 Thomas, 13(2), 22, 36,
  41(2), 62
 Thomas A., 146
 Virginia Ann, 147
 W., 13, 274(2)
 William, 13, 22, 36,
  41(3), 62, 125, 145, 195,
  218, 257, 258, 311
WATTERSON,
 Daniel S., 274
 Keziah, 274
 Mary D., 274
 R. S., 274
 William S. C., 274
WATTS & MINAFER, 19
WATTS & MINIFREE, 35
WEALLY,
 Nelson, 40
WEAVER,
 H. B., 384
 H. O., 384
 M. B., 384
 Hattie, 384
 S. I., 4
 S. J., 30
 S. L., 384(2)
 Seaborn J., 5
WEEDEN,
 E. B., 360
WEIR,
 Martha A., 391, 409, 412,
  426
WELCH,
 Elizabeth M., 200
WELDON,

 E. B., 388, 426
WELLBORN,
 A. R., 313
 Spencer T., 95
WELLIN,
 S. T., 297
WESLEY,
 M. A., 390
WEST,
 Allen, 152
 Ann Jane, 238
 Araminta, 231
 Brittain, 208
 Britton, 213, 228, 238
 Isam, 208
 Joseph, 208
 Lucinda, 331
 Martha, 389
 Paschal, 227
 Seaborn J., 262
 Susanah, 128, 227, 268,
  279
 Susannah, 122, 247, 250,
  264, 297
 T. J., 268
 Thomas, 331
 Widow, 208
 Willis, 208
 windham, 208
 Windom, 213, 228, 238
WESTBROOK,
 B., 8, 13
 Cany, 62
 Elizabeth, 54
 F. L., 385
 G., 8, 13, 331
 Gain, 351
 Gainey, 23, 35, 154
 Gainy, 16, 35, 187, 304,
  306(3), 329, 344, 345, 363

 M. H., 54
 M. O., 351
 Malissa O., 351
WESTBROOKS,
 Marshal H., 65
WESTLEY,
 Evans, 201, 203

WESTLY,
 G. L., 203
 Jackson, 203
 William S., 203
WESTMORELAND,
 C. F., 46
 C. L., 68
 C. S., 46, 68(2), 81
 Calvin S., 81
 E., Mrs., 46
 Elizabeth, 46, 68
 J. G., 232
 John, 19, 44, 46(2), 47,
  68(2), 72
 M., 23, 32, 46, 68
 M. F., 232
 M. J., 46
 M. W., 46(2)
 Mark, 46
 Mark W., 44, 68, 72
 Robert J., 68
 S. J., Miss, 72
 Sarah J., 68
 Thomas, 47
 Westley, 46, 68
WHALEY,
 Charles, 32, 85
 Daniel, 85
 Elizabeth, 1, 4
 Hiram, 17
 John, 19, 85
 Josiah, 1, 4, 17, 53
 Mabry, 262
 Madison, 85
 Mary, 19
 S. D., 53
 S. R., 17
 Samuel, 1, 4, 17
 William, 1, 7
 William P., 4, 17(2), 53
WHATLEY,
 Johnston, 57, 152
 William, 3, 8, 19, 30, 76,
  149, 152(2), 158, 166,
  226, 404, 21
WHATLY,
 Johnston, 315
 Mary W., 315

INDEX

WHEATLEY,
  I. T., 17(2)
WHEELIS,
  Emeline, 271(2)
  Tempy, 271
WHITAKER,
  Andrew J., 130, 289, 295
  B. F., 307(2)
  Benjamin F., 130, 289(2), 295
  Frances, 289
  Isabella, 295
  J. A., 316
  J. I., 39
  Jared, 235
  Jared I., 9(2), 65(2), 67, 69, 75, 99, 295
  Jared J., 42(2), 46
  John, 178, 244
  John I., 15, 89(2), 90, 94(2), 95, 98, 106, 113(2), 114, 118, 129, 130, 133, 134(2), 140, 155, 176, 186(2), 194, 207, 221, 245(3), 249, 259, 260(2), 272(2), 278, 286, 289(2), 292, 293(2), 315, 320, 322, 329, 338(3), 342
  John J., 307
  John L., 143
  John R., 256
  Levicy, 329, 342
  Mrs., 320
  S. F., 307
  S. T., 81, 215, 230, 231, 261(2)
  S.T., 38
  Sarah F., 295, 307
  Sarah Francis, 130
  Simon T., 74, 75, 80, 89(2), 90, 98, 118, 130, 185, 193, 209, 249, 256(2), 272, 295(2), 296
  Thomas, 74
  Thomas S., 307
  W. L., 176
  W. R., 134, 178, 186(2),
    256, 289, 320, 342
  W. S., 307(2)
  William L., 289, 296
  William S., 130, 307
  Willis, 113, 289
  Willis R., 130, 133, 140, 143, 155, 272, 277, 295(2), 296, 307
  Willis S., 113
WHITE,
  Isam, 271
  Margaret, 317
  Margaret J., 396
  Martha M., 407
WHITLEY,
  T. D., 21
  T. H., 16
  Thomas H., 10
WHITLOCK,
  Beasly, 159
  C. M., 397, 401, 402, 418
  Charlie, 406
  Daniel, 159
  E. A., Miss, 418, 424, 430, 434, 436, 439
  Eugene A., 397
  Eugenia, 418
  Eugenia A., 401, 402, 406, 418
  J. A., 310, 317, 401, 406, 409, 415, 418(2)
  J. L., 401(2)
  J. R., 397, 401, 402(2), 418
  John, 348
  John A., 397, 402
  John I., 318
  Robert, 348
  Robert H., 159
WHITLOVK,
  M. V., 333
  R. H., 333
WHITLOW,
  M. E., 276, 289
  Martha E., 117, 258(2)
  W. H., 290
  W. M., 276
  Warren, 105, 117, 225,
    240, 258(2), 276, 289, 290
  William, 276
  William M., 105, 225, 240, 258
WICKETTE,
  Jane, 52
  John, 52
WIGGINGS,
  William, 73
WIGGINS,
  William, 73
WILBORN,
  Spencer T., 122
WILBOURN,
  Spencer T., 291
WILERFORD,
  Chares W., 63
  Wilson A., 63
WILEY,
  Thomas H., 228
WILEY BANKS & C., 65
WILIFORD,
  Charles, 34
  Charles W., 78
  Wilson A., 78
WILKIINS,
  Samuel, 391
WILKINS,
  Eliza, 357
  Eliza F., 241
  Exer, 357
  Helen, 357
  Henry, 357
  John W., 19, 71
  Mary, 357
  Sallie, 357
  Samantha, 357
  W. H., 357
  W. W., 186
  William W., 146, 147, 262
WILKINSON,
  Elbert, 157
  Martha, 157
  Martha E., 63
  Mary, 256
  William J., 256
  William R., 121, 250, 256

INDEX

WILKSON,
  John S., 238
WILKY,
  I. W., 219
WILLERFORD,
  Charles W., 63
  Wilson A., 63
WILLIAMS,
  A. B., 9, 18, 23, 32, 46, 48
  A. G., 12
  Allie, 425
  Avington B., 8, 63, 236, 249
  C., Miss, 233
  Celesta, 46
  Cintha, 46
  Collecta, 197
  Elizabeth, 46
  Elizabeth L., 197
  Gilbert, 323
  I., 10
  I. C., 17
  J. C., 336
  J. H., 71
  James B., 236
  James H., 12, 18(2), 23, 46, 56, 63, 79, 194(2), 205, 237
  John, 6, 10, 23, 117, 230, 231
  John H., 36, 43, 194
  Jordan, 89, 235
  Joseph, 35
  Joseph B., 219(2)
  Kizzie, 425
  Lewis, 367
  M. L., 249
  Marcey, 46
  Marcus L., 197, 232, 249
  Mary E., 413
  Moses, 18, 194, 205, 237
  P., 23
  Penelope, 232
  Thomas J., 36, 43
  W. H., 48
  W. L., 187, 188(2), 191, 317, 335, 340, 358, 363, 368, 383
  W. T., 425(2)
  Z., 46
WILLIAMSON,
  I. B., 238
WILLIFORD,
  J. H., 406
WILSON,
  Ann, 393
  Annie, 388, 396, 402(2)
  John, 79
  Nancy, 79, 220
  S. E., 68
  Stephen D., 46
  Stephen E., 68
  W., 315
  Washington, 79, 220, 279
  William W., 320
WINN,
  G. O., 303
  O., 303
WISH,
  Susan, 115(2)
WOOD,
  J. J., 25
  James, 3
WOODRUFF,
  Solomon, 58
WOODS,
  F. A., 300, 377
  L. F., 392, 419
  M. E., 419
  Mary E., 392
  R. H., 373, 377(2), 381, 392, 398
WOOTON,
  Lucinda, 201
  William B., 201
  William H., 128
  Young L., 110, 111, 123, 217, 259, 267
  Z. L., 253
WOOTON & CO., 67
WOOTTON,
  Lucinda, 54, 267
  Nancy L., 267
  Tanissa, 142
  William B., 54, 267
  William H., 131, 155, 267, 290, 293
  Wilson L., 267
  Young L., 54, 124, 142, 246, 247, 275
WORD,
  J. M., 23
WRIGHT,
  Martin, 282
WYATT,
  James, 32
  Mag, 415
  Mansell, 232
  William, 232, 314
WYCHE,
  Matilda, 413
WYNN,
  J. H., 310, 408
  J. O., 430
  O., 300

-Y-

YANCEY,
  Mattie, 442
YANCY,
  A. F., 200
YARBOUGH,
  C., 203
  George, 203
  Thomas, 203
YATES,
  A. N., 201
  Eliza A., 311
  Emily M., 98
  Emily Martha, 273
  F. S. C., 365
  G. A., 201
  G. M., 211
  George M., 99, 237, 273(2)
  J. B., 291
  J. C., 147
  Joseph G., 148, 155, 156(2), 159(3)
  M., 342
  M. L., 179, 223, 238, 311, 332, 352, 359, 360
  Martha, 417

INDEX

Mathew, 47, 56, 62, 98,
  99, 201, 203, 211, 237,
  262, 333, 381
Matthew, 98, 171, 262,
  273, 376, 385, 388, 391,
  396(2), 402, 409, 430
S. F. C., 376, 391, 430(2)
S. F. C., Mrs., 396, 402,
  409, 417
S. F., Mrs., 405
S. Francina, 388
S. T., 385
S. T. C., 372, 380
Sophrona J., 98
Sophrona Jane, 273
YOUNG,
  Elizabeth, 377
  James, 195, 377
YOUNGBLOOD,
  B. F., 303
  Hiram, 379
  John, 203
  Martha, 203
  Sarah F., 356

-Z-

ZELLARS,
  S., 219
  Simeon, 112
ZORN,
  E., 407
  William, 407

NEGROES (BY TESTATOR'S SURNAME)

-A-

ANTHONY,
  Caroline, 34
  Haley, 34
  James, 34
  Jane, 34
  Jenny, 34
  Kesiah, 34
  Matilda, 34, 226
  Micajah, 34, 226
  Milly, 34(2)
  Philis, 34

-B-

BARGAMY,
  Bill, 286
  Bob, 286
  Charles, 286
  George, 286
  Lindy, 286
  Mike, 286
  Kit, 286
  Nel, 286
  Wat, 286
BEALL,
  Ben, 13
  Lizi, 13
  Violet, 13
BEARDEN,
  Alek, 24
  Caroline, 24
  Cintha, 24
  Jane, 24
  Jim, 24
  Lena, 24
  Mary, 24(2)
BRASSELL,
  Caroline, 203
  Charles, 285
  Dan, 285
  Docl, 203
  George, 203
  Gidon, 285
  Hannah, 285
  Isaac, 285
  Joseph, 203
  Looney, 285
  Madison, 285
  Mary, 285
  Milton, 285
  Moses, 285
  Peter, 203
  Ruffin, 285
  Simon, 285
  Sopa, 203
  Thena, 285
  Tilda, 285
BROOKS,
  Angeline, 232
  Break, 232
  Caroline, 208
  Francis, 232
  Jeff, 208
  Jim, 208
  Moses, 208
  Sharlot, 208
  Toby, 208
  William, 232
BUFFINGTON,
  Ann, 292
  Clary, 292
  Harry, 292
  Peter, 292

-C-

CARROLL,
  Allen, 30
  Ben, 3, 4, 5
  Bob, 5
  Bobb, 4
  Clark, 3, 4
  Feb, 4, 30
  Frank, 3, 4
  George, 3, 4, 5, 30
  Guy, 3, 4(2)
  Harry, 5
  Harvey, 4
  Jesse, 4, 5
  Jourdan, 4
  Leny, 3
  Lezzy, 4
  Lizzie, 5
  Matilda, 30
  Rachel, 30
  Tab, 4, 5
CLARKE,
  Adam, 326
  Barry, 326
  Charles, 326
  Henry, 326
  infant, 326
  James, 326
  Martha, 326
  Mundy, 326
  Roxy, 326
  Susan, 326
CLEMENTS,
  Anthony, 257, 293
  Anthony (little), 257, 273
  Caroline, 257
  Easter, 257, 273
  Emily, 257, 273
  Hester, 257
  Ike, 257, 273
  Jac, 257
  Jack, 273
  Jane, 257, 293
  Jim, 257
  Julia, 257, 273
  Lettia, 257
  Lezza, 257
  Mandy, 257, 273
  Mary, 273
  May, 257
  Melia, 273
  Mellia, 257
  Nancy, 257, 273
  old man, 273
  Sterling, 257, 273
  Tobe, 273

NEGROES (BY TESTATOR'S SURNAME)

CLEMENTS (continued)
  Warren, 273
  Wenia, 257
  William, 257
COLLINS,
  Aaron, 69
  Aron, 39
  Bill, 39, 69
  Charles, 39, 69
  Frank, 69
  Harriet, 39
  Katy, 69
  Peter, 39, 69
  Rhoda, 39, 69
  Sally, 39, 69
  Stephen, 39, 69
  Taressa, 39
  Teresa, 69
  William, 39, 69
COOK,
  Jane, 210
  Laurence, 210
  Tom, 210
CYRUS,
  Abram, 286
  Andy, 286
  Dick, 286
  Ellen, 286
  Georgian, 286
  Harriett, 286
  Malissa, 286
  Milly, 286
  Nancy, 286
  Sally, 286

-D-

DEVAUGHN,
  Asbury, 298
  George, 298
  Jack, 298
  Margtha, 298
  Nelly, 298
  Rose, 298
  Sandy, 298
  Simon, 298
DORMAN,
  Ann, 38

  Betsey, 38
  Ceasor, 38
  Dinah, 38
  Isaac, 38
  John, 38
  Leroy, 38
  Lewis, 38
  Liusa, 38
  Liza, 38
  Margaret, 38
  Sarah, 38
  Vilet, 38
DUFFELL,
  Hindy, 288
  Roda, 288

-E-

EASTIN,
  Emeline, 290
  George, 55, 207, 257, 290
  Jordan, 55, 290
  Lucy, 55, 257, 290
  Reese, 55
  Run, 290
  Sarah, 290
  Simon, 55, 207, 257(2), 290
ELDER,
  Clemency, 19
  Daniel, 19
  Mariah, 19
  Pamelia, 19
  William, 19
EMILY,
  Jim, 47
EVANS,
  Fanny, 219
  Jim, 219
  John, 219
  Louisa, 219
  Nancy, 219
  Phillip, 219
  Sophronia, 219
  Tom, 219
  Willes, 219
  Wlter, 219

-F-

FAULKNER,
  Berry, 210
  Clara, 210
  Lucy, 210
  Ned, 210
  Sarah, 210
  Warren, 210

-G-

GENTRY,
  Annah, 195
  John, 195
  Kisey, 195
GRIGGS,
  Allen, 192
  Sutton, 192

-H-

HALES,
  Isham, 218
  Mahala, 218
  Mahaly, 218
  Martha, 218
  Matilda, 218(2)
  Minea, 218
  Nelson, 218(2)
  Richard, 218(2)
  Tamer, 218(2)
HEAD,
  Ann, 48
  Ceans, 48
  Ceasor, 48
  Dinah, 48(2)
  Elijah, 48
  Elizabeth, 48
  Isaac, 48
  Leroy, 48
  Lewis, 48
  Margaret, 48
  Viney, 48(2)
HENDERSON,
  Abraham, 35
  Bill, 52

NEGROES (BY TESTATOR'S SURNAME)

Caroline, 35
Daniel, 35
Easter, 52
Eastern, 35
Elizabeth, 35
Harriett, 35
Isaac, 35
isaac, 35
Joseph, 35, 52
Malissa, 35
Mariah, 35
Mary, 52
mary, 35
Nancy, 35, 52
Paul, 35, 52
Randson, 35
Robert, 35
Thomas, 35
William, 35
Willis, 35
HERRING,
   Charles, 33(3)
HILL,
   Linus, 219(2)
   Rockaway, 254
HUGHS,
   Aggy, 13

-I-

IKENER,
   Adam, 3
   Betsey, 3
   Bill, 3
   Bob, 3
   Bull, 3
   Caly, 3
   Ceasor, 3
   Doctor, 3
   Elleck, 3
   Eve, 3
   George, 3
   Hannah, 3
   Hardy, 3
   Harry, 3
   Harvey, 3
   India Ann, 3
   Jacob, 3

Jesse, 3
Jim, 3
Jinney, 3
John Henry, 3
Leman, 3
Lucinda, 3
Marah, 3
Mark, 3
Martha, 3
Mary, 3(2)
Mitchell, 3
Nancy, 3
Nelly, 3
Reuben, 3
Roan, 3(2)
Sarah, 3
Spencer, 3
Suckey, 3
Tilpha, 3
Viney, 3

-J-

JENNINGS,
   Aaron, 29
   Alfred, 29, 39
   Augustus, 39
   Bastin, 39
   Bostin, 232
   Boston, 29
   Caroline, 29, 39
   Charles, 29(2), 39(2)
   Dick, 29, 39
   Gust, 29
   Hailey, 29
   Haney, 39
   Hannah, 29, 39
   Harriet, 29
   Harriett, 39
   Henry, 29, 39
   Jack, 29, 39
   Jenny, 29
   John, 29
   Lucas, 29
   Mac, 29
   Mahala, 39
   Mariah, 29, 39
   Mark, 39

   Martha, 29
   Mary, 29, 39
   Milly, 29(2), 39
   Nelly, 39
   Philis, 29
   Phillis, 29
   Philly, 39
   Rose, 29
   Simm, 29
   Simon, 232
   Squin, 29
   Susan, 39
   ThelseyJane, 39
JINNINGS,
   Andrew, 196
   Dennis, 196
   Dick, 196
   Dilsey, 196
   Jerry, 196
   Jesse, 196
   Josiah, 196
   Julia Ann, 196
   Landy, 196
   Lendy, 196
   Mary, 196(2)
   Phillip, 196
   Polly, 196
   Prince, 196
   Sarah, 196
   Squire, 196
   Sterling, 196
   Wiley, 196
JONES,
   Flora, 234
   Jeff, 234
   Mike, 234
   Polly, 234

-L-

LASSETER,
   Eliza, 20
LOYD,
   Aggey, 27
   Aggy, 35, 51
   Anthony, 27, 35, 51
   Henry, 27, 35, 51
   Jane, 27, 51

NEGROES (BY TESTATOR'S SURNAME)

LOYD (continued)
  Lewis, 35, 51
  Luois, 27
  Mary, 51
  Nelson, 27, 35, 51
  Nicey, 27
  Nicy, 35, 51

-M-

MACKY,
  Abner, 258
  Ann, 258
  Asbury, 258
  Ben, 258
  Cidney, 258
  Clark, 258
  Easter, 258
  Eliza, 258
  Harriet, 258
  Jane, 258(2)
  Jefferson, 258
  Jim, 258
  Julian, 258
  Leroy, 258
  Leta, 258
  Levin, 258
  Lila, 258
  Lola, 258
  Manda, 258
  Mandy, 258
  Minerva, 258
  Morgan, 258
  Polly, 258
  Rosa, 258
  Wash, 258
MCLANE,
  Anthony, 194
MCLEAN,
  Roland, 40
  Salene, 40
  Stephen, 40
MCLEROY,
  Ann, 237
  Billy, 237
  Colbert, 237
  Jane, 237
  Louisa, 237

  Martha, 237
  Matilda, 237(2)
  Sarah, 237
MARTIN,
  Ann, 7, 47
  Bob, 47
  Caroline, 47
  Crawford, 47
  Eady, 7
  Ebenezer, 7, 47
  Ede, 47
  Emilia Ann, 47
  Emily, 7
  Francis, 47
  Frank, 7(3)
  Hannah, 7, 47
  harriet, 47
  Henry, 47
  Hiram, 7, 47
  Jim, 47(2)
  John, 47(2)
  Manena, 47
  Margaret, 47
  Mariah, 47
  Martha, 47
  Nancy, 47
  Peter, 7, 47
  Pheba, 47
  Phebea, 7
  Polly, 7
  Qean, 47
  Rachael, 7(4)
  Rachel, 47
  Randall, 7
  Randle, 47
  Rhoda, 47
  Sarah, 47
  Stephen, 7, 47
  Susan, 47
  Tom, 47
  Warren, 47
  Wesley, 47
MEADORS,
  Fannie, 12
  Fassey, 12
  Nancy, 18
  Robert, 12(2), 18(2)
MILES,

  Andy, 277
  Ann, 277
  Caroline, 277
  Chany, 277
  Dick, 277
  Drew, 277
  Ellen, 277
  Fayette, 277
  Henny, 277
  Jesse, 277
  Jim, 277
  Len, 277
  Lewis, 277
  Liza, 277
  Martha, 277
  Monroe, 277
  Peggy, 277
  Rhoda, 277
  Tom, 277
MILLSAPS,
  Andrew, 1(2)
  Anny, 1
  Any, 1
  Arthur, 1(2)
  Auston, 1
  Delah, 1
  Eveline, 1(2)
  George, 1(2)
  Green, 1(2)
  Lissy, 1
  Melissa, 1
  Sarah, 1
  Silsey, 1
MILNER,
  Anthony, 6
  Antony, 12
  Burrell, 6, 12
  Charity, 12
  Frank, 12
  Henry, 12
  Lemas, 12
  Lucy, 12
  Squire, 6, 12
  William, 6, 12
MURPHY,
  America, 286
  Ben, 43
  Benjamin, 34

NEGROES (BY TESTATOR'S SURNAME)

Benny, 34
Charles, 34, 286
Cheely, 43
Dennis, 286
Dock, 43
Eliza, 43
Ellen, 43
Faney, 286
Green, 34, 43
Hannah, 34
Henry, 34, 43, 286
Jack, 34
Jane, 34, 43
Jason, 34, 43
Liza, 34
Margaret, 34, 43
Mariah, 286
Mary, 34, 43(2)
Nancy, 34, 43
NHannah, 43
Quin, 34
Samuel, 34
Susan, 34
Tom, 43(2)
Wiley, 286

-P-

PERSONS,
 Abram, 27
 Antionette, 27
 Calvin, 27
 Delila, 27
 Elizer, 27
 Evarlina, 27
 Isaak, 27
 Jesse, 27
 John, 27
 Mariah, 27
 Mary, 27
 Phil, 27
 Silvey, 27
 Stephen, 27
 Texanah, 27
 Tide, 27
 Washington, 27
PORTER,
 Abram, 286

Jerry, 286
Peter, 286
Tom, 286
Walker, 286
PRICE,
 Anna, 17
 Charlotte, 17
 Esther, 17
 James, 17
 Jordan, 17
 Lewis, 17
 Lucinda, 17

-S-

SCALES,
 Anthony, 256
 Dianah, 256
 Handy, 256
 Jack, 256
SELLERS,
 Andrew, 53
 Bob, 37, 52(2)
 Caroline, 37, 52
 Caty, 37(2), 52(2)
 Ceasor, 37, 53
 easor, 52
 Faby, 37
 Fanny, 37, 52
 Fenly, 52, 53
 Isaac, 53
 Mary, 37, 52, 53
 Peter, 52, 53
 Rachel, 53
 Singleton, 53
 Thomas, 53
SMALLWOOD,
 Charles, 57(2)
 Eady, 57
 Edom, 57
 Eliza, 57
 Henry, 57
 James, 57
 John, 57
 Lizes, 57
 Mills, 57
 Patsey, 57
 Saline, 57

Wesley, 57
SHARP,
 Aarron, 15
 Ailsey, 15
 Bashr, 15
 Delila, 15
 Eliza, 15
 Emma, 15
 Hamilton, 15
 Harriet, 15
 Henry, 15
 Isabela, 15
 Joseph, 15
 Malissa, 15
 Mary, 15
 Nelson, 15
 Sally, 15
 Tour, 15
 Winston, 15
SMITH,
 Adaline, 216
 Ann, 216
 Bob, 219
 Caroline, 216
 Charles, 219
 Cinda, 219
 Clary, 26
 Davy, 216
 Dick, 216
 Elizabeth, 216, 219
 Frank, 219
 Hannah, 219
 Harriet, 216
 Henry, 26, 219
 Herriet, 219
 Jackson, 216
 Madison, 216
 Missouri, 219
 Nancy, 219(2)
 Rachel, 26
 Sallie, 219
 Sarah, 216
 Vena, 219
 William, 216
 Willis, 26
SPRATLIN,
 Ann, 288
 Carry, 288

NEGROES (BY TESTATOR'S SURNAME)

SPRATLIN (continued)
  Click, 288
  Dorsey, 288
  Eastern, 288
  Elijah, 288
  John, 288(2)
  Letty, 288
  Louisa, 288
  Mariah, 288
  Peter, 288
  Salina, 288
  Silvey, 288(2)
  Stephen, 288
  Viney, 288
STUBBS,
  Bill, 56
  Bob, 56
  Caty, 56
  Ellick, 56
  Henry, 56
  Jane, 56
  Jincy, 56
  Louisa, 56
  Mack, 56
  Mary, 56
  Nancy, 56
  Sarah, 56
  Spencer, 56
  Wright, 56
  Zilphey, 56

-T-

TILGHMAN,
  Ellick, 7
  Joe, 7, 30
  Richmond, 7, 30
  Sandford, 7
TURNER,
  Catherine, 56
  Ellen, 48, 56
  Joe, 56
  John, 48, 56
  Sarah, 48, 56

-W-

WARE,

Anna, 66
Ben, 26, 49
Big Jim, 26, 49
Bill, 49
Book, 49
Booker, 26
Daniel, 49
Fanny, 26, 49, 60, 223
Foley, 49
Gabe, 26
Gale, 49
Harriet, 26, 60
Harrriet, 49
Jack, 49, 60
Jacob, 26
Jim, 49
Joe, 26, 49
John, 26, 49, 63
Lamb, 26, 66
Liddy, 26, 49
Little Jim, 26
Lucy, 49
Martha, 26, 49
Mary, 26, 49
Nelly, 26, 49, 60
Peter, 26, 49, 60, 223
Polly, 26, 49
Sam, 66
Susan, 49(2)
Tob, 66
Toby, 26
Tom, 49, 63
William, 26
Willie, 26
WATERSON,
  Green, 33
  Hanson, 33
  Lena, 33
  Lise, 33
  Mary, 33(7)
  Sarah, 33
WATSON,
  Ann, 218, 279
  Hughy, 218
  Laura, 218
  Martha, 218

Milton, 22
WEST,
  Ike, 250
  Isaac, 264
  Jacob, 250, 264
  John, 250, 264
  Joshua, 250, 264
  Rhoda, 264
  Rhody, 250
WESTMORELAND,
  Alna, 46
  Bill, 46
  Caroline, 46
  Daniel, 46
  Dice, 46
  Dudley, 46
  Edi, 47
  Elizabeth, 46
  George, 46
  Hal, 46
  Henry, 46
  Jack, 46
  Julia, 46
  Martin, 47
  Mary, 46(2)
  Nice, 46
  Olive, 46
  Rose, 46
  Sam, 46
  Steward, 46
  Tom, 46
  Ziletha, 46
WHITAKER,
  Amanda, 256
  Betsy, 256
  Caroline, 256
  Dan, 256
  Eliza, 256(2)
  Emily, 256
  Henry, 256(2)
  Jesse, 256
  Juda, 256
  Louisa, 256
  Luisa, 256
  Mandy, 256
  Mariah, 256
  Marth, 256
  Martha, 256(3)

NEGROES (BY TESTATOR'S SURNAME)

Mon, 256
WILLIAMS,
  Alsey, 8
  Bile, 8
  Bill, 48
  Caroline, 8, 48
  George, 48
  Hannah, 8, 48
  Henry, 8, 48
  Morris, 8
  Viney, 8, 48

Other Heritage Books by Jeannette Holland Austin:

1860 Paulding County, Georgia Census

Alabama Bible Records

DeKalb County, Georgia Probate Records

*Fayette County, Georgia Probate Records: Volume II
Annual Returns, Inventories, Sales, Bonds, 1845–1897*

Georgia Bible Records, Supplement, 1772–1940

Georgia Obituaries, 1740–1935

Georgia Obituaries, 1905–1910

Jackson County, Georgia Tombstones
Jeannette Holland Austin and Dorothy Holland Herring

Masters of the Low Country: A History of the Georgia Colony

North Carolina–South Carolina Bible Records

The Georgians Database: Genealogical Notes

Virginia Bible Records

www.ingramcontent.com/pod-product-compliance
Lightning Source LLC
Chambersburg PA
CBHW050423240426
43661CB00055B/2259